Palaeography of Orissa

Palaeography of Orissa

Subrata Kumar Acharya

D.K. Printworld (P) Ltd.
New Delhi

Cataloging in Publication Data — DK
[Courtesy: D.K. Agencies (P) Ltd. <docinfo@dkagencies.com>]

Acharya, Subrata Kumar, 1962-
Palaeography of Orissa / Subrata Kumar Acharya.
p. 29 cm.
Revision of the author's thesis (Ph. D.) — Sambalpur University, 1992.
Includes bibliographical references (p.)
Includes index.
ISBN 8124603065

1. Palaeography — India — Orissa. I. Title.

DDC 417.409 541 3 21

ISBN 81-246-0306-5
First Published in India in 2005

The publication of this book has been financially supported by the Indian Council of Historical Research. The responsibility for the facts stated or opinions expressed is entirely of the author and not of the Council.

Published and printed by:
D.K. Printworld (P) Ltd.
Regd. office : *'Sri Kunj'*, F-52, Bali Nagar
New Delhi - 110 015
Phones : (011) 2545-3975; 2546-6019; *Fax* : (011) 2546-5926
E-mail: dkprintworld@vsnl.net
Web: www.dkprintworld.com

Foreword

I DEEM it a privilege to be asked to write a foreword to Dr. Subrata Kumar Acharya's *magnum opus* **Palaeography of Orissa**. It is only rarely that such a lucidly written research work on such a technical subject gets written and published. I can say with confidence that I am yet to come across such a thorough and comprehensive treatment of the history of palaeographical developments in a given region of the subcontinent. In 10 well-planned chapters (Chapters 2 to 11) Dr. Acharya has unfolded various stages of the evolution and development of Early, Middle and Modern Orissan scripts beginning from the Imperial Mauryan Brāhmī Script. Special as well as regular features of successive intermediate stages of Later Brāhmī, Middle Kaliṅga Script, Box-headed characters of South Kośala, the Toṣalī, Utkala and Koṅgoda scripts, the Kuṭila script, the Orissan Proto-Nāgarī script, the Mixed Kaliṅga writing and the Proto-Oriya script are all competently discussed; the author has taken care to provide palaeographical charts wherever necessary to strengthen the line of his presentation. A welcome feature of this laudable academic venture is that Dr. Acharya has succeeded in blending authentic political history with the palaeographical history of Orissa.

I have no doubt that this meticulously researched, well documented book, which is highly technical and lucid too, will be received and read with great interest by the world of Indologists. But what I would like to mention particularly is that the researchers of the younger generation ought to adopt Dr. Acharya's methodology as role model for preparing similar monographs for other palaeographical segments of our country.

I congratulate Dr. Subrata Kumar Acharya for this rare accomplishment.

Mysore
16-7-2003

K.V. Ramesh
Formerly Director (Epigraphy and
Jt. Director General (Retd.)
Archaeological Survey of Indian, and Presently
Honorary Director, Oriental Research
Institute, Mysore

Dedicated to the Memory of

J.G. Bühler, G.H. Ojha, D.C. Sircar,

and other Savants to whose writings the
Author owes his little knowledge of
Indian Epigraphy and Palaeography

Preface

THIS is a thoroughly revised version of my thesis which was approved for the degree of Doctor of Philosophy by Sambalpur University in 1992. The theme of this study first engaged my attention in the mid-1980s and the major part of the work was done in the late 1980s of the last century. Earlier I had studied the Palaeography of Orissa from the third century BC to the twelfth century AD. But later I extended the scope of my study up to the seventeenth century. The present study tries to trace the evolution of the regional script of Orissa from the Brāhmī script to the advent of the modern Oriya script through various intermediate stages. For this purpose several hundreds of copper-plate and stone inscriptions have been examined.

In writing the palaeography of Orissa I have tried to establish the evolutionary character of the Oriya script. The Brāhmī script has been indisputably acknowledged as the parent of most of the regional scripts of India including the Oriya. While selecting nomenclatures for the scripts prevalent in the different sub-regional kingdoms of ancient Orissa, I have followed the dominant stylistic peculiarities which distinguishes one style from the other, although they were all offshoots of the Brāhmī. The box-headed, the acute-angled, the Kuṭila script, etc., which are some of the well-known writing styles prevalent in broader palaeographical zones made their flow into different sub-regional kingdoms and sufficiently reinforced their existing local styles. It has been, therefore, emphasized that the geo-political forces are the major determinants for shaping the writing style of a given region/sub-region. In the subsequent course of scriptal development, palaeographical segmentation ran parallel with linguistic segmentation. The advent of the proto-regional and regional script of Orissa is studied in the backdrop of this process. The seventeen palaeographical charts appended to this book trace the historical evolution of the scripts used in the epigraphic records of Orissa. The text should, therefore, be studied in conjunction with these charts. The letter-forms have been reproduced from the facsimiles of the original inscriptions published in different journals. Estampages of a majority of Oriya inscriptions have been consulted either in the office of the Director (Epigraphy), Mysore or in the collection of late Dr. K.B. Tripathi. Legends on coins, seals, sealings, terracotta objects, etc., which are not inscriptions in real sense have not been taken into consideration. While the work was in progress many new districts were formed, but whenever there is reference to a district, it should be understood as an undivided district. Photographs of some select inscriptions have been included in each chapter in order to acquaint the readers with the prevalent characters.

In the preparation of this book, I have received help and guidance of Dr. S.N. Rajaguru, Dr. S.C. Behera and Dr. S.C. Panda. I owe my special obligations to all of them. My thanks are also due to Prof. E.C.L. Duning Caspers (Institute Kern, Leiden) and Prof. R.N. Mishra (Jiwaji University, Gwalior) who examined my thesis and offered valuable suggestions. I am indebted to Dr. K.B. Tripathi who was kind enough to lend me the photocopies of the estampages of some of the Oriya inscriptions, which I consulted in this work with great profit. I am happy to acknowledge the financial help I received from the ICHR for publication of this work and the cooperation I received from the authorities of the National Library, Kolkata, the Asiatic Society, Kolkata, the Archaeological Survey of India, New Delhi, the Office of the Director (Epigraphy), Mysore, the Orissa State Museum, Bhubaneswar and the Indian Institute of Advanced Study, Simla. My special thanks are due to the Director (Epigraphy), Mysore, for supplying the photographs of a majority of inscriptions included in this book. I am beholden to Dr. K.V. Ramesh who has been so kind to write a foreword to this work. I feel it my duty to thank the publishers, M/s D.K. Printworld (P) Ltd., New Delhi, who did their best to being out the book as nicely as possible. And finally, I would wish to thank my wife Geeta for constant encouragement.

Subrata Kumar Acharya

Contents

Abbreviations

AGI	:	Ananta Gumphā Inscription
ASI	:	Archaeological Survey of India
ASSI	:	Archaeological Survey of Southern India
ASWI	:	Archaeological Survey of Western India
BE	:	Bhauma Era
BI	:	Bhadrak Inscription of Mahārāja Gaṇa
BPL	:	*Bhāratīya Prācīna Lipimālā*, G.H. Ojha, Delhi, 1959.
CHI	:	Choṭa Hāthīgumphā Inscription
CII	:	*Corpus Inscriptionum Indicarum*
CPIAPGM	:	*Copper Plate Inscriptions of Andhra Pradesh Goverment Museum, Hyderabad*, 2 vols., N. Ramesan, Hyderabad, 1962 & 1970.
EA	:	*Epigraphia Andhrica*
EI	:	*Epigraphia Indica*
ELOS	:	*The Evolution of Oriya Language and Script*, K.B. Tripathi, Cuttack, 1962.
GE	:	Gupta Era
GY	:	Gaṅga Year
HCIP	:	*History and Culture of Indian People*, ed. R.C. Mazumdar, Bombay, 1951-57.
HGI	:	Haridās Gumphā Inscription
HI	:	Hāthīgumphā Inscription
IA	:	*Indian Antiquary*
IC	:	*Indian Culture*
IHQ	:	*Indian Historical Quarterly*
IHRC	:	Indian Historical Records Commission
IP	:	*Indian Palaeography*, G. Bühler, Calcutta, 1959; *Indian Palaeography*, A.H. Dani, Delhi, 1986.

ISGO	:	*Inscriptions of the Sūryavaṁśī Gajapatis of Orissa*, R. Subrahmanyam, New Delhi, 1986.
ITPOSPJ	:	*Inscriptions of the Temples of Puri and Origin of Śrī Puruṣottama Jagannāth*, I. S. N. Rajaguru, Puri, 1992.
JAHC	:	*Journal of Andhra History and Culture*
JAHRS	:	*Journal of Andhra Historical Research Society*
JAIH	:	*Journal of Ancient Indian History*
JAS	:	*Journal of the Asiatic Society*
JASB, L	:	*Journal of Asiatic Society of Bengal, Letters*
JASB, NS	:	*Journal of the Asiatic Society of Bengal, New Series*
JBORS	:	*Journal of the Bihar and Orissa Research Society*
JBRS	:	*Journal of the Bihar Research Society*
JESI	:	*Journal of the Epigraphical Society of India*
JGI	:	Jambeśvara Gumphā Inscription
JKHRS	:	*Journal of the Kalinga Historical Research Society*
JNSI	:	*Journal of the Numismatic Society of India*
JOA	:	*Journal of Orissa Academy*
JOH	:	*Journal of Orissa History*
JOR	:	*Journal of Oriental Research*
JORS	:	*Journal of the Orissa Research Society*
JPASB	:	*Journal and Proceedings of the Asiatic Society of Bengal*
JRAS	:	*Journal of the Royal Asiatic Society* (Bombay Branch)
JRASB, L	:	*Journal of the Royal Asiatic Society of Bengal, Letters*
MASB	:	*Memoirs of the Archaeological Survey of India*
MBIs	:	Minor Brāhmī Inscriptions
MGI-US	:	Mañcapurī Gumphā Inscription — Upper Storey
MGI-LS	:	Mañcapurī Gumphā Inscription — Lower Storey
NAHO	:	*New Aspects of History of Orissa*
NI	:	Nanaghat Inscription
OHRJ	:	*Orissa Historical Research Journal*

OUBK	:	*Orissa Under the Bhauma Kings*, B. Mishra, Calcutta, 1934.
PIHC	:	*Proceedings of Indian History Congress*
RED	:	Rock Edicts at Dhauli
REJ	:	Rock Edicts at Jaugada
RY	:	Regnal Year
S.	:	Śakābda (Śaka era)
SGI	:	Sarpa Guṁphā Inscription
SBI	:	Sitabinji Boulder Inscriptions
SII	:	*South Indian Inscriptions*
SRED	:	Separate Rock Edicts at Dhauli
SREJ	:	Separate Rock Edicts at Jaugada
TGI	:	Tatowā Guṁphā Inscription
TGR	:	*Three Grants from Ragolu*, N.M. Rao, Hyderabad, 1982.
VGI	:	Vyāghra Guṁphā Inscription
VS	:	Vikrama *Saṁvat* (era)

Key to Transliteration

अ *a* (but)	आ *ā* (palm)	इ *i* (it)
ई *ī* (beet)	उ *u* (put)	ऊ *ū* (pool)
ऋ *ṛ* (rhythm)	ए *e* (play)	ऐ *ai* (high)
ओ *o* (toe)	औ *au* (loud)	ऌ* ḷa
क *ka* (skate)[1]	ख* *kha* (blockhead)[1]	ग *ga* (gate)[1]
घ *gha* (loghut)[1]	ङ *ṅa* (sing)[1]	
च *ca* (chunk)[2]	छ* *cha* (catch him)[2]	ज *ja* (john)[2]
झ *jha* (hedgehog)[2]	ञ *ña* (bunch)[2]	
ट *ṭa* (start)[3]	ठ* *ṭha* (anthill)[3]	ड *ḍa* (dart)[3]
ढ* *ḍha* (godhead)[3]	ण* *ṇa* (under)[3]	
त *ta* (path)[4]	थ *tha* (thunder)[4]	द *da* (that)[4]
ध* *dha* (breathe)[4]	न *na* (numb)[4]	
प *pa* (spin)[5]	फ* *pha* (loophole)[5]	ब *ba* (bin)[5]
भ *bha* (abhor)[5]	म *ma* (much)[5]	
य *ya* (young)	र *ra* (drama)	ल *la* (luck)
ळ* ḷa	व *va* (vile)	
श *śa* (shove)	ष *ṣa* (bushel)	
स *sa* (so)	ह *ha* (hum)	
क्ष *kṣa* (kṣatriya)	त्र *tra* (trishūl)	ज्ञ *jña* (jñāni)

अं (˙) *ṁ* (*saṁskṛti*) *ṁ anusvāra* (nasalisation of preceding vowel)

अः *ḥ* (*prātaḥ*) *ḥ visarga* (aspiration of preceding vowel)

* No exact English equivalents for these letters.

[1] guttural [2] palatal [3] lingual [4] dental [5] labial

List of Photographs

List of Plates

Pl. XV : Proto-Oriya Script : Inscriptions of the later Somavaṁśīs, the Telugu-Coḍas, the Bhañjas, the Imperial Gaṅgas, etc. (eleventh-fourteenth centuries AD).

Pl. XVI : Proto-Oriya Script : Inscriptions (stone) of the time of the Imperial Gaṅgas (twelfth-fifteenth centuries AD).

Pl. XVII : Early and Modern Oriya Script : Inscriptions of the Sūryavaṁśī Gajapatis, the Ministerial Dynasties and others (fifteenth-seventeenth centuries AD).

1

Introduction

I

PALAEOGRAPHY of Orissa cannot be studied in isolation. The subject is better understood in the broader context of Indian palaeography. Of course, in view of the diversity and multifaceted cultural milieu of Indian civilization, the subject offers an intricate and complex problem. But diversity of scripts in India is only a later development. Whereas all the regional scripts used today, as has been popularly believed, are evolved out of an originally homogeneous script, i.e., the Brāhmī script. The script was more popularly used in a greater part of India under the Mauryas (third century BC) and is now acknowledged as the parent of all the regional scripts of India. The scriptal transformations took place in several successive stages through the centuries. Even if the stages are well-defined they are not applicable uniformly throughout the sub-continent. Individual or local mannerisms very often distinguished a particular script from the other leading to palaeographical ramification and zonalization. Among the mannerisms include application of different types of headmarks, addition of tails, cursiveness or angularity of the letter-forms, ornamental or simplified engravings, etc. Moreover, the geo-physical and political forces often led to the flow of writing traditions from one region to the other and displacement of a particular writing style by another. The same process further occasionally promoted isolationistic tendencies and determined the perpetuation of its existing mannerisms for quite sometime. This is particularly true at least up to the advent of the proto-regional scripts. But subsequently the proto-regional and regional scripts took shape consequent upon the emergence of powerful regional polities in different linguistic segments and thereby established the relationship between language medium and script. The evolution of the regional script of Orissa largely confirms to this process.

II

Orissa was never a homogeneous unit at any point of her past history. It was inhabited by the peoples of Kaliṅga, Oḍra, Toṣali, Koṅgoda, Kośala, Trikaliṅga, Utkala, etc. They were the different geographical entities that existed at different periods of history. In the pre-Christian centuries the whole of the present Orissa and a part of territories in the north up to the river Ganga and another in the south up to the Godavari was known as Kaliṅga with its nuclear area comprising of the Puri and Ganjam districts. The antiquities belonging to Aśoka (third century BC) and Khāravela (first century BC) are found in this area. In the early centuries of Christian era the whole of Orissa was parcelled into smaller principalities, each ruled by a ruling dynasty.

Even if the political boundaries of these kingdoms and principalities fluctuated from time to time according to the power of the ruling dynasties, the topography of their centres and their spatial distributions remained almost unchanged from the fourth-fifth to eleventh-twelfth centuries. It was during this period, the Eastern Gaṅgas, the Bhaumakaras and the Somavaṁśīs respectively carved out independent sub-regional kingdoms like Kaliṅga, Toṣalī and South Kośala and established comparatively powerful polities. The "nuclear areas" of these sub-regional kingdoms mostly located in the river valleys that assured an economic base for the powers. Each of these sub-regional powers had a number of satellite principalities ruled by local chieftains in the tribal hinterland of their kingdom. One of the significant trends of the period is that these powers vied with each other in expanding their frontiers at the expense of other neighbouring kingdoms/principalities and in getting control of the "nuclear areas" of other "sub-regional kingdoms." This political process continued throughout the ninth-thirteenth centuries culminating in the formation of a regional state by Anaṅgabhīmadeva III (AD 1211-38) of the Gaṅga family. Along the process of regional state formation moved the process of socio-cultural and linguistic assimilation of the erstwhile sub-regional kingdoms imparting a sense of regional identity to its people.

Kaliṅga, the original homeland of Gaṅgas, had become their southern border region whereas the fertile Mahānadī delta arose as the natural centre of their empire. No doubt it could impart a regional identity to its people. But this had serious consequences because the history of Orissa of the subsequent centuries is characterized by competition for power among the Andhras and the Oriyas, internal treachery, dissensions, army over-powering the civil authority, etc., exposing the internal weakness of a loosely structured political system. Taking advantage of these weaknesses the external forces threatened the integrity of the empire from time to time and ultimately the Afghans were successful in sealing the fate of the independence of Orissa in AD 1568. Closely following the Afghans, the Moguls (1593-1751) and later on the Marathas (1751-1803) and the Britishers (1803-1947) invaded and subjugated Orissa.

Thus, in spite of the political and to some extent economic forces operating against the cohesiveness of the Oriyas at different points of history, the distinctive character of the Oriyas as a separate society having their own way of life, custom, language and religion has long been acknowledged. The advantageous geographical location of Orissa largely contributed her for maintaining this distinctive character. Situated between the impassable Vindhyas in the west and the Bay of Bengal in the east, it was the gateway between the Uttarāpatha and Dakṣiṇāpatha. The culture-currents of the north not only infiltrated into it but traditions from the south made their flow to this region in reverse direction. This landscape was, therefore, a meeting ground of diverse traditions from the north and the south. The intermediary geographical location of Orissa helped her assimilating and absorbing most essential elements of society and culture within its fabric and thereby creating a milieu that was quite novel and original.

III

Palaeographical research on Orissa can be traced back to time of James Prinsep. Credit goes to this learned man who by his ingenious scholarship for the first time could succeed in deciphering the Brāhmī alphabet. He had successfully deciphered the script without the help of any bilingual or biscriptal inscription and had established that the script was written from left to right like the other modern Indian scripts. As the script was written from left to right, Prinsep inclined to believe that the Brāhmī script originated from the Greek.

The inscriptions in the Khandagiri and Udayagiri caves were noticed in 1820 but not until 1837 they had been successfully deciphered.[1] In this year Prinsep took up the study of the inscriptions and published his readings along with the facsimiles prepared by Kittoe in the *Journal of the Asiatic Society*, Bengal under the title "Notes on the inscriptions at Udayagiri and Khandagiri in Cuttack in Lat characters."[2] Next year he examined Kittoe's lithograph of the Dhauli cave inscription of the time of Aśoka and published it in the same journal.[3]

By this time a large number of inscriptions had been discovered and the Asiatic Society of Bengal was taking onerous responsibility of publishing them in its journal. But until Prinsep took up the task of decipherment of Brāhmī inscriptions, epigraphical studies were restricted to decipherable records only. Again, to him credit goes for preparing a palaeographical chart under the title "Modification of the Sanskrit Alphabet from 543 BC to AD 1200." To this chart he added a note saying:

> The table furnishes a curious species of palaeographical chronometer, by which an ancient monument may be assigned with considerable accuracy to the period to which it was written, even though it possesses no actual date.[4]

The copies of another important inscription at Jaugada of the time of Aśoka were taken in 1850 by Sir Walter Elliot and subsequently the first purely mechanical estampages of the rock were prepared by Burgess. Kern and Senart edited the Jaugada edicts but the improved reading along with the photolithographs were published by Bühler in the *Archaeological Survey of South India*.[5] At this stage the epigraphic-palaeographic research on India was at its infancy and most of the scholars held the rudimentary conception that the letter-forms were ends in themselves.

In 1872 a new non-official journal called the *Indian Antiquary* started publishing under the editorship of James Burgess. The journal was started with an object of supplementing the existing

1. A. Sterling was first to notice the inscription in the Hāthīgumphā of Udayagiri hill and in 1820 he requested Col. Mackenzie to prepare a lithograph of the inscription. The lithograph facsimile was published by Sterling in the *Asiatic Researches*, 15, 313ff.
2. *Journal of the Asiatic Society of Bengal (JASB)*, 6 (1837), 1072-91, pl. 58.
3. *Ibid.*, 7 (1838), 436 ff.
4. *Essays on Indian Antiquities*, ed. E. Thomas, London, 1858, 39.
5. *Archaeological Survey of South India*, I, 144.

Journal of the Asiatic Society of Bengal which gave fresh stimulus to the epigraphic-palaeographic study. In the very first volume of the *Journal*, John Beams edited the Balasore copper axe-head grant of Gajapati king Puruṣottamadeva written in Oriya language and script.[6] When A.C. Burnell wrote his *Elements of South Indian Palaeography*, he was immensely benefited by studying the already published inscriptions in the existing journals. He preferred to include the Jaugada edicts of Aśoka for his south Indian palaeographical enquiries.[7] His scheme of dividing the characters of the epigraphic records Kaliṅga into western and eastern branches along the two dynasties of the Cāḷukyas is confusing.[8] According to him:

> The Nandināgarī (South Indian Nāgarī) is directly derived from the N. Indian Devanāgarī of about the eleventh century, but it is from the type that prevailed at Benares and in the west, and not from the Gauḍī or Bengal.[9]

He further opined that a few inscriptions of the Gaṅgas of Kaliṅganagar belonging to the tenth century were written in a variety of south Indian Nāgarī script and the origin of the Oriya alphabet should be traced to that source.[10]

Sir Alexander Cunningham systematically arranged all the edicts of Aśoka and brought out the first volume of his *Corpus Inscriptionum Indicarum* in 1877.[11] In the same volume he made a further improvement on the reading of the Hāthīgumphā inscription by James Prinsep. But the zinco-photographs of the inscriptions appended to the volume are quite defective and unreliable. In part II of the volume Cunningham studied the alphabetic characters of the Aśokan edicts in general. He made a comparison of the different symbols with the different members of human frame and maintained the theory of pictorial origin of the old Indian alphabet.[12] Later on E. Hultzsch published a revised edition of his corpus in 1925, in which all Aśokan records discovered till then were ably edited.[13]

Another contemporary Indologist, R.L. Mitra published *The Antiquities of Orissa* in two volumes in 1875 and 1880 respectively. In the second volume he noticed the inscriptions on the jambs of the doorway leading to the Audience Chamber of the Jagannāth temple at Puri and appended the translations of the legible records. He remarked:

6. *Indian Antiquary (IA)*, 1 (1872), 355.
7. A.C. Burnell, *Elements of South Indian Palaeography (from the 4th to the 14th century* AD), 2nd edn., London, 1878; Indian edition, Delhi, 1968, 11.
8. *Ibid.*, 23.
9. *Ibid.*, 52-53.
10. *Ibid.*, 53.
11. A. Cunningham, *Corpus Inscriptionum Indicarum* (CII), I, *Inscriptions of Aśoka*, London, 1877; Indian edn., Vanarasi, 1961, 15-20, 65-81, 88-93, pls. VIII-XIII (for Dhauli and Jaugada edicts).
12. *Ibid.*, 49-63.
13. E. Hultzsch, *CII*, I, *Inscriptions of Aśoka*, Varanasi, 1969.

> These are in the Uriya language and character, written in most corrupt orthography and syntax, and so faulty in construction that ordinarily-educated Uriyas can scarcely make out their meaning.[14]

Later on in 1893 M.M. Chakravarti edited all these inscriptions along with the inscriptions of the Liṅgarāja temple at Bhubaneswar without estampages in *Journal of the Asiatic Society of Bengal*.[15]

Following Cunningham, J.F. Fleet produced the third volume of the *Corpus Inscriptionum Indicarum* in 1888 where he incorporated all the known inscriptions of the Guptas and their contemporaries. Fleet took care of editing some of the inscriptions of the Śarabhapurīyas and Pāṇḍuvaṁśīs of South Kośala.[16] He was the first scholar to propound geographical designations for the scripts — the northern and the southern. While editing the copper-plate inscriptions of the above ruling families he writes, "The characters belong to the southern class of alphabets; and give another specimen of box-headed variety of the Central Indian alphabet."[17] It was during this time Rudolf Hoernle[18] argued for two separate varieties (a western and an eastern) in the Fleet's "northern characters" and along with Fleet paved the way for the study of the regional scripts in north India. Fleet and Hoernle were the two earliest authorities to define the palaeographical terminologies and to explain the regional differences with the help of test letters.

In 1886, E. Hultzsch became the Government Epigraphist. Since then he took a regular survey of the Madras presidency and collected a number of inscriptions. Between 1887 and 1903, he published a few volumes in order of their collection in the series *South Indian Inscriptions.* In volume V (1926) and VI (1928) of this series some hundreds of inscriptions of the Imperial Gaṅgas and the Sūryavaṁśī Gajapatis found from the temples of Mukhalingam, Srikurmam and Simhancalam had been incorporated.[19] But the volumes remained practically inaccessible to scholars who were not conversant with the south Indian languages. However, about 40 Oriya inscriptions published in these volumes were in the Devanāgarī script. But they are less significant for palaeographical study.

Although the *Indian Antiquary* was maintaining its popularity and serving the cause of Indian epigraphy, the need was felt to start an official journal solely devoted to the publication of inscriptional records. So in 1892, another quarterly journal called the *Epigraphia Indica* was started publishing under the editorship of James Burgess. In these volumes every inscription

---

14. R.L. Mitra, *The Antiquities of Orissa*, II, Calcutta, 1880, 120.
15. *JASB*, 62 (1893), 88-104.
16. J.F. Fleet, *CII*, III, *Inscriptions of Early Gupta kings and their Successors*, rev edn., Calcutta, 1971, Nos. 40, 41, 81.
17. *Ibid.*, 192, 196 & 291.
18. *JASB*, 1891, pt. I, 82.
19. Some of these inscriptions were also listed in V. Rangacharya, *Inscriptions from the Madras Presidency*, 3 vols., Madras, 1919, 666-710, 1674-90.

edited had some introductory paragraphs dealing with its characters, languages and orthography which later on served the cause of Indian palaeography. Regular contributions of prominent scholars like Fleet, Hultzsch, Kielhorn and others on some important epigraphical records of Orissa to these volumes sufficiently enriched the knowledge about this region.

Gaurisankar Hiralal Ojha made a pioneering effort of writing a comprehensive book called *Bhāratīya Prācīna Lipimālā* (*The Palaeography of India*) in Hindi in the year 1894. Judging from the mature and utilitarian stage that Brāhmī had attained, Ojha was not in favour of ascribing its origin to any external source or influence.[20] He suggested the continuation of the script without any significant change roughly from 500 BC to AD 350 whereafter two separate streams of writing (a northern and a southern) diverged from its main source. The northern stream was classified into the Gupta, the *Kuṭila,* the Nāgarī, the Śāradā and the Bengali scripts while the southern stream into the western, the Central Provincial, the Telugu-Kannaḍa, the Grantha, the Kaliṅga and the Tamil scripts.[21] Ojha believed that the Oriya script was derived from the Bengali which itself began to diverge from the Nāgarī in about AD 1000.[22] According to him the Kaliṅga script was used in the copper-plate grants of the Eastern Gaṅgas from the seventh to the eleventh centuries. Although initially the script resembled to the square-headed (also known as box-headed) characters of the Central Provinces, later on a peculiar variety in which the Nāgarī, the Telugu-Canarese and the Grantha characters were mixed together. Ojha's book was revised and enlarged in 1918.[23]

J.G. Bühler wrote a book on the origin of the Brāhmī script (1895) and argued in favour of its Semitic origin.[24] In the next year he published his *magnum opus Indische Palaeographie* in German, the English translation of which was made by Fleet and published as an appendix to the *Indian Antiquary*, vol. XXXIII, 1904. Bühler was a first rate authority on all questions of palaeography and his work remained to this day as the standard work on the subject. In the writings of the Aśokan edicts, he distinguished at least two local varieties, the northern and the southern and talked of a third one, the Drāviḍī (Bhaṭṭiprolu) script. About the Dhauli and Jaugada edicts, he writes:

> The southern variety is most strongly expressed in the Girnar and Siddhapura edicts, less clearly in the Dhauli and Jaugada edicts, by differences in signs for *A, Ā, kha, ja, ma, ra, sa,* the medial *i* and the ligatures with *ra*.[25]

---

20. G.H. Ojha, *Bhāratīya Prācīna Lipimālā* (*BPL*), 3rd edn., Delhi, 1959, 30.
21. *Ibid.*, 42-44.
22. *Ibid.*, 43.
23. *Ibid.*, 44.
24. J.G. Bühler, *On the Origin of the Indian Brāhma Alphabet*, 3rd edn., Vanarasi, 1963, 4.
25. Bühler, *Indian Palaeography* (*IP*), Calcutta, 1959, 60.

On the basis of the broadening of the lower parts of some of the letters, thickening of the top of the upper verticals and of the use of the so-called serif, he grouped the inscriptions of Khāravela and his descendants under the old Kaliṅga script.[26] From the middle of the fourth century AD, he classified the northern script into the Gupta alphabet of the fourth-fifth centuries (having two sub-divisions, eastern and western), the Acute-angled or *Siddhamātṛkā* (Fleet's *Kuṭila*), the Nāgarī, the Śāradā, the proto-Bengali, the hooked alphabet of Nepal and the arrow-head type (*Bhaikṣukī lipi* of Al-beruni). He attributed the origin of cursive forms of the northern alphabets to the Aśokan edict VI of Dhauli, edicts of Kalsi and the Jaina votive inscriptions of the Kuṣāṇa period.[27] The southern alphabets have been classified into western, central Indian (box-headed), Telugu-Canarese, later Kaliṅga (north-eastern coast of former Madras Presidency between Chicacole and Ganjam), Grantha and Tamil. Like Ojha, Bühler too opined that in the Later Kaliṅga script of the Eastern Gaṅgas of the seventh-twelfth centuries, the Nāgarī, the Telugu-Canarese and the Grantha characters were mixed together.[28]

Bühler went a step further and explained:

> The Kingdom of the Gaṅgas of Kaliṅga lay between the districts in which the Nāgarī and the Kanarese-Telugu scripts were used, and it was not far from the territory of Grantha. Its population was probably mixed, and used all these scripts, as well as in earlier times, those employed in the older western and central-Indian inscriptions. The professional clerks and writers of course had to master all the alphabets.[29]

Kielhorn attributed the mixed style of Kaliṅga to "the variety of royal scribes, who wished to show that they were acquainted with a number of alphabets."

Bühler was one of the earliest authorities to use certain palaeographical terminologies like wedges, *serifs*, block-heads, arrow-heads, hooks, cursive or angular forms, horn-like protuberances, etc., some of which were taken as standard terms by the later palaeographers in explaining the scriptal development and ramification. Besides, the palaeographical charts appended to the volume served as the most dependable index for the younger generation of epigraphists not only to decipher the newly discovered records but also to deduce their relative chronology. The numerical charts furnished by Ojha and Bühler have not been superseded and supplemented so far. The monograph of S.L. Gokhale is only a compilation of the works of the two earlier palaeographers.[30]

Since the nineteenth century palaeographers recognized that palaeography supplied a clue to ascertaining the relative chronology of the undated articles, need was felt for accurate copying

26. Bühler, *Indian Palaeography* (*IP*), Calcutta, 1959, 68.
27. *Ibid.*, 74-77.
28. *Ibid.*, 98.
29. *Ibid.*, 108-09.
30. S.L. Gokhale, *Indian Numerals*, Poona, 1966.

of the letter-forms from the facsimiles and estampages of the epigraphs from the original. Bühler's greatest contribution lies in the accurate reproduction of the letters from the original facsimiles, estampages and cuttings. But one thing that misled the nineteenth century palaeographers is that they looked to the forms of the letters as ends in themselves. Even Bühler who made a scientific approach to the subject failed to perceive the relationship between the wedges, *serifs*, hooks, heads, etc., with the actual form of the letters.

From 1910 onwards a great controversy raged among the scholars like Fleet, Bhagawanlal Indraji, R.D. Banerji, K.P. Jayaswal and B.M. Barua on the date, content and palaeography of the Hāthīgumphā inscription of Khāravela. This was culminated in the publication of a book called *Old Brahmi Inscriptions in the Udayagiri and Khandagiri Caves* by B.M. Barua. The book contains a note on "The Letter Forms" of the cave inscriptions where Barua observed that the occurrence of the different types of Brāhmī alphabet in the Hāthīgumphā inscription was due to the employment of different scribes representing different localities.[31]

Until R.D. Banerji brought out his book *The Origin of the Bengali Script* (1919), the study of the regional scripts of India was in a desideratum. He traced the evolution of the Bengali script from the fourth century BC to the fifteenth century AD. He divided the Mauryan alphabet into Older and Younger. According to him, "The edicts of Dhauli and Jaugada though relegated to the southern variety of the Older Mauryan alphabets, stand in an intermediate position."[32] Further, he included the inscriptions of Khāravela in the Younger Mauryan alphabet.[33] Following Hoernle, Banerji divided the northern alphabet into two varieties, eastern and western, and held that after the sixth century the eastern variety of the northern alphabet was used in Bengal. Two dated inscriptions of Orissa — (a) Patiakella plate of Śivarāja of GE 283 (AD 602) and (b) Ganjam grant of Śaśāṅka of GE 300 (AD 619) — have been grouped under this variety.[34] Moreover, he maintained that the modern Oriya script developed out of the Bengali after the fourteenth century.[35] Since this observation of Banerji was not substantiated by adequate discussion and illustration, a fresh controversy began to take the field.

Sir Hugh McPherson in a short article entitled "The Oriya Alphabet," remarked:

> The Oriyas following their neighbouring nation the Telugus, Tamils, etc., developed in a peculiar formation their provincial 'Kuṭila' characters. As the palmleaves were the only writing materials in ancient Orissa as in other parts of the sea-coast provinces of southern India, an iron stylus (called stilus) was employed for scratching in the characters, and this gave rise to the rounded shape of the Oriya characters which originally sprung from the Kuṭila characters.[36]

31. B.M. Barua, *Old Brāhmī Inscriptions in the Udayagiri and Khandagiri Caves*, Calcutta, 1929, 145-53.
32. R.D. Banerji, *The Origin of the Bengali Script*, Calcutta, 1919, 11.
33. *Ibid.*, 12.
34. *Ibid.*, 37.
35. *Ibid.*, 6.
36. Sir Hugh McPherson, "The Alphabet," *JBORS*, 10, pt. 1-2 (1924), 168-70.

A few years later, Grierson observed:

> The Maithili and Bengali alphabets are directly derived from Bühler's proto-Bengali. The Oriya alphabet, on the contrary, derived from Nāgarī, and probably reached Orissa directly from the west. It is differentiated from the ordinary Nāgarī type by its use of curved lines instead of horizontal strokes. This is due to the old custom of writing on strips of the leaf of the talipot palm instead of paper. The characters are scratched upon this with an iron stylus, the writing being along the line of the fibres of leaf. In such writing horizontal straight lines must be avoided, as such would infallibly tend to to cause the leaf to split.[37]

Compared to McPherson, Grierson's observations were based on his critical analysis of Indo-Āryan languages and northern scripts. Subsequently when P.L. Paul (1936) [38] and S.N. Chakravarti (1938) [39] wrote about the development of Bengali script, they did not mention anything about the Bengali parentage of the early Oriya script.

Pandit Binayak Mishra was one of the early Oriya scholars who evinced some interest in the study of epigraphy. In 1933 he prepared a dynastic list of inscriptions of Orissa of the seventh-eleventh centuries under the title *Dynasties of Medieval Orissa*.[40] In the very next year, he published another monograph, *Orissa under the Bhauma Kings*.[41] In this book the author edited 14 inscriptions of the Bhaumakara dynasty and appended facsimiles of a few of them. But the books are of little interest from palaeographical point of view.

The publication of the *Indian Antiquary* was discontinued in 1934. But the *Epigraphia Indica* still maintained its high standard of scholarship before the young epigraphists. A number of epigraphists evinced tremendous interest in editing and interpreting the inscriptions discovered in this part of the sub-continent. Mention must be made of a few of them, viz., Hiralal, R.D. Banerji, B.C. Mazumdar, Y.R. Gupte, T.C. Rath, R.C. Mazumdar, B.C. Chhabra, V.V. Mirashi, N.P. Chakravarti, L.P. Pandeya, N.G. Mazumdar, R.K. Ghosal, D.C. Sircar, K.C. Panigrahi, P. Acharya and others. The palaeographical notes given in the introductory paragraphs are invaluable additions to the existing knowledge on the subject. While classifying the characters of the inscriptions under different scripts, the learned editors followed Bühler's work as the basis. Apart from the *Epigraphia Indica* other learned journals like the *Journal of Bihar and Orissa Research Society* (1915), the *Indian Historical Quarterly* (1925) and the *Journal of Andhra Historical Research Society* (1926) started publishing from Patna, Calcutta (Kolkata) and Rajahmundry respectively. In the volumes of these journals the inscriptions of Orissa were edited and re-edited from time to time by the scholars like H.P. Shastri, Binayak Mishra, H. Pandey, N. Tripathy,

37. Grierson, "On the Modern Indo-Aryan Vernaculars," *IA*, 1932, 134.

38. P.L. Paul, "The Development of the Bengali Script," *IHQ*, 12 (1936), 309-34.

39. S.N. Chakravarti, The Development of the Bengali Alphabet from the fifth century AD to the End of the Muhammadan Rule, *JRASB, Letters*, 4 (1938), 351-91.

40. B. Mishra, *Dynasties of Medieval Orissa*, Calcutta, 1933.

41. *Orissa Under the Bhauma Kings* (*OUBK*), Calcutta, 1934.

A. Banerji, G. Ramdas, L.N.H. Jagadeb, C.N. Rao, R. Subba Rao, G.V. Sitapati and others. In the second quarter of the twentieth century there was a growing interest among the Oriya scholars to unfold the history, culture and archaeology of Orissa. But there was not a single indological/historical journal in English in Orissa to cater to their needs. A few Journals such as *Prachi* (1931), The *Journal of the Orissa Academy* (1939) and the *Journal of the Kalinga Historical Research Society* (1946) published respectively from Cuttack and Bolangir could not survive for long, and were discontinued after the publication of a few volumes. But some of the important inscriptions of Orissa were published in these volumes. The *Orissa Historical Research Journal* with its beginning in 1952 incorporated varied articles on history, culture and archaeology of Orissa. Newly discovered copper-plates and stone inscriptions of Orissa were edited from time to time in the volumes of this journal. In the early volumes of this journal, a majority of the inscriptions were edited by S.N. Rajaguru and a few by K.C. Panigrahi, B.V. Nath, K.B. Tripathi, S.C. De, P. Acharya, S.N. Das, and others. Except for a few, most of the scholars editing epigraphs in these journals could not maintain the standard set by the *Epigraphia Indica*. In spite of improper and uncritical editing they had a yeoman's contribution to the study of Orissan epigraphy by bringing back to light the vast mass of inscriptional literature of Orissa which otherwise could have gone into oblivion. Again in spite of the richness of epigraphical material for the study of the palaeography of Orissa, no sincere effort was made by the scholars in that direction.

R.B. Pandey's *Indian Palaeography* (1952) deals more with epigraphy than palaeography.[42] In *The Alphabet* (1953), Dravid Diringer largely followed the scheme prepared by Bühler and incorporated some of his observations on the evolution of the regional scripts. He preferred to subscribe to the view that the Oriyas developed their written characters from the proto-Bengali source.[43] Sometime after the same view was held by Hans Jensen (1970).[44]

The advanced palaeography of the Buguda and Puri plates of the Śailodbhava king Mādhavavarman had aroused some problem to settle the genealogy and chronology of the family. The difference in the palaeography of the Ganjam and Khurda plates on the one hand and the Buguda and Puri plates as well as the characters issued by the son and grandson of the issuer of the Buguda and Puri records on the other led Hultzsch and Kielhorn to suggest that the issuer of the first group was a remote ancestor of that of the second.[45] Later on R.G. Basak[46] and R.C. Mazumdar[47] offered their own solutions to the problem. The publication of the Orissa Museum plates of Mādhavavarman, the introductory part of which resembled to the second

42. R.B. Pandey, *Indian Palaeography*, pt. I, Benares, 1952.
43. D. Diringer, *The Alphabet*, London, 1953, 267.
44. H. Jensen, *Sign, Symbol & Script*, London, 1970, 379-81.
45. *EI*, 6, 144; *ibid.*, 7, 102.
46. *Ibid.*, 23, 126-27.
47. *JAHRS*, 10, 1-15.

group of records and the characters to the first group, quite satisfactorily answered the palaeographical objection to the identification of the issuer of the Ganjam and Khurda plates with that of the Buguda and Puri plates. D.C. Sircar in his article Palaeography of the Śailodbhava Grants published in *OHRJ* (1954) established this identification. While examining the characters of the records of Dharmarāja, he pointed out that the Nivina and Banapura plates of the king were written in a script similar to the Ganjam, Khurda and Orissa Museum plates and the rest of the plates similar to the Buguda and Puri plates of Mādhavavarman. According to Sircar:

> . . . in the seventh-eighth centuries, the normal East Indian alphabet and a modified form of the Northern Alphabet were both prevalent side by side in the southern parts of Orissa.[48]

Subsequently when S.C. Behera (1982) prepared a book on the history of this dynasty he devoted a chapter on "Palaeography and Language in Śailodbhava Charters." Although he was one with Hultzsch in stating that the characters belonged the "acute-angled type with nail heads which formed the transition from Gupta to Nāgari," he tried to prove that they were "a development of the Māṭhara script with usual Gupta influence."[49]

K.B. Tripathi studied the palaeography of the early Oriya inscriptions and published his findings in three instalments in the subsequent volumes of *OHRJ* (1955-60).[50] As his main purpose was to study the script of the early Oriya inscriptions (AD 1051-1568), his treatment of the characters of the inscriptions of Orissa before the middle of the eleventh century was synoptic. He classified the scripts of Orissa into the Brāhmī, the Gupta, the acute-angled, the proto-Bengali, the early Oriya and the modern Oriya scripts. He observed that the acute-angled script (seventh-tenth centuries) as prevalent in the eastern parts of north India progressed and by the end of the tenth century assumed distinct features leading up to the modern Bengali and, therefore, the script can be called as the proto-Bengali. This proto-Bengali characters were prevalent in the charters of the Somavaṁśīs, the Imperial Gaṅgas and other contemporary ruling families. He traced the evolution of the early Oriya script to three sources, like the proto-Bengali, the Nāgarī and the Later Kaliṅga script. According to him, "the Oriya script is more akin to the proto-Bengali than to the modern Bengali. It has preserved many proto-Bengali forms which Bengali has discarded."[51] He examined the formation of individual letter-forms (vowels and consonants) as well as the medial vowels and ligatures. All these findings of Tripathi have been incorporated in his *The Evolution of Oriya Language and Script* (1962).[52] The twelve palaeographical charts appended to this book are illustrative of the evolution of the early Oriya script. Thus, Tripathi

---

48. D.C. Sircar, Palaeography of the Śailodbhava Grants, *OHRJ*, 3 (I), 33.
49. S.C. Behera, *Rise and Fall of the Śailodbhavas*, Calcutta, 1982, 146-54.
50. K.B. Tripathi, "The Palaeography of the Early Oriya Inscriptions," *OHRJ*, 4 (1-2), 11-27; 5 (3-4), 144-55; 8 (3-4), 187-93.
51. K.B. Tripathi, "The Palaeography of the Early Oriya Inscriptions, 4 (1-2), 18.
52. *The Evolution of Oriya Language and Script* (*EOLS*), Cuttack, 1962, Ch. 4A-4D, 36-81.

made a laudable effort and his work has not been superseded to this day. In 1960, S.N. Rajaguru made a preliminary study of the Oriya script in his book *Oḍiā Lipira Kramavikāśa* (*The Evolution of the Oriya Script*) in Oriya. Although the book is of elementary nature, yet the broad framework in which he traced the evolution of the Oriya script is instructive. The various stages through which the script evolved has been given like this: Mauryan Brāhmī (300 BC), Later Brāhmī (100 BC-AD 300), Gupta (AD 300-700), Medieval Kaliṅga (AD 600-1100), Box-headed (AD 400-800), and Modern Oriya (AD 1400 onwards) scripts. Rajaguru believed that the modern Oriya script was evolved out of the proto-Oriya which was already there in the ninth century.[53]

An improved version of his work also appeared in instalments in the Oriya journal *Koṇārka*.[54] Between 1958 and 1976, Rajaguru published all the inscriptions of Orissa (except the Bhaumakaras and their feudatories) in five volumes.[55] The sixth volume of the series containing the inscriptions of the Bhañjas was edited by S. Tripathy in 1974.[56] From palaeographical point of view they are of little interest.

The earlier supposition that there existed regional varieties in the Mauryan Brāhmī was strongly refuted by C.S. Upasak in his *History and Palaeography of the Mauryan Brāhmī Script* (1960). According to him:

> A conscientious study of the formation of each letter has shown that no regional variety as such can be found in the Aśokan inscriptions. The difference that we notice is mainly due to the individual stylistic characteristic either in engraving or in writing the draft which was copied by the engraver. Regional forms of writing cannot be traced, since there exist fundamental varieties in the inscriptions of the same area, even sometimes in the same inscriptions.[57]

A.H. Dani brought the study of Indian Palaeography (1963) to a scientific footing and made a comprehensive analysis of the subject up to the eighth century AD. The twenty-three plates in which he illustrated the characters of different varieties of scripts are quite, exhaustive. Dani made a significant departure, both at the conceptual and analytical level, from the earlier palaeographers. To him "the letter-forms are a part of culture and palaeography defines them within that culture."[58]

Dani supplemented the theory of Upasak that no regional variety did exist in the Aśokan Brāhmī.[59] He included the Hāthīgumphā inscription of Khāravela in the Provincial Brāhmī

53. S.N. Rajaguru, *Oḍiā Lipira Kramavikāśa* (in Oriya), Bhubaneswar, 1960, 16-26.
54. "Oḍiā Lipi," *Koṇārka* (Oriya), Journal of the Orissa Sahitya Academy, Bhubaneswar, 4 (3), 1969, 43-60.
55. S.N. Rajaguru, *Inscriptions of Orissa*, I (2)-5, Berhampur and Bhubaneswar, 1958-76.
56. S. Tripathy, *Inscriptions of Orissa*, 6, Bhubhaneswar, 1974.
57. C.S. Upasak, *History and Palaeography of the Mauryan Brāhmī Script*, Nalanda, 1960, 29-30.
58. A.H. Dani, *Indian Palaeography* (*IP*), 2nd edn., Delhi, 1986, xix.
59. *Ibid.*, 35.

script used in eastern India.[60] The script used in the inscriptions of the Māṭharas, the Śarabhapurīyas and the Eastern Gaṅgas to the end of the seventh century have been grouped under proto-regional Deccani style, whereas the script used in the inscriptions of Eastern Gaṅgas after the seventh century have been classified under the proto-regional Andhra style.[61] Thus localization of the writing styles and their affiliation to various cultural regions was the guiding principle of Dani for the study of the Indian palaeography. For that reason he discarded the earlier terminologies like acute-angled, box-headed, arrow-headed, etc. The line of argument initiated by Dani that the differences in the selection of the writing tool and the technique often changed the face of the letters was later on examined by T.P. Verma while studying the *Palaeography of Brāhmī Script in North India* (1971). As regards the palaeographical peculiarities of the Hāthīguṁphā inscription, he explained that "Orissa was less informed of the new developments (the 'new-pen style') and kept adhering with the older forms for sometime."[62]

In his article "Indian Epigraphy and Palaeography" published in the *Journal of Ancient Indian History* (1970-71), D.C. Sircar preferred to substitute the term Gauḍī for Bühler's proto-Bengali on the authority of Al-beruni and held that "Gauḍī, i.e., the East Indian derivative of the Siddhamātṛikā alphabet, was used in Bengal, Bihar, Nepal, Assam and Orissa between the 10th and 14th centuries."[63] He further believed that the Oriya alphabet was a derivative of the Gauḍī and its development was complete in the records of about the fourteenth century.[64] Sircar held this opinion even while editing a number of copper-plates and stone inscriptions of the Imperial Gaṅgas of twelfth-fourteenth centuries in the *Epigraphia Indica* volumes 28-33.

In a separate chapter in her book *Early Stone Temples of Orissa* (1979) Vidya Dehejia made a scholarly excercise on the evolution of the scripts of Orissa up to the tenth century AD. By giving comparative palaeographical charts of the inscriptions of the Śailodbhavas, the Bhaumakaras, the Bhañjas and also some of the temple inscriptions of the period, she justified her claim that such an exercise on the subject had not been undertaken before. Dehejia apprehended the danger of fixing dates on the basis of palaeography. But she was hopeful of deducing relative chronology of the undated records based on the evolution of the scripts.[65] In his book *Khāravela* (1984), N.K. Sahu devoted a separate chapter on palaeography of the Hāthīguṁphā inscription.[66] But the descriptions made on the abstract shapes of the vowel and consonant signs of the inscription are of elementary nature.

---

60. A.H. Dani, *Indian Palaeography (IP)*, 2nd edn., Delhi, 1986, 57-59.
61. *Ibid.*, 176-91.
62. T.P. Verma, *Palaeography of Brāhmī Script in North India*, Varanasi, 1971, 90.
63. D.C. Sircar, "Introduction to Indian Epigraphy and Palaeography," *JAIH*, 4 (1-2), 1970-71, 120.
64. *Ibid.*, 122.
65. V. Dehejia, *Early Stone Temples of Orissa*, Delhi 1979, 154-72.
66. N.K. Sahu, *Khāravela*, Bhubaneswar, 1984, 262-79.

In *Indian Epigraphy* (1984), K.V. Ramesh believed in "disciplined and sequential pattern" in which the Mauryan Brāhmī was transformed to different regional scripts. He emphasized that "comparative palaeography" as well as "urban and rural strains of palaeography" should be the major determinants for arriving at a relative chronology of the undated inscriptions.[67] He contested Dani's concept "development of writing as a part of the evolution of the culture" as an unhistorical assumption. On the other hand, he maintained that geo-physical and political factors created ideal conditions in which the regional languages and their respective scripts blossomed.[68] Following Sircar he too held that the Gauḍīya script was the forerunner of more than one regional script of eastern Indian and said,

> . . . taking a narrower view of the particular linguistic region of its provenance, the script could be dubbed as proto-Bengali which does not deny the fact of its being proto-Assamese or proto-Oriya or proto-Maithili.[69]

Thus, basically Ramesh tried to make certain changes at the conceptual level for the palaeographical studies in India.

Recently the ICHR has undertaken the ambitious programme of the publication of the inscription of India. In this series, the inscriptions of some of the ruling families of Orissa have already been published. The efforts of R. Subrahmanyam,[70] A.M. Shastri[71] and S. Tripathy[72] in this direction are praiseworthy.

IV

The richness of the epigraphical materials and the palaeographical features of the inscriptions of different kingdoms of ancient and medieval Orissa offer a good perspective for a systematic and comprehensive study of the palaeography of Orissa. The sustained efforts of a good number of scholars no doubt make the task easier, but the subject has not yet received the attention it deserves.

Our approach to the subject is completely different from the earlier works, in a sense that we have discarded the earlier conception of the independent value of palaeography. Palaeography has little independent value. It is a variable factor and dates assigned to the undated epigraphs on its sole evidence admit of wide divergence. It is precisely for this reason that the overemphasis of the old palaeographers on the letter-forms as supplying chronological

---

67. K.V. Ramesh, *Indian Epigraphy*, I, New Delhi, 1984, 51-62.
68. *Ibid.*, 71.
69. *Ibid.*, 75.
70. R. Subrahmanyam, *Inscriptions of the Sūryavaṁśī Gajapatis of Orissa* (*ISGO*), New Delhi, 1986.
71. A.M. Shastri, *Inscriptions of the Śarabhapurīyas, Pāṇḍavaṁśīns and Somavaṁśīns* (*ISPS*), 2 pts, New Delhi, 1995.
72. S. Tripathy, *Inscriptions of Orissa*, I (*Circa Fifth-Eighth centuries* AD), New Delhi, 1997.

clues for ascertaining infallible dates has been set aside. The letter-forms are not ends in themselves. The substance working on, the writing tool and the professionals representing different localities are some of the determining factors which largely governed the palaeographical changes in a given locality and at a particular point of time. But the different traits or distinguishing features of the writing style of a locality or kingdom largely depended on geo-physical and political forces.

Initially these forces led to the emergence of well-defined broad palaeographical zones with minimum variation in style and technique, but with the proliferation of kingdoms and with the insular character of some of these kingdoms, local mannerisms began to assume leading to further scriptal ramification and zonalization. The hypothesis that palaeographical segmentation ran parallel with linguistic segmentation has been fruitfully tested in the Orissan context. The vernacular played an important role in shaping the script of the region. Finally we have discarded the dynastic appellations as unconvincing and misleading, and instead preferred to subscribe to the stylistic nomenclatures as more acceptable and scientific.

2

Imperial Brāhmī Script in Orissa

HISTORICAL period in India starts from the third century BC. It is in this century that we come across the indisputably datable specimens of writing. The royal proclamations of Aśoka engraved on rocks, pillars and caves are the first set of historical records so far discovered in India. They are written in the local script. Those found in the Indus valley region are in the Kharoṣṭhī script; elsewhere in India they are in the Brāhmī script. Thus, the Brāhmī script travelled over an extensive area of the subcontinent. Imperial scribes were directed to carry the message to the far-flung areas and with them the writing tradition made a flow from the centre. The royal edicts thus engraved have a uniformity of purpose, language, content and character. Hence, the script is often termed "Imperial" or "Aśokan" Brāhmī.

By the time Aśoka employed the script, the Brāhmī was fully perfected and standardized. This seems that writing had a long history before Aśokan inscriptions. The problem of origin of the Brāhmī script has been hotly debated by the Indologists, in India and abroad. It is needless to delve into the problem, which itself requires a special treatment.

In Orissa two sets of Aśokan Rock Edicts have been discovered at Dhauli and Jaugada. Dhauli (ancient Toṣālī) is situated near Bhubaneswar in Puri district whereas Jaugada (ancient Somapā) is a ruined fort near Berhampur in Ganjam district of Orissa. A series of fourteen edicts are generally found at other places and they constitute the Rock Edicts of Aśoka. But at Dhauli and Jaugada the Rock Edicts XI, XII, and XIII have been omitted and they have been replaced by two special edicts. They are called Separate Rock Edict I and Separate Rock Edict II. Most probably the omission of Rock edicts is due to political expediency. Because Kaliṅga was a newly-conquered territory where people needed greater attention from the imperial court.

The Aśokan inscriptions at Dhauli are arranged in three parallel columns. The eleven Rock Edicts have been arranged in the whole of the middle column and one-half of the right column. The separate Edicts I and II are added, the former occupying the right-hand column and the latter filling the whole of the left-hand column.

The Jaugada inscriptions are written on three different tablets on the vertical face of the rock. The first tablet contains, the first five edicts; the second the next five edicts to which is added the XIV or closing one of the fourteen Rock Edicts; the third contains duplicates of the two separate edicts engraved at Dhauli.

Standard Aśokan Brāhmī script (*fig.* I) diffused to various parts of the country exhibits a homogeneous character. This homogeneity was due to the uniform political system of the Mauryas throughout their empire. The Mauryan rulers had devised a highly centralized administrative system in which the officers or bureaucrats were functioning according to the directions from the centre. As such the centre had full control over the provincial administration. The royal proclamations were also written by the imperial scribes at the direction of the emperor and therefore they exhibit uniformity of purpose, content, language and script. Minor variations

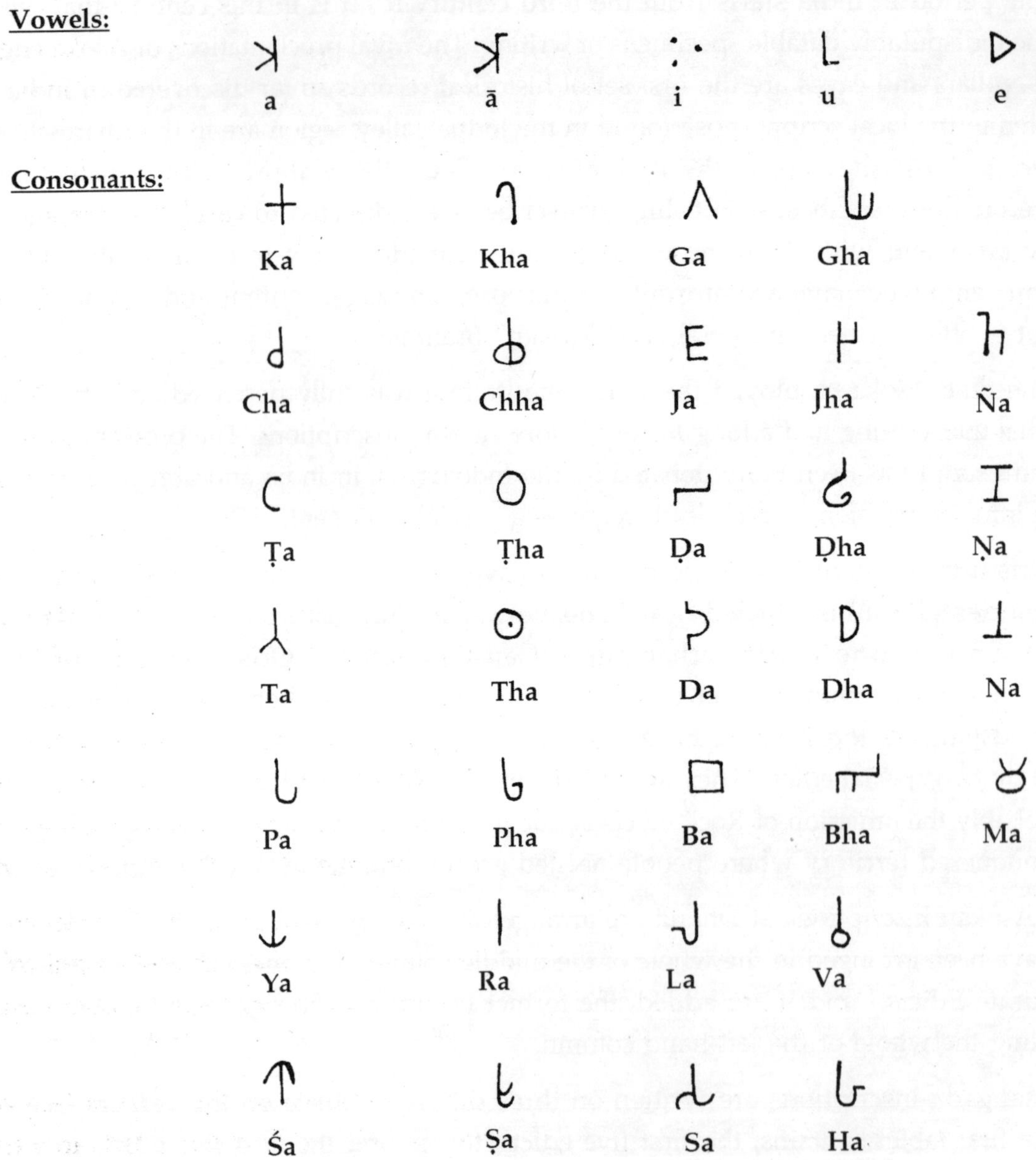

***fig.* I: Standard Aśokan Brāhmī**

though cannot be ruled out, they agree in their essential characters. On the strength of this peculiarity of letter-forms, scholars tempt to advocate the existence of regional varieties. By the close of the nineteenth century, Bühler noticed the northern and southern varieties of Aśokan Brāhmī alphabet. He classified the Dhauli and Jaugada edicts under the southern variety. According to Bühler,

> The Southern variety is most strongly expressed in the Girnar and Siddhapura edicts, less clearly in the Dhauli and Jaugada edicts, by differences in the signs for *A, Ā, kha, ja, ma, ra, sa,* the medial *i* and the ligatures with *ra.*[1]

R.D. Banerji went a step further and wrote,

> The edicts of Dhauli and Jaugada though relegated to the Southern variety of the older Maurya alphabet, stand in an intermediate position.[2]

He attributed the peculiar cursive characters to the importation from the north.

C.S. Upasak who made an intensive examination of individual letters of Aśokan Brāhmī rightly concluded that no regional variety as such could be found in Aśokan inscriptions.[3] Aśokan inscriptions are engraved on different materials, viz., rocks, pillars and caves. Engraved pillars are mostly confined to north India whereas rocks bearing royal edicts are usually distributed in the Deccan and south India. The polished and rounded surface of the pillars made them suitable for cursive engraving. But angular forms are commonly found on the rocks. Angularity or cursiveness of the letter-forms is further depended on the nature of the surface of the rock. Letters engraved on a smooth surface exhibited accurate and artistic forms than those on a rough surface.

To the earlier palaeographers letter-forms are ends in themselves and they based their conclusions on the letter-forms alone. They were not at all concerned with the materials on which the edicts were engraved. They failed to notice the distinction between the engravings on the writing materials like pillars and rocks, and erroneously derived broad geographical designations for the variant Aśokan Brāhmī alphabets. Angular characters have been drawn side by side with cursive forms in the edicts at Dhauli and Jaugada. This led R.D. Banerji to christen an intermediary variety of Aśokan Brāhmī in this part of the country.

Not only writing materials, very often employment of different hands and use of different kinds of writing tools determine the shape of the letters. Moreover, the existence of fundamental variations in the letter-forms of the inscriptions of the same area and often of the same inscription blurs the possibility of regional varieties.

---

1. Bühler, *IP*, 60.
2. R.D. Banerji, *The Origin of the Bengali Script*, Calcutta, 1919, 11.
3. C.S. Upasak, *The History and Palaeography of Mauryan Brāhmī Script*, Nalanda, 1960, 29.

In Dhauli and Jaugada edicts minor variations are seen in the reversible characters of some letters, e.g., ⁝· or ·⁝, for *i*, ˥ or ʃ for *o*, D or Ɑ for *dha*, ⊥ or ⊥ for *no*, and in the addition of a loop or circle to the bottom of the hooked *kha*. All these peculiarities except the second form of *o* are occasionally found in Orissan edicts and they are met with at other places too. But the reversed *o* is exclusively seen in Dhauli and Jaugada REs. The reversed *i* is optionally noticed in REs at Girnar and Kalsi, in the minor REs at Rupanath and Bairat, and the in the pillar edicts at Sarnath and Allahabad-Kosam. The reversed *dha* which is rarely seen in the SRE at Dhauli and exclusively in the SRE at Jaugada is also found in the minor REs at Rupanath, Erragudi, Maski and Gujjara, and in the pillar edicts at Delhi-Topra. The reversed medial vowel *o* in *no* is found in the REs at Girnar and Erragudi, in the minor REs at Rupanath and Gujjara, and in the pillar edicts at Delhi-Topra and Allahabad-Kosam. The loop or circle attached to the bottom of the hooked *kha* which is seen only in SRE at Jaugada is also noticed in the REs at Kalsi, in the minor REs at Maski and Sasaram, in the pillar edicts at Lauriya-Nandangarh and Lauriya-Araraj, and in the minor pillar edicts at Sarnath. As shown above, no one style can be attributed to a particular region. Dani has rightly pointed out, ". . . but except for the second form of *o*, which is peculiar to the Dhauli and Jaugada RE, no regional classification is possible."[4] It is, therefore, difficult to reduce the Aśokan edicts at Dhauli and Jaugada to a regional variety merely on the strength of the above digressions.

The lines are straight and parallel. They run from left to right. In the reversed *o* and *dha* of Jaugada, Bühler noticed the survival of "boustrophedon writing." These stylistic peculiarities are perhaps due to slovenliness on the part of the engraver than anything else. The letters are all of uniform size. The height of the letters is usually equal; and sometimes even in the conjuncts an equal height is maintained by making the second letter smaller in size.

Punctuation marks like straight vertical lines and grouping of the words for sense-demarcation in a sentence are not followed in Aśokan rock-edicts in Orissa. But the idea was not altogether absent in these inscriptions. Each edict starts on a fresh line, leaving the space blank at the end of the preceding line. Beside, the commencement of edicts is invariably marked by a horizontal dash. The two separate edicts on the Jaugada rock are kept within a space enclosed by lines. The upper portion of this space is marked out by two *svastika* symbols at the top of each corner of SREJ-II. They have curved arms and direction of these arms vary in each case — 卐.卍. The lower portion has one *svastika* and three taurine figures along the line of separation. The taurine figure having a dot in the centre of its circle could be read as *maṁ* and possibly denote *maṅgala*, meaning auspicious. As these symbols are definitely auspicious marks, the attribution of alphabetic meaning to one of them seems to be far-fetched. Thus, the Jaugada separate edicts bear the earliest specimen of such symbols. According to Cunningham, "These Orissa and Ganjam inscriptions are the most carefully and neatly engraved of all the rock edicts."[5] Coming to the

4. A.H. Dani, *IP*, 48.

5. A. Cunningham, *CII*, I, *Inscriptions of Aśoka*, Varanasi, 1961, 19.

script proper, we find they are in conformity with the Aśokan Brāhmī alphabets engraved at other places of the sub-continent. The engravers followed the imperial direction of engraving the inscriptions in the standard form of the Brāhmī. In the following pages an attempt is made to examine the characteristics of the letter-forms. In *Pl.* I the letter-forms of the individual letters of the Dhauli and Jaugada edicts have been produced. The fascimiles of the inscriptions appended to Hultzsch's *Corpus Inscriptionum Indicarum*, vol. I has been consulted for the purpose. For convenience and easy reference, the exact place from where the letter-forms are reproduced in the plates are mentioned in the text. At first the abbreviated forms of the place where the edict is found is mentioned followed by the number of edict, the line of edict and finally the word in which the letter appeared.

Vowels

In Aśokan Brāhmī only six initial vowels are used. They are *a, ā, i, e, u* and *o*. All these vowel signs are also found in the Dhauli and Jaugada edicts. Upasak studied the signs individually whereas Dani grouped them in pairs, viz., *a* and *ā*, *i* and *e* and *u* and *o*. According to Dani, "Of these, three are basic, *a, i,* and *u*; while three others, *ā, e* and *o* are secondary forms."[6]

***A*:** The initial vowel *a* has a number of varieties in the Aśokan edicts. Modern palaeographers have recognized three main groups of the forms of this letter — (a) angular, (b) cursive, and (c) mixed. All these forms are found in the Orissan edicts. The angular form of the letter consists of two slanting strokes touching each other in the middle of the vertical to the right as in *Pl.* Ia.1, 2 and 3 (RED-V-2 — *apatiye*; REJ-1-3 — *anudivasaṁ*). When the angular lines meet each other before touching the middle of the vertical bar, a small horizontal dash is added to join the two, e.g., 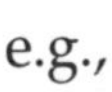 in RED-III-2 — *athā*; REJ-VI-6 — *athāye*; SREJ-II-15 — *anucātuṁ* (*Pl.* Ia.1, 3 and 4). In the cursive variety of this letter, the two slanting strokes are turned into curves and they join to the vertical at a point  as in *Pl.* Ia.1 and 3 (RED-V-3 — *ativaṁtaṁ*; REJ-VI-2 — *aṁte*). Occasionally they touch the vertical at two different points  as in *Pl.* Ia. 2 and 4 (SRED-II-15 — *apāye*; SKEJ-II-12 — *asvāsanāye*). In the third group, the angular and cursive features are mixed together and thereby change the face of the letter. Of the two arms, if the lower one is rounded then the upper one is angularly drawn and vice versa.

***Ā*:** The initial *ā* is a horizontal dash added to *a*. The initial *ā* has almost all the standard and peculiar forms of *a* with a horizontal tick attached either to the top or middle of its vertical line. In the Orissan edicts the tick is invariably seen applied to the middle — 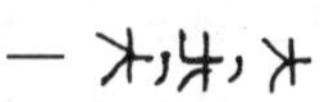 . In the angular *ā*, the tick is drawn from the middle where the two strokes meet each other. But the cursive form of the letter is more interesting. When the two arms meet the vertical at two different points, they have a space in between and one of the arms crosses the vertical on the right. Projection of the upper arm is more frequent than that of the lower one.

6. Dani, *op. cit.*, 36.

I **:** The initial *i* is simply represented by three dots arranged trianglewise. In the standard Aśokan Brāhmī the two dots are placed one above the other and the third one is marked to the middle right. This is also the common form in the edicts at Dhauli and Jaugada. Optionally the position of the third dot is reversed and it is placed to the left as in *Pl.* Ia.1 and 4 (RED-V-6 — *iyaṁ*; SREJ-I-10 — *iyaṁ*).

***U*:** The initial *u* is formed by a long vertical joined by a short horizontal bar to its bottom right, thereby forming a right angle. This is also the standard Aśokan Brāhmī form. But sometimes the vertical line is drawn in a slanting manner and, therefore, an acute angle is formed at the bottom as in *Pl.*Ia. 1, 2 and 3.

***E*:** The letter *e* is indicated by a triangle. In the standard Aśokan Brāhmī it is drawn in the form of a triangle with its tip on the right. This variety is seen only in SREJ-I-7— *eve* (*Pl.* Ia.4). While in a majority of cases this letter-form is reversed and the tip of the triangle faces to the left as in *Pl.* Ia. 1, 2 (second), 3, 4 (second). Optionally, the tip of the triangle faces to the top, e.g., SRED-I-8 — *eka* (*Pl.* Ia.2).

***O*:** In the Aśokan Brāhmī the letter *o* has occurred very rarely. For this reason we notice only a few varieties of this letter. It is usually seen in the form of a vertical to which a horizontal line is joined to its top right and another to its bottom left. This may be termed as angular *o*. It is altogether absent in Dhauli and Jaugada edicts. Instead we come across the reversed version of the standard Asokan *o* which is peculiar to these places alone. The letter-forms in *Pl.* Ia.1 and 3 are reproduced form RED-VI-2 and REJ-VI-2 respectively.

Consonants

All total twenty-nine consonants are noticed in the Dhauli and Jaugada edicts. The very rare letter *ña* occurred only for once. The semi-vowel *ra* does not make appearance in these edicts at all and is always indicated by the sign for *la*. Though the three sibilants are found in the Aśokan Brāhmī, the dental *sa* is most commonly used. In the edicts of Dhauli and Jaugada, the dental *sa* is used exclusively. Upasak has observed several varieties of the individual letters in these Orissan edicts and accounted the engraver for them. However, a majority of the consonants strictly confirm to their respective standard Aśokan Brāhmī forms as seen in the edicts from other parts of the subcontinent.

***Ka*:** The letter *ka* is a simple cross. Both the horizontal and the vertical lines are of equal size. They intersect each other at right angle. This simple cross type of *ka* is the standard form and is also traceable in the Orissan edicts (*Pl.* Ia). Occasionally the vertical of the letter is lengthened as in *ka* in the word *tilake* in SRED-I-16 (*Pl.* Ia.2) and *ka* in *kaṭaviye* in REJ-I-2 (*Pl.* Ia.3). Upasak explained that the engraver first drew the vertical line, but since he had not left a proportionate space for the horizontal line to its left, he had to make the horizontal line short.[7] Another

7. Upasak, *op. cit.*, 55.

peculiarity is noticed in *kaṁ* in the word *hakaṁ* in SREJ-II-1 (*Pl.* Ia.4) where the horizontal stroke of *ka* is found curved upwards. In another corrupt form of the letter the left and right halves of the horizontal mid-bar look like two different strokes as in RED-X-2 — *palakamati;* REJ-VI-5 — *kamatalā;* and SREJ-II-1 — *vacanika*. In such cases, the vertical is drawn first and then the two halves of the horizontal line separately. In yet another corrupt form of the letter the upper and lower halves of the vertical line look like two different strokes as in RED-VI-1 — *atikaṁtaṁ* and REJ-II-2 — *cikisā*. In these cases, the horizontal is drawn first and then the two halves of the vertical line.

***Kha*:** In the standard Aśokan Brāhmī, the letter *kha* is formed like a hook with either a dot or circle at its foot. In the Orissan edicts the hooked letter with a dot is more commonly found (*Pl.* Ia). The other variety with a circle or an oval is optionally noticed in SREJ-I (*Pl.* Ia.4). In a few cases, the letter-form is devoid of the dot or circle as in *Pl.* Ia.2 (SRED-I-22 — *akhakhase*).

***Ga*:** The letter *ga* consists of two slanting strokes diverging downwards from the same point and thereby forming an acute angle at the top. This is the standard form regularly found in the edicts at Dhauli and Jaugada. Optionally, the top of the letter instead of becoming angular is rounded as in *Pl.* Ia.1 (RED-VII-2 — *vucalāgā*). It is believed that when the engraver failed to join the two slanting strokes at the top, he tried to join them by a curve.

***Gha*:** *Gha* is shaped like a fishing hook to which a stroke is added in the middle that makes it as three prongs, the one to the extreme left being elongated. This may be termed as the three pronged *gha*. In the Orissan edicts both the angular and cursive forms of the letter are noticed. In the angular variety the rounded bottom of the letter is flattened and the three prongs are drawn straight as in *Pl.* Ia.1 (second) (RED-IV-2 — *bhelighosa*). In *Pl.* Ia.1 (first), the right arm merges with the central prong and gives a rounded look. This is reproduced from RED-XIV-1 — *ghaṭite*.

***Ca*:** The letter *ca* is a semi-circle drawn to the bottom left of a vertical line. Optionally a square takes the place of the semi-circle as in the case of *cā* (*Pl.* Ia.4, SREJ-I-4 — *kecā*). Occasionally the semi-circle is also seen in the form of a triangle. However, in all such cases the vertical is drawn first and then the semi-circle, square or the triangle.

***Cha*:** It is believed that the letter-form of *cha* is developed out of the rudimentary form of *ca* by duplicating the semi-circle on the right. This makes a full circle at the bottom. Sometimes the circle is changed into an ellipse at the base and, therefore, it can be called as elliptical *cha*. In the Orissan edicts both the features are met with.

***Ja*:** "The letter *ja* has two basic forms, the angular with three arms and the round with double curves; the latter is most common and the first is optional in many inscriptions."[8] The double-curved *ja* is regular in the Orissan edicts. The angular *ja* with three arms opening to the

8. Dani, *op. cit.*, 39.

right also appears optionally as in *ja* in the word *pajāye* in SREJ-II-3 (*Pl.* Ia.4). In another peculiar form, the double-curved *ja* has obtained a dot in the middle 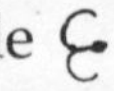 (RED-III-3; REJ-IV-6) which reminds us of the same type of *ja* in the word *jane* in Delhi-Topra pillar edict VII-15 and of a slightly different one with a circle instead of a dot in the Lauriya-Nandangarh pillar edict IV-2 — *lajūke*. Although Upasak has attributed it to make a distinction between *ja* and *jā*, it seems quick engraving of the curves in one action resulted in the formation of a circle or dot in the middle.

Jha: *Jha* is a rare letter in the Aśokan inscriptions. It is indicated by a vertical from the middle of which a horizontal bar goes to the right and then a small vertical darts up. This may be termed as the angular *jha*. This form of the letter is noticed throughout. But in some cases minor variations are noticed either in shortening the right vertical as in *Pl.* Ia.4 or placing it in a slanting manner as in *Pl.* Ia.3.

Ña: *Ña* is another rare letter the form of which is obtained by inverting the angular *jha* and adding a small horizontal dash to its top left as in *Pl.* Ia.2 (SRED-II-6 — *paṭiñā*). This may be termed as angular *ña*.

Ṭa: The letter *ṭa* is a semi-circle opened to the right. Sometimes the top or bottom arms of the semi-circle are flattened.

Ṭha: *Ṭha* is a perfect circle used throughout the Aśokan edicts. A peculiar form has occurred in the word *aṭhasi* in SRED-II-2 (*Pl.* Ia.2).

Ḍa: The letter *ḍa* in the Aśokan Brāhmī is represented by a horizontal line with two vertical strokes at its either end, the left pointing downwards and the right upwards. This may be termed as angular *ḍa*. This type is also found in the Dhauli and Jaugada edicts without any mutilation (*Pl.* Ib).

Ḍha: The letter *ḍha* is denoted by a curve opening to the right, the upper end of which is surmounted by a vertical bar while the lower one slightly curling in. This is the standard form also used in the Dhauli edicts (*Pl.* Ib.1) and may be called as round-backed *ḍha*. At times the curve of the letter is compressed as in *Pl.* Ib.1 (second). Besides, optionally the letter is drawn angularly as in *Pl.* Ib.3 (REJ-VIII-2— *vuḍhā*).

Ṇa: The letter *ṇa* has occurred only on three occasions in the Dhauli and Jaugada SREs. It is formed by a vertical line with two horizontal strokes, one at the top and the other at the bottom. This angular type of *ṇa* has little variations.

Ta: In the Dhauli and Jaugada edicts a number of varieties of the letter *ta* are met with. The monumental form is represented by a vertical stroke from the lower end of which two slanting strokes project in two different directions and thereby form an angle  (*Pl.* Ib). Variations of the letter-form are made either by reducing the height of vertical as in *ta* (*Pl.* Ib.4) or by reducing the size of the inclining strokes as in *te* (*Pl.* Ib.4). In another variety, an inclined straight line is

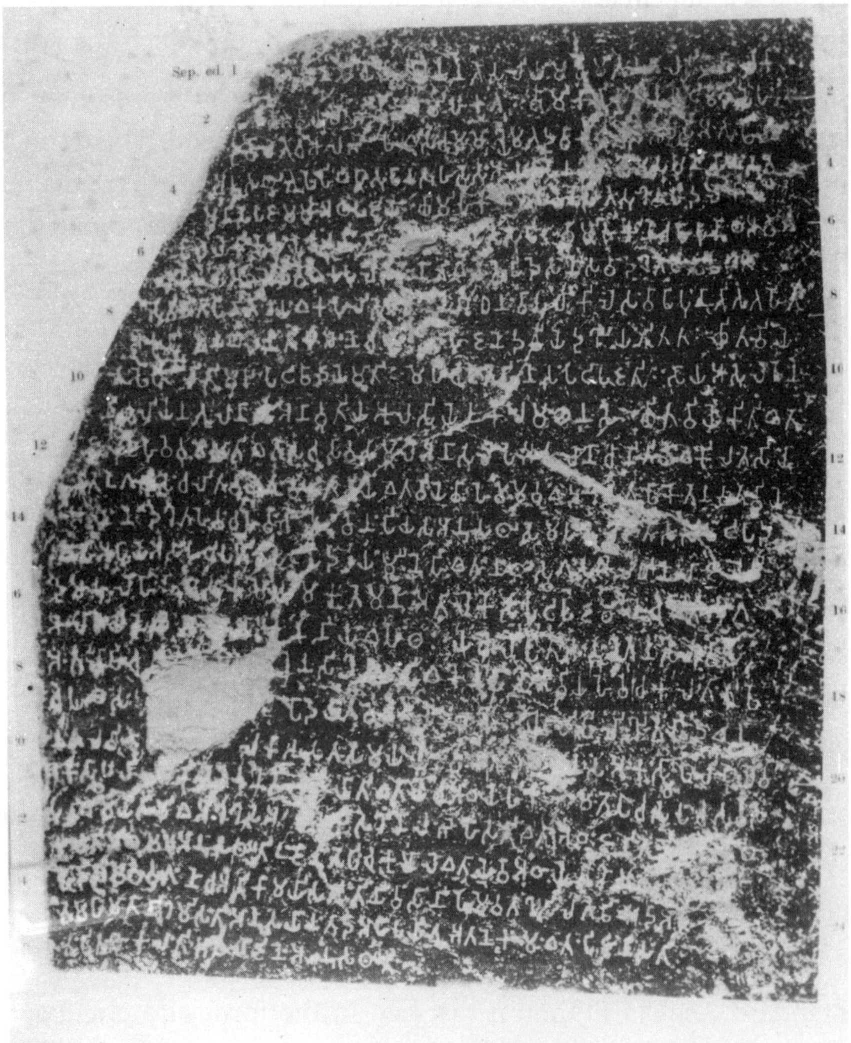

Photo 2.1 : Dhauli Separate Rock Edit-I.

drawn from the middle of which another short stroke is drawn at an angle either to the left or right, e.g.,  or  (*Pl.* Ib.2). In yet another variety, the two slanting strokes projecting from the end of the vertical are turned into a curve and facing down as in *ta* in the word *mokhiyamata* in SREJ-I-2 (*Pl.* Ib. 4, third). This type of the letter-form of *ta* is also seen in the edicts at Erragudi, Brahmagiri and Kalsi. This may be termed as down-facing curve type of *ta*.

Tha: The letter *tha* is a full circle with a dot in the middle. Sometimes the circle is not perfectly drawn and this may be due to the rough surface of the rock on which the edicts were written.

Da: In the standard Aśokan Brāhmī the letter-form of *da* is represented by a semi-circle opened to the left with the addition of a small vertical at either end. This round-backed type of *da* is regularly found used in the Orissan edicts as well. Among the other notable forms mention may be made of the one having an angular back as in *di* (*Pl.* Ib.3) and a pointed back as in *da* (*Pl.* Ib.4). Both these sub-varieties are also noticed at Girnar and Kalsi.

Dha: *Dha* is formed by a semi-circle with its diameter to the left (*Pl.* Ib). In the other variety the letter-form is reversed as in *Pl.* Ib.2 (first) and 4 (reproduced respectively from SRED-II-9 — *ālādha*, and SREJ-II-7 — *ālādha* and 8 — *ālādhi*). The reversed variety is exclusively used in SREJ. It is also used in the minor rock-edicts at Maski, Gujjara and Erragudi.

Na: The letter-form of *na* is represented by a horizontal base-line with a vertical placed on it. The letter-form resembles to that of *ṇa* without the top horizontal bar. Optionally the base-line becomes bigger in size than the vertical as in *ṇu* (*Pl.* Ib. SREJ-I-8 — *anusathi*). This may be termed as the horizontal base type of *na*.

Pa: The letter-form of *pa* resembles a fish-hook and is uniform throughout (*Pl.* Ib).

Pha: *Pha* is the same as *pa* with an additional curl or dash at its lower end as in *Pl.* Ib.

Ba: In the standard Aśokan Brāhmī, the letter *ba* is drawn like a small square and this form is found in the Orissan edicts without any alteration (*Pl.* Ib).

Bha: The letter-form of *bha* is the same as *ḍa* with an additional vertical drawn parallel to the lower one . This may be termed as angular *bha*.

Ma: In the standard Aśokan Brāhmī *ma* is seen in the form of a circular loop to which a semi-circle is added at its top. This circular loop type of *ma* is also frequent in the Orissan edicts. Besides, it has a number of corrupt forms such as the one having either two straight strokes instead of a semi-circle as in *mū* (*Pl.* Ib.2, SRED-I-12 — *mūle*) or curves as in *me* (*Pl.* Ib.1, RED-V-8 — *ca me*); and the other where the semi-circle does not touch the circular loop 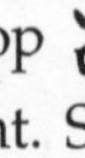 (SRED-I-16 — *pajamīne*). In all such cases the loop is drawn first and then the top element. Sometimes the letter is drawn in one action starting from the left arm to the end of the right arm as in *mū* (*Pl.* Ib.3, REJ-VI-5 — *mūle*). This may be due to quick engraving.

Ya: "The letter *ya* has two basic forms, one crescentic and the segmantic."[9] The first is made by drawing a vertical at the centre of the crescent 𑀬. In the second variety the crescent is divided into two segments touching the upright at the centre 𑀬. Both the varieties are regularly met with in the Orissan edicts. According to Bühler, "In writing the notched *ya* (Dani's segmented *ya*) the left half of the sign has been made first and the right half has been added afterwards."[10] In *Pl.* Ib.2. (SRED-II-4 — *siyā*, 9 — *aṭhāye*) the crescent is turned into an angle.

La: The letter *la* is seen in the form of a vertical with an upturned curve and a small tick on the left. This may be termed as round bottomed *la*. The rounded bottom of the letter is sometimes drawn angularly as in *le* (*Pl.* Ib.2, SRED-I-23 — *kumāle*) and *lu* (*Pl.* Ib.3, REJ-VI-1 — *puluve*). In some cases the tick is waived and an angle is formed at the bottom, e.g., *laṁ* (*Pl.* Ib.3, REJ-VI-1 — *kālaṁ*). This is peculiar only to the edicts at Jaugada and also occasionally met with in the edicts at Girnar (XIV-6 — *lipi*) and Kalsi (VI-20 — *palake*). This may be due to the carelessness on the part of the engraver.

Va: The letter *va* is a circle with a vertical placed centrally on its top. In the Orissan edicts this circular base type of *va* is engraved without any modification (*Pl.* Ib). Variations of this letter are very few, except that the circle becomes oval or flat. Upasak has erroneously traced in RED-XIV-I that "the circle *va* is replaced by a loop to the right of the vertical."[11]

Sa: As has been pointed out above, of the three sibilants only the dental *sa* is exclusively found in the edicts of Dhauli and Jaugada whereas the other two sibilants are conspicuous by their absence. The letter-form is indicated by a vertical with an upturned curve on the right and another down-facing curve on the left. This may be termed as double-curved type of *sa*. A minor variation in the letter-form is noticed where the cursive left limb is drawn angularly. Such angular engravings are frequent in the Jaugada SREs I and II (*Pl.* Ib.4), and less frequent in other edicts, e.g., *sū* (*Pl.* Ib.I, RED-I-3 — *sūpaṭhāye*).

Ha: *Ha* is the exact reversed form of *la*, i.e., the left-facing upturned curve of *la* totally shifts to the right. No significant change in the basic form is marked in the Orissan edicts. But some peculiarities are noticed in the Jaugada SREs. Sometimes its rounded bottom is extremely angularized with its tick facing downwards as in *hi* (*Pl.* Ib.4. SREJ-I-3 — *hitasukhena*); at others the entire lower limb is denoted by a down-going curve as in *he Pl.* Ib.4, SREJ-I-6 — *nahevaṁ*).

Medials

Medial vowels are added to the consonants and conjuncts. Phonological change in the consonants and conjuncts is concomitant with the evolution of a system of diacritical notation for expressing the medial vowels. Upasak has rightly pointed out, "It was apparently of purely indigenous

9. Dani, *op. cit.*, 42.
10. Bühler, *op. cit.*, 63.
11. Upasak, *op. cit.*, 97.

evolution, and perhaps the Sanskrit grammarians were its originators."[12] Dani contended that the signs for the medial vowels are based on the three basic initial vowels *a*, *i* and *u*, and from these basic forms other signs are developed. It is the general rule that the medial signs are drawn only after the engraving of the consonants. Since the medial *a* is inherent in all the consonants, no separate diacritical notation is required for expressing this.

Just as the vowel *ā* is a secondary sign evolved out of the basic *a*, so also the medial vowel *ā* is only a horizontal dash attached to the consonant where *a* is present. The dash is attached either to the top right or in the middle right according to the verticality or roundedness of the top of the alphabets. In the case of *kā, gā, cā, chā, ḍā, ḍhā, tā, dā, nā, pā, bhā, mā, yā, lā, vā, sā* and *hā* the horizontal dash is attached to the top right of the letters. In the letters having rounded top the medial vowel is placed in the middle, e.g., *jā, ṭhā* and *tha* (*fig*. II.3, 4 & 6). In other cases like *ṇā, bā*, etc., the vowel mark is also placed in the middle (*fig*. II.5 & 7).

Medial *i* is a horizontal dash from the terminal of which a vertical is darting up and thereby forming an angle. This angular mark is commonly placed at the top right of the consonants. In the letters having round shape this sign is placed in the middle right as in *ṭhi* and *thi* (*fig*. II.3 & 4). In the case of letters *ja, ṭa*, and *ṇa* only a vertical is placed at the top. The long medial vowel *ī* is represented by doubling the vertical top stroke of *i*.

The medial *u* is expressed by adding either a horizontal stroke to the bottom of the vertical as in *ku, cu*, etc., or a vertical to the curved end as in *ṭu, thu, pu, mu*, etc. (*fig*. II). There are still some letters, the lower portions of which are neither curved nor vertical such as *kha, na*, etc., and in such cases a vertical stroke is added to the bottom (*fig*. II.2, 6). The diacritical notation for the long vowel *ū* is expressed by doubling either the horizontal or the vertical stroke, as the case may be, of medial *u*. Sometimes the double verticals for *ū* is noticed in a peculiar manner. Instead of going parallel to each other they slant from the bottom of the letter and thereby form an angle, e.g., *ṭū, ṭhū, mū, vū, sū*, and *hū* (*fig*. II).

The medial *e* is a horizontal bar added to the top left of the consonant as in most cases like *ke, ge, te, ye*, etc. But in a few letters whose top portions are rounded the vowel mark is attached to the middle as in *ṭhe* and *the*. In the case of *kha* it is projected from the terminal of the hook (*fig*. II.2).

As in initial *o* where two horizontal lines are found, one attached to the top left and the other to the bottom right of the vertical, so also in medial *o* the two horizontal lines retain the same positions with the stroke to the bottom lifted to the middle of the top half of the consonant. This is commonly found in *to, no, yo*, etc. In the letters like *kho, jo* and *bo* the medial sign is noticed in the middle of the two sides of the consonant (*fig*. II.1, 2 and 6).

In Dhauli and Jaugada REs, as has been referred to earlier, the initial *o* is totally reversed. For this reason, in the REs, the reversion of the diacritical notation is also very frequent. When

12. Upasak, *op. cit.*, 105.

***fig.* II: Medials in the Aśokan Brāhmī Script in Orissa**

the medial is reversed the top left horizontal line takes the place of top right of the vertical whereas the right stroke shifts its place to the left as in *gho, co, do, no, lo,* etc. Sometimes the medial strokes slant and portray different look, e.g., *no*. This is perhaps due to carelessness of the engraver.

The initial vowels *ai* and *au* are not traceable in the Aśokan edicts. As such no medial signs for the above letters are found. Of the Aśokan inscriptions, only at Girnar and Brahmagiri the medial sign for *ai* is used optionally.

The *anusvāra* is a dot that mostly stands on the right side top of the letter. But in connection with the medial *i*, it is placed regularly inside the angle of the vowel as in *kiṁ* and below the medial sign as in *tiṁ*.

Conjuncts

The conjuncts are formed by placing one consonant upon another without any change. The letter of which the phonetic value is to be derived is normally placed below the first consonant. In Aśokan Brāhmī a tendency has developed to shorten both the letters of the conjunct and maintain equal height with the consonants proper. Generally, the second letter is more shortened than the first consonant. In the edicts of Dhauli and Jaugada the sound elements of only three letters, viz., *ma, ya* and *va* have been used. Though the letter *ra* is conspicuous by its absence in the Orissan edicts, Hultzsch erroneously conclued its occurrence in conjunction with other consonants at least four times in Jaugada REs.

According to Hultzsch the horizontal strokes attached to the bottom right *ta* in the word *savatra* (ṚEJ-II-4; Hultzsch, *CII*, I, p. 102) and *da* in the word *piyadrasine* (REJ-I-3; Hultzsch, *CII*,

I, p. 101), to the top left of *pa* in the word *pratívedayaṁtu* (REJ-VI-2, Hultzsch: *CII*, I, p. 106) and attached to the top and bottom right of *da* in the word *drakhati* (REJ-I-2; Hultzsch : *CII*, I, p. 101) may be possibly intended for the sound element of *ra*. But such contentions of the learned scholar hold no ground for *ra* is always inserted in the vertical of the consonant.

The conjuncts having the sound elements *ma* are only found in the Dhauli and Jaugada SREs. *Ma* is drawn below the right limb of the first component *sa* and thereby form the conjunct *smā* (*Pl.* Ic.2, SRED-I-9, 20, 21 — *akasmā*). Sometimes the medial sign *a* is placed in the right limb of *ma* vide *smā* (*Pl.* Ic.4). This may be an orthographical peculiarity.

In Dhauli and Jaugada edicts the phonetic value *ya* is invariably added to the bottom of the consonants like *kha, na, ma, va,* and *sa*. In each case *ya* is drawn fully and equal height is maintained between the first component and the sound element. In the case of the rounded bases of *ma* and *va* and dotted *kha*, it is placed exactly below the circle or dot, e.g., *mya* (*Pl.* Ic.1, RED-IX-3 — *saṁmya*), *vye* (*Pl.* Ic.4, SREJ-I-7 — *saṁcalitavye*) and *khya* (*Pl.* Ic.2, SRED-I-3, II-2 — *mokhyamata*), in the case of the double curved base of *sa* below the right curve, e.g., *sye* (*Pl.* Ic.4, SREJ-I-6 — *ālasyena*); and in the case of angular *na* it is placed to the bottom left as in *nye* (*Pl.* Ic.4, SREJ-I-5 — *anye*).

When *va* becomes an adjunct of other letters, it loses its vertical and only the circle is drawn at the bottom right of the consonants, e.g., *tvā* in the word *tadatvāye* (*Pl.* Ic.1 and 3, RED and REJ-X-1) and *sva* (*Pl.* Ic.3, REJ-IX-6 — *svage*; 4, SREJ-II-6 — *asvaseyu*). Sometimes *va* is fully represented beneath the consonants, e.g., *sva* (*Pl.* Ic.1, RED-VI-6 — *svagaṁ*), *hve* (*Pl.* Ic.4, SREJ-I-6 and II-5 — *hveyū*), etc.

From the above analysis it has been made clear that no regional variety as such did exist in the Aśokan Brāhmī. The scribes followed the imperial command of engraving the edicts in the standard form of the Brāhmī. The peculiar reversible characters of two or three letters in the edicts at Dhauli and Jaugada are not followed regularly and this digression is possibly due to the slovenliness on the part of the engraver than anything else. The cursive engraving of a few of the letter-forms which prompted some to reduce the script to an intermediate variety of the Brāhmī also appears to be untenable. This may be attributed to the surface of the rock on which the writing was made. Alternatively, this may be due to the employment of the local engravers to copy the draft of the original edicts on the surface of the rocks.

Bibliography

Hultzsch, E., *CII*, I, *Inscriptions of Aśoka*, 2nd edition, Varanasi, 1969, 84-117 & pls.

3

Transitional and Later Brāhmī Script in Orissa

THE imperial character of the Aśokan Brāhmī alphabet, as has been discussed in the preceding chapter, commanded uniformity in the writing style and, therefore, it can hardly be reduced to regional varieties. But with the collapse of that imperial fabric, imperial hand was also abruptly arrested and more and more people took interest to acquire technical knowledge of the art of writing. This diffusion was further accelerated by the introduction and circulation of coins by various authorities in the centuries succeeding Mauryan rule. The Brāhmī script thus entered into a stage of transition from royalty to popularity.

During this period the north-western India was frequently exposed to the foreign invaders who brought along with them traditions alien to this land. The Greeks introduced their coin technology and palaeography which considerably influenced the Brāhmī script. The limited space on the surface of the coins demanded reduction in the verticals of the letters and approximate equalization of their length and breadth. The Brāhmī script was much to be influenced by this new technique. But not until the Śaka-Kṣatrapas popularized this system the developement was rather slow. The change hitherto effected was confined only to the coin legends whereas traditional tool and technique largely dominated for engraving the inscriptions on stone.

By the close of the first century BC the Śaka-Kṣatrapas established themselves in north-western India and brought revolutionary changes in the art of writing the Brāhmī script. They used a "new-edged pen" for writing which gave altogether a new face to the Brāhmī letters.[1] The tapering thickness of the verticals, the definite head-formations with a dot or a dash, the equalization of the verticals of the letters like *pa, la, sa,* and *ha,* the angularization of the curves of the letters and the curved flourish of the medial vowels are some traits of this period from which the new pen style was inspired. In spite of these notable changes effected in the writing style, very little fundamental differences are noticed in the essential characters of the letters.

North India was bound to get the first impulse of this new style because of its proximity to the north-western highways through which the exotic elements infiltrated into this sub-continent. As such after much experiment the style got assimilated and significant changes occurred in writing the Brāhmī script. The touch of this new style is not felt in Orissa because of two important

1. A.H. Dani, *IP*, 52; T.P. Verma, *Palaeography of Brāhmī Script in North India*, Varanasi, 1971, 82.

reasons. Firstly, Orissa was not subjugated by any of the foreign powers such as the Indo-Greeks, the Śaka-Kṣatrapas or the Kuṣāṇas. Secondly, the new tool technique was not introduced to Orissa. But there is no denying the fact that certain changes occurred in writing the Brāhmī and they are due to the influence of the coin technology and palaeography popularized in north India. The Hāthīgumphā inscription of Khāravela and the other minor Brāhmī inscriptions of his supposed successors, chief queen, officers, ascetics, etc., in the Udayagiri hill no doubt point to the popularization of the Brāhmī script in this part of India. The characters of all these records appear to be a stage in the development of the Brāhmī in Orissa. They can very well be said as the "transitional stage," even if the archaic features are still retained to some extent.

But the real problem arises when we try to handle the palaeographical features of the inscriptions of the early centuries of the Christian era. The history of Orissa for three or four centuries after the fall of the Cedi power appears to be hazy and obscure. No systematic records relating to the history of the period have been made available so far. Piecing together the bits of facts it is now held by some scholars that the Sātavāhanas had extended their sway over the southern part of Kaliṅga and a portion of South Kośala sometime in the first half of the second century AD.[2] But there is no direct proof of the continuity of their supremacy over Kaliṅga and South Kośala after the second century. The earlier supposition of a phase of Kuṣāṇa domination over Kaliṅga on the strength of some numismatic finds seems to be untenable.[3] The imitation copper coins are assigned to a period when the Kuṣāṇa empire had become a thing of the past. According to K.C. Panigrahi, "Orissa was perhaps under the supremacy of the Muruṇḍas who were responsible for the currency in Orissa of the coins that have distinctly imitated the Kuṣāṇa coin types."[4] A gold coin found from Sisupalgarh excavation[5] bearing the legend *mahārājadhasa dhamadāmadharasa*) (Skt. *mahārājādhirāja dharmadāmadharasya*) in the Brāhmī characters of the third century AD led A.S. Altekar to think that Dharmadāmadhara was a Muruṇḍa king ruling a part of Bihar and Orissa.[6]

To this period belong the Bhadrak inscription of *mahārāja* Gaṇa and the boulder inscriptions at Sitabinji. On palaeographical grounds the Bhadrak inscription is assigned to the third century AD. There are a number of votive inscriptions on the boulders and also a short-painted label containing one line of writing, *mahārāja śrī diśābhañja*, in a rock-shelter called *rāvaṇachāyā* at Sitabinji. Although there is a good deal of controversy among scholars regarding the palaeography

2. N.K. Sahu, *Utkal University History of Orissa*, I, Bhubaneswar, 1964, 415-18.
3. S. Tripathy, *Early and Medieval Coins and Currency System of Orissa Circa 300 BC to 1568 AD*, Calcutta, 1986, 57.
4. *History of Orissa*, Cuttack, 1981, 42.
5. B.B. Lal, *Ancient India*, 5, 1949, 62-105.
6. *Journal of the Numismatic Society of India* (*JNSI*), 12, 3.

and date of this painted label,[7] we are inclined to place the record in the seventh century on the basis of the letters *ra* and *śa*. The addition of a stroke at the bottom of *ra* and the type of *śa* and *śrī* are never used in Orissa before seventh century. So far as the boulder inscriptions are concerned, they are incised earlier than the painted label. They are written in Prakrit language and their characters resemble those of south India of the fourth century.

The Bhadrak inscription and the Sitabinji boulder inscriptions exhibit no homogeneous characters. The change in the face of certain letter-forms, the application of head-marks and the long flourishes of the medial vowels in these inscriptions led us to group them under the later Brāhmī script in Orissa. But in view of the absence of any other epigraphical material which can properly be fitted to the early centuries of the Christian era at least up to the fourth century AD, the characters of the above insciptions should not be considered as a true index of the connected development of the Brāhmī in Orissa.

In *Pl.* II, the characters of the following inscriptions have been reproduced.

1. Hāthīguṁphā Inscriptions of Khāravela (HI).
2. Minor Brāhmī Inscriptions in the caves of Udayagiri hill (MBIs).
   (i) Mañcapurī Guṁphā Inscription-Upper Storey (MGI-US).
   (ii) Mañcapurī Guṁphā Inscription-Lower Storey (MGI-LS).
   (iii) Sarpa Guṁphā Inscription-A (SGI-A).
   (iv) Sarpa Guṁphā Inscription-B (SGI-B).
   (v) Haridās Guṁphā Inscription (HGI).
   (vi) Vyāghra Guṁphā Inscription (VGI).
   (vii) Jambeśvara Guṁphā Inscription (JGI).
   (viii) Choṭa Hāthīguṁphā Inscription (CHI).
   (ix) Ananta Guṁphā Inscription-A (AGI-A).
   (x) Ananta Guṁphā Inscription-B (AGI-B).

---

7. T.N. Ramachandran has assigned the characters of the *Rāvaṇachāyā* inscription to about the forth century AD and the boulder inscriptions to the sixth century AD. According to him, "these inscriptions on boulders are in a 'South Indian *Lipi*', while the painted inscription on *Rāvaṇachāyā* is of the eastern variety of the Northern alphabet like the Susunia rock, Bengal." (*JAHRS*, 19, 193) Later on R.C. Mazumdar observed, "the characters of the short record at Sitabinji can by no means be regarded as later than those of the characters of the early kings of Kaliṅga who have been unanimously referred to the fifth century AD." (*The Age of Imperial Kanauj*, 4, 73-74), D.C. Sircar, on the other hand, thinks that the characters of the inscription belong to a much later date, between the eighth and eleventh century AD (*EI*, 35, 47-50).

(xi) Tatowā Gumphā Inscription-A (TGI-A).

(xii) Tatowā Gumphā Inscription-B (TGI-B).

3. Bhadrak Inscription of Mahārāja Gaṇa (BI).

4. Sitabinji Boulder Inscriptions (SBI).

The abbreviations mentioned at the end of the inscriptions have been used in their proper places in the following discussion. For our convenience we have divided this chapter into two sections. In Section I, the transitional Brāhmī script as represented in HI and MBIs is studied while in Section II, the later Brāhmī characters as seen in BI and SBIs have been taken into consideration.

I

The Nanaghat inscription (NI) of Nāganikā[8] and the Hāthīgumphā inscription (HI) of Khāravela are the two largest inscriptions after Aśokan records in western and eastern India respectively. The internal evidence in the latter also demonstrate the fact that Sātakarṇi was an older contemporary of Khāravela.[9] In view of the contemporaneity of the two records, scholars studied the palaeography of the two inscriptions in order to arrive at a tentative date. R.P. Chanda made a comparative study of both the epigraphs and on palaeographical grounds assigned them to the first century BC. He maintained that NI is definitely anterior to HI and pointed out that the following are the most notable characteristics of the Hāthīgumphā alphabet :

> (1) A considerable number of letters with thick-headed vertical or serif; (2) *ka* with the lower part of the vertical prolonged; (3) invariably rounded *ga*; (4) *ca* of the butterfly type with two loops; (5) *ta*'s having in most cases rounded lower part.[10]

Supporting Chanda, D.C. Sircar opined,

> The angular forms and straight bases of letters like *va*, *ma*, *pa*, *ha* and *ya*, which are usually found in the Hāthīgumphā epigraph, suggest a date not much earlier than the beginning of the first century AD. On grounds of palaeography, it is to be placed later probably than the Nanaghat records and certainly than the Besnagar inscription of Heliodoros.[11]

R.D. Banerji[12] who has made a detailed analysis of the palaeography of both the records refuted

---

8. *Archaeological Survey of Western India* (*ASWI*), 5, 60 & 86.
9. In the second regnal year of his reign, Khāravela disregarding Śātakarṇi, despatched a vast army to the west which marched up to the river Kanhavemnā (Krishna) and stormed the city of Musika (Asika). The Śātakarṇi has been identified with the Sātavāhana king Śātakarṇi I, husband of queen Nāganikā, the issuer of the Nanaghat inscription.
10. *Memoirs of the Archaeological Survey of India* (*MASI*), 1, 10.
11. Sircar, *Select Inscriptions*, I, 213, n. 1.
12. *Memoirs of the Asiatic Society of Bengal* (*MASB*), 11 (3), 131-46.

Photo 3.1 : Hāthīguṁphā Inscription of Khāravela.

the views of R.P. Chanda and inclined to place them in the second century BC. He observed that all the *ga*'s in Khāravela's inscription are not arched; that the lower part of all the *ta*'s are not invariably rounded; that it has a number of letter-forms bearing the characteristic features of the alphabet of the Mauryan inscriptions. He further concluded that some of the letters of HI are earlier than those of NI while a few letters of the former belonged to the later period than those of the latter. The use of initial *a* with its two left strokes joining the vertical straight line at different points, the right-angled form of *ja* and *da*, the form of *bha* having its left vertical shorter than the right and the angular form of *ma* are certainly later than those used in NI. Except these differences, the transitional forms of other letters in both the inscriptions appear to be similar and indicate that their dates are not wide apart. Thus the difference in the forms of letters used in these inscriptions are so very few that the occurrence of certain later forms in any one of them cannot be taken to indicate a later date of that particular inscription; specially in view of the fact that the record, in which such later forms of characters were used, lies about a thousand miles distant from the other. Palaeographical examination is not possible with inscriptions lying more than thousands miles apart.

Banerji inclined to explain the occurrence of different types of the Brāhmī letters in Khāravela's inscription because he noticed the engraving of three separate hands in the same piece of stone. Supporting Banerji's view, B.M. Barua[13] believed that the scribes employed to incise the inscription represented different localities.

A.H. Dani pointed out that even though the advanced letter-forms are commonly met with in HI, some of the archaic forms still persist optionally. The occurrence of the advanced forms is not due to the belief that the scribes were acquainted with the new technical knowledge rather the letter-forms have been copied from the Śaka-Kṣatrapa inscriptions of Mathura. According to him, "This is bound to be the case in such a remote region as Orissa, where the new technical tradition could not get a foothold for a longer time."[14] Following Dani, T.P. Verma[15] also believed that the use of the new pen was not known to the writers of HI. However, both of them fixed the date of epigraph in the first half of the first century AD on the basis of palaeography.

The HI of Khāravela is the earliest and the most important record in the whole series of inscriptions found in the Khandagiri and Udayagiri hills. On account of its worn out condition scholars have put forth divergent views regarding its palaeography and date. Although a majority of letters such as the initial *u*, the medial vowels *ā, u, e, o* and the consonants *ka, ca, cha, ṭa, ṭha, ḍa, ṇa, tha, da, dha, na, ba, sa*, etc., do not deviate from their Aśokan Brāhmī counterparts, the characters of the rest of the letters show great variety. The transitional letter-forms are drawn side by side with their old Brāhmī forms. The transitional forms are seen in the letters, viz., *a*,

13. B.M. Barua, *Old Brāhmī Inscriptions in the Udayagiri and Khandagiri Caves*, Calcutta, 1929, 152.

14. Dani, *op. cit.*, 58.

15. Verma, *op. cit.*, 85.

kha, ga, gha, ja, ta, pa, bha, ma, la, va, ha, etc. (*fig.* 1). In such cases the verticals are found reduced in size, angles are formed in place of curves and existing angular letters are transformed into curves. Some of the letters display partly angular and partly cursive engraving. Sometimes the letter-forms are much more developed as in *gha, pa, bha, ma, la, ha,* etc., where there is an attempt to approximate equalization of the verticals. But nowhere in HI do we find the tapering thickness of the letters. There is absolutely no trace of the use of the so-called "new-edged pen," but some of the forms are very suspicious as they recall those of the new technique. It is, therefore, very difficult to date the inscription on the basis of palaeography. The new tool technique was popularized in Mathura centre by the Śakas only in the first century AD. Prior to that Śaka coin technology and palaeography was much influenced by the Greeks. The date of HI is now believed to be somewhere in the later half of the first century BC, so it is very likely that the scribes employed to engrave the inscription were possibly brought from Mathura who tried to imitate coin palaeography on stone. Had there been any imitation of the new tool technique, there would also have been the imitation of the tapering thickness of the letters which is an important outcome of the style. There is cogent reason to believe that the scribes thus employed were brought from Mathura and they were allowed to engrave the inscription along with the local artists in traditional tool.

It should be remembered that whatever stylistic peculiarities penetrated into this region during the reign of Khāravela did not outlive the existing local mannerisms. In the MBIs in the caves of the two hills, issued by the chief queen of of Khāravela, his son and grandson, some important officers, monks and merchants, we still notice the continuation of the archaic features with a preference for angularity of the letter-forms except *kha, ga* (optionally), *ta, pa, ma,* etc. In the circular or broad loop of *kha,* the rounded or angular back of *ga,* the equalization of the verticals of *la* and *ha* and in the softening of the angle of the medial *i* we see transitional and developed characteristics. The MBIs are decidedly later than the HI of the later half of the first century BC and their lower limit can be fixed in the middle of the first century AD.

The other inscriptions which are supposed to be the younger contemporaries of HI and MBIs on the basis of their palaeography are the Guntupally Brāhmī inscriptions of the time of Mahāmeghavāhana Siri Sada,[16] the Velpuru inscription of the time of *Aira Mahārāja* Manasada,[17] the Gunji rock inscription of the time of Kumāravaradatta,[18] and the Kirari wooden pillar inscription.[19] Guntupally and Velpuru are located in West Godavari and Guntur districts of Andhra Pradesh respectively while Gunji and Kirari are situated in Bilaspur district of

---

16. R. Subrahmanyam, *The Guntupally Brāhmī Inscriptions of Khāravela*, Epigraphical Series no. 3, Government of Andhra Pradesh, Hyderabad, 1968, 1-7 & pls.; D.C. Sircar, *JAIH*, 3 (1-2), 30-36.
17. P.S. Shastri, *Journal of Andhra History and Culture* (*JAHC*), 1 (2), 64; D.C. Sircar, *EI*, 32, 82-87.
18. L.P. Pandeya, *JKHRS*, 1 (3), 217-18; V.V. Mirashi, *EI*, 27, 48-52; D.C. Sircar, *JAS, L*, 19 (1), 59-61.
19. H. Sastri, *EI*, 18, 152-57.

Chhatisgarh. Except Guntupally, the other three inscriptions are later than HI by at least two centuries. In point of time and space they are thus removed from the group of inscriptions found in the hills of Khandagiri and Udayagiri, and their characters also show considerable variety.

The Guntupally Brāhmī inscriptions exhibit more rounded letter-forms. The transitional forms are also totally absent, verticals are not reduced in size and in general they show a local development from the Aśokan Brāhmī on the other side of the river Godavari without any outside impingement. The general cursive style of engraving, the elongated verticals of *ka* and *ra* with their lower ends curving to the left and the addition of the definite solid triangular head-marks in the Velpuru inscriptions have much resemblance with the later Sātavāhana records from Amaravati. The Gunji rock inscription shows an acquaintance with line head-mark but does not give it regularly. The equalization of the verticals is maintained to some extent but the verticals of *a, ka* and *ra* are elongated. Some change is effected to the letter-forms of *da, bha, va, sa,* etc. The characters of the Kirari inscription are more developed than the Gunji rock inscription. They are characterized by solid triangular head-marks, and the medial vowels follow the Deccani style and show ornamental curves in the case of *i*. The verticals of *a, ka,* and *ra* are gently curved. *Ya* is of the tripartite form. The straight base-line of *ṇa* and *na* are curved. The triangle of *kha, ma* and *va* are retained. The left vertical of the square type of *ba* is shrunken. On the basis of palaeography, Dani fixed the dates of the Gunji and Kirari inscriptions in the early and middle part of the third century AD respectively.[20] Therefore, there seems to be no point in comparing these inscriptions with the inscriptions of Khandagiri and Udayagiri hills. Palaeographical comparison is possible only in the case of a particular group of inscriptions from a particular locality.

However, it cannot be doubted that the script used in HI and MBIs are posterior to the Aśokan Brāhmī. Notwithstanding the minor variations here and there, they agree in their essential characters and may be grouped as a stage in the development of the Brāhmī in Orissa. As palaeography is a variable factor and dates assigned to the undated epigraph on its sole evidence admit of wide divergence, it is safe to keep them within the broad time-bracket, i.e., *circa* 100 BC and AD 100.

Vowels

Among the initial vowels *a, u, e, ai* and *o* are found in the inscriptions. The diphthong *ai* is an important addition where both the initial and medial forms of *e* are combined together as in *ai* (*Pl.* IIa.1, HI-1 — *airena;* MGI-LS-A — *airasa*). The letter *a* is represented by its cursive variety with its two curves meeting the vertical at two different points. Optionally the upper curve is drawn angularly. The initial *a* is not found and *i* occurred once in HI but the letter is not distinct.

20. Dani, *op. cit.*, 92.

The other vowels like *u*, *e* and *o* have shown no deviation from the Aśokan Brāhmī type, except in some cases the point of *e* tend to become a curve, e.g., *e* (*Pl.* IIa.1, HI-8 — *etina*). As has been referred to in the preceding chapter the sign for the initial *o* is reversed in RED and REJ. But in HI the letter-form resembles the standard Aśokan *o* with its vertical slightly bent.

Consonants

One of the marked features in this stage of developement of the Brāhmī is that the vertical of the letters are reduced in size. This is the case in a majority of letters in HI but in MBIs we seldom find this feature. In the letters *ka*, *na* and *ha* in MBIs the verticals are optionally found reduced. Another feature is that the angular letters are becoming cursive and vice versa. In place of the pointed top of *ga*, angular *ta* and *bha*, curves have been formed. Similarly angular formations are noticed in the curved bases of the letters like *kha*, *pa*, *ma*, *la*, *va* and *ha*. It has been conjectured by some that in HI the verticals of the letters are thickened and knobes (Bühler's serif) are created at the top of the main verticals. After a close scrutiny of the letter-forms we fail to notice this feature anywhere in HI. Moreover, in Dhauli and Jaugada edicts *ra* is invariably written as *la*, whereas both *ra* and *la* signs are available in all the inscriptions under discussion. Finally, of the three sibilants only dental *sa* is used throughout the texts of these inscriptions. This does not mean that the writers were not aware of the other two sibilants. The table of alphabets discovered in TGI-B[21] contains six lines of the Brāhmī alphabets and the three sibilants are written separately and they are repeated thrice. K.P. Jayaswal and R.D. Banerji have traced a palatal *śa* in the word *viniśr̥to* (HI-17). But the correct reading of this word is *vinisito*. In fact, palatal *sa* does not occur in HI.

As has been discussed above, no significant change is noticed in letter-forms of *ka*, *ca*, *cha*, *ja*, *ṭa*, *ṭha*, *ḍa*, *ṇa*, *tha*, *da*, *dha*, *na*, *ba*, *sa*, etc., from the Aśokan Brāhmī. *Ka* is the same cruciform type with its vertical commonly found reduced in HI and optionally in MBIs. *Gha* is of three-pronged type but occasionally its rounded bottom is flattened. *Ca* is of semi-circular loop type. In one instance the semi-circle is turned to make a full circle (*Pl.* IIa.2, SGI — A-*ca*). The letter *cha* is elliptical. The three-armed *ja* is predominant throughout. But optionally the double-curved *ja* is also noticed. *Ṭa* is still a semi-circle opened to right. *Ṭha* is a perfect circle. *Ḍa* has retained its old angular form. The top and bottom horizontal lines of the angular *ṇa* are perfectly straight and parallel. Occasionally they are longer than the vertical joining them in the middle (*Pl.* IIa. 2, AGI-A—*samaṇa*). *Tha* is a full circle with a dot at its centre. In a majority of cases the back of *da* is drawn angularly. *Dha* is a broad semi-circle attached to the right upright. The base-line of *na* is still straight. *Ba* is either a square or a rectangle. *Ya* is crescentic. The double-curved type of *sa*

21. This inscription was noticed for the first time by J.D. M. Beglar in 1882. The whole inscription is written or painted on the back wall of the inner chamber of the cave. It is a repetition of the Indian (Brāhmī) alphabet. Possibly some young monk was trying to improve his knowledge of the alphabet by writing on the back wall of the cell.

is still current with its vertical reduced in size. *Ṇa*, *jha*, and *dha* do not appear at all. The rest of the letters show considerable variety; their old forms are drawn side by side with their transitional and advanced forms.

Kha: The letter *kha* has many variants. The old Aśokan Brāhmī form with a dot at the base of the vertical is nowhere traceable. Another old variety with a circle at the bottom is optionally appeared in HI. At times the circle is replaced by a triangle as in *Khāravelena* (*Pl.* IIa.1, HI-1). Another form is without having any appendage in its lower part, e.g., *khi* (*Pl.* IIa.1, HI-5 — *nikhita*). In MBIs the circle is represented in a peculiar manner and the letter is bigger in size, vide *Pl.* IIa. 2.

Ga : The older angular *ga* pointed at the top has been changed. Its pointed top is either rounded or flattened. Sometimes the sloping limbs are straightened and thereby form a different look as in *ga* in the word *kaliṅgā* (*Pl.* IIa.2, MGI-LS-A).

Ta : The angular *ta* with two slanting strokes making an angle is retained. Occasionally the vertical is reduced in size and the two strokes are either retained as in *ta* (*Pl.* IIa.1, HI-5 — *ahata*) or rounded as in *to* (*Pl.* IIa.1, HI-12 — *janeto*). In MBIs the vertical is not reduced but the angle is turned to be a definite curve, e.g., *to* (*Pl.* IIa.2, HGI — *pasāto*).

Pa : A number of varieties of the letter-form of *pa* are noticed in HI and MBIs. The hooked *pa* is still current in the epigraphs of the period, e.g., *pa* (*Pl.* IIb.2, SGI-B — *pasādo*; HGI — *pasāto*). Among the notable changes in the form of this letter mention may be made that its vertical is reduced in size and its rounded bottom is turned into a firm base-line as in *pu* and *pa Pl.* IIb.1, HI-5 — *puvarāja* and 2, MGI-US-1 — *pasādāya*, MIG-LS-A — *kudepa*). Further the letter has maintained equal height of its both the arms as in *Pl.* IIb.1, HI-9 — *kaparukho*; 2, MGI-US-2 — *papotasa*.

Bha : The angular *bha* is still current. One important change is noticed in the lower right arm which is now shifted exactly below the upper right arm and forms one single vertical line as in *bhiṁ* (*Pl.* IIb.1, HI-6—*bhiṁgāre*). In the other variety, the two lower limbs are drawn equal in height. In *bhū* (*Pl.* IIb.2, VGI-2 — *bhūtino*) the lower portion is totally rounded.

Ma : Two different forms of *ma* are noticed. One is the older form in which the lower part of the letter consists of a circle and the upper part of two well rounded curves. This circular loop type is regularly used in the HI and MBIs. Only optionally the transitional form is found in which the circle is turned into a perfect triangle but the two upper curves are retained, e.g., *ma* (*Pl.* IIb.1, HI-3 — *mahārāja*; 2, AGI-A — *samaṇa*; TGI-A — *kusuma*).

La : The hooked *la* is commonly found in MBIs. In a majority of cases in HI the right vertical is found reduced in size but the lower part is still curved. But occasionally the base-line is flattened and right angles are formed on both the sides as in *li* (*Pl.* IIb.1, HI-6 — *tanasuliya*) and *le* (*Pl.* IIb.2, MGI-LS-1 — *leṇaṁ* and VGI-2 — *leṇaṁ*).

Va : The letter *va* has at least two forms. The circular base type of *va* is still retained but its vertical is reduced in size as in *va* (*Pl.* IIb.1, H-11 — *puvarāja*). In the other form the circle is changed into a triangle, vide *va* (*Pl.* IIb.1, HI-6—*vāṭa*). This latter form is commonly found in HI. In MG-LS-2—*vadukhasa*, the circle of the letter *va* is drawn like an ellipse (*Pl.* IIb.2).

Ha : The archaic form of *ha* with its lower part fully rounded and the left vertical longer than the right is noticed in JGI—*mahāmadā* (*Pl.* IIb.2). In another variety, the letter is seen in flattening the bottom but not equalizing the height of the verticals, vide *ha* (*Pl.* IIb.1, HI-13—*hathī*). In the latest form there is an attempt to equalize the verticals and the letter is totally angularized as in *hi* (*Pl.* IIb.1, HI-4—*sehi*) and *hā* (*Pl.* IIb.2, MGI-LS-1—*mahārāja*).

Medials

Minor changes are noticeable in the application of the diacritical notations to the consonants especially in *i* and *ī*. Otherwise the rest of the medial vowels do not make any significant deviation from the old fashion. *Ā* is still a horizontal bar to top right. *E* is just the reverse of *a*. *U* is a small horizontal bar to the bottom right or below the consonants. In the older form the medial is attached below when the consonants have rounded bases. But as we have seen above, in the transitional phase those rounded lower parts of the letters are replaced by flattened bottoms and, therefore, the scribes now preferred to apply the medial sign exactly below the right vertical, e.g., *pu* (*Pl.* IIb.1). The long *ū* is obtained by doubling the sign for *u*. The old form of the medial *i* with a right angle at the top right is largely predominated in the present group of inscriptions. But changes are noticed in softening the right angles into curves as in *khi* and *dhi* (*Pl.* II.1) or totally making it as a slanting stroke as in *dhi* (*Pl.* II.2). The medial sign for *ī* has undergone total change. It is expressed by two slanting bars or curves emerging from the top of the letter; its use is solely confined to HI. The medial *o* is a single horizontal line attached centrally to the top of the letters like *ka*, *ga*, *ta*, *pa*, *ya*, etc. Once in HI the horizontal is found completely detached from the letter as in *go* (*Pl.* IIa.1). In the case of *ma*, the sign is either a straight line in the middle or two horizontal bars one placed on the top of the right limb and the other in the middle left as in *mo* (*Pl.* IIa.1, HI-1—*namo*). In the case of *no* the old sign is still used but unlike the reversed placing in the Dhauli and Jaugada edicts we find here its correct expression. The usual horizontal sign could be drawn by the writer, but in that case it could not have been distinguished from the consonant *ṇa*. Perhaps this difficulty compelled him to retain the archaic sign. The *anusvāra* is always seen in the form of a dot or a circle placed at the top right of the consonant.

Conjuncts

Only one conjunct, i.e., *nha* has occurred in HI where the consonant *ha* is placed below the right terminal of the base-line of *na* without any physical change (*Pl.* IIb.1, HI-4—*kanhaveṁṇā*). However, some scholars conjectured the occurrence of the subscript *ra* in conjunction with other consonants in HI[22] and MBIs.[23]

From the above discussion it is clear that the characters of MBIs show a perference for archaic forms which are optionally met with in HI. In HI there is a tendency to reduce the verticals and angularize the cursive letters. The general duct of writing does not eliminate the archaic letter-forms. This shows that possibly HI was incised at a time when the verticals had yet not been turned into of equal heights and when the curves had just begun to become angularized.

From the internal evidences it is also clear that MBIs are posterior to HI. But the most curious fact is that while some development is noticed in the letter-forms in HI, the other inscriptions preferred to retain the old Brāhmī forms. Besides, in none of the above inscriptions the "new-edged pen" is employed. The tapering thickness of the letters which is mainly effected by this technique is conspicuous by its absence. Dani who unnecessarily speculated that the non-introduction of the new technical tradition immediately after its introduction in north India is due to the provenance of the record in a remote region as Orissa, has probably erred because he assigned a later date to HI. In fact, the new technical tradition was not introduced to Orissa. It was popularized in north India only in the first century AD by the Śaka-Kṣatrapas. The possible explanation for the occurrence of both the archaic and advanced letter-forms is due to the bringing of group of scribes from Mathura by Khāravela to engrave the inscription in co-operation with the existing royal scribes of the court circle. They tried to imitate the coin technology and palaeography on stone with the help of the traditional tool and technique. We are one with the scholars who on the basis of occurrence of different types of the Brāhmī letters opined that in Khāravela's inscription the engraving of more than one hand is visible and they represented different localities.

The predominance of the old Brāhmī letter-forms in the minor inscriptions can also be explained in the light of the fact that while the royal scribes were instrumental in engraving HI, a majority of the minor inscriptions were the works of private individuals who were less acquainted with the innovations in writing styles in other parts of the country and preferred to stick to the local style. Unlike north India where popularization of the script was mostly due to coin technology and palaeography of Greeks and subsequently to the introduction of the "new-edged pen" by the Śaka-Kṣatrapas, in Orissa it was perhaps the teacher-taught relationship that preserved the art of writing. The TGI-A is a case in point where the table of the Brāhmī alphabet is engraved or painted on the backwall of the inner chamber of the cave. Some young monk had used the wall as a copy book and improved his knowledge of the alphabet by writing on it.

---

22. At one place in line 11 of HI, Jayaswal read *tra* in the word *tramira* but later on the reading was amended by Barua for *timira*.
23. In SGI-A and HGI the subscript *ra* is distinctly attached to the letter *ka* in the word *culakramasa*. This has been rightly deciphered by R.D. Banerji but later on scholars read it as *culakamasa*.

II

By the third-fourth centuries AD, the Brāhmī script has undergone some notable changes. The changes are noticed especially in the application of the head-marks, the diacritical notations, the cursive forms and in the ornamental flourishes. All these changes or elaborations imparted new faces to the individual letter-forms. They are on account of quick engraving and a fondness on the part of the engraver for the ornate style. But this is not the case everywhere. During this period certain regional variations have already appeared in different zones and each zone has a separate identity in the sense that a particular style of writing continued to dominate or develop in that zone with or without outside reinforcement. In Orissan context, it becomes difficult to trace the evolution of the Brāhmī roughly from the middle of the first to the middle of the third century AD, as no important epigraphical material can properly be fitted to this time-bracket.

Whatever inscriptions available to us so far point to a stage where some new features have already made their appearance. In the unusually thick and big size of letters in the BI and in the solid triangular headed and flattened bottom of Sitabinji letters we find no uniform style. This is obvious because the characters of the BI are developed locally whereas those of the SBIs are definitely intruded into this region from the south, especially from Andhra. The solid triangular head-mark, the long flourishes of the medial *i* and *u*, and the length of the vertical *ra* are some of the traits of these boulder inscriptions at Sitabinji which closely resemble those of the Ikṣvāku inscriptions of late third century AD. But the advanced features are seen in the addition of head-marks to both the limbs of *pa* and *ma* and also in the notched bases of some of the letters such as *ca, tha, dha, pa, ma,* etc. The SBIs should, therefore, be assigned to a date slightly later than the Ikṣvāku inscriptions, very likely to the fourth century AD. A few inscriptions[24] seem to be written in Sanskrit language. The type of the medial *i*, the conjunct *kṣa*, and the subscript *ya* used in them further confirm our contention that the script of the SBIs is decidedly brought from Andhra. One possible explanation for the intrusion of this script to north Orissa is that Sitabinji was a centre of Śaiva worship and the Śaiva ascetics and even the pilgrims might have come to this place from the south and perhaps they were responsible for engraving on these boulders. They are the works of the Śaiva ascetics is proved by the fact that a number of rock shelters have been discovered around Sitabinji and its neighbourhood which perhaps served as abodes of these ascetics. An inscription reading *purudhasa chicha maruta,* i.e., Maruta, the disciple of Purudha, incised on a boulder in the same site also points to the same direction.

Coming to the script proper, we find that only the characters of the BI are developed locally. In the BI, for the first time we come across the application of head-marks. Small horizontal lines are added to the top of the letters except *ga* and *ja*. In the case of *a, pa,* and *ma* it is applied to both the limbs while in *gha* it is noticed on all the three limbs. Of the vowels only *a* is used in this

24. T.N. Ramachandran, *JAHRS*, 19, 191-202, Nos. 13 & 14.

inscription where it has a cursive upper half and straight line below joining the right upright by a horizontal straight line. The old *ka* is used with its cross-bar slightly curved. *Ga* has a broad back and also a foot-mark at its left arm. *Gha* is totally rounded with its three prongs maintain equal height. *Ja, ra,* and *sa* are of the old type. *Ḍa* and *da* have angular backs. The verticals of *ta* and *va* are not seen. *Na* has a broad loop in the left and is terminal is seen in the right. The two verticals of *pa* are of equal height and it has also a firm base-line. The old form of *ma* occurred only once where the circle has turned into a square and the upper curves into straight bars. The other variety is a tailed *ma. La* and *ha* have developed a down-going curve at the bottom. The looped *na*, the tailed *ma*, the hooked *la* and *ha* are almost as developed as the Allahabad pillar inscription of Samudragupta. But the rest of the letter-forms so also the medial vowels *a, e* and *u* still recall the old style.

The solid triangular head-mark is an important feature of the SBIs. It is usually attached to the top of almost all the letters. In the case of *pa* and *ma*, it is found on both the limbs, in *sa* on the middle and right, and in *ya* only on the middle limb. One peculiarity is noticed in the addition of head-mark to *ga*. Sometimes the head-mark does not touch the main body of the letters and appears to be detached as in *ga, tha, da, ra,* etc. (*Pl.* IIa and b.4). The letter-forms seem to be angularly drawn and this resulted in the flattening of the bottom. The thickness of the middle of the base-line tempts us to remark that the writers actually tried to notch the base-line. At times, it becomes difficult to distinguish between *dha* and *va, pa* and *ma, ya* and *sa*. The other peculiarities are : *ga* has an inward bend at the bottom of both the strokes, *tha* is a triangle with a thick dot in the middle, *ya* has an inward bend in its left limb, the vertical of *ra* is unusually elongated and has a small curl to bottom left, *sa* is more angularly drawn with its right half drawn in one action while the left half is detached from the rest of the letter. The medial vowels *i* and *u* are only used. The medial *i* is either a broad curve to left as in *dhi* or a curve that springs from the head-mark and falls to the left even beyond the letter as in *si* (*Pl.* IIb.4). The medial *u* is a long vertical with a small curve to left as in *pu* (*Pl.* IIb.4).

Bibliography

PLATE-II

The following list follows the arrangement of the plates illustrated.

1. Hāthīguṁphā inscription of Khāravela, D.C. Sircar, *Select Inscriptions*, I, Book II, 213 ff. & pls. XXXVII-XXXVIII.
2. Minor Brāhmī inscriptions in the caves of Udayagiri hill, R.D. Banerji, *EI*, 13, 159-66 & pls.
3. Bhadrak inscription of Mahārāja Gaṇa, D.C. Sircar, *ibid*, 29, 169-74 & pl.
4. Sitabinji boulder inscriptions, T.N. Ramachandran, *JAHRS*, 19, 191-202 & pls.

4

Median Kaliṅga Script

IN the fourth and fifth centuries AD a major political development took place in Orissa leading to the emergence of small independent local powers in various sub-regional kingdoms such as Kaliṅga, South Kośala, Toṣalī, etc. Of these Kaliṅga was the earliest sub-regional kingdom where some local powers assumed leadership sometime in the middle of the fourth century AD. Kaliṅga, which was a part of the centralized administrative system under Aśoka and which was an independent state under Khāravela, passed on to the Sātavāhanas in the second century AD and the Muruṇḍas in the third century AD. The Muruṇḍa rule was voilently intercepted by *circa* AD 300 after which Kaliṅga plunged into a state of political chaos giving rise to the centrifugal forces which brought division and disunity. The weak and divided Kaliṅga was invaded by Samudragupta[1] and closely following his invasion she emerged as a homogeneous kingdom. By the time her political boundary shrank alarmingly and reduced her to a sub-regional kingdom comprising of a portion of Ganjam district of Orissa, and Srikakulam, Visakhapatanam and East Godavari districts of Andhra Pradesh.

As many as seventeen copper-plate grants so far discovered from this area supply the information that there existed several royal families claiming lordship of Kaliṅga.[2] Of these

1. The Allahabad pillar inscription (Fleet, *CII*, III, 1-17) makes us believe that Samudragupta in course of his south Indian campaign defeated the rulers of twelve kingdoms. The kingdoms conquered by him included among others, Koṭṭūra, Piṣṭapura, Eraṇḍapalla and Devarāṣṭra which are known to have been located in different parts of the Kaliṅga kingdom. Koṭṭūra is identified with modern Kothoor about 12 miles to the south of the Mahendra hills. Piṣṭapura is identified with Pithapuram in East Godavari district. Eraṇḍapalla and Devarāṣṭra have been identified with Erandapalli and Yellamanchili respectively in Visakhapatnam district (J. Dubreuil, *Ancient History of the Deccan*, 58-60 and 160), Eranḍapalla has been mentioned in the Siddhantam plates of Devendravarman and Devarāṣṭra finds mention in the Sringavarapukota plates of Anantavarman of Kaliṅga.

2. Scholars have not succeeded so far in reconstructing a comprehensive dynastic, genealogical and chronological account of these rulers. D.C. Sircar suggests that there were three separate dynasties, namely, the Pitṛbhaktas, the Māṭharas and the Vaśiṣṭhas (*The Successors of the Sātavāhanas*, New Delhi, 74). B.V. Krishna Rao is of the opinion that the Māṭharas and the Vaśiṣthas were two ruling families in Kaliṅga (*A History of the Early Dynasties of Andhradesa*, 386). This has been accepted by N.K. Sahu (*Utkal University History of Orissa*, I, 467-74) and K.C. Panigrahi (*History of Orissa*, 46). S. N. Rajaguru reduces them to only one dynasty, i.e., the Māṭhara dynasty (*Inscriptions of Orissa*, I, pt. II, 68-69). S. Tripathy has recently advocated the existence of three separate dynasties (*Inscriptions of Orissa*, I, 4-15) which can be accepted with slight emendation.

royal families, some rulers claim to be scions of the Māṭhara dynasty of Kaliṅga, some are known to belong to the Vaśiṣṭha-*kula* and others style themselves as Pitṛbhaktas (devoted to father), instead of referring to the name of a specific royal family to which they belonged. In the absence of any dynastic name of the last group of rulers, we prefer to call them Pitṛbhaktas in our subsequent discussion. The provenance of the records of all these ruling families as well as the internal evidence furnished by them apparently indicate that the Māṭharas and the Pitṛbhaktas ruled more or less contemporaneously in the territory between the river Risikulya in the north and the Godavari in the south. A majority of their copper-plate grants were issued from Siṁhapura and as such it became a bone of contention between the two families and continued to dominate their history. However, with the end of the rule of the Vaśiṣṭhas, the Rāma-Kāśyapa *gotras*[3] held sway over Yellamanchili-Pithapuram area of Andhra Pradesh while Singupuram was temporarily occupied by one Śatrudamana of an unknown family. Although the chronology of none of these ruling houses is forthcoming, yet it is generally accepted that they existed between *circa* AD 350 and 600.

Towards the closing years of the fifth century AD, the Eastern Gaṅgas were seen ruling over Trikaliṅga with their base of power at Dantapura. In course of time they claimed sovereignty over entire Kaliṅga and it was Hastivarman who used the title *sakala-Kaliṅgādhipati* in his charters for the first time which was incorporated in the Gaṅga *praśasti* and used by each king of the dynasty in a conventional manner. The Eastern Gaṅgas continued to rule over Kaliṅga for more than five centuries and a majority of copper-plate grants were issued from Kaliṅganagara identified with modern Mukhalingam on the bank of river Vamsadhara in Srikakulam district of Andhra Pradesh. Thus, the Vamsadhara basin formed as a potential resource base or the "nuclear area" of the sub-regional kingdom of Kaliṅga. Unlike the records of their predecessors in Kaliṅga, the Eastern Gaṅga copper-plate grants are dated in Gaṅga era, the initial date of which has been now accepted as AD 498.[4]

The Pitṛbhaktas and the Māṭharas were the earliest ruling houses in Kaliṅga to start the practice of creating the rent-free *agrahāras* in favour of pious brāhmaṇas, reputed for their learning and scholarship in different branches of study.[5] The practice was also continued by the Eastern Gaṅgas and Brahmanical settlements began to multiply in Kaliṅga. Brāhmaṇas not only in their individual capacity received land grants, but also collectively enjoyed tax-free holdings in the same village or villages.

3. Pṛthivi-Mahārāja who issued his Tandivada and Gallavalli plates from Piṣṭapura is stated to have belonged to Śrī-Rāma-Kāśyapa *gotra*, and, therefore, scholars preferred to call his family as Rāma-Kāśyapa.

4. V.V. Mirashi fixed the date of commencement of Gaṅga era as the 14 March, AD 498. He based his argument on the astronomical details found in the Gaṅga records (*EI*, 27, 1927ff).

5. Perhaps the practice had already been started sometime before these ruling houses. Because the Brihatprostha grant of Umāvarman makes us believe that there existed thirty-six *agrahāras* in Kaliṅga by the time of Umāvarman.

Another notable development of the period is that Prakrit no longer served as the language of the inscriptions and it was replaced exclusively by Sanskrit. From this time onward till the end of the Gaṅga rule (later branch) about the middle of the fifteenth century Sanskrit continued to be the official language. It was also the state language of other sub-regional kingdoms of early Orissa.

In the records of these dynasties at least up to the close of the seventh century AD a peculiar script is used. The script is peculiar in the sense that no uniform character was in vogue in these inscriptions. In the squat and rounded forms of essential characters, in the ornamental and simplified medial vowels, and in the varied forms of head-marks ranging from the dotted or double-dotted to the broad or notched rectangles, frequent alterations were made in the epigraphic palaeography of this sub-regional kingdom of Kaliṅga. Perhaps no other palaeographical sub-zone of early India had adopted so many writing styles as is found in Kaliṅga in this period. Such inconsistent and irregular characteristics make it altogether difficult to select a stylistic or dynastic appellation. Most of the editors of the copper-plate grants of this period and authorities on palaeography classify them either under "Southern variety"[6] or "Box-headed characters."[7] There is some validity in the first remark. But we see no reason why the script used in the inscriptions of the early ruling houses of Kaliṅga and the early Eastern Gaṅgas should be classified under "Box-headed characters."

A.H. Dani has attributed the style of Māṭhara inscriptions to the square-headed script (same as the box-headed script) of Vākāṭakas.[8] He explained three stages by which the square-headed characters infiltrated into this region and subsequently how a new form was evolved out of it. In the first stage the Māṭharas borrowed the style directly from the Vākāṭakas. Next, Indravarman I, the issuer of the Jirjingi plates, probably borrowed the script from the Māṭharas. Finally, the script took a new shape under the rulers starting from Hastivarman of GY 79 to Devendravarman of GY 183. During this period the solid square head-marks transformed into "broad rectangles."

Theoretically, these stages of development furnish a good technique to check the influences and counter influences of the scripts used by different dynasties ruling contemporaneously. But their generalization conveys many serious inconsistencies. However, Dani is the first scholar to notice a distinct variety of "broad rectangles" in the inscriptions of the early Eastern Gaṅgas.

The early ruling houses of Kaliṅga did not necessarily borrow the solid box-headed characters from the Vākāṭakas. In the whole range of inscriptions of these families only three copper-plate

6. J.F. Fleet, *IA*, 16, 131; E. Hultzsch, *EI*, 17, 330; R. C. Mazumdar, *ibid.*, 23, 56; R.K. Ghoshal, *ibid.*, 25, 194, 218; 26, 62, 132; 27, 33; M. Venkataramayya, *ibid.*, 28, 226, 298; R. Subrahmanyam, *ibid.*, 28, 175; 30, 37; D.C. Sircar, *ibid.*, 30, 112; 31, 89; G.S. Gai, *ibid.*, 37, 337.

7. Bühler, *IP*, 107; C. Sivaramamurti, *Indian Epigraphy and South Indian Scripts*, Madras, 1966, 198-99; P.R. Srinivasan and R. Subrahmanyam, *EI*, 37, 159ff.

8. Dani, *IP*, 177.

grants of Umāvarman and one copper-plate grant of his successor Nanda-Prabhañjanavarman, exhibit some letters, though not all, in the above script. The head formation is only a fashion and has not at all affected the existing local forms of the letters. Except the said charter of Nanda-Prabhañjanavarman, the head formations in the others show a peculiar "thickset ductus of writing." Angularity of the letters which is an important feature is not seen in these records except in the letters *a*, *ka* and *ra*. The characters have in all cases a tendency to assume a squat and rounded shape. Of the early Eastern Gaṅga records only the Ponnuturu plates of Sāmantavarman of GY 64 exhibit both solid squares and angular characters. In the subsequent charters although the angularity is retained to some extent, the head-mark changed a lot. The double-dotted head-formation which was peculiar to Kaliṅga appeared again and in gradual process assumed broad rectangular shapes. The notching of the base lines and other limbs of the letters is an inspiration derived from the Viṣṇukuṇḍins. It is for these reasons, therefore, the script prevalent in Kaliṅga from the middle of the fourth to the close of the seventh century should not be classified under the square-headed characters.

On the other hand, the characters prevalent in Kaliṅga during the period under discussion closely resemble to the contemporary south Indian script as used in the inscriptions of the Śālaṅkāyanas and Viṣṇukuṇḍins who were ruling the territory on the other side of the river Godavari with Veṅgī as their seat of power. The definite impingement of the script of this palaeographical zone on the script of Kaliṅga though cannot be ruled out, at the same time there is reason to believe that the script had maintained some peculiar traits which can be distinguished from that of the Śālaṅkāyanas and the Viṣṇukuṇḍins. Compared to the latter where the head-mark is less significant and the letter-forms more rounded, in Kaliṅga we come across different types of head formations and less rounding of the letter-forms. There is such a paucity of material for the period before the fourth century AD that it becomes difficult to hazard any conclusion as to how and when the southern variety of script infiltrated into this area. One possible explanation is that the Sātavāhanas who held sway over the southern part of Kaliṅga in the second century AD were instrumental for the infiltration of the southern variety of the Brāhmī to this area and thereafter it developed locally. Unlike Kaliṅga, the connected development of the Brāhmī up to the fourth century AD on the other side of the lower Godavari valley appears to be satisfactory in the sense that the Ikṣvākus who succeeded Sātavāhanas in the area made remarkable progress in the writing tradition which they inherited from their predecessors. There is cogent reason to believe that the writers and scribes in Kaliṅga continued the writing style which once penetrated from the south during the Sātavāhana domination and that they were not unaware of the developments made by the Ikṣvākus and later on by the Śālaṅkāyanas and Viṣṇukuṇḍins on the other side of the lower Godavari valley. The retrogression in the symmetrical writing of the Ikṣvākus and the preference for a simpler style of writing in the inscriptions of the Śālaṅkāyanas, and similar simpler style of engravings in Kaliṅgan inscriptions of the fourth-fifth centuries warrant that the professionals in Kaliṅga were more inspired by the Śālaṅkāyanas of Veṅgi. The so-called southern variety of script travelled over an extensive region and its influence is also felt in the Deccan. The Vākāṭaka and Gupta inscriptions of the Deccan exhibit a character that is pre-eminently south Indian. But for the box head-marks and the angularity of the letter-forms, they are grouped under a different style. Similarly, the script prevalent in Kaliṅga can only be affiliated to the broad palaeographical zone of south Indian, but its peculiar traits definitely developed locally and independently.

The so-called "Kaliṅga script" has already gained currency among the palaeographers. By Kaliṅga script G.H. Ojha makes us understand as the script that was prevalent in Kaliṅga from the seventh to the twelfth century AD.[9] Bühler[10] and David Diringer[11] divided the script into two groups such as "Early Kaliṅga script" and "Later Kaliṅga script."[12] Hans Jensen called them as "Elder Kaliṅga script" and "Younger Kaliṅga script." In the opinion of all these scholars the early or elder Kaliṅga script is the script used in the Hāthīguṁphā and subsequent inscriptions up to the fourth century AD whereas the script used in the copper-plate grants of the Eastern Gaṅgas has been characterized as late or younger Kaliṅga script. To them the later Kaliṅga script is the script where no homogeneous character is discerned and the letter-forms show all manner of mixed forms. Bühler has shown a difference in the writing style of the documents of the Eastern Gaṅgas up to GY 183 from that of their later inscriptions. In the preceding chapter we have preferred to call "Transitional Brāhmī script" and "Later Brāhmī script" to the Hāthiguṁphā inscription of Khāravela and other cave inscriptions of his successors, and the subsequent inscriptions discovered in Orissa up to the fourth century AD respectively. The later variety is seen in the mixed style of writing in the Eastern Gaṅga and Śvetaka Gaṅga records which derived its source from *Kuṭila*, proto-Nāgarī, Telugu-Canarese and Grantha characters. This later variety will be dealt with in Chapter 9. Between these two groups the records of the minor ruling houses of Kaliṅga and the early Eastern Gaṅgas up to close of the seventh century intervened. They exhibit a great variety in the application of head-marks, in the addition of notches to the base-lines and to other limbs of the letters, in the placing of the medial vowels and in the general angularity of the letter-forms. These are the peculiar traits which distinguish the script from the early and later group of writing styles prevalent in Kaliṅga. The script was in vogue right up to the time of Devendravarman I of GY 192 (AD 690). It will not be improper, therefore, if we call the style of the inscriptions of this intervening period as the "Median Kaliṅga Script."

In *Pl.* III and IV, the characters of almost all the known inscriptions of the minor ruling houses and the early Eastern Gaṅgas of Kaliṅga respectively have been reproduced. The characters of a few inscriptions of the Gaṅgas of Śvetaka have also been incorporated in *Pl.* IV.

9. Ojha, *BPL*, 92-94.
10. Bühler, *op. cit.*, 107-09.
11. D. Diringer, *The Alphabet*, London, 1953, 300.
12. Hans Jensen, *Sign, Symbol and Script*, London, 1970, 399.

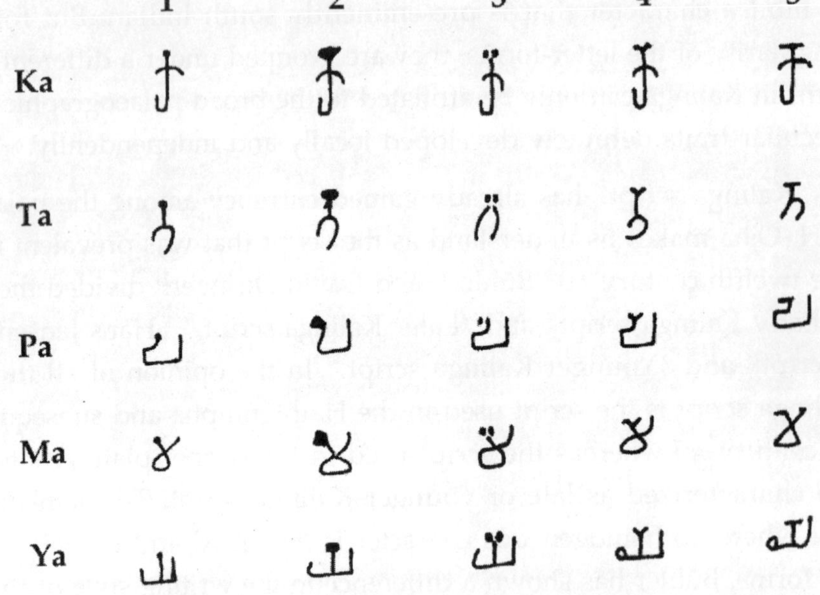

fig. 1a: **Development of head-marks in the inscriptions of the early ruling houses of Kaliṅga**

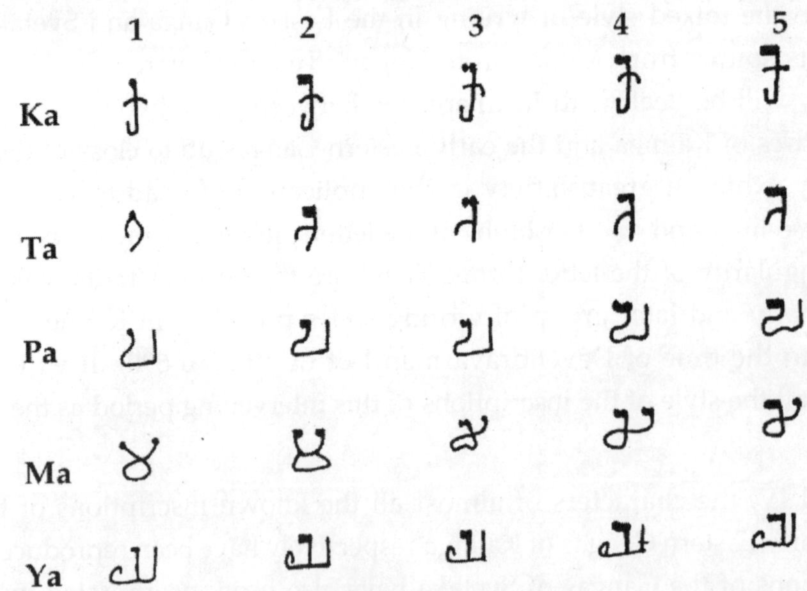

fig. 1b: **Development of head-marks in the inscriptions of the early Eastern Gaṅgas of Kaliṅga**

As has been said in the preceding Chapter, the head-marks became an important feature of the letter-forms in the third and fourth centuries AD. A close scrutiny of the head-marks used in the inscriptions of Kaliṅga reveals that they exhibit a great variety. In the Koroshonda copper-plate grant of Viśākhavarman the head-marks are small dots on the top of the letters, probably a development of the so-called serif used in the inscriptions of the early centuries of the Christian era. Except the Baranga plates, where the head-mark is less significant, in the rest of the copper-plate grants of Umāvarman the head-mark is deeply cut. They are the peculiar "thick-set ductus of writing" which will be henceforth called as "block head-marks." At the first glance they seem to resemble to the solid box head-marks as used in the inscriptions of the Pallavas of the third and fourth centuries AD,[13] but in actual sense the writers tried to imitate the head formations of the Pallavas which was never perfectly employed on the copper-plates and hence the outcome of the block head-marks (*fig.* Ia.2). In other words, there is an interplay of solid box and block head-marks in the inscriptions of Umāvarman. Similar engraving is also noticed in the Ragolu plates of Śaktivarman who was ruling over Kaliṅga from Pithapuram. In all these records the head-marks are employed either on the top left or on the top of the verticals of the letters. The latter peculiarity is just the beginning which subsequently became more regular in the records of Kaliṅga. Usually the head-mark is seen on the left verticals of *a, pa, pha, ma, sa* and on the middle vertical of *ya*. Optionally it is attached to both the limbs of *ma* and even seen on the rounded tops of *ga, dha* and *śa*. The initial *i, e*, the consonants *kha, ja, ṇa, ba* and *la* are devoid of the head-mark. Very rarely it is attached to *la* (*Pl.* IIIb.2) and *ba* (*Pl.* IIIb.8).

The head-marks in the three copper-plate grants of Nanda-Prabhañjanavarman vary widely. The three documents appear to be written by three different hands. The serif of the Chicacole plates does not call for special remarks. In the Baranga plates there is no uniformity in its application; thick and thin lines are usually found but at the same time some block head-marks appear here and there. The Ragolu plates of the king is dated in his 24th regnal year and written by the same Mātṛvara, son of Haridatta, who caused to have written the Brihatprostha and Temburu plates of Umāvarman. The inscription display solid box-headed characters and the block formations are only sparsely met with. One more peculiarity is that the head-marks are mostly placed centrally on the top of the verticals. *A* and *ma* have head-marks on both the limbs. The other features are the same as noticed in the inscriptions of Umāvarman and Śaktivarman.

In the Komarti plates of Caṇḍavarman the head-mark is represented either by dots or solid box heads but in the Bobbili plates small horizontal lines usually appear on the top of the letters while occasionally a dot is placed to the left of the vertical. This is probably an inspiration derived from the Māṭharas. In the Ningondi plates of Prabhañjanavarman and in the Andhavaram plates of Anantaśaktivarman another peculiar variety of serif is noticed which is not known to have prevailed in any part of the country. It is represented by two small dots

13. *IA*, 5, 50ff; N. Ramesan, *Copper Plate Inscriptions of Andhra Pradesh Government Museum* (*CPIAPGM*), I, Hyderabad, 1962, 211-38 & plates.

placed either one on each side of the vertical or to its left (*fig.* Ia.3). The rounded tops of *ga*, *dha* and *śa* have given room to such head-marks. The head-mark is less distinct in the Ningondi plates but deep and clear in the Andhavaram plates. One important point is that the latter are written by the same Mātr̥vara who discarded the earlier practice of applying block or solid box heads and preferred to apply double-dotted head-marks.[14] This frequent change in the application of the head-marks without altering the essential characters of the letters evidently point to the conclusion that the head-mark does not necessarily affect the essential characters. But this is partly true in the sense that more often cursiveness or angularity of the letter-form largely depended on the head-mark.

Anantavarman and Pr̥thivī-Mahārāja who ruled over the southern part of Kaliṅga used line head-marks in their charters, whereas Śatrudamana who held sway over the northern part of Kaliṅga used dotted head-marks. The Srungavarapukota plates of Anantavarman is an exception because in this record there is a dip at the centre of the line exactly on the top of the vertical and, therefore, it resembles a wavy line (*fig.* Ia.4). Similar head formations are also noticed in the inscriptions of the Pallavas.

Except the Jirjingi plates of Indravarman I and the Chicacole plates of Indravarman III, where the head-mark is a small dot, almost all the early copper-plate grants of the Eastern Gaṅgas up to the year 133 (AD 631) exhibit the double-dotted head-marks. In all probability the Eastern Gaṅgas borrowed this stylized feature from the Māṭharas. But now a tendency has developed to draw the two dots closely and whenever there is any gap it is filled in by repeated scratching. As a result sometimes we notice solid box heads at the top of the letters. Optionally when the surface is not perfectly scooped out there appears a wavy line either on the top or bottom line of such head formations (*fig.* Ib.4). The striking similarity of the head-marks and also the letter-forms in the inscriptions of Sāmantavarman, Hastivarman and Indravarman II up to the GY 91 (AD 589) is due to the fact that they were all written by Vinayacandra, the son of Bhānucandra.[15] Vinayacandra's son Ādityamañci also continued the same duct of writing in the Urajam plates of Indravarman II. In the Andhavaram plates of Indravarman III, a majority of letters display the old type of double-dotted head-mark without any attempt on the part of the scribe to scratch the surface between the dots. So far as the head-mark is concerned, the

---

14. The Brihatprostha and the Temburu plates of Umāvarman, The Ragolu plates of Nanda-Prabhañjanavarman and the Andhavaram plates of Anantaśaktivarman are issued from Siṁhapura and prepared by Māṭr̥vara, son of Haridatta. The Bobbili plates of Caṇḍavarman are also issued from Siṁhapura and written by Māṭr̥vara's son Rudradatta. This would indicate that Māṭr̥vara and his family were residing at Siṁhapura and holding the office of *deśākṣapaṭalādhikr̥ta* in continuous succession.

15. The Trilingi grant of Indravarman I is also written by Vinayacandra, son of Bhānucandra. This is the single plate of a missing set. The date portion of the plate reads *aṣṭāviṁśati*, meaning 28. This may not be impossible but seems to be improbable that Vinayacandra served under the Eastern Gaṅgas for such a long time.

inscription has a close resemblance to the Andhavaram plates of Anantaśaktivarman referred to above and as such one may easily jump to the conclusion that the double-dotted head-mark is a peculiar trait confined to Andhavaram alone. But in the foregoing discussion we have made it clear that a good number of inscriptions of the Māṭharas and the early Eastern Gaṅgas discovered from different places also represent the same characteristic. Head-marks are generally attached to the top left of the verticals. They are found on the left limb of *a, gha, pa, pha, ṣa, ha,* etc., on the middle limb of *ya,* and on both the limbs of *ma* and *a* (optionally). In the case of *ga, ṭha, dha* and *śa,* it is less distinct. The letters *i, kha, ja, ṇa* and *la* are devoid of the head-mark.

In the process the style attained its climax in the Purle and the Tekkali plates of Indravarman III of year 137 (not 149) and 154 respectively. Both the plates are written by *Sarvādhikṛta* Śāmbapuropādhyāya, the son of *Hastādhyakṣa* Dharmacandra, and, therefore, they resemble closely. The head-mark is seen in the form of a broad solid rectangle. Occasionally, a wavy line is formed on the top surface of the rectangle. We are inclined to believe that the broad solid rectangle is an offshoot of the double-dotted head-mark. In the three grants of Devendravarman I we notice a retrogression in the style.

The characters of almost all the inscriptions under study belong to the southern class of alphabets. In the upturned curves at the bottom left of the verticals of *a, ka, ra*; in the broad loops of *e, kha, ca, ma, va, ṣa*; in the inward curves in the left arm of *gha, ṅa, pa, pha, ba, ṣa, ha*; and in the peculiar letter-forms of *ṇa, ta, na, bha,* etc., we notice definite traces of the southern duct of writing. The letter *ṇa* has developed a loop at its base and its stem is branched off into two downward curves. Henceforth it will be called as looped *ṇa*. This type of *ṇa* is usually seen in the Deccan. Optionally, the letter *ta* has a loop and resembles the looped variety of *na*. This looped *ta* is seen in the early Pallava records and also used by the Viṣṇukuṇḍins. In the early records the letter *bha* is represented by a notched left arm and in the Eastern Gaṅga grants it has developed a straight right upright. The former will be called as notched *bha* and the latter as angular *bha*. Another important characteristic of the period is the frequency in notching the horizontal base lines of most of the letters. In the early records of Kaliṅga we seldom notice this feature. But roughly from the middle of the fifth century this tendency has developed in this sub-region. This became a regular feature in the copper-plate grants of the early Eastern Gaṅgas. The use of stylus as the tool for writing on the copper-plate is primarily responsible for effecting such forms to the letters. On the other side of the river Godavari, the later Śālaṅkāyanas, the Viṣṇukuṇḍins, and even the Eastern Cāḷukyas continued the practice in their copper-plate grants. Since such peculiarities are due to stylus engraving, by no stretch of imagination it should be conjectured that the professional writers and scribes borrowed this feature from their counterparts on the other side of the lower Godavari valley.

The northern influence is traceable in the letters *ṇa, ta* and *na*. *Ṇa* has a double-curved top with either a sloping or a straight base line. Henceforth it will be called as double-curved *ṇa*. The left arm of *ta* is a curved hook added to the right vertical. In the subsequent discussion it will be

fig. II

called as hooked *ta*. The loop of *na* is shifted to the left and joined to the right vertical medially by a line. The northern characters are more frequent in the early Eastern Gaṅga records than in the inscriptions of the minor ruling houses of Kaliṅga.

Although the cursive style of writing is prevalent in the inscriptions of the early ruling houses of Kaliṅga, yet in the early Eastern Gaṅga records angularity of the letter-forms became a marked trait. The Koroshonda copper-plate grant of Viśākhavarman exhibits a type of letters free of extraneous imprint and developed locally. Barring the elongated verticality of *a*, *ka* and *ra*, all letters show the alignment to a definite size and proportion. They are compressed and rounded as in the inscriptions of the Śālaṅkāyanas of Veṅgī. The later inscriptions of Umāvarman show a preference for partial angularization of the letters, especially in the lower parts of *a*, *ka*, *ra* and the medial *u*. But a majority of letters are still rounded and do not significantly deviate from the general trend of cursive engraving that prevailed in Kaliṅga. Similar angular features are also seen in a number of inscriptions of the Pitṛbhaktas, the Māṭharas and the Vaśiṣṭhas. It is very likely that the professionals who received some inspirations from the Pallavas in imitating the solid box-headed characters also tried to alter the faces of the letters by angularizing them. But they never succeeded either in perfectly applying the solid box heads or in fully angularizing the letter-forms. However, the charters of Śatrudamana and Pṛthivī-Mahārāja show a strong preference for cursive engraving.

In all probability, the Eastern Gaṅgas inherited the writing traditions from their predecessors in Kaliṅga. Except the Jirjingi plates of Indravarman I (the plates are written in a sloping style and closely resemble to the similar style of engraving in the Siripuram plates of Anantavarman), the rest of their grants upto the GY 192 and Pherava grant of the Śvetaka Gaṅga Sāmantavarman exihibit a uniform style. Angularization of the letter-forms is more pronounced in these inscriptions. *A*, *ka*, *ra*, and the medial *u* are still angularly drawn. Besides, the two stems of *ga*, *dha* (optionally) and *śa* are straightened. In the letters such as *ta*, *na*, *bha*, etc., right uprights are seen in place of curves. But *ṭa*, *ḍa*, *tha*, *da* and *la* still retained the rounded features. It is difficult to account for the continuation of the same type of script for an appreciably longer period. It is perhaps the insular nature of the sub-regional kingdom of Kaliṅga and also the holding of the offices of *rāhasika* and *hastādhyakṣa* by the members of a single family with their names ending "candra" in continuous succession resulted in the continuation of the same duct of writing up to the time of Devendravarman I, son of Guṇārṇava.[16] In the early copper-plate grants of Kaliṅga, there is no specific reference to the name of the scribe although the name of the writer finds mention on several occasions. The early Eastern Gaṅga records up to the year 97 do not make any reference to the scribe. But there are examples where it has been clearly stated that the same person was responsible for writing and engraving on the copper-plates.[17]

It is not out of place to refer to the fact that this median Kaliṅga script had also travelled to South Kośala. The Terasinga plates of *mahārāja* Tuṣṭikara[18] is a case in point where the characters fully resemble to the Kaliṅga variety of script of the sixth century AD and to be more particular to the Jirjingi plates of Indravarman I. Although the box-headed characters are commonly found in the charters of South Kośala roughly up to the middle of the ninth century, this is only the extant specimen written in Kaliṅga variety of script. It seems that Sadgāmaka who had written the document with the cognisance of *Rāhasika* Subandhu possibly migrated from Kaliṅga. An interesting feature of the record is that the main document is written in the Kaliṅga variety of script while the outer side of the first plate is written in box-headed characters of the fifth century which exhibit utter carelessness on the part of the engraver.

The period witnessed the beginning of some new features in the inscriptions. The copper-plate grants usually start with an invocatory verse preceded by an auspicious symbol, i.e., *oṁ* or *siddhaṁ* which is represented by a spire with its tail falling either to the left, right or bottom. Dani has made a classification of the various types of *oṁ* into northern, southern and western.[19] If this classification is to be accepted then we find that a majority of such signs closely resemble

16. Bhānucandra, Vinayacandra, Āditya-māñci (-candra), Devacandra, Dharmacandra, Mātṛcandra and Pallavacandra possibly belonged to the same Apūrvanaṭa family of Eraṇḍapalli.

17. Vide *likhitam-utkirṇaṁ ca* in the Trilingi plate of Indravarman I (l.1 of reverse) and the Ponnuturu plates of Sāmantavarman (l.27).

18. *EI*, 30, 274-78 & pls.

19. Dani, *op. cit.*, 121.

to the southern type whereas towards the end of our period one or two examples display the northern variety (*fig*. II.7 and 8). Another peculiar development of the period is the use of *jihvāmūlīya* (*visarga* in combination with *ka*) and *upadhmānīya* (*visarga* in combination with *pa*). In south India, the *jihvāmūlīya* is a looped *ma* attached to the top left of *ka*, but in north India the loop of *ma* is converted into a triangle with its top opening closed by a horizontal stroke and it is placed above the letter *ka*. Dani has called the latter as north Indian "dumb-bell" form of *jihvāmūlīya*.[20] Only in one instance the "dumb-bell" form is found in Kaliṅga whereas on most occasions the southern type is found used. In the southern type, the head-mark is seen attached to the left arm or to both the arms of *ma* while *ka* is devoid of such head formations. The *upadhmānīya* is a simple cross within a rough square or oblong joined to the top of the left limb of *pa*. In course of time, the rough square or oblong is replaced by an oval with its top making a dip at the centre and the lower vertical of the cross is either retained or omitted (*fig*. II.3 and 4). In one instance, the upper portion is represented by two different curves coming in and joining the middle bar at two different points. Towards end of our period, a cerebral *ṣa* is used in place of *ma* in the *jihvāmūlīya* (*fig*. II.6) as in the Dharmalingesvara plates of Devendravarman and the same sign is also seen for denoting the *upadhmānīya* (*fig*. II.9) as in the Trilingi plates of Devendravarman.

The use of the final forms of *ta, na* and *ma* is altogether a new feature that we come across in the inscriptions of Orissa in this period. Usually the final forms of these letters are indicated by reducing their size and suppressing the head-marks. In such cases the consonant is devoid of the vowel inherent in it. In the Pherava grant of Sāmantavarman of year 185 (AD 683), a small tick (*halanta*) is added at the bottom of the final *t*. One peculiar type of final *m* is noticed at the end of the Narasingapalli plates of Hastivarman of GY 79, where it is seen in the form of two loops one above the other and a dot in the centre of the lower loop.

Interpunctuation and punctuation marks are used in these inscriptions. But they are not always correctly used. The sign for interpunctuation is either a small horizontal or vertical stroke or a dot. At times short curves are also seen in place of straight strokes. The punctuation marks are represented by double verticals or curves. In *fig*. II.5, an additional tick is added to the first vertical. In *fig*. II.6, a peculiar type of punctuation mark is seen where the first vertical has a rounded top and a dot inside. This peculiar type is reproduced from the Jirjingi plates of Indravarman I. At the end the copper-plate inscriptions are marked by a number of signs as in *fig*. II.

Vowels

The initial *a* has a hook and a straight or slanting bar on its top which join the right vertical slightly above the centre. There is an inward curl at the bottom left of the vertical. This type of *a* is regularly found to have been used in the inscriptions of Kaliṅga. Occasionally the letter is

20. Dani, *op. cit*., 158.

totally rounded and the small curl at the bottom appears to be a big curve as in *Pl.* IIIa.12. *Ā* is a downward curve springing from the lower part of the right vertical of *a*. *I* consists of a horizontal with its two ends go down a little over the two dots or circles. Sometimes the horizontal line is notched in the middle. This is called as the roof type of *i*. In the records of the early dynasties, the initial *u* is occasionally seen where it is represented by a simple hook but later on it developed into a broad curve opening to right. This has been defined as broad back type of *u*. *E* is in the form of a broad loop with a definite right vertical. Optionally the left arm is detached from the right stem (*Pl.* IIIa.9 and *Pl.* IVa.7) and the base-line is notched. The initial *ṛ* seems to be used once in the word *ṛpyavatī* in line 11 of the Tekkali plates of Indravarman of GY 154.

Consonants

Ka **:** The letter *ka* has a small upward stroke joined to the left of the lower end of the vertical. The middle horizontal is curved with its right end very often goes down. At times the small upward stroke goes up to the height of the middle curve but does not touch it (*Pl.* IIIa.11, 12; IVa.9).

Kha **:** The hooked *kha* has a line foot-mark is early inscriptions of Kaliṅga. Later on this line is replaced by a broad loop. The broad looped *kha* has occurred in *Pl.* IIIa.9 and 11 but it is regularly found used in the Eastern Gaṅga grants (*Pl.* IVa). In a majority of cases in *Pl.* IVa the base of the broad loop of *kha* is notched. In one instance, the terminal of the top hook curls in as in *khi* (*Pl.* IVa.7). In another example, the hook is doubly curved (*Pl.* IIIa.7).

Ga **:** *Ga* is having either a rounded or a flat top with its two arms maintaining equal height. Sometimes the two stems do not meet each other at the top. Optionally the left foot of *ga* is terminally curling in as in *Pl.* IIIa.10, 11 and *Pl.* IVa.7, 8, 9, 10. The later peculiarity is usually seen in the Viṣṇukuṇḍin inscriptions.

Gha **:** The letter *gha* is hardly seen in the inscriptions of the minor ruling houses of Kaliṅga. But in the records of the early Eastern Gaṅgas we find a number of examples where the three pronged *gha* has an important change in its left limb. The left limb slightly curls in and goes up.

Ṅa **:** The guttural nasal *na* is never used alone; it is always found in conjunction with other letters of its class and also with palatal *śa*. In the early inscriptions it is represented by a simple curve opening to the right and in most cases there is an inward dip at its left arm. In the early Eastern Gaṅga records it is seen in the form of a square opened to the right. The latter may be called as square variety of *ṅa*.

Ca **:** The letter *ca* is broad looped type, having in most cases a right stem and in others the stem gets a round shape. In one instance, the broad loop is drawn like a perfect square as in *cā* (*Pl.* IIIa.3). Occasionally the top left portion of the letter curves doubly and in such cases the small vertical upright between the head-mark and the broad loop is missing (*Pl.* IIIa.5, 11, and *Pl.* IVa.1).

Cha : The elliptical *cha* is seen used in *Pl.* IVa.4. In the other variety the letter has a loop on each side of the vertical as in *Pl.* IIIa.4 and 7. In the subsequent discussion this variety will be called as the butter-fly type.

Ja : The three-armed *ja* is still retained in the inscriptions under study. Minor changes are noticed in the left vertical and in the upper and lower arms of the letter. Sometimes the top half of the left vertical is rounded and slightly shifts to the left while the upper and lower arms are often drawn in an undulating manner.

Jha : *Jha* is a rare letter which looks like *ra* with an additional upward stroke to the right of the vertical. The letter-form is angularly drawn. *Jha* in *Pl.* IVa.4 is reproduced from line 13 of the Urajam plates of Indravarman of GY 97.

Ña : The palatal nasal *ña* is also never used alone. It is always found in conjunction with other consonants of its class. It consists of a terminally curved top horizontal attached to the right vertical and an angular right hook projecting downwards from the centre of that vertical. Like *a, ka,* and *ra,* the letter has also an upturned curve to the bottom left of the vertical. Towards the end of our period the top horizontal makes a double bend and occasionally an inward curve is noticed in top left of the horizontal.

Ṭa : The old form of the semi-circular *ṭa* still persists largely, but optionally a right angle is formed at the base. This angular feature is generally noticed in the inscriptions of the minor ruling houses whereas in the early Eastern Gaṅga records the letter has developed a broad back with its opening to the right.

Ṭha : The letter *ṭha* is only noticed in the inscriptions of the Māṭhara king Anantaśaktivarman where it is either represented by a simple circle or square (*Pl.* IIIa.8 and 9). One peculiarity is that in the circular type of *ṭha* a head-mark is attached to the top of the letter.

Ḍa & Da : It becomes very difficult to make a distinction between *ḍa* and *da*. Both the letters are having broad backs with their opening to the right. The only difference is that *da* has both angular and cursive back while *ḍa* has only the cursive back. The letter-forms can be termed as broad back type of *ḍa* and *da*.

Ṇa : Both the north Indian and the Deccanese letter-forms of *ṇa* are met with in the inscriptions of our period. We have traced out at least two varieties of north Indian *ṇa* in Kaliṅga : (a) In the first variety a loop is drawn at the left of the base and the letter has two outer curves as in *ṇi* (*Pl.* IIIa.2). This is reproduced from the Baranga plates of Umāvarman and similar form of the letter is also seen in the Allahabad pillar inscription, the Susunia rock inscription and also in the Asanapat image inscription. (b) In the second variety, a small base line from the ends of which two curves branch off in two different directions as in *Pl.* IIIa.11, and *Pl.* IVa.1, 7, 8, 9, 10, 11. The second variety is regularly found used after the Purle plates of Indravarman III. In the subsequent discussion the first and second variety of the north Indian *ṇa* will be called as

Photo 4.1 (a): Andhavaram plates of Anantaśaktivarman (i)

Photo 4.1 (b): Andhavaram plates of Anantaśaktivarman (ii a)

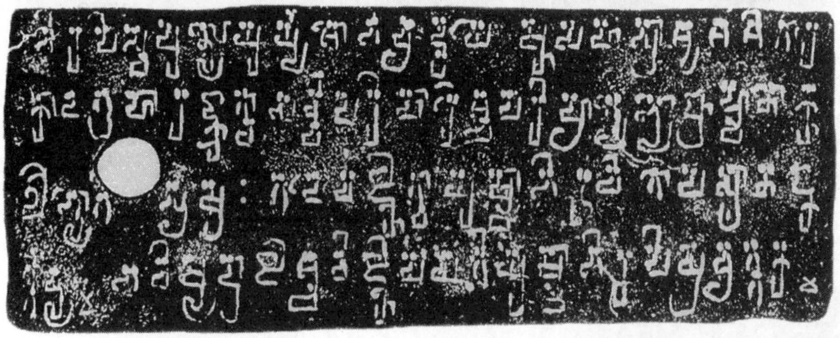

Photo 4.1 (c): Andhavaram plates of Anantaśaktivarman (ii b)

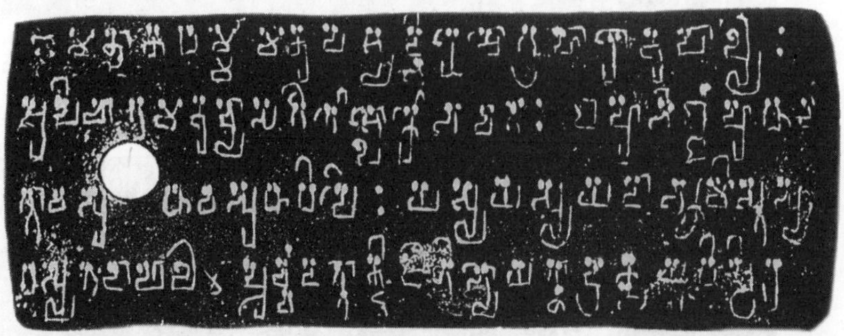

Photo 4.1 (d): Andhavaram plates of Anantaśaktivarman (iii a)

Photo 4.1 (e): Andhavaram plates of Anantaśaktivarman (iii b)

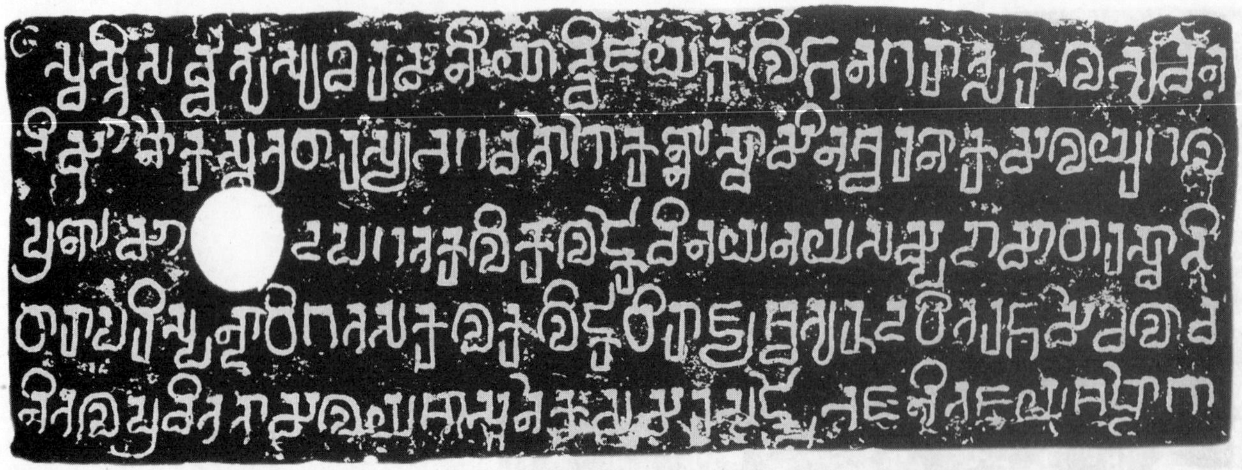

Photo 4.2 (a) : Urajam plate of Indravarman, GY 97 (i).

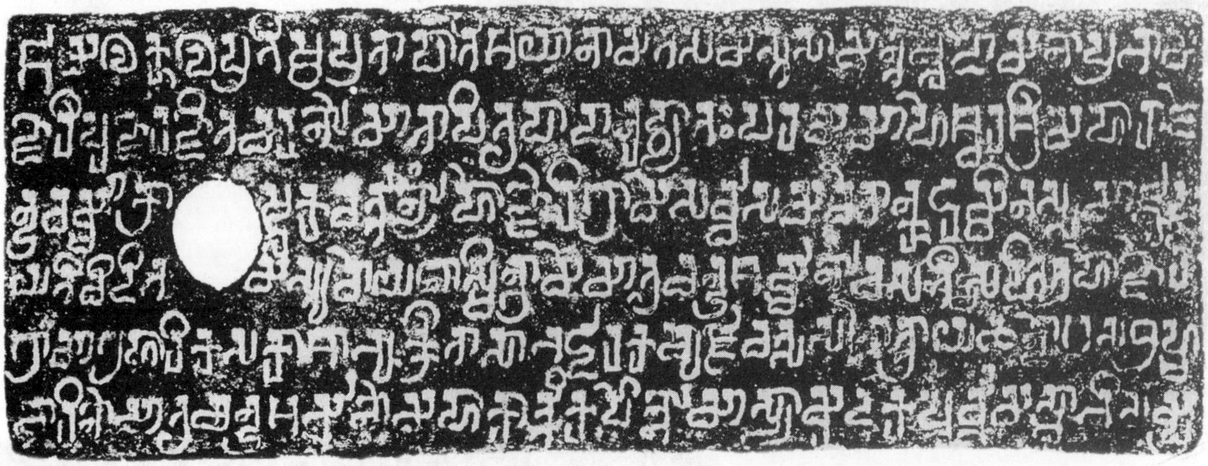

Photo 4.2 (b) : Urajam plate of Indravarman, GY 97 (ii a).

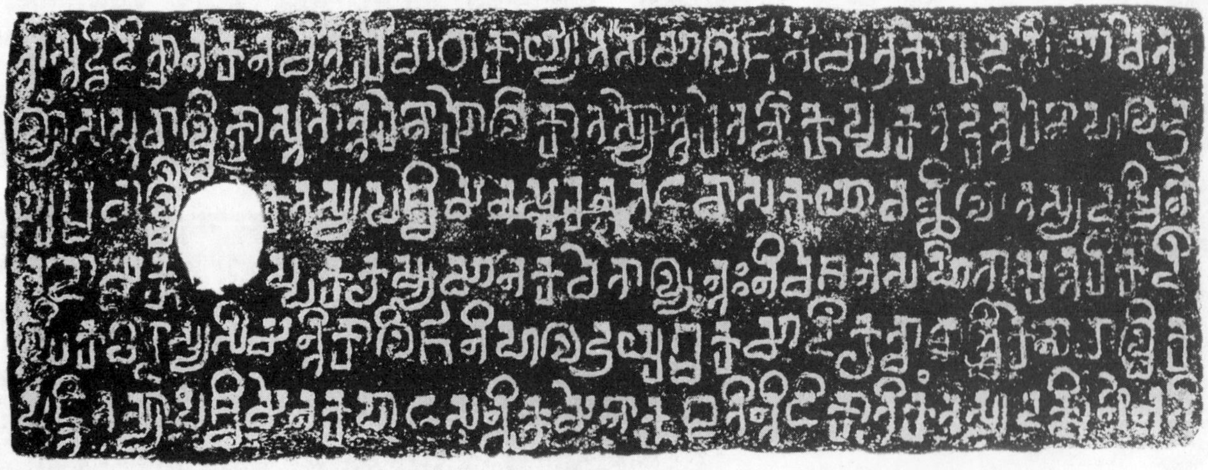

Photo 4.2 (c) : Urajam plate of Indravarman, GY 97 (ii b).

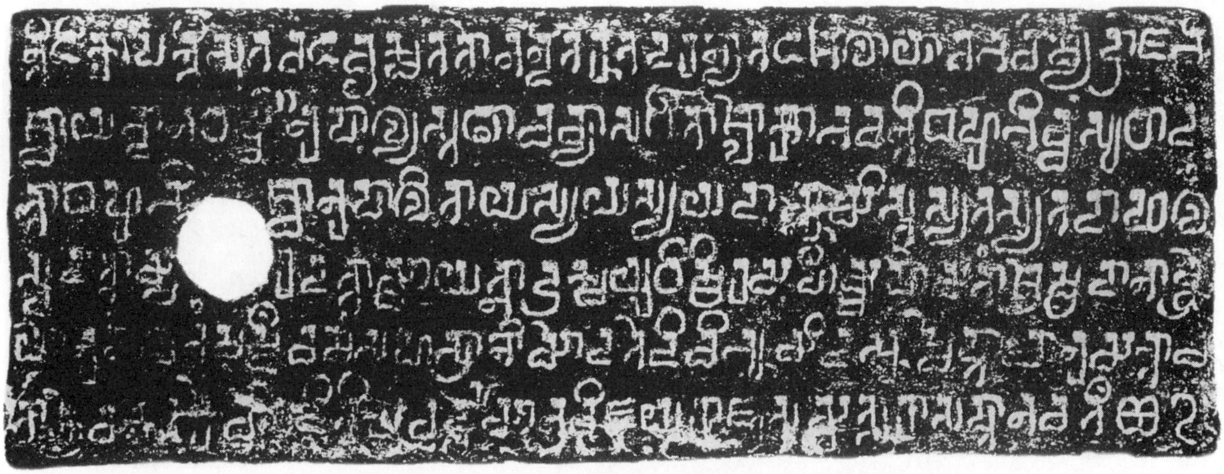

Photo 4.2 (d) : Urajam plate of Indravarman, GY 97 (iii a).

Photo 4.2 (e) : Urajam plate of Indravarman, GY 97 (iii b).

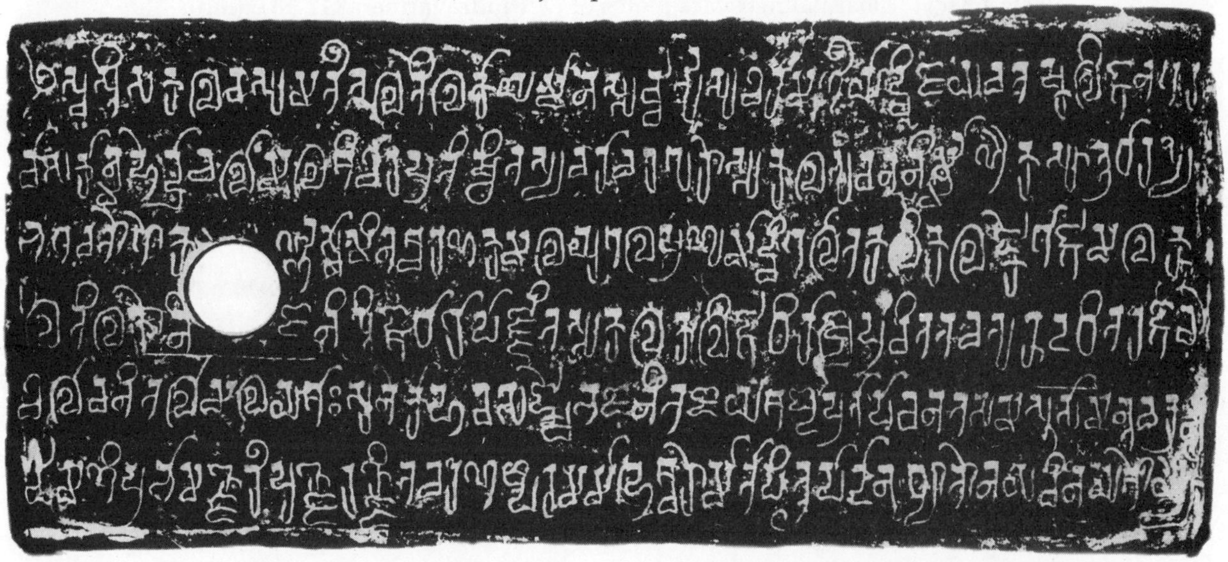

Photo 4.3 (a) : Dharmalingesvara plates of Devendravarman, GY 184 (i).

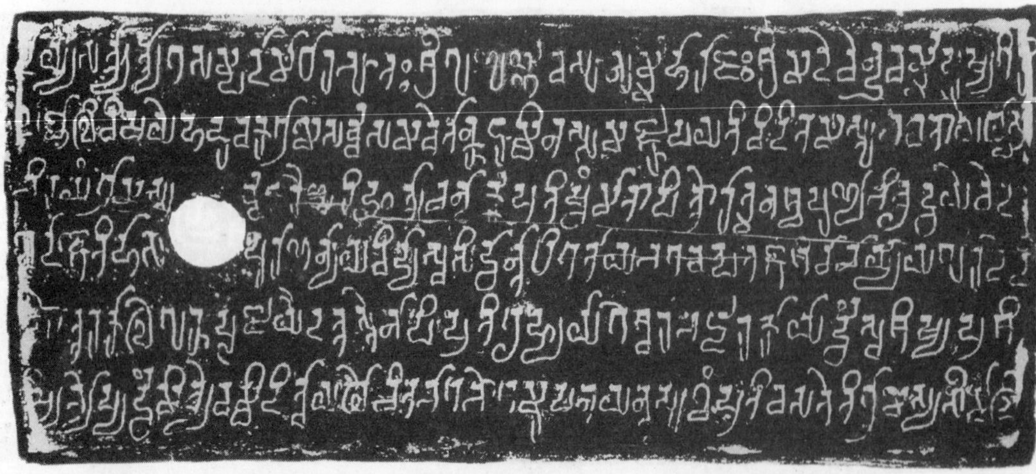

Photo 4.3 (b) : Dharmalingesvara plates of Devendravarman, GY 184 (ii a).

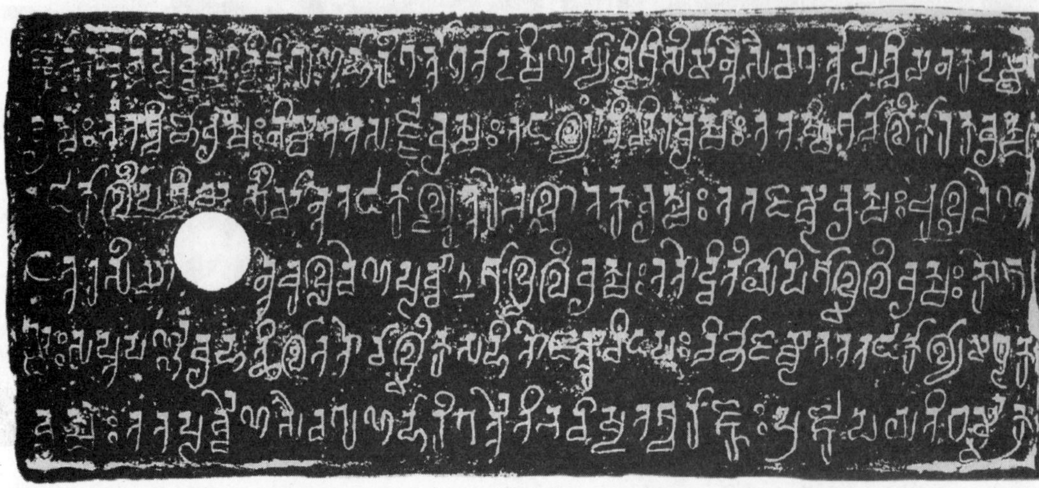

Photo 4.3 (c) : Dharmalingesvara plates of Devendravarman, GY 184, (ii b).

Photo 4.3 (d) : Dharmalingesvara plates of Devendravarman, GY 184 (iii).

"looped variety of the north" and "double curved variety" respectively. The Deccanese letter-form of *ṇa* is represented by a loop at the base and a short stem above which branches off into two downward curves from the top. This Deccanese form is used in the inscriptions of the minor ruling houses of Kaliṅga but later on under the early Eastern Gaṅgas, a definite right vertical is formed and the loop is shifted to the left and joined to the vertical by a small dash. Some peculiarities are noticed in closing the loop as in *Pl.* IIIa.2, 5, 10, 12, and in lengthening the outer curves up to the base as in *Pl.* IIIa.5 and 10. Hereafter this Deccanese letter-form of *ṇa* will be called as looped *ṇa*.

Ta : The archaic *ta* with its angular or rounded lower appendage still persists in the inscriptions of the minor ruling houses. Sometimes the small vertical is missing and the appendage meets the head-mark directly. Optionally, the appendage is disjointed at the top and thereby looks as two different strokes (*Pl.* IIIa.6 and 8). In the early Eastern Gaṅga records a definite vertical is formed and a slanting stroke or curve is drawn to its left. In one or two examples, the letter-form resembles to the looped *na* as in *tṛ* (*Pl.* IIIa.9) and *ti* (*Pl.* IVa.5). Similar looped from of *ta* is regularly found to have been used in Western Gaṅga and Viṣṇukuṇḍin records. Towards the end of our period the right vertical is found missing and the curve shifts to the right (*Pl.* IVa.8, 9, 10 and 11).

Tha : The circle of *tha* is represented in various manners and the central dot is retained in some cases but a tendency has now been developed to draw a loop at the bottom in place of the dot. In the later inscriptions the outer curves and the loop are drawn in one action. Hereafter this variety of the letter will be called as looped *tha*. In one or two Śvetaka Gaṅga records a horizontal mid-line is drawn inside the circle (*Pl.* IVa.11).

Dha : *Dha* is more or less shaped like an oblong or a rough square in the early inscriptions. Later on it assumed a somewhat rectangular shape standing heightwise with its top flattened and thickened (*Pl.* IVa.).

Na : The letter *na* is of looped variety. At times the loop is completely filled in as in *Pl.* IIIb.6, 10 and 12. In the early Eastern Gaṅga records although the looped *na* is retained to some extent in a majority of cases the loop is found attached to the right vertical by an additional line. In the early Śvetaka Gaṅga records the looped *na* is exclusively found used.

Pa & Pha : The old form of *pa* is seen in the letter *pi* (*Pl.* IIIb.5). One important change is made in the left limb of the letter which bends midway and then darts up as in *gha*. This variety of *pa* will be called in the subsequent discussion as "bent arm type" of *pa*. Sometimes the letter bulges out. In the later inscriptions of Kaliṅga the base line is notched. *Pha* is an additional limb curling in from the top end of the right vertical of *pa*. Initially it is represented as a small curl but later on it joins the base line and thereby forms a closed loop.

Ba : The square type of *ba* is optionally used in these inscriptions. Like *gha, pa,* etc., it left arm bends midway as in *Pl.* IIIb.6 and 7. But in most cases an inward dip is formed at its left arm. In the early Eastern Gaṅga records the base-line is notched.

Bha : The letter *bha* has a number of varieties. The first variety is represented by a slanting or straight stroke to the right and doubly curved arm to the left (*Pl.* IIIb.1, 2, 4, 8, 9 and *Pl.* IVb.1, 5). This variety of the letter-form will be called as 'double curved type' of *bha*. In the second variety an angular left limb joins the right upright medially as in *Pl.* IIIb.3, 7, 10 and *Pl.* IVb.2, 3, 4, 6. In the subsequent discussion such form of the letter will be called as angular *bha*. Still another variety is found in the form of a broad cursive appendage joined to the head-mark by a small vertical as in *Pl.* IIIb.5, 6, 11 and *Pl.* IVb.7, 8, 9, 10, 11. This will be called as 'broad type' of *bha*.

Ma : The letter *ma* is of the broad looped type. The loop is formed variously — square, oblong, elliptical, triangular, rectangular, etc. One important development is that the two side strokes on the top of the loop are removed to the extreme right. The base-line of the broad loop is often notched.

Ya : The tripartite *ya* with its shortened left limb is still noticed in the inscriptions of the Pitṛbhaktas and the Māṭharas. But later on there appeared an inward curl in the left limb. Sometimes the curl joins the base-line and therefore forms a loop as in *Pl.* IIIb.10, 12 and *Pl.* IVb.3, 7. Henceforth this variety of *ya* will be called as the looped *ya*. In the early Eastern Gaṅga and Śvetaka Gaṅga charters the left half of the base-line is notched while the right half is either angular or cursive.

Ra : Like *ka*, the letter *ra* has also developed a short upward stroke to the bottom left of the vertical. In *Pl.* IIIb.10, 11 and *Pl.* IVb.9 the stroke is further extended.

La : The letter *la* has at least three important varieties. In the first variety it is represented by a hook facing left and joined to the right upright by a horizontal base-line as in *Pl.* IIIb.1, 2, 7, 11 and *Pl.* IVb.1. This may be called as the hooked *la*. In the second variety the top of the right upright curves to the left and often it is extended downwards. The upper arm is either flattened or rounded and sometimes the base-line is notched. This is the standard type of the letter used in the median Kaliṅga script and may be termed as hooked *la* with an extended upper curve. In the third variety the hook is either facing left or down with a curve encircling it as in *Pl.* IIIb.9 and IVb.5, 10, 11. Hereafter this variety will be called as the 'circular type' of *la*.

Va : The letter *va* is either a small square or triangle with a definite right upright. Optionally it is rounded. In *Pl.* IVb, we find a number of examples where the base-line is notched.

Śa : The palatal *śa* resembles *ga* with an additional mid-line joining the two uprights slightly above the centre. The two uprights are of equal height. The top of the letter is either flattened or rounded and at times also crowns a head-mark. In *Pl.* IIIb.10, 11 and *Pl.* IVb.7, 8, 10, the left foot curls in and only on one occasion it touches the mid-line.

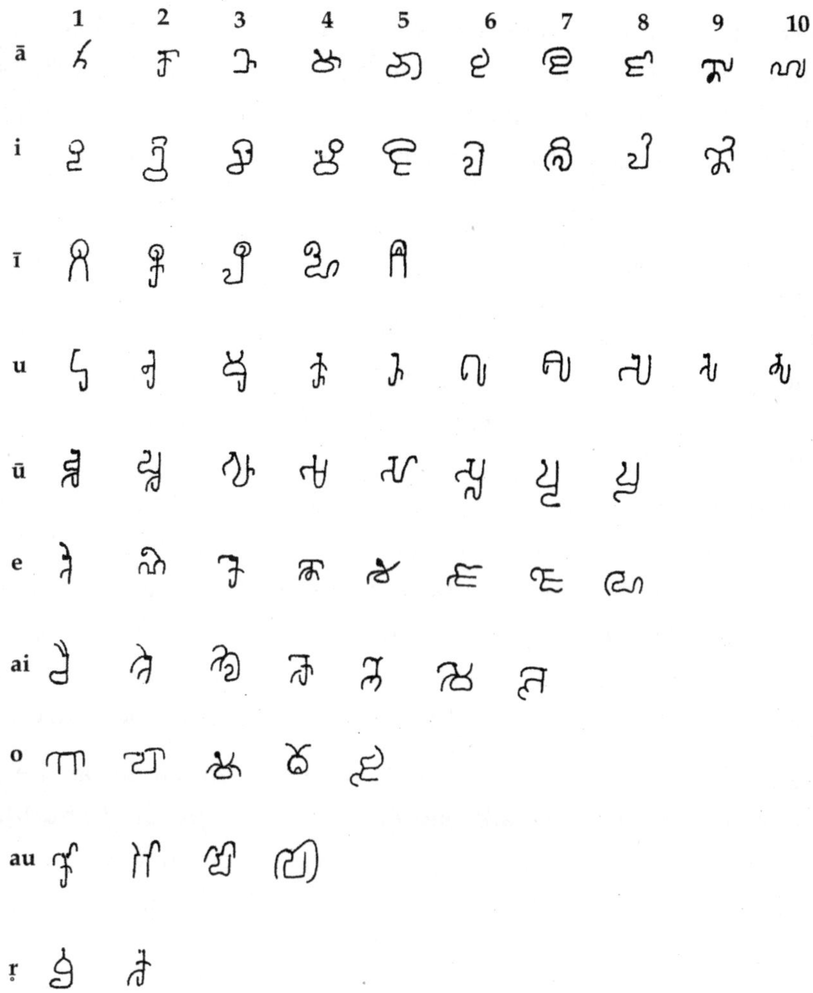

fig. **III: Medials in the Median Kaliṅga Script**

Ṣa : The cerebral *ṣa* resembles the bent arm type of *pa* with an additional line joining the two limbs medially.

Sa : The dental *sa* has developed a hook in its left limb while the right limb is represented by a broad upturned curve almost equal the height of the middle stem. In the subsequent discussion this variety will be called as hooked *sa*. At times a firm base-line is formed in its right limb. When the left hook is broadened the letter-form resembles *bhu* (angular *bha* with the medial *u*). In some of the early inscriptions, the letter is extremely angularly drawn as in *Pl.* IIIb.3, 7 and 8. In one instance it has developed an acute angle in its right limb (*Pl.* IIIb.7).

Ha : The letter *ha* resembles the letter-form of *pa* with its right vertical terminally curved out and moved down. In a majority of cases the right vertical is reduced in height and towards the end of our period it is totally missing. There are a number of examples where the body of the letter is bulged and rounded. In *Pl.* IVb.8, the bent arm in the left limb is not found.

Kṣa : In modern Oriya *kṣa* is considered as a consonant. It is for this reason we prefer to place the letter under the consonants. It is a combination of *ka* and *ṣa*. The superscript *ka* is devoid of its curve to the left and the vertical is also reduced in size. The left limb of *ṣa* joins the lower end of *ka* and the head-mark of the former is absent. Only occasionally, the head-mark is found attached as in *Pl*. IIIb.2 and 8.

Medials

The medial *ā* has a number of varieties. In the first variety it is seen in the form of a slanting stroke above the head-mark. In the second variety the old type of the medial with a horizontal to the top right is seen and it has developed an additional downward tick as in *kā* (*fig*. III.2). This is the usual form of the medial *ā* used in the inscriptions of Kaliṅga of our period. Sometimes the downward tick is extended unusually vide *cā* (*fig*. III.5). Optionally it is attached to the middle of the letters such as *kha* and *ma*. The third variety is represented by an upturned curve as seen *ṇā* (*fig*. III. 9 and 10). The medial *ā* while attached to the letter *ja* is applied variously. In one instance it is an upturned curve emerging from the middle prong. The curve is often unusually extended to the back of the letter and is of the broad curve type, e.g., *jā* (*fig*. III.7). In another example it first goes up from the terminal of the upper prong and then curves down (*fig*. III.8).

The common sign for the medial *i* is a small circle or semi-circle on the top of the letter. Sometimes it is noticed in the form of a broad curve as in *ji* (*fig*. III.8 and 9). The medial *ī* is indicated by an additional tick, hook or curl given inside the circular type of *i*. At times a small semi-circle is drawn inside the semi-circular type of *i* in order to denote its length, e.g., *gī* (*fig*. III.5).

At least three important varieties of the medial *u* are found in the inscriptions of Kaliṅga. The first variety is derived from the vertical type of the medial *u* used in the preceding period where the vertical has got a curved tip to the left as in *tu, nu, mu*, etc. The second variety is noticed only in the letters *ka* and *ra*. Since the curved tip already exists in the body of these letters, the medial sign is an angular hook running down from the right side of the vertical (*fig*. III.4 and 5). The third variety is represented by an upturned curve to the right as in *gu, tu* (optionally), *nu* (optionally), *bhu* and *śu*. The medial *ū* is an additional slanting stroke to the left in the case of the curved tip type of the medial *u* as in *cū* and *pū* (*fig*. III.1 and 2)., and a small hook on the right side of the upturned *u* as in *bhū* (*fig*. III.3). Sometimes a mid-line is drawn between the vertical and the upturned curve as in *bhū* (*fig*. III.4). The medial sign is often drawn as a gentle curve to right as in *bhū* (*fig*. III.5) or to left as in *sū* (*fig*. III.6). There are other examples where the medial sign is a broad curve either facing right (*fig*. III.7) or facing down (*fig*. III.8).

The medial *e* is either a slanting stroke or a terminally curved horizontal to the top left. These are the usual type of medial signs regularly found used in Kaliṅga. Optionally it is noticed in the form of a small curve running down from the top as in *je* (*fig*. III.7) or from the middle as in *ne, me*, and *je* (*fig*. III.4, 5 and 6). Towards the end of our period in one or two inscriptions we find the curve from the top totally covers the left half of the letter, e.g., *he* (*fig*. III.8). This may be termed as the broad curve type of the medial *e*. The two signs that individually denote *e* conjointly denote *ai*. Some peculiar signs are found in the form of a terminally curved horizontal and a curve from the middle vide *kai* and *mai* (*fig*. III. 4 and 6). The curve is often attached to the bottom of the letter vide *tai* and *bhai* (*fig*. III.5 and 7).

The medial signs for *ā* and *e* are combined together to express the medial *o*. Its peculiar application is noticed in *jo* (*fig*. III.5) where the medial *ā* is represented by an upturned curve from the middle prong of *ja* and the medial *e* by a downward curve attached to the lower left side of the letter, and in *mo* (*fig*. III.3) where both the signs are attached to the middle of the letter above the loop. It is also seen in the form of two curves springing from the head-mark in two different directions as in *tho* (*fig*. III.4). The diacritical notation for *au* is a downward curve or a slanting stroke to the top left and a hook to the top right. This will be called as the hooked type of the medial *au*.

R̥ is a broad curve opened to the left with a small inward curl usually attached to the bottom of letters. But in *kr̥*, it is a downward curve from the middle left of the vertical of *ka*.

Anusvāra is a dot or a small circle usually seen on the top right of the letters. Optionally it is drawn on the top of the letters as in *sṭiṁ* (*Pl*. IVc.4 and 9). *Visarga* is represented by two similar dots or circles one above the other on the right side of the letter.

Conjuncts

With the increasing use of Sanskrit as the language of the inscriptions more and more conjuncts are formed to suit its grammar and phonetics. In the conjuncts of this period, two consonants are placed one above the other without any significant change. As such the size of a conjunct is double the size of the consonants. Normally the second element is devoid of the head-mark. First of all we take into consideration the nasals. They are joined to the consonants of their respective classes (*vargas*) as superscripts. The guttural nasal *ṅa* joins the consonants of its class like *ka*, *ga* and *gha* normally at the terminal of its base. But *ga* very often merges its flat top with the base line of the superscript *na* (*Pl*. IVb.4 and 7) or both the letters are joined together by a small vertical on the right side (*Pl*. IIIb.2).

The palatal nasal *ña* in conjunction with the letters of its class is devoid of its upturned curve to the left and the second elements are appended to the bottom left of its vertical. In *Pl*. IVb.9 and 10, when the curve is retained, the subscript *ja* slightly shifts to the right. The conjunct *ñca* looks like *khā* (broad looped *kha* with medial *ā*). In the case of the looped *ṇa*, the subscripts *ṭa* and *ḍa* are joined to the outer curve of its loop; of the looped *ṇa* with a definite right vertical, to the lower end of the vertical; and in the case of the double-curved *ṇa*, to the right side of its firm base-line. On the first occasion, the loop and the subscript are drawn in one action. One peculiar feature is that sometimes the second element directly meets the top curve as in *ṇṭa* and *ṇḍi* (*Pl*.

IIIb. 10 and IV b. 7). This lingual nasal is often doubled vide *Pl.* IVb.2, 5, and 10. In *Pl.* IVb.2, although the flat roof of the second element is absent, in the other examples the subscript *ṇa* is fully drawn without any mutilation. Like the looped *ṇa,* the looped *na* also joins the subscripts of its class with the outer curve of its loop. In the early Eastern Gaṅga grants when a right stem is appeared in the looped *na,* it joins the subscripts at the lower end of its stem. *Pa* and *ba* are found attached to *ma* as second elements. *Pa* joins its left arm on the right side of the loop of *ma* and *ba* is drawn exactly below the loop of *ma* with or without an additional bar joining the two on the right side. In *Pl.* IVb.2, 3, and 9, the top horizontal of *ba* merges with the base-line of the loop of *ma.*

After the nasals we prefer to reproduce some of the conjuncts with *ka, ca, ja, ṭa, ta, da, pa, ba, śa, ṣa, sa,* etc., as superscripts. Of these *ka, ca, ja, ṭa, ta, da* and *pa* are sometimes doubled and they are not to be treated as orthographical peculiarities. Except *ka,* the other letters when doubled do not call for special remark. In *kka,* two horizontals intersect the vertical at two different points and there is no other change in the conjunct. *Ka* in conjunction with *ta* is devoid of the upturned curve to the left and the latter joins the lower end of the former either as two slanting strokes or a curve or hook. *Cha* is seen as a subscript of *ca. Ja* with its subscript *ña* forms the conjunct *jña* where the top horizontal bar of *ña* is often found merged with the lower prong of *ja* and its lower curve is fully represented. The superscript *ta* has a number of subscripts such as *ka, tha, pa, ma, sa,* etc. In each case the second element is engraved without any change in the main body of the letter. The first element *da* is found in conjunction with *ga, dha, ba, bha,* etc. The subscripts *dha* and *ba* are sometimes joined to *da* by an additional small vertical on the right side. In *pta,* ths subscript *ta* is found below the right arm of *pa.* In *bda* (*Pl.* IVc), the upper stem of *da* is attached to the right upright of *ba.* The palatal *śa* with the subscript *ca* is commonly found in almost all the inscriptions of our period. In one instance, *cha* is used as subscript of *śa* as in *śche* (*Pl.* IVc.3). The subscripts *ka, ṭa* and *ṭha* are usually found attached to the superscript *ṣa* exactly below its right vertical with or without an additional bar. The subscript *ṇa* is found just below *ṣa.* In the early Eastern Gaṅga grants, the upper portion of the subscript *ṭha* is often merged with the base-line of *ṣa.* The dental *sa* has a number of subscripts such as *ka, ta, tha, pa,* etc., and they are joined to the superscript without any mutilation.

There are some important subscripts such as *na, ma, ya, ra, la* and *va* which later on suffered so much change as to become totally different from their corresponding radical signs. At this stage of development only *ya* and *ra* have made some notable change. The subscript *ya* is a broad curve which first moves to left from the right arm of the first member and then again curves to right and moves up. Optionally it moves up to the height of the superscript. In *Pl.* IIIc.7, it is totally angularized. The subscript *ra* is represented by a left going curve from the right arm of the superscript. These two subscripts are also found attached to the existing conjuncts as third members. The second element *la* is normally devoid of its upper curve. But the cursive variety of *la* is always represented fully. In *Pl.* IIIc.12, it is drawn in a peculiar manner.

The *repha* is a small angle above the head-mark of the letters. Sometimes the sign also crowns a head-mark and the medial vowels are also attached to it.

Orthography

There are a number of orthographical peculiarities in the inscriptions of the period which deserve notice. They are : (a) use of the *jihvāmūlīya* and the *upadhmānīya*; (b) use of the guttural nasal *ṅa* in place of *anusvāra* especially before *śa* and *ha*; (c) use of *anusvāra* in place of final *m*; (d) use of *ṛ* in place of *ri*; (e) doubling of *dha* in conjunction with a following *ya*; (f) doubling of a consonant after *repha*; (g) occasional doubling of a consonant before *r*; (h) occasional doubling of the consonants like *ka, ta, pa, sa*, etc., and (i) occasional expression of *ba* and *va* by the sign for the latter. Besides, the rules of *sandhi* are not properly observed in a few cases and at times instances of incorrect syntax are found.

Bibliography

PLATE III

1. Koroshonda plates of Viśākhavarman, G. Ramdas, *EI*, 21, 23-25 & pls.
2. Plates of Umāvarman
   (a) Baranga plates of Umāvarman, S.C. Behera, *OHRJ*, 6 (2-3), 106-09 & pls.
   (b) Tekkali plates of Umāvarman, M. Venkataramayya, *EI*, 27, 298-302 & pls.
   (c) Dhavalapeta plates of Umāvarman, R.K. Ghosal, *ibid.*, 26, 132-35 & pls.
   (d) Brihatprostha plates of Umāvarman, E. Hultzsch, *ibid.*, 12, 4-6 & pls.
   (e) Temburu plates of Umāvarman, G.S. Gai, *ibid.*, 37, 337-40 & pls.
3. (a) Baranga plates of Nanda-Prabhañjanavarman, S.C. Behera, *OHRJ*, 6 (2-3), 109-14 & pls.
   (b) Chicacole plates of Nanda-Prabhañjanavarman, J.F. Fleet, *IA*, 13, 48-50 & pls.
4. Ragolu plates of Nanda-Prabhañjanavarman, N.M. Rao, *TGR*, 1-7 & pls.
5. Plates of Caṇḍavarman
   (a) Bobbili plates of Caṇḍavarman, R.K. Ghoshal, *EI*, 27, 33-36 & pls.
   (b) Komarti plates of Caṇḍavarman, E. Hultzsch, *ibid.*, 4, 142-45 & pls.
6. Ragolu plates of Śaktivarman, E. Hultzsch, *ibid.*, 12, 1-3 & pls.
7. Ningondi plates of Prabhañjanavarman, D.C. Sircar, *ibid.*, 30, 112-18 & pls.
8. Andhavaram plates of Anantaśaktivarman, R. Subrahmanyam, *ibid.*, 28, 175-79 & pls.
9. Madras Museum plates of Anantaśaktivarman, M. Venkataramayya, *ibid.*, 28, 226-35 & pls.
10. Plates of Anantavarman
    (a) Siripuram plates of Anantavarman, S.V. Srinivasa Rao, *ibid.*, 24, 47-52 & pls.
    (b) Srungavarapukota plates of Anantavarman, R.C. Majumdar, *ibid.*, 23, 56-61 & pls.
11. Pedda-Dugam plates of Śatrudamana, D.C. Sircar, *ibid.*, 31, 89-93 & pls.
12. Plates of Pṛthivī-Mahārāja

(a) Tandivada plates of Pṛthivī Mahārāja, R.S. Panchamukhi, *ibid.*, 23, 88-98 & pls.

(b) Parlakimedi (also known as Gallavalli) plates of Pṛthvī Mahārāja. S.C. De, *ibid.*, 35, 221-24 & pls.

PLATE IV

Eastern Gaṅgas

1. Jirjingi plates of Indravarman, GY 39, R.K. Ghoshal, *EI*, 25, 281-88 & pls.
2. Ponnuturu plates of Sāmantavarman, GY 64, M. Somasekhara Sarma, *ibid.*, 27, 216-22 & pls.
3. Plates of Hastivarman
   (a) Narasingapalli plates of Hastivarman, GY 79, R.C. Majumdar, *ibid.*, 23, 62-67 & pls.
   (b) Urlam plates of Hastivarman, GY 80, E. Hultzsch, *ibid.*, 17, 330-34 & pls.
4. Plates of Indravarman
   (a) Acyutapuram plates of Indravarman, GY 87, E. Hultzsch, *ibid.*, 3, 127-30 & pls.
   (b) Santa-Bommali plates of Indravarman, GY 87, R.K. Ghosali, *ibid.*, 25, 194-98 & pls.
   (c) Urajam plates of Indravarman, GY 97, P.R. Srinivasan & R. Subrahmanyam, *ibid.*, 37, 159-62 & pls.
5. Chicacola plates of Indravarman, GY 128, J.F. Fleet, *IA*, 13, 119-22 & pls.
6. Andhavaram plates of Indravarman, GY 133, R. Subrahmanyam, *EI*, 30, 37-42 & pls.
7. (a) Purle plates of Indravarman, GY 137, G. Ramdas, *ibid.*, 14, 360-63 & pls.
   (b) Tekkali plates of Indravarman, GY 154, E. Hultzsch, *ibid.*, 18, 307-11 & pls.
8. Chicacole plates of Indravarman, GY 138, J.F. Fleet, *IA*, 13, 122-24 & pls.
9. (a) Chicacole plates of Devendravarman, GY 183, E. Hultzsch, *EI*, 3, 130-34 & pls.
   (b) Dharmalingesvara (also known as Sudava) plates of Devendravarman, GY 184, R.K. Ghoshal, *ibid.*, 26, 62-65 & pls.
10. Trilingi plates of Devendravarman, GY 192, L.N.H. Jagadeb, *IHQ*, 11, 300-03 & pls.

Śvetaka Gaṅgas

11. Pherava plates of Sāmantavarman, GY 185, R.C. Majumdar, *EI*, 27, 108-15 & pls.

5

Box-Headed Characters in South Kośala

THE early history of South Kośala appears to be obscure. No systematic account pertaining to her history at least up to the middle of the fourth century AD can be possible from the available sources. No doubt the Purāṇas and the *Mahābhārata* furnish information about the existence of Kośala or South Kośala as a contiguous territory of Mekalā or Vidarbha, and lying to the north of Dakṣiṇāpatha. But the earliest epigraphic reference to South Kośala is made in the Allahabad pillar inscription of Samudragupta. The topography of this sub-regional kingdom was roughly comprising of Raipur, Bilaspur and Raigarh districts of Chhatisgarh and Sambalpur, Bolangir and Kalahandi districts of Orissa. The territorial extent of South Kośala was almost identical from the fourth to the ninth century AD. The upper Mahanadi valley and its tributaries formed its main resource base and contributed to the material prosperity of this sub-regional kingdom. Besides, the river Mahanadi served as the main artery that connected the hinterland of South Kośala with the coastal plains of Orissa.

In the middle of the fourth century, Samudragupta defeated the king of Kośala and passed through it to more southernly kingdoms of Dakṣiṇāpatha.[1] As the emperor had no intention of political subjugation of the conquered kingdoms of Dakṣiṇāpatha, so sometime after his exit the Nalas, the Rājarṣitulyakulas, the Parvatadvārakas and later on the Śarabhapurīyas and the Pāṇḍuvaṁśī-Somavaṁśīs tried to extend their sway over different parts of South Kośala. It is strange to note that none of these ruling families except the Pāṇḍuvaṁśīs claimed themselves as the rulers of South Kośala.

The Nalas were one of the earliest ruling houses in South Kośala to make rent-free land grants to the learned brāhmaṇas and registering the deeds on copper-plates. From the provenance of their inscriptions and coins it is believed that they rose to prominence in Koraput-Bastar area with their capital at Puṣkarī, identified with modern Podagarh in Koraput district of Orissa. The area did never form a part of South Kośala and the Nalas never mentioned in their records as rulers of Kośala or South Kośala. But the type of script prevalent in their inscriptions and the Puranic evidences induce us to group them with other ruling houses of South Kośala.[2]

1. J.F. Fleet, *CII*, III. 7.
2. In the *Vāyu* and *Brahmāṇḍa* Purāṇas it has been stated that the descendants of Nala would rule over Kośala. F.E. Pargiter (ed.), *Purāṇa Texts of the Dynasties of the Kali Age*, Oxford, 1913, 51.

Contemporaneous with the Nalas, the Rājarṣitulyakulas and the Parvatadvārakas had established their hold over the western and eastern parts of South Kośala respectively. The Nalas had entered into a conflict with the Vākāṭakas and this Nala-Vākāṭaka struggle continued to dominate their history in the fifth century AD.[3] The political confusion that was created in the wake of this struggle prompted the Śarabhapurīyas to grab political power at the cost of other ruling lineages in South Kośala. The Śarabhapurīyas held sway over South Kośala roughly up to the middle of the sixth century and then they were succeeded by the Pāṇḍuvaṁśīs. A large number of copper-plate grants of the Śarabhapurīyas and Pāṇḍuvaṁśīs have been discovered so far and most of them were issued from their capital Śrīpura, identified with Sirpur in modern Raipur district.

The script prevalent in South Kośala is characterized by the box-headed variety of the Deccan. In the fourth century AD, a new style of writing was evolved in Eastern Malwa and Vidarbha and the Vākāṭakas were mainly responsible for developing this. The chief characteristic of this, as Fleet recognized a century ago, is "the peculiar box-head tops of the letters, formed by sinking four short strokes in the shape of a square and leaving a block of stone or copper in the centre of them."[4] Dani selected a new nomenclature, i.e., "square head-mark" and reclassified it into two sub-varieties, viz., "solid square" and "hollow square" head marks.[5] But due to some obvious reasons, as will be shown later in this chapter, we prefer to subscribe to the old term "the box-headed variety." However, these peculiar head formations, as has been rightly pointed out by Dani, is "natural neither to pen nor to stylus."[6] He further suggested that it was a development of the new pen style or writing that was seen from the first century onwards in the north. Be that as it may, these head-marks are only ornamental limbs having no essential connection with the letter-forms. In the letter-forms, the southern influence predominated over the northern. The southern characters had penetrated into this region long before with the Sātavāhana advance into the north. At the same time, the intermediary character of this zone allowed the northern ideas to pass through it to more southern regions. The "Deccanese style," therefore, absorbed some elements of the north but they were not so forceful to outlive the existing southern duct of writing. The "Deccanese style" had spread over a wider area and became the accepted form of writing everywhere. It reached South Kośala sometime in the fifth century and remained as the

3. The Rithapur plates of Bhavadattavarman issued from the Vākāṭaka capital Nandivardhana makes us believe that the Nalas had invaded the Vākāṭaka kingdom, occupied Nandivardhana and established themselves for a time in Vidarbha. This incident took place during the reign of Narendrasena (*c.* AD 440-60). This is again confirmed by the statement in the Balaghat plates (*EI*, 9, 271) that Pṛthvīsena (*c.* AD 460-80) succeeded in retrieving the fortunes of the family. The Nala political power suffered a great set-back at the hands of the Vākāṭaka king Harisena (*c.* AD 480-500) towards the end of the fifth century.

4. Fleet, *op. cit.*, 19.

5. Dani, *IP*, 81.

6. *Ibid.*, 171.

standard script of this sub-regional kingdom roughly up to the middle of the ninth century. The early inscriptions exhibit both solid and hollow box-headed characters, notwithstanding the fact that a large majority of the records of the Nalas, the Śarabhapurīyas and the Pāṇḍuvaṁśīs are in hollow box-headed variety alone. As the box-head is a distinguishing feature of the Deccan and it was directly imported from there to South Kośala and remained as the standard script for a fairly long period, it is reasonable to christen the style as the "Box-headed Characters of the Deccan in South Kośala."

In *Pl.* V all the known inscriptions of South Kośala written in box-headed characters have been included for study of their palaeography.

Chronologically the Rithapur plates of Bhavadattavarman is the earliest known record of South Kośala to use the box-headed characters. The hollow box-head-marks are usually found on the top left of the letters and they are seen in the form of perfect squares (*fig.* I.3). Since the grant was issued from the Vākāṭaka capital Nandivardhana and its characters closely resemble to the Siwani[7] and the Pattan[8] plates of Pravarasena II, it appears to be more probable that Bhavadattavarman was much inspired by the writing style of the Vākāṭakas and he allowed the writers and scribes to follow the writing traditions prevalent in Vidarbha. In the Kesaribeda plates of his son and successor *mahārāja* Arthapati the scribe preferred to engrave in the solid or "scooped out" variety of the box head-mark as used in the Chammak copper-plate inscription of Pravarasena II.[9] The box does not always represent a square or rectangle but at times appears to be a circle or thick dot (*fig.* I.1). One important point that merits consideration here is that both the Rithapur and Kesaribeda plates were drafted by the Privy Councillor (*rahasyādhikṛta*) Culla. In view of the difference in head-mark as well as the general appearance of the essential characters of the letters, it seems that the documents were engraved on copper by two different hands although they were drafted by the same officer. The Podagadh stone inscription is also written in the solid box-headed characters. This is the only example of stone inscriptions in South Kośala written in the said variety. Owing to the nature of the substance working on, in the case of inscriptions on stone, the central blocks of the hollow box head-marks would obviously be very liable to injury both in the process of engraving and from the ravages of time. Therefore, the scribes did never prefer to incise the hollow square head-marks on stone. This is also the case in Central India where on a few specimens of earlier period such as the Nachne Ki Talai stone inscription of Pṛthvīsena,[10] etc., the scribes employed the technique but later on they discarded the practice altogether. Compared to this, on copper both the sub-varieties are well preserved and clearly recognizable.

---

7. Fleet, *op. cit.*, 243-49 & pl. XXXV.
8. *EI*, 23, 81-87 & pls.
9. *IA*, 12, 239ff.; Fleet, *op. cit.*, 235-43 & pl. XXXIV.
10. *Ibid.*, 233-35 & pl. XXXIII, A & B.

***fig.* I: Development of the Box head-marks in the inscriptions of South Kośala**

The additional endorsement in four lines on the outer side of the first plate of the Terasinga plates of Tuṣṭikara is written in hollow box-headed characters which exhibit utter carelessness on the part of the engraver. According to D.C. Sircar,

> The facts that it was engraved at the beginning of the main document in the box-headed script, perhaps to give it an earlier look, and that it exhibits numerous errors in both drafting and engraving may suggest that the endoresment is a forgery.[11]

The Śarabhapurīyas who stepped into political power of South Kośala in the beginning of the sixth century perhaps borrowed the writing tradition from the Nalas. *Mahārāja* Narendra, the earliest known ruler of the dynasty who is known to have issued three copper-plate grants, used both the sub-varieties of the box-headed character in his charters. His Pipardula plates are written in solid box-headed characters while his Khurud and Rawan plates are engraved in

11. *EI*, 30, 275.

hollow box-headed variety. The head-marks in a majority of cases in these plates are drawn in the form of solid rectangles (*fig.* I.2). Similarly, hollow rectangles are commonly found used in the Khurud and Rawan plates of the king. The Pipardula grant is the only record of the Śarabhapurīyas written in the said style, although the feature optionally appeared in the Khurud plates. It should be remembered that both the plates were engraved by the same scribe named Śrīdatta. As there is difference only in the application of the head-mark and no significant departure in the essential characters, we should rest content with the suggestion that the head-marks are only ornamental features without having any connection with the letter-forms. In the subsequent charters of the dynasty, the hollow box-headed characters continued to dominate the epigraphic alphabet of South Kośala. Unlike the charters of Narendra, the box-head is always seen in the form of a square or oblong in these inscriptions at least up to the time of Sudevarāja I. All the charters of Jayarāja and Sudevarāja I were inscribed by Acalasiṁha and Droṇasiṁha respectively. Golasiṁha, who very likely belonged to the same family of scribes, caused to have engraved the plates of Pravararāja and Sudevarāja II. Golasiṁha effected some change in the hollow box heads. The top horizontal line of the box is now slightly projected on both the sides and optionally the two strokes also go beyond the top horizontal. Besides, the left stroke is often drawn in a slanting manner (*fig.* I.4). These peculiarities are less clearly visible in the charters of Pravararāja but more clearly recognizable in the grants of Sudevarāja II. These may be considered as individual traits of the scribe in the superfluous part of the letters which in no way did affect the main body.

The Pāṇḍuvaṁśīs, who usurped the throne of the Śarabhapurīyas, ultimately adopted the existing writing style of the kingdom for another century and a half. In the copper-plate grants of Tīvaradeva, Nannarāja II and Mahāśivagupta Bālārjuna, the hollow box-headed characters as noticed in the later Śarabhapurīya records have been imitated. The top horizontal stroke of the box is still projected on both the sides and the left side stroke is still drawn in a slanting manner (*fig.* I.5). These features supply another specimen of excellent calligraphy in hollow box-headed characters. Thus, the hollow box-headed characters survived long in the upper Mahanadi valley in the plates of the Śarabhapurīyas and the Pāṇḍuvaṁśīs and this amply demonstrates the insular character of South Kośala.

As has been stated earlier, the box head-marks are invariably attached to the top left of the letters. In *Pl.* V.3, they are optionally found on the top of the verticals. In the case of the letters showing two verticals on the top such as *a, ā, pa, ṣa, ha*, etc., it is normally found attached to the left vertical; in the case of *ga, ca, tha, dha, śa*, etc., it is found above their flat tops; and in the case of *ya* it is joined to the middle vertical. When the box head-mark is attached to the flat tops it resembles a rectangle. The letter *gha* has the head-mark on its left limb and *ma* has it either on its left or right limb or on both the limbs. Occasionally it is also noticed in *kha* (*Pl.* Va.6, 10), *ja* (*Pl.* Va.1) and *la* (*Pl.* Vb.6). The initial vowels *i, e* and the consonants *kha, ja, ṇa, ba, la*, etc., are normally devoid of the head-mark.

The characters of the inscriptions under study belong to the southern class of alphabets. As has been pointed out above, the south Indian characters penetrated into the Deccan with the Sātavāhana advance into the north and they could hardly be outlived by any other force in the subsequent two or three centuries. The letter-forms of the Vākāṭakas of Vidarbha are pre-eminently south Indian and in them we see a development of the style of writing known in the late Sātavāhana records. "The hands show a mixed tendency to both angular and round shapes."[12] As in the use of both the sub-varieties of the head-mark, so also in the essential characters of the inscriptions of the Deccan and South Kośala, there is no appreciable difference except the greater stress on angularity of the letter-forms in the case of the latter. The southern duct of writing was also popularized in Kaliṅga and this may tempt one to attribute the style of South Kośala to that of Kaliṅga. No doubt the main grant of Terasinga plates of Tuṣṭikara is decidedly written in the median Kaliṅga script of the sixth century, but the script was not powerful enough to displace the existing writing tradition of South Kośala. Moreover, palaeographical tests have little independent value and, therefore, much to be construed on the strength of internal and circumstantial evidences. At the moment we subscribe to the view that the renewed contact of the Nalas with the Vākāṭakas in the fifth century AD led the former to popularize the script of the Deccan in their dominion. In the upturned curves to the left of the elongated verticals of *a*, *ka* and *ra;* in the bent arm type of *gha, pa, pha, ba, ṣa, ha,* etc., in the broad looped *ka, ca, va, ma,* etc., in the looped *ṇa;* and the broad curve type of *la* we notice unmistakable representation of southern characteristics. The north Indian peculiarity is seen in the letter *ta* where it is represented by either a curve or hook or a simple line attached to the right vertical medially. In the circle type of the medials *i, ī,* broad rectangular *kha,* simple lined *ta* and broad curve type of *la,* Dani has proved definite influences from the Gurjaras.[13] But in our opinion, these peculiarities could either be local developments or an inspiration derived from Kaliṅga.

Extreme angularity of the letter-forms is a characteristic trait of the inscriptions of South Kośala. It seems that the box-head is primarily responsible for imparting angularity to the letter-forms. In a sense the box head-mark led to the creation of angular forms. As such in most cases the curves are converted into angles. The loops of *e, kha, ca, ṇa, na, ma, va,* etc., are angularized and closely resemble a square or rectangle. The letters *u, ṭa, tha, dha, la,* etc., still prefer a round shape in the early inscriptions but they are also angularized optionally in the Śarabhapurīya and Pāṇḍuvaṁśī charters. The Kesaribeda plates of Arthapati exhibit a character which is less angular in comparison with the Rithapur plates of Bhavadattavarman and the Podagadh stone inscription of Skandavarman. The letter-forms are more rounded and their general appearance resembles to that of the Chammak plates of Vākāṭakas King Pravarasena II. The Śarabhapurīya charters are written in an angular manner. But the letter-forms in the Pāṇḍuvaṁśī records are more angular and elongated than those of the plates of the Śarabhapurīyas and much more so

12. Dani, *op. cit.*, 174.

13. *Ibid.*, 176-77.

than those of the Siwani and Pattan plates of Pravarasena II and the Balaghat plates of Pṛthvīsena II.[14]

Contraction of the breadth of the letters is another peculiarity of the box-headed script of South Kośala. This feature is clearly recognizable in the charters of the Pāṇḍuvaṁśīs, although in the earlier records the letter-forms are broad based. The tendency for elongation of a few letters as noticed in the later inscriptions is a direct offshoot of the contraction of the breadth of the letters. However, the Pāṇḍuvaṁśī copper-plate grants are very carefully engraved and they exhibit a highly ornate style.

Both the spiral and curled forms of the auspicious sound *oṁ* are used in the epigraphs of this period. The southern type of the spiral *oṁ* is frequently found used in the inscriptions of the Nalas and the Śarabhapurīyas while its northern type with a curled head is popularized in the Pāṇḍuvaṁśī charters (*fig.* II.6, 7 and 8). The *jihvāmūlīya* and the *upadhmānīya* are indicated by a looped *ma* joined to the top left of *ka* and a cross within a circle or quadrangle attached to the top left or top of *pa* respectively. In the case of the *jihvāmūlīya* the head-mark is invariably found attached to the left arm of *ma* and the second element *ka* is devoid of it. In the Śarabhapurīya charters the loop of *ma* is converted into a square or rectangle (*fig.* II.3). The peculiar type of the *upadhmānīya* in *fig.* II.4 is reproduced from line 14 of the Mallar plates of Pravararāja. Similar type of the *upadhmānīya* is also seen optionally in the Chicacole plates of the Eastern Gaṅga king Devendravarman of GY 183 (AD 681).

The final forms of *ta*, *na* and *ma* are used in the inscriptions under discussion. In the early inscriptions they are seen in their miniature forms at the bottom of the preceding letter. But later on they are drawn equal in size and proportion with other letters. In the Thakurdiya and Mallar plates of Pravararāja, the final *t* is represented by a curve falling to the right and two small verticals springing up from its round top. The right arm is bent gently medially  in *kuṭila* style. In the later Śarabhapurīya and in almost all the Pāṇḍuvaṁśī charters the *halanta* mark is applied to the final *t* and *m*. In the line 28 of the Bonda plates of Mahāśivagupta Bālārjuna, the final *t* is seen in the form of a small left facing curve and another big curve encircling it. The same sign also denotes the numeral 9 in contemporary epigraphs.[15]

The mark of interpunctuation is indicated either by a vertical, horizontal or a small dash. The last two signs are usually found in the Śarabhapurīya grants. In the Pāṇḍuvaṁśī charters the vertical is bent medially as in *fig.* II.5 or has developed a hook at the top left of the vertical as in *fig.* II.6. Two parallel strokes or a pair of horizontal strokes or dashes, one above the other, have been employed to indicate the mark of punctuation. Optionally a horizontal stroke with a dot both above and below has been used as a mark of punctuation, vide *fig.* II.3. This is reproduced

14. *EI*, 9, 267-71 & pls.

15. *Ibid.*, 33, 155-58 & pls.; 7, 102-07 & pls.

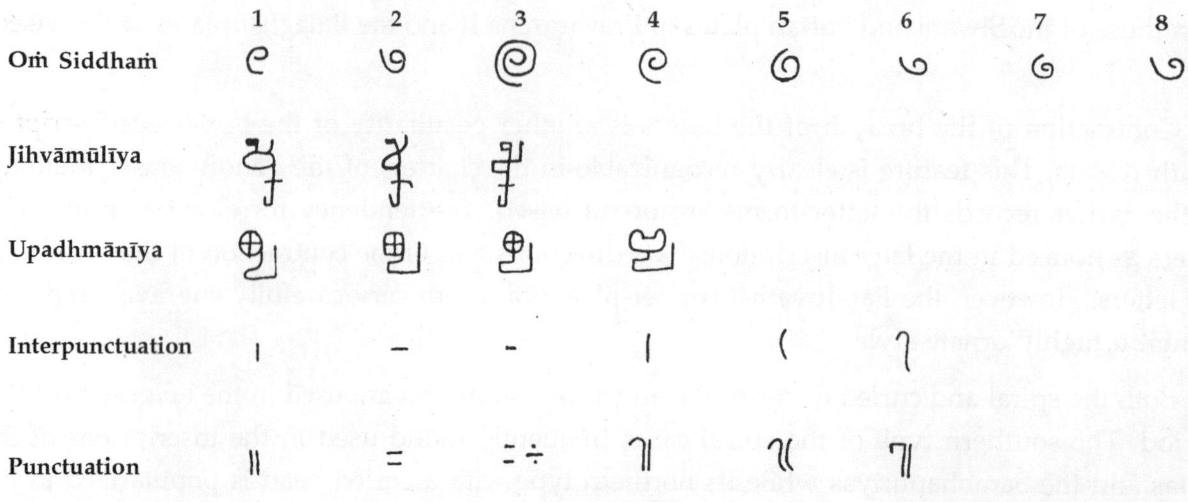

fig. II

from lines 12, 16 and 22 of the Mallar plates of Jayarāja of regnal year 5. In the later Śarabhapurīya and Pāṇḍuvaṁśī records, punctuation is shown by means of a vertical line with its top bent towards the left and followed by another vertical line (*fig.* II.4). In *fig.* II.5 and 6, the rounded top of the curve is flattened.

The Rithapur plates of Bhavadattavarman and the Lodhia plates of Mahāśivagupta Bālārjuna are removed from each other by nearly four centuries, yet in the characters of these two inscriptions we do not notice any significant difference. The long survival of the box-headed characters in the upper Mahanadi valley obviously point to the insular character of the sub-regional kingdom of South Kośala. A number of contemporary powers no doubt tried to break the insular position of South Kośala but they were not successful in their attempts. Even the characteristics peculiar to the grants of the Eastern Gaṅgas of Kaliṅga, the Pāṇḍavas of Mekalā and those of the Parivrājakas and the Ucchakalpas of Bhagelkhand in Central India made their flow to this kingdom in the sixth-seventh centuries but they had a very short life and died a natural death. The characters of the main document of the Terasinga plates of Tuṣṭikara, as has been discussed in the last chapter, are decidedly written in the median Kaliṅga script of the early sixth century. It is needless to repeat them here. However, the unusual and isolated occurrence of the Kaliṅga type of script in this part of Orissa is perhaps to be explained as the work of a Kaliṅga scribe who found himself in this region.

The characters of the Arang plates of Bhīmasena II belong to the northern class of alphabets and they closely resemble to those of the plates of the Parivrājakas and the Ucchakalpas in general and the Khoh plates of *mahārāja* Hastin of GE 163 (AD 482)[16] and the Karitalai plates of *mahārāja* Jayanātha of (Gupta) era 174 (AD 493)[17] in particular. The head-mark is indicated by a

16. Fleet, *op. cit.*, 100-05 & pl. XIII.

17. *Ibid.*, 117-20 & pl. XVI.

Photo 5.1 (a): Mallar plates of Jayarāja, RY 5 (i)

Photo 5.1 (b): Mallar plates of Jayarāja, RY 5 (ii a)

Photo 5.1 (c): Mallar plates of Jayarāja, RY 5 (ii b)

Photo 5.1 (d): Mallar plates of Jayarāja, RY 5 (iii)

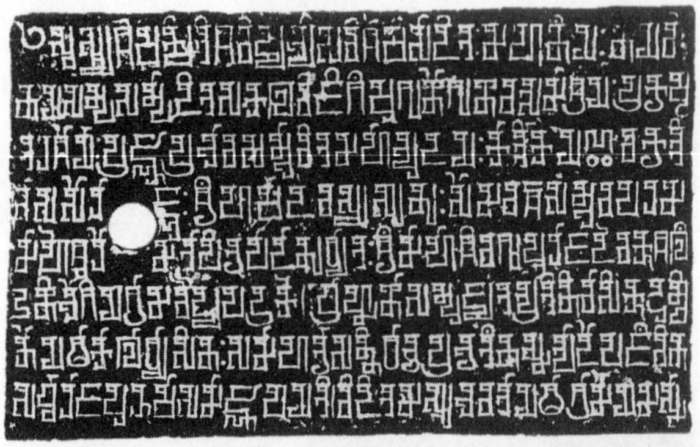

Photo 5.2 (a): Lodhia plates of Mahāśivagupta, RY 57 (i)

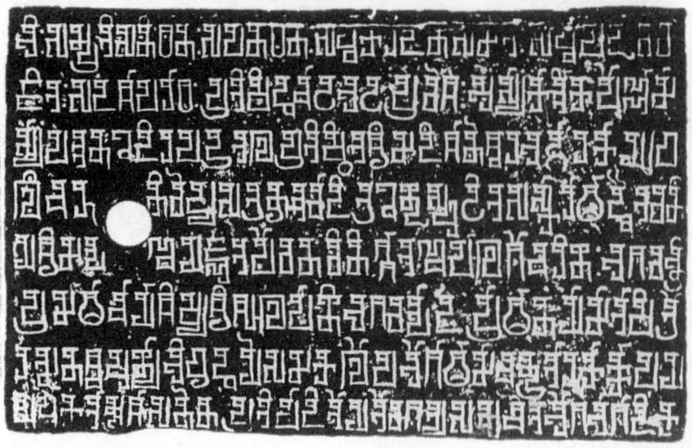

Photo 5.2 (b): Lodhia plates of Mahāśivagupta, RY 57 (ii a)

Photo 5.2 (c): Lodhia plates of Mahāśivagupta, RY 57 (ii b)

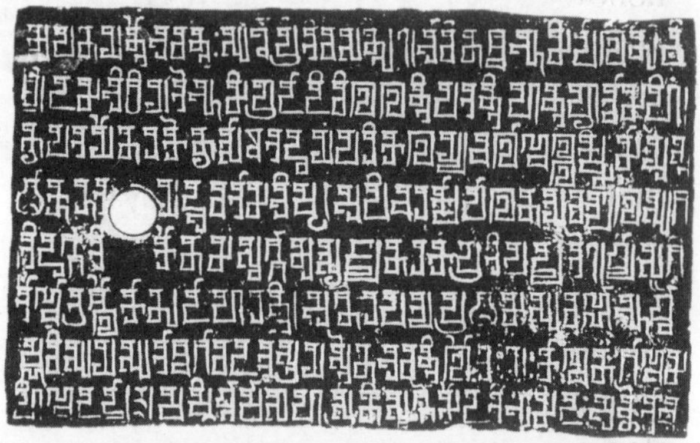

Photo 5.2 (d): Lodhia plates of Mahāśivagupta, RY 57 (iii)

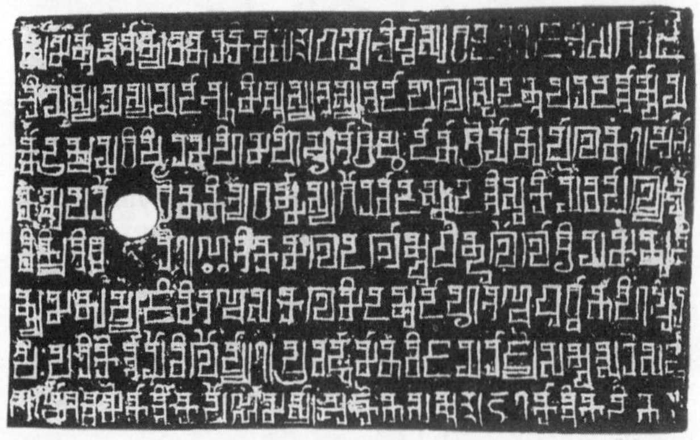

simple line. The most conspicuous of the test letters stamping the characters of the inscription as the northern class of alphabet, are the initial *ā* and the consonants *ka*, *ṇa*, *ra* and *sa*. The letters *ga* and *śa* have line foot mark in their left limbs; and the medial vowels are more simplified. There is no trace of acute-angle in the right side of the letters, but the letter-forms are more angular.

Another inscription which makes a significant departure from the box-headed characters of South Kośala is the Mallar plates of Vyāghrarāja of the Amarārya *kula*. The characters belong to the southern class of alphabets and on palaeographical grounds may be assigned to the seventh century. They represent a very rare type, in which the top of each letter, as a rule, consists of a small triangle with its apex downwards, and which, one that account, has appropriately been named "nail-headed." The nail head is of linear or hollow type and not of the "scooped-out" variety. According to Fleet, this nail-headed variety is a variation of the box-headed characters.[18] The known instances of the particular variety are the Poona plates of Prabhāvatīgupta,[19] the Majhgawan plates of the Parivrājaka king Hastin of year 191,[20] the Bamhani[21] and Mallar[22] plates of Pāṇḍava king Śūrabala, and the Malga plates of *sāmanta* Indrarāja[23] of an unknown family. Except the plates of Śūrabala, where we find an interplay of hollow triangular and box head-marks, in the rest of the inscriptions cited above the head-mark is always represented by a hollow or linear triangle. The characters of the Majhgawan and the Malga plates are exclusively written in the northern class of alphabets while those of the plates of Śūrabala and of Vyāghrarāja are pre-eminently in the southern class and those of the Poona plates are found to be a mixture of both.[24] However, the script of the Mallar plates of Vyāghrarāja bears striking resemblance to that of Bamhani and the Mallar plates of Śūarabala. This is obviously accounted for by the comparative proximity between the two : they belong more or less to one and the same period and their find-spots are not far removed from each other. The hollow triangular head-marks are not seen on *i*, *ja*, *ṇa*, *ba* and *la*. The flat tops of *ga*, *tha*, *dha* and *śa* are pointed at the top while crowning the head-mark. The test letters *ka*, *ja*, *ma*, *ra*, *la* and *sa* and the medials *i* and *ī* bear the stamp of southern characteristics. The letter-forms are more roundish than those of the plates of Śūrabala and they exhibit notch formations in the base-line of the letters such as *tha*, *pa*, *ma*, *ṣa*, etc. At the present stage of our knowledge, it is quite inexplicable how these peculiarities particularly the extreme cursive engraving and notch formations reached here from the south.

18. Fleet, *op. cit.*, 19.
19. *EI*, 15, 39ff & pl.
20. Fleet, *op. cit.*, 106-09 & pl. XIV.
21. *EI*, 27, 132-45 & pls.
22. *St ıdies in Indian Epigraphy*, 3, 183-93 & pls.
23. *EI*, 33, 209-14 & pls.
24. From an analysis of the script of the Poona plates of Prabhāvatīgupta it would be very difficult to ascertain whether the northern or southern characters predominate there.

The Pipalpadar plates of Nandarāja, the Rajim stone inscription of the Nala King Vilāsatuṅga and the numerous stone inscriptions of the time of Mahāśivagupta Bālārjuna are written in a different script. The plates of Nandarāja are written in the acute-angled script as prevalent in the records of the Śailodbhavas and, therefore, may be assigned to the seventh century AD. The palaeographical peculiarities of the plates have been studied in Chapter 6. The characters of the stone inscriptions of Vilāsatuṅga and Mahāśivagupta Bālārjuna are written in the *kuṭila* script of the eighth-ninth centuries. They have been included in Chapter 7.

In the foregoing discussion it has been made clear that the characters of the inscriptions of South Kośala of the period under review are pre-eminently south Indian and it is also held that similar characters also made their way to Kaliṅga from the south and continued to dominate the epigraphic alphabet of the kingdom up to the close of the seventh century or slightly later. In the essential characters of the inscriptions of the two sub-regional kingdoms, therefore, we do not find any marked difference except the greater stress on the angularity of the letter-forms of the box-headed script of South Kośala. Unlike the median Kaliṅga script where the notching of the base line and the cursive engraving are the marked traits, in the box-headed characters of South Kośala, the notch formation is completely absent and the curves are more often straightened.

Vowels

Of the initial vowels, *a*, *ā*, *i*, *u*, *e* and *au* have been found used in the inscriptions under discussion. The letter-forms of *a* and *ā* fully agree with those of their counterparts in the inscriptions of Kaliṅga. The only change effected here is the development of a horizontal with its left terminal slightly curling in place of the two curves as noticed in Kaliṅga. In *Pl.* Va.10, the letter *a* has a redundant curve added to the vertical on the right. In fact, the addition of this curve makes it *ā*, but here *ā* has a medial mark at the top in spite of having the curve on the right. In the case of *a*, the curve is redundant and in the case of *ā* the medial mark is unnecessary. A similar curve is also seen in *kha*. However, such peculiarity is only noticed optionally in the Bonda plates of Mahāśivagupta Bālārjuna of year 22. The roof type of the initial *i* with or without the central dip is found optionally in the early inscriptions of South Kośala. But later on it has developed a definite base-line in the middle and two curves on its both sides. When the curves are angularized it results in the form as noticed in *Pl.* Va.8 and 10. The two dots of the initial *i* are retained up to the close of the Śarabhapurīyas but in the charters of the Pāṇḍuvaṁśīs they are invariably represented by two small circles. In *Pl.* Va.6, they are seen in the form of two small dashes. In *Pl.* Va.1 and 2, the vowel *u* has a long slanting stroke and a hook attached to the bottom right. In the later inscriptions it is found in broad back type and opened to the right. In *Pl.* Va.8, it opens to the left. The letter-form of the broad backed *u* can hardly be distinguished from those of *ṭa* and *da*. The initial *e* is broad looped type and it has a right upright. In *Pl.* Va.10, it has a broad triangle at the top. The peculiar letter-form is reproduced from the Lodhia plates of Mahāśivagupta Bālārjuna of year 57. The triangle appears to be redundant. The rare letter *au* (*Pl.* Va.6) is used only once in line 10 of the Raipur plates of Sudevarāja I of year 10. It has a broad back, opened to the right and a horizontal top stroke from the right terminal of which another curve springs up.

Consonants

The letter-forms of a majority of consonants closely resemble to those of the consonants used in the median Kaliṅga script. It is needless to repeat them there. The letter *ka* has a horizontal corss bar. The broad loops of *ka, ca, ma, va,* etc., are seen either in the form of a square, oblong or rectangle. The top of *kha* is flattened and its left terminal slightly curls in. The letters *ga* and *śa* have two equal arms and have flattened tops. *Gha, pa, pha, ṣa* and *ha* are bent arm type. The inward limb of *pha* either joins the base-line or remains half-way. But in *Pl.* Vb.6, it moves out. In the case of *ha,* the outward limb goes up to the height of the head-mark and then runs down to the base. *Cha* is of butterfly type. The letters *ṭa, ḍa, ḍha* and *da* are broad back type and are opened to the right. The broad back of *ṭa, ḍa* and *ḍha* are either rounded or angular but the back *da* is always drawn angularly. At times when the letter *ta* is angularized, it becomes difficult to distinguish between *ṭa* and *da. Ḍa* has an appendage at its lower end while *ḍha* has a loop (*Pl.* Va.7) or an inward curve at its lower end (*Pl.* Va.8 and 10). The letter *ta* has a right stem and its left curve often turns into a small horizontal dash with or without a short downward tick. The lower end of the vertical is also slightly bent to the left. The pot bellied *dha* is used in the early inscriptions but later on it is compressed and elongated. The tripartite *ya* is never getting a loop at its left arm. In the early inscriptions of South Kośala *la* is with or without having a broad curve to the left, but later on the top of the broad curve is flattened and it also covers the entire left half of the body of the letter. The dental *sa* has an angular hook in the left and a parallel line in the right joined to the middle stem by a small horizontal base-line. *Ra* and *kṣa* do not deviate from their respective forms used in the median Kaliṅga script.

The consonants which call for special remark are *ṅa, ja, jha, ña, ṇa, tha, na, ba, bha* and *ma*. Of these consonants, *jha, ṅa* and *ña* are never used alone; they are always found in conjunction with other letters.

Ṅa : In *Pl.* Va.1, the guttural nasal *ṅa* is seen in broad type, opened to the right with its top and left arm notched in the middle. The square variety of the letter-form with an opening to the right is also used in *Pl.* Va.5. In the inscriptions of the Śarabhapurīya kings Jayarāja and Sudevarāja I, a step formation is made in the top left of the subscript and in one or two instances it resembles *ja* (*Pl.* Va. 6). In the later documents of South Kośala, the subscript is very much compressed and the left arm joining the two horizontals is reduced in height (*Pl.* Va.7 and 8).

Ja : The three armed *ja* is regularly found used without any mutilation in the inscriptions of the Nalas and the early Śarabhapurīya rulers. Occasionally with the application of the head-mark to the left of the letter, the upper arm is reduced in size and joined to the middle bar at a different point (*Pl.* Va.1). In *Pl.* Va.3 and 5, the upper arm is optionally notched. In the subsequent epigraphs, the upper arm is reduced in size and a step formation is obtained on the top left of the letter, vide *Pl.* Va. 5, 6, 7, 8, 9 and 10.

Jha : The secondary form of the rare letter *jha* is exclusively found in the inscriptions of Tīvaradeva. In *jjha* (*Pl.* Va.8), it is drawn angularly. The upward hook to the right has an acute angle while the upturned curve added to the left of the lower end of the vertical is replaced by a small tick.

Ña : The palatal nasal *ña* is expressed in the same way as in the early Eastern Gaṅga grants of Kaliṅga. The left end of the flat top has an inward curve and the right hook is often replaced by a small dash. Changes are noticed from the close of the Śarabhapurīya rule where we find the flat top is doubly bent as in *ñca* (*Pl.* Vb.7) and *jñā* (*Pl.* Va.7). In the Pāṇḍuvaṁśī charters, the top portion of the letter resembles to that of the initial *i* of the same charters, vide superscript *ña* in *Pl.* Vb.8, 9 and 10 and subscript *ña* in *Pl.* Vc.8, 9, and 10. Sometimes the right hook is absent.

Ṇa & Na : The looped *ṇa* is used exclusively in the charters of South Kośala exhibiting box-headed characters. For sometime the letter-form as used in the inscriptions of the minor ruling houses of Kaliṅga is retained. But from the time of Jayarāja changes are made in its doubly curved roof and also in the circular loop at the base. The roof is flattened with its two ends slightly go down and the loop is converted into a square. The outer curve of the square is also angularized. Except the flat roof, the stem above the square, the square itself and the outer curve to the right are drawn in one action. Unlike the early Eastern Gaṅga grants where the loop is often attached to the right upright by an additional horizontal stroke, here in South Kośala it is regularly found at the base. The looped *na* is the same as looped *ṇa* without its flat top.

Tha : The letter *tha* is seen in the form of a circle or oval with a dot or dash at its centre. Sometimes a loop or curve is noticed at the base as in *Pl.* Va.4, 5 and 6. In the later inscriptions the circle or oval of the letter is compressed at the top and the base is broadened as in *Pl.* Va.7, 8, 9 and 10. The letter-form looks like a jar.

Ba : In the inscriptions of the Nalas and also in those of the Śarabhapurīya king *mahārāja* Narendra, the square type of *ba* is used with or without notching its top or left arm. In *Pl.* Vb.5, the left arm has developed a definite inward curve. In *Pl.* Vb.7, the square type of *ba* is perfectly represented. But in a majority of cases the top arm is reduced in size and a step formation is obtained at its top left.

Bha : The double-curved type of *bha* is noticed in *Pl.* Vb.2 and its broad type is seen in *Pl.* Vb.3 and 4. In the rest of the grants the angular *bha* is invariably used. The angular hook attached to the right upright makes an inward curl and from the time of Pravararāja a new element is added to it. Like *a, ka, ña* and *ra*, the letter had also obtained an upturned angle at its bottom left, see *bha, bhā* and *bho* in *Pl.* Vb.7, 8 and 10 respectively. This new element appears to be superfluous.

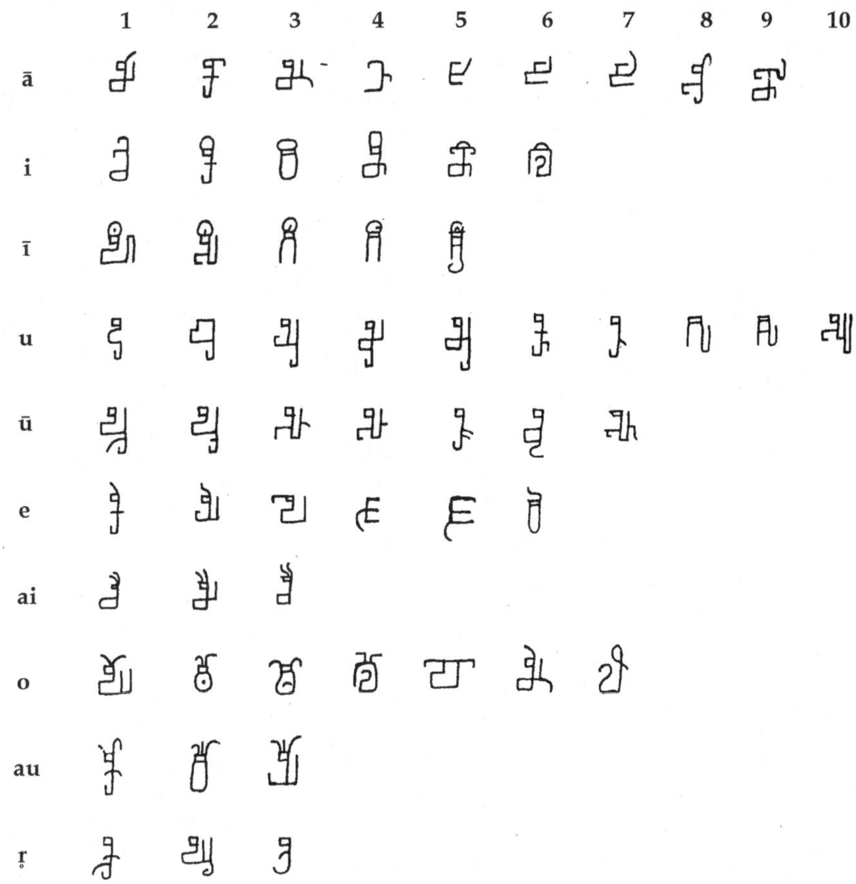

fig. **III: Medials in the Box-headed Characters in South Kośala**

Ma : The archaic form of *ma* with a broad loop and two strokes above it are met with in *Pl.* Vb.1 and 2. But in *Pl.* Vb.1, optionally we notice that the loop of the letter is turned into a square or rectangle and the two strokes are shifted to the extreme right. In the later records this variety is regularly found used. More often the left stroke merges with the right vertical of the square or rectangle and the right stroke moves upward (*Pl.* Vb.6, 7, 8, 9 and 10). From the head-mark to the upward stroke in the right, the letter is drawn in one action.

Medials

All the varieties of the medial signs discussed in the median Kaliṅga script are regular in the box-headed characters of South Kośala. The medial *ā* has a number of varieties such as a slanting stroke above the head-mark as in *mā* (*fig.* III.1), a horizontal with a downward tick as in *kā*, *mā* and *khā* (*fig.* III.2, 3 and 4 respectively), an upturned curve as in *ṇā* (*fig.* III.9) or a down facing curve to top right as in *bhā* (*fig.* III.8). In the case of *ja* it is always seen attached to the middle prong in the form of a straight or slanting bar or a curve.

The medial *i* is indicated by a small circle, semi-circle, curve or an angular hook on the top of the letter. Its length is obtained by inserting a dot at the centre of a small tick or curve at the base of the circular type of the medial *i*. In *fig*. III.4, the small tick is seen attached to the right side of the circle. The peculiarity is optionally noticed in the Raipur plates of Sudevarāja I.

We come across all the three varieties of the medial *u* as used in the median Kaliṅga script. In *cu, ṭu, du, dhu, nu* (optionally), *pu, bu, mu, yu, su, hu, kṣu*, etc., it is an upturned curve to the bottom left; in *gu, tu, nu, śu* and *su* it is an upturned curve to the right, often it goes up to the height of the letter; and in *ku* and *ru* it is a hook or a slanting stroke facing down (*fig*. III). In the Pāṇḍuvaṁśī records the hook is often bent medially. At times it becomes difficult to distinguish between *bhu* and the dental *sa*. The length of the medial is denoted by adding a slanting stroke or a small dash to the middle left as in *pū* and *pū* (*fig*. III.1 and 2) or the middle right as in *bhū* and *bhū* (*fig*. III.3 and 4). In the case of *rū*, the slanting stroke for the diacritical notation of *u* is doubled, vide *rū* (*fig*. III.5) and in the case of *cū* it is seen in the form of a broad curve facing right. The broad curve type is reproduced from line 1 of the Thakurdiya plates of Pravararāja. However, this is the only instance of such type found in the box-headed characters of South Kośala.

The medial *e* is just the reversed form of the medial *ā*. In the case of *ja*, it is seen either on the middle or bottom left. In the Pāṇḍuvaṁśī records, the slanting stroke is doubly bent, e.g., *ye* and *dhe* (*fig*. III.2 and 6) and thereby appears to be more ornate. When *e* is doubled it forms *ai*.

The medial *o* is represented by the top stroke for *a* and *e*. In *mo* the sign for *o* is partly exhibited by a top and partly by a foot stroke (*fig*. III.6) and in *lo* (optionally) a loop is formed at the top of the right upright (*fig*. III.7). *Au* is tripartite (*fig*. III.2 and 3) and optionally it has a slanting stroke to left and a down facing hook to right as in *kau* (*fig*. III.10). *R̥* is of broad curve type as in median Kaliṅga script.

The *anusvāra* and the *visarga* retain their respective forms as used in Kaliṅga. Optionally they are seen in the form of small horizontals.

Conjuncts

In the conjuncts practically no mutilation is made to the letter-forms. Compared to the superscipts, the subscripts are smaller in size and generally devoid of the head-mark.

The guttural nasal *ṅa* joins the consonants of its class normally at the terminal of its base with or without an additional line. At times the second elements are drawn exactly below the nasal as in *ṅkha, ṅgo* and *ṅke* (*Pl*. Vb.5, 8 and 10 respectively). In the case of *ṅgo*, the box head-mark is retained. The subscript *ca* is noticed in conjunction with *ña* where the lower curve of the latter is missing. The broad loop of *ca* meets the right and upright *ña* on the left and often it appears that the conjunct is drawn in one action vide *Pl*. Vb.7 (second) and 9. In the case of the superscripts *ṇa* and *na*, the subscripts are regularly found attached to the outer curve of the loop. The letter *ba* in conjunction with the superscript *ma* is found just below with or without an additional line. Optionally its upper arm is merged with the lower arm of *ma*. In the later inscriptions, *pa, ba* and *bha* are joined to the outer angle of *ma* on the right.

The conjuncts with *ka, ca, ja, ta, da, pa, śa, ṣa* and *sa* as superscripts have been shown in *Pl.* Vc and they are almost the same as used in the median Kaliṅga script. Except the sibilants, all other consonants referred to above are doubled to form the conjuncts. In the early inscriptions, the roof of *ña* often joins the horizontal base of the superscript *ja*, vide *Pl.* Vc.2, 6 and 7 (first) while in the later inscriptions when the nasal has developed double angular bends at the top it is always represented fully. The palatal *śa* with the subscript *ca* is commonly found in almost all the inscriptions. The cerebral *ṣa* has *ka, ṭa, ṭha* and *ṇa* as subscripts. *Ṭha* is a perfect circle in many cases while *ṇa* in *Pl.* Vc.7 and 8 is represented in its north Indian form of double curved type. In *sthā*, the second element *tha* has a horizontal bar in the middle of a circle.

The use of *na, ma, la* and *va* as second elements do not call for special remark except that the letter *la* is devoid of its top curve or angle in the early records. The subscript *ya* has a curved base and an upturned vertical almost covering the right side of the superscript. In the inscriptions of the Pāṇḍuvaṁśīs the cursive base is angularized. The subscript *ra* is a broad curve to the left.

The *repha* is a small angle on the top and in most cases it has a head-mark. The medial vowels usually applied to the top of the letters are sometimes seen diverging from the head of the *repha*.

Orthography

Of the common orthographical peculiarities, as noticed in the epigraphs under study, mention may be made of the following : (1) The *jihvāmūlīya* and the *upadhmānīya* have been used on many occasions in the early records and their lower limits can be seen respectively in the Baloda plates of Tīvaradeva and the Mallar plates of Pravararāja. (2) The consonants preceding *repha* and following *r* have been reduplicated. (3) Similarly *dha* in conjunction with *ya* and *va* after *anusvāra* have been doubled. (4) *Ba* and *va*, medial *i* and *ī*, and *ri* and medial *ṛ*, have been wrongly interchanged. (5) The palatal *śa* wrongly appears for the lingual *ṣa* and the dental *sa* for the palatal *śa*. (6) *Anusvāra* before *śa* and *sa* has sometimes been wrongly changed into the guttural nasal. (7) Occasionally *anusvāra* is used instead of the dental *na*. (8) *Anusvāra* and *visarga* have often been unnecessarily used while they are omitted in many cases. (9) The rules of *sandhi* have not always been observed. (10) Such mistakes as *siṅgha* for *siṁha*, *tāmbra* for *tāmra*, *muha* for *mukha*, etc., are either cases of Prakritism or due to wrong pronunciation.

Bibliography

PLATE V

Nalas

1. Rithapur plates of Bhavadattavarman, Y.R. Gupta, *EI*, 19, 100-04 & pls.

2. Kesaribeda plates of Arthapati, D.C. Sircar, *ibid.*, 28, 12-17 & pls.
3. Podagadh stone inscription of Skandavarman, C.R. Krishnamacharlu, *ibid.*, 21, 153-57 & pl.

Śarabhapurīyas

4. Pipardula plates of Narendra, D.C. Sircar & L.P. Pandeya, *IHQ*, 19, 139-46 & pl.
5. (a) Khurud plates of Narendra, M.G. Dikshit, *EI*, 31, 263-66 & pls.
   (b) Rawan plates of Narendra, Usha Jain, *JESI*, 6, 44-45 & pl.
6. Plates of Jayarāja and Sudevarāja I
   (a) Amgura plates of Mahā-Jayarāja, RY 3, D.C. Sircar & J.P. Singh Deo, *Indian Museum Bulletin*, 11 (1), 57-59 & pls.
   (b) Arang plates of Mahā-Jayarāja, RY 5, J.F. Fleet, *CII*, 3, 191-95 & pls.
   (c) Mallar plates of Jayarāja, RY 5, D.C. Sircar, *EI*, 33, 155-58 & pls.
   (d) Mallar plates of Jayarāja, RY 9, G. Bhattacharya and M. Sivayya, *ibid.*, 34, 28-31 & pls.
   (e) Khariar plates of Mahā-Sudevarāja, RY 2, Sten Konow, *ibid.*, 9, 170-73 & pls.
   (f) Sirpur plates of Mahā-Sudevarāja, RY 7, S.L. Katare, *ibid.*, 31, 103-08 & pls.
   (g) Arang plates of Mahā-Sudevarāja, RY 8, L.P. Pandeya, *ibid.*, 23, 18-22 & pls.
   (h) Raipur plates of Mahā-Sudevarāja, RY 10, J.F. Fleet, *CII*, 3, 196-200 & pls.
   (i) Sarangarh plates of Mahā-Sudevarāja, Hiralal, *EI*, 9, 281-85 & pls.
7. (a) Thakurdiya plates of Mahā-Pravararāja, RY 3, V.V. Mirashi, *ibid.*, 22, 15-23 & pls.
   (b) Mallar plates of Mahā-Pravararāja, RY 3, G. Bhattacharya, *Ibid.*, 34, 51-52 & pls.
   (c) Mahasamund plates of Mahā-Sudevarāja II, RY 3, B.C. Jain, *JESI*, 5, 93-97 & pls.
   (d) Kauvatal plates of Mahā-Sudevarāja II, RY 7, A.N. Lahiri, *EI*, 31, 314-16 & pls.

Pāṇḍuvaṁśīs

8. Plates of Tīvaradeva
   (a) Bonda plates of Tīvaradeva, RY 5, D.C. Sircar, *ibid.*, 34, 111-16 & pls.
   (b) Rajim plates of Tīvaradeva, RY 7, J.F. Fleet, *CII*, 3, 291-99 & pls.
   (c) Baloda plates of Tīvaradeva, E. Hultzsch, *EI*, 7, 102-07 & pls.
   (d) Tiruvanantapuram plates of Tīvaradeva, M.J. Sharma, *JESI*, 22, 51-55 & pls.
9. Adhabhara plates of Mahā-Nannarāja, B.C. Jain, *EI*, 31, 219-22 & pls.
10. Plates of Mahāśivagupta Bālārjuna
    (a) Bardula plates of Mahāśivagupta Bālārjuna, P.B. Desai, *ibid.*, 27, 287-91 & pls.
    (b) Mallar plates of Mahāśivagupta Bālārjuna, V.V. Mirashi & L.P. Pandeya, *ibid.*, 23, 113-22 & pls.
    (c) Bonda plates of Mahāśivagupta Bālārjuna, V.V. Mirashi & L.P. Pandeya, *ibid*, 35, 60-65 & pls.
    (d) Lodhia plates of Mahāśivagupta Bālārjuna, L.P. Pandeya, *ibid.*, 27, 319-25 & pls.
    (e) Another Mallar plates of Mahāśivagupta Bālārjuna, B.C. Jain, *Prachya Pratibha*, 5(1), 54-56 & pls.

6

Acute-Angled Alphabet in Toṣalī, Utkala and Koṅgoda

LIKE Kaliṅga and South Kośala, the history of Toṣalī in the early centuries of the Christian era is shrouded in mystery. We do not have much information about her history until we come to the rule of the Vigrahas and the Mudgalas sometime in the second half of the sixth century AD. But Toṣalī is found mentioned in ancient Indian literature and the *Nāṭyaśāstra* of Bharata makes us believe that Toṣalī as a territory was distinct from Kośala and Kaliṅga. A good number of copper-plate grants belonging to the Vigrahas, the Mudgalas and the Dattas refer to Uttara and Dakśiṇa Toṣalī and there is, therefore, reason to believe that it was divided into two territorial units and the river Mahanadi probably formed a dividing line between the two. The epigraphic evidence to Toṣalī or Ubhaya Toṣalī can be pushed back in point of time to the Asanapat inscription of *mahārāja* Śatrubhañja.[1] Uttara Toṣalī (north Toṣalī) was roughly comprising of the Mayurbhanj, Balasore and Cuttack (northern part) districts of Orissa while Puri and parts of Cuttack and Ganjam (up to Risikulya) districts of Orissa formed the kingdom of Dakṣiṇa Toṣalī (south Toṣalī). In the early seventh century, north Toṣalī was redesignated as Utkala and south Toṣalī was known as Koṅgoda. This arrangement remained so until the advent of the Bhaumakaras in the first half of the eighth century and did not necessarily affect the territorial extent of the undivided Toṣalī. It is well known that Koṅgoda was ruled by the Śailodbhavas roughly from the beginning of the seventh to the middle of the eighth century AD. Thus, the political history of the north-central Orissa between fifth and eighth centuries was characterized by the appearance of various ruling lineages, some of whom very short lived because of the displacement and subjugation of the old by the new lineages and this resulted in a constant change in geographical contour and foci of kingdoms.

The minor ruling families of Toṣalī such as the Vigrahas, the Mudgalas and the Dattas had started the practice of registering land grants to the brāhmaṇas and the religious establishments on copper-plates. Taken together at least a dozen of copper-plate grants of these rulers of the dynasties have been discovered so far. Some of them are also dated in an unspecified era. That

---

1. The inscription in thirteen lines is written on stone below the image of Śiva Naṭarāja in *tāṇḍava* dance posture. It was discovered from a small village named Asanapat in Keonjhar district. Aniruddha Das (*OHRJ*, 12, pt. 2, 1-8) believed that the inscription belonged to the fourth century AD while S. Tripathy (*JOH*, 1, 2, 5-10) ascribed it on the grounds of the plaeography of the inscription and iconography of Naṭarāja image to the sixth century AD.

the era in question refers to the Gupta era has been well accepted among scholars. The Śailodbhavas of Koṅgoda are also known to us from more than fifteen copper-plate grants issued by their rulers. One of the Śailodbhava charters is dated in Gupta era 300 (AD 619) and refers to Śaśāṅka of Gauḍa as the overlord of the Śailodbhava king Mādhavavarman II. In the inscriptions of these families an altogether different type of script was prevalent.

Unlike Kaliṅga and South Kośala, where the general duct of writing was mainly inspired by the south Indian script, in Toṣalī the north Indian alphabet was popularized. Starting from the Asanapat inscription, which may be taken as the earliest in the series of inscriptions dealt with in this chapter, almost all the inscriptions of the north-central Orissa roughly up to the middle of the eighth century exhibit a character which is closely akin to that prevalent in north India. In the opinion of D.C. Sircar, the characters of the Sumandala plates of Dharmarāja and the Kanas plate of Lokavigraha belong to the class commonly characterized as the Gupta script.[2] N.G. Mazumdar,[3] while editing the four Soro plates, and R.D. Banerji,[4] while editing the Patiakella plate, remarked that their character belong to the northern class of alphabets. R.C. Mazumdar makes us believe that the alphabet of the two Midnapur plates belongs to the type used in the north-east India during the period AD 550-650.[5] Haridas Mitra believes that the alphabet of the Balasore grant of Bhānudatta belongs to the eastern variety of the north Indian alphabet.[6] So far as the charters of the Śailodbhavas are concerned, scholars widely differ regarding their characters. In the words of Hultzsch, "The alphabet is acute-angled type with nail heads which forms the transition from Gupta to Nāgarī."[7] The palaeography of the Śailodbhava charters is termed by Kielhorn as the "Ganjam variety of the Northern alphabet."[8] D.C. Sircar held the view that some of the inscriptions were written in the normal east Indian alphabet of the seventh century and some of them exhibit a slightly modified script prevalent in the same age in the southern areas of Orissa.[9] In the opinion of N.P. Chakravarty[10] and S.N. Rajaguru,[11] some of the inscriptions are written in early or old type of the Nāgarī script. Y.R. Gupte believes that the characters of the Kondedda plates are written in the northern variety of Nāgarī.[12] While tracing the development of the palaeography of the Śailodbhava grants S.C. Behera finds "Śailodbhava

2. *EI*, 28, 80 and 329.
3. *Ibid.*, 22, 198.
4. *Ibid.*, 9, 285.
5. *JRASB*, *L*, 11 (1945), 1.
6. *IHQ*, 11 (4), 611-26.
7. *EI*, 6, 143.
8. *Ibid.*, 7, 101
9. *Ibid.*, 30, 265 and 269.
10. *Ibid.*, 21, 34.
11. *JBORS*, 16, 177.
12. *EI*, 19, 265.

script is but a development of Māṭhara with the usual Gupta influence."[13]

In the fourth-sixth centuries, the Guptas had dominated a wide area of north India and the script used in the inscriptions of the Gupta rulers, their subordinates and contemporaries throughout north India was popularly known to the old palaeographers as the Gupta script.[14] Hoernle,[15] Bühler,[16] R.D. Banerji[17] and others have recognized several varieties in the Gupta alpbhabet. But long ago Fleet had discarded this dynastic appellation as unsatisfactory and misleading.[18] This seems to be true in the sense that the characters were not confined to the inscriptions of the Guptas alone and that the inscriptions of Guptas were by no means written exclusively in this alphabet. In central India, we have Gupta inscriptions written in box-headed characters. Moreover, the real beginning of the so-called Gupta alphabet may be traced to very early times even to the days of the Kuṣāṇas and the Kṣatrapas. Fleet has, therefore, suggested, "It is perfectly plain that the alphabets varied, not according to dynasties, but according to localities; and in establishing any system of comparative palaeography, we must select territorial, not dynastic names."[19] He proposed the general north Indian alphabet for the scripts used in the inscriptions of the Guptas.

The use of this broad geographical nomenclature "north India" is also not convincing because of the regional variations of the scripts in north India itself. It is, therefore, that the old palaeographers have rightly recognized two major palaeographical zones in north India such the eastern and western. A.H. Dani too has set aside the broad geographical nomenclature on the ground that the features are neither confined to a particular division, north or south, nor co-extensive with the two.[20] On the other hand, he localized and affiliated the scripts of the entire subcontinent into nine "cultural regions." In north India, he has seen at least three such regions : (i) Middle Ganges Valley, (ii) Eastern India, and (iii) Mathura and north-western region.[21] Dani has further observed that the script of the Middle Ganges valley influenced that of Orissa

---

13. S.C. Behera, *Rise and Fall of the Śailodbhavas*, Calcutta, 1982, 148.
14. Bühler, *IP*, 76; G.H. Ojha, *BPL*, 60.
15. Hoernle, basing himself on the letter *ma*, recognized two main varieties in the monumental Gupta character, a southern and a northern, the latter having two sub-varieties (the test letter being *ṣa*), an eastern and a western, (*JASB*, 1891, pt. 1, 81).
16. According to Bühler, the main varieties of the Gupta character are the western and the eastern, and the differences between them appear in the signs for *la*, *ṣa* and *ha* (*IP*, 77).
17. Banerji recognizes four main varieties, namely : the eastern, the western, the southern and the central Asian; the first two of them mainly appearing in the inscriptions of the early Gupta emperors. (*The Origin of the Bengali Script*, Calcutta, 1919, 23-25).
18. Fleet, *CII*, III, 3.
19. *Ibid.*, 4.
20. Dani, *IP*, 108.
21. *Ibid.*, 109-10.

(possibly he meant north Orissa). Although he has been criticized on the ground that his classification of the palaeographical zone is "arbitrary" and that he assumed a common boundary for the segmentation of cultures and scripts,[22] yet his observation that the easy movement of the literates and scribes from one region to another, the quick movement of technical skills and styles of writing consequent upon the use of Sanskrit as the language medium and that the flow of palaeographical peculiarities from one region to another and the subsequent ouster or replacement of the existing local style by intruding one as a result of the growth of powerful polities or the political changes are unimpeachable. However, Dani's zonalization of the eastern variety of the northern alphabet into the Middle Ganges Valley and eastern India is unwarranted because there may be differences in the ornamentation or simplification of the scripts, but in the essential characters there is no perceptible difference. Besides, the occasional appearance of the ornamental palaeographical traits in the epigraphs outside the Middle Ganges valley (i.e., Bengal and Orissa) cannot be explained satisfactorily and, therefore, renders impossible to accept Dani's zonalization.

The epigraphic alphabet of north India of the fourth-seventh centuries posits a challanging problem to the palaeographers for palaeographical zonalization because of the fact that the features are not confined to a particular zone and that they are in a constant flux. It is well known that by the fourth century AD, the north Indian script shows two varieties, an eastern and a western. The test letters *ma, la, ṣa, sa* and *ha* exhibit marked differences in the two varieties. In the western variety, the letter-forms of *ma* and *sa* are archaic; *la* and *ha* are having firm bases-lines and *ṣa* has a definite mid-line. In the eastern variety, *ma* is tailed, *sa* is looped, *la* and *ha* have hooks and *ṣa* has also a loop on the left. The differences between the varieties persisted in spite of the Gupta hegemony over a major part of north India. Rather the imperial domination fostered an easy and quick flow of technical skills from one zone to the other along with mobility of the scribes, prefessionals, monks, brāhmaṇas and merchants. Since the base of power of the Guptas was located in the Middle Ganges valley, it formed an important spring-board in eastern India for the dispersal of the duct of writing to Malwa, Bengal, Nepal and Orissa. But with the fall of the Guptas, the Maukharīs stepped into the valley and along with them the traditions peculiar to Malwa and Kanauj began to influence and modify the writing style of the Middle Ganges Valley. This gave rise to the characters of the Bodh-Gaya inscription of Mahānāman (AD 588).[23] This new type of script has been described by Bühler as the "acute-angled script." The chief characteristics of this script are that the letters slope from left to right, the head-marks are denoted by solid triangles, the medials turn into ornamental flourishes with the interplay of thick and thin lines and the formation of acute angles on the right by lowering the base-line to the right. Besides, some of the letter-forms display significant development. *Ka* has obtained a loop, *gha* has a cursive left and an angular right half, *ja* has suppressed its upper arm, *ṇa* has

22. K.V. Ramesh, *Indian Epigraphy*, I, New Dehi, 1984, 71.

23. Fleet, *op. cit.*, 274-78, pt. XLIA.

dropped the loop, *tha* and *dha* have obtained a definite right upright, *kha*, *ga*, *bha* and *śa* have a triangle in the left foot, *ya* is bipartite, *ra* has a tick at the bottom, *sa* has a triangular loop and so on.

According to Bühler these changes which ultimately led to the form of the Bodh-Gaya inscription of Mahānāman can be traced in the records of western India. Hoernle also made a similar remark and stated that the eastern alphabet was entirely displaced by the western alphabet in the sixth century. However, it seems that the process of impingement from the western script started as early as the beginning of the sixth century and by the close of the same century sufficiently enriched the existing style of the valley. In the subsequent stage of the scriptal development in eastern India it has been noticed that the acute-angled script further progressed in the direction of bending the right uprights of the letters. This feature has been termed as the *kuṭila* style and can aptly be called as the parent of the Nāgarī. It grew to its full extent in the Madhuvan[24] and Bansekhra[25] plates of Harṣavardhana and continued to dominate the epigraphic alphabet of eastern India for a long time. The characters of the Faridpur grant of Samācāradeva,[26] the Nidhanpur plates of Bhāskaravarman[27] and the Tipperah plates of Lokanāth[28] are exclusively written after the Bodh-Gaya inscription of Mahānāman and the plates of Harṣavardhana. Thus, there is a uniform pattern of development of the script in the Middle Ganges Valley and eastern India and it is futile to take them as separate palaeographical zones.

Coming to Orissa, excepting the Asanapat inscription, the inscribed slabs of Ratnagiri and the Jeyrampur plate of the time of Gopacandra (all these inscriptions belong to *circa* AD 450-550), we do not get any other important epigraph from Toṣalī as yet until we come to AD 570, the date of the Sumandala plates of Dharmarāja. The paucity of epigraphical sources precludes us from framing a true index of palaeographical development in Toṣalī. The characters of the Sumandala grant exhibit an advanced palaeography while compared to those of any inscription of eastern India. The exclusive use of the looped *ka* and the bipartite *ya* is not even known from the Haraha stone inscription of Īśāṇavarman (AD 554).[29] *Tha* and *śa* optionally have their top curves being detached from the right uprights, a tendency which did not occur in any inscription of eastern India before the date of the Sumandala plates. But at any rate these peculiarities should not be taken as common traits of the epigraphic alphabet of Toṣalī by this date. From the other records of this locality belonging to the late sixth and early seventh century, it is evident that the old forms of *ka* and *ya* still survived until they are finally displaced in the Ganjam plates

24. *EI*, 7, 157-58 & pl.
25. *Ibid.*, 4, 210-11 & pl.
26. *JASB*, 6, 1910, 435-36 & pl. The inscription has been placed by N.K. Bhattasali towards the end of the sixth century AD (*EI*, 18, 74).
27. *Ibid.*, 12, 73-76 & pl.
28. *Ibid.*, 15, 306-09 & pl.
29. *Ibid.*, 14, 115-18 & pl.

of Mādhavavarman of AD 620. The general duct of writing of a majority of records belonging to this period seems to have been inspired by the acute-angled script of eastern India. In the less prominent solid triangular head-marks, in the foot-marks attached to the bottom of the vertical of the letters and in the formation of acute angles by sloping the base-lines of the letters, we notice a simplified version of the script prevalent in eastern India. The floridity in the ducts of writing is absent and the *kuṭila* type of bending the right uprights of the letters is not yet favoured.

The Sumandala plates and the Ganjam plates are separated from each other exactly by half a century and the characters of the latter can be termed as a stage of development from those of the former. Once the style of writing transmitted into Toṣalī, it completely displaced the existing local style within half a century. In the characters of the Ganjam plates we clearly notice the completion of the process of displacement. E. Hultzsch has very rightly pointed out that the alphabet of the Ganjam plate is "acute-angled type with nail heads" (by nail head he possibly meant the solid triangular head-mark). Although the triangle is less prominent in the inscriptions of north-central Orissa, yet the acute angles are seen more or less in all the records up to the middle of the eighth century. The survival of this script in the characters of the Śailodbhavas led Kielhorn to believe that the script has an individuality of its own and, therefore, he christened it as "the Ganjam variety of the northern alphabet." No doubt the script maintained its individuality and developed locally in the sub-regional kingdom of Koṅgoda up to the middle of eighth century without any reinforcement from the north, but it cannot be denied that the script is a logical development of the style that began to transform the characters of the inscriptions of Toṣalī in the latter half of the sixth century. Thus, there is sufficient reason to select the stylistic appellation "the acute-angled alphabet" for the script used in the eprigraphs of Toṣalī, Utkala and Koṅgoda in the sixth-eighth centuries. For our convenience we preferred to include the inscriptions from Asanapat, Ratnagiri as well as the Jeyrampur plate of the time of Gopacandra for establishing any system of connected development of the palaeography of north Orissa.

In *Pl.* VI we have included almost all the inscriptions of Toṣalī and Utkala between fifth and seventh centuries AD, while in *Pl.* VII we have incorporated all the records of the Śailodbhavas of Koṅgoda. Besides, the characters of some of the contemporary records showing acute-angled alphabet have also been reproduced in these plates. Chronologically one or two of them may go beyond our time-bracket, but they need not necessarily affect the process of palaeographical development.

The Buguda, Puri and Purusottampur plates of Mādhavavarman II and the Nivina plates of Dharmarāja II exhibit advanced palaeography. The characters of the Buguda plates offer a little later look than those of the Puṛi and Purusottampur plates. In the application of the horizontal head-marks covering the entire breadth of the letters, in the *kuṭila* style of bending the right uprights, in the definite tail to the lower right extremities of the letters, in the advanced type of the medial vowels and in the letter-forms of *ṇa*, *ma* and *la*, the Buguda plates no doubt display decidedly later appearance. These peculiarities tempt us to believe that the record was engraved in the tenth century. The enigma presented by this set of plates has led to much debate among scholars. Hultzsch and Kielhorn believed that the issuer of the Buguda plates was a remote descendant of the issuer of the Ganjam plates. R.G. Basak, however, suggested that the Buguda and Puri plates were issued by the grandson of the issuer of the Ganjam and Khurda plates. Guided by the palaeographical differences, R.C. Mazumdar divided the Śailodbhava family into two groups the early Śailodbhavas (*c.* AD 550-700) and the later Śailodbhavas (*c.* AD 850-1000). In this connection it is worthy to record our opinion about the incongruity presented by the palaeography of the Buguḍa plates of Mādhavavarman II. The above suggestions of scholars were made before the publication of the Purusottampur and the Orissa Museum plates of the king. After the publication of these two plates the identity of Mādhavavarman of all these plates is no longer questioned. But the period of time that intervened between the plates of Mādhavavarman (especially the Ganjam, Khurda and the Orissa Museum plates) on the one hand and Buguda plates of the same king on the other may be satisfactorily explained by the fact that, in the case of the latter, the original inscription was beaten in and re-engraved on the same plates at a later date. Long before, Kielhorn and N.P. Chakravarty have also recognized the traces of an older inscription on the same set of plates.

Like the Buguda plates, the Nivina grant of Dharmarāja II also exhibits advanced palaeography and their characters bear much resemblance to those employed in the Buguda plates. Palaeographically the date of these two records are not far removed from each other. As in the case of the Buguda plates so also in the Nivina plates the identity of the issuer with the issuer of the other charters of Dharmarāja II, cannot be doubted. But the advanced characters of the grant prompt us to record that the inscription was copied at a later date when the original was mutilated or broken due to some reason or other, a practice of which there are several well-known examples. While writing a paper on the "Palaeography of the Ṣailodbhava grants," D.C. Sircar without noticing this fact, observes that there is a distinction between the Banpur and Nivina plates of Dharmarāja on the one hand and those of the Kondedda, Puri and the Chandesvara plates of the same king on the other hand, and that the former group of records exhibits an alphabet which is the same as that employed in the Ganjam, Khurda and the Orissa Museum plates of Mādhavavarman II.[30] This observation of Sircar is not at all convincing for the reasons that the Banpur and Nivina plates do not resemble each other, and that the Nivina plates were written at a later date as evidenced from the peculiarities already enumerated in the case of the Buguda plates. This fact renders it impossible to accept the suggestion of S.C. Behera that the alphabet of the Nivina and Chandesvar plates closely resemble each other and these two plates were copied from the original in the ninth-tenth century AD. We rest satisfied with the position that the Nivina plates alone were written at a later date while all other plates of Dharmarāja II were written in the acute-angled alphabet that was current in Koṅgoda in the seventh and early eighth century AD. We, therefore, deem it fit not to include the Buguda and

30. *OHRJ*, 3 (1), 31-34 & corrigendum.

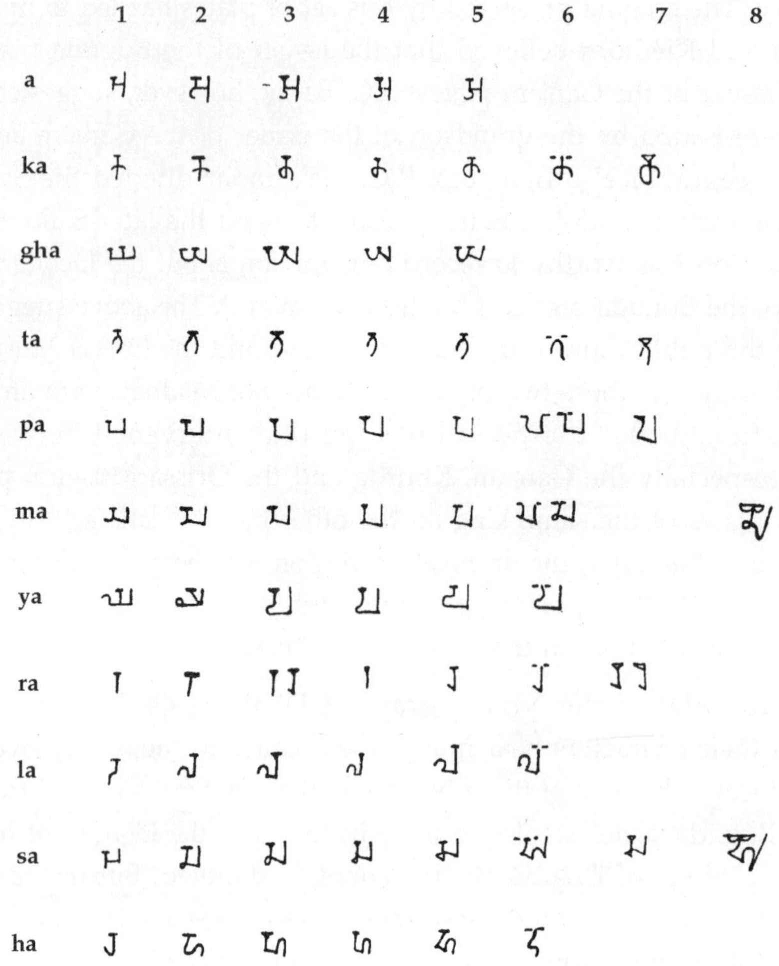

fig. I: Head-marks in the Acute-Angled Alphabet of Toṣali, Utkala and Koṅgoda

Nivina plates in the palaeographical chart because of their advanced characters.

There is another point of incongruity in the palaeography of the charters of Mādhavavarman II. Besides the Buguda plates, which as noted down above, is a clear case of palimpsest, the other charters of the king can be divided into two groups on the basis of their palaeography. The first group is represented by the Ganjam, Khurda and Orissa Museum plates and the second group by his Puri and Purusottampur plates. In the style of writing the first group is quite dissimilar to the second. In the former the letters are formed by continuous lines, the head-marks are solid triangles and the right limbs are indicated by straight verticals, while in the latter they are formed by sharp and detached strokes, the head-marks are marked by "two wings" and the right limbs exhibit gentle bends in *kuṭila* fashion. The alphabets of the second group of records cannot, therefore, be regarded as quite normal. They seem to be engraved at a slightly later date and in the essential characters they closely resemble to those of the plates of Dharmarāja II. The letters *ṇa, tha, la, ha*, etc., can stand the test very well. Upendrasiṁha, the writer of these plates, is also known to us from the Orissa Museum plates, but there is a marked difference in their palaeography. The peculiar head-mark, the *kuṭila* tendency and the above test letters are sufficient to militate against the postulation that they belonged to the first half of the seventh century. We incline to believe that these two plates were copied from the original sometime in the first half of the eighth century.

The acute-angled script is also used in the Dhenkanal plate of Jayasiṁha of an unknown family, the Russelkonda plates of Neṭṭabhañja of Drumarāja family, the Baud plates of Neṭṭabhañja of Aṅgulakapāṭana, and the Pipalpadar plates of Nandarājadeva. Besides, the Paraśurāmeśvara temple inscription and the stone inscriptions from Bankada are also written in this script. All these inscriptions belong to the seventh-eighth centuries.

In the inscriptions of Toṣalī and Utkala the head-marks are very irregular. They are represented by either thick lines, samll solid triangles or simple lines. In the Asanapat inscription and in the Khondalite stone slab inscriptions the head-marks are either solid triangles or thick lines. In the Jeyrampur plate of Acyuta, thick lines are drawn on the top of the letters. This exclusive use of the thick line head-mark is also noticed in the Mallasarul plate of Vijayasena,[31] the Damodarpur copper-plate inscriptions of the Gupta period[32] and in the inscriptions of the Magadha Maukharīs.[33] All these records belong to the first half of the sixth century AD. From the Sumandala plates onwards a majority of inscriptions of Toṣalī display solid triangular head-marks. They are more clearly marked in the Sumandala plates while in the other records they are less distinct. The head-marks in the obverse of the Erbang plate of Śambhuyaśa are denoted by notches, quite uncharacteristic of the inscriptions of Toṣalī. This is in contrast with the simple line head-marks applied to the letters of the reverse of the same plate. Besides the head-marks, the difference in the general cursive and angular style of engraving, in the letter-forms of *da*, *bha*, *ya* and *ra*, and in the difference in signs for the medial *i* and *ī* are noteworthy. In our opinion, the writing on the obverse and the reverse of the Erbaṅg plate is made by two different hands. The head formations in the inscriptions of the Dattas are represented by thick lines and they recall those of the Jeyrampur plate. Coming to the Śailodbhava charters, the Ganjam plates of Mādhavavarman represent the most distinct and beautiful specimens of solid triangular head-marks. Similar head formations are also seen in Khurda and Orissa Museum plates of the same king. But the Puri and Purusottampur plates display two strokes or lines on the top of he letters. They are not exactly placed on the top but on both sides of the limbs. Optionally, the right limbs also adorn the head-mark and even the letters having flat tops such as *kha*, *ga*, *śa*, etc., we have them on their left. In the Median Kaliṅga script we have already seen how the double-dotted head-mark appeared in some of the inscriptions. The scribes of Koṅgoda possibly borrowed the

31. *EI*, 23, 159-61 & pl.
32. *Ibid.*, 15, 130-38 & pls.
33. Fleet, *op. cit.*, 222-27 & pls., *EI*, 10, 50-51 & pl.

stylized head-marks from their next door neighbours, the Eastern Gaṅgas of Kaliṅga and instead of double dots preferred to use double strokes or lines. The nearest resemblance of this type of head-mark is traceable in the Pipalpadar plates of Nandarāja, where it is very prominently employed. This may be considered as the westward expansion of the style prevalent in Koṅgoda. In the characters of Madhyamarāja I, Dharmarāja II and Madhyamarāja III the simple line head-marks are used, but optionally the solid triangles and thick lines appear here and there. This is also true in the case of the Russelkonda plates of Neṭṭabhañja, Baud plates of Neṭṭabhañja and the Dhenkanal plate of Jayasiṁha. The head-marks used in the Paraśurāmeśvara temple inscriptions (1 & 3) and the Bankada inscriptions (1, 5, 10) are noteworthy in the sense that they are indicated by hollow triangles. This is possibly due to the reason that after marking the triangle, the inciser left the central block unscooped. In the Paraśurāmeśvara temple inscription no. 4 and in the Bankada inscription no. 8 another peculiar head formation is met with where a broad curve facing up with an inward dip at the centre joins the top horizontal. In the former the central dip does not touch the horizontal above but in the latter it touches the horizontal and thereby forms two loops.

The head-marks are usually found attached to the top of the letters. In the letters having two limbs such as *a, ā, pa, pha, ma,* bipartite *ya, ṣa* and *sa,* they are found on the top of their left limb. In the three-pronged *gha,* it is seen on the left and middle prongs while in the tripartite *ya* it is found on the middle limb. Although in the early inscriptions the top arm of *ja* is fully represented, later on it is reduced to a mere head-mark. The letters *i, e, kha, ga, ña, ṭa, ṭha, ṇa, tha, dha, ba, śa,* etc., are devoid of the head-mark. In the subscripts also we do not notice the application of head-marks.

Another important feature is the addition of foot-marks to the left limb of the letters such as *kha, ga* and *śa.* They are seen in the form of either solid triangles or thick or thin lines. The foot-marks normally varied according to the head-marks. If the head-marks are thick lines, the foot-marks are also indicated by similar signs. In this connection attention may be drawn to the Paraśurāmeśvara temple inscription no. 4 and the Bankada inscription no. 8 where the foot-marks are essentially shaped after the stylized head-marks. However, this is particularly true in the case of the inscriptions of the fifth-eighth centuries, but later on these letters have developed curves or loops in the left limbs and they have absolutely no connection with the head-mark above. The application of thick or thin-lined foot-marks is possibly due to simplification that was imparted to the letter-forms. Such lines are also drawn in the epigraphs of Bengal in eastern India. Besides, the letter *bha* has obtained a triangle at its left limb. In the Asanapat inscription it is represented as a thick head while in the Jeyrampur plate there is no trace of any mark in the left foot of *bha.* Gradually this solid triangle is developed into a triangular loop and then the loop is opened up. For the first time the triangular loop is met with in the two Midnapur plates of Śubhakīrti and Somadatta. Excepting a few early Śailodbhava grants, in almost all their plates the loop is opened up. One more common feature of the fifth-sixth century inscriptions of Toṣalī is lengthening of the right limbs of *kha, ga, ta, bha* and *śa.*

The thickening of the lower tips of the verticals of some of the letters is another peculiarity noticed in some of the records under discussion. In the lower tips of the right limbs of *a, ā, kha, ga, ta, bha, śa, ha,* etc., of the vertical type of *ka, ra* and the medial *u* there are definite traces of foot-marks. But this peculiarity is only short-lived in the inscriptions of Toṣalī and Utkala. The Jeyrampur plate of Acyuta, the Khondalite slab inscriptions of Ratnagiri, the Sumandala plates of Dharmarāja, the Soro plate of Śambhuyaśa, the two Midnapur plates of Śubhakīrti and Somadatta, and the Olasing plate of Bhānudatta are some of the examples where this peculiarity is noticed. This is also to be attributed to pen style of engraving. In the Śailodbhava charters this feature is totally absent.

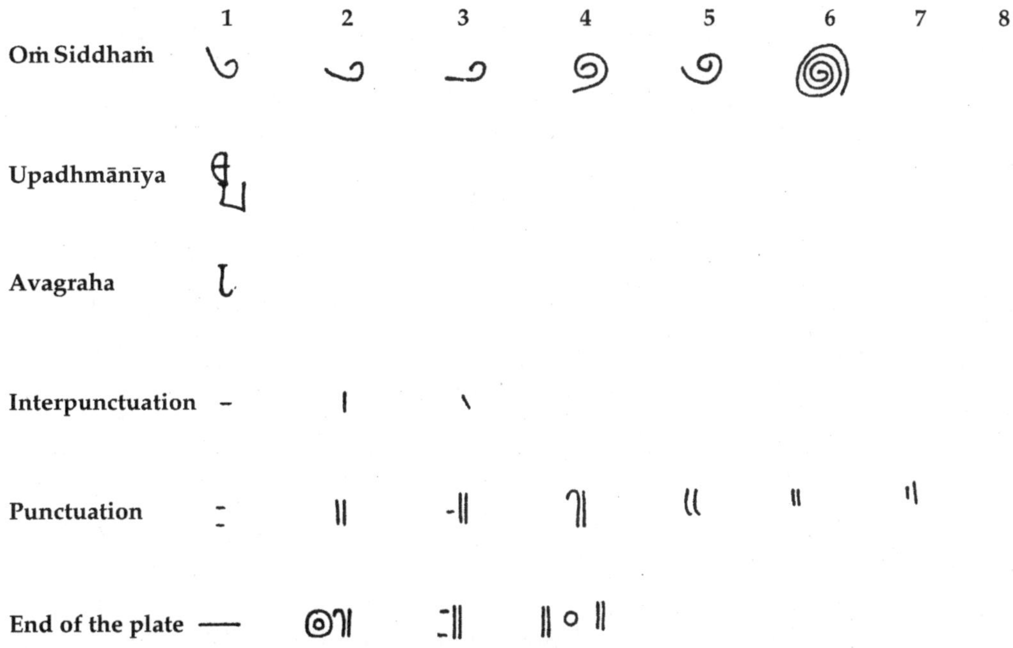

fig. II

Formation of acute angles at the lower part of the right limbs of the letters is an important trait of this alphabet. This is a development from the firm base-lines of some of the letters such as *gha, ṇa, pa, pha, ma, ya, la, ṣa, sa, ha,* etc. In such cases the base-line first slopes and then meets the right upright at an acute angle. In the fifth and early sixth-century inscriptions this feature is not so much popularized. In the Asanapat inscription only *ma* has developed acute angle while in the Jeyrampur plate both *ma* and *gha* have shown acute angles. In the slab inscriptions of Ratnagiri, the base-line of *ma* and *sa* optionally join the right upright at an acute angle. The Sumandala plates exhibit acute angles in the letter-forms of *gha, da, ma,* bipartite *ya* and *sa.* Although *ṇa, pa, pha, ṣa, la* and *ha* have firm base-lines in a majority of cases yet optionally they are also written in acute-angled style. In the epigraphs of the Mudgalas and the Dattas this feature is seen in almost all the letters except *la* and *ha.* Only occasionally these two letters retain the acute angles but on most occasions *la* has maintained a firm base-line and the back of *ha* is rounded. In the Ganjam, Khurda and Orissa Museum plates the acute angles are drawn beautifully. In the subsequent charters of the Śailodbhavas they are also followed but not so elegantly applied. The Chandesvara plates of Dharmarāja II is a case in point where the letters are formed of sharp and detached strokes. This is mainly due to lifting of the pen after drawing each stroke. In other words, the letters are not drawn in one action. A similar style of engraving is traceable in the Pipalpadar plates of Nandarāja.

The *kuṭila* tendency which is not so much popularized in the Orissan records of the seventh and early eighth centuries, finds its restricted use in the charters of the Śailodbhavas of Koṅgoda. In the plates of Dharmarāja II, for the first time we come across its use in the gentle bends in the right arms of *ta* and *bha* and in the particular sign for the medial *i* covering the entire right side of the letter. In Puri and Purusottampur plates of Mādhavavarman II the right vertical lines of the letters are bent medially in *kuṭila* style, but the head-marks are not denoted by solid triangles. We have already opined that both the plates were copied from the originals at a later date, possibly in the eighth century. The scribe not only acquainted himself with the *kuṭila* tendency but also borrowed the peculiar head formation from Kaliṅga.

Angularity of the letter-forms is a characteristic feature of the acute-angled alphabet. The formation of acute angles has itself imparted much angularity to the letter-forms. Moreover, in the flattening of the top of *kha*, *ga* and *śa*; in the development of right verticals in the letters *tha* and *dha*; in some of the medial vowels such as *ā*, *e* and *u*; and in the subscripts *ya* and *ra* we find definite traces of angularization. However, there are some inscriptions of Toṣalī and Utkala such as the Kanas plate of Lokavigraha, the Patiakella plate of Śivarāja and the Erbang plate (obverse) of Śambhuyaśa, all belonging to the beginning of the seventh century, the characters of which are written in a cursive style. The angles in the left arm of *pa*, *pha*, *ṣa*, *sa* and *ha*, and the flat top of *kha*, *ga*, and *śa* are invariably rounded. This may again be attributed to the process of simplification. In spite of the fact that most of the Śailodbhava charters display angular drawing, yet the above letter-forms are optionally engraved cursively. Another example of cursive engraving is seen in the Russelkonda plates of Neṭṭabhañja and the Baud plates of Neṭṭabhañja.

The auspicious sound *oṁ* is usually denoted by a curve with its opening to the left. Optionally it has the spiral form, the terminal of which either faces down or left. The spiral form of *oṁ* in *fig*. II.6 is reproduced from the Patiakella plate of Śivarāja.

The sign of interpunctuation is generally a short horizontal or a slightly curved stroke in the early inscriptions. But later on it is indicated by a small vertical. In the Russelkonda plates of Neṭṭabhañja, interpunctuation marks are indicated often by a slightly curved stroke. There is a similar mark at the end of some lines (cf. ll. 6, 10, 13, 19, 20) which according to Sircar, "apparently used as a hyphen as done in English and a *daṇḍa* in certain later inscriptions."[34]

34. Fleet, *op. cit.*, 28, 259.

Full stop is sometimes indicated by two small horizontals, one above the other, not differing much from the sign for *visarga;* but the usual form of double vertical is employed in a majority of cases. In the double vertical type of full stop at least two subvarieties are found. Firstly, an additional tick is drawn to the left of the first vertical as in *fig*. II.3. This peculiarity is noticed in the Soro plate (C) of Somadatta. Secondly, a curve is drawn to the top left of the first vertical as in *fig*. II.4. This has been reproduced from the Kanas plate of Lokavigraha.

The signs indicating the completion of the record at the end of the charters are also applied variously. The signs in *figs*. II.1, 2, 3 and 4 have been reproduced from the the Sumandala plates of Dharmarāja, Kanas plate of Lokavigraha, the Soro plate (C) of Somodatta and the Olasing plate of Bhānudatta respectively.

The use of *jihvāmūlīya* is not found in the inscriptions under study. The *upadhmānīya* is used twice in lines 5 and 17 of the Ganjam plates of Mādhavavarman II where the mark above the letter *pa* resembles to the letter-form of *tha* with a horizontal mid-line.

The Russelkonda plates of Neṭṭabhañja is one of the earliest epigraphs where we come across the use of *avagraha* (the sign showing coalescence of *a*, short or long, with preceding *a*, short or long, or with preceding *e* or *o*) in line 11. The sign is a simple vertical below the head-mark and its lower tip generally curves to the right. However, it is wrongly used in the inscription. The same record also supplies the earliest reference to pagination. The inscribed faces of the plates have been numbered consecutively in the left hand margins.

The final forms of *k*, *t*, *n* and *m* are used in the inscriptions of this period. The period also witnessed the use of *halanta* (i.e., vowelless consonant) in this part of Orissa. It is seen in the form of a straight or slanting bar at the bottom of the letter. The upper limit of the use of *halanta* may be traced to the Soro plate (A) of Śambhuyaśa of 579-80. Prior to the application of this mark, the final form of *m* is expressed by the Arabic numeral 3 facing down on in l. 42 of the Jeyrampur plate of Acyuta. Of all the final letters referred to above, *t* has a number of variants. In the first variety, the letter *ta* is doubled and it resembles to the conjunct *tta;* in the second variety, the *halanta* mark is applied to the bottom of the letter; in the third variety, the final *t* is seen in the form of a double curve that moves left and after covering the entire left half either stops at the top or falls down to the right. The first two varieties are found in the records of Toṣalī and Utkala, while the third one is the standard form used in the charters of the Śailodbhavas of Koṅgoda.

Vowels

The initial *a* consists of two verticals of unequal length joined together by a horizontal line in the middle. The lower end of the left limb makes an inward curl in an early inscription, e.g., *a* in *Pl.* VIa.2, but in the rest of the inscriptions it has developed a curve facing left. At times an additional tick is added at the right foot, vide *Pl.* VIIa.5. The letter *ā* is the same as *a* with an additional curve facing left attached to the lower end of the right upright. When a tick mark is applied at the right foot the length is denoted by an additional vertical on the right as in *Pl.* VIIa.2 and 5. However, this feature is seen only toward the later part of our period. At times the left limb is doubly curved as in *Pl.* VIa.5 and VIIa.8. The initial *i* is indicated by two dots or small circles with a horizontal dash or curve drawn below. This is the standard form regularly found used in the epigraphs under discussion. The archaic letter-forms of *u* are noticed in *Pl.* VIa.1 and 2. Later on a broad curve is drawn to right and it faces left. This is the standard form used in most of the inscriptions under study. The letter-form in *Pl.* VIIa.7 is possibly intended for long *u*. The archaic letter-form of *e* is seen in *Pl.* VIa.2, but later on it is invariably denoted by a triangle with its tip facing down. The reversed form used in *Pl.* VIa.6 may be due to carelessness on the part of the engraver. The rare letter *au* as seen in *Pl.* VIa.10 and VIIa.5 is reproduced from line 6 of the Dhenkanal plate of Jayasiṁha and line 52 of the Kondedda plates of Dharmarāja II. The letter-form in both the cases is represented by a double curve to right with an additional stroke emerging from the junction of the two curves.

Consonants

During this period notable changes took place in the essential characters of a majority of consonants. At the same time some of the letters retained their respective earlier forms and among them mention may be made of the elliptical *cha*, the semi-circular type of *ṭa* opening to the right, the circular *ṭha*, the letter *dha* with a broad curve joined to the right vertical, the square type of *ba*, etc. It is needless to repeat their individual forms. As in Kaliṅga and South Kośala, so also in Toṣalī, Utkala and Koṅgoda, the guttural and palatal nasals are never used alone. They are always found in conjunction with other letters of their respective classes.

Ka : The letter *ka* has two broad varieties. The old form of the letter with a vertical and a cross-bar is still noticed. The cross-bar is drawn either straight or cursively. But from the middle of the sixth century a new type of *ka* with a triangular or rounded loop on the left has appeared and became the standard form in Toṣalī, Utkala and Koṅgoda. The letter-form as reproduced in *Pl.* VIa.5 (second) and VIIa.7 (second) may be due to the slovenliness on the part of the engraver than anything else.

Kha : Besides the foot-mark or triangular head-mark on the left, the letter *kha* has developed a triangular loop on the right foot. At times a broad triangle is drawn and it covers the entire right limb as in *Pl.* VIa.5 and VIIa.4, 7, 8. In the earlier inscriptions this triangular loop is not so prominent, vide *Pl.* VIa.1 and 2. The top of *kha* is invariably flattened and therefore we may call it as flat-topped *kha* with a triangular loop on the right.

Ga : The letter *ga* is almost the same as *kha* minus the triangular loop on the right. It has a perfect right upright larger than the left limb and its top is flattened. This variety of the letter-form can be termed as flat-topped *ga* with an extended right arm.

Gha : The letter *gha* is represented in the form of a cursive left half and an angular right half in almost all the inscriptions. The right half has displayed an acute angle because of the lowering of the base-line and, therefore it can be called as the acute-angled *gha*.

Ṅa : The guttural nasal *ṅa* is broadly of two types. The square variety of *ṅa* is mostly favoured in the earlier inscriptions but later on it is indicated by a simple curve to left. In *Pl.* VIIb.8, the curve is turned into an acute angle.

Ca : The letter *ca* has a number of varieties. In the first variety it is indicated by a rounded top as in *Pl.* VI a.2, 6 and may be termed as looped *ca*. In the second variety, the loop is pointed on the left as in *Pl.* VIa.3, 10 and may be termed as beaked *ca*. In the third variety, it is seen in the form a triangular loop joining to the head-mark with or without an additional bar and may be called as triangular *ca*. This is the common form in the acute-angled alphabet of the seventh-eighth centuries. There is still another variety where the top of the triangle is opened up and the left and right arms join the head-mark separately as in *Pl.* VIIa.8, 9.

Ja : The three-armed *ja* is still used in the earlier inscriptions, vide *Pl.* VIa.1, 2, 6, 8, 9. Its use is also seen in one inscription of the eighth century, vide *ja* in *Pl.* VIIa.9. But from the close of the sixth century, a change is effected to this letter with its lower arm being placed in a slanting manner as in *Pl.* VIa.3, 4, 7. In the seventh-eighth century records another development is made by suppressing the upper arm and adding a head-mark on the top of the letter as in *Pl.* VIa.10 and VIIa.1, 2, 3, 4 (first), 5 (first), 7 (second), 10 (second). Towards the end of our period, a downward curve is drawn from the terminal of the lower arm vide *Pl.* VIIa.4 (second), 5 (second).

Ḍa : The letter *ḍa* is mostly drawn angularly. It consists of two strokes, a cursive or slanting stroke to the left and a slanting stroke to right. The letter-form has thus developed an angular back and in the subsequent discussion may be called as angular *ḍa*. In one instance it has a rounded back and the base-line curves down, e.g., *ḍi* in *Pl.* VIa.7.

Ḍha : *Ḍha* has a rounded back on the left and a loop to the right.

Ṇa : In *Pl.* VIa.1, the letter *ṇa* is seen in the form of the looped variety of the north where the loop is completely filled in. This is chiefly due to the fact that the inscription is written on stone and that the loops are liable to injury at the time of incising especially when the space is limited. But the intention was obviously to draw a loop. This looped variety of *ṇa* of the north is also met with in the Khondalite slab inscriptions of Ratnagiri. The loop of *ṇa* in these inscriptions is quite prominent. This is also the case in the triangular loop of *kha*, the looped *ca*, the looped *va* and the left loop of the dental *sa*. The lower limit of its use in any record of India is fixed in the later part of the fifth century. The double-curved type of *ṇa* which has already been discussed in the median Kaliṅga script is a northern peculiarity infiltrated into Kaliṅga. This letter-form appeared in the inscriptions of Toṣalī from the beginning of the sixth century AD. There is no doubt that this double-curved *ṇa* developed out of the looped variety of *ṇa* of the north by suppressing the loop and extending the outer curves downwards. On most occasions the base-line is firm but on others it slants and meets the right upright at an angle, e.g., *ṇo* (*Pl.* VIa.3), *ṇā* (*Pl.* VIIa.1), *ṇe* (*Pl.* VIIa.3), *ṇā* (*Pl.* VIIa.9), etc. This may be termed as the acute-angled *ṇa*. At times the entire letter is angularly drawn as in *Pl.* VIIa.5, 7 or it is drawn in the form of a cursive left half and an angular right half as in *Pl.* VIIa.4 (first), 5 (second), or it has a curve in the place of a firm or sloping base-line as in *Pl.* VIIa.4 (second), 5 (first). The last two characteristics are particularly important for the development of the proto-Nāgarī *ṇa* and, therefore, may be called as the transitional types of *ṇa*.

Ta : The letter *ta* is a curve facing down and touching the head-mark with or without a short vertical. The curve is often angularized and is indicated in the form of two slanting strokes drawn from the head-mark or the short vertical. In *Pl.* VIa.10 (first), the curve is attached to the left vetical.

Tha : The letter *tha* is an oval or a circle or square or rectangle with a mid-line. Often it has a broad cursive back like *dha* with a mid-line. In due course, the letter is opened at the top but the mid-line remained in tact as in *Pl.* VIa.9, 10. Towards the close of the seventh century, the mid-line is suppressed and the top curve curls in to form a loop, vide *Pl.* VIIa.2, 4 (second), 5 (third), 9, 10. Its occurrence in *Pl.* VIa.3 is accidental.

Da : In the early epigraphs the letter *da* has a cursive back but gradually it resembled to the form of the angular *da* and distinguished from the latter by the addition of a small upturned tick at the end. In due course the tick is extended down. Like angular *da* this can also be termed as angular *da*. In one instance, e.g., *da* in *Pl.* VIb.5 (first), it is expressed in broad backed type as used in the Median Kaliṅga script.

Na : The looped *na* is the standard form regularly found used in the inscriptions of the period. Among the other varieties mention may be made of the letter-form used in *Pl.* VIb.7, 9 which resembles to that of *ta*. In later Śailodbhava charters it is represented by two downward strokes from the head-mark with the left stroke getting a loop in its lower extremity vide *Pl.* VIIb.4 (second), 5 (second). In another variety the loop is joined to the right upright medially as in *Pl.* VIIb.5 (third), 7 (second). There is still another peculiar form where the loop is replaced by a small dash as in *Pl.* VIb.10 (third), VIIb.8 (second).

Pa : The letter *pa* is opened at the top and is perfectly angular. The two verticals are of equal height and its base-line slopes down to meet the right upright at an acute angle. This is the standard form of the letter and may be termed as acute-angled *pa*. Towards the end of our period the base-line again becomes firm and resembles to its archaic form.

Pha : The letter *pha* is the same as *pa* with its right upright curling in or out at the top. Sometimes a cursive or an angular loop is formed covering the entire right side as in *Pl.* VIb.2, 3, 5, 7, 9 and VIIb.4, 5, 8. In *Pl.* VIIb.7, the loop is seen on the top right of the right vertical.

Photo 6.1 (a): Kanas plate of Bhānudatta, RY 5 (Obverse)

Photo 6.1 (b): Kanas plate of Bhānudatta, RY 5 (Reverse)

Photo 6.2 (a): Orissa Museum plates of Mādhavavarman, RY 50 (i)

Photo 6.2 (b): Orissa Museum plates of Mādhavavarman, RY 50 (ii a)

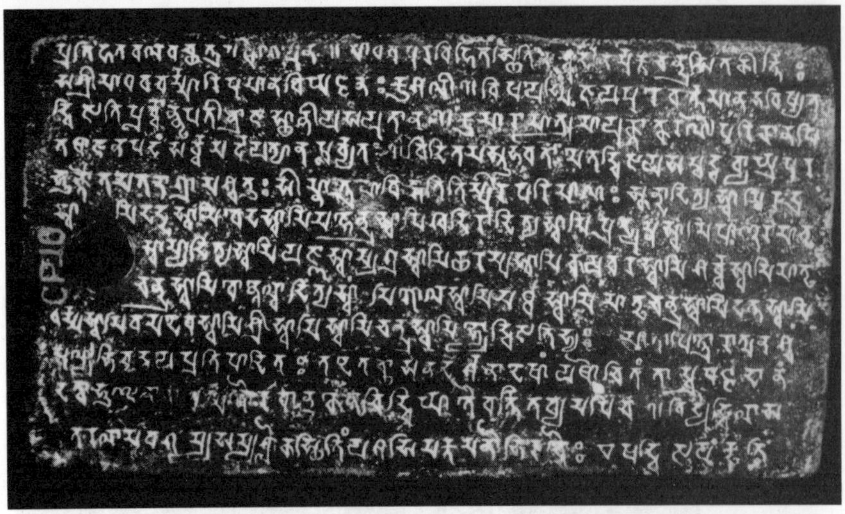

Photo 6.2 (c): Orissa Museum plates of Mādhavavarman, RY 50 (ii b)

Photo 6.2 (d): Orissa Museum plates of Mādhavavarman, RY 50 (iii)

Bha : *Bha* consists of two slanting strokes moving down from the head-mark with the left stroke forming a solid triangular head at its lower end as in *Pl.* VIb.1, 3, 7. In the next stage the solid triangle is turned into a triangular loop as in *Pl.* VIb.8. Later on this loop is opened up and a sharp acute angle is formed in the lower part of the letter because of the sloping of the base of the triangle, see *Pl.* VIb.9, 10, and VIIb.2, 3, 4, 5, 6 (first), 9. This may be called as acute-angled *bha*. Its appearance in *Pl.* VIb.5 (second) may be accidental. The double-curved type of *bha* as used in the median Kaliṅga script is also noticed in *Pl.* VIb.5 (first). In the two Bhañja records discussed in this chapter, the acute-angled *bha* is only optionally used while in most cases the angles are rounded (*Pl.* VIIb.7, 8).

Ma : The firm base-line of the tailed *ma* is now drawn in a slanting manner and thereby form an acute angle on the bottom right. This is the standard form used throughout the period. Like *pa, pha, bha*, etc., this can also be termed as an acute-angled *ma*. In one instance the tail is replaced by a small loop on the left as in *Pl.* VIIb.9.

Ya : The tripartite *ya* with its left limb curling out is usually found in the earlier epigraphs. Another archaic variety of the letter with a loop in the left is also noticed in at least one epigraph of early sixth century, e.g., *ya* in *Pl.* VIb.2. In *Pl.* VIb.4 (second), 5 (first), the letter is split into two parts having two vertical strokes with a curvature on each side at the bottom of the vertical. In *Pl.* VIb.5 (second and third), the letter has a cursive left half and an angular right half. In the case of the latter an acute angle is formed at the bottom right. All these pecularities appeared in the inscriptions only up to the beginning of the seventh century. Thereafter the letter is invariably expressed by its bipartite form with a firm or sloping base-line.

Ra : The vertical type of *ra* is seen in the records of the Mudgalas, the Vigrahas and the Dattas, with an exception of the Erbang plate of Śambhuyaśa. But in the records of the Śailodbhavas of Koṅgoda and also in almost all other records studied here the letter has developed a tick at its bottom left. In the later Śailodbhava charters an advanced variety of the letter-form has already appeared where the vertical is shortened and an additional slanting stroke is drawn at the bottom as in *Pl.* VIIb.3 (second), 4 (second), 5 (second).

La : The standard form of the letter *la* is indicated by a hook joined to a diminutive right vertical by a slanting base-line which forms an acute angle on the right side. This may be termed as acute-angled *la*. However, optionally a firm or curved base-line is also seen. The letter-form in *Pl.* VIb.1 is archaic.

Va : The letter *va* is mostly drawn in the form of a triangle and resembles to the triangular *ca*. This variety of *va* may be called as triangular *va*. In one instance a perfect circle is seen attached to the head-mark by an additional short vertical, e.g., *vi* in *Pl.* VIb.5. In the later inscriptions of our period a definite right upright is drawn and a broad curve is added to it on the left as in *Pl.* VIIb.8, 9.

Śa : The palatal *śa* is of the flat-topped variety with an extended right arm. In the second variety the flat top is rounded and the mid-line slopes from right to left and thereby form a loop at the top as in *Pl.* VIb.3 (second), 10, and VIIb.1 (first), 4, 8. In *Pl.* VIb.5, the mid-line stops half-way and this feature may be not be considered as a variety. The letter-form in *Pl.* VIb.3 (first), is a rare one.

Ṣa : In the early inscriptions, the cerebral and the dental sibilants are expressed by the sign for the latter cf. *ṣa* and *sa* in *Pl.* VIb.1 and 2. This feature is also seen in the slab inscriptions of Ratnagiri. This is a peculiarity of the inscription of eastern India belonging to the fifth-sixth centuries. But the standard form of the cerebral *ṣa* is seen from the middle of the sixth century where it is the same as the acute-angled *pa* with an additional mid-line. Only occasionally it has a rounded base as in *Pl.* VIb.5 (first), 6.

Sa : In *Pl.* VIb.1, the dental *sa* has a solid triangle at the bottom left and the base-line slopes to meet the right vertical at an acute angle. In the subsequent development the solid triangle is turned into a triangular loop as in *Pl.* VIb.3, 4, 5 (second), 6, 7, 8, 9, and VIIb.5 (first), 9 (first). From the beginning of the seventh century the triangular loop is opened at the top, but the loop is still retained in one or two late records. In *Pl.* VIb.2 and VIIb.7 (second), a circular loop is seen below the head-mark. In the two Bhañja records, vide *Pl.* VIIb.7, 8, the left limb of the letter is rounded. The letter-form in *Pl.* VIb.5 resembles to the later variety of *ma* with a loop in the left limb.

Ha : In *Pl.* VIb.1, the letter *ha* is a curve added to the bottom left of the vertical. In the rest of the inscriptions the vertical is joined to a hook on the right by a sloping base-line and an acute angle is formed in the right. At times the base-line is rouned as in *Pl.* VIb.2, 6 and VIIb.2, 4 (second), 5 (second), 7, 8.

Kṣa : The letter *kṣa* is still formed of the superscript *ka* and the subscript cerebral *ṣa*. Although the looped *ka* is regularly used in the epigraphs from the seventh century, yet its archaic form is retained while placed as a superscript not only in *kṣa* but also in other conjuncts. However, the letter-form in *Pl.* VIb.7 and VIIb.4, 5 is represented by a looped *ka* and below it the cerebral *ṣa*.

Medials

A number of varieties of the medials reproduced in *fig.* III of this chapter are also known from the documents of the other sub-regional kingdoms like Kaliṅga and South Kośala. The three important varieties of the medial *ā* such as (a) a slanting stroke, (b) an upturned curve, and (c) a horizontal with a downward tick as noticed in the median Kaliṅga script are also used in the acute-angled script as used in Toṣalī. Utkala and Koṅgoda. Towards the end of our period, the tick of the last variety touches the horizontal medially as in *ṇā*. (*fig.* III.7).

The semi-circular type of the medial *i* is found on a number of occasions but an important northern variety has already appeared in these inscriptions with a curve falling to the left and covering a major portion of the letter vide *ti* and *ri* (*fig.* III.1 and 6). The type of the medial used

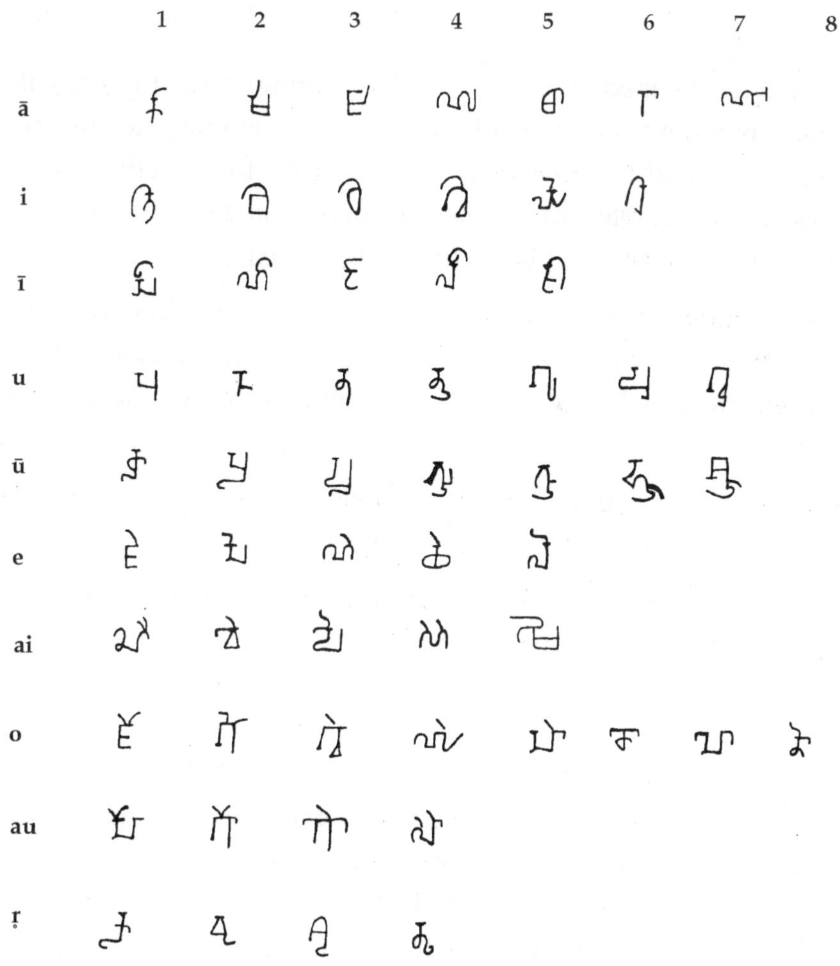

***fig.* III: Medials in the Acute-Angled Alphabet of Toṣalī, Utkala and Koṅgoda**

in *fig*. III.5 with an angular back to right is another peculiarity noticed in some inscriptions under study. The long *ī* is denoted by a curve falling right. In another variety it is seen in the form of a curve falling to the right and like the short medial *i* it covers a major part of the body of the letter, vide *jī* (*fig*. III.5).

The vertical type of the medial *u* is used in the early records, but later on a small tick is added to the bottom left of the vertical as in *yu* and *khu* (*fig*. III.6 and 7). The last variety is also seen in other consonants such as *da, pa, ma, śa, sa, ha,* etc. The other variety with an upturned curve to the right of the letter is not so much popularized in these inscriptions. But one important northern feature of the medial *u* which is frequently found used in these inscriptions is a curve facing left attached to the lower end of the letters, e.g., *nu* in *fig*. III.4. The length of the medial *u* is indicated either by a horizontal line to the left of the vertical type of *u* with its end curling down as in *kū, pū* and *yū* (*fig*. III.1, 2 and 3) or an additional upturned curve, dash or slanting stroke attached to the right of the letter in the case of the left-facing curve type of the medial *u* as in *bhū, bhū, bhū* and *śū* (*fig*. III.4, 5, 6 and 7).

The archiac variety of the medial *e* with a stroke slanting to the top left still persists largely. Of the new varieties, mention may be made of the one resembling to the angular type of the medial *i* as in *me* (*fig*. III.2) and the other with a short stroke to left with its ends twisted as in *le* (*fig*. III.5). The medial *e* is doubled to denote the medial *ai*. The medial *ai* in *ṇai* (*fig*. III.4) is interesting where a slanting stroke is placed on the top of each curve of *ṇa*.

The medial *o* is a combination of the medial signs for *ā* and e. The medial sign for *au* is the same as that for *o* with an additional horizontal attached to the top right as in *mau* and *gau* (*fig*. III.1 and 2) or with an additional horizontal or curve attached to the top left as in *gau* or *tau* (*fig*. III.3 and 4).

R̥ is a curve opened to the right and joined to the lower end of the letters. The type of *r̥* used in *kr̥* (*fig*. III.1), resembles to the medial *u* as seen in *pu* (*fig*. III.2).

The *anusvāra* and the *visarga* are the same as noticed in other sub-regional kingdoms. The sign of *visarga* in the Sumandala plates of Dharmarāja is expressed by two small horizontals, e.g., *nuḥ* in *Pl*. VIb.3.

Conjuncts

In the conjuncts two consonants are placed one above the other and the size of the subscript is compressed and its head-mark dropped. The guttural nasal *ṅa* joins the consonants of its class such as *ka* and *ga* normally at the terminal of its base. The letter *ka* as second element is regularly expressed in its looped form except the one reproduced in *Pl*. VIb.8. The secondary *ga* is either flattened or rounded at the top. At times when the flat-topped *ga* is used more often it merges its top with the base-line of the superscript *ṅa*.

The palatal nasal *ña* joins the letters of its class such as *ca, cha,* and *ja* usually below its right arm. The second element *ca* is triangular type but in one instance it is expressed by a perfect rectangle as in *Pl*. VIb.4. The secondary *cha* is mostly elliptical but a new feature has already appeared in *Pl*. VIIb.4 where the left loop of the ellipse is opened up and the right one is retained with the mid-vertical projecting down. This may be termed as the spiral type of *cha*. In the subseqent centuries this type of *cha* is found used independently. In *ñcha* (*Pl*. VIIb.5 second), the secondary *cha* is placed exactly below the superscript without any additional line. The second element *ja* in combination with *ña* usually slopes from right to left.

The double-curved or the acute-angled *ṇa* is regularly found as first element in the records of our period at least up to the beginning of the seventh century. Thereafter, the letter is doubly bent at the top and resembles to the letter-form of *ña*. The subscript *ḍa* in conjunction with it is normally of the angular type, *ṭa* faces down (*Pl*. VIc.4) and *ṭha* is in the form of an ellipse (*Pl*. VIIb.1).

The letter *tha* in conjunction with the superscript *na* looks like an elliptical *cha* (*Pl.* VIIb.2) or a looped *ka* with its outer curve moving down (*Pl.* VIc.10).

The secondary *pa* and *bha* are drawn in continuation with the right upright of *ma*.

Except the sibilants, the letters like *ka, ca, ja, ta, da, pa*, etc., are often doubled. The subscript *ta* is found in conjunction with *ka; cha* with *ca; ña* with *ja; ka, pa, pha* and *sa* with *ta;* and *ta* with *pa*. The secondary *ña* in conjunction with *ja* either faces left or down and the secondary *ṭa* with *ṭa* either faces right or down. The subscript *dha* in conjunction with *ga* merges its right upright with that of the latter. The letters *ga, pa* and *bha* are seen joined to *la* as second elements in *Pl.* VIIc.3, 4, 5, 7. The letter *ca* in *śca* is mostly a triangle but occasionally a rectangle. *Ṭa, ṭha* and *ṇa* are joined to the superscript *ṣa*. Similarly the dental *sa* has *ka, ta, tha*, etc., as second elements.

The secondary *na, ma, la* and *va* do not call for special attention except the point that *ma* drops its tail on a number of occasions. The subscript *ya* is mostly angularly drawn in the fifth-sixth century documents but later on it is drawn cursively and much more restrained in its size. Like *ya*, the subscript *ra* is also much more restrained in the later records of our period.

The *repha* is a small vertical on the top of the letters crowned by a solid triangular wedge or a line head-mark.

Orthography

As regards orthography, the following peculiarities require attention : (1) The *upadhmānīya* is occasionally used and its lower limit in this part of Orissa is fixed in the Ganjam plates of Mādhavavarman of GE 300 (AD 619-20). (2) The guttural nasal *ṅa* is used in place of *anusvāra* before *sa* and *ha*. (3) Final *na* is sometimes changed into *anusvāra*. (4) Occasionally the sign for *visarga* is omitted. (5) The lower limit of the use of *ba* is seen in the Soro plate of Śambhuyaśa of GE 260 (AD 579-80). Thereafter *ba* is throughout represented by the sign for *va*. (6) A consonant following or preceding *r* is occasionally doubled. The excepted doubling of *ja* and *la* in this position has not been made. (7) The medial *i* and *ī*, and *ri* and medial *r̥* have been wrongly interchanged. (8) The rules of *sandhi* have been neglected on a number of occasions. (9) Except the Russelkonda plates of Neṭṭabhañja, the sign of *avagraha* is never used. (10) A number of local Prakrit words have been used in the midst of high flown Sanskrit verses in the Śailodbhava charters.

Bibliography

PLATE VI

1. Asanapat Naṭarāja image inscription of Śatrubhañja, D.C. Sircar, *EI*, 40, 121-26 & pl.
2. Jeyrampur plate of the time of Gopacandra, P.R. Srinivasan, *ibid.*, 39, 141-48 & pl.
3. Sumandala plates of the time of Pr̥thivīvigraha, GE 250, D.C. Sircar, *ibid.*, 28, 79-85 & pls.
4. Soro plate of Śambhuyaśa, GE 260, N.G. Majumdar, *ibid.*, 23, 201-02 & pl.

5. Erbang plate of Śambhuyaśa, S.N. Rajaguru, *OHRJ*, 12 (3), 113-22 & pl.
6. (a) Kanas plate of Lokavigraha, GE 280, D.C. Sircar, *EI*, 28, 329-31 & pl.
   (b) Patiakella plate of Śivarāja, R.D. Banerji, *ibid.*, 9, 285-88 & pl.
7. Two Soro plates of Somadatta, N.C. Majumdar, *ibid.*, 23, 202-03 & pls.
8. (a) Midnapore plate of Somadatta, R.C. Majumdar, *JRASB*, *L*, 11, 7-8 & pl.
   (b) Midnapore plate of Śubhakīrti, *ibid.*, 9 & pl.
9. Plates of Bhānudatta.
   (a) Kanas (also known as Olasing) plate of Bhānudatta, D.C. Sircar, *EI*, 28, 332-34 & pl.
   (b) Soro plate of Bhānudatta, N.G. Majumdar, *ibid.*, 23, 203 & pl.
   (c) Balasore plate of Śrī-Bhānu, R.K. Ghoshal, *ibid.*, 26, 239-40 & pl., Haridas Mitra, *IHQ*, 11 (4), 611-26 & pl.
10. Dhenkanal plate of Jayasiṁha, H.P. Shastri, *JBORS*, 2 (4), 417-19 & pl.

PLATE VII

1. Ganjam plates of Mādhavarāja, GE 300, E, Hultzsch, *EI*, 6, 143-46 & pls.
   Khurda plates of Mādhavarāja, G.M. Laskar, *JASB*, 73 (1), 282-86 & pls.
2. (a) Purusottampur plates of Mādhavavarman, D.C. Sircar, *EI*, 30, 264-69 & pls.
   (b) Puri plates of Mādhavavarman, R.G. Basak, *ibid.*, 23, 122-31 & pls.
3. Orissa Museum plates of Mādhavavarman, N.G. Mazumdar, *ibid.*, 24, 148-53 & pls.
4. Plates of Madhyamarāja I
   (a) Banpur plates of Madhyamarāja, D.C. Sircar, *ibid.*, 29, 33-38 & pls.
   (b) Parikud plates of Madhyamarāja, R.D. Banerji, *ibid.*, 11, 281-87 & pls.
5. Plates of Dharmarāja
   (a) Banpur plates of Dharmarāja, D.C. Sircar, *ibid.*, 29, 38-43 & pls.
   (b) Puri plates of Dharmarāja, S.N. Rajaguru, *JBORS*, 16 (2), 176-88 & pls.
   (c) Chandesvar plates of Dharmarāja, D.C. Sircar, *EI*, 30, 269-73 & pls.
   (d) Kondedda plates of Dharmarāja, Y.R. Gupte, *ibid.*, 19, 265-71 & pls.
6. Tekkali plates of Madhyamarāja, H.P. Shastri, *JBORS*, 4 (1), 162-67 & pl.
7. Russelkonda plates of Neṭṭabhañja, D.C. Sircar, *EI*, 28, 258-63 & pls.
8. Baud plates of Neṭṭabhañja, B. Mishra, *JBORS*, 17 (1), 104-18 & pls.
9. Pipalpadar plates of Nandarājadeva, S.S. Iyer, *EI*, 42, 171-73 & pls.
10. (a) Paraśurāmeśvara temple inscriptions, A. Ghosh, *ibid.*, 126-27 & pl.
    (b) Ten Fragmentary Stone Inscriptions from Bankada, B.K. Rath & S.K. Acharya in H.C. Das & *et al.* (eds.), *Kṛṣṇa Pratibhā, Studies in Indology, Prof. Krishna Chandra Panigrahi Commemoration Volume*, Delhi, 1994, 61-68 & pls.

7

Kuṭila Script in Tosalī

IN the first half of the eighth century a new ruling lineage known as the Bhaumakaras came to power in north Tosalī. Although nothing definite is known about their origin, yet the internal and circumstantial evidences suggest that they had a tribal origin and that they possibly came from Assam.[1] Initially with their hold over north Tosalī, they gradually extended their political authority over south Tosalī and Koṅgoda. The existence of Koṅgoda as an independent kingdom was no more recognized and it became an administrative unit of South Tosalī under the Bhaumakaras. No less than twenty copper-plate inscriptions of this family have so far come to light. All the Bhaumakara charters are issued from Guheśvarapāṭaka or Guhadevapāṭaka, identified with Gohira Tikira about 5 miles from modern Jajpur on the Vaitaraṇī river.[2] They are recorded in an unspecified era, the initial year of which has now been accepted as AD 736.[3]

The Bhaumakara inscriptions of the eighth-ninth centuries are written in a style quite dissimilar to the duct of writing that was prevalent in Tosalī, Utkala and Koṅgoda in the preceding centuries. The solid triangular wedge which was not so prominently applied in the acute-angled alphabet appeared prominently. The straightened right vertical limbs of the letters are now bent inward medially. The straight base-lines of the letters like *gha, pa, pha, bha, ma, ya, la, ṣa, ha,* etc., and the flat tops of *kha, ga, śa* are rounded. The acute angles are seen only in the letters like *ma, ya* and *sa*. The ends of the medial vowel *e* are now twisted and the medial *ā* and *ī* drawn to the right of the letters are also bent medially. Thus, the points of difference are many and in general appearance too the script used in the Bhaumakara charters appears to make a complete departure not only from the simplified version of the acute-angled script as used in Orissa but also from the script that was current in the epigraphs of their contemporaries and feudatories

1. Pt. Binayak Mishra (*OUBK*, 81) suggested that the Bhaumakaras originally belonged to an aboriginal tribe called Bhuyans, living in the hilly tracts of Orissa. In the opinion of R.D. Banerji (*EI*, 15, 2), the Bhaumakaras of Orissa most probably claimed their descent from Naraka, the demon king of Prāgjyotiṣapura, as the kings of Kāmarūpa did. This view of Banerji has been accepted by K.C. Panigrahi (*History of Orissa*, Cuttack, 1981, 66-69), U. Subudhi (*The Bhaumakaras of Orissa*, Calcutta, 1978, 33-34) and B. Das (*The Bhaumakaras and Their Times*, Delhi, 1978, 25-39).
2. K.C. Panigrahi, *Chronology of the Bhauma-Karas and the Somavaṁśīs of Orissa*, Bhopal, 1961, 22.
3. S.N. Rajaguru, "The Dasapalla Copper plate grant of Rāṇaka Śatrubhañja Deva, Saṁvrat 198," *OHRJ*, 1 (3), 1952, 208-12; K.C. Panigrahi, *op. cit.*, 1961, 8-9.

ruling in other parts of Orissa. The new features are peculiar to the *kuṭila* style of engraving and hence we prefer to call the characters of the Bhaumakara records as *kuṭila* script. The script is also known as the *siddhamātṛkā*. It is regularly found used in the Bhaumakara charters up to BE 158 (AD 894) and after that the Kumuranga plate of Daṇḍimahādevī of BE 187 (AD 923) is also written in the same style.

There are two important points which deserve attention here: (a) firstly, the reason for the late arrival of the *kuṭila* script to Orissa, and (b) secondly, the probable source region wherefrom the characters transmitted to Orissa. In the preceding chapter we have made it fairly clear that the acute-angled script which made a flow to Orissa from eastern India sometime in the middle of the sixth century survived late at least up to the middle of the eighth century in the inscriptions of the Śailodbhavas of Koṅgoda. In the absence of the solid triangular wedges and the use of less ornamental features the script became a local mannerism of Koṅgoda and did not allow any change in the existing writing style. It is for this reason the use of the *kuṭila* script in Orissa was delayed. With the commencement of the Bhaumakara rule in Toṣalī, the *kuṭila* script made its flow to Orissa. It is evident that the Middle Ganges Valley in eastern India was the area where the script appeared for the first time. The Bodh-Gaya inscription of Mahānāman of AD 588[4] supply us the earliest example of certain characteristics which later on progressed in the direction of the *kuṭila* script. The copper-plate grants of Harṣavardhana of early seventh century,[5] the Apshad inscription of Ādityasena of late seventh century[6] and the Nalanda stone inscription of Yaśovarman of early eighth century[7] are some of the representative specimens of this style of engraving. The style did not confine to the valley alone; it reached Bengal (and Assam) as early as the beginning of the seventh century and Nepal in the later part of the same century. The Nidhanpur plates of Bhāskaravarman (*c.* AD 600-50)[8] and the Ashrafpur grant of Devakhaḍga (*c.* AD 670-85) of Bengal[9] and the inscriptions dated between (Harṣa ?) years 60 and 159 of Nepal[10] are unmistakably written in the above style. It may be repeated here that there is no significant difference between the scripts of the Middle Ganges Valley and eastern India except that the ornamental features are meagrely used in the inscriptions of the latter. Hence the style of engraving of the Valley can conveniently be included in the broader palaeographical segment of eastern India. The marginal differences in style within the broader palaeographical segment may be considered as local mannerisms. It is, therefore, very difficult to determine the source from which the scribes and the engravers of the Bhaumakara charters derived inspiration. Since

4. *CII*, III, 279 & pl.
5. *EI*, 4, 210-11 & pl.; 7, 157-58 & pl.
6. *CII*, III, 202-05 & pl.
7. *EI*, 20, 43-44 & pl.
8. *Ibid.*, 12, 73-76 & pl.
9. *MASB*, 1(6), 89-91 & pl.
10. R. Gnoli, *Nepalese Inscriptions in Gupta Characters*, Roma, 1956, LIX-LXXXI.

we subscribe to the observation of the scholars that the Bhaumakaras of Orissa claimed their descent from the Bhauma-Naraka family of Kāmarūpa (Assam), it may be presumed that the *kuṭila* script as prevalent in eastern India made a flow to Orissa in the eighth century and regularly used up to the close of the following century without significant modification. A possible explanation in support of the preservation of the *kuṭila* style of engraving in the Bhaumakara charters can be made in the following lines. In fact, till the advent of the Bhaumakaras in the eighth century AD Mahāyāna Buddhism is known to have thrived more on popular support then on any court patronage. But with the coming of the Bhaumakaras to Orissa royal patronage was extended to the Buddhist monasteries and establishment. Not far from their base of power a number of Buddhist monasteries flourished with the active support of the royal authorities and in course of time some of them grew up into famous universities. They were the seats of culture and education in the country and erudite scholars and teachers used to impart here both religious and secular instructions to the people. They might have attracted pupils and scholars from far and wide. In addition to this the Tāntric form of Buddhism which developed in the seventh-eighth centuries in the universities at Ratnagiri, etc., facilitated for an exchange of scholars between the universities of Orissa and those of eastern India Prājña,[11] Rāhularūci,[12] Luipā[13] and other Buddhist *siddhācārya*s who had earlier studied or taught in the famous universities like Nalanda, Vikramaśilā, Odantapura, etc., also visited the universities of Orissa and studied or taught here different sections of Tāntric Buddhism. It appears that with the coming of these *siddhācārya*s the *kuṭila* script of eastern India got transmitted to the famous monastic establishments close to the base of power of the Bhaumakaras and then from there it entered into the royal court through the scribes. The early Bhaumakaras who directly patronized

11. Yuan Chao in his "Catalogue of the new Translations made during the period Cheng-Yuan" (Cheng Yuan Sin ting Shet Kia mou lou, *c.* XVII, Tokyo, XXXVIII, 70, 71, 86) states, "Prājña was born in Kāpisa, the western verge of the Indian world, had commenced his studies in northern India, had thus passed eighteen years in learning; afterwards he had settled in 'the monastery of the king of Wu cha (Uda, Orissa) of southern India' to study Yoga." The monastery of the king of Wu cha appears to be no other than the monastery of Ratnagiri, which was famous for the study of Yoga philosophy, and Prājña had to study there after completing his studies in different institutions of India including the University of Nalanda. (N.K. Sahu, *Buddhism in Orissa*, Utkal University, 1958, 88).

12. An image of Padmapāṇi Avalokiteśvara preserved in the Orissa State Museum contains an inscription in the pedestal which reveals that *Mahāmaṇḍalācārya Paramaguru* Rāhularūci installed that image during the reign of King Śubhākaradeva. (*EI*, 26, 247). Rāhularūci of the inscription has been identified by S.C. De (*PIHC*, 1949, 66ff.) with Rāhuldeva of the Tibetan traditions. For sometime he was the high priest of the University of Nalanda and it is also known that Nāgārjuna was educated at Nalanda under Rāhuladeva.

13. According to Lama Taramath, Luipā, the disciple of Savaripā, was a writer of the king of Uḍḍiyān named Sāmanta Śubhā. (Pag Sam Jon Zang, 124 and 135). But in the opinion of Rāhula Sānkṛtayāyana he belonged to Magadha and was in his youth a scribe (Kāyastha) to king Dharmapāla who flourished in AD 769-809. Since Luipā was a disciple of Savaripā and the latter a disciple of Nāgārjuna; it is apparent that all of them had their training and education in the University of Nalanda.

the Buddhist establishments possibly requisitioned the services of some erudite scholars for drafting the official charters. Not only the script but also the ornate language and rhetorical style of composition of the verses in these records prove that the scribes like Brahmadatta, Ānandanāga, Haravara, Nāgaḍḍadeva, Devapyā, Sakrasena and others were scholars of repute and had their training and education under well-known teachers engaged in these monasteries. Thus, the above analysis gives credence to our hypothesis that the *kuṭila* script travelled to Orissa from eastern India.

In *Pl.* VIII the characters of all the copper-plate grants of the Bhaumakaras up to the BE 158 (AD 894) except the Talcher plate of Śubhākaradeva IV of BE 141 (?) have been reproduced. The Kumuranga plate of Daṇḍimahādevī of BE 187 (AD 923) is also written in this style. The Talcher of Śubhākaradeva IV and other later grants of the family are written in the characters closely resembling to the inscriptions of their contemporaries and feudatories in different parts of Orissa. We shall discuss them in the next chapter. Outside Toṣalī, the impact of the *kuṭila* script was felt in one Bhañja record of the eighth century and also in the stone inscriptions of Rajim-Sirpur area, all belonging to the period *circa* AD 750-850. The Jangalpadu grant of Śatrubhañja ascribed to the eighth century is written in characters akin to the *kuṭila* script as prevalent in the Bhaumakara charters. The Rajim stone inscriptions discovered in and around Sirpur and belonging to the time of Mahāśivagupta Bālārjuna are also written in this script. In the Rajim inscription of Vilāsatuṅga, the *kuṭila* trait of bending the right upright is not so prominent but the solid triangular wedge and the twists in the medial *a* and *e* induced us to group the inscription under the *kuṭila* script. The latter peculiarities may be due to the indirect influence of the script of Toṣalī. But the *kuṭila* traits are more pronounced in the Sirpur inscriptions of the time of Bālārjuna. It is difficult to explain how the stylized script reached as far as Sirpur in the upper Mahanadi Valley. In this connection it may be said that Mahāśivagupta was a Śaiva by faith and had assumed the title of *paramamaheśvara*. He had granted some lands to Śaiva ascetic, Śivācārya by name, who migrated from Āmardaka and to another named Sadāśivācārya.[14] The place has been identified by S.N. Rajaguru with Amarda in Mayurbhanj district of Orissa.[15] King Bālārjuna was a great patron of Buddhism and the Sirpur inscription of his time opens with a stanza in praise of Buddha.[16] He had allowed one Alakā,[17] wife of Koradeva, and Ānandaprabha,[18] a Buddhist Bhikṣu, to construct monasteries and alms-houses for the monks residing in those monasteries. It appears that the establishment of these monasteries and alms-

14. *EI*, 31, 31-36.
15. *Inscriptions of Orissa*, 4, 349-50n. Also see L.K. Panda, "Identification of Āmardakatīrtha," *JOH*, 4 (2), 1982, 1-3. V.V. Mirashi, however, has identified it with Amod in Madhya Pradesh (*CII*, IV, pt. 1, introduction, cli-cliv).
16. *EI*, 31, 197-98.
17. *Ibid.*, 23, 113ff.
18. *Ibid.*, 31, 197-98.

fig. **I: Head-Marks in the Kuṭila Script of Toṣalī**

houses under the liberal patronage of king Bālārjuna might have attracted a number of Buddhist monks and scholars from Toṣalī and other places. Moreover, some of the Sirpur inscriptions reveal that they were written by one Sumaṅgala, the son of Tāradatta.[19] The name Tāradatta reminds us about *mahākṣapaṭalādhikṛta* Tāradatta, the *dūtaka* or executor of the Terundia plate of Śubhākara II of BE 100 (AD 836). Since Bālārjuna ruled over South Kośala for about sixty years roughly in the later part of the eighth and first half of the ninth century, it is not unreasonable to believe that he was a contemporary of Śubhākara II of AD 836; that *mahākṣapaṭalādhikṛta* Tāradatta was the same as Tāradatta, the father of Sumaṅgala; and that this scribal family either in the lifetime of Tāradatta or of his son Sumaṅgala migrated to South Kośala. None of the above arguments may be conclusive; but taken together, they appear to make a strong point in favour of our presumption that the writing style peculiar to the Bhaumakara records of Toṣalī made a flow to South Kośala along with the migrant monks, scholars and scribal families. However, the script remained short-lived in South Kośala and with the advent of the Somavaṁśīs in the last decades of the ninth century we come across fully developed forms of the proto-Nāgarī script.

19. *EI*, 31-36, 197-98; *IHQ*, 33, 229-34.

The solid triangular head-mark is an important characteristic of the *kuṭila* script. This head-mark is invariably seen in almost all the inscriptions under review. It is seen on the top of the initial *u* and the consonants *ka, ca, cha, ja, ḍa, ḍha, ta, da, na, bha, ra, la, va, ha,* etc. The top curve above the two small circles of the initial *i* is often replaced by a solid triangular wedge. In the letters having two limbs such as *a, ā, pa, pha, ma, ya, ṣa, sa,* etc., it is found on the top of the left limb. In the Bhaumakara inscriptions of the ninth century, the wedges are found attached to both the limbs of these letters apparently due to the influence of the proto-Nāgarī current in other parts of Orissa. The letter *gha* which has now suppressed the middle prong has obtained head-marks on both the limbs. With the opening of the top of *tha,* the wedge is applied to the right limb. Optionally it is also seen on the top of the vertical type of the medial *ā*. The initial *i, e,* the consonants *kha, ga, ṭa, ṇa, tha, dha, śa,* and the subscripts of the conjuncts and compounds are devoid of the head-mark.

The application of simple line or solid triangular foot-mark to the left limb of *kha, ga* and *śa* is still continued. But often it is represented by a triangular or circular loop. The last feature is regularly found in the proto-Nāgarī script.

The inward bend in the right vertical of *a, ā, kha, ga, gha, ca, ṭa, ṇa, tha, dha, pa, pha, ma, ya, la, va, śa, ṣa, sa,* etc., is peculiar to the *kuṭila* style of engraving. Similar bend is also seen in the right arm of the initial *e* (optionally); in the outer curves of looped *ka* and *na;* in the middle stem of the elliptical *cha;* in the right arm of *ta, bha,* and *ha;* in the lower tick of *da;* in the vertical type of the medial *ā;* and in the medial *ī*. Optionally, the slanting stroke of the medial *u* and *ū* in the case of *ru* and *bhū* respectively are also bent medially in *kuṭila* style. The medial *a* and *e* indicated by top strokes running respectively to right and left, have developed twists at the ends. The

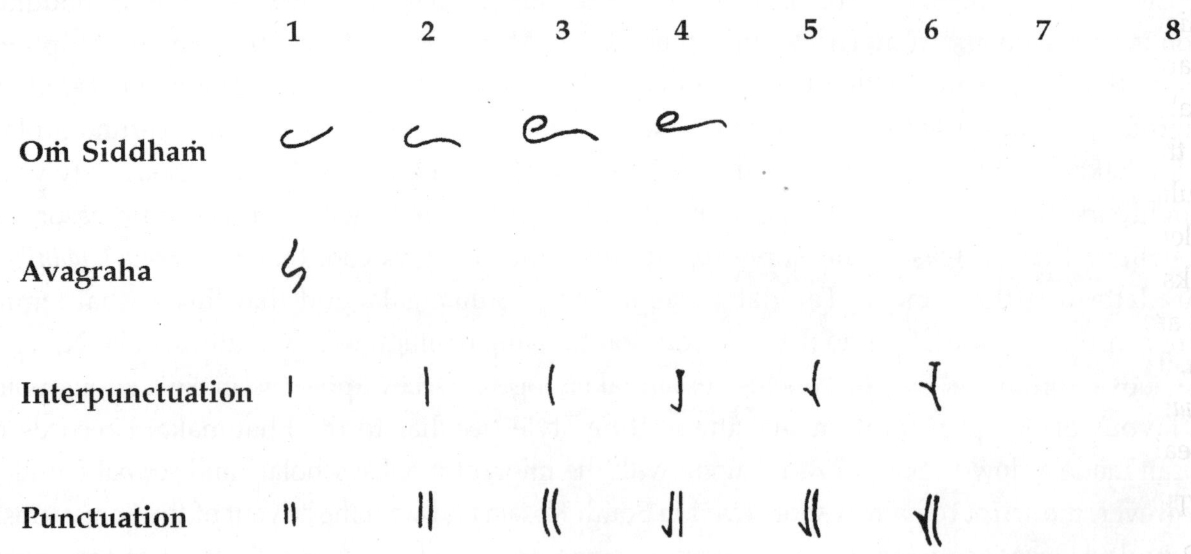

fig. **II.**

kuṭila style of engraving is also noticed in the Jangalpadu plates of Śatrubhañja and in the Sirpur and Senakapat inscriptions of the time of Mahāśivagupta Bālārjuna. But the trait is absent in the Rajim stone inscriptions of Vilāsatuṅga where the right limbs are mostly drawn straight except the medial *ī*, and the top stroke type of the medial *ā* and *e* which have shown twists at their ends.

The acute angles in the lower right limbs of the letters are not so prominent in the records of the Bhaumakaras. This is mainly due to the rounding of the base-lines of *gha, pa, pha, ya, ṣa,* etc. However, a few letters such as *ma, ya,* and *sa* have still retained the feature to some extent. In this connection attention may be drawn to the Rajim stone inscription of Vilāsatuṅga where the base-line of some of the letters are not yet rounded and they meet the right uprights at an acute angle. The acute angles are noticed in the lower right arm of *gha, ma, ya, la, ṣa, sa,* etc. In the Sirpur and Senakapat inscriptions of the time of Bālārjuna, this feature is also noticed optionally. It appears that the surface of the rock on which these inscriptions were incised possibly did not allow the stone-cutters to incise the rounded or twisted features so accurately.

Another notable feature of the period is that the right limbs of most of the letters like the initial *e* (optionally), the consonants *gha, ca, tha, dha, pa, pha, ma, ya, la, va, ṣa, sa,* etc., and even the middle stem of *ka* (optionally), *cha* are slightly projected at the bottom.

It has already been seen that in the simplified version of the acute-angled alphabet as appeared in the inscriptions of Orissa in the sixth-eighth century AD the angular features are maintained to some extent. But in the *kuṭila* script of the eighth-ninth century there is a marked tendency of rounding the letters. Besides the bending of the right arms of the letters in *kuṭila* fashion and rounding of the base-lines of some of the letters already referred above, most of the medial vowels are also drawn cursively. The flat tops of *kha, ga* and *śa* are invariably rounded; the angular back of *ḍa* and *da* are optionally drawn cursively; and the triangular type of the initial *e* has also developed a rounded back. But the back of the letters like *bha, sa, ha* (optionally) and the type of the letter-form of *ra* have shown angular features. Thus, on the whole, the use of angular features is considerably minimized in the *kuṭila* script, but even in the rounded forms of the letters and the medial vowels, and above all in the application of the solid triangular head-marks, the records of the Bhaumakaras display excellent draftsmanship and highly ornate style. The angularity of the letter-forms are preserved in the stone inscriptions of the Rajim-Sirpur area. The triangular type of the initial *e*; the flat top of *kha, ga, śa*; the angular back of *ḍa, da, bha, sa, ha*; and the base-line of *gha, ṇa, pa* (optionally), *ma, la,* etc., deserve attention. But in general appearance, they too seem to be more ornamental.

The sign for *siddhaṁ* is a curve with its left end curling in. Gradually, the curl turns into a loop as in *fig*. II.4. The spiral form of the auspicious sign is completely absent in the epigraphs under discussion.

The sign for *avagraha* is used in the two Baud grants of Pṛthivīmahādevī dated in BE 158. It is denoted by a double curve as in *fig*. II.1.

The interpunctuation is indicated by a short or long vertical stroke. But in most cases the vertical makes an inward bend in the middle apparently due to the influence of *kuṭila* style of engraving. In *fig*. II.4, 5 and 6, a peculiar type of interpunctuation mark is seen which is represented by a small projection to the left either from the bottom or middle of the bent vertical. In the inscriptions of the time of Mahāśivagupta Bālārjuna the projection is seen at the bottom but the vertical is straight as in *fig*. II.4. The full stop is indicated by two parallel strokes either drawn straight or bent medially in *kuṭila* fashion. As in interpunctuation so also in punctuation mark the first vertical has developed a slight projection to the left either from its bottom or middle and another bent vertical is added to it. In the Rajim-Sirpur inscriptions the verticals are almost straight.

It is interesting to note here that the Senakapat inscription of the time of Bālārjuna supplies one of the earliest examples of writing in paragraphs. The entire record is written in 30 verse in 23 lines. The first 21 verses from the beginning to line 17 are written in one paragraph and the rest of the verses are written in another paragraph. The second paragraph begins after a space for six *akṣaras* (letters) blank.

The final forms of *ka, ṭa, ta, na, ma*, etc., are used in the inscriptions under study. Except final *t*, final form of letters are represented by adding a *halanta* sign at the bottom. Most of these final forms with the *halanta* mark have occurred in the Sirpur and Senakapat inscriptions. The final *t* is indicated by a spire with its terminal moving up or down. In the ninth century records of the Bhaumakaras, the spire is replaced by a curve with its outer curve bent medially in *kuṭila* style.

Vowels

The initial *a, ā, i, e, u*, etc., have developed from their respective letter-forms as seen in the acute-angled alphabet. The small vertical in the left limb of *a* is either retained or dropped and its curve is either facing left or down. In a majority of cases, a small tick is added at the bottom of its right vertical. Although in one of the early inscriptions the length of *a* is denoted by an additional curve drawn at the lower end of the right vertical, in the subsequent records it is indicated by an additional vertical on the right either stops half-way or of the same length as the right vertical. In the early inscriptions of the Bhaumakaras and also optionally in the stone inscriptions of South Kośala the type of *i* as noticed in the acute-angled script with two small dots or circles and a curve below is written. But in most of the later epigraphs of the Bhaumakaras the curve is shifted to the top of the two dots and more often it is seen in the form of a solid triangle. The letter *u* is of broad curve type with its left facing curve going up. The triangular type of the initial *e* is retained for sometime in the Bhaumakaras inscriptions of Rajim-Sirpur area. But an important development is seen in the drawing of a definite right upright and the angles at the top are rounded to form a cursive back as in *Pl*. VIIIa.2 and 3. In *Pl*. VIIIa.5, there is a small projection on the left of the letter and in *Pl.* VIIIa.6, there is an opening on the left with a hook at the top.

Consonants

The consonants of the *kuṭila* script of the eighth-ninth centuries are a stage of development from the acute-angled alphabet of the preceding centuries. No doubt with the *kuṭila* style of bending of the verticals and with the rounding of the angles, some of the letters such as *ka, ṅa, cha, ḍa, ḍha, dha, na, pa, pha, bha, ya, ra, ṣa*, etc., display a different look, but in the essential characters they do not make any significant change. The letter *ka* is looped throughout with its outer curve slightly elongated in *kuṭila* style and its middle stem is also bent gently. This may be called as *kuṭila* type of *ka*. Occasionally, the loop is absent as in *Pl.* VIIIa.8 and 10. The letter *ṅa* has a rounded back and often resembles *da* without its cursive appendange at the bottom. The letter *cha* is elliptical. The letter *ḍa* is having an angular back in the early Bhaumakaras inscriptions and also in the inscriptions of the Rajim-Sirpur area while in the rest of the records its back is rounded and its cursive appendage is prominent. The letter *ḍha* is also having a rounded back but its loop to the right is replaced by an inward curl. *Dha* is broad backed type throughout. *Na* is looped but in some cases the loop is filled in as in *Pl.* VIIIb.1, 2, 3, 4 and its outer curve is bent in *kuṭila* style. Optionally the loop is reduced to a mere tick joined to the right vertical medially, vide *Pl.* VIIIa.4, 5, 11. The base-lines of *pa, pha, ya* and *ṣa* are rounded and they join to the bent vertical on the right and, therefore, may be called as the *kuṭila* type of *pa, pha, ya* and *ṣa*. The open-mouthed *bha* has still retained its angular back and sloping base-line. But its outer curve is bent in *kuṭila* style. The letter *ra* with a small vertical and a slanting stroke at its bottom as noticed in the later Śailodbhava charters became more frequent. Optionally its earlier form, i.e., a long vertical with a small tick to the left is also seen in *Pl.* VIIIb.7. 10, The rest of the letters.

Kha **:** The solid foot-mark on the left limb of the letter *kha* is still retained in the stone inscriptions of Toṣalī and South Kośala and optionally in the copper-plate grants of Toṣalī. But in most of the grants the closed loop is distinctly drawn. In one instance, e.g., *kha* (*Pl.* VIIIa.5), the loop is circular. The archaic features of adding a line at the left foot is noticed in *Pl.* VIIIa.1 and 9. Except the stone inscriptions of Rajim-Sirpur area, in the rest of the records under review the roof of the letter is rounded. The triangular or rounded loop at the right foot of the letter is also retained but occasionally it covers the entire right half.

Gha **:** The base of the letter *gha* is doubly curved and there is an inward dip at its centre. The letter has now obtained a bipartite form. The acute-angled type of the letter-form with a cursive left half and an angular right half is still to be found in *Pl.* VIIIa.9. The three pronged *gha* is seen in *Pl.* VIIIa.11.

Ca **:** The letter *ca* is of triangular type with its tip facing to the left and, therefore, there is a definite right vertical. The beaked *ca* is found in *Pl.* VIIIa.8.

Ja **:** As in the acute-angled script so also in the *kuṭila* style, the upper arm of *ja* is suppressed and a head-mark is applied to the letter. The standard *kuṭila* variety of the letter is represented by an elongated right arm drawn in *kuṭila* fashion and the left arm forming a curl below. In one instance, an advanced form of the letter is seen where the lower arm is indicated by a curve facing left, e.g., *ji* (*Pl.* VIIIa.6). The letter-form in *Pl.* VIIIa.9 (first) is archaic.

Ña **:** As in the acute-angled script so also in the *kuṭila* script of the eighth century there is hardly any difference between the letter-forms of *ña* and *ṇa*. But in the ninth century inscriptions of the Bhaumakaras of Toṣalī an important change is noticed where the doubly bent roof of *ña* is reduced to a mere hook and an additional limb resembling the English numeral 3 is joined to its right as in *Pl.* VIIIb.2 (second), 3, 4, 5, 6. This form of *ña* is seen when used as a superscript but as a subscript the hook is dropped and only the sign resembling the English numeral 3 is indicated, vide *ja* (*Pl.* VIIIc). In one instance, e.g., *jñaḥ* (*Pl.* VIIIc.5), the letter-form is fully represented.

Ṭa **:** The semi-circular type of *ṭa* with its opening to the right is still found in some of the inscriptions of our period but an important addition is made now on the right side of the letter. It has obtained a vertical to the right usually attached to the upper curve as in *Pl.* VIIIa.1 and 8. The vertical makes an inward bend. A second variety is also seen in the ninth century inscriptions of the Bhaumakaras of Toṣalī where the semi-circle is doubled as in *Pl.* VIIIa.3, 4, 5 and 6.

Ṇa **:** The standard form of *ṇa* is represented by a doubly bend curve with its right arm elongated. There is no doubt about it that this form of the letter is evolved out of the transitional *ṇa* of the earlier epoch. Since the right arm is bent in *kuṭila* fashion, the letter-form may be termed as *kuṭila* variety of *ṇa*. The double-curved type of *ṇa* with a firm base-line and the acute-angled *ṇa* are seen in *Pl.* VIIIa.9 and 10 respectively.

Ta **:** The letter *ta* is a down facing curve usually touching the head-mark directly and its right arm is elongated in *kuṭila* fashion. The letter-form is beautifully drawn in a majority of inscriptions. It can be called as the *kuṭila* variety of *ta*.

Tha **:** The letter *tha* has a number of variants. In the first variety, the broad cursive back of the letter now makes a double bend at its centre as in *Pl.* VIIIa.3, 4. In the second variety, the letter is seen in bipartite form where the top of the letter is opened up and the left limb has a small circle at its top as in *Pl.* VIIIa.5, 6. This variety is a further development from the type of *tha* with an inward curl or loop noticed in the acute-angled script of the preceding period. The latter variety is also retained in the stone inscriptions of the Rajim-Sirpur area.

Da **:** The letter *da* consists of two beautiful curves meeting each other and forming an acute angle on the left, and a tail is added on the right. The letter-form is most artistically drawn and uniform throughout. The tail is bent in *kuṭila* fashion.

Photo 7.1 (a): Neulpur plate of Śubhākara (Obverse)

Photo 7.1 (b): Neulpur plate of Śubhākara (Reverse)

Photo 7.2 (a): Baud plate of Tribhuvanamahādevī, BE 158 (Obverse)

Photo 7.2 (b): Baud plate of Tribhuvanamahādevī BE, 158 (Reverse)

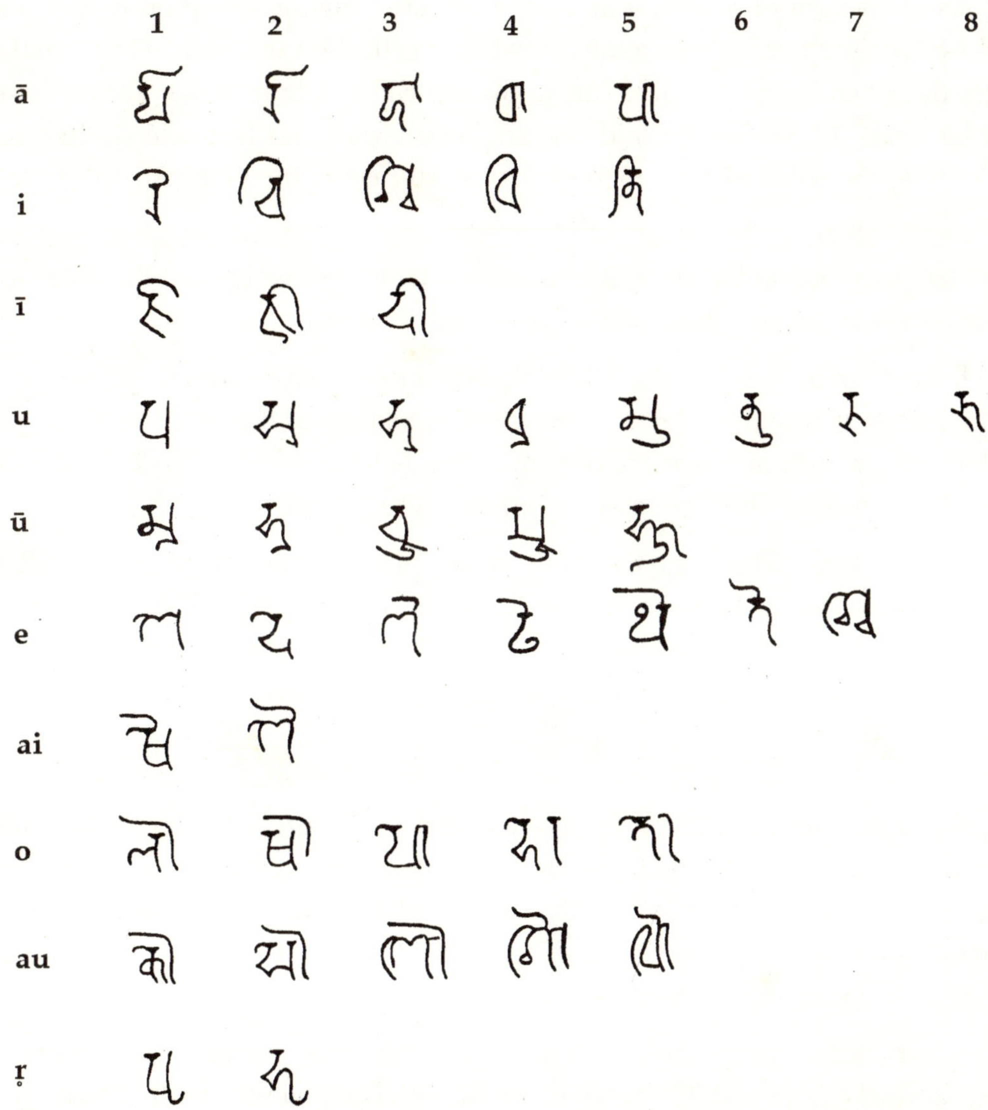

***fig.* III: Medials in the Kuṭila Script of Toṣalī**

Ma : The letter *ma* has developed a loop in the lower part of the left limb. Its base-line is either firm or sloping and the right upright makes an inward bend. This variety of *ma* can be termed as *kuṭila* type. The acute-angled *ma* is seen in *Pl.* VIIIb.9. The letter-form in *Pl.* VIIIb.11, is more archaic.

La : The acute-angled *la* is still retained in the early inscriptions of the Bhaumakaras and also in the stone inscriptions of Rajim-Sirpur area (*Pl.* VIIIb.1, 7, 9, 10), but later on the hook of *la* is drawn in the form of a double curve joining the right vertical medially.

Va : The letter-form of *va* is not easily distinguished from that of *ca* and the only difference is that in the case of the former, the tip of the triangle to the left is rounded.

Śa : The standard form of *sa* is indicated by a left arm having a loop on its top and a solid triangular foot-mark, with or without joining the bent vertical on the right. The formation of the loop is chiefly due to shifting of the mid-line to the top right. A transitional variety is seen in *Pl.* VIIIb.6, 8, 9 (second), 10, where the mid-line stops half-way and hence looks like an inward curl. In *Pl.* VIIIb.6, the solid triangular foot-mark is turned to be a circular loop. The archaic letter-form with a flat top is seen in *Pl.* VIIIb.9 (first).

Sa : The triangular loop in the left arm of *sa* is invariably opened up and the letter-form looks more angular. This variety may be called as open-mouthed *sa*.

Ha : The letter-form of *ha* is not easily distinguished from that of *bha* except that the angle in the left of the former is rounded. Perhaps this close similarity of the forms of these two letters prompted the scribe to add at tail at the bottom of the letter as in *Pl.* VIIIb.2, 3, 4, 5, 6, 7, 10 in order to distinguish it from *bha*. This may be termed as tailed *ha*.

Kṣa : The letter *kṣa* is still a combination of *ka* and *ṣa*. Excepting the one (*Pl.* VIIIb.9), in the rest of the records the loop of *ka* is not seen at all and its outer curve to the right is extended to the right of the subscript. Another change is seen in lowering the mid-line of *ṣa* and suppressing its right arm as in *Pl.* VIIIb.4, 5, 6.

Medials

The medial *ā* has a number of varieties. Firstly, it is seen in the form of a top stroke with its ends twisted as in *yā* and *rā* (*fig.* III. 1, and 2). Secondly, it has a bent vertical joined to the horizontal medially on the left as in *hā* (*fig.* III.3). Thirdly, the size of the horizontal is reduced while that of the bent vertical is lengthened as in *dhā* (*fig.* III.4). Finally, the bent vertical is further lengthened and drawn equal the size of the letter proper.

The earlier varieties of the medial *i* such as a curve facing or falling to the left are also used in the inscriptions of this period. Of the other notable developments mention may be made of the lengthening of the curve and covering the entire left half of the letter as in *khi* and *dhi* (*fig.* III.3 and 4). In *ni* (*fig.* III.5), the lower end of the long curve is twisted. The length of *i* is denoted by a curve facing to the right as in *jī* (*fig.* III.1) or a curve falling to the right and covering the entire right half with an inward bend in *kuṭila* style as in *jī* and *dī* (*fig.* III.2 and 3).

The old type of a small vertical or a small vertical with a leftward tick at the right foot of the letter are also used in the inscriptions of this period. A common variety of the medial is a curve opened to the left as in *mu* and *nu* (*fig.* III.5 and 6). In the case of *ru*, it is still a slanting stroke and often the stroke is twisted in *kuṭila* fashion, vide *ru* (*fig.* III.8). The length of *u* is indicated either by a horizontal with its end curling down as in *mū* (*fig.* III.1) or a left going tick slightly curling down as in *bhū* (*fig.* III.2). The latter variety is also optionally used in order to denote the medial *u* and, therefore, often it becomes difficult to distinguish the two. In another variety, the length is indicated by adding a slanting stroke above the "left facing curve type" of the medial *u* as in *cū* and *mū* (*fig*. III.3 and 4). This is more regularly used in the inscriptions under discussion. The twists at the end of the curve and slanting stroke in *bhū* (*fig*. III.5) are due to the influence of the *kuṭila* style of engraving.

The earlier variety of the medial *e* with a slanting stroke to the top left is now drawn in the form of either a small curve joined to the left of the letters as in *ṇe* and *de* (*fig*. III.1 and 2) or a left going curve joined to the top of the letter as in *ṇe*, *ḍhe* and *the* (*fig*. III.3, 4 and 5). In *te* (*fig*. III.6) the top curve is twisted in *kuṭila* style. In another latest variety, the medial is a broad curve covering the left half of the letter, e.g., *khe* (*fig*. III.7). The sign of *ai* is expressed partly by a small curve joining to the left of the letter and partly by a left going curve from the top of the letter, vide *ṣai* and *ṇai* (*fig*. III.1 and 2).

The medial *o* is a combination of the medial signs for *ā* and *e*. It has at least two important varieties. In the first variety, it has a leftward curve on the top and a vertical on the right of the letter, and both signs are drawn in one action as in *lo* and *ṣo* (*fig*. III.1 and 2). In the second variety, it is seen in the form of a small curve to the left and a vertical to the right. More often, the vertical is detached from the letter as in *bho* and *to* (*fig*. III.4 and 5). The medial *au* is the same as the medial *o* with an additional small curve to the left as in *kau* and *sau* (*fig*. III.1 and 2) or a broad curve covering the left half of the letter as in *ṇau* (*fig*. III.3). In *gau* and *dhau* (*fig*. III.4 and 5), the left going curve on the top of the letter is drawn separately and twisted in *kuṭila* style. The sign of *ṛ* is a curve to the bottom right. The *anusvāra* and the *visarga* are the same as noticed in the records of the earlier centuries.

Conjuncts

As in the acute-angled script so also in the *kuṭila* script of the eighth-ninth century, the consonants are placed one above the other to form the conjuncts and no significant mutilation is allowed in the subscripts. The size of the subscript is reduced and its head-mark dropped. A tendency has now developed to compress the subscripts such as *pa*, *tha*, *ya*, etc., and extend their right arm up to the height of the superscript. Towards the end of our period the extended right arm of these letters received solid triangular wedges, vide *lpa*, *nma* and *dya* in *Pl*. VIIIc.5.

The nasals do not call for special attention except that *ṅa* has developed a small dot or circle on its top right as in *ṅga* and *ṅku* (*Pl*. VIIIb.3 and 6). In many cases, *ka* as first element is devoid of its loop but as second element the loop is retained. The letter *ṭa* which has obtained two semi-circles facing right in the Bhaumakara charters when doubled either retains its total form as in *Pl*. VIIIc.4 or turns its lower semi-circle that now faces down as in *Pl*. VIIIc.3 and 4. While the old form of *ṭa* with a semi-circle facing right is used, another semi-circle either facing right or down is drawn in order to indicate *ṭṭa*. As a subscript, the nasal *ṇa* is seen in the form of the English numeral 3. At times it faces down as in *ṣṇoḥ* and *ṣṇā* (*Pl*. VIIIc.9 and 10). The subscript *ya* is of rectangular type in *Pl*. VIIIc.1, 7, 9, 10 or is a gentle curve to the right in *Pl*. VIIIc.2, 3, 4,

5, 6. The other conjuncts and the *repha* are almost the same as noticed in the acute-angled script and, therefore, it is needless here to repeat their individual forms.

Orthography

In respect of orthography, the only points that call for special notice are as follows : (1) The letter *va* has been used throughout for *ba*. (2) A consonant following or preceding *r* is occasionally doubled. (3) Optionally, the guttural nasal *ṅa* is used for *anusvāra* and vowel *i* for *ī*. (4) The *anusvāra* and the *visarga* are sometimes omitted. (5) Often the medial *i* and *ī*, the medial *u* and *ū*, the letter *śa* and *sa*, the conjunct *tsa* and *ccha*, and *ṛ* and *ri* have been wrongly interchanged. (6) Except the Baud plate of Pṛthivīmahādevī, the sign of *avagraha* is nowhere used. (7) Occasionally, the rules of *sandhi* have been ignored. (8) The words such as *pṛthī* or *pṛthvī*, *puṣya* for *pauṣa*, *peḍā* for *peṭa*, etc., strongly recall the influence of Oriya pronunciation in the midst of Sanskrit texts while the words *goherī*, *joṭa*, *valitvā*, etc., occurring in the grant portion of the plates seem to be Sanskritized Oriya expressions.

Bibliography

PLATE VIII

1. Neulpur plate of Śubhākara, R.D. Banerji, *EI*, 15, 1-8 & pl.
2. (a) Terundia plate of Śubhākara, BE 100, D.C. Sircar, *ibid*, 28, 211-16 & pl.
   (b) Hindol plate of Śubhākara, BE 103, Binayak Mishra, *JBORS*, 16 (1), 69-83 & pl.
   (c) Dharakote plate of Śubhākara, BE 103, S.N. Rajaguru, *JAHRS*, 4 (3-4), 189-94 & pl.
3. Dhenkanal plate of Tribhuvanamahādevī, BE 110, H.P. Sastri, *JBORS*, 2 (4), 419-27 & pl.
4. Two Talcher plates of Śivakaradeva, BE 149, B. Misra, *OUBK*, 40-51 & pl.
5. Two Baud plates of Tribhuvanamahādevī, BE 158, S.C. De, *EI*, 29, 216-19 & pl.
6. Kumurang (also known as Banpur) plates of Daṇḍimahādevī, BE 187, H. Panday, *JBORS*, 5 (4), 564-81 & pl.
7. Two inscriptions from Jaipur, D.C. Sircar, *EI*, 28, 180-85 & pl.
8. Jangalpadu (also known as Tekkali) plates of Śatrubhañja, D.C. Sircar, *ibid*., 30, 250-54 & pl.
9. Rajim stone inscription of Vilāsatuṅga, V.V. Mirashi, *ibid*., 26, 49-58 & pl.
10. Sirpur inscriptions of the time of Mahāśivagupta Bālārjuna,
    (a) S.L. Katare, *IHQ*, 33, 229-34 & pl.
    (b) F. Kielhorn, *IA*, 18, 179-81 & pl.
    (c) Hiralal, *EI*, 11, 184-201 & pl.
    (d) S. Sankarnarayanan & B.C. Jain, *ibid*., 39, 149-56 & pl.
    (e) B.C. Jain, *ibid*., 38, 59-62 & pl.
11. Senakapat inscription of the time of Śivagupta Bālārjuna, M.G. Dikshit & D.C. Sircar, *ibid*., 31, 31-36 & pl.

8

Proto-Nāgarī Script in Orissa

Contemporaneous with the Bhaumakaras a number of minor ruling houses began to rule in small territorial units known as *maṇḍala*s. They are (1) the Śulkis of Kodālaka-maṇḍala, (2) the Tuṅgas of Yamagartta-maṇḍala, (3) the Nandas of Airāvatta-maṇḍala, (4) the Mayuras of Boṇāi-maṇḍala, (5) the Bhañjas of Khiñjali-maṇḍala, (6) the Bhañjas of Khijjiṅgakoṭṭa-maṇḍala, (7) the Gaṅgas of Śvetaka-maṇḍala, and (8) the Nalas of Khiḍiṅga-śṛṅga-maṇḍala. The use of Bhauma era in some of their charters and the subordinate titles such as *rāṇaka, māṇḍalika, samādhigata-pañcamahāśavda*, etc., by the rulers of these ruling lineages indicate that at one time or other they owed allegiance to the Bhaumakaras. But to all intents and purposes, they ruled independently and issued charters without evern referring to their overlords. It may be noted, however, that excepting a few, most of these ruling lineages flourished in the ninth-tenth centuries. While the Gaṅgas of Śvetaka and the Nalas of Khiḍiṅgaśṛṅga ruled over parts of Ganjam district in south Orissa, the other minor ruling houses carved out small principalities mostly in north and central Orissa. The period is also synchronized with the emergence of another powerful ruling house in western Orissa known as Somavaṁśīs. The Somavaṁśī rulers followed an expansionist policy and united north and central Orissa with western Orissa both politically and culturally. After the middle of the tenth century neither do we find any evidence of Bhaumakara rule in Toṣalī nor do we trace the rule of the most of the ruling families referred to above. Thus, the political history of Orissa in the ninth-tenth centuries is characterized by the proliferation of kingdoms all over Orissa, the rise to power of new lineages, the emergence of powerful polities and carving out of relatively larger kingdoms at the expense of other minor ruling families.

The period is also characterized by the issue of nearly 150 copper-plates and a number of stone inscriptions. The characters of these records reveal an altogether different variety. The learned editors of different grants remarked differently about their characters which make it very difficult to group them under a particular style or nomenclature. So far as the later Bhaumakara charters are concerned, F. Kielhorn (editor of the Ganjam plate of Daṇḍimahādevī) points out that the characters belong to the "northern part of Eastern India;" D.C. Sircar and P.R. Srinivasan (editors of the Santiragrama plate of Daṇḍimahādevī and a grant of Vakulamahādevī respectively) observed that the characters are "eastern variety of north Indian Alphabet;" Priyatosh Banerji (editor of Angul plate of Dharmmamahādevī) remarked that they belong to a variety of the northern alphabet of *c.* tenth-eleventh century and may be called an "admixture of Nāgarī and proto-Bengali letters;" and G.S. Das and K.C. Panigrahi (joint editors of the Taltalai plate of Dharmmamahādevī) are of the opinion that the characters are "northern type of alphabet."

Regarding the characters of the Śulki charters, D.C. Sircar and P. Acharya (joint editors of the Hindol plate of Kulastambha) held the view that they are "east Indian Variety of northern alphabet;" those of the Tuṅgas, D.C. Sircar (editor of the Talcher plate of Gayāḍatuṅga) and P.R. Srinivasan (editor of the Khadgaprasad plate of Vinītatuṅga) opined that they are "Siddhamātṛkā alphabet of Eastern India;" and those of the Nandas, K.C. Panigrahi and D.C. Sircar (editors of the Baripada and Jurerpur plates of Devānandadeva respectively) observed that they belonged to the northern class of alphabet. The Angul plates of Śāntikaradeva and the charter of Vīrapracaṇḍadeva have been grouped under the "eastern variety of north Indian alphabet" by S. Tripathy and P.R. Srinivasan respectively.

D.C. Sircar, P.R. Srinivasan, C.C. Das Gupta, and S. Tripathy who edited a number of inscriptions of the Bhañjas of Khiñjali-maṇḍala almost agree in their observation about the characters and say that they belong to the "eastern variety of the north Indian alphabet." Hiralal, who has edited three records of this family, opines that they are written in "Nāgarī" characters. But A. Banerji (editor of the Baud plates of Raṇabhañja) remarked that the characters belonged to the "Ganjam variety of northern alphabet" while J.K. Sahu (editor of the Samabalpur University Museum plates of Raṇabhañja) is of the opinion that the characters are of *kuṭila* type.

Similarly, H.P. Shastri and R.C. Majumdar who edited the Khandadeuli plate of Raṇabhañja and the Adipur plates of Narendrabhañja held the view that the characters are "late *kuṭila* type" and "northern type" respectively. Very recently S. Tripathy (editor of the Panasi plate of Rāyabhañja) remarked that the characters of the inscription belong to the "eastern variety of north Indian alphabet."

J.F. Fleet who has edited six charters of the early Somavaṁśīs and F. Kielhorn who edited the Kudopalli plates of the time of Bhīmaratha pointed out that the characters of these inscriptions are "Nāgarī of the northern class." A.M. Shastri and S. Tripathy who have recently published the three Gopalpur plates of Janmejaya I also held the same view and said that they can be rightly said to mark a "transition between the older *siddhamātṛkā* alphabet and the present Nāgarī script" while D.C. Sircar and P.C. Rath (joint editors of the Kalibhana plates of Janmejaya I) remarked that they are "a peculiar type of the northern class — an admixture of proto-Bengali and Devanāgarī." In the opinion of D.C. Sircar, the Patna Museum plates of Yayāti I are written in the "eastern variety of northern alphabet." The characters of some of the charters have been characterized by B.C. Chhabra (Sonepur plates of Janmejaya I) as "northern type;" by S.N. Rajaguru and M.P. Das (Gaintala plates of Janmejaya I) as "northern type of Kuṭilākṣara;" by J.K. Sahu (Sambalpur University Museum plates of Janmejaya I) as "*kuṭila* type;" by L.P. Pandeya (Mahakosala Historical Society's plates of Bhīmaratha) as "acute-angled type of

Northern script attributable to the seventh-eighth century AD;" by P.R. Srinivasan (Mahulpara plates of Dharmaratha) as "Nāgarī as prevalent in Kaliṅga in the eleventh century AD;" and by K.B. Tripathi as "ordinarily called *kuṭila* but may be called proto-Oriya (or proto-Bengali after Bühler)."

About the characters of the later Gaṅgas of Śvetaka branch F. Kielhorn (Ganjam plates of Pṛthvīvarmadeva), C.C. Das Gupta (Indian Museum plates of Indravarman), and P.N. Bhattacharya (Badakhemundi plates of Indravarman) suggested that they are "Nāgarī as written in Orissa and neighbouring parts of east India," "south Indian Nāgarī" and "Nāgarī" respectively.

D.C. Sircar, the editor of the Pandiapathar plates of Nala King Bhīmasena remarked that their characters belong to the "east Indian alphabet." S. Subrahmanya Iyer and S. Tripathy who jointly edited the Orissa State Museum plates of Narendradhavala are of the opinion that their characters resemble to the Kaliṅga alphabet of the eleventh century AD.

A majority of the copper-plate grants of the eastern and Imperial Gaṅgas (up to Anantavarman Coḍagaṅgadeva) and those of their lineal descendants in the adjoining areas have been edited by Sten Konow, G.V. Ramamurti, C.N. Rao (jointly with R. Subba Rao), R. Subba Rao, T.N. Ramachandran, R.C. Mazumdar, R. Subrahmanyam, N. Ramesan, N.M. Rao, S. Tripathy and others, and they held the view that their characters are old Nāgarī or Nāgarī. D.C. Sircar, who re-edited the Chidivalasa plates of Devendravarman, opined that the characters of these plates belonged to the "eastern variety of northern alphabet." G.S. Gai and M. Krishna Kumari also held the similar view while editing the Arsavalli plates of Vajrahasta and the Yudhepura plates of Rājarāja I respectively. Again, D.C. Sircar and R.C. Majumdar who have edited some of the charters of Vajrahasta III and Rājarāja I observed that they are written in Gauḍīya alphabet. Moreover, S.N. Rajaguru believed that the alphabet of the Nirakarpur plates of the time of Eastern Gaṅga king Devendravarman are in "north Kaliṅga type," while that of the Simhapura plates of Dharmakheḍi is in "*kuṭila* type."

From the above observations of the learned scholars, it can be surmised that the characters of the inscriptions of Orissa of ninth-eleventh centuries can be characterized as either "northern type of alphabet" or "eastern variety of northern alphabet," or "Nāgarī of the northern type" or "*kuṭila* type" or "old Nāgarī type." Of the other observations mention may be made of (a) "the Ganjam variety of the northern alphabet," (b) "the acute-angled alphabet of seventh-eighth centuries," (c) "the *siddhamātṛkā* alphabet," (d) "north Kaliṅga type," (e) "Kaliṅga Nāgarī," (f) "south Indian Nāgarī," etc.

A. Banerji who edited the Baud plates of Raṇabhañja makes us believe that the characters are the "Ganjam variety of the northern alphabet." The idea was possibly borrowed from F. Kielhorn who had for the first time made such a remark on the characters of the Ganjam copper-plate grant of Mādhavavarman of GE 300 (AD 619-20). In Chapter 6 we have already invalidated this nomenclature and preferred to call the script as acute-angled alphabet and considering the gap of about 250 years that intervened between the Ganjam plates of Mādhavavarman and the Baud plates of Raṇabhañja, it appears to be incongruous to christen the style of the latter as the "acute-angled script." L.P. Pandeya's observation that the characters of the Mahakosala Historical Society's plates of Bhīmaratha are in acute-angled script attributable to the seventh-eighth century AD again seems to be wholly erroneous and misleading. From the internal and circumstantial evidences it is apparent that Bhīmaratha flourished in the latter part of the tenth century and from the palaeographical point of view it can hardly be believed that the "acute-angled alphabet" survived in any part of India as late as the tenth century AD. The horizontal head-marks covering the entire breadth of the letters; the firm or rounded base-lines of *pa, pha, ma, ya, ṣa*, etc., and the advanced letter-forms of *kha, ga, ja, ṭa, ṇa, ma, la, śa, ha*, etc., negate the possibility of attributing the style to the "acute-angled script" of the seventh-eighth centuries. The characters of the Tuṅga inscriptions have been categorized by D.C. Sircar and P.R. Srinivasan as "Siddhamātṛkā type." None of the characteristic of the *siddhamātṛkā* such as angularity of the letter-forms, solid triangular wedges forming as head-marks and sloping of the letters from left to right can be traced in the inscriptions of the Tuṅgas who supposed to have ruled in the late ninth and early tenth century AD.

Besides the alphabet of some of the documents of the Gaṅgas of Kaliṅga have been taken by the learned editors as "north Kaliṅga type" or "Nāgarī as used in Kaliṅga" or "Kaliṅga Nāgarī" or "south Indian Nāgarī." What has been termed by scholars as Kaliṅga Nāgarī or Nāgarī as used in Kaliṅga in the eleventh-twelfth century AD is in fact an admixture of the proto-Nāgarī and the proto-Oriya. The proto-Oriya characters began to appear in the epigraphic alphabet of the eleventh century. Kaliṅga appears to be one of the palaeographical zones/sub-zones where some peculiar traits have been noticed in the existing proto-Nāgarī script and the regular use of those traits in the subsequent period ultimately led to the evolution of the proto-Oriya script. As will be shown later, the proto-Oriya evolved out of the proto-Nāgarī and the characters of the inscriptions of Kaliṅga of the eleventh-twelfth centuries exhibit a transition from the proto-Nāgarī to the proto-Oriya. As it happens in every transitional alphabet that in the evolutionary process the traits of a new script got mixed up with the existing script of the locality, so also in the inscriptions of Kaliṅga of the said period certain peculiar features began to appear in the proto-Nāgarī script which in due course of time progressed in the direction of the proto-regional script of Orissa. It is, therefore, wrong to believe that the proto-Nāgarī as used in Kaliṅga was a distinct variety and what is true is that the proto-Oriya script was mixed up with the proto-Nāgarī script.

In the historical development of the epigraphic palaeography of north India, the *kuṭila* script or the *siddhamātṛkā* alphabet and its variations were in use in different localities of north and central India in the sixth-eighth century AD. It is also learnt that the script has some ornamental traits in the solid triangles, medial vowels, gentle bend in the lower right limb of the letters and in the sloping of the letters from left to right. But in the next century some localities began to prefer to draw the letters in a more simplified manner. The solid triangular wedges are now turned into simple line head-marks, the ornamental flourishes of the medial vowels are considerably restrained, the bending of the right upright or the right limb is straightened, and the tendency to slope the letters from left to right is no longer traceable. These changes made in the letter-forms gave altogether a new look to them. But it should be remembered that the scribe did not alter the essential characters rather he followed the same accepted forms of the letters already achieved by a particular technical process in the preceding centuries. The desire was obviously to reduce the time taken in producing the complex form without sacrificing its individuality. Moreover, the tendency of simplification was found in the hands of some writers while others preferred to keep up the taste for ornamentation. It is possibly for this reason that the writing style of a particular locality is simplified compared to that of other. Here, the individual taste, not the writing material, is responsible for difference in the style of writing.

Thus, the process of simplification applied to the *kuṭila* script led to the development of the incipient stages of the northern Nāgarī, the fully developed forms of which as has been suggested by V.S. Sukhthankar[1] may be seen in the Kauthem (Miraj State) copper-plate grant of the Cāḷukya king Vikramāditya V (AD 1009).[2] The distinguishing features of the Nāgarī script are the addition of the horizontal top strokes covering the entire breadth of the letters instead of solid triangular wedges of the *siddhamātṛkā* and the formation of straight verticals in the place of bent right limbs of the letters. Although the *kuṭila* script in its later development became more and more akin to the Nāgarī script, yet the process of transition from the *kuṭila* to the Nāgarī script took sometime and this transitional stage may be called as the proto-Nāgarī.

In this transitional script, the solid triangular wedges are flattened and they are drawn in the form of horizontal covering lines. In the *kuṭila* script, the letters *a, ā, gha, pa, ma, ya, ṣa* and *sa* have already obtained two limbs and the wedge is applied to the top of the left limb and occasionally to both the limbs. But in the next stage of development with the flattening of wedges, the covering line at first remained half way but subsequently it joined to the right limb and the breadth of this line equalled to the size of the letters. In the proto-Nāgarī alphabet we also notice other changes in the head-marks such as hollow triangles, hooks, etc., which, as will be shown below, led to the birth of several proto-regional characteristics. Another important trait is that the right limb still maintained the inward bend in the middle and after sometime although the limb is straightened a tail formation is made at its lower end. Some of the letter-forms such as *a, ā, u, o, au, ka, ga, gha, tha, da, na, pa, ma, ya, ra, la, va, ṣa*, etc., can be easily recognized as the Nāgarī. In due course of time the Nāgarī forms of the other letters except *i, ī, kha, dha*, etc., have also been developed. The medial vowels of the Nāgarī are traceable in *ā, i, ī, u* and *ū* and in a majority of cases they are used throughout the period but the medials like *e, ai, o,* and *au* are different.

1. V.S. Sukhthankar, "Palaeographic Notes," *R.G. Bhandarkar Commemoration Volume*, Bhandarkar Oriental Research Institute, Poona, 1917, 309.
2. *IA*, 16, 15ff. & pl.

The above characteristics of the transitional script are seen in a greater part of northern India in the ninth-eleventh centuries. But palaeographers widely differ on the question of the earliest use of the script in India. Bühler[3] is inclined to believe that the most ancient document, written throughout in Nāgarī, is the Samangarh grant of the Rāṣṭrakūṭa king Dantidurga of AD 754[4] and that the characters of the Kanheri inscriptions Nos. 15 and 43 which are respectively incised in AD 851 and 877 during the reign of the Śilāhāra princes Pullaśakti and Kapardin II[5] are of the same type as those of the Samangarh grant. Bühler has further held the view that the Samangarh and the Kanheri inscriptions, together with some others of the ninth century show the archaic variety of the southern Nāgarī, the fully developed form of which is exhibited in the Kauthem plates of AD 1009 already referred to above. In northern and central India, Bühler[6] has noticed that the Nāgarī script at first appeared on the Bengal Asiatic Society's plate of the Pratihāra king Vināyakapāla[7] to which he has wrongly assigned the date AD 794. In his opinion, the chief difference between the southern and northern Nāgarī is that the absence of the small tails slanting to the right from the end of the verticals of the letters in the southern variety of the Nāgarī. According to G.H. Ojha[8] in north India, the Nāgarī script began to be used from the beginning of the tenth century AD and appeared for the first time in the Dighva-Dubauli plate of Pratihāra king Mahendrapāla of Kanauj of VS 955 or AD 898.[9] He remarked that in south India, the Nāgarī script resembling to modern Nāgarī appeared even before its development in northern India, may be in the eighth century AD. The inscriptions which he relied for this view form the following series : (a) the Samangarh grant of Dantidurga of Ś. 675 (AD 754), (b) the Dhulia plates of Govindarāja II of Ś. 701 (AD 780),[10] (c) the Paithan[11] and Vanigaon[12] plates of Rāṣṭrakūṭa Govinda III of Ś. 713 (AD 794) and Ś. 730 (AD 808) respectively, (d) the Baroda plates of Rāṣṭrakūṭa Yuvarāja Dhārāvarṣa of Ś. 757 (AD 853),[13] (e) the plates of Amoghavarṣa,[14] and (f) his Śilāhāravaṁśī feudatory Pullaśakti I and II found from Kanheri of Ś. 765 (AD 843) and Ś. 773 (AD 851).[15]

3. Bühler, *IP*, 83.
4. *IA*, 11, 108-15 & pl.
5. *Ibid.*, 13, 135ff. & pl.
6. Bühler, *op. cit.*, 84.
7. *IA*, 15, 138-41 & pl.
8. Ojha, *BPL*, 68-70.
9. *IA*, 15, 105-13 & pl.
10. *EI*, 8, 182-87 & pl.
11. *Ibid.*, 3, 103-10 & pl.
12. *IA*, 11, 159-61 & pl.
13. *Ibid.*, 14, 200ff. & pl.
14. *EI*, 6, 98-108 & pl.; 18, 235-57 & pl.; 26, 59-62 & pl. 35, 85-88 & pl. 37, 129-34 & pl.
15. *IA*, 13, 135ff.

Both Bühler and Ojha took the Samangarh grant of Dantidurga as the earliest specimen of the Nāgarī or Southern Nāgārī. A.H. Dani also relied on this inscription and said that the Rāṣṭrakūṭas were responsible for introducing the proto-Nāgarī script in the Deccan.[16] But long back, V.S. Sukhthankar in his palaeographical notes questioned the authenticity of the grant. According to him,

> In the case of the Samangad grant, however, the outstanding consideration for suspecting its authenticity is the circumstance that it contains not merely advanced forms, but that these are used to the entire exclusion of others which must have been current at the epoch. The use of advanced forms is not arbitrary: the regularity with which they recur shows that they had become fixed types at the time the document was concocted.[17]

In fact, in the Samangarh plates we find neither the slightest trace of the wedge formation nor the bending of the right verticals in *kuṭila* fashion, but on the other hand, the frequent use of top covering strokes and of the straightened right limbs are the characteristic peculiarities of the Nāgarī. Sukhthankar has made a comparison between the alphabets of these plates and those of the Daulatabad plates of Rāṣṭrakūṭa Śaṅkaragaṇa, *Ś*. 715 (AD 793),[18] the Radhanpur[19] and Vani[20] plates of Rāṣṭrakūṭa Govinda III of AD 808, and has pointed out that the alphabet of the alleged grant of Dantidurga occupy a very isolated position in the progressive development of Nāgarī. Moreover, the decimal system of notation used in expressing the date of the grant has been seriously challenged as uncharacteristic of the period and locality in question. Taking all into consideration, he held the opinion that the balance of evidence points strongly to the conclusion that the Samangarh grant is a spurious document. On the other hand, he believed that the very earliest dated inscriptions which are written throughout in Nāgarī (proto-Nāgarī) characters are the Kanheri cave inscriptions (AD 851 and 877) of the Śilāhāra feudatories Pullaśakti and Kapardin II. These show (i) the top stroke covering the entire breadth of the letter, and (ii) rectangular corners. However, the transitional stages leading up to these forms can be traced to the inscriptions of the Rāṣṭrakūṭas of the first half of the ninth century. But they can hardly be grouped under proto-Nāgarī or Nāgarī, as the wedges are not yet fully flattened and the acute angles are not turned into right angles. However, it is quite obvious that the Rāṣṭrakūṭas were responsible for introducing the *kuṭila* script of Central India and Rajasthan into Western Deccan which in due course of time developed into proto-Nāgarī by their feudatories. The subsequent course of development of the proto-Nāgarī in western India can be traced with the help of the inscriptions of the Rāṣṭrakūṭas of Lāṭa and Malkhed belonging to *circa* AD 850-950 . After the Śilāhāra princes, the Rāṣṭrakūṭas of Gujarat branch used the proto-Nāgarī alphabet in their

16. Dani, *IP*, 165.
17. Sukhthankar, *op. cit.*, 317.
18. *EI*, 9, 193-98 & pl.
19. *Ibid.*, 6, 239-51 & pl.
20. *IA*, 11, 156ff & pl.

inscriptions. The Bagumra plates of Dhrubarāja II *alias* Dhārāvarṣa of Ś. 789 (AD 867)[21] and the Bagumra plate of Kṛṣṇarāja *alias* Akālavarṣa of Ś. 810 (AD 888)[22] are representative specimens of the Gujarat branch of the Rāṣṭrakūṭas written in the said characters. Shortly after the date of the second grant, the Rāṣṭrakūṭas of Gujarat were swept away by the main branch of the Rāṣṭrakūṭas of Malkhed and the latter continued the use of the script current in the locality and carried it to further south. In the Bagumra plates of Indra III of Ś. 836 (AD 914),[23] the Cambay plates of Govinda IV or Ś. 852 (AD 930),[24] the Sangli plates of Govinda IV of Ś. 855 (AD 933),[25] and the Salotgi pillar inscription of the reign of Kṛṣṇa III *alias* Akālavarṣa of Ś. 867 (AD 945),[26] the proto-Nāgarī characters show a definite progressive movement when compared to those of the records of the Śilāhāras and of the Rāṣṭrakūṭas of Gujarat.

So far as the earliest use of the proto-Nāgarī in northern and central India is concerned, Bühler is substantially right in saying that the script first appeared in the Bengal Asiatic Society's plates of Vināyakapāla. All the traits of the proto-Nāgarī are fully represented in these plates. About the date of the grant, Bühler has erroneously supposed it as AD 794-95, but it has now been accepted as Vikrama *Saṁvat* 988 (AD 931). However, the transition from the *kuṭila* to the proto-Nāgarī script in northern and central India is not an abrupt one. The earliest forms of the transition are seen in the Dighva-Dubauli plates of Pratīhāra Mahendrapāla I of AD 898. Although the term Nāgarī or proto-Nāgarī can be applied to this record with doubtful propriety, yet the mixture of the solid triangles and flat strokes as head-marks and the sporadic presence of straightened right limbs show that it has got the earliest touch of the process of simplification in this part of north India leading to the fully developed proto-Nāgarī characters in the Bengal Asiatic Society's plates of Vināyakapāla. Later on in the inscriptions of the same region, the Paramāras of Malwa, the Candellas of Jejākabhukti and in those of the Rāṣṭrakūṭas of Kanauj, the script was used.

Now the question arises whether the development of the proto-Nāgarī characters in Western Deccan, and in northern and central India was made in isolation or whether there was any inter-zonal influences between the two important palaeographical zones of the ninth-tenth centuries. These questions can be answered in the backdrop of the political activities and social changes of the period under review. Politically, the period witnessed a tripartite struggle between the Rāṣṭrakūṭas, the Gurjara-Pratīhāras and the Pālas for the domination of northern India, and Kanauj was the bone of contention. With varying degrees of success the members of these

21. *IA*, 12, 181ff. & pl.
22. *Ibid.*, 13, 65ff. & pl.
23. *EI*, 9, 24ff. & pl.
24. *Ibid.*, 7, 26-47 & pl.
25. *IA*, 12, 249ff. & pl.
26. F. Kielhorn, *A List of the Inscriptions of Southern India from about* AD *500*, Appendix to *EI*, 7, No. 94.

ruling lineages tried to subjugate Kanauj and to extend their sphere of influence over entire northern part of India. Although the Gurjara-Pratīhāras achieved initial success in capturing the city of Kanauj, they received reverses at the hands of the Rāṣṭrakūṭa king Kṛṣṇa II (*c.* AD 878-914) and his feudatory Kṛṣṇarāja (the last known member of Gujarat branch of the Rāṣṭrakūṭas), sometime before AD 888, the date of the Bagumra plates of the latter. The next Rāṣṭrakūṭa king Indra III (*c.* AD 914-27) also claimed that he had captured and devastated the city of Kanauj and defeated Mahīpāla *alias* Vināyakapāla I (*c.* AD 912-42) in an engagement.[27] It is also learnt that Vināyakapāla I survived the terrible shock and regained the lost territories and later on extended his empire up to Saurāṣṭra (Kathiawar peninsula) in the west. In the train of conquests, the proto-Nāgarī script which was popularized by the Rāṣṭrakūṭa feudatories in Western Deccan could have been introduced to northern India in the late ninth and early tenth centuries. The movement of the brāhmaṇas, the artisans, the traders and other professional groups along the route from Gujarat to Kanauj could have hastened the process. The dates of the Dighva-Dubauli plates of Mahendrapāla I and the Bengal Asiatic Society's plates of Vināyakapāla I further give credence to this hypothesis. Thus, the changes effected in the writing style of Western Deccan (west Maharashtra and south Gujarat) in the later part of ninth century got transmitted into northern India in the late ninth and early tenth centuries and considerably influenced the epigraphical alphabet of the north and central India.

Coming to eastern India, the Pālas who had established themselves in Bengal in the latter half of the eighth century AD gradually extended their kingdoms in the west and this resulted in a political union of a major part of Bengal and Bihar. The political union paved the way for a uniform pattern of writing in the epigraphic alphabet of eastern India. In the inscriptions of the Pālas of this period, although the right arm is straightened, the acute angle is still noticed on account of sloping of the base-line and the wedge formation gets more prominence. This is particularly true in the case of the Khalimpur grant of Dharmapāla[28] and Mungir grant of Devapāla.[29]

But the proto-Nāgarī character had not yet appeared in the inscriptions of eastern India until the tenth century AD. There is a reason to believe that the script of Bengal in the early part of tenth century received some impingement from that of north and central India where the proto-Nāgarī script was slowly taking shape. The Paharpur (Rajashahi district, East Pakistan) and the Mahisantosh (Dinajpur district, East Pakistan) image inscriptions of the Gurjara-Pratīhāra king Mahendrapāla I (*c.* AD 885-910) or regnal year 5 and 15 respectively evidently make it clear that the king had occupied wide areas of Bengal and Bihar by defeating his

27. R.C. Mazumdar (ed.), *History and Culture of Indian People* (*HCIP*), IV, *The Age of Imperial Kanauj*, Bombay, 1964, 11-12 & 35-36.

28. *JASB*, 1894, pt. 1, 53-58 & pl. III.

29. *EI*, 18, 304-07 & pl.

contemporary Pāla ruler Nārāyaṇapāla (*c.* AD 854-910).[30] It seems, the domination of Mahendrapāla over Bengal for more than a decade (*c.* AD 890-900) led to the introduction of certain changes in the writing style of eastern India. Its impact was felt in the Badal pillar inscription of Nārāyaṇapāla (*c.* AD 900). The letter forms of *gha, ja, ṇa, ta, da, ma, ra, va, śa, ha,* etc., may stand the test well. Later on a few documents of the Pālas of the tenth-eleventh century and those of the Candras of east Bengal of the same time are written in the proto-Nāgarī script. One important characteristic of the proto-Nāgarī script of Bengal is that the wedge is only marginally flattened to cover the entire breadth of the letters and is still traceable. At times it has got a hollow in the wedge. But in the essential characters, in the straightening of the right limbs and in the application of the medial vowels, they resemble to the proto-Nāgarī alphabet of other parts of northern India. Probably, it is for this slight variation in the formation of the head-marks in the proto-Nāgarī script of Bengal some scholars have termed the script as "eastern variety of northern India." But we prefer to call it a peculiarity of the proto-Nāgarī script. This is, however, a matter of nomenclature.

Thus, from the above analysis it is understood that the proto-Nāgarī script first appeared in the epigraphic alphabet of western Deccan in the second half of the ninth century which gradually travelled to Kanauj along the route of Rāṣṭrakūṭa invasion sometime in the late ninth century. From Kanauj it moved to eastern India and considerably influenced the prevalent script. It has also become clear that political activities of the three major powers such as the Rāṣṭrakūṭas, the Gurjara-Pratīhāras and the Pālas in the eighth-tenth centuries as well as the mobility of the brāhmaṇas, the artisans, the traders and the other professional groups removed the major disparities which existed in the writing styles of different palaeographical zones of northern, western and eastern India and paved the way for a nearly uniform script in a major part of northern India. The proto-Nāgarī script is, therefore, considered as the parent of a number of other proto-regional scripts in northern, western and eastern India.

In the preceding chapter we have studied the *kuṭila* script that was current in central Orissa in the eighth-ninth centuries AD. It is also learnt that besides the early records of the Bhaumakaras, a few other inscriptions of their contemporaries have been written in the said alphabet. But from the beginning of the tenth century the script was substituted by the proto-Nāgarī and the characters of most of the subsequent charters of the Bhaumakaras are in the proto-Nāgarī script. Of course, the Talcher plate of Śubhākaradeva of BE 141 (AD 877) is written in the proto-Nāgarī characters. This may be considered as one of the earliest specimens of the proto-Nāgarī script in Orissa but may not be the earliest. In the ninth century, while the stylized *kuṭila* script was used by the Bhaumakaras in their charters, their feudatories preferred to write the documents in a more simplified manner. The process of simplification that was initiated by the feudatories essentially led to the birth of the proto-Nāgarī. We have at least three different ruling lineages ruling over three different localities or *maṇḍala*s (feudal pockets) where the process of

30. D.C. Sircar, *Epigraphical Discoveries in East Pakistan*, Calcutta, 1973, 2.

simplification was already in operation. They were: (1) the Gaṅgas of Śvetaka-maṇḍala, (2) the Bhañjas of Khiñjali-maṇḍala, and (3) the Śulkis of Kodālaka-maṇḍala. This shows that the proto-Nāgarī was current in the charters of the feudatories before its popularization in the later Bhaumakara records. A proper investigation into the palaeographical peculiarities of the inscriptions of these feudal powers lands us on a surer ground about the earliest use of the script in any of the Orissan epigraphs.

Although the characters of the Vishmagiri plates of Śvetaka Gaṅga Indravarman II (who is in our chronological scheme ruled from *circa* AD 800-20) are grouped under the mixed Kaliṅga script, the stage of development of the northern characters in this set of plates can aplty be labelled as proto-Nāgarī. In the application of the horizontal covering lines on the top of the letters, substitution of uprights on the right of the letters and in the use of certain medial vowels, we notice unmistakable occurrence of the proto-Nāgarī features. Besides, letter-form of *a, ā, ka, ṇa, da, ma, ya, va, sa, ha*, etc., are exclusively written in the proto-Nāgarī. The initials *a* and *ā* are having two curves facing left. The looped *ka* has lengthened its outer curve downwards. *Ṇa, da* and *va* have obtained a definite right upright. The letters having two limbs such as *pa, ma, ya, sa*, etc., have been closed at the top by a horizontal line. Of the medials, *ā* (optionally) is developing into a full length vertical, *i* and *ī* cover the entire left and right sides of the letters respectively; and *u* is normally a curve open to the left. In the two subsequent charters such as the Indian Museum plates of Jayavarman and the Badakhemundi plates of Bhūpendravarman although the horizontal line head-mark covering the entire breadth of letters is not employed uniformly, yet certain letter-forms such as *na* (optionally), *pha, ra, la, śa* and *ṣa*, etc., can easily be recognized as the proto-Nāgarī. Further, in the Indian Museum plates of Indravarman III (*circa* AD 880-900) there is no trace of the mixed style of engraving and the characters can aptly be grouped under proto-Nāgarī. The letter-forms of *a, u, ka, kha, ga, gha, ca, cha, ṇa, tha, da, pa, pha, ma, ya, ra, la, va, śa, ṣa, sa, ha*, etc., are of proto-Nāgarī type. Besides, the medials *a, i, ī* and *u* also conform to the proto-Nāgarī type of the medials. The characters of the Pandiapathar plates of the Nala king Bhīmasena of BE 159 (AD 895) closely resemble to those of the Indian Museum plates of Śvetaka Gaṅga Indravarman III referred to above. Bhīmasena ruled over Khiḍiṅga-śṛṅga-maṇḍala. A comparison of the language and palaeography of the Śvetaka Gaṅga grants and the Pandiapathar grants makes it evident that the writer of the latter got inspiration from his counterpart in the Śvetaka Gaṅga court. Not only the characters of the Pandiapathar plates bear close resemblance with the northern characters which occurred in Śvetaka Gaṅga grants of ninth century but also the draft of the introductory part of the Nala grant was adapted from the introductory section of the documents of the Gaṅga rulers of Śvetaka. Taking all into consideration it can be argued that the process of simplification of the northern characters has already been started in the Vishmagiri grant belonging to the early ninth century which ultimately led to the birth of the proto-Nāgarī in the Indian Museum plates of Indravarman III and Panddiapathar plates of Bhīmasena in the latter part of the same century. Thus, Chikiti-Khodasing area of Ganjam district (ancient Śvetaka and Khiḍiṅga-śṛṅga-maṇḍalas) is one of the earliest localities where the proto-Nāgarī script began to appear as early as the ninth century.

The next important locality where the proto-Nāgarī script was developing in the first half of the ninth century is Khiñjali-maṇḍala or modern Baud-Phulbani area on the right side of the middle Mahanadi Valley. Śatrubhañja, the earliest known member of the family, is known from his Kumurukela and Sonepur copper-plate grants. The two plates are written by two different hands. The former exhibits a more ornate style compared to the latter and in it we trace an early attempt on the part of the scribe to reduce the wedges into small thick lines and the bent right limbs into perfect uprights with a tail like formation at the bottom. The small line head-marks are applied to both the limbs in the case of the letters having two limbs such as *a, ā, gha, pa, ma, ya, ṣa, sa,* etc., and optionally in *a* and *ya* they join together to form a total covering line as in the proto-Nāgarī. The top of *kha* and *ga* have been flattened; the letters *ca, na,* and *va* have got right uprights; *ha* is tailed; *ja* has its curve opened to the left; and the medial *ā* is developed into a full length vertical, *i* and *ī* cover the entire left and right side of the letters respectively, *e* is always denoted by a *śiro-mātrā* (top stroke). But the medial *u* has still retained its archaic form with a small tick at the lower end of the letters. On the whole, the characters of the Kumurukela plates represent a transitional alphabet and the process of simplification in these plates is restricted only to the head-marks and right limbs of the letters and in other respects they retain the ornate style.

The palaeography of the Sonepur plates of the same king is decidedly advanced when compared to the Kumurukela plates. The wedges on the top of the letters is considerably flattened to cover the entire breadth of the letters and the right uprights are also noticed in a majority of cases. In the case of the letters having two limbs (except *pha*), the flattened wedge covers the top but the wedge is faintly visible on the left limb and on the top in the rest of the letters where the head-mark is applied. The cursive engraving is traceable in the rounding of the top of *kha, ga,* of the right side of *ca, ṇa, ta, na, pa, la, va, ṣa* (optionally), and in the gentle twist of the curves of *a, ā, u* and of the lower right limbs of *ka, ca, ṇa, ta, na, la, va, ha,* etc. The medial vowels are the same as appeared in the Kumurukela plates with the exception of *u* which is no longer a tick but a curve opened to the left as in the Nāgarī. The same duct of writing is also noticed in the charters of Raṇabhañja, the son and successor of Śatrubhañja.

The Sonepur plates of Śatrubhañja as well as the plates of Raṇabhañja at least up to his 50th regnal year are written in a uniform style. In none of the above charters we do come across the mention of the names of the writers. But the names of the engravers are invariably referred to and they were Śivanāga, Jaināga and Padmanābha. All of them claimed themselves as the sons of one Paṇḍi, who was a merchant (*vaṇika*) and a goldsmith (*suvarṇakāra*), and a resident of Gandhaṭapāṭi (modern Gandharadhi near Baud). It appears that the members of this family of professional engravers had developed a local mannerism in the writing style and that they received formal training under a particular teacher. In view of the absence of the names of the

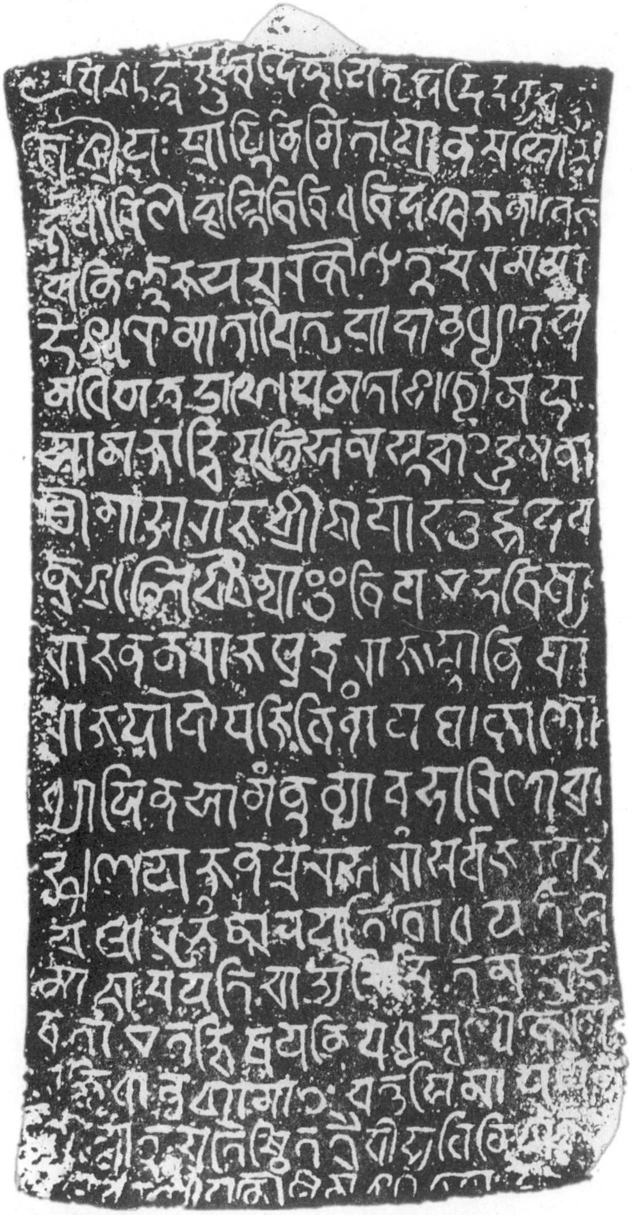

Photo 8.1 (a): Talcher plate of Gayāḍatuṅga (Obverse)

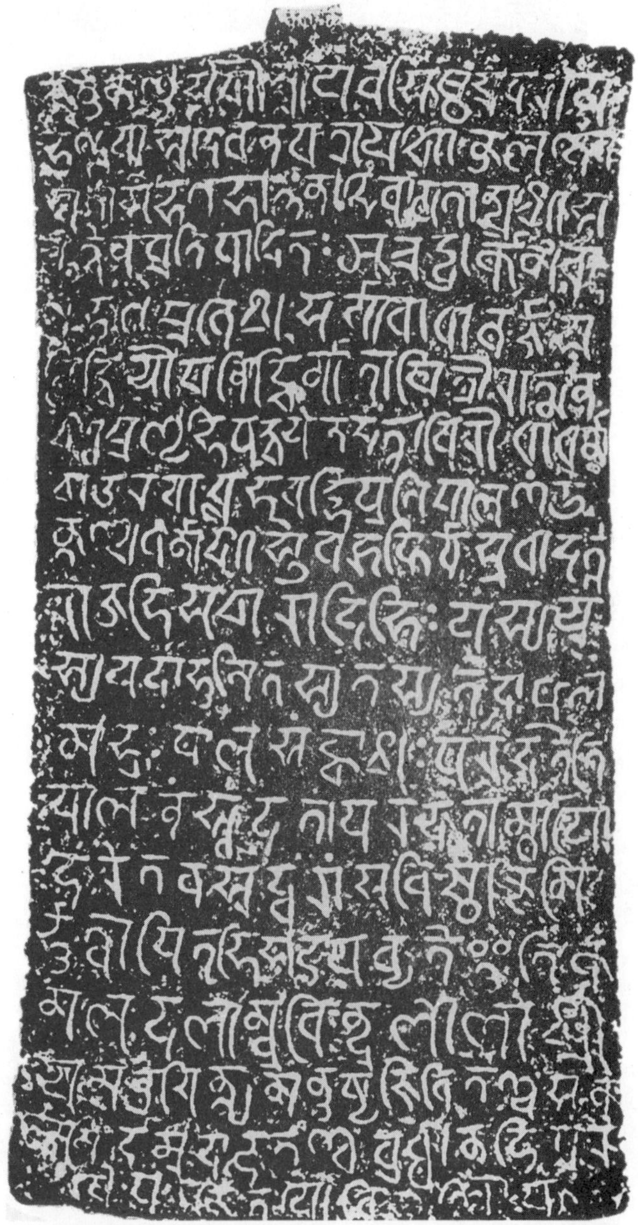

Photo 8.1 (b): Talcher plate of Gayāḍatuṅga (Reverse)

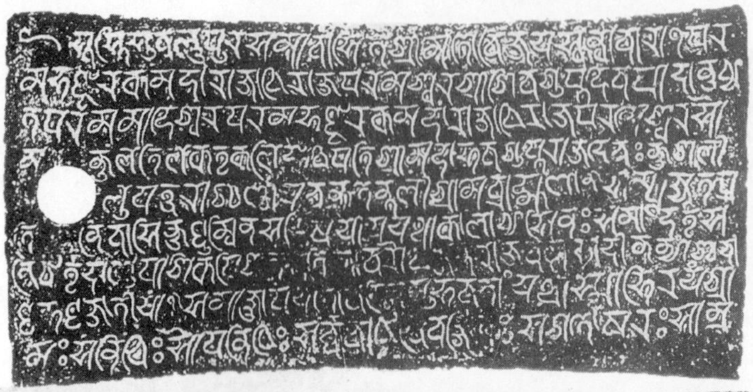

Photo 8.2 (a): Vakratentali plates of Janmejaya I, RY 3 (i)

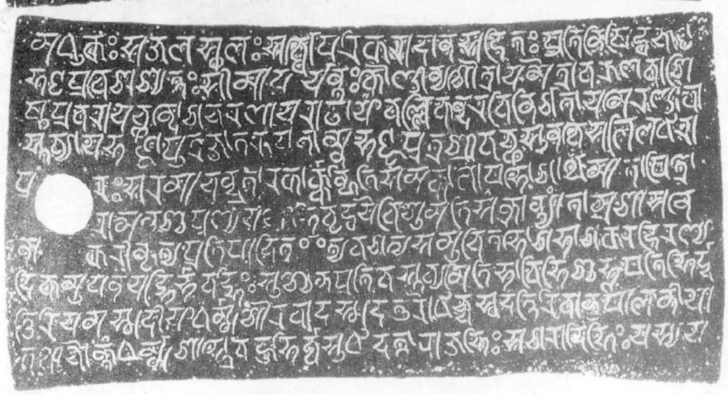

Photo 8.2 (b): Vakratentali plates of Janmejaya I, RY 3 (ii a)

Photo 8.2 (c): Vakratentali plates of Janmejaya I, RY 3 (ii b)

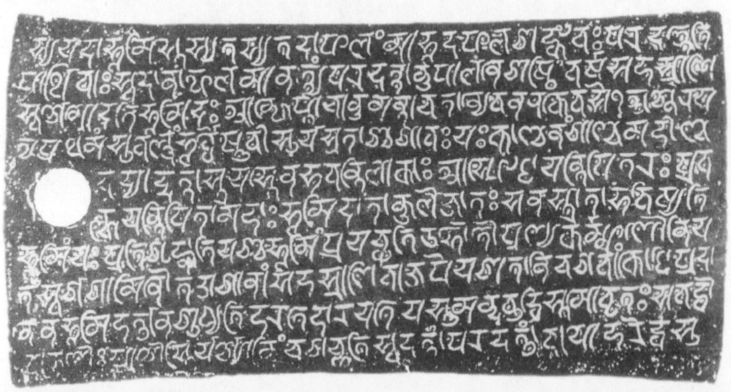

Photo 8.2 (d): Vakratentali plates of Janmejaya I, RY 3 (iii)

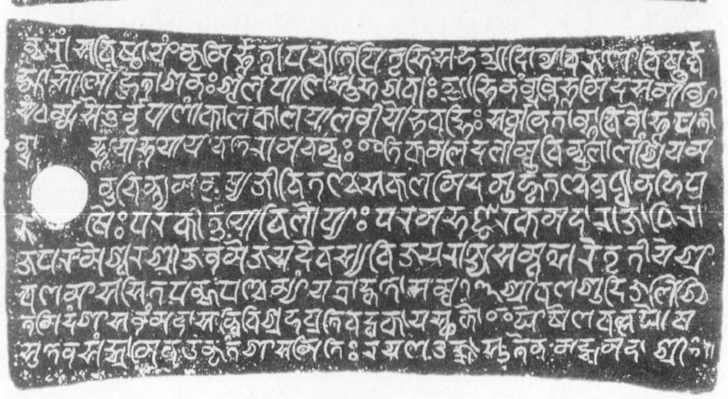

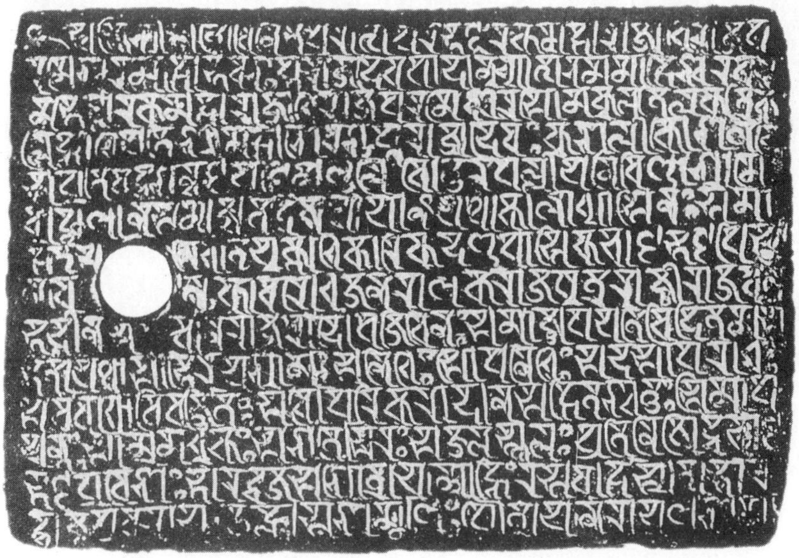

Photo 8.3 (a): Nibinna plates of Yayāti I, RY 15 (i)

Photo 8.3 (b): Nibinna plates of Yayāti I, RY 15 (ii a)

Photo 8.3 (c): Nibinna plates of Yayāti I, RY 15 (ii b)

Photo 8.3 (d): Nibinna plates of Yayāti I, RY 15 (iii)

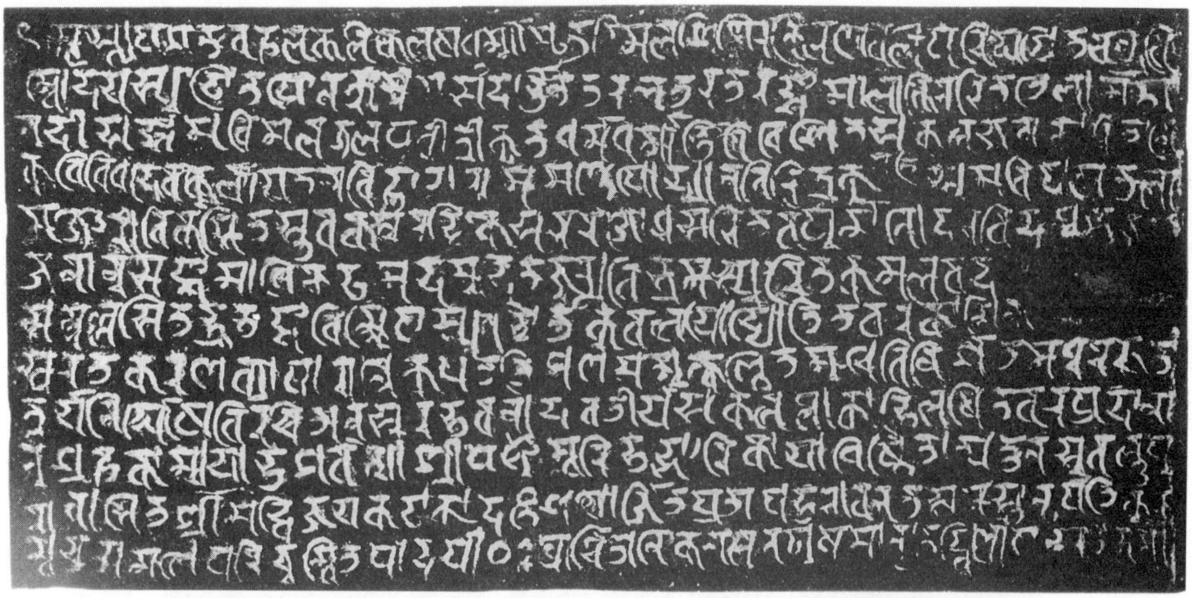

Photo 8.4 (a): Maranja-Mura plates of Mahāśivagupta Yayāti II, RY 3 (i)

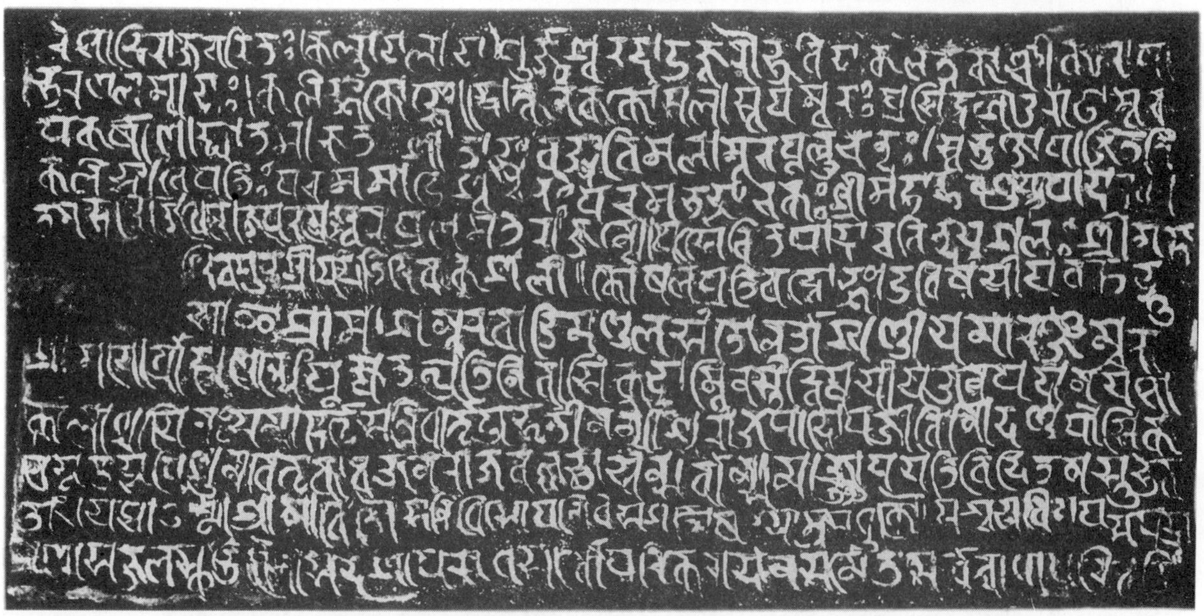

Photo 8.4 (b): Maranja-Mura plates of Mahāśivagupta Yayāti II, RY 3 (ii a).

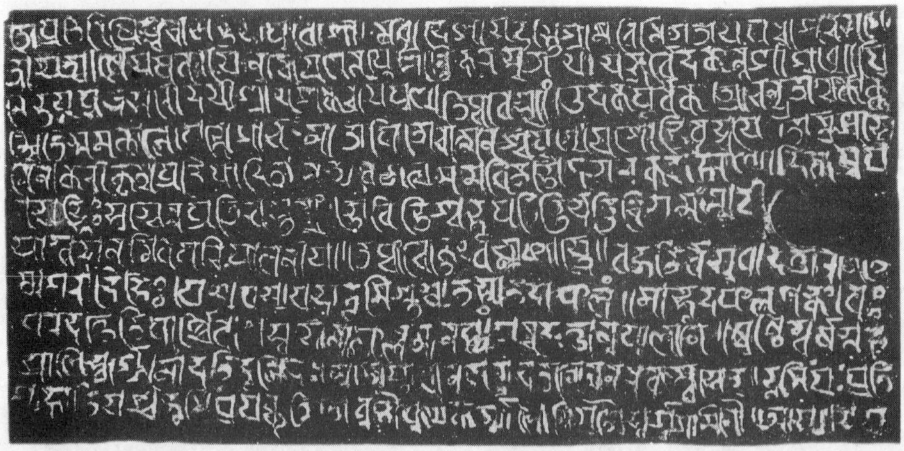

Photo 8.4 (c): Maranja-Mura plates of Mahāśivagupta Yayāti II, RY 3 (ii b).

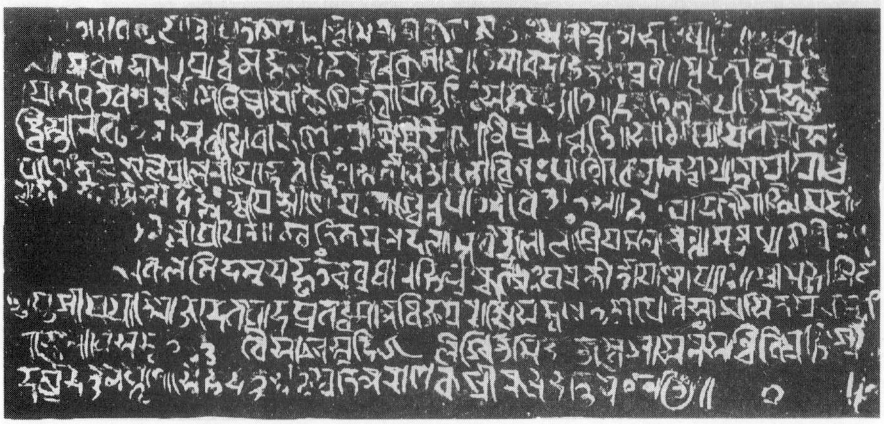

Photo 8.4 (d): Maranja-Mura plates of Mahāśivagupta Yayāti II, RY 3 (iii).

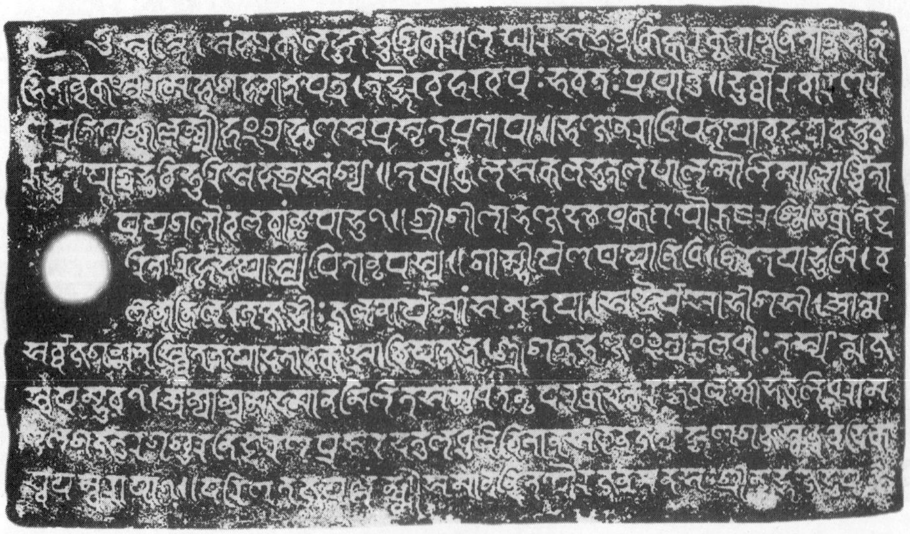

Photo 8.5 (a): Orissa State Museum plates of Raṇabhañja, RY 50 (i)

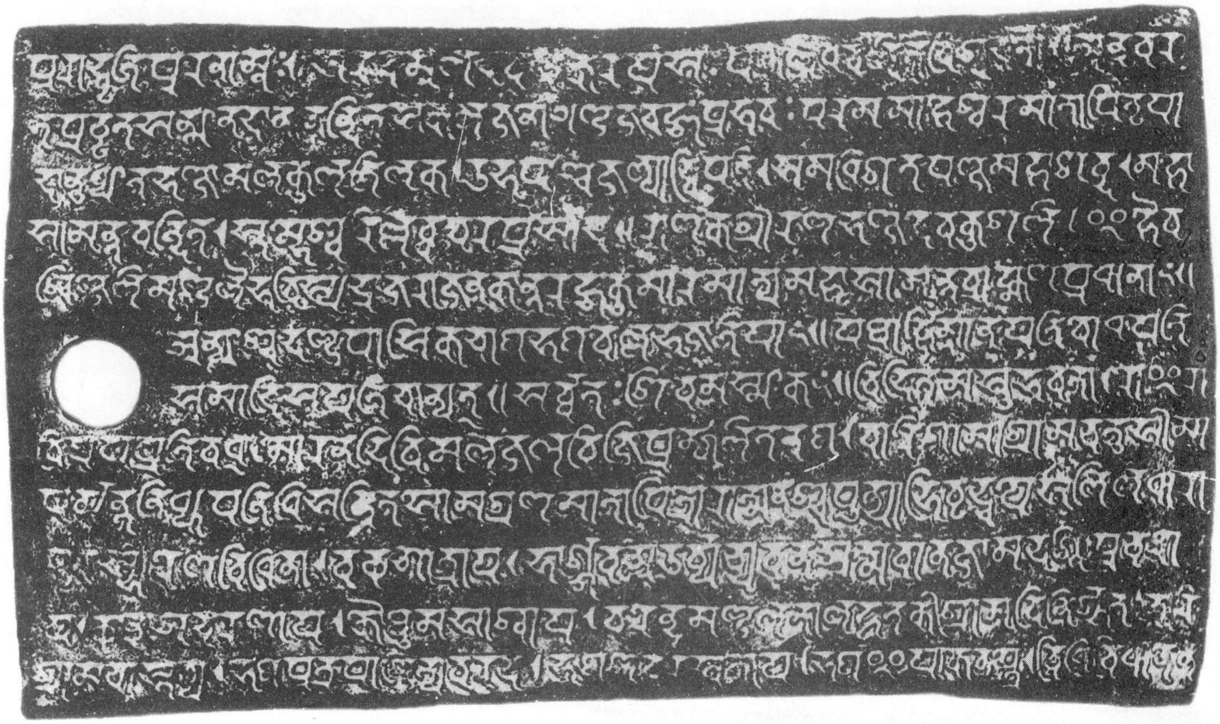

Photo 8.5 (b): Orissa State Museum plates of Raṇabhañja, RY 50 (ii a)

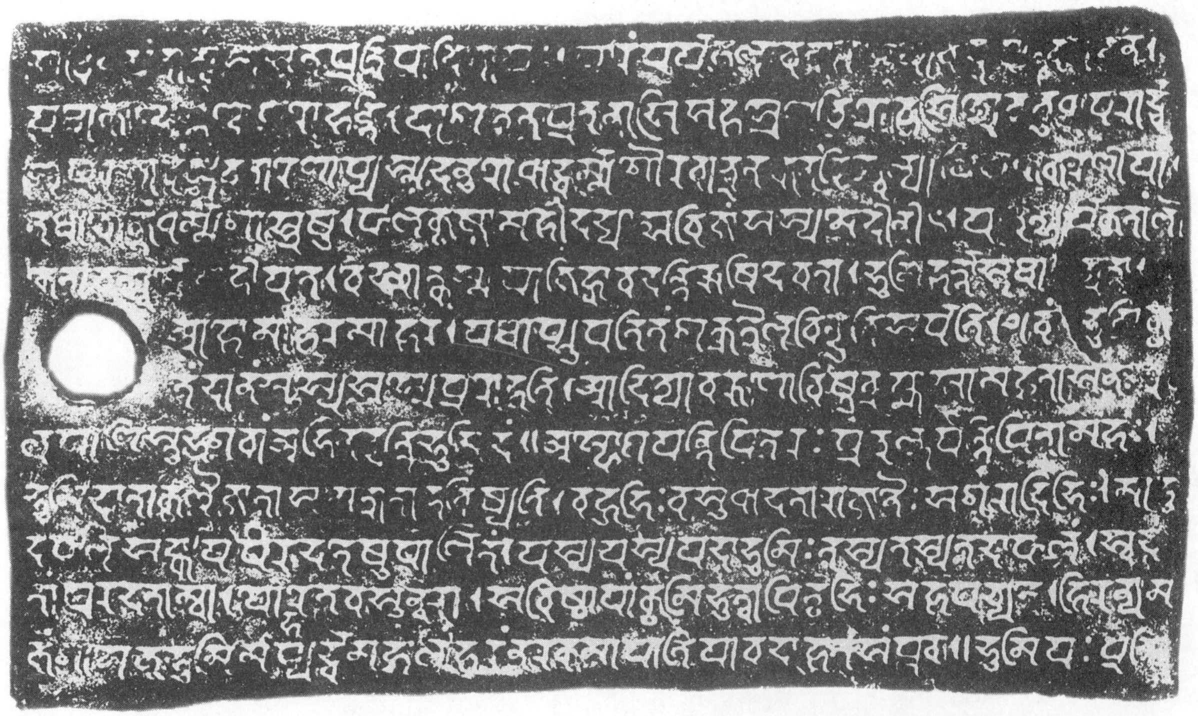

Photo 8.5 (c): Orissa State Museum plates of Raṇabhañja, RY 50 (ii b)

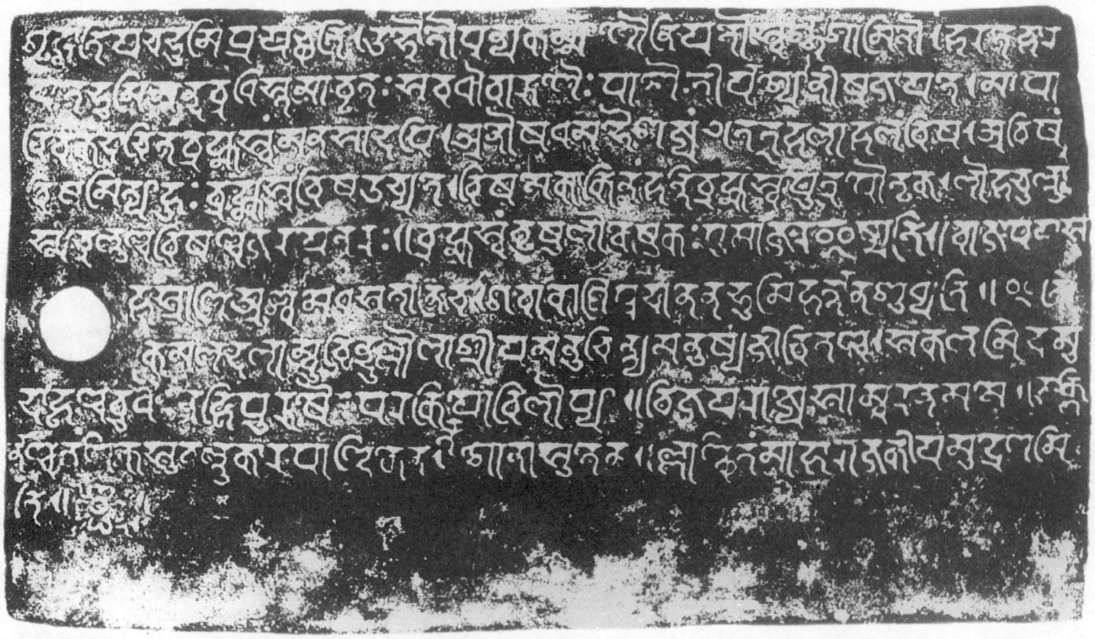

Photo 8.5 (d): Orissa State Museum plates of Raṇabhañja, RY 50 (iii)

Photo 8.6 (a): Arsavalli plates of Vajrahasta III, Ś. 982 (i)

Photo 8.6 (b): Arsavalli plates of Vajrahasta III, Ś. 982 (ii a)

Photo 8.6 (c): Arsavalli plates of Vajrahasta III, Ś. 982 (ii b)

writers and occurrence of a uniform style of writing in these records, it can also be inferred that the members of this family were responsible both for drafting the documents and engraving them on copper-plates. The prevalence of the same style of engraving in the Madras Museum plates of Narendradhavala, written by the same Padmanābha, the son of Paṇḍi, and a resident of Gandhaṭapāṭi, gives strength to our inference. This is further indicative of the fact that this family of professional writers and engravers left the royal court of the Bhañjas probably at the time of their ouster from Dhṛtipura by the Somavaṁśīs of South Kośala, and sought the patronage of the Nalas of Khiḍiṅga-śṛṅga-maṇḍala in the early tenth century AD. This is a strong case to point that often the mobility of such professional families determined the flow of stylistic peculiarities from one region to the other.

The Kodālaka-maṇḍala or the Angul-Dhenkanal-Bhuban area in the Brahmani valley is yet another locality where the proto-Nāgarī script began to appear as the epigraphic alphabet roughly from the second quarter of the ninth century. The Śulkis who ruled over the territory were one of the earliest ruling houses to start the process of simplification in the existing duct of writing in this part of Orissa. Raṇastambha, the earliest known member of the family, is known to us from his four copper-plate grants, one of which (the Dhenkanal plate) is dated in *saṁvat* (Bhauma) 103 or AD 839. The characters of this inscription exhibit a transition from the acute-angled to the proto-Nāgarī script. Although the head-mark is denoted by horizontal lines and the right arm is always indicated by a vertical, yet acute angles are still seen optionally in the letters like *da, pa, pha, ma, ya, sa, ha,* etc. The letter-forms of *ka, ja, ṇa, tha, na, la, ha,* etc., show archaism. The other grants of Raṇastambha as well as those of his successors are written in a style which can very appropriately be called as the proto-Nāgarī. The letter-forms of *a, ā, ka, pa, ma, ya, ra, la, va, ṣa,* etc., can be easily recognized as the Nāgarī. Of the medials, *ā* is optionally drawn as a full vertical on the right; the Nāgarī forms of *i, ī, u, ū* and *e* are also seen side by side with their archaic forms. The characters of the Dhenkanal plate of Jayastambha and the Puri plate of Kulastambha exhibit a slight difference because of the flattening of the wedges.

Thus, in Orissan context, the earliest occurrence of the proto-Nāgarī can be traced to the inscriptions of the Gaṅgas of Śvetaka-maṇḍala, the Bhañjas of Khiñjali-maṇḍala (Dhṛtipura branch) and in those of the Śulkis of Kodālaka-maṇḍala. Since the Vishmagiri grant is dated in AD 825, and one of the Śulki grants of Raṇastambha is dated in AD 839, and since Śatrubhañja's rule is fixed in the first half of the ninth century AD, it is legitimate to believe that the proto-Nāgarī took birth in Orissa in the first half of the ninth century AD almost simultaneously in these three localities. When we opine this, we are fully conscious about the period of advent of the proto-Nāgarī in other regions of India. It is learnt that the script first appeared in the inscriptions of the Śilāhāras and Rāṣtrakūṭas of Gujarat branch in western Deccan from the middle of the ninth century and subsequently it travelled to more northernly regions and influenced the existing script. In north India it first appeared in the Bengal Asiatic Society plates of Vināyakapala of AD 931. Compared to this, Orissa appears to be the earliest region where the proto-Nāgarī took birth in the second quarter of the ninth century almost independent of any extraneous influence.

One common point about the three ruling lineages who initiated the process of simplification is that all of them were feudatories under the Bhaumakaras and ruled over small *maṇḍalas*. While the ornate *kuṭila* script was current in the charters of the Bhaumakaras, the feudal chiefs did not follow the scripts of their overlords, but obliged to get their inscriptions engraved in a more simplified manner which led to the birth of the proto-Nāgarī. Compared to the acute-angled or the *kuṭila* script, the proto-Nāgarī is decidedly a progressive movement in the historical evolution of the script in India. This development was chiefly due to the ideosyncrasies of the scribes than anything else. From empirical evidence it can be said that scribes of exceptional merit sought the patronage of the royal court of the overlords but not of the feudal lords. Thus, while the imperial courts requestioned the services of the scribes of exceptional merit who could draft the documents carefully in ornate language and in excellent calligraphy, the feudal courts were content to recruit scribes and engravers who had less expertise and technical skill in drafting the documents. This is evident from the careless engraving, corrupt language and incorrect orthography incorporated in most of the documents of the Nalas, the Bhañjas, the Śulkis and other feudatories of the Bhaumakaras. It may be noted here that the difference in palaeography of the official charters of the Bhaumakaras and their feudatories is due to the urban and rural strains of palaeography. But while the urban is ornate and conservative the rural is simple and progressive. Moreover, application of the solid triangular wedges and bending of the right limbs in *kuṭila* fashion indeed involved great draftsmanship on the part of the scribe. But when the scribe was less acquainted with the style he preferred to draw simple lines in place of the wedges and twisted limbs without altering the accepted forms of the letters. These changes no doubt gave a different look to the letters and they appear to be careless in engraving. The simplified script as well as the corrupt language of the inscriptions give strength to our view that the scribes in the feudal courts were often less acquainted with the expertise and technical skill in drafting the documents. It is probably for this reason, the scribes in the feudal courts on most occasions did not prefer to mention their names in the official charters. Excepting a few, in a majority of documents of the Bhañjas, the Śulkis and other minor ruling houses of the ninth and tenth centuries, we do not come across the reference to the name and designation of the scribes. Alternatively, it is also possible that these documents could have been drafted and engraved by the merchants, goldsmiths or braziers, whose names frequently find mention in these charters.

However, the changes so effected made a definite progressive movement and this was not achieved by a conscious attempt on the part of the scribe or the engraver. This is true especially in the incipient stage of development of the proto-Nāgarī. But when it became a local mannerism, the scribes of the royal courts began to emulate the script and in this way it could become the standard script of the locality or region. The proto-Nāgarī script that involved quick engraving might have provided an additional incentive for its popularization as the epigraphic alphabet of a greater part of Orissa in the subsequent centuries.

This process of development is also true in the case of western Deccan where the Śilāhāra feudatories first started the process of simplification in the existing duct of writing. Here again, the scribes made an unconscious attempt in writing the inscriptions in a script which became the parent of a majority of proto-regional characters of northern India. It is not merely due to the personal ideosyncrasies of the writers but also due to the writing material the birth of the proto-Nāgarī was possible in western Deccan. The surface of the rock on which the inscriptions were incised probably did not allow the stone-cutters (*sūtradhāras*) to inscribe in an ornate style and may be the reason for which they preferred to a more simplified script.

The subsequent course of development of the script can be obtained from the inscriptions of almost all the ruling houses of Orissa of the ninth-eleventh centuries.

In south Orissa, the Gaṅgas of Śvetaka, the Nalas of Khidinga-śṛṅga-maṇḍala and the Eastern and Imperial Gaṅgas of Kaliṅga used the script in their official charters. The later members of the Śvetaka Gaṅgas such as Pṛthivīvarman, Indravarman III and Dānārṇava who ruled in the second half of the ninth and early decades of the tenth century AD discarded the mixed alphabet of Kaliṅga and preferred to use the proto-Nāgarī script in their records. The facsimile of the Ganjam plates of Pṛthivīvarman has not been published. But the reference to names of the writer and the brazier respectively as *sāndhivigrahika* Śrī Sāmanta and Svayambhū, the son of Napa, who were also caused to have written and engraved the two copper-plate grants of Indravarman III, makes it apparent that all the three inscriptions were engraved by the same hand and that the characters closely resembled to those of the grants of Indravarman III. All the traits of the proto-Nāgarī are seen in these inscriptions, except the medial *ā* which is still denoted by a small tick, the medial *e* which is optionally indicated by a small curve to the left, and of course, occasional representation of a crescent in place of a horizontal line on the top of the letters. Of the other palaeographical peculiarities mention may be made of the initial *e* and the consonants *kha*, *ga*, *tha*, *ha*, etc. All these letters except *ha* resemble to their respective proto-Oriya counterparts. The characters of the Badakhemundi plates of Dānārṇava are also the same except that the wedges are flattened to cover the entire breadth of the letters as in the case of the Sonepur plates of Śatrubhañja and the plates of Raṇabhañja (up to RY 50) of Khiñjali-maṇḍala. Another peculiarity is the formation of a tail in the lower extremities of the letters and also of the medials *ā* and *ī*.

There is a marked difference between the characters of the Madras Museum plates and the Orissa State Museum plates of (Bhauma) *Saṁvat* 189 (AD 925) of Narendradhavala. While the former is engraved carefully with a preference for ornamentation especially in the medial *e*, the punctuation and the inter-punctuation marks and also in the tail-like formations in the lower extremities of the letters, the latter is written carelessly by a separate hand. From the palaeographical point of view, the letter-forms of *pa, pha, ya, ra, la, va,* etc., and the medial *ā* and *i* of the Orissa State of Museum plates are particularly interesting. Occasionally, the letter *pa* is square-shaped, top of *pha* and *ya* are totally rounded, *ra* is triangular, *la* is archaic with its base-line sloping down, *va* is looped, and the medial *ā* is an upturned curve and *i* is semi-circular.

At times *pa* and *ya* so also *ca, ra* and *va* are indistinguishable. The semi-circular type of the medial *i* was current in the locality in the preceding century and its use was possibly due to the reinforcement from the Telugu-Canarese and the Pallava-Grantha alphabet. In the subsequent centuries, this semi-circular type of the medial *i* was preferred in the proto-Oriya and modern Oriya script.

So far as the Eastern Gaṅgas are concerned, we do not find the occurrence of the proto-Nāgarī characters in any record, until we come to the Chicacole plates of Satyavarman of GY 351 (AD 849). Like most of the charters of the Eastern Gaṅgas of the eighth-ninth centuries, this document is also written in the mixed alphabet of Kaliṅga, but some letters have attained their respective proto-Nāgarī forms. The letters *a, gha, pa, pha, ma, ya, ṣa,* etc., have got total covering lines; *kha, ga* and *śa* have obtained circular loops in their left limbs and the letter-forms of *ca, bha, ra* and *va* are decidedly written in the proto-Nāgarī. Prior to the date of this charter, in none of the grants of the Eastern Gaṅgas we do come across these peculiarities. It seems that the scribes in the royal court of the Eastern Gaṅgas received some inspiration from their counterparts in those of their nextdoor neighbours, the Śvetaka Gaṅgas and the Nalas. Subsequently, the proto-Nāgarī characters are only optionally mixed up with the characters derived from other sources. The undated Chicacole plates of Anantavarman are particularly interesting because not only some of the letter-forms such as *a, i, u, cha, ta, tha, da, dha,* etc., are exclusively written in the proto-Nāgarī, but also the second plate second side and the third plate first side of the grant are in the proto-Nāgarī characters while the rest is in the mixed Kaliṅga script.

An index of the palaeographical development in the records of the Eastern Gaṅgas of Kaliṅga of the latter half of the ninth century AD, makes it apparent that the northern characters predominated mostly which ultimately displaced the mixed alphabet of Kaliṅga in the later part of the same century. The Chidivalasa plates of Devendravarman of GY 397 (AD 895) and the Nirakarpur plates of Udayakheḍī of the time of Devendravarman are written throughout in the proto-Nāgarī script. The characters of these two inscriptions resemble to those of the Śvetaka Gaṅga King Indravarman III already referred to above. The next stage of development of the script in Kaliṅga is seen in the grants of the later Gaṅgas. Vajrahasta II, who ruled in the last decades of the tenth century, preferred to use both the proto-Nāgarī and the mixed Kaliṅga script in his grants. Except the Mandasa plates dated in Ś. 917 (AD 995) and the Ramapuram plates dated in GY 495 (AD 993) the rest of his grants are in the proto-Nāgarī. There is a gap of nearly a century between Devendravarman IV and Vajrahasta II. Inscriptions of the intervening period are not forthcoming.

After the Śulkis, the Tuṅgas, the Nandas and the other minor ruling houses who ruled over the territories in the Brahmani valley used the proto-Nāgarī script in their charters. The Talcher plate of Gayāḍatuṅga and the Talcher plate of Vinītatuṅga are decidedly written in the proto-Nāgarī. The head-marks are always denoted by horizontal covering lines and the right limbs by straight verticals. In respect of other palaeographical peculiarities they share those of the Śulkis. The characters of the rest of the plates of Gayāḍatuṅga are akin to those of the Dhenkanal plate of Jayastambha and the Puri plate of Kulastambha already referred to above. The process of flattening the wedges and covering the entire breadth of the letters as well as the formation of a tail at the lower extremities of the right limbs of the letters are suggestive of the transitional stage of development of the script. The Khadgaprasad plate of Vinītatuṅga which is dated in (Bhauma) *saṁvat* 161 (AD 897) is written in a manner that was current in the charters of the Bhañjas of Khiñjali-maṇḍala (Dhṛtipura branch) and peculiar to the scribal family of Paṇḍi, a resident of Gandhaṭapāṭi. The Khadgaprasad plate does not supply the name of the scribe, but *vaṇika* Duvadāsa, the engraver of the record, could have received his training under Paṇḍi or his sons.

The records of the Nandas are almost written in a uniform style. The letters *a, ā, ka, pa, ma, ya, ra, la, va, ṣa*, etc., can be easily recognizable as the Nāgarī. The initial *e* and *ai*, and the consonants *ca* and *va* have obtained right uprights and at times the last two are indistinguishable. The letters *kha* and *ga* are flattened at the top. *Na* has two forms, one of which has two limbs and resembles a compressed *ma*. Of the medials, *a* is either a short or long vertical to the right, *i* is either a curve to the left or a semi-circle on the top, *u* is either a small tick or a curve open to the left and *e* is indicated by either a *śiro-mātrā* (top stroke) or a *pṛṣṭha-mātrā* (side stroke). Palaeographically, the Nanda grants can be ascribed to the first half of the tenth century AD. The Hindol plate of Vīrapracaṇḍadeva, the Bonai plate of Udayavarāha and the Angul plates of Śāntikaradeva of an unknown family are not dated. But the characters of these inscriptions closely resemble to those of the Nandas and later Bhaumakaras. There is no trace of flattening of the wedges and the head-marks are simple lines covering the entire breadth of the letters. The right uprights are perfectly drawn and there is no slightest trace of the tail formation. The other palaeographical peculiarities remain the same.

So far as the Bhaumakara inscriptions are concerned, the Talcher plate of Śubhākaradeva IV dated in BE 141 (AD 877) is written in the proto-Nāgarī script. In the application of the small lines in the lower extremities of the left limbs of *kha, ga, śa*; in the tripartite *ja*; and in the angular *ḍa* we notice some archaism. But the letter-forms of *ḍha, tha*, and *ha* are fully developed and the letters *ca* and *va* have obtained right uprights. However, this is the only inscription of the Bhaumakaras of the ninth century written in the said script while the rest of the inscriptions are in the *kuṭila* script. It appears that the scribe of the plate under review got inspired by the proto-Nāgarī script that was current in the charters of the feudatories ruling in different localities for more than half a century. Very likely the inspiration was derived from the Śulkis who were ruling in close neighbourhood of Guheśvarapāṭaka, the base of power of the Bhaumakaras. But it was not favoured by the other scribes until the reign of Daṇḍimahādevī. Excepting the Kumuranga plate (AD 923), the characters of which have been suggested as the last survival of *kuṭila* alphabet in Orissa, the rest of the charters of the queen make a strong preference for the proto-Nāgarī script. By the time Daṇḍimahādevī preferred the script for her official records, the script was already popularized in the documents of the different ruling lineages for nearly a century or so.

The copper-plate grants of Daṇḍimahādevī exhibit wide variety. In the Kumuranga plate, the transition from the *kuṭila* to the proto-Nāgarī is apparent in the retaining of the solid triangular wedges and the sloping of the letters. The right limb has developed a tail at its bottom. The Ganjam and the Santiragrama plates, both dated in BE 180 (AD 916) are written in a uniform style and they are unmistakably in the proto-Nāgarī script. The covering lines are perfect horizontals and the right uprights are devoid of the tail. The undated Ganjam plates shows another peculiarity where the head-marks are represented by crescents and the lines of the letters so also the medial vowels are disjointed. The characters of the grant of Vakulamahādevī (AD 940) display yet another example of transitional alphabet. It is interesting to note here that the Ganjam plate, the Kumuranga plate and the grant of Vakulamahādevī are written by the same *mahākavi* (great poet) Jambhala, son of Jayātmana and engraved respectively by Sambhaka, Dāmodara and Kumāraka. Taking into account the stylistic difference in the three epigraphs, it may be suggested that although Jambhala had drafted the documents, yet the engravers while copying the drafts on the copper-plates had incorporated some features according to their choice without altering the essential characters of the letters. This is yet another example to show that ideosyncrasies of the engravers often determine the stylistic differences of the inscriptions of the same period and locality. However, the characters of the plates of Dharmmamahādevī, the last known ruler of the family, do not call for special remark except that the wedges are substituted by lines and the tails are totally dropped.

In the middle Mahanadi valley the Bhañjas of Khiñjali-maṇḍala (Dhṛtipura branch) had already started the use of the proto-Nāgarī script. But the later records of Raṇabhañja as well as those of his successors who ruled from Vañjulvaka exhibit some archaism in writing. In the latter records of Raṇabhañja the wedges are retained as in the *kuṭila* script but the right limbs are straightened. Similarly in the charters of his successors, the wedges are flattened to form straight top strokes but the inward bend in the right limbs are retained. Most of the grants of Śilābhañja II, Neṭṭabhañja I, Vidyādharabhañja and Neṭṭabhañja II are written in this style. The Buguda plates of Mādhavavarman II and the Nivina plates of Dharmarāja II, both belonging to the Śailodbhava family, are undoubtedly palimpsests and they are possibly re-engraved during the late ninth and early tenth centuries because their characters closely resemble to those of the records of the Bhañjas of Vañjulvaka already referred to above. Occasionally, it becomes difficult to decide how a particular inscription with a mixture of solid triangular wedges and right uprights or of straight top strokes and twisted right limbs is to be classed. Again it becomes difficult to explain about the preference for such archaic traits. At this stage of our knowledge it can only be conjectured that the scribe or the engraver had an obsession for some traits of the earlier script possibly with an intention to retain the ornate style although he was aware of the progressive movement in the development of the script that was current in the locality. However, this happens in all transitional alphabets.

The two grants of Śatrubhañja II (AD 934) and the Orissa Museum plates of Neṭṭabhañja III (AD 949) are written in the proto-Nāgarī throughout.

The Somavaṁśīs who had established themselves in the middle Mahanadi Valley in the late ninth century gradually extended their sphere of influence to the coastal Orissa sometime before the middle of the tenth century. The palaeography of the inscriptions of the family presents a truer index of development of the the proto-Nāgarī in Orissa roughly from the latter part of the ninth to the close of the eleventh century AD. By the time the Somavaṁśīs took up the script for their official charters, it was popularized in a major part of Orissa. It seems that the Somavaṁśīs initially followed the proto-Nāgarī script as used in the charters of the Bhañjas of Dhṛtipura branch. The characters of the early records of Janmejaya I share with those of the Bhañja rulers Śatrubhañja I and Raṇabhañja. Except for some noticeable difference in the letter-forms of *a*, *ā*, *ja*, *tha*, etc., the rest of the letters as well as the medial signs are the same as in the Bhañja records. The initials *a* and *ā* consist of two curves in place of only one as in the early Bhañja charters. *Ja* is developed with its lower limb curving to the left and the upper slanting down. The letter *tha* has developed a circular loop at the top left and it is not joined to the right vertical. The letter *ḍha* is of Nāgarī type. Two types of *na* appear, the one having two limbs is not joined in the middle. The top of *kha* and *ga* is rounded. The straight top stroke of *gha*, *ma*, *sa*, come nearer the right limb but not joined to it while in the rest of the letters having two limbs, it totally covers the top.

In the subsequent charters of the family the same duct of writing appeared with certain changes in the head-marks and the right limbs. The head-marks are represented by either straight top strokes or solid or hollow triangles. The right limbs are seen either in the form of straight verticals or lines sloping from left to right and developing a tail in their lower extremities. Optionally, there is a preference for cursive engraving. Judging from the different types of head-marks, the formation of tails in the right limbs and also the general cursive engraving, it can be said that the proto-Nāgarī script in the tenth-eleventh centuries is no longer a simplified script, rather with its popularization it became a standard script of Orissa, and the scribes and engravers had a strong preference for the ornate style. Except the Mahakosala Historical Society's plates of Bhīmaratha and Kudopalli plates of the time of the same ruler, the rest of the records starting from the later years of Yayāti I down to Uddyotakeśarī are written in an ornate style. About the palaeography of the two plates of the time of Bhīmaratha, it is learnt that the scribe of the first set of plates is *mahāsāndhivigrahika* Śrī Rudradatta son of Devadatta, who migrated from

Ayoddhyāpura, identified with modern Ayodhya in the Faizabad district of U.P. The script of the record might be current in Ayodhya in the latter half of the tenth century AD. Of the palaeographical peculiarities of the record mention may be made of the initial *e*, the consonants *ja, ḍa, tha, na, va*, etc., and the medial *e*. The initial *e* is still a triangle, the lower limb of *ja* is yet to turn to left, *ḍa* has an angular back, the loop of *tha* is not yet formed, *na* is archaic and *va* is rounded. The medial *e* is either a slanting stroke or a beautiful twisted curve on the top of the letters. The head-mark is always drawn as a perfect line. Thus, the characters of the plate exhibit some archaism. The second set of plates is issued by one *rāṇaka* Śrī Puñja son of Voḍā, belonging to the Māṭhara family of Vāmaṇḍāpāṭi and written by Pūrṇadatta, son of Śrī Kiraṇa, who was a merchant (*śreṣṭhin*) of Leṇapura. Vāmaṇḍāpāṭi is the same as Bamanda or Bamra in Sundargarh district of Orissa while Leṇapura is not yet identified. But the script is regular for the period and locality. Of palaeographical interest, mention may be made of simple lines in the lower left limbs of *kha, ga* and *śa*; the angular back of *tha*; the disjointed loops of *na* and *ma*; and the left limbs of *ja* and *śa*. On most occasions, the line head-marks do not join the body of the letters. On the whole, the inscription is very carelessly written.

Elsewhere it is noticed that the letter-forms of *ka, gha, ḍha, da, pa, ma, ya, ra, la, va, ṣa*, etc., are easily recognizable as the Nāgarī. Besides these letters, in the Somavaṁśī records of the tenth-eleventh centuries notable developments are made in some of the letter-forms leading them to the modern Nāgarī. The letter *ja* has obtained a right vertical, the upper curve of *ṭa* is gradually reduced to a slanting bar to join the head-mark above, the lower limb of *ḍa* fully curves to the left, *ta* optionally gets a right upright and the loop of *na* joins the right vertical medially. All these letters closely resemble to their respective modern Nāgarī forms. Optionally, when the top of *ga* is flattened and when the left limb of *tha* has obtained a loop, they also resemble to their Nāgarī forms. But in the case of the letter, the head-mark is not yet applied. Of the medials *ā, i*, and *ī* strictly conform to their Nāgarī forms; only the medial *e* is drawn in two different ways as noticed earlier. Except *u, o* and *au*, the rest of the initials do not make any significant development in the direction of the Nāgarī script, rather they move in the direction of forming the proto-regional forms.

With the extension of the Somavaṁśī control over Utkala and a portion of Kaliṅga, a large part of Orissa become united by cultural and linguistic bonds. K.C. Panigrahi has very convincingly proved how the art and architecture of Kośala with its transmitting centre at Baud travelled to Utkala in the tenth century to initiate a revival of artistic conceptions which with some modifications and improvements became the hall-mark of Orissan architecture.[31] It is not unreasonable to suppose that along with art and architecture, the writing traditions current in the official charters of the Somavaṁśīs of Kośala made a flow to the coastal part of Orissa and supplied a fresh reinforcement to the existing writing style. The Bhañjas of

31. K.C. Panigrahi, *Archaeological Remains at Bhubaneswar*, Calcutta, 1961, 157-59 & 251.

Khijjiṅgakoṭṭa and the later Gaṅgas of Kaliṅga might have derived the inspiration from the proto-Nāgarī script as used in the Somvavaṁśī records of the tenth and early eleventh century. The characters of most of the records of the Bhañjas of Khijjiṅgakoṭṭa are akin to those of the Somavaṁśīs. But unlike the latter where the head-marks are indicated variously, in the Bhañja charters they are drawn as simple lines extending all the way across the letters. Only occasionally in one or two inscriptions, the tail is totally dropped, while in the rest of the letters they are distinctly applied. In the Kesari plates of Śatrubhañja, the tail is extended further. The charter also exhibits the semi-circular type of the medial *i* and its use is seen in the Nuapatana plates of Dharmaratha of the time of Janmejaya II (*circa* AD 1065-85).

But more important is the flow of the proto-Nāgarī script as used in the charters of the Somavaṁśīs to Kaliṅga. It has been observed elsewhere in this book that the mixed alphabet of Kaliṅga was displaced by the proto-Nāgarī script in the late ninth century and in spite of the popularization of the latter, some of the scribes had an obsession to draft the documents in the former. The Mandas a plates of Vajrahasta II dated in Ś. 917 (AD 995), written in the mixed style, is a case in point. This may be due to the local need because the population of Kaliṅga was a composite one speaking different dialects and acquainted with a variety of scripts current then. But after this record, the mixed alphabet was not favoured by the scribes or the engravers and each inscription either on stone or copper-plate was written in a particular script, may be in proto-Nāgarī, proto-Telugu or in proto-Oriya. Of course, for sometime the proto-Nāgarī was used in the princely charters on copper-plates but gradually the proto-regional characters appeared in the copper-plates and stone inscriptions. Since the population of the locality was basically consisting of two different dialectical groups such as the Telugus and the Oriyas, each group preferred to get its inscriptions written in its own language and script. In the next chapter we shall discuss this point in a greater detail.

Thus the survival and continuity of the proto-Nāgarī script in Kaliṅga is largely due to the fresh reinforcement of the script during the Somavaṁśī domination over a portion of Kaliṅga in the late tenth and early eleventh century AD. The characters of the Simhipura plates of the Kadamba feudatory Dharmakheḍi of the year 520 (AD 1018) and some of the plates of Vajrahasta III are decidedly in the proto-Nāgarī script as appeared in the Somavaṁśī charters. The stage of development of the letter-forms and the medial vowels are almost the same. But in these inscriptions, the head-mark does not show a great variety; they are regularly denoted by simple lines and the right limb is a perfect vertical without any trace of the tail. In the Simhipura plates, the letter *cha* has develped a definite loop at the end, *ja* is nearer to its Nāgarī form and *na* is perfectly of the Nāgarī type. In the plates of Vajrahasta III, the letters *ka, gha, ja, ṭa, ḍha, ta, da, pa, ma, ya, ra, la, va, ṣa*, etc., and the medial *ā, i, ī, u, ū*, etc., appear to be modern Nāgarī. The letter *na* having two limbs joined in the middle is exclusively used. The letters *kha, ga*, and *śa* have opened up their loops in the left limbs. Except *u*, the other initial vowels are developing in the direction of the proto-regional characters. The Narasapatam plates of Vajrahasta III is written carelessly as is evident from the letter-forms of *u*, *e*, *ka* (optionally), *ca*, *ḍha*, *da*, *ha* and the medials *ā*, *u*. At times the letter-forms of *ca* and *ja* exhibit archaism. The letter *ḍa* appears to be Telugu-Canarese.

The Gunupur plates of *rāṇaka* Dānārṇava of Ambāvāḍī-maṇḍala, the Upalada plates of *rāṇaka* Rāmadeva of Tailapa family, the Madagam plates of Devendravarman and Bhīmakheḍi, and the Kambakaya plates of Devendravarman are some of the other inscriptions of south Orissa which are also written in the proto-Nāgarī. On the basis of palaeography, they can be assigned to the eleventh century. The first record do not call for any special remark except that the letter *pa* is rounded, and that the letters *na* and *la* have two forms each. In the second and third inscriptions, occasionally the head-marks are represented by hollow triangular wedges as in the Navamuni and the Lalatendu Kesari cave inscriptions of the time of Somavaṁśī Uddyotakeśarī. Palaeographically, the dates of the Gunupur plates and the Veerabhadrapur rock inscription are not far removed from that of the cave inscriptions of the time of Uddyotakeśarī. In the Gunupur plates another peculiarity is noticed, i.e., the letters *ca*, *dha*, *pa*, *pha*, *ma*, *ṣa*, etc., slope down to join the right upright at an acute angle. Moreover, the letters *ca*, *ṇa*, *ta*, *da*, *na*, *ra*, *va*, etc., have more than one form.

Of the other inscriptions of Orissa written in the proto-Nāgarī script mention may be made of the Parśurāmeśvara temple inscription (southern doorway), the temple inscriptions of Paikapada, the Buddhist tract in a stone inscription in Orissa Museum, the Buddhist Dharani from Soro, the three inscriptions from Baripada, the Someśvara temple inscription at Ranipur-Jharial, the two inscribed stelae found from Monastery I of Ratnagiri, etc.

The development of the proto-Nāgarī in Orissa through the acute-angled and the *siddhamātṛkā* or the *kuṭila* scripts and its survival and continuity for more than two centuries can be attributed to a number of factors. In the early medieval period, the elementary education was primarily controlled by the educational institutions such as the *agrahāra*s, the temples and the *maṭha*s attached to the temples. The educated families and the professional families of scribes and engravers are other important units of imparting education to the pupils. The teachers engaged in such institutions usually taught to their pupils different subjects in Sanskrit language and in the script which was already accepted through a technical process. In doing so very often they preferred to use certain ornamental, simplified or cursive traits without sacrificing the individuality of the letter-forms. Although outwardly there may be some difference in the style of writing but by and large they remain the same and do not exhibit any significant deviation. Thus education had effected standardization of the letter-forms used in each centre and the art of writing got transmitted from one generation to the other through this teaching-learning process. But its survival and continuity with certain changes in time and space is largely due to the reinforcements which it received from the northern part of India from time to time.

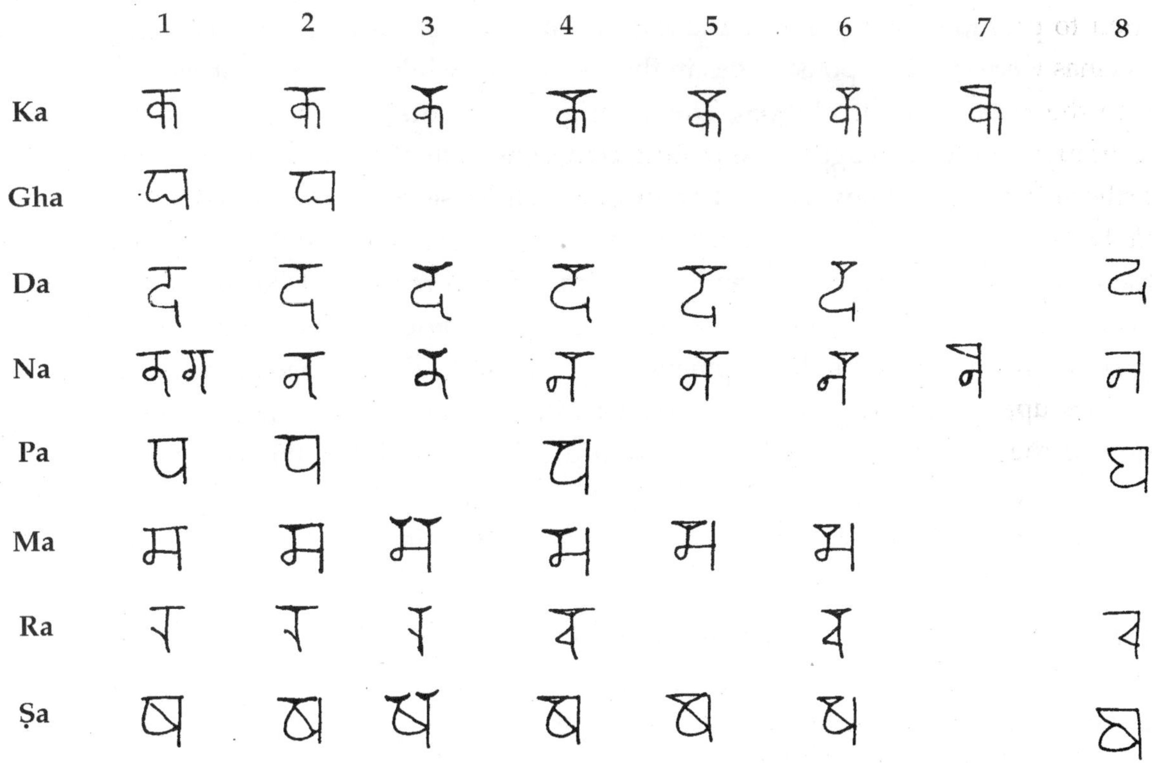

fig. **I: Head-Marks in the Proto-Nāgāri Script of Orissa**

Orissa seems to have been one of the important regions which attracted a large number of brāhmaṇas from northern India in the eighth-eleventh centuries.[32] The inscriptions of Orissa belonging to *circa* AD 750-1050 furnish the evidence of the emigration of a number of brāhmaṇa families to different kingdoms of Orissa from Ṭakkāri, Kolāñca, Hastipada, Mathura, Ahicchatra, Muktāvattu, Śrāvastī, etc. The places of migration of some of the brāhmaṇa families are not specifically mentioned but the countries to which they belonged have been referred to in the inscriptions. Such families mostly came from Madhyadeśa, Rāḍha, Varendrī, Puṇḍravardhana, etc. It is interesting to note that except one or two examples, the rest of the places are admittedly in modern U.P., Bihar and West Bengal. Moreover, judging from the names and the *gotra*s of a number of brāhmaṇa beneficiaries it can be inferred that there was an influx of "non-local" upper class people in its majority to Orissa during this period. The political changes in northern India, the royal oppressions, the need for a better economic life consequent upon famines or other natural calamities, and the desire to prove their merit in a more congenial atmosphere are some of the reasons which might have compelled them to migrate to safer regions.[33] The rulers of Orissa followed the policy of inviting these brāhmaṇas and donating them lands with an

32. Swati Datta, *Migrant Brāhmaṇas in Northern India*, Delhi, 1989, 37-52.

33. *Ibid.*, 84-115.

intention to promote their political and cultural ambitions.[34] It is learnt that only a few such brāhamaṇas were given responsibilities in the royal court while a majority of them were granted lands in the rural areas or villages. These emigrate brāhmaṇas who permanently settled in Orissa brought the knowledge of the writing traditions current then in their original homelands in northern India. The knowledge of writing which these educated "non-local" upper class people brought to Orissa was not fundamentally different from those that was prevalent in the traditional educational institutions and also in the official records of Orissa. It is probably for this reason that the northern characters survived throughout the period and facilitated for a progressive movement in the development of the script. Had there been any substantial influx of educated upper class to Orissa from southern India spanning over three hundred years, the existing northern characters could have been displaced by either the Telugu-Canarese, the Grantha or the Tamil script. In *Pl.* IX, X, XI and XII, the proto-Nāgarī script as used in the inscriptions of different ruling families of Orissa of the ninth-eleventh centuries have been reproduced.

In a majority of inscriptions of Orissa of the ninth-eleventh centuries, the head-marks are denoted by straight top strokes covering the total breadth of the letters. This type of head-formation is seen in the charters of the Śulkis, the Tuṅgas, the Nandas, the later Bhaumakaras, the Gaṅgas, the Bhañjas of Khiñjali-maṇḍala (Vañjulvaka branch), the Bhañjas of Khijjiṅgakoṭṭa and in those of the other minor ruling families. Some of the Somavaṁśī charters as well as the temple inscriptions of the period also exhibit this type of head formation. The letters having two limbs are now closed at the top while the letters *i, e, o, au, kha, ga, ṭha, na, tha, dha,* etc., are devoid of the head-mark. Towards the end of our period the letter *ta* has occasionally obtained a head-mark and resembled to its Nāgarī form. The second variety of the head-mark is represented by the flattening of the solid triangular wedges into straight top strokes (*fig.* I.2) and this is exclusively used in the records of the Bhañjas of Khiñjali-maṇḍala (Dhṛtipura branch) and in a few records of the Śulkis, the Tuṅgas, the Nalas and also of the Somavaṁśī king Janmejaya I. With the flattening of the wedges the same effect is produced as in the case of drawing the straight lines but there is faint trace of the wedge in the middle and it is also traceable in the left limb of the letters having two limbs. The other peculiarities in the application of the head-marks are restricted to the official charters of the Somavaṁśīs. In the three Chaudwar plates of Janmejaya I (RY 31), the solid triangular wedge is seen with an inward dip at the centre (*fig.* I.3). From the later part of the reign of Janmejaya I, the hollow triangular wedges with their heads pointing down are applied to the letters (*fig* I.4). This is also seen in the inscriptions of Yayāti I, Dharmaratha and in the cave inscriptions of the time of Uddyotakeśarī. Its influence was also felt in some of the inscriptions of Kaliṅga, e.g., the Gunupur plates of *rāṇaka* Dānārṇava and the

34. According to Swati Datta, "Anyway, the invitation if there was any, was made after the Brāhmaṇas had already migrated. Definitely the migration did not take place as a result of the invitation." (*ibid.*, 93).

rock inscription of Veerabhadrapura. Optionally, the top line of the inverted triangle is elongated and the side strokes are compressed. However, in all such cases, the head-mark is only applied to the left limb of the letters like *a, ā, gha, pa, pha, ma, ya, ṣa, sa,* etc. But in the Khandapara plates of Dharmaratha all such letters except *ma* have got straight lines and at times the top of *pa, pha, ya* and *ṣa* are extremely rounded. The Maranja-Mura plates of Yayāti II exhibit yet another peculiarity where the inverted hollow triangle totally shifts to the left and merges its side stroke with the right vertical of the letter (*fig.* I.7). In the Nuapatana plates of the time of Janmejaya II, the straight top stroke totally shifts to the left as in *da, na, va,* etc. This peculiarity is also noticed in the eleventh-twelfth century records of the Kalacūris,[35] the Paramāras[36] and in the Deopara stone inscription of Vijayasena[37] (*c.* AD 1096-1159).

It is believed that the proto-Nāgarī alphabet developed out of the process of simplification of the ornate *kuṭila* script of the eighth-ninth centuries. The simple line head-marks and the straightening of the right limbs are sufficient indicators of the tendency of simplification applied to the script. But when the simplified script was popularized and accepted as the standard script over a wider area, the scribes and engravers preferred to use some traits which imparted an ornamental look to the letter-forms. Like the varieties of head-marks used in the Somavaṁśī charters of the tenth-eleventh centuries, the right limb of the letters are also drawn differently and occasionally there is a strong preference for cursive engraving. The right limb is usually straightened on most occasions but at times it bends in *kuṭila* fashion as in the case of the records of the Bhañjas of Vañjulvaka branch or a tail is formed in the lower extremities as in the records of the Somavaṁśīs. The tail is very prominent in the Patna plates of Yayāti I, the Cuttack plates of Bhīmaratha and in the Kesari plate of Śatrubhañja of Khijjiṅgakoṭṭa. Besides the right limb of the letters, it is also noticed at the end of the curve of *ka, bha, ha,* etc., of the small vertical of *da,* of the triangular or circular loops of *kha, ga,* and *śa,* of the medial *ā* and *ī,* and of the interpunctuation and punctuation marks. The lower part of a majority of letters such as *u, e* (optionally), *o, au, gha, ja, ṭa, ḍa, ḍha, tha, da, dha, pa, pha, bha, ya, va, ṣa, sa, ha, kṣa,* etc., exhibit cursive engraving. At times the top of *kha, ga,* and *śa* are also rounded. Towards the end of our period, the letters *pa, pha, ya,* etc., have got an inward dip in the left limb. This trait is traceable in the eleventh century records of the Somavaṁśīs of Utkala and the Later Gaṅgas of Kaliṅga. It is also seen in some of the Tuṅga records of the late ninth century and in the Orissa State Museum plates of Narendradhavala of AD 925. However, in the Khandapara plates of Dharmaratha the rounding of the letters is more prominent and some of the letters such as *kha, ga, tha, pa, pha, ya, śa, ṣa,* etc., can be recognized as belonging to the Oriya script. Moreover, the triangular loops of *kha, ga* and *śa* are at times turned into circles and only optionally they are opened. Sometimes they are drawn as simple lines as in the case of the Talcher plate of

35. V.V. Mirashi, *CII*, IV, pt. 1, 236-309 & pls. XXXVIII, XL, XLI, XLIII, XLV, XLVI, XLVII.

36. *EI*, 1, 234ff. & pls.

37. *Ibid.*, 305ff. pls.

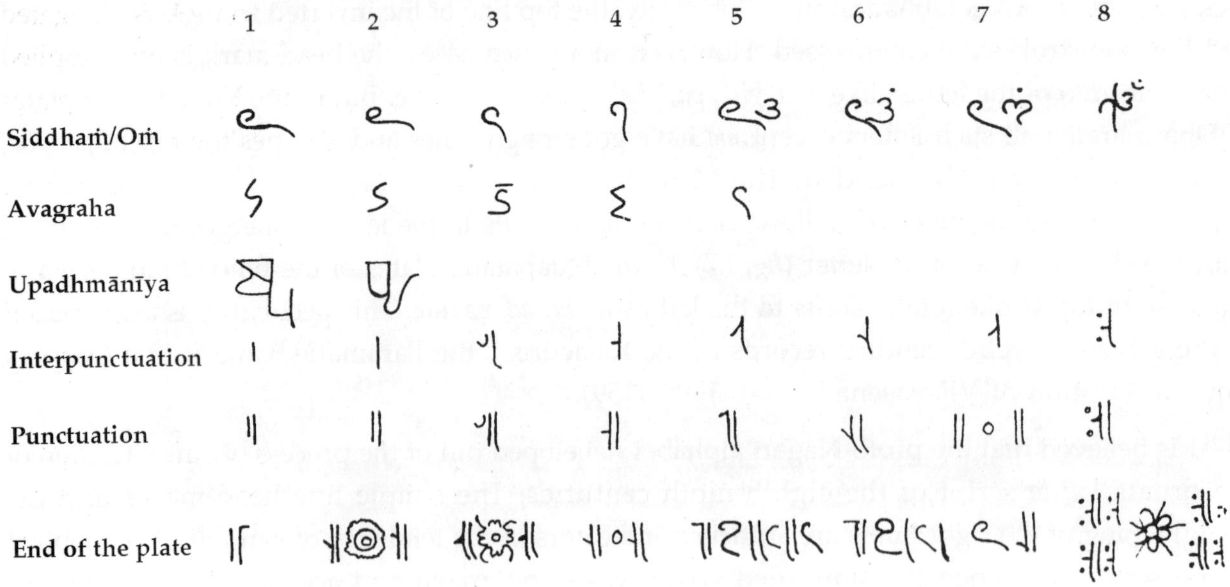

fig. II

Śubhākaradeva IV of BE 141, the plate of Rāyabhañja, the Ukhunda plate of Pṛthvībhañja and the Kudopalli plates of the time of Bhīmaratha.

The auspicious sign of *siddhaṁ* is represented by the usual form of a horizontal or a curve with its ends developing into beautiful curls. Very often a loop formation is made at the left end. In another variety, the curl is seen on the top and it runs down. But of special interest is the advent of the sign of *oṁ*. In the records of the Bhañjas of Khiñjali-maṇḍala (Dhṛtipura branch) we come across the use of the sign of *oṁ* after *siddhaṁ*. The sign for *oṁ* resembles that of the initial *o* with a dot or circle over it (*fig*. II.6). A similar type of *oṁ* is also noticed in the Dasapalla plates of Śatrubhañja of BE 198 (AD 934). In the Somavaṁśī inscriptions the same sign is noticed but its dot or circle is dropped (*fig*. II.5). The fully developed form of the sign can be traced in the Brāhmeśvara temple inscription where a crescent with a dot in its middle is seen above the initial *o* (*fig*. II.8). This form of *oṁ* is usually found in the Devanāgarī and also in modern Oriya script. The crescent with a dot in its middle is the earliest occurrence of the *candrabindu*.

The *avagraha* is correctly used in a number of inscriptions of the Somavaṁśīs, the later Bhaumakaras and in those of the Bhañjas of Khijjiṅgakoṭṭa. Its use is also noticed in the Baripada plate of Devānandadeva (l.8) and in the Badakhemundi plates of the Śvetaka Gaṅga Dānārṇava (ll.15, 21). In most cases it is drawn in the form of the English capital letter S, although at times it has got a horizontal line on the top as in *fig*. II.3 (vide the Kesari plate of Śatrubhañja, l.9) or it is drawn angularly as in *fig*. II.1 (vide the grant of Vakulamahādevī, l.34) or resembles to the sign of *siddhaṁ* as in *fig*. II.5 (vide the Adipur plate of Narendrabhañja, l.25) or doubly curved as in *fig*. II.4 (vide Badakhemundi plates of Dānārṇava).

The sign for the *upadhmānīya* in *fig.*I.1 and 2 have been reproduced respectively from l.24 of the Pandiapathar plates of Bhīmasena and l.13 of the Chidivalasa plates of Devendravarman of GY 397 (AD 895). However, the latter supplies the lower limit of the use of the *upadhmānīya* in the inscriptions of Orissa.

The sign for interpunctuation is usually a simple vertical stroke (*fig.* II.1, 2). The other variety with a small projection or tick attached either to the top, middle or bottom of the vertical is also used in a majority of inscriptions (*fig.* II.4, 5, 6, 7). Sometimes they are drawn in a slanting manner. Among the other interesting varieties mention may be made of (a) a small curve at the top left of the vertical as in *fig.* II.3 (vide the two plates of the Śvetaka Gaṅga King Indravarman III), and (b) a small tick in the middle left of the vertical with a *visarga*-like sign before it as in *fig.* II.8 (vide the Madras Museum plates of Narendradhavala).

The punctuation mark is normally indicated by drawing two parallel lines; but whenever the projection or the tick mark is applied it is only applied to the first vertical and the second one is devoid of any such mark. In one instance, e.g., l.28 of the Santiragrama plate of Daṇḍimahādevī, the *visarga*-like sign is found before two *daṇḍa*s. This reminds us of the interpunctuation mark as used in the Madras Museum plates of Narendradhavala. However, the *visarga*-like sign is quite superfluous and its use before the interpunctuation or punctuation marks is only intended for the floridity of writing. There is yet another variety of the sign for full stop, e.g., a circle or a circle with a dot at the centre placed between two punctuation marks (*fig.* II.7).

The end of the charters are generally indicated by the signs for interpunctuation and punctuation marks. In some of the grants of the Somavaṁśīs, the Śvetaka Gaṅgas, the Bhañjas of Khiñjali-maṇḍala and in those of the Bhañjas of Khijjiṅgakoṭṭa, it is often seen in the form of a circle or a floral design between two punctuation marks (*fig.* II.2, 3, 4). In some of the grants of Bhañjas of Vañjulvaka branch and of the Nalas, the sign of *siddhaṁ* is noticed before or after the punctuation mark (*fig.* II.5, 6, 7). The end of the Madras Museum plates of Narendradhavala is represented by a number of *daṇḍa*s with a floral design at the centre (*fig.* II.8).

The final forms of *ta*, *na* and *ma* are found used with a number of varieties. There are two regular forms in which either the letters are devoid of the head-mark or they are drawn fully with a *halanta* sign added at the bottom. Besides, the final *t* is also expressed by a double curve either facing down or facing right as in Ganjam plates (H) of Neṭṭabhañja (l.7) and the Pandiapathar plates of Bhīmasena (l.1) respectively. Occasionally it resembles the initial *o*. In the Somavaṁśī charters, the final *n* is seen in the form of a loop or circle with a curve on its stop , , . The sign for final *n* is reproduced from l.16 of the Khandapara plates of Dharmaratha. Final *m* is represented by a small circle with a *halanta* below it. The sign is also used as an optional form of the *anusvāra* in a majority of inscriptions of the period under review. The signs and for final *m* are reproduced from the Cuttack plates of Bhīmaratha (l.35) and the Aida plates of Raṇabhañja (l.18). Moreover, the latter grant supplies the use of the final forms of *ca* (l.26) and *tha* (l.3), while the final *ka* is found used in l.28 of the Narasapatam plates of Vajrahasta III Ś. 967.

Vowels

Of the initials *a, ā, i, u, e, ai, o, au* and *ṛ* are found used in the inscriptions of the period. The small vertical of the initial *a* that joins the head-mark above and the left-facing curve below is either replaced by an additional curve or suppressed totally. Its replacement by an additional curve ultimately resulted in the birth of its proto-Nāgarī or Nāgarī form as in *Pl.* IXa.4, 5, 8, 10; XIa.6, 8; XIIa.3. The total suppression of the vertical and the small tick or tail at the bottom right of the letter played an important role in the development of the proto-regional characters. The small tick in course of time changed into a triangle and subsequently it is opened at the top and joined to the left-facing curve (*Pl.* Xa.9; XIa.9, 10; XIIa.7, 8, 9). The letter-form of *ā* is indicated by a full length vertical added to the right of *a*. Of all the initials the form of *i* exhibits a great variety. It has at least three broad forms. (a) In the first variety, a triangle, a line or a curve is placed on the top of the two small circles. In *Pl.* Xa.10 (second) both the ends of the top curve join the two circles and the curve itself has an inward dip. (b) In the second variety, a curve either facing down or left is subjoined to the two circles. Sometimes it is doubly curved and resembles the initial *o* (*Pl.* IXa.7; XIa.3, 5, 6, 7). (c) In the third variety, both the top and bottom elements are retained, e.g., (*Pl.* IXa.6; Xa.3). However, it took some more time to develop the proto-Nāgarī and Nāgarī forms of this letter. The left-facing broad curve of *u* is still retained largely but optionally the small vertical is transformed into a curve and resembles to the Nāgarī *u* (*Pl.* XIIa.1, 3). The triangular type of *e* with its tip facing down is retained in a few inscriptions of the period. But in a majority of cases, the left limb is curved and joined to the right upright at the bottom. Sometimes, the right upright is slightly projected downwards. The letter-form is apparently an intermediate stage in the evolution of its Nāgarī form. The letter-form in *Pl.* XIIa.3 and 11 resembles to its modern Oriya counterpart. Another variety of this letter is represented by a cursive top and an opening in the left limb. This peculiarity is noticed only in the inscriptions of south Orissa. There is yet another form of this initial vowel which is exclusively found in the Somavaṁśī charters where the left-facing curve is separately drawn and detached from the right upright. There is only one example of the initial vowel *ai* which has an additional slanting stroke at the top of the proto-Nāgarī type of *e* referred to above. The letter-form of *o* is denoted by two left-facing curves as in *Pl.* Xa.1, 3, 8, 9. It is still current in the Nāgarī alphabet. *A* has an additional curve darting up from the middle right of the letter *o*. The rare letter *ṛ* is used once in the Baud plates of Ranabhañja of year 54 (*Pl.* XIa.3).

Consonants

With the application of the horizontal head-marks covering the entire breadth of the letters and with the straightening of the right verticals, the consonants like *ka, pa, ma, ya, la, va* and *ṣa* have already assumed the Nāgarī forms. The same features when applied to *pha, bha, sa* and *ha* further resulted in the evolution of their respective proto-Nāgarī forms. The proto-Nāgarī *pha* is the same as the Nāgarī *pa* with a small curl facing downwards or loop joined to the top right. The old form of adding the head-mark only to the left limb of the letter is seen in a number of examples. The other peculiar forms of the letter such as an inward dip at the centre of the left limb (*Pl.* IXb.7, 11; Xb. 7, 9, 10, 11; XIb.9, 10; XIIb.10) and the replacement of the flattened head-mark by a curve (*Pl.* Xb.7), clearly demonstrate the coming of the proto-regional characters in vogue. The proto-Nāgarī *bha, sa* and *ha* are undoubtedly developed out of the open-mouthed *bha, sa* and the tailed *ha* respectively. In a few records of the Nalas and Gaṅgas of Śvetaka, the proto-Nāgarī *ha* is devoid of the tail and the letter is more cursively drawn (*Pl.* XIIb.1, 3, 4, 5, 6). The letter-forms of *gha, ḍa, ḍha,* etc., are in the process of development from the proto-Nāgarī to the Nāgarī script. *Gha* gets closer to the Nāgarī form but the inward dip at the centre of its base-line is yet to be shifted to the left in order to get its modern form. The cursive appendage in the lower limb of *ḍa* is in the process of developing a full leftward curve. In some of the tenth-eleventh century inscriptions of Orissa, *ḍha* has already obtained a broad curve at its back and as small tick below the head-mark. The consonants like *ṇa* and *ta* do not call for special remark except that their elongated right arms drawn in *kuṭila* fashion are now straightened. But in a few inscriptions of the Somavaṁśīs of Utkala and the Imperial Gaṅgas of Kaliṅga of the eleventh century the Nāgarī form of *ta* is seen (*Pl.* Xa.9; XIIa 10). In *Pl.* Xa. 11, the letter-form resembles to the proto-Bengali *ta.* Although the angular back of *da* is retained on most occasions, yet a tendency has developed in this period to draw the two curves in one action and thereby forming a rounded back. Its Nāgarī form is obtained by putting a tick below the head-mark. The archaic shape of the letter *ṭha* with a simple circle is still retained. The class nasals such as *ṅa* and *ña* do not appear independently and they are always found attached to the letters of their respective classes. *Ṅa* is regularly found used as a curve opening to the right with or without a dot or a small circle to the top left. *Ña* is represented by a down-facing curve or a double curve with the initial *o* added to its right. While *ṅa* is used only as a superscript, *ña* is used both as a superscript and a subscript. The rest of the consonants exhibit some peculiar varieties.

Kha : The standard proto-Nāgarī *kha* is indicated by a looped (circular, triangular or beaked) foot-mark, a rounded top and another loop at the bottom of the right upright. But optionally the foot-mark is indicated by a small tick as in *Pl.* IXa.1; Xa. , 8, 11; XIa.9; the loop is opened as in *Pl.* XIa.2; XIIa.9, 10; and the roof is flattened as in *Pl.* IXa.8; Xa.3, 6, 7, 8, 10, 11. There has been a tendency to broaden the inner loop and at times it covers the entire right arm. Sometimes this closed inner loop is opened at the top as in *Pl.* IXa.1, 11; Xa.2, 4, 5, 7, 9; XIa.4, 6, 7, 8, 9; XIIa.1, 2, 3, 7, 8, 9, 10. In *Pl.* XIIa.8 (second), the letter-form can easily be recognized as modern Oriya *kha*.

Ga : Like *kha,* the letter *ga* has also a looped foot-mark and a rounded top attached to the right upright. Optionally the foot-mark is denoted by a small tick as in *Pl.* IXa.1; Xa.8, 11; XIa.9;

and the rounded top is flattened as in *Pl.* IXa.3; Xa.3, 8, 10; XIa.1, 3, 7. In *Pl.*XIa. 2, 4; XIIa.10; the loop is opened up.

Ca : The letter-form of *ca* has a number of varieties. The archaic form of the letter with a triangle or a loop is found in a number of inscriptions. The triangular type of *ca* with its apex pointing to the left is seen in some of the records of Bhaumakaras and their feudatories (*Pl.* IXa. 3, 6, 10). The notched type of *ca* is still survived in Kaliṅga (*Pl.* XIIa.9). In the inscriptions of the Bhañjas, the letter is more cursively drawn. The upper half of its left limb marks an inward bend while the lower half makes an outward bend and they join to the right limb (*Pl.* XIa. 2-10). In yet another example, the left limb does not touch the right arm and is drawn separately from the head-mark (*Pl.* Xa.5, 6, 7, 9). The influence of this form of the letter is noticed in the records of the Nalas and Gaṅgas of Kaliṅga, vide *Pl.* XIIa.1, 5, 7, 10.

Cha : There are two broad varieties of this letter. The elliptical *cha* is mostly found used in the inscriptions of the period. But in the southern part of Orissa, in the records of the Bhañjas of Vañjulvaka, Eastern Gaṅgas, Śvetaka Gaṅgas and Imperial Gaṅgas there is an opening in the ellipse and a loop is formed in the right (*Pl.* XIa.4; XIIa.1, 3, 8, 9). It is also seen in the Bonai plate of Udayavarāha (*Pl.* IXa.10). The formation of this loop is an important stage in the development of its Nāgarī counterpart. However, this may be termed as the open-mouthed type of *cha*.

Ja : The letter-form of *ja* has undergone significant changes during this period. The *kuṭila* variety of *ja* is used on most occasions with its right arm straightened. But an important development that is made in this stage is that the small curl below the left arm is now grown into a full left-facing curve. This has further progressed in the direction of forming a curve facing up and then again curving down. The entire lower half of the letter is cursively drawn in one action and joins the head-mark by an additional tick. This may be called as proto-Nāgarī *ja* and is aptly the precursor of the Nāgarī *ja*. Towards the end of our period the Nāgarī letter-form of *ja* has already appeared in one or two records of Orissa (*Pl.* Xa.11; XIIa.10).

Jha : The rare letter *jha* is noticed in a few records of the Somavaṁśīs. The letter is represented by the suppressed upper arm type of *ja* with an additional line drawn on its right and a tail below. In *Pl.* Xa.9, the tail is missing probably due to inadvertence of the engraver.

Ṭa : The single curve type *ṭa* with a line on the right is retained in a few inscriptions. But the double-curve type *ṭa* with a line on the right is most regularly found used in the inscriptions of the period. Subsequently the top curve is flattened and an acute angle is formed at its back. This variety is seen in some of the inscriptions of the Somavaṁśīs of the eleventh century (*Pl.* Xa.8, 10). The letter-form may be termed as proto-Nāgarī *ṭa*. Its Nāgarī form is obtained by shifting the slanting stroke, joining the head-mark and the curve below, to the middle and by suppressing the line on the right. This modern Nāgarī letter-form is noticed in the inscriptions of Imperial Gaṅgas of Kaliṅga (*Pl.* XIIa.10).

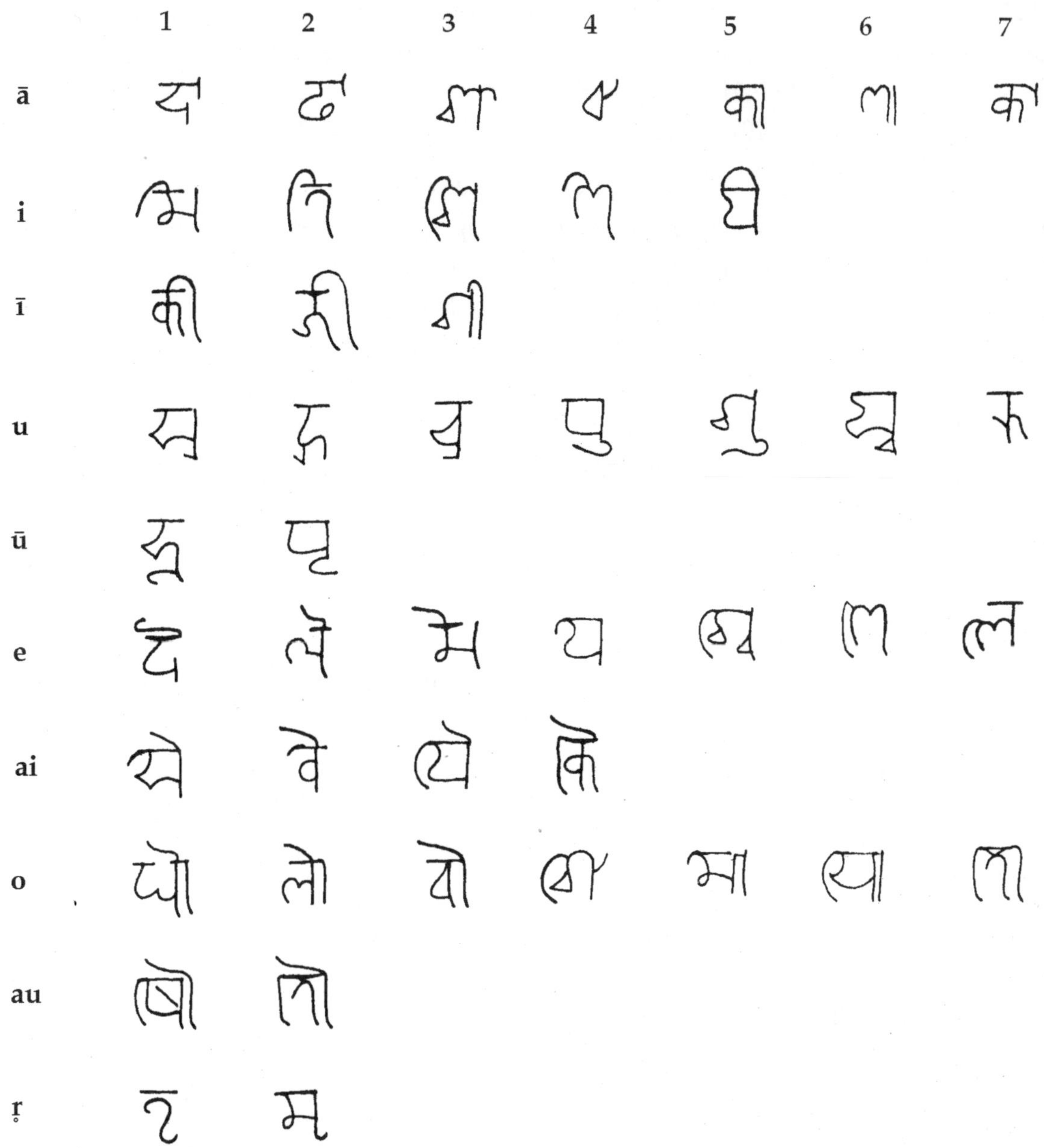

fig. **III: Medials in the Proto-Nāgārī Script of Orissa**

Tha : The archaic shapes of this consonant such as the inward loop or curl type (*Pl.* XIIb.1, 7 first) and the doubly curved back type (*Pl.* IXb.8; Xa.5, 8, 11; XIa.2, 3, 4, 7, 9) are still retained in the inscriptions of the period. The bipartite *tha* with a closed loop or with its loop opened is more frequently used. In one instance, the opened loop of the bipartite *tha* is facing to the left and the lower limb is angularly drawn (*Pl.* XIIb.7 second). In *Pl.* IXb.9, 10 and *Pl.* XIIb.3, the letter is very carelessly drawn.

Dha : The broad-backed type of *dha* is regularly appeared in the inscriptions of the period. Optionally the broad curve is angularly drawn and, therefore, the letter resembles a triangle as in *Pl.* IXb.2, 9. In the official charters of Vajrahasta III of Kaliṅga there is a small opening in the upper limb of the letter (*Pl.* XIIb.9, 10).

Na : The looped variety of *na* is more popularly used in the inscriptions of the period. In another variety the loop or dot is placed beside the right upright as in *Pl.* Xb.6, 8; XIb.1. In *Pl.* IXb.3; Xb.10, it is joined to the right upright. The double-armed variety of the letter which at first appeared in the acute-angled script of the sixth-seventh centuries is also seen in the inscriptions of Orissa of the ninth-eleventh centuries. Yet another peculiar variety of this letter is found used in the inscriptions of the Gaṅgas of Kaliṅga and the Bhañjas of Khiñjali-maṇḍala, where a mid-line is added to the double-armed variety of *na*. The letter form is often confused with *ma*. This may be termed as double armed with a mid-line type of *na*. The Nāgarī form of this letter represented by the loop joining to the right upright by an additional line is seen in *Pl.* Xb.4, 7, 9, 11; XIb.11; XIIb.8. But because of the different types of head-marks applied to this essential character of the letter, it can be appropriately called as proto-Nāgarī type of *na*.

Ra : The archaic forms of this letter such as a vertical with a tick or a slanting stroke at the bottom are still retained. The latter variety is apparently the precursor of the Nāgarī *ra*. Another important variety of this letter is denoted by a tick or a slanting stroke joined to the left of the right upright medially. In yet another variety a hollow triangle is formed on the left and this variety is the precursor of *ra* in many proto-regional scripts of eastern India. Its earliest occurrence is traced in the inscriptions of the Somavaṁśīs of the tenth century (*Pl.* Xb.3 onwards).

Śa : Like *kha* and *ga,* the foot-mark of *śa* is also denoted by a closed (circular, triangular or beaked) loop. The roof of the letter is doubly curved before it meets the right upright. The archaic form of the letter with an inward curl on the top is also used in a few inscriptions vide *Pl.* IXb.3, 7, 8; Xb.5, 6, 7; XIb. 4; XIIb.4 and the representation of the foot-mark by a small tick to the left is also found in a few examples, vide *Pl.* IXb.1; Xb.8, 11; XIb.9. Optionally, the loop is opened as in *Pl.* IXb.10; IXb.2, 4; XIIb.2, 6, 10.

Kṣa : The old form of the letter expressed by a superscript *ka* and a subscript *ṣa* is survived in a few inscriptions of south Orissa, vide *Pl.* XIIb.1, 5. But during this phase this superscript *ka* is changed into a distinct loop or a down-facing curve on the left and its outer curve joins the letter *ṣa* below; another downward curve is drawn as the right. Optionally, this downward curve merges with the mid-line of *ṣa* as in *Pl.* IXb.8; Xb.3, 11; XIb.7, 10; XIIb.6-10. In the inscriptions of the eleventh century, the right upright of the letter darts up and touches the line head-mark. The base-line of the letter is either rounded or firm.

Medials

The medial *ā* is denoted by a small downward tick or curve on the top right or a full length vertical on the right. Occasionally it is seen in the form of an upturned curve as in *dhā* (*fig*. III.4). *I* is a curve falling on the left from the centre of the head-mark of the letters. While occasionally it stops half-way (*fig*. III.1), regularly it covers the entire left of the letters (*fig*. III.2, 3). In a few inscriptions of the eleventh century, the medial *i* is seen in the form of a down-facing curve applied on the top of the letters (*fig*. III.4, 5). This is closely akin to the modern Oriya medial *i*. The medial *ī* is a curve falling on the right from the centre of the head-mark. Like *ā* it covers the entire right of the letters. The medial *u* is drawn in three different ways : (a) a small tick, (b) a small triangle and (c) a left-facing curve attached to the bottom left of the right upright. In the case of the letters without having a right upright it is drawn below the letters and in the case of *ha* it is joined to its tail (*fig*. III.2). In the case of *ra*, the sign is a downward curve attached to the right of the letter (*fig*. III.7). Of the three varieties of *u*, the left-facing curve type is more regularly used in the proto-Nāgarī script of Orissa and it is also retained in the Nāgarī script. Its length is denoted by a down-facing curve as in *bhū* (*fig*. III.1) or a right-facing curve as in *pū* (*fig*. III.2). In the proto-Nāgarī script the medial *e* is indicated by either a *śiro-mātrā* (a left going curve joined to the top of the letters) as in *de, le, me* (*fig*. III.1, 2, 3) or a *pṛṣṭha-mātrā* (a broad curve covering the left half of the letter) as in *khe, ṇe* (*fig*. III.5, 6). The old form of the sign with a small down-facing curve on the left is also survived (*fig*. III.4). In *fig*. III.7, the broad curve is applied to the lower half of the letter. While the *śiro-mātrā* is clearly recognized as a Nāgarī sign for *e*, the *pṛṣṭha-mātrā* is popularized in the proto-regional characters of eastern India. The sign of *ai* is expressed partly by a *śiro-mātrā* and partly by a *pṛṣṭha-mātrā* in the left. The medial *o* is a combination of the medial signs for *a* and *e*. The sign in *gho, lo, vo* (*fig*. III.1, 2, 3) consisting of a leftward curve on the top and a vertical on the right of the letter is prevalent in modern Nāgarī script while the sign in *yo, to* (*fig*. III.6, 7) represented by a broad curve on the left and a full length vertical on the right of the letters is the precursor of the proto-regional characters of eastern India. Besides, the antiquated forms of this medial are also survived during this period as in *go, mo* (*fig*. III.4, 5). The medial *au* is expressed by *pṛṣṭha-mātrā*s on each side of the letter and a *śiro-mātrā* as in *ṣau, tau* (*fig*. III.1, 2). The sign of *ṛ* is a curve to the bottom right of the letters. The archaic forms of the *anusvāra* and the *visarga* continued to be used during this phase as well. But at times the *anusvāra* has obtained a *halanta* like stroke as in *tāṁ* (*Pl*. XIa.5).

Conjuncts

The conjuncts are as usual and do not call for special remark. The tendency of reducing the size of the subscripts, and dropping their head formation as well as extending their right arms up to the head-marks of the superscripts which have already been noticed in the earlier scripts have been continued in the proto-Nāgarī script as well. The subscripts *ña* and *ṇa* look alike, cf. *ṇṇa* in *Pl*. Xb.3, 10 and *jña* in *Pl*. Xc.1, 2, 4, 5, 6. The letter-form of *ta* when doubled resembles the subscripts of above conjuncts. The subscript *ṭa* is on most occassions expressed by a down-facing curve and resembles the subscript *ta*, cf. *ṭṭa* and *pta* in *Pl*. IXc.1, 2,4. The subscript *tha* is represented either by its own form as in *stha* (*Pl*. IXc.3, 7, 10; Xc.3 (first); XIc.3 (second); XIIc.1,

3, 7, 9) and *ttha* (*Pl.* XIIc.7) or by an ellipse as in *stha* (*Pl.* IXc.1, 4; Xc.2, 3, 7; XIc.1; XIIc.2) and *ntha* (*Pl.* Xb.9). When it is elliptical it resembles the subscript *cha*, cf. *stha* in *Pl.* IXc.1, 4 and *ccha* in *Pl.* IXc.2, 3. The ornamental flourish of the diacritical notations for *ya* and *ra* of the *kuṭila* script is considerably simplified. The subscript *ya* is a simple upturned curve with its base-line rounded or firm. *Ra* is a simple left going stroke at the bottom. The *repha* is a simple angle.

Orthography

In addition to the orthographical peculiarities mentioned in the chapter on the *kuṭila* script there are a few more interesting points such as: (a) the *anusvāra* is often substituted for final *n*; (b) the difference between the vowels like *a* and *ā*, *i* and *ī*, and *u* and *ū* is not well marked; (c) the sibilants are promiscuously used and there are several cases of interchange of sibilants; (d) the occasional use of double nasals, e.g., *ṣaṁmpati*; and (e) the omission and commission of letters and even words in the body of the text. Moreover, the inscriptions often exhibit the influence of the local dialect. The words such as *sātami* for *saptamyāṁ*, *dui* for *dvi*, *visae* for *viṣaye*, *pāthara* for *prastara*, *vardhae* for *vṛddhaye*, *siṅgha* for *siṁha*, *kanva* for *kāṇva*, *tṛbhuvana* for *tribhuvana*, *krimi* for *kṛmi*, *māhārāja* for *mahārājā*, *tāmvra* for *tāmra*, *jasya* for *yasya*, *bhitare* for *abhyantare* and so on as appeared in the Sanskrit inscriptions of the period apparently demonstrate the strong influence of local pronunciation.

Bibliography

PLATE IX

1. Talcher plate of Śubhākara, BE 141 (5), B. Mishra, *OUBK*, 32-39 & pl.
2. Plates of Daṇḍimahādevī

   (a) Two Ganjam plates of Daṇḍimahādevī, BE 180, F. Kielhorn, *EI*, 6, 133-42 & pls.

   (b) Santiragrama plate of Daṇḍimahādevī, BE 180, D.C. Sircar, *ibid.*, 29, 79-89 & pl.

   (c) Arual plate of Daṇḍimahādevī, BE 183, From the photograph in B. Das, *The Bhaumakaras and their Times*, New Delhi, 1978, pl. 6a. and 6b.
3. A Grant of Vakulamahādevī, BE 204, P.R. Srinivasan, *EI*, 36, 307-12 & pl.
4. Plates of Dharmmamahādevī

   (a) Angul plate of Dharmmamahādevī, P. Banerji, *JASB*, L, 17 (3), 245-50 & pl.

   (b) Taltali plate of Dharmmamahādevī, G. Das & K.C. Panigrahi, *IHQ*, 21, 213-22 & pl.
5. Plates of the Śulkis

   (a) Seven Copper-plate Records of Land Grants from Dhenkanal, H.P. Shastri, *JBORS*, 2 (4), Nos. A, B, D, E, 395-405 & 409-17 & pls.

   (b) A Grant of Raṇastambha, H.P. Shastri, *ibid.*, 4 (2), 168-71 (without plate).

   (c) Talcher plate of Kulastambha, R.D. Banerji, *EI*, 12, 156-59; Plate published in N.N. Vasu, *Archaeological Survey of Mayurabhanj*, I, 157-60 & pls. 101-02.

   (d) Hindol plate of Kulastambha, D.C. Sircar & P. Acharya, *EI*, 28, 107-14 & pl.

(e) Puri plate of Kulastambha, M.M. Chakravarti, *JASB*, (1895), 64 (1), 125-27.

6. (a) Dhenkanal plate of Jayastambha, H.P. Shastri, *JBORS*, 2 (4), No. C, 405-09 & pl.

   (b) Puri plate of Kulastambha, D.C. Sircar, *EI*, 29, 164-69 (without plate).

7. Plates of the Tuṅgas

   (a) Grants of Gayāḍatuṅga, D.C. Sircar, *ibid.*, 34, 91-104 & pls.

   (b) A copper-plate grant of Gayāḍatuṅga, S. Tripathy, *JESI*, 7, 120-27 & pl.

   (c) Two grants of Vinītatuṅga, P.R. Srinivasan, *EI*, 38, 124-31 & pls.

   (d) Bonai plate of Vinītatuṅga, H.P. Shastri, *JBORS*, 6 (2), 236-40 & pl.

8. Plates of the Nandas

   (a) Two plates of Devānandadeva, D.C. Sircar, *EI*, 27, 325-34 & pls.

   (b) Baripada Museum plate of Devānandadeva, K.C. Panigrahi, *ibid.*, 26, 74-82 & pl.

   (c) Dasapalla plate of Devānandadeva, (BE) 184, D.C. Sircar, *ibid.*, 29, 183-89 & pl.

   (d) Tamra plate of Devānandadeva, S.N. Rajaguru, *OHRJ*, 15 (1-2), 115-20 & pl.

   (e) Talmul plate of Devānandadeva, K.S. Behera, *EI*, 40, 240-44 & pl.

   (f) Jayapura (also known as Talmul) plate of Dhruvānandadeva, N. Tripathy, *JBORS*, 16 (3-4), 457-72; plate published in *ibid.*, 15, 89-100.

9. Hindol Plate of Vīrapracaṇḍadeva, P.R. Srinivasan, *EI*, 38, 63-65 & pl.

10. Bonai plate of Udayavarāha, P. Acharya, *JBRS*, 31 (3), 159-71 & pl.

11. Angul plates of Śāntikaradeva, S. Tripathy, *EI*, 40, 113-18 & pl.

PLATE X

1. Plates of Janmejaya I (up to RY 23) and his feudatories.

   (a)Three Gopalpur plates of Janmejaya I, A.M. Shastri & S. Tripathy, *OHRJ*, 39, 93-146 & pl.

   (b)Vakratentali plates of Janmejaya I, RY 3, B.C. Mazumdar, *EI*, 11, 93-95 & pls.

   (c)Kalibhana plates of Janamejaya I, RY 6, D.C. Sircar & P.C. Rath, *IHQ*, 20, 238-44 & pls.

   (d)Patna plates of Janmejaya I, RY 6, J.F. Fleet, *EI*, 3, 340-44 & pls.

   (e)Patna plates of Janmejaya I, RY 6, G.M. Laskar, *JASB, NS*, I, 4-6 & 12-13 & pls.

   (f)Nagpur Museum plates of Janmejaya I, RY 8, E. Hultzsch, *EI*, 8, 138-43 & pls.

   (g)Gaintala plates of Janmejaya I, RY 17, S.N. Rajaguru & M.P. Dash, *OHRJ*, 11 (3), 192-97 & pls.

   (h)Sonepur plates of Janmejaya I, RY 17, B.C. Chhabra, *EI*, 23, 248-55 & pl.

   (i)Sambalpur University Museum plates of Janmejaya I, RY 23, J.K. Sahu, *JOH* 2 (1), 1-5 & pls.

   (j)Degaon plates of Mugdhagondaladeva of the time of Janmejaya I, S. Tripathy & B.K. Rath, *JORS*, 3, 29-34 & pls.

2. Cuttack (also known as Chaudwar) plates of Janamejaya I, RY 31, J.F. Fleet, *EI*, 3, 345-51.

3. (a) Kalibhana plates of Janmejaya I, RY 34, D.C. Sircar & P.C. Rath, *IHQ*, 20, 245-50 & pls.

   (b) Orissa State Museum plates of Yayāti I, RY 4, P.R. Srinivasan, *EI*, 38, 186-89 & pls.

   (c) Bolangir Museum plates of Yayāti I, RY 8, D.C. Sircar, *JASB, L*, 19 (2), 117-24 & pls.

   (d) Cuttack plates of Yayāti I, RY 9, J.F. Fleet, *EI*, 3, 95-98. For plates see A.M. Shastri, *ISPS*, pt. II, pls. CXXXVI-CXL.

(e) Nibina plates of Yayāti I, RY 15, B.C. Mazumdar, *ibid.*, 11, 95-98 & pls.

(f) Patna plates of Yayāti I, RY 24, G.M. Laskar, *JASB, NS*, 1, 7-8 & 16-18. For plates see A.M. Shastri, *ISPS*, pt. II, pls. CXLV-CXLVIII.

4. (a) Patna plates of Yayāti I, RY 28, G.M. Laskar, *JASB, NS*, 1, 8-12, 19-23. For plates see A.M. Shastri, *ISPS*, pt. II, pl. CXLIX-CLIII.

   (b) Cuttack plates of Bhīmaratha, RY 3, J.F. Fleet, *EI*, 3, 355-59 & pls.

   (c) Banpur plates of Indraratha, RY 6, K.S. Behera, *JESI*, 15, 37-46 & pls.

5. Mahakosala Historical Society's plates of Bhīmaratha, RY 11, L.P. Pandeya, *EI*, 22, 135-38 & pls.
6. Kudopali plates of the time of Bhīmaratha, RY 13, F. Kielhorn, *ibid.*, 4, 254-59 & pls.
7. Mahulpara (also known as Khandapara) plates of Dharmaratha, RY 11, P.R. Srinivasan, *ibid.*, 37, 225-32 & pls.
8. Maranja-Mura (also known as Jatesinga and Dungri) plates of Yayāti II. B.C. Mazumdar, *JBORS*, 2 (1), 45-59 & pls.
9. (a) Narasingpur (also known as Balijhari) plates of Uddyotakeśarī, RY 4, B. Mishra, *ibid.*, 17 (1), 1-24 & pls.

   (b) Sankhameri plates of Uddyotakeśarī, RY 4, A.M. Shastri, *ISPS*, pt. II, Supplement, 345-57 & pls. CCVII-CCXI.

10. (a) Brāhmeśvara temple inscription of the time of Uddyotakeśarī, RY 18, P. Acharya, *JRASB, L*, 18 (2), 63-74 & eye copy.

    (b) Lalatendukesari & Navamuni cave inscriptions of the time of Uddyotakeśarī, R.D. Banerji, *EI*, 13, 65-66 & pl. III.

    The follwing inscriptions have also been consulted :

    (a) Paraśurāmeśvara temple inscription, *ibid.*, 26, 126-27 & pl.

    (b) Paikapada inscriptions, R.P. Mohapatra, *Archaeology in Orissa*, I, Delhi, 1986. 253 (without plate).

    (c) A stone inscription in Orissa Museum, A. Ghosh, *EI*, 26, 171-74 & pl.

    (d) A Buddhist Dharani from Soro, S.C. De, *OHRJ*, 1 (4), 271-73 & pl.

    (e) Three inscriptions from Baripada, D.C. Sircar, *EI*, 33, 82-86 & pls.

    (f) Someśvara temple inscription at Rānīpur-Jharial, A. Cunnimgham, *ASI Reports*, 13, 128-37 & pls. XI-XVI.

    (g)Two inscribed stelae from *Ratnagiri*, D. Mitra, Ratnagiri, I, 212-15 & pls. CLXIII, CLXIV & CLXXXVII.

11. Nuapatana plates of the time of Janamejaya II, K.S. Behera, *JORS*, 1, 29-33 & pls.

PLATE XI

Bhañjas of Khiñjalimaṇḍala

1. Kumurukela plates of Śatrubhañja, B.C. Majumdar, *JBORS*, 2 (4), 429-35 & pls.
2. (a) Sonepur plates of Śatrubhañja, B.C. Majumdar, *EI*, 11, 98-104 & pls.

   (b) Tasapaikera (also known as Binka) plates of Raṇabhañja, RY 16, B.C. Majumdar, *JBORS*, 2 (2), 167-77 & pls.

   (c) Daśapalla plates of Raṇabhañja, RY 24, Benoytosh Bhattacharya, *ibid.*, 6 (2), 266-79 & pls.

(d) Baud plates of Raṇabhañja, RY 26, R.D. Banerji, *EI*, 12, 325-28 & pls.

(e) Phulbani plates of Raṇabhañja, RY 28, S.S. Iyer, *ibid.*, 42, 65-71 & pls.

(f) Patna Museum plates of Raṇabhañja, RY 41, R.D. Banerji, *EI*, 20, 100-04 & pls.

(g) Sonepur (also known as Singhara) plates of Raṇabhañja, RY 50, B.C. Mazumdar, *JBORS*, 6 (4), 481-86 & pls.

(h) Orissa Museum (also known as Aida) plates of Raṇabhañja, RY 50, P.R. Srinivasan, *EI*, 37, 257-63.

(i) Phulbani plates of Raṇabhañja, RY 50, S. Tripathy, *JESI*, 5, 115-25 & pls.

3. (a) Sambalpur University Museum plates of Raṇabhañja, RY 52, J.K. Sahu, *NAHO*, 2, 5-13 & pls.

   (b) Baud plates of Raṇabhañja, RY 54, R.D. Banerji, *EI*, 12, 322-25 & pls.

   (c) Baud plates of Raṇabhañja, RY 58, Adris Banerji, *IHQ*, 10 (3), 473-77 & pls.

4. (a) Four Bhañja copper-plate Grants, Hiralal, *ibid.*, 18, Nos. H, I, J, 282-98 & pls.

   (b) Ghumsar plates of Neṭṭabhañja, James Princep, *JASB*, 6, (1837), 667-69 & pls.

   (c) Komanda plates of Neṭṭabhañja, K.C. Panigrahi, *EI*, 24, 172-75 & pls.

   (d) Pettasara plates of Neṭṭabhañja, C.C. Das Gupta, *ibid.*, 27, 337-40 & pls.

   (e) Malingi plates of Neṭṭabhañja I, S. Tripathy & R. Mishra, *OHRJ*, 37, 216-36 & pls.

   (f) Orissa Museum plates of Śilābhañja, D.C. Sircar & P. Acharya, *EI*, 28, 272-78 & pls.

   (g) Orissa Museum plates of Vidyādharabhañja, F. Keilhorn, *ibid.*, 9, 271-77 & pls.

   (h) Orissa Museum plates of Neṭṭabhañja II, P.R. Srinivasan, *ibid.*, 37, 263-68 & pls.

5. (a) Dasapalla plates of Śatrubhañja (BE), 198, D.C. Sircar, *ibid.*, 29, 189-94 & pls.

   (b) Ganjam plates of Śatrubhañja, (BE), 198, S.N. Rajaguru, *OHRJ*, 4 (3-4), 67-76 & pls.

6. Orissa Museum plates of Neṭṭabhañja III, (BE), 213, D.C. Sircar & P. Acharya, *EI*, 28, 278-83 & pls.

Bhañjas of Khijjiṅgakoṭṭa

7 (a) Bamanghati plate of Raṇabhañja, (BE), 188, P.C. Ghosh, *JASB*, 40 (1), 161-67 & pl.

   (b) Khandadeuli plate of Raṇabhañja, H.P. Shastri, *JBORS*, 4 (2), 172-77 & pl.

8. Adipur plates of Narendrabhañja (BE) 193, R.C. Mazumdar, *EI* 25, 147-61 & pl.

9. (a) Bamanghati plate of Rāyabhañja, P.C. Ghosh, *JASB*, 40 (1), 168-69 & pl.

   (b) Panasi plate of Rāyabhañja, S. Tripathy, *JORS*, 4, 43-51 & pl.

   (c) Ukhunda plate of Pṛthvībhañja, B. Mishra, *IHQ*, 13 (3), 427-29 & pl.

10. (a) Kesari plate of Śatrubhañja, R.C. Mazumdar, *EI*, 25, 161-64 & pl.

    (b) A grant of Rāyabhañja, J. Sundaram, *ibid.*, 37, 233-36, 238-40 & pl.

PLATE XII

Nalas

1. Pandiapathar plates of Bhīmasena, (BE) 159, D.C. Sircar, *EI*, 34, 233-38 & pls.

2. (a) Orissa Museum plates of Narendradhavala (BE) 189, S.S. Iyer & S. Tripathy, *ibid.*, 41, 148-53 & pls.

   (b) Madras Museum plates of Narendradhavala, D.C. Sircar, *ibid.*, 28, 44-50 & pls.

Śvetaka Gaṅgas

3. Indian Museum plates of Indravarman, C.C. Das Gupta, *ibid.*, 26, 165-71 & pls.
4. Ganjam plates of Dānārṇava, S.N. Chakravarti, *ibid.*, 23, 263-65 & pls.

Eastern Gaṅgas

5. Chidivalasa plates of Devendravarman, GY 397, D.C. Sircar, *JAS, L*, 18 (2), 77-81 & pls.
6. (a) Nirakarpur plates of the time of Devedravarman, S.N. Rajaguru, *JBRS*, 35 (1-2), 1-10 & pls.
   (b) Doora plates of Udayakheḍi, S.S. Iyer & S. Tripathy, *EI*, 41, 61-67 & pls.
7. (a) Ponduru plates of Vajrahasta II, GY 500, *JAHRS*, 11, 7-12 & pls.
   (b) Andhavaram plates of Vajrahasta II, R. Subrahmanyam, *EI*, 31, 202-04 & pls.
8. (a) Simhipura plates of Kadamba king Dharmakheḍi, S.N. Rajaguru, *JAHRS*, 3 (2-4), 171-80 & pls.
   (b) Chicacole plates of Madhukāmārṇava, G. Ramdas, *JBORS*, 18, 272-95 & pls.
9. Narasapatam plates of Vajrahasta III, *Ś.* 967, Sten Konow, *EI*, 11, 147-53.
10. Plates of Vajrahasta III & Rājarāja
    (a) Chicacole plates of Vajrahasta, *Ś.* 971, C.N. Rao & R.S. Rao, *JAHRS*, 8 (2-3), 163-66, 171-76 & pls.
    (b) Nadagam plates of Vajrahasta, *Ś.* 979, G.V. Ramamurti, *EI*, 4, 183-93 & pls.
    (c) Nandabalaga plates of Vajrahasta, *Ś.* 981, C. Somasundar Rao, *EA*, 4, 25-32 & pls.
    (d) Ragolu plates of Vajrahasta, *Ś.* 981, N.M. Rao, *TGR*, 8-14 & pls.
    (e) Chikkalavalsa plates of Vajrahasta, Ś. 982, D.C. Sircar, *EI*, 33, 141-46 & pls.
    (f) Arasavalli plates of Vajrahasta, Ś. 982, G.S. Gai, *ibid.*, 32, 310-16 & pls.
    (g) Danta plates of Vajrahasta, *Ś.* 982, N. Ramesan, *CPIAPGM*, 137-52 & pls.
    (h) Peddabammadi plates of Vajrahasta, *Ś.* 982, R.C. Majumdar, *EI*, 31, 305-08 & pls.
    (i) Boddapadu plates of Vajrahasta, *Ś.* 982, G.S. Gai, *ibid.*, 34, 42-44 & pls.
    (j) Madras Museum plates of Vajrahasta, *Ś.* 984, Sten Konow, *ibid.*, 9, 94-98 & pls.
    (k) Ganjam plates of Vajrahasta, *Ś.* 991, R.C. Mazumdar, *ibid.*, 22, 67-73 & pls.
    (l) Mattura plates Rājarāja, *Ś.* 995, N. Ramesan, *CPIAPGM*, 153-59 & pls.
    (m) Chicacole plates of Rājarāja, *Ś.* 998, C.N. Rao & R.S. Rao, *JAHRS*, 8 (2-3), 166-68, 176-80 & pls.
    (n) Galavalli plates of Rājarāja, *Ś.* 998, D.C. Sircar, *EI*, 31, 191-96 & pls.
    (o) Yuddhapura plates of Rājarāja, *Ś.* 998, M. Krishna Kumari, *JESI*, 13, 52-58 & pls.
    (p) Devukavadakuru plates of Rājarāja, *Ś.* 998, N.M. Rao, *EA*, 5, 77-82 & pls.
11. Gunupur plates of *rāṇaka* Dānārṇava, S. Tripathy, *OHRJ*, 16 (4) -22 (1), (single issue), 30-35 & pls.
    The following inscriptions have also been consulted:
    (a) Upalada plates of *rāṇaka* Rāmadeva of Tailapa family, B. Ch. Chhabra, *EI*, 23, 141-43 & pls.
    (b) Madagam plates of Devendravarman and Bhīmakheḍi, R.C. Mazumdar, *ibid.*, 31, 45-52 & pls.
    (c) Kambakaya plates of Devendravarman, T.N. Ramachandran, *JBHS*, 4 (1), 27-39 & pls.

9

Mixed Kaliṅga Script

WHILE dealing with the median Kaliṅga script in chapter 4 of this book we have made it fairly clear that the reign of Devendravarman I formed a land-mark in the development of alphabet in Kaliṅga. The inscriptions of the Eastern Gaṅgas and their feudatories (mainly the Kadambas) from the end of the seventh to the end of the tenth century as well as those of the Śvetaka Gaṅgas of the eighth-ninth centuries show a fundamental difference in the style of writing than those seen in the early group of inscriptions discovered in the same locality. The points of difference between the two groups are : (a) that the broad rectangular head-marks of the earlier script are substituted by short horizontal strokes; (b) that the angularity of the letter-forms are discarded in favour of extreme cursiveness; (c) that the stylistic engraving is more pronounced in the notched bases of the letters, and (d) that *ka, ta, na, ra,* etc., and the medial *u* and *ū* are replaced by altogether new forms. But the most important characteristic of the present group of inscriptions is the representation of the same letter in several different forms prevalent in the neighbouring kingdoms of Kaliṅga. From the view of diversity in the writing style of this sub-regional kingdom, it becomes difficult to affiliate the script of Kaliṅga of this period to any particular style or to any palaeographical zone.

The old palaeographers, Ojha[1] and Bühler,[2] upheld the view that the Eastern Gaṅga inscriptions of the seventh-twelfth centuries were written in Kaliṅga or later Kaliṅga script. Following them P. Banerji,[3] V.V. Mirashi[4] and D.C. Sircar,[5] who edited a number of plates of the Eastern Gaṅgas and their contemporaries in Kaliṅga, have extended similar opinion regarding their characters. Another group of scholars including Fleet,[6] R.K. Ghoshal,[7] G. Ramdas[8] and others believed that their characters belonged to the southern class of alphabets.

---

1. Ojha, *BPL*, 44.
2. Bühler, *IP*, 107-09.
3. *EI*, 31, 317.
4. *Ibid.*, 30, 23-24.
5. *Ibid.*, 32, 201; 33, 187.
6. *IA*. 18, 143.
7. *EI*, 26, 174.
8. *Ibid.*, 13, 212.

The opinion of the scholars that the characters of the Gaṅga inscriptions of Kaliṅga belonged to the southern class of alphabets is misleading and erroneous. In the seventh-tenth centuries no homogeneous script was prevalent in south India. In the seventh century a significant transformation took place in the epigraphic alphabet of southern and western Deccan. The new script is widely admitted as the precursor of the Telugu and Canarese script, and hence the term Telugu-Canarese.[9] In the beginning the script was noticed in the inscriptions of the Western Cāḷukyas but later on it was borrowed by the Rāṣṭrakūṭas and the Eastern Cāḷukyas. The simple line head-marks, the formation of notches at the base of the broad loops of the letters and the extreme cursive engraving are some of the characteristics peculiar to the Telugu-Canarese script. The general cursiveness of the letters and the notch formations are exclusively attributable to the definite stylistic engraving. Besides, the letters *a, ka, kha, cha, ja, ṇa, ta, na, ba, ma, ya, la, sa,* etc., have developed some new features which can be easily recognized as Telugu-Canarese. Most of the new features of these letters have appeared in the inscriptions between *circa* AD 650 and 950. The period has been characterized by Bühler as the middle stage in the development of the Telugu-Canarese.[10] The curl to the left of *a* soars up to the head-mark in a beautiful curve. The cross-bar and the compressed hook-shaped lower end of the vertical of *ka* together form a rectangle or oblong with a pronounced serif above. In the lower end of the hooked *kha* a loop is formed with its terminal inclined to the right and then shoots up. *Cha* consists of two loops, the left one being a little raised than the right one and touches the line head-mark above. The letter *ja* has maintained its earlier form for a longer time but later on a new feature has developed with its top curve curling to left, middle and moving upwards and its lower one making a total curve. The perpendicular line is thus totally absent. From the curl to the lower arm the letter is drawn in one action and then the upturned curve is added. The letter *ṇa* has developed a loop to the top left. The letter *ta* is a broad curve to right with its opening in the left. A tail is added to *da* and often it turns up. The loop to the left of *na* is replaced by a similar curve attached to the right stem. *Ba* is opened at the top in the inscriptions of the Eastern Cāḷukyas from the ninth century. The upper part of *ma* is drawn to the right and placed nearly on the same level as the lower one. *Ya* has a loop at its left limb. The vertical of *ra* is doubled and closed at the top by a horizontal head-mark. The hook of *la* faces either to the left or down. Its outer curve extends downwards and makes almost a circle. *Sa* is devoid of the middle stem and the two curves are drawn in one action.

The period was also synchronized with the appearance of a special style, known as the Grantha style in the inscriptions of the Pallavas, the Coḷas and the Pāṇḍyas for writing Sanskrit. The Grantha alphabet of the seventh-eighth centuries is popularly known as Pallava Grantha for the Pallavas were exclusively using the script in their Sanskrit inscriptions. The monumental

---

9. A.C. Burnell, *Elements of South Indian Palaeography*, 15ff, A.H. Dani has termed the script as proto-Kannaḍī, (*IP*, 111).

10. Bühler, *op. cit.*, 104-09.

Grantha characters of the seventh-eighth centuries have been preserved in the lithic records at Kanchi, Mamallapuram, Trichinapalli, etc., and they display great draftsmanship in the execution of their individual forms. The precursor of this special style is not exactly known. From the letter-forms it appears that the Grantha script itself is a curious mixture of various elements derived from the north and the Deccan. However, Bühler has suggested three stages — the archaic, the middle and the transitional — in which the Grantha alphabet was evolved.[11] According to him, the characters of the archaic Grantha in general agree with those of the archaic Telugu-Canarese, but show a few peculiarities in the letter-forms of *tha, śa* and *ṣa* which remain constant in the later stages. The dot in the middle of *tha* is missing and a loop or curve is noticed in the right stern. The cross-bars of *śa* and *ṣa* have been reduced to mere lines or curves joined to the right limbs. The archaic Grantha characters are found up to the middle of the seventh century. From the middle of the seventh to the close of the eighth century, the Grantha style entered into its second stage. Most of the lithic records from Kanchi,[12] Mamallapuram[13] and Trichinapalli[14] have been assigned to this period. Besides, the Kuram plates of Parameśvara I[15] and the Kasakudi plates of the time of Nandīvarman[16] have also shown more advanced type of letter-forms. Although simple line head-marks are generally noticed in these inscriptions, occasionally they are indicated by forks as in the Kailāśanāth temple inscription of Kanchipuram of king Rājasiṁha and also in the Kasakudi plates of the time of Nandīvarman. Among the other peculiarities mention may be made of the doubling of the verticals of *a, ā, ka, ra* and also the medials *u, ū*. The opening of the top of the double vertical type of *a, ā, ka* and *ra* is another trait of this style. The roof of the initial *i* makes a double bend and then either turns down vertically to join the right dot below or obliquely to join the left dot. The letters *ga* and *śa* have developed an upturned curve at the left and they are much more rounded; *tha* and *dha* are opened at the top; *ja* and *ba* have shown the same double bend at the top and obliquely turning to the left as in the initial *i*, while a loop is formed at the bottom of *ja*, the base-line and the right upright of *ba* remained constant. The dental *ta* is looped and the dental *na* is devoid of the loop and now it has a curve to the bottom right. The northern forms are seen especially in the letters *bha* and *sa*. The frequent separation of the medial *ā, e, ai, o* and *au* from the consonants is another notable feature of the script. From the close of the eighth century, the Grantha style entered into its transitional phase and in this phase certain new developments are made in some letter-forms. Notable among them are *i, e, kha, gha, ca, ḍa, ṇa, tha, dha, pa, ma, ya, va, ṣa, sa, ha*, etc. An outer curve to the top left of the letters is a common characteristic found in a number

11. Bühler, *op. cit.*, 109-12.
12. Hultzsch, *SII*, 2(3), pl. IX.
13. *EI*, 10, 6-12 & pls.
14. Hultzsch, *op. cit.*, pl. X.
15. *Ibid.*, pls. XI-XII.
16. *Ibid.*, pls. XIII-XIV.

of letters such as *kha, gha, ca, ḍa, pa, pha, ṣa, sa, ha,* etc. The last remaining dot of the initial *i* is suppressed. The initial *e* is more cursively drawn and often it has obtained a loop at the top. The letter *ṇa* has also developed one or two loops on the left side. The letters *tha* and *dha* are completely opened at the top and their base-lines are doubly curved. *Ma* is closed at the top. The letter *va* is also opened and it has obtained a curve to the left hence it closely resembles to the letter-form of *pa*. The Udayandiram plates of Pallava Nandīvarman[17] and Gaṅga Pṛthvīpati II[18] are representative specimens of the transitional Grantha alphabet used in south India.

In addition to the Telugu-Canarese and Grantha characters, the Tamil and Vattelutu scripts had also developed respectively in the Tanjore-Madura region and southern Malabar in the seventh-eighth century. Since they are least important for our study, we refrain from discussing their characteristics in detail. The period is also synchronized with the advent of the proto-Nāgarī script in south India. The Rāṣṭrakūṭas and the Śilāhāras were chiefly responsible for the innovation and introduction of this script in western Deccan and Konkan. The script is the precursor of south Indian Nāgarī or Nandī-Nāgarī and it differs from the northern variety mainly "by the want of the small tails slanting to the right from the ends of the verticals, and in general by stiffer forms."[19] In the preceding chapter we have discussed at length the advent of proto-Nāgarī script in the inscriptions of the Rāṣṭrakūṭas and Śilāhāras and it is, therefore, needless to repeat them here.

Thus, by the seventh-eighth centuries, the entire south India was divided into a number of well-defined palaeographical segments and in each segment the proto-regional characters have been taking shape. It is further true that this process of palaeographical segmentation was running parallel to linguistic segmentation in south India.

In the backdrop of this when we consider the palaeographical peculiarities of the inscriptions of Kaliṅga of the seventh-tenth century, it becomes difficult for us to accept that the characters of the inscriptions are of "southern class of alphabets." The Tamil and Vaṭṭeḷutu scripts prevalent in far south did not cast any impact on the style of this locality. Besides, it can hardly be believed that the scribes of Kaliṅga came under the spell of the proto-Nāgarī script as used in the inscriptions of the Rāṣṭrakūṭas and their contemporaries in western Deccan and Konkan, while the script was also prevalent in the territories to the north of Kaliṅga.

The script used in Kaliṅga from the close of the seventh to the close of the tenth century is a curious mixture of all the traits prevalent in the neighbouring palaeographical zones of Kaliṅga. It has been suggested elsewhere that geography is a determining factor in the development of script of a given locality/region. The kingdoms of Kaliṅga lay between the broad palaeographical zones in which the northern scripts such as *siddhamātṛkā/kuṭila* or its offshoot the proto-Nāgarī

17. *IA*, 8, 168-69 & pls.
18. Hultzsch, *op. cit.*, pl. XVI.
19. Bühler, *op. cit.*, 84.

and the Telugu-Canarese scripts were used. It was also not far form the territory where the Grantha alphabet was in vogue. Hence in the script of Kaliṅga the characteristics peculiar to proto-Nāgarī, Telugu-Canarese and Grantha characters are inextricably mixed together. To add to this geo-physical factor, there is also a socio-linguistic factor which largely contributed to this mixed style of engraving. The population of the locality was probably a mixed one and therefore they were acquainted with languages and scripts prevalent on both sides of the their locality. In this respect, this palaeographical segment can rightly be considered as an overlapping zone. Throughout its history, the people of this zone tried to master the languages and scripts current in both the broad linguistic-palaeographical zones on its side. It has already been noticed that in the median Kaliṅga script, the scribes had a tremendous inclination towards the scripts of the Deccan and more precisely to the lower Godavari Valley. And similarly during this phase they looked for the inspiration from the Telugu-Canarese source which was brought to the lower Godavari valley by the Eastern Cāḷukyas of Veṅgī. The introduction of the Telugu-Canarese script to the north of the lower Godavari valley by the Eastern Cāḷukyas from the closing decades of the seventh century can also be attributed to the Gaṅga-Cāḷukya conflict and establishment of the Madhyama-Kaliṅga branch by the Cāḷukyas with their capital at Elamanchili identified with Yellamanchili in the Visakhapatanam district of Andhra Pradesh. Elamanchili remained as a bone of contention between the ruling families as is evident from the inscriptions that the Eastern Gaṅgas were successful in expelling the Cāḷukyas from Elamanchili and retrieving the lost territory sometime in the late eighth and early ninth century AD. However, of all the scripts concocted by the scribes of Kaliṅga, the Telugu-Canarese has a greater share followed by the proto-Nāgarī and the Grantha. This situation continued at least up to the middle of the ninth century and subsequently the use of the proto-Nāgarī script is more pronounced compared to other scripts. The proto-Nāgarī script as used in the inscriptions of Kaliṅga was not an import from the Rāṣṭrakūṭas but a simplified version of the *kuṭila* script as used in the records of the Bhaumakaras of Toṣalī. The script had not taken its birth by the close of the seventh century. But the Śvetaka Gaṅgas who were probably the feudatories of the Bhaumakaras for sometime simplified the *kuṭila* script in their charters of the late eighth and early ninth century AD and as a result some of the letter-forms roughly resembled to the proto-Nāgarī. In the chapter of the proto-Nāgarī script this point has been elaborately dealt with. But from the middle of the ninth century the use of the proto-Nāgarī is much more pronounced in the inscription of the Gaṅgas of Kaliṅga and their feudatories as well as the Gaṅgas of Śvetaka. The transmission of the Grantha characters to Kaliṅga and Śvetaka is difficult to explain. But it might have travelled to this part of Orissa along with the pilgrims, saints, religious teachers, traders and merchants. In addition to all these scripts, the existing local style of Kaliṅga survived for sometime in the inscriptions of the Eastern and Śvetaka Gaṅgas. Thus, the scribes of Kaliṅga had developed an independent school where the royal charters were drafted in all manners of mixed forms and the script may aptly be designated as the Mixed Kaliṅga Script. The opinion of Kielhorn that the mixed style of writing is due to the variety of the royal scribes, who wished to show their acquaintance with a number of contemporary alphabets may not appear to be sound. The geo-physical and political forces and the socio-linguistic composition of this small locality drove the professional scribes to master all the alphabets. Thus, it was not due to the vanity of the scribes but due to the local need the scribes had to acquaint themselves with all the contemporary alphabets.

In *Pl.* XIII we have reproduced the characters of almost all the published documents of the Eastern Gaṅgas of Kaliṅga while in *Pl.* XIV all the records belonging to the Kadambas and the Śvetaka Gaṅgas exhibiting the mixed style of writing have been taken into account.

We have traced out at least six important varieties of head-marks used in the mixed Kaliṅga script. The short horizontal line head-mark (*fig.* I.1) is most regularly found used in the inscriptions under study. In the chapter on the median Kaliṅga script we have already pointed out that the broad rectangular head-marks as seen in the grants of Indaravarman III were considerably simplified in the charters of his successor Devendravarman I. This process of simplification possibly resulted in drawing line head-marks in the Siddhantam plates. But there is also reason to believe that this short line head-mark was possibly derived from the Telugu-Canarese script as used in the grants of the Eastern Cāḷukyas of Veṅgī. Because the Siddhantam grant of the king is not only the earliest to use this type of head-formation but also it is the earliest to borrow certain letter-forms peculiar to the Telugu-Canarese. However, this short line head-mark is widely used in a majority of records of Kaliṅga starting from the close of the seventh century. It is added to the left limbs of *a, pa, pha, ṣa* and to the middle limb of *ya*. It is also seen optionally on the rounded top of *ga* and *ta* as in *ga* and *ta* in *Pl.* IIa.1. The letters *i, e, o, kha, ga, ṅa, ja, ña, ṭa, ṇa, tha, dha, ma, ta* and *śa* are devoid of the head-marks. In the northern form of the initial *u* and the consonants *ma, la,* etc., this type of head-mark is used.

The Andhvaram plates of Anantavarman of GY 216 display a peculiar type of forked head-mark. It is also noticed in the Chicacole plates of Satyavarman of GY 351 and the Gallavalli plates of Manujendravarman of GY 393. It normally replaces the short line head-mark in a majority of letters already noted down above. But occasionally it is seen on the rounded top of *ga, ta, dha, śa* and *sa,* vide *Pl.* I.7 and 10. This forked head-mark is a peculiarity of the Pallava-Grantha and it is noticed in the seventh century inscriptions at Kanchi, Mamallapuram and Trichinapalli. Andhavaram plates of Anantavarman prove beyond doubt that the Pallava-Grantha characteristics were imported to Kaliṅga as early as the beginning of the eighth century. The pilgrims from Kaliṅga to these religious centres of south India were possibly instrumental in carrying the knowledge to their homeland. This forked head-mark was not only used in some of the epigraphs of Kaliṅga but also it made its way to Veṅgī and other areas where the Telugu-Canarese script was prevalent. From the later records of the Eastern Cāḷukyas, it is evident that the forks show a tendency to become an arc. This arc-shaped head-mark is also met with in Kaliṅgan inscriptions, vide *Pl.* II. 1, 9, 10. The addition of an arc to the top of the circular type of *ṭha* in *ṭhya* (*Pl.*IIc.9) is interesting.

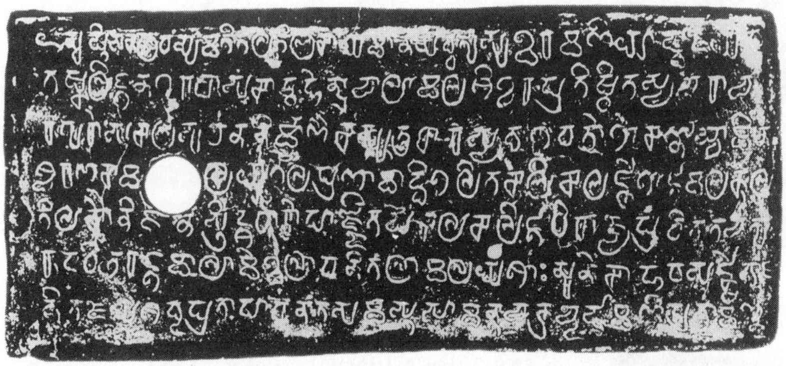

Photo 9.1 (a): Siddhantam plates of Devendravarman, GY 195 (i)

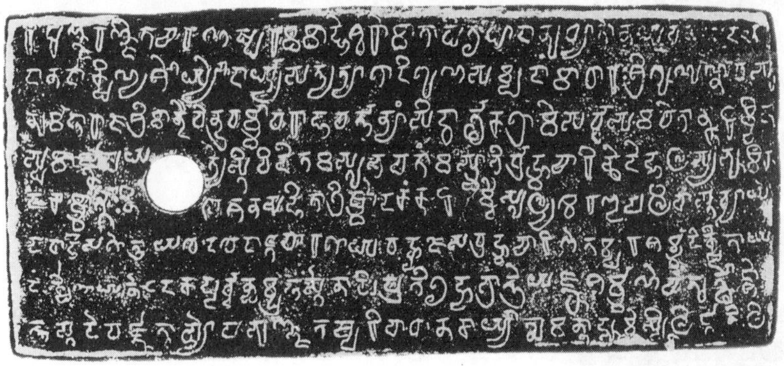

Photo 9.1 (b): Siddhantam plates of Devendravarman, GY 195 (ii a)

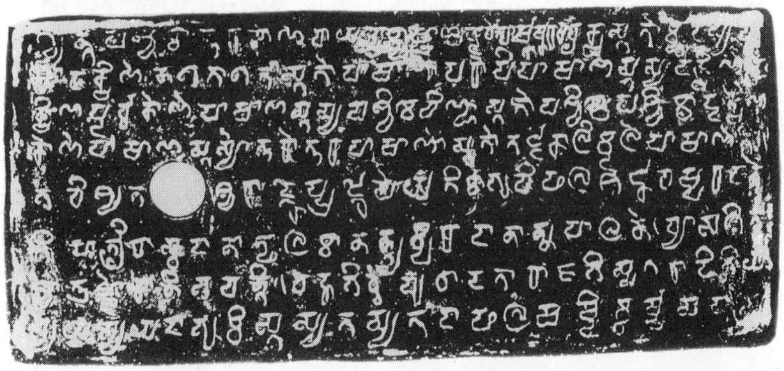

Photo 9.1 (c): Siddhantam plates of Devendravarman, GY 195 (ii b)

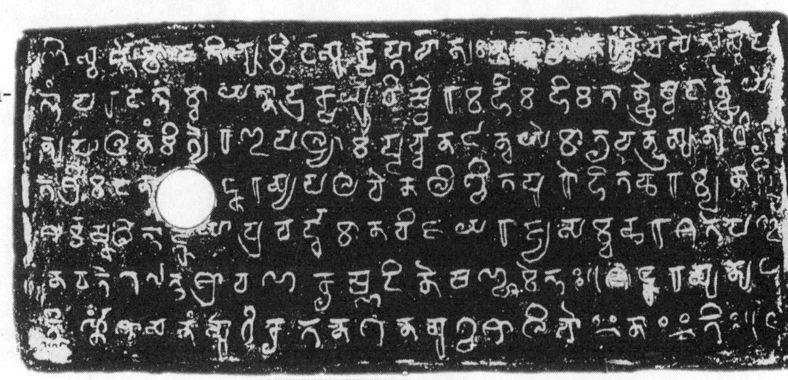

Photo 9.1 (d): Siddhantam plates of Devendravarman, GY 195 (iii)

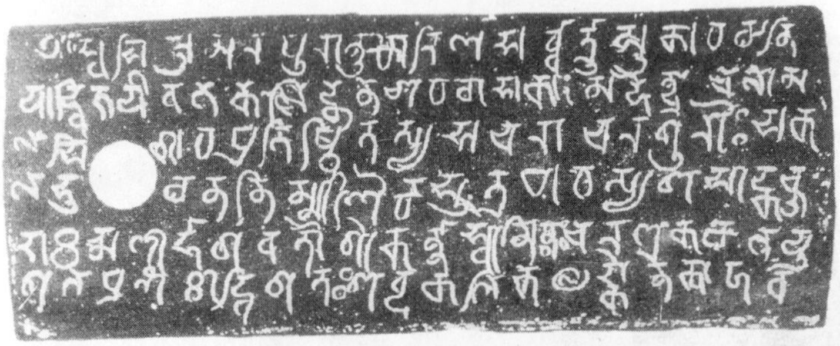

Photo 9.2 (a): Chicacole plates of Satyavarman, GY 351 (i)

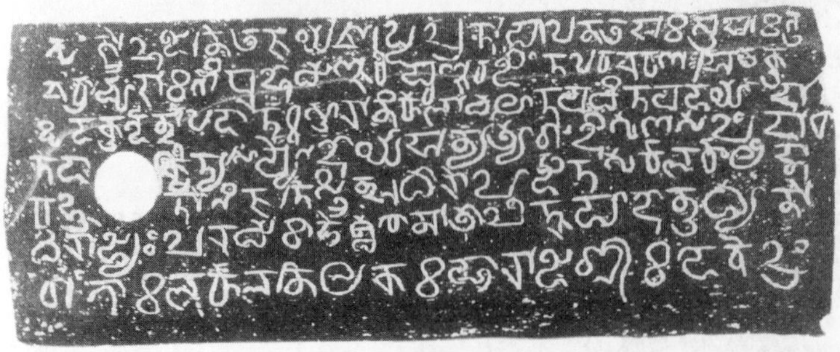

Photo 9.2 (b): Chicacole plates of Satyavarman, GY 351 (ii a)

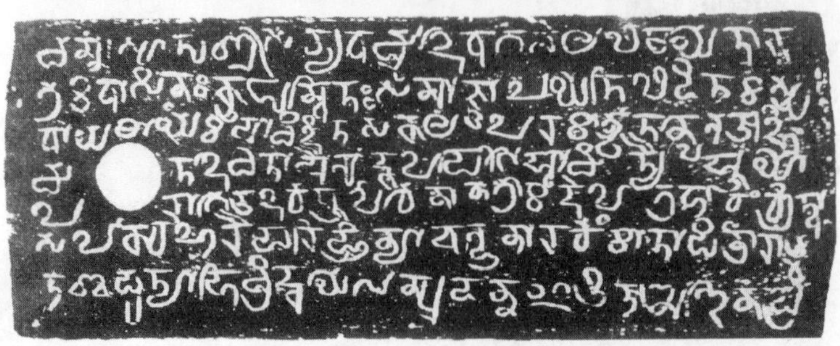

Photo 9.2 (c): Chicacole plates of Satyavarman, GY 351 (ii b)

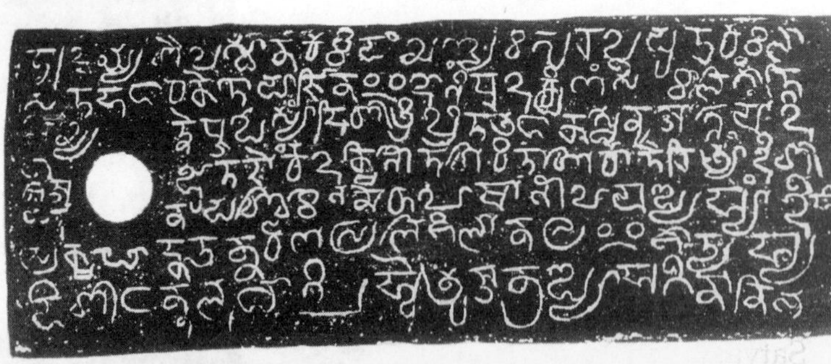

Photo 9.2 (d): Chicacole plates of Satyavarman, GY 351 (iii a)

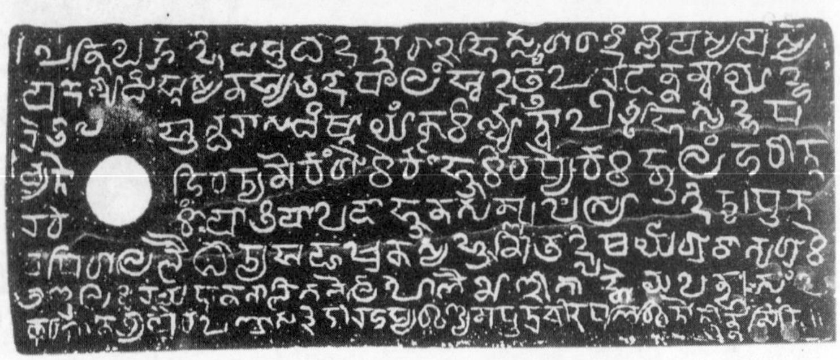

Photo 9.2 (e): Chicacole plates of Satyavarman, GY 351 (iii b)

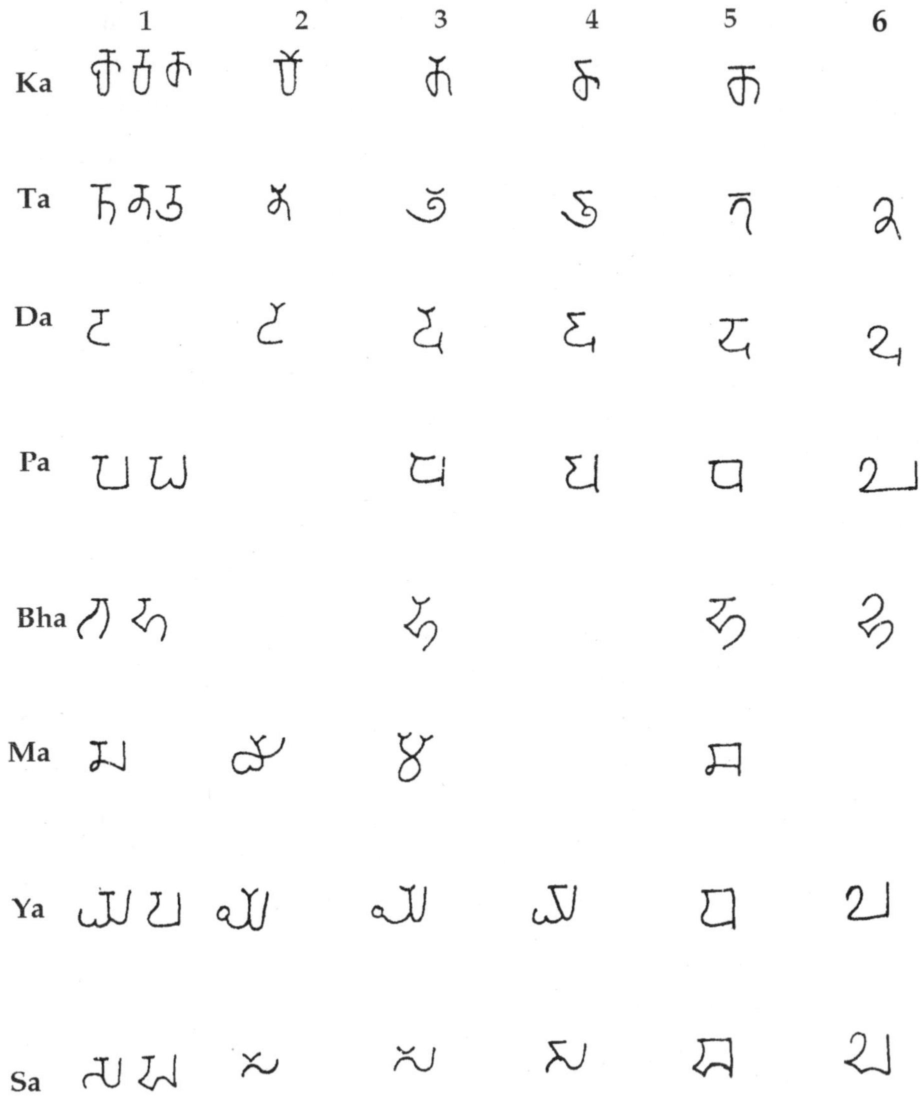

fig. **I: Head-Marks in the Mixed Kaliṅga Script**

The addition of a curve to the top left (*fig*. I.6) is another type of head formation which is also derived from the Grantha source. This peculiarity is confined only to the Chicacole plates of Satyavarman of GY 351 and the Gallavalli plates of Manujendravarman of GY 393 (*Pl.* XIII.7 and 10 respectively). It is also seen occasionally in the undated charter of Anantavarman (*Pl.* XIII.11). Besides the letters shown in *fig*. I.6, the other letters such as *ca, va* and *ha* have similar curves on their tops.

From the beginning of the ninth century the head-mark is represented by a horizontal line covering the entire breadth of the letters. This feature appeared for the first line in the Vishmagiri plates of the Śvetaka Gaṅga King Indravarman II (*circa* AD 800-20). It could be due to simplification of the wedge used in *kuṭila* style of engraving. A few decades after its introduction in the records of the Śvetaka Gaṅgas, the Eastern Gaṅgas got inspired by this new feature and the Chicacole plates of Satyavarman of GY 351 is supposed to be the earliest to use this type of head-mark. But the short horizontal line head-mark still survived a bit longer and from the close of the ninth century the head-mark is regularly indicated by a horizontal line covering the entire breadth of the letters. This is an important feature of the proto-Nāgarī or Nāgarī script and as such the Nāgarī letter-forms of *gha, pa, pha, ma, ya, ṣa, sa*, etc., having two limbs, a left and a right one, are now totally covered by the horizontal line at the top.

The head formation in *fig*. I.4 is the same horizontal line but the vertical below it is shifted to its left end and connects lower part of the letter in a slanting manner. It has thus developed an acute angle at the top left. This type of head-mark is only optionally noticed in the Chicacole plates of Satyavarman of GY 351, the Gallavalli plates of Manujendravarman of GY 393 and the Parlakhemundi plates of Vajrahasta. The origin of this type of head-mark can be traced back to the Chicacole plates of Devendravarman of GY 251, where we find the vertical bar remained intact while the short horizontal line is shifted to the right. This resulted in a right angle at the top. In this particular document, the Telugu-Canarese letter-forms of *ta* and *ga* have only displayed this tendency. We believe that the formation of an acute angle at the top by slanting the vertical bar is a development from the shifting of the line head-mark to the right. This feature is a local development and is very important for the development of the proto-regional characters in the subsequent centuries.

A marked change is noticed in the cursive engraving of the letters. Compared to the median Kaliṅga script the letter-forms in the mixed Kaliṅga script are abnormally rounded and often they bulge out. Excepting the northern variety of letters which are to some extent angularized, the angles are not seen at all. The letters *ga* and *śa* are represented by flat tops only occasionally. But on most occasions they are rounded. The notching of the base-line in the broad loops of *kha, ca, ma* (optionally), *va, ṣa, kṣa*, etc., is an important trait of this period. These broad-looped letters with notched base-lines were also seen in the median Kaliṅga script and they continued to be used in the mixed Kaliṅga script for sometime. The vertical of *ṅa, ja* and also the left limb of *ba* are often notched. We have already referred to above that the notch formation is an important feature of the Telugu-Canarese. But by no stretch of imagination it should be conjectured that the scribes of Kaliṅga borrowed this from the Telugu-Canarese. Rather the tendency started in Kaliṅga much before the Eastern Cāḷukyas introduced it in their charters. What is of the Telugu-Canarese import is the formation of an inward dip at the centre of the lower part of the letters such as *kha, ca, pa, pha, ma, va, ṣa, sa, ha, kṣa*, etc. However the general cursive engraving, the notch formation and the application of an inward dip can chiefly be attributed to stylistic engraving.

Elsewhere in this chapter we have remarked that the existing local style of Kaliṅga survived for sometime in the epigraphs of the Eastern Gaṅgas and their contemporaries in Kaliṅga. In this connection attention may be drawn to a few letters prevalent in the mixed Kaliṅga script. The initial *a* and *ā* with an appendage at the bottom left of their verticals, the roof type of the initial *i*, the broad-backed type of the initial *u* and the consonants *ṭa, ḍa, da*, etc., the broad looped *kha, ca, ma, va*, etc., the letters *ga* and *śa* with an inward curl in their left limbs, the elliptical *cha*, the three-armed *ja* with its upper and lower arms notched, the double-curved *ṇa*, the looped *tha*, the letters *pa, pha* and *ṣa* with notched base-lines, the angular and broad types of *bha*, the hooked *la* without its outer curve, the letter *sa* with a hook facing down to left and an upturned curve to right, etc., are some of the letter-forms already discussed in the median Kaliṅga script of the fourth-seventh centuries have also appeared in the mixed Kaliṅga script. Moreover, most of the medials used in this mixed style of writing are not unknown to the Kaliṅga scribes. Some of these letter-forms survived up to the beginning or middle of the ninth century. An investigation into the question of late survival of the letter-forms of the existing local style of Kaliṅga makes it apparent that they resemble to some extent to those of their respective Telugu-Canarese or northern counterparts.

The Telugu-Canarese script is by far the most important source which substantially influenced the mixed Kaliṅga script. Almost every inscription of Kaliṅga from the close of the seventh to the close of the tenth century derived some features from this source. The Siddhantam plates of Devendravarman I is the earliest to incorporate some features from this source. The doubling of the vertical of *ka, ra* and the medial *u*; the slanting stroke type of the medial *ā* with its tip bent down; the formation of an inward dip in the lower parts of *pa, ma, ha* and in the left loop of *cha*; the curving of the right upright of the angular *bha*; the hook of *la* either facing left or down and its outer curve making a complete circle (this feature is termed as the circular type of *la* and is also seen in other records of the same king and also in the Pherava grant of the Śvetaka Gaṅga king Sāmantavarman of GY 185); a second type of *la* with its hook facing down and doubly bent; and the type of *ya* with its left half doubly bent and the right half turned up in the form of a broad curve are unmistakably the inspiration derived from the Telugu-Canarese.

Once the script infiltrated into Kaliṅga it dominated the epigraphic alphabet of the region for at least three centuries. Besides the Telugu-Canarese peculiarities already noted down in connection with the Siddhantam grant, the other features which were imported to Kaliṅga from time to time may be taken into consideration. The initial *a and ā* with a broad curve to left springing from the lower end of their right vertical and covering the entire left half, the initial *i* with its roof gently bend down at the ends are of Telugu-Canarese import. Of the consonants, the letter *ka* with a rectangular or oblong loop in the left; *kha* with a loop at the bottom left and its outer curve darting up; the totally rounded *ga*; the letter *ja* with an outer curve to top left and an upturned middle arm; the addition of a small curve to the lower end of the broad back type of *ḍa* and *da*; the letter *ṇa* with a loop at the top; the cursive appendage of *ta* with its opening to the left; the letter *dha* with a circle and its base notched; the type of *na* with its hook or curve to left; the broad-looped *ma* with its loop shifting to the left and the upper strokes to the right; the type of *ya* with its left limb doubly bent and a loop at the end; the totally rounded *ra*; and the letter *sa* with two curves, the left one facing down and the right one facing up can be attributed to the Telugu-Canarese. The type of letter-form of *ṇa*, *dha*, *ya*, *ra*, etc., can be grouped under Bühler's transitional stage of development of the Telugu-Canarese.

Compared to the Telugu-Canarese, the Grantha script is not so much popularized in the mixed Kaliṅga script. Its use is restricted to a few documents. Palaeographically, the Andhavaram plates of Anantavarman I of GY 216 is an important document because this is the earliest record in which we come across the impingement from the Grantha style. The type of the initial *i* with its one arm joining the dot below; the initial *ī* resembling the double vertical type of *ra* with a dot in middle left; the initial *o* opened at the top with an outer curve to left and the base-line notched; the letter *kha* without the loop at the base; the letter *ṇa* with a curl in its left arm; the looped *ta*; the superscript *ṅa* with its roof doubly bent; etc., are some of the peculiarities which can be affiliated to the Grantha style. From the forms of letters exhibiting traces of this peculiar style, it is apparent that they belonged to Bühler's middle variety of development of the Grantha. After the Andhavaram plates, we do not come across any other record using the Grantha features for about eight decades or so. In the undated Munjeru grant of Anantavarman II, which has been assigned to the close of the eighth or the beginning of the ninth century, atleast two letters *ma* and *ya* are written in this style. The looped *ma* is closed at the top by a curve and it resembles number 8 in English. The letter *ya* is split into two parts, having two vertical strokes with a curvature on each side at the bottom. This variety of *ya* is not so common in the Grantha; it is noticed in the Omgadh plates (no. 2) of Siṁhavarman and the Chura plates of Vijaya Viṣṇugopavarman. A similar letter-form is also seen in the Soro and Erbaṅg plates of Śambhuyaśa of the Mudgala family. But we believe that the scribes of Kaliṅga borrowed this variety of *ya* from the Grantha source. However, these two letter-forms are seen in a number of subsequent charts of the Eastern Gaṅgas of Kaliṅga.

In the five sets of copper-plate grants of Devendravarman III, all of which are written by an identical hand, optionally we notice curling in of the left curve of *ṇa*, the looped *ta*, the letter *tha* with its loop shifted to the left, the letter *na* with a hook joined to the right of the verical, etc. The Munjeru plates of Anantavarman II and the five plates of Devendravarman III are not far removed in point of time and the occurrence of the Grantha characters after the lapse of about eight decades from the Andhavaram plates of Anantavarman of GY 216, makes us believe that it was the second wave of the Grantha characters that infiltrated into Kaliṅga in the close of the eighth or beginning of the ninth century AD. Considering the Grantha letter-forms used in the plates of Anantavarman II and Devendravarman III, it can be surmised that they belonged to Bühler's transitional variety of the Grantha. The Grantha letter-forms of *da*, *na*, *ta*, *ma*, *ya*, etc., survived longer in Kaliṅga.

At any rate the mixed Kaliṅga script received a fresh reinforcement from the Grantha source about the middle of the ninth century. Of the new varieties of the Grantha letters, mention may be made of *ga*, *ca*, *ja*, *ṭa*, *ṇa*, *dha*, *pa*, *ba*, *ya*, *ra*, *va*, *sa*, *ha*, etc. *Ga* has an upturned curve at the left limb. The letters *ca*, *pa*, *ya* and *va* are represented almost by a uniform sign with a curvature to the left, a firm base-line and a right upright. The letter-forms of *dha* and *ba* are also similarly drawn but their base-lines are notched. The letter *ja* has a double bend at the top; *ta* has an additional vertical at the top; *ṇa* has loops in its left; *ra* is a perfect rectangle standing heightwise; *sa* has a curve to the left and the rest of the features resemble to its northern form; and *ha* resembles to its Telugu-Canarese form with the outer curve to the right covering the entire lower part of the letter. Besides, the frequent separation of the medial *ā*, *e*, and *o* in the Mandasa plates of Anantavarman of Ś. 917 (AD 995) is another trait of the Grantha which inspired the scribe of this particular charter. The Śvetaka Gaṅga records do not furnish much evidence about the use of the Grantha characters.

It is not out of place to refer to a very archaic letter-form of *ka* optionally noticed in the Mandasa plates of Anantavarman of Ś. 917 (AD 995). The letter is represented by a simple vertical and a cross-bar. This variety of *ka* is more frequently used in the Tamil inscriptions of the ninth-tenth century. It is not unreasonable to believe that the scribe of the said plates borrowed this from the Tamil source. However, this is the only letter which can be attributed to the Tamil script.

The northern characteristics as used in the coastal regions of Orissa have also inspired the writing style of Kaliṅga from time to time. Neither the acute angles nor the *kuṭila* traits did make any substantial impact on the mixed Kaliṅga script. Although the acute angles are not seen at all, the new varieties of the letter-forms which developed in Toṣalī, Utkala and Koṅgoda in the sixth-eighth centuries have made their flow to Kaliṅga. The type of *a* with a curve facing left attached to the lower end of the left limb, the initial *i* with two dots or small circles above and a curve or line below, the initial *u* with a broad curve facing left, the triangular type of *e*, the looped *ka*, the flat-topped *kha* with its left limb developing a solid triangular head-mark, the letter *ja* with its top arm reduced to a mere line head-mark and the other two arms sloping down from the slanting stem, the angular *ḍa* and *da*, the letter *tha* with a mid-line, the letter *dha* with a broad curve joining to the right vertical, the letter *bha* with its triangular loop in the left limb opened up, the bipartite *ya*, the letter *ra* with a tick joined to the bottom left of the vertical, the hooked *la* with a firm base-line, etc., are definitely borrowed from the neighbouring kingdoms in the north. The northern varieties of *a*, *ā*, *i*, *u*, *ka*, *ja*, *dha*, *bha*, etc., already noted down survived longer in the mixed Kaliṅga script. Besides, some of the medial signs which were not known to the scribes of Kaliṅga of the earlier period now found their appearance in the mixed Kaliṅga script. The type of *ā* with a horizontal and a small curve or vertical attached to it medially on the right, the type of *i* with a curve falling to the left and covering the entire left half, the type of *ī* with a curve falling to the right and covering the entire right half, the medial *u* with a small tick at the end of a vertical joined to the lower part of the letters, another type of the medial with a curve opening to the left, the type of *ū* with an additional stroke or curve placed above the second type of the medial *u* just referred to, the medial *ṛ* with its opening to the right, etc., are of nothern import.

Like the acute angles, the *kuṭila* traits are also not so much popularized in the mixed Kaliṅga script. Optionally the outer curves of the looped *ka, na,* the right arm of *ta* and the curve of the medial *ī* covering its right half are medially bent inward in *kuṭila* style but the flattening of the wedge on the top of the letters *ka, ta, na,* etc., evidently make us believe that they belonged to the proto-Nāgarī. The proto-Nāgarī script which is a logical development of the acute-angled script made its flow to Kaliṅga sometime in the eighth century. The Svalpavelura plates of Anantavarman (*circa* AD 780-800) of the Śvetaka Gaṅga family is the earliest to use the proto-Nāgarī features. The letter *kha* with a triangular loop in its left limb, angular *da* with a downward tick, the letter *ma* with a loop in its left limb, etc., can be attributed to the proto-Nāgarī script. In the Vishmagiri plates of Indravarman (*circa* AD 800-20), the head-mark is represented by a horizontal stroke covering the entire breadth of the letters. As a result of this the letters usually opened at the top such as *pa, pha, ma, ya, sa,* etc., are totally closed. In the subsequent charters of the family the proto-Nāgarī characters became more pronounced. The letters *kha, ga,* and *śa* have developed loops in their left limbs, the letters *ca, cha, ja, ṇa, ta, tha, da, na, la, ha, kṣa,* etc., have also obtained their respective proto-Nāgarī characters. However, after the middle of the ninth century, the proto-Nāgarī script completely displaced the mixed style of engraving in the epigraphs of the Śvetaka Gaṅgas.

The proto-Nāgarī characters transmitted to the Eastern Gaṅga records through the Śvetaka Gaṅgas and by the beginning of the ninth century, we come across a number of letters written in the said characters. In the five sets of copper-plate grants of Devendravarman III, the letters *kha, ca, ja, ṇa, ta, pha, ma, la,* etc., are shown in their proto-Nāgarī forms. The letter *kha* has triangular loops on both the limbs, the triangular type of *ca* is opened up at the top and joined to the horizontal line head-mark separately, *ja* has a curve opened to the left, the right arm of *ṇa* is extended, the right arm of *ta* is bent medially, *pha* is closed at the top, *ma* has a loop in its left limb and *la* is doubly bent and attached to the right stroke. By the middle of the ninth century the mixed style of engraving of Kaliṅga received a fresh reinforcement from the proto-Nāgarī script. In this connection attention may be drawn to the Chicacole plates of Satyavarman of GY 351 (AD 849). This is the earliest inscription where *kha, ga, śa* have obtained circular loops in their left limbs, the letters *a, gha, pa, pha, ma, ya, ṣa,* etc., are optionally closed at the top by the horizontal line head-mark, the letter *ra* having a short vertical with a slanting stroke below, the medial *ā* with its short vertical extended to the bottom of the letter, the medial *i* and *ī* falling to left and right respectively, the medial *u* with a curve facing to the left are distinctly of proto-Nāgarī origin. Excepting the Chidivalasa plates of Devendravarman IV of GY 397 and the Nirakarpur plates of the time of the same king which are written in proto-Nāgarī characters, in the rest of the charters of the Eastern Gaṅgas up to the close of the tenth century these proto-Nāgarī characters are inextricably mixed up with the characters derived from other sources. Among the other proto-Nāgarī features used in these epigraphs mention may be made of the letter *tha* with a curve opened to the top left and joined to the right upright by another curve,

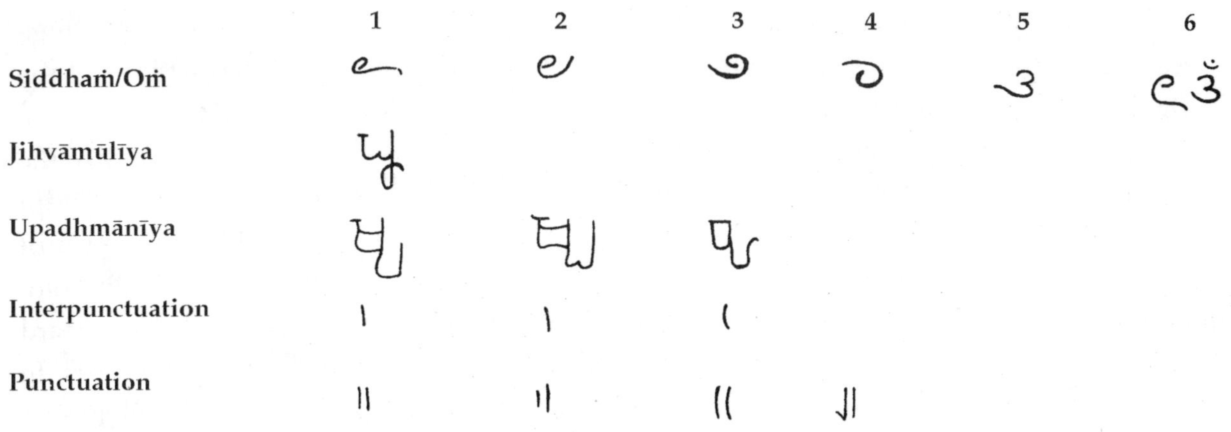

fig. II

the letter *ha* with a tail at its bottom, the letters *ca, pa, pha, ma, ya, va, ṣa, sa,* etc., with their right upright projecting beyond the base-line and the letter *ga, ṇa, śa,* etc., with their right upright developing "horn-like protuberance" at the top.

A few peculiarities have been observed in the Chicacole plates of Satyavarman of GY 351 (AD 849) and the undated Chicacole plates of Anantavarman. The first plate second side of the former is written in proto-Nāgarī characters while the rest of the plates display the mixed style of engraving. Similarly the second plate second side and third plate first side of the latter are in the proto-Nāgarī characters while the first plate second side and second plate first side are in the mixed Kaliṅga script. Besides, the proto-Nāgarī script is used in the whole of the Ramapuram plates of Anantavarman GY 495 (AD 993) while the lines 6-7 and 43-44 are written in the Telugu-Canarese script.

It is noteworthy here to refer to a few varieties of the letters, viz., *ja, ṇa, dha* and *ma* which cannot be affiliated to any other source and in our opinion they developed locally and independently. The letter *ja* has a number of varieties such as the omission of the stem to the left; the shortening of the stem and addition of the upper and lower arms at its the back; and the cursive projections to the left from the upper and lower arms are peculiar to Kaliṅga alone. The base-line of the double-curved *ṇa* is suppressed and both the curves meet each other at a point in the middle. The broad curve to the left of *dha* is doubly curved and this variety is more frequent in the mixed Kaliṅga script. The looped *ma* is closed at the top by a horizontal line. This type of closing the top of the looped *ma* by a curve is a peculiarity of the Grantha style of the ninth-tenth century. But the occurrence of this type of *ma* as early as the close of the seventh century proves it beyond doubt that this peculiarity developed in Kaliṅga locally. Since the Grantha script itself is a curious mixture of different traits prevalent in the Deccan and south India, it would not be a matter of surprise if it is held that the closing of the top of the looped *ma* was incorporated in the Grantha style from Kaliṅga.

The sign for *siddhaṁ* is represented by a curve facing either left, right or down. In some of the Śvetaka Gaṅga records it is seen in the form of a horizontal line with its left end curving up and right end twisted (*fig.* II). This variety is commonly found in the inscriptions written in the *kuṭila* script. The *jihvāmūlīya* and the *upadhmānīya* are indicated by almost an identical sign, i.e., a cerebral *ṣa* on the top of *ka* and *pa* respectively. The lower limit of the use of *jihvāmūlīya* in Kaliṅga can be fixed at GY 195 or AD 693, the date of the Siddhantam plates of Devendravarman I while the *upadhmānīya* is occasionally found used up to GY 397 or AD 895, the date of the Chidivalasa plates of Devendravarman IV, where it is seen in the form of *pa* instead of *ṣa*. The punctuation and interpunctuation marks do not call for special mark except the one reproduced in *fig.* II, where a tick is joined to the lower end of the left vertical. The use of this peculiar punctuation mark is confined to the Svalpavelura plates of the Śvetaka Gaṅga king Anantavarman.

In the final form of *ta*, the letter is devoid of its head-mark and a *halanta* mark is joined at its bottom. At times it is drawn in continuation with the letter but normally it is indicated by a separate stroke. The type of *t* as used in line 15 of the Svalpavelura plates is already noticed in the acute-angled script. *Avagraha* is not used at all.

Vowels

A : The upturned curve type of *a* which was popular and regularly used in the median Kaliṅga script survived in *Pl.* XIII.2. In *Pl.* XIIIa.1, it has developed a loop. Subsequently, the upturned curve is doubled and the right arm does not always form an upright as in *Pl.* XIIIa.4 (first), 5. This variety along with the one having a round curve on the left (*Pl.* XIIIa.6, XIVa.1 second) are clearly recognized as Telugu-Canarese types. The extreme rounded forms of this letter as seen in *Pl.* XIIIa.3 (second), 4 (second), 7 (second) are other sub-varieties of the Telugu-Canarese form. In each case the letter-form is carelessly drawn. The letter-form with two verticals of unequal length joined by a mid bar with a left-facing curve attached to the left limb is found on many occasions as in *Pl.* XIIIa.3 (first), 7 (first) and so on. This variety is popularly used in the acute-angled script of the Śailodbhavas of Koṅgoda and their contemporaries in Ganjam (e.g., Russelkonda plates of Neṭṭabhañja) in the seventh-eighth centuries. The letter-form in *Pl.* XIIIa.7 (third), 10; XIVa.1 (first), 3 (first), 4 (second), 8, 9, 10 can undoubtedly be grouped under the proto-Nāgarī. The left limb in all these cases exhibits two distinct left-facing curves. Another variety of the proto-Nāgarī *a* as used in the inscription of the Somavaṁśīs of the tenth century began to appear in the inscriptions of the Gaṅgas of Kaliṅga and their feudatories from the close of the same century. Its use in the Ramapuram and Mandasa plates of Anantavarman Vajrahasta II (*Pl.* XIVa.3 (third) and 4 (first)) lends support to this. Another form of this letter resembling to the letter-form of the initial *o* appears in *Pl.* XIIIa.8 (second) which cannot be affiliated to any script.

Ā : The letter-form of *ā* is the same as *a* with an additional down facing curve or a small line in the right. The small line is often developed into a full length vertical as in *Pl.* XIVa.1. In *Pl.* XIVa.4 the letter-form is peculiarly drawn.

I & Ī : The notched roof type of *i* with two dots or small circles below which appeared in the median Kaliṅga script continued to be used in the mixed Kaliṅga script (*Pl.* XIIIa.2, 5; XIVa.1). Optionally, it is expressed by only the notched roof and the dots/circles and at the bottom are suppressed (*Pl.* XIIIa.6, 10; XIV.2). This variety is also used in the Telugu-Canarese script. In *Pl.* XIIIa.2, it is seen in the form of a flat roof with its one end joining the dot below. The other variety with two dots/circles and a curve below is noticed in a number of inscriptions of Kaliṅga of the period. It is the standard form in the acute-angled script as popularized in Orissa. Later on the same variety is also optionally used in the *kuṭila* and proto-Nāgarī script. The length of this variety of *i* is denoted by an additional stroke on the top as in *Pl.* XIVa.1, 4. The letter-form in *Pl.* XIVa.7 (first) is of southern type and its length is indicated by an additional top stroke as in *Pl.* XIIIa.2; XIVa.2.

U : The broad-backed type of *u* survived in the mixed Kaliṅga script at least up to the close of the ninth century. The left-facing broad curve type of *u* which is distinctly a northern variety began to be used in the records of Kaliṅga from the middle of the eighth century. As in the proto-Nāgarī script, so also in the mixed Kaliṅga script, this variety progressed in the direction of developing two left-facing curves with a head-mark (*Pl.* XIVa.3, 8, 9, 10). Chronologically, the scribes under Śvetaka Gaṅgas were the earliest to introduce this change. The letter-form is getting closer to its modern Nāgarī form.

E : The broad-looped type of *e* with a notched base-line is seen in *Pl.* XIVa.1. The letter-forms in the Gautami plates of Indravarman and Badakhemundi plates of Jayavarman (*Pl.* XIVa.5 and 6) is very peculiarly drawn and may be called as the corrupt form of the broad-looped type of *e*. The triangular type of *e* is seen in *Pl.* XIIIa.3, 7. The proto-Nāgarī form of *e* is noticed in *Pl.* XIVa.3, 4, 9. The letter-form in *Pl.* XIVa.10 is a northern variety and often seen in the *kuṭila* script.

O : The initial *o* in *Pl.* XIIIa.2 is reproduced from line 21 of the Andhavaram plates of Anantavarman and it is apparently belonging to the Telugu-Canarese and Grantha script of the seventh-eighth centuries. The other variety as seen in *Pl.* XIV.3 is of proto-Nāgarī type.

Consonants

In the mixed Kaliṅga script of the seventh-tenth centuries it is not easy at several places, except with the help of the context, to distinguish one letter from the other. The broad-looped type of *ca* is liable to be confounded with that of *va*, the angular *ḍa* with that of *da*, the broad-backed type of *ḍa* with that of *da*, the elliptical *cha* with that of *tha*, the looped *ta* with that of *na*, the medial *i* with *ī*, *u* with *ū*, and the superscript *ña* with *ṇa*. *Gha*, *ṭa*, *ṭha*, *ḍa*, *ḍha* and *da* do not call for special remarks. *Gha* has suppressed its middle prong and the line head-mark is applied either on the left limb or on the entire top of the letter. *Ṭa* is broad-backed type. Optionally it is represented by two curves. *Ṭha* is of circular type. *Ḍa* is broad-backed type with or without its base-line notched. The angular *ḍa* of the acute-angled script is also seen used. In *Pl.* XIIIa.5 (second), 6 (second), 11 (first), the letter-form is devoid of the head-mark and its ends curl in. *Ḍha* is broad-backed type with its lower end curling in. *Da* is again broad-backed type with or without its base-line notched. The angular *da* of the acute-angled script with or without a tail is also notched. The rest of the letters exhibit a great variety.

In the Chicacole plates of Satyavarman and the Mandasa plates of Anantavarman, an attempt has been made to distinguish between the dental and palatal *la*. The proto-Nāgarī form of the letter is used for the latter while the Telugu-Canarese form is used for the former. But the engravers of the plates were not consistent in the use of these two sound symbols. Moreover, the Parlakhemundi plates of Vajrahasta furnish the rare Telugu-Canarese letter-forms for *ṟ* in *Eṟayamarāja* (l.13), *ḷ* in *Coḷa* (l.10), and *ḻ* in *Śeḻuśeḻāgaḍḍi* (l.18) and *ḻomka* (l.20).

Ka : The upturned curve type of *ka* of the median Kaliṅga script is now totally displaced by the Telugu-Canarese *ka* where there is a deliberate attempt to merge the upturned curve with the cross-bar. When the curve merges with the cross-bar it results in the formation of roughly a broad rectangular loop standing heightwise. One of the best examples of this variety is reproduced from line 26 of the Pattali plates of Yuvarāja Rājendravarman (*Pl.* XIIIa.6, first). Optionally the curve does not meet the left end of the cross-bar and hence the scribe makes a deliberate attempt to join the two. This is resulted in the formation of an inward dip in the left limb as in *Pl.* XIIIa.3 (second), 7 (first) and so on. In the next stage this Telugu-Canarese form is progressed in the direction of shifting the pronounced serif and the small tick below it to the centre of the loop as in *Pl.* XIIIa.10 (second), 11 (fourth); XIVa.7 (first). In *Pl.* XIIIa.10 (third and fourth), the loop is extremely rounded. The letter-form in *Pl.* XIIIa.7 (fourth) without its forked head-mark confirms to the Grantha *ka*. The Tamil form of the letter is noticed in *Pl.* XIVa.4 (first). The letter-form in *Pl.* XIVa.1 (first), 5, 6 is archaic. The looped *ka* of the northern type is seen on many occasions. In *Pl.* XIIIa.2 (second), the outer curve is not prominent; in *Pl.* XIIIa.7 (second), the outer curve is bent in *kuṭila* fashion; and in *Pl.* XIVa.10 (first), the letter-form resembles to the proto-Nāgarī or Nāgarī form. Optionally the outer curve makes an angular bend and shoots up as in *Pl.* XIIIa.1 (second), 6 (third).

Kha : The broad-looped type of *kha* with its base-line notched of the earlier epoch is still noticed in the mixed Kaliṅga script. In *Pl.* XIIIa.2 (third), the loop is opened up at the top. The Telugu-Canarese form of the letter with a loop to the left and the inclining stroke shooting up is noticed in *Pl.* XIIIa.3 (third), 6, 7 (first) and so on. The flat-topped *kha* with a triangular loop on the right which was current in the acute-angled script of the Śailodbhavas of Koṅgoda occurred in *Pl.* XIIIa.3 (second). As in the northern script so also in the mixed Kaliṅga script this form of the letter progressed in the direction of forming a triangular or circular foot-mark on the left limb and its flat top extremely rounded as in *Pl.* XIIIa.5 (second), 7 (second), 9 and so on. In *Pl.* XIVa.7, the flat top is retained. At times, the foot-mark and even the loop on the right limb are opened up as in *Pl.* XIIIa.5 (third), XIVa.8. The letter-form in *Pl.* XIIIa.7 (third), 11 (third), XIVa.10, can clearly be recognized as proto-Nāgarī. However, while drawing these northern forms of this letter, scribes have rounded them so much that they display altogether different looks.

Ga **:** The flat-topped *ga* with an inward curl in the left foot is retained for sometime in the mixed Kaliṅga script. Among the other varieties mention may be made of (a) the Telugu-Canarese type with a round top as in *Pl.* XIIIa.3 (third), 4 (second), 7 (first), 10 (first) and so on; (b) the Grantha type as in *Pl.* XIIIa.10 (fifth); (c) the flat or round topped *ga* with a triangular foot-mark as in *Pl.* XIIIa.3 (first), 10 (fourth), 11 (third), XIVa.5 (second); (d) the proto-Nāgarī type as in *Pl.* XIIIa.7 (second), 9 (first), 10 (third), XIVa.1 (third), 3 and so on.

Ca **:** The broad-looped *ca* with its base-line notched is survived up to the close of the ninth century. Another sub-variety of this type of letter is indicated by the opening of its broad loop at the top and its two arms join the line head-mark separately. This is more regularly used in the mixed Kaliṅga script. The letter-form in *Pl.* XIIIa.10 (third) and XIVa. 4 (second) is used in the transitional Grantha script of the eighth-tenth centuries. Of the northern varieties, the triangular type is used in *Pl.* XIIIa.7 (third), 10 (second). In another variety, the left and right arms of the letter meet the head-mark separately as in *Pl.* XIIIa.5 (first), 9 (first) and so on. This form of the letter is more cursively drawn in *Pl.* XIIIa.5 (second).

Cha **:** The elliptical *cha* is more frequently used in the inscriptions of the period under review. The open-mouthed type of *cha* has also appeared from the beginning of the ninth century as in *Pl.* XIIIa.4 (second), 11; XIVa.4, 9, 10. In another variety the head-mark is joined to the left loop of the elliptical *cha* (*Pl.* XIIIa.1, 3 and so on). This is a Telugu-Canarese peculiarity.

Ja **:** The three-armed *ja* is still retained in the mixed Kaliṅga script. Often the upper and lower arms are notched as in *Pl.* XIIIa.3 (second, fourth), 6 (second), XIVa.1 (third) and so on. This notched type of *ja* is also seen in the Telugu-Canarese and Pallava Grantha scripts of the seventh-eighth centuries. From this notched variety two separate letter-forms evolved. The one having an outer curve on the top left as seen in *Pl.* XIIIa.5 (second), 7 (second) and so on; and the other having a double-curved roof as in *Pl.* XIVa.4 (second) are easily recognized as Telugu-Canarese and Grantha *ja* respectively. The letter-form in *Pl.* XIVa.9. (second) cannot be affiliated to any script. The northern forms of this consonant is represented by the suppressed upper arm type. The proto-Nāgarī type of *ja* with a definite left-facing curve at the bottom has also appeared, vide *Pl.* XIVa. 4 (first). Sometimes it is more rounded as in *Pl.* XIIIa.5 (third).

Ṇa **:** The double-curved *ṇa* with a firm base-line is continued to be used in the mixed Kaliṅga script. Optionally the right curve is lengthened and the left curve makes an inward bend, e.g., *Pl.* XIIIa.5 (second). But during this period another peculiar tendency has developed which led to the suppression of the base-line and formation of two down-facing curves as in *Pl.* XIIIa.1 (second), 3 (second) and so on. When the right arm is elongated and became a vertical with a horn-like protuberance at the top it resembles to the proto-Nāgarī form of *ṇa*, vide *Pl.* XIIIa.5 (third), 7 (second) and so on. The letter-form in *Pl.* XIIIa.7 (first), 10 (third), 11 (third), XIVa.1 (fourth), 2 (first), 3 (first) is of Telugu-Canarese while the letter-form in *Pl.* XIIIa.10 (fourth) is of Grantha type.

Ta : The face of the letter *ta* has changed a lot from the earlier script. Now a tendency has developed to shorten and straighten its left curve and lengthen its right curve. This has resulted in the formation of a left-facing curve as in *Pl.* XIIIa.3 (second), 5 (first) and so on. This is the standard Telugu-Canarese form. The looped type of *ta* as used in *Pl.* XIIIa.2 (second), 5 (second), 7 (third), etc., can be recognized as belonging to the Grantha script. This looped *ta* can easily be confounded with the looped *na*. Another variety of *ta* is found in this period which is indicated by a vertical with a hook or curve on its right as in *Pl.* XIVa. (first) and 8 (first). The northern form of *ta* such as the down-facing curve type (*Pl.* XIIIa.1) and the *kuṭila* type (*Pl.* XIIIa.4, 5) are also occasionally met with.

Tha : The earlier varieties of the letter expressed by a circle with either a curve or loop at the bottom or a horizontal mid-line are still used in the inscriptioins of the period. Subsequently the circle is opened at the top as in *Pl.* XIIIa.2 (second). In *Pl.* XIIIa.5 (second) it is opened on the right and in *Pl.* XIIIa.6 it has obtained a head-mark. In one instance, e.g., *Pl.* XIIIa. 3 (first) the letter-form resembles the elliptical *cha*. This is reproduced from line 28 of the Visakhapatanam plates of Devendravarman. The letter-forms in *Pl.* XIVa.7, 9, 10 are extremely rounded. The northern forms of this letter is seen in *Pl.* XIIIa.11; XIVa.3, 4, 8.

Dha : The northern varieties of the letter *dha* such as the broad-backed type and the double-curved type are regularly found used in the mixed Kaliṅga script. Among the other varieties mention may be made of the circular type with a notched base-line as in *Pl.* XIIIb.7 (third), 10 (second); XIVb.1 (second), 2 and the open-mouthed type with a notched base-line as in *Pl.* XIVb. 4 (second) which can be recognized as Telugu-Canarese and Grantha *dha* respectively. In *Pl.* XIIIb.4 (second) the letter-form is a triangle.

Na : The looped *na* is more frequently used in the inscriptions of the period. The Telugu-Canarese form of the letter with a hook attached to the left of the right vertical is seen in *Pl.* XIIIb.3 (second), 10 (second), XIVb.2 (first). In the Grantha script the hook is attached to the right as in *Pl.* XIIIb.7 (second). The double-armed with a mid-line type of *na* is appeared in *Pl.* XIVb.1 (second), 6 (third). The letter-forms in *Pl.* XIVb.5, 7 and 10 are of nothern type. The letter-form in *Pl.* XIVb.4 is a rare one.

Pa : The bent arm type of *pa* with a notched base-line which had already appeared in the median Kaliṅga script became more frequent and this form is also used in the Telugu-Canarese script. Occasionally the bent arm is straightened. The letter-form in *Pl.* XIIIb.7 (second), 10 (third) is borrowed from the transitional Grantha alphabet. *Pa* in *Pl.* XIIIb.5 (second) is acute-angled. The open-mouthed *pa* is also used in the inscriptions of the Gaṅgas of Śvetaka (*Pl.* XIVb.5). Subsequently the proto-Nāgarī *pa* with a horizontal covering line on the top began to be used in the inscriptions of the Gaṅgas of Śvetaka and Kaliṅga.

Pha : Like the bent arm type of *pa,* the bent arm type of *pha* with a notched base-line is still retained in the mixed Kaliṅga script. This is the standard form in the Telugu-Canarese script of the seventh-tenth centuries. Optionally, the bent arm is straightened as in *Pl.* XIIIb.3, 5 (first), XIVb.6; the notch is missing as in *Pl.* XIVb.1; and the right arm has an outward curl or loop as in *Pl.* XIVb.7 (second). The open-mouthed *pha* with its right arm drawn in *kuṭila* fashion is seen in *Pl.* XIVb.7 (first). In *Pl.* XIIIb.5 (second), 7 (second), 10, XIVb.9, 10 its mouth is closed by a horizontal covering line and it has either a circle or down-facing curve on the right.

Ba : The forms of the letter *ba* in *Pl.* XIVb.1 and 2 are of Telugu-Canarese type. In most of the inscriptions of the period *ba* is expressed by the symbol for *va.*

Bha : All important varieties of the median Kaliṅga script have been retained in the mixed Kaliṅga script. The double-curved type and the broad type with its notched curves are also used in the Telugu-Canarese script. The letter-form in *Pl.* XIIIb.5 (third), 7 (third), 10 (third), 11 (third) are of Grantha type. The proto-Nāgarī form of the letter is seen in *Pl.* XIIIb.7 (second) and so on.

Ma : The letter *ma* is of broad-looped type with or without its base-line notched. This type of the letter is continued from the median Kaliṅga script. Among the other varieties mention may be made of (a) the Grantha type with a covering line or curve at the top as in *Pl.* XIIIb.1, 4 (second) and so on; (b) the Telugu-Canarese type as in *Pl.* XIIIb.7 (fifth), 10 (third), XIVb.1 (third), 2 (first); (c) the looped type of the northern script as in *Pl.* XIIIb.5 (third), etc., and (d) the proto-Nāgarī type as in *Pl.* XIIIb.7 (second) and so on.

Ya : The tripartite *ya* with its left limb curling in and making a notch at the base is the regular form used in the mixed Kaliṅga script. Optionally a circular loop is formed on the left limb as in *Pl.* XIIIb.5 (third), 7 (first), 10 (first), XIVb.1 (second). These forms are also current in the Telugu-Canarese script of the seventh-tenth centuries. In another variety the two cursive limbs meet the head-mark separately as in *Pl.* XIIIb.4 (second), 6 (third), 8 and so on. This form of the letter is peculiar to Kaliṅga alone. The letter-form in *Pl.* XIIIb.2 (second), 3 (third), 5 (first and second) is devoid of the line head-mark. In *Pl.* XIIIb.10 (third), the letter-form resembles the Grantha *pa.* But in the Grantha script we do not come across of this type of *ya.* It is very likely that the similarity between the open-mouthed *pa* and the bipartite *ya* of the northern script led the scribe to approximate the form of *ya* with Grantha *pa.* Of the northern varieties, the letter-form in *Pl.* XIIIb.3 (first) is acute-angled type; in *Pl.* XIVb.1 (third), 7 (second) is of bipartite type; in *Pl.* XIIIb.7 (second), XIVb. 3 (first), 4 (second), 8, etc., it is of proto-Nāgarī type.

Ra : The upturned curve type of *ra* is survived at least up to the close of the ninth century. But a tendency has already been started from the close of the seventh century to merge the upturned curve with the head-mark. With the merging of this curve, the letter roughly resembles a rectangular standing heightwise, vide *Pl.* XIIIb.1, 2 (first) and so on. Sometimes this variety is drawn more cursively and resembled a broad loop as in *Pl.* XIIIb.3 (second), XIVb. 1 (first), 2 (second), 3 (first). Both these varieties of *ra* are seen in the Telugu-Canarese script of the eighth-tenth centuries. The northern forms of this letter such as the vertical with a tick type and the vertical with a slanting stroke type appeared in the mixed Kaliṅga script from the beginning of the ninth century.

La : The hooked *la*, the hooked *la* with an extended upper curve, and the circular type of *la* which appeared in the median Kaliṅga script continued to be used in the mixed Kaliṅga script. Of these, the circular type of *la* is more frequently used during this period. It is also clearly recognized as the standard Telgu-Canarese form. The letter-forms in *Pl.* XIIIb.5 (second) and 10 (third) are exceptional and peculiar to Kaliṅga alone. The down-facing curve type of *la* as seen in *Pl.* XIVb.7 (second), is survived from the acute-angled script. In *Pl.* XIVb.9 (second) and 10 (second), its base-line is considerably rounded. The proto-Nāgarī form of the letter appears in many inscriptions of the ninth-tenth centuries.

Va : The broad-looped type of *va* with or without its base-line notched is the regular form used in the mixed Kaliṅga script. Optionally, it has got a right upright on which the line head-mark is joined, e.g., *Pl.* XIVb.1 (second). This form is apparently an import from the Telugu-Canarese source. The letter-form in *Pl.* XIIIb.7 (third) and 10 (second) resembles the transitional Grantha form of *va*. In *Pl.* XIIIb.5 (second), the letter is expressed by a broad loop with a mid-line. The proto-Nāgarī form of the letter has appeared from the ninth century.

Śa : Like *ga*, the flat top of *śa* is also invariably rounded and the left limb curls in as in *Pl.* XIIIb. 1, 2 and so on. This form along with the one having no curl were current in the Telugu-Canarese script. Occasionally the cross-bar is reduced to a small horizontal as in *Pl.* XIIIb.3 (second), 4, 8, or totally suppressed as in *Pl.* XIIIb.5 (third), 6 (first). The letter-forms in *Pl.* XIIIb.5 (second) and XIVb.4 (second) are rare ones. The proto-Nāgarī form of the letter is used from the ninth century.

Ṣa : The bent arm type of *ṣa* with or without its base-line notched is the standard form used during this period. It is also popularly used in the Telugu-Canarese script. The Grantha Type of the letter has appeared in one instance, e.g., *Pl.* XIIIb.5 (first). In *Pl.* XIIIb.11, 8 (first) the reduced corss-bar is curved and joined to the line head-mark on the right. In *Pl.* XIIIb.7, 9, 10; XIVb.9, 10, the letter-form is distinctly of proto-Nāgarī type.

Sa : The hooked type of *sa* of the earlier epoch retained mostly during this period. Optionally the two limbs are separated and joined the head-mark at different points as in *Pl.* XIIIb.1 (first), 3 (third), 8, XIVb.1 (first). In *Pl.* XIIIb.6 (second), 7 (third), 9 (second), XIVb.3 (first) the middle

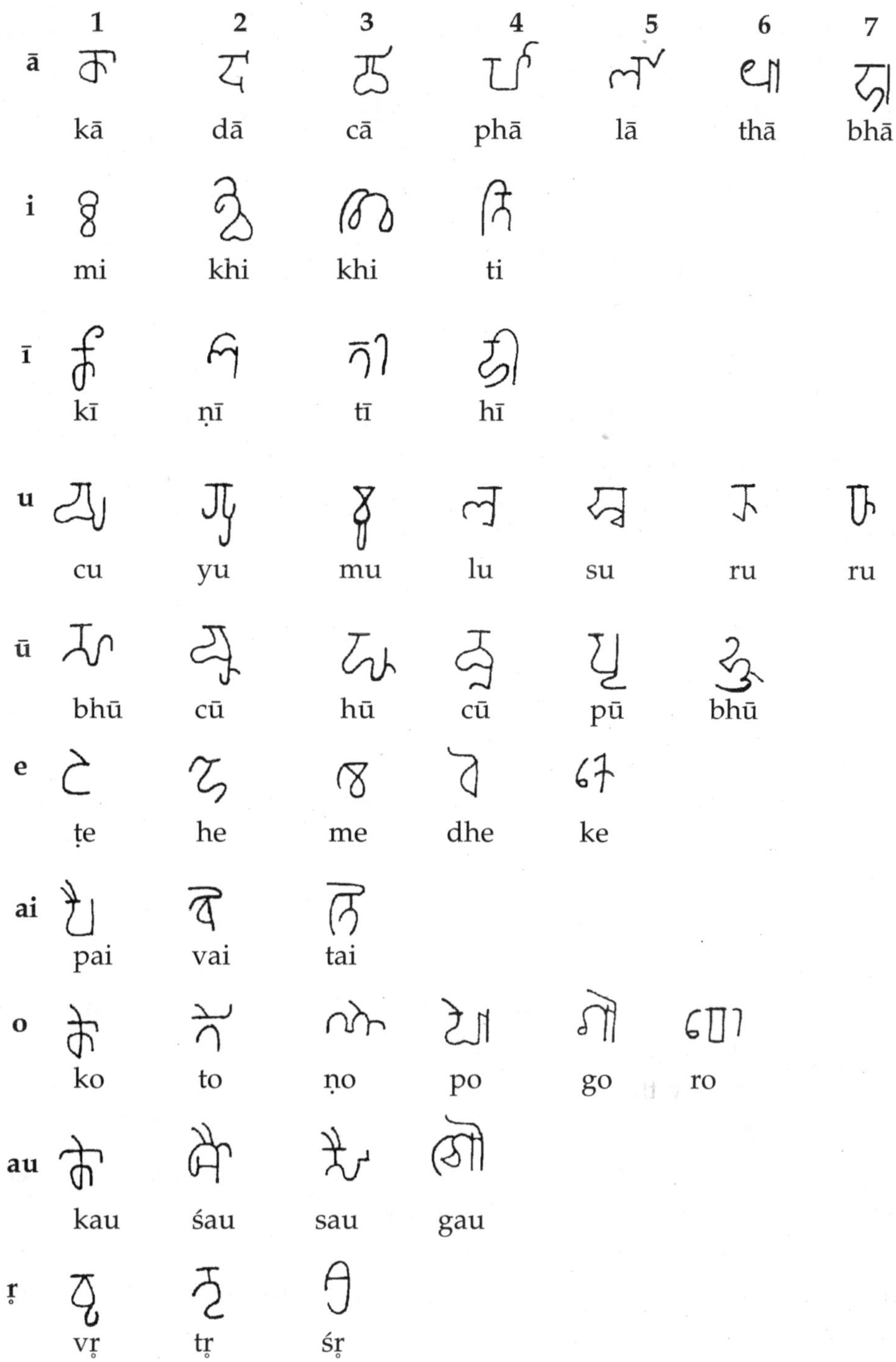

***fig.* III: Medials in the Mixed Kaliṅga Script**

stroke joining the head-mark and the hook below is suppressed. This form is undoubtedly belonging to the Telugu-Canarese script. In *Pl.* XIIIb.5 (second), XIVb.2 (second), 4 (second), even the head-mark is dropped. In *Pl.* XIIIb.5 (second), the hooked *sa* came under the impact of the acute-angled script and, therefore, its right limb exhibits a perfect acute angle. The open-mouthed *sa* which is popularly used in the scripts of northern India is also used simultaneously, vide *Pl.* XIIIb.1 (second), 5, (first) and so on. In *Pl.* XIIIb.10 (second), XIVb.3 (second), 4 (first), 8, 9, the letter-form is admittedly of proto-Nāgarī type. These northern varieties often came under the influence of the general cursive engraving of the locality, e.g., *sa* in *Pl.* XIIIb.2 (second), 5 (third). The letter-form in *Pl.* XIIIb.10 (third) is a Grantha peculiarity.

Ha : The bent arm type of *ha* of the earlier epoch is no longer favoured and the outer curve is now more pronounced. The letter has also a notched base-line as in *Pl.* XIIIb.1 (second), 4 (second) and so on. This form of the letter is regularly found used in the Telugu-Canarese script. The letter-form in *Pl.* XIIIb.10 (second) is recognized as belonging to the Grantha script. The letter-form with an angular back as in *Pl.* XIIIb.4 (first), 9 (second) resembles the open-mouthed *bha*. The letter having its right arm bent in *kuṭila* fashion and having a tail can be affiliated to the northern script.

Kṣa : *Kṣa* is still largely a combination of *ka* and *ṣa*. The letter-forms in *Pl.* XIIIb.10, XIVb.1, 2, 3 (first), 9 (second) are of southern type. In the ninth-tenth centuries, the subscript *ka* has reduced to a mere loop and joined to *ṣa* below as in *Pl.* XIIIb.11 and so on. This is also met with in the proto-Nāgarī script of Orissa.

Medials

The diacritical notations for the medial vowels as used in the different scripts of India up to the tenth century are also found used in the mixed Kaliṅga script. It is needles to repeat them here. Of the new notations mention may be made of (a) the medial *ā* in *lā* (*fig.* III.1) where it forms an angle on the right; (b) *u* in *mu* (*fig.* III.4) where the upturned curve touches the base of the letter; (c) *e* in *ke* (*fig.* III.6) where the curve on the left has obtained a loop at its bottom; (d) *o* in *ro* (*fig.* III.8) where the above variety of *e* is used on the left and a vertical is drawn on the right; and (e) the medial *ṛ* in *śṛ* (*fig.* III.10), where it is denoted by a curve to the left. Most of the peculiarities referred to above are borrowed either from the Telugu-Canarese, or Grantha or from the Tamil scripts. It is interesting to note here that of those the notations for *e* and *o* as well as the semi-circular type of the medial *i* as in *mi* (*fig.* III.2) are popularized in modern Oriya script. One of the important features of the mixed Kaliṅga script is that even in each inscription the signs for the medial vowels exhibit great variety. The Parlakhemundi copper-plate grant of the time of Vajrahastadeva is a case in point where the signs for *u*, *ū*, *e* and *o* are written in four, five or six different ways.

Conjuncts

As in the scripts of the preceding centuries so also in the mixed Kaliṅga script of the seventh-tenth centuries, the conjuncts are represented by the consonants placed one above the other and the second elements are usually devoid of the head-mark. Compared to the superscripts the subscripts are smaller in size.

Of the nasals, the guttural nasal *ṅa* when joined to the letters of its class is either a right-facing curve or an angle. As in the early Eastern Gaṅga inscriptions, so also in the inscriptions of the later rulers of the Eastern Gaṅgas, the curve has an inward dip at its back as in *Pl.* XIIIb.3 (second), 5 (second). The superscript *ṅa* in *Pl.* XIIIb.3 (first) resembles to the Telugu-Canarese *ja* while in *Pl.* XIIIb.2 (first), it is drawn closely after *ña*. It has peculiar forms in *Pl.* XIIIb.2 (first), 10 (first) and XIVb.6 (second). In a majority of inscriptions of the period, the subscript *ña* and *ṇa* are denoted by a uniform type which is very much akin to the double-curved type of *ṇa* with or without a firm base-line. Subsequently when this type of *ṇa* is changed into two down-facing curve type, the superscripts also changed their forms accordingly. In *Pl.* XIIIb.10, 11, the superscript *ṇa* is of Telugu-Canarese type. In *Pl.* XIIIb.2 (second) and XIVb.9 (second), the superscript *ña* has obtained an additional initial *o* sign on its right. The other nasals like *na* and *ma* when used as superscripts do not call for special remark. The letter *ña* when used as a second element is fully represented in some of the inscriptions of the seventh and early eighth century as in *Pl.* XIIIc.1, 2 (second), XIVc.6. Later on it is used in the Parlakhemundi plates of Vajrahasta (Pl. XIVc.1), which may be considered as the lower limit of the use of this type of *ña*. In the other cases it is represented by double curve type or two left-facing curve type as in *jña* (*Pl.* XIIIc.4) and *jñā* (*Pl.* XIIIc.6).

The broad-backed type of *ṭa* when doubled is expressed by two broad-backed curves facing right as in *ṭṭa* in *Pl.* XIIIc and XIVc. As a subscript the letter is often drawn as a down-facing curve as in *sṭi* (*Pl.* XIII c.9). The subscript *tha* is regularly expressed by its full form. In one instance, e.g., *sthā* in *Pl.* XIIIc.3 it is indicated by an ellipse with a mid-line. The diacritical notations for *ya* and *ra* are seen in the form of broad curves. The broad curve of *ya* is occasionally notched as in *thya* (*Pl.* XIIIc.4), *nya* (*Pl.* XIIIc.5) and so on. The *repha* has still maintained an angle at the top.

Orthography

The orthographical peculiarities of the inscriptions of the period call for no special remarks. They have appeared in the inscriptions from other localities of Orissa up to the tenth-eveventh centuries, and have already been dealt with in the preceding chapters. It is not necessary therefore, to repeat them here.

Bibliography

PLATE XIII

1. Siddhantam plates of Devendravarman, GY 195, G. Ramdas, *EI*, 13, 212-16 & pls.
2. a) Dharmalingesvara plates of Anantavarman, GY 204, R.K. Ghoshal, *ibid.*, 26, 65-68 & pls.
   b) Andhavaram plates of Anantavarman, GY 216, R. Subrahmanyam, *ibid.*, 31, 199-202 & pls.
3. a) Chicacole plates of Devendravarman, GY 251, J.F. Fleet, *IA*, 13, 273-76 & pls.

b) Visakhapatanam plates of Devendravarman, GY 254, *ibid.*, 18, 143-46 & pls.

4. a) Alamanda plates of Anantavarman, GY 304, E. Hultzsch, *EI*, 3, 17-21 & pls.

   b) Munjeru plates of Anantavarman. O. Ramachandraiya & C.S. Rao, *KAN Sastri Felicitation Volume*, 117-24 & pls.

5. Plates of Devendravarman

   (a) Salantari (also called Musunika) plates of Devendravarman, GY 306, V.V. Mirashi, *EI*, 30, 23-28 & pls.

   (b) Bangalore plates of Devendravarman, Lewis Rice, *EC*, 9, 140 & pls.

   (c) Chicacole plates of Devendravarman, D.C. Sircar, *JASB*, *L*, 18 (1), 17-20 & pls.

   (d) Badakhemundi (also known as the Indian Museum) plates of Devendravarman, GY 308, B. C. Chhabra, *EI*, 23, 73-78 & pls.

   (e) Tekkali plates of Devendravarman, GY 310, E. Hultzsch, *ibid.*, 18, 311-13 & pls.

6. a) Pattali plates of Yuvarāja Rājendravarman, GY 313, D.C. Sircar, *ibid.*, 32, 201-06 & pls.

   b) Nampali plates of Yuvarāja Rājendravarman, GY 314, KAN Sastri, *JOR*, 9, 50-63 & pls.

7. Chicacole plates of Satyavarman, GY 351, J.F. Fleet, *IA*, 14, 10-12 & pls.

8. Tekkali plates of Anantavarman, GY 358, R.K. Ghoshal, *EI*, 26, 174-77 & pls.

9. Chipurupalli (also known as Kalahandi) plates of Anantavarman, GY 383, P. Banerjee, *ibid.*, 31, 317-22 & pls.

10. Gallavalli plates of Manujendravarman, GY 393, D.C. Sircar, *ibid.*, 187-91 & pls.

11. Undated Chicacole plates of Anantavarman, D.C. Sircar, *JASB*, *L*, 18 (1), 47-51 & pls.

PLATE-XIV

Kadambas

1. Parlakimedi plates of Vajrahasta, F. Kielhorn, *EI*, 3, 220-24 & pls.
2. Napitavataka plates of Devendravarman, G.S. Gai, *ibid.*, 34, 189-92 & pls.
3. Ramapuram plates of Anantavarman, GY 495, N.M. Rao, *JAHRS*, 35, 177-82 & pls.
4. Mandasa plates of Anantavarman, *Ś*. 917, G. Ramdas, *JBORS*, 17 (2-3), 175-88 & pls.

Śvetaka Gaṅgas

5. Gautami plates of Indravarman, K.G. Goswami, *EI*, 24, 180-83 & pls.
6. Badakhemundi plates of Jayavarman, S.N. Chakravarti, *ibid.*, 33, 261-63 & pls.
7. Svalpavelura plates of Anantavarman, B. C. Chhabra, *ibid.*, 24, 129-37 & pls.
8. Vishmagiri plates of Indravarman, T.C. Rath, *ibid.*, 19, 134-37 & pls.
9. Indian Museum plates of Jayavarman, BE 100, S.N. Chakravarti, *ibid.*, 23, 267-69 & pls.
10. Badakhemundi plates of Bhūpendravarman, *ibid.*, 265-67 & pls.

10

Proto-Oriya Script

STUDY of the palaeography of the inscriptions of Orissa of the next three and half centuries starting from the closing decades of eleventh century is the most perplexing and enigmatic one. Among the inscriptions of Orissa of the period mention may be made of the stone inscriptions which are several hundreds in number and more than two dozens of copper-plate grants of the Imperial Gaṅgas. Besides, there are another dozen of copper-plate grants of the contemporaries of the Gaṅgas such as the later Somavaṁśīs, the Telugu-Coḍas, the later Bhañjas and others. The copper-plates grants of the period are invariably written in Sanskrit language but their scripts vary greatly. Of the thirteen charters of Anantavarman Coḍagaṅgadeva (AD 1077-1147) so far discovered, six are in northern (proto-Nāgarī or old Nāgarī) characters while the rest of the charters are engraved in southern (old Telugu or Canarese) scripts. The charters issued by the subsequent rulers of the family up to the close of the fourteenth century are written in proto-Nāgarī as used in Orissa or Nāgarī with an admixture of proto-regional characters like proto-Bengali or proto-Oriya. Similarly the charters issued by the contemporaries of the Imperial Gaṅgas are either written in proto-Nāgarī or Nāgarī scripts or exclusively in the proto-regional characters of Orissa. The lapidary inscriptions of the time of the Imperial Gaṅgas are mostly engraved on the walls of the temples of Bhubaneswar, Puri, Mukhalingam, Srikurmam, Simhanchalam, Draksaram and others. They are written in Sanskrit, Telugu, Oriya, and Tamil languages and in proto-Nāgarī, Nāgarī, Telugu, Tamil, proto-Bengali and proto-Oriya scripts. The Oriya inscriptions of this period discovered so far are comparatively few and some of them are written in Telugu, Nāgarī and proto-regional characters. The inscriptions of the Imperial Gaṅgas written in the southern scripts such as old Telugu, Canarese or Tamil are apparent and easily recognizable, and therefore do not invite any incongruity. They can easily be assigned to a definite palaeographic-linguistic zone.But the epigraphs written in the proto-Nāgarī and its derivatives posit a serious confusion when we attempt to trace the origin of the proto-regional script of Orissa. It is well-known that the Oriya script was fully developed by the time of Kapilendradeva (AD 1435-67) of the Sūryavaṁśī Gajapati dynasty and this fact is sufficient enough to warrant that the script had its precursor in the preceding centuries. Unlike the other proto-regional scripts of eastern India, particularly proto-Bengali, the incipient stage of proto-Oriya appears to be hazy and obscure due to more than one reason.

It has just been referred to above that at least six charters of Anantavarman Coḍagaṅgadeva are written in the northern characters. The editors preferred to call them as old Nāgarī or south Indian Nāgarī script.[1] A majority of the later official documents of the Imperial Gaṅga rulers have been edited by D.C. Sircar (either independently or jointly with others) and invariably on each and every occasion he observed that, "the characters belonged to the class usually termed proto-Bengali, although a more appropriate name of the script ought to be Gauḍi."[2] While editing the Sankarananda Math plates of Narasiṁhadeva, he remarked that the characters are "Gauḍī influenced by Nāgarī, though a few letters have forms approaching those of the letters of modern Oriya."[3] S.N. Rajaguru and A.K. Rath who have edited a few charters of the family are of the opinion that their characters belonged to a period when Nāgarī and Oriya scripts were on their way of moulding.[4] Apart from these Gaṅga charters there are a number of copper-plate grants of their contemporaries ruling in subordinate capacity over small territorial pockets of Orissa. Palaeographically they are assigned to the eleventh-thirteenth centuries and their characters are said to have belonged to different scripts by different authorities. D.C. Sircar, the editor of the Polasara plates of Arkeśvaradeva of *Kali* era 4248 (AD 1147-48) opined that, "The characters belong to that variety of the east Indian script of the early medieval period which is usually called proto-Bengali, although, . . . a more appropriate name for the script is Gauḍī."[5] B.C. Mazumdar echoed a similar opinion while editing the Mahada plates of Yogeśvaradevavarman and said, "the main characters agree with or strongly resemble, the modern Bangali letters."[6] But at the same time he preferred to ascribe a few letters to the modern Nāgarī or Oriya script. S.N. Rajaguru and G. Ramdas the editors of the Phūlasara plates of Kīrttirājadeva and Kumarisimha plates of Someśvaradeva respectively believed that the alphabet employed in these plates belonged to the old Nāgarī type.[7] T.C. Rath, who edited the Antirigam plates of Jayabhañja, also believed that the characters of the inscription are highly specialized form of old Nāgarī type," but "they very closely resemble the Uriya characters."[8] K.C. Panigrahi who edited and examined the palaeography of a number of copper-plate grants of the later Somavaṁśīs and their feudatories, the later Bhañjas and the Telugu-Coḍas observed that characters belonged to the proto-Oriya script.[9] Commenting on the alphabet of the Kamalpur plates of the time of Karṇadeva, Panigrahi stated, "The characters used in the record are proto-

1. G.V. Sitapati, *JAHRS*, I (I), 40; Fleet, *IA*, 18, 161 & 172; R. Subba Rao, *JAHRS*, 12 (I), 9; C.N. Rao and R. Subba Rao, *ibid.*, 8 (2-3), 191; N. Ramesan, *CPIAPGM*, I, Hyderabad, 1962, 137ff.
2. *EI*, 28, 236.
3. *Ibid.*, 302.
4. *OHRJ*, 5 (1-2), 4; 12 (4), 165.
5. *EI*, 28, 63.
6. *Ibid.*, 12, 218.
7. *JAHRS*, 3 (I), 30; *JKHRS*, I (3), 229.
8. *EI*, 19, 42.
9. *JOH*, I (I), 1-5; *EI*, 25, 172-73; 26, 276-79.

Oriya and may be classed with those of the Adipur plate of Durjayabhañja, Mahada plates of Yogeśvaradevavarman, the Patna Museum plates of Someśvara, Baud plates Kanakabhañja, Baud plates of Saloṇabhañja and the Ratnagiri charter of Karṇadeva. Some of the letters appear with the rounded tops which are an outstanding characteristic of the modern Oriya scripts."[10] Hiralal[11] and R.D. Banerji[12] further remarked that the characters of the Antirigam plates of Jayabhañja and the Patna Museum plates of Someśvara are written in, "Oriya style of writing" and "Oriya of the fourteenth or fifteenth century AD" respectively.

There are a large number of stone inscriptions belonging to the Gaṅga rulers written either in Sanskrit or Oriya language and in the proto-regional characters. A majority of these inscriptions have been edited by D.C. Sircar who held the opinion that they are all written in proto-Bengali or Gauḍīya characters.[13] But at places he admitted the influence of the characteristics peculiar to the Oriya script. D.C. Sircar and S.R. Sharma who jointly edited the Algaum inscription of the time of Coḍagaṅgadeva remarked, "The characters belong to a cursive form of the Gauḍīya class, commonly called proto-Bengali and may be assigned to about the twelfth century AD or even later."[14] The characters of the Liṅgarāja temple inscription of Rājarāja II of Ś. 1094 (AD 1172) have been assigned to the Gauḍīya alphabet but, in some cases exhibit the development of early Oriya characteristics.[15] Similarly, the Sonepur inscription of Bhānudeva I is said to have been written in Gauḍīya with certain characteristics of the Oriya alphabet.[16] A few inscriptions of the thirteenth-fourteenth centuries which are edited by S.N. Das, K.B. Tripathi and B.V. Nath are said to be written in proto-Oriya characters.[17] D.C. Sircar and K.B. Tripathi who edited the Siddheśvara temple inscription of Narasiṁha IV are of the opinion that the inscription is written in Oriya script.[18] B. C. Chhabra, the editor of the Cāṭeśvara temple inscription remarked that the characters of the inscription are proto-Bengali.[19] F. Kielhorn while editing the Megheśvara temple inscription of Svapneśvardeva and the eulogy of Bhaṭṭa Bhavadeva believed that their palaeography belonged to the "ordinary Nāgarī alphabet used in northern India during the twelfth and thirteenth centuries AD."[20]

---

10. *JOH*, I (I), 1.
11. *EI*, 18, 284.
12. *Ibid.*, 19, 97-98.
13. *Ibid.*, 30, 18, 30, 91, 198, 231; 32, 229; 33, 41, 182; 35, 115.
14. *Ibid.*, 29, 44.
15. *Ibid.*, 35, 118.
16. *Ibid.*, 32, 325.
17. S.N. Das, *OHRJ*, 1 (4), 301-305; 2 (3-4), 53-55; K.B. Tripathi, *Indian Linguistics*, 17 (1957), 47; B.V. Nath, *OHRJ*, 3 (3), 146-49.
18. *EI*, 29, 105.
19. *Ibid.*, 122.
20. *Ibid.*, 6, 198.

Thus, the epigraphic records of Orissa under review have been grouped under either proto-Bengali (Gauḍī) or proto-Oriya or (old) Nāgarī script. There has been a lot of controversy among scholars regarding the origin of the proto-Bengali script. Bühler and Ojha, the old palaeographers almost expressed an identical opinion and attributed it to an off-shoot of the Nāgarī. According to Bühler, "Towards the end of the eleventh century, the Nāgarī inscriptions of Eastern India show such distinct traces of changes leading up to the modern Bengali writing, and these changes become so numerous in the twelfth century, that it is possible to class their alphabets as Proto-Bengali."[21] The script of the Deopara inscription of Vijayasena,[22] belonging to the later part of the eleventh century has been taken to be one of the earliest specimens of the proto-Bengali where the letter-form of *e*, *kha*, *ña*, *ta*, *tha*, *ma*, *ra*, *la*, and *sa*, differ form their contemporary Nāgarī forms prevalent in other parts of northern India.

Later on the proto-Bengali characters became more pronounced in the Kamauli plate of Vaidyadeva of AD 1142[23] and in the Cambridge MSS. No. 1699, I, 2 of AD 1198-99.[24] On the other hand, R.D. Banerji, S.N. Chakravarti and D.C. Sircar attributed the origin of the proto-Bengali to the eastern variety of the northern alphabet with or without the influence of proto-Nāgarī and believed that in the Bangarh grant of Mahīpāla I,[25] ascribable to the later half of the tenth century, the proto-Bengali characters were met with for the first time. Acccording to R.D. Banerji., "in the Bangarh inscription of Mahīpāla we find the latest form of the tenth century alphabet of the North-East. In this inscription we come across the pure Bengali alphabet for the first time which is further developed in another century."[26] In the opinion of S.N. Chakravarti,

> In the 10th century, it (the eastern variety of Northern alphabet) came to be influenced by the Nāgarī, which appeared first on the copper plate grant of Vināyaka-Pāla (VE 988) and found its way into Bengal during the domination of the Gurjara-Pratīhāra kings. But from the time of Mahīpāla I onwards, the influence of the Nāgarī alphabet gradually declined and we find towards the end of the tenth century the birth of the proto-Bengali alphabet. In the Irda grant of the Kamboja king Nayapāladeva and the Bangarh grant of Mahīpāla I we come across the Proto-Bengali alphabet for the first time. The latter inscription shows the well-developed Bengali forms of the letters *a*, *u*, *ka*, *kha*, *ga*, *cha*, *dha*, *va*, and *ha*. In the case of *ja* we find, however, the complete Bengali form. The Deopara inscription of Vijayasena which is assigned to the end of the eleventh or commencement of the twelfth century AD, shows the further progress of the Proto-Bengali alphabet.[27]

21. Bühler, *IP*, 92-93.
22. Metcalfe, *JASB*, 34 (1), 128-54; F. Kielhorn, *EI*, 1, 305-15; N.G. Mazumdar, *Inscriptions of Bengal, III*, Rajshahi, 1929, 42-56.
23. *EI*, 2, 347.
24. Bühler, *op. cit.*, 93, n. 274.
25. *EI*, 14, 324-30.
26. R.D. Banerji, *The Origin of the Bengali Script*, Calcutta, 1919, 74.
27. S.N. Chakravarti, "Development of the Bengali Alphabet from the Fifth Century AD to the End of the Muhammadan Rule," *JRASB*, *L*, 4, 1938, 365.

D.C. Sircar has gone a step further and remarked that in eastern India, the *siddhamātṛkā* gave rise to the proto-Bengali script, sometime in about the tenth century from which ultimately sprang the regional alphabets of Bengal, Bihar, Nepal, Assam and Orissa. He preferred to substitute the term Gauḍī for Bühler's proto-Bengali on the authority of Al-beruni. He further stated, "the letters of this alphabet sometimes exhibit a hook like sign at the top which developed out of the hollow-triangular type of the top *mātrā* referred to above. This is designated by some scholars as 'the Nepalese hook,' though it is also found in other regions of the Gauḍī using area outside Nepal. In Orissa the same sign ultimately developed into the curved top *mātrā* of the letters of the Oriya alphabets."[28] Thus, the controversy among scholars chiefly rests on two points, firstly the source from which the proto-Bengali script originated and secondly the date of its origin.

The chief characteristics of the proto-Bengali are (a) the small triangles with the rounded lower side, the "Nepalese hooks" or the line head-marks attached to the left of the top of various letters; (b) the initial *i* iwith a definite right upright; (c) the opening of *e* and *ai*; (d) the opening of the loops of *kha*, *ga*, *tha*, and *śa*, (e) the left-facing curve type of *ta*; (f) the slanting horizontal base-line of *na* and *ma*; (g) the triangular type of *ra*; (h) the formation of a solid wedge on the left of *sa*; (i) the triangular type of the medial *u*; etc.

The *siddhamātṛkā* or the *kuṭila* script continued to be used in Bengal up to the ninth century and progressed in the direction of forming proto-Nāgarī characters in the tenth century. The domination of the Gurjara-Pratīhāras over the western parts of the Pāla kingdom might have contributed to the introduction of the proto-Nāgarī features into Bengal. From the tenth-eleventh century inscriptions of Bengal it is abundantly clear that the solid triangular head-mark of the *kuṭila* script is replaced by flattened tops; that the bipartite letter forms of *gha*, *pa*, *ma*, *ya*, *ṣa*, *sa*, etc., are now covered with the flattening lines; that the *kuṭila* type of bending the right limbs of the letters is discarded in favour of uprights; that a definite tail is seen attached to the bottom right of most of the letters; that a majority of letters such as *ka*, *gha*, *ṭa*, *ṭha*, *ḍha*, *ṇa*, *ta*, *da*, *na*, *pa*, *ba*, *ma*, *ya*, *ra*, *la*, *va*, *ṣa*, etc., as well as most of the medial vowels are clearly recognized as belonging to the Nāgarī alphabet. It is further observed that none of the proto-Bengali characteristics except the opening of the left loops of *kha*, *ga* and *śa*, do not make their way into the script. In the inscriptions of the later Pālas, Candras and those of the Kamboja king Nayapāladeva, we come across this type of scripts which can appropriately be designated as proto-Nāgarī. It may be said here that the inference of Banerji and Chakravarti that the Bangarh grant of Mahīpāla I marked the advent of the proto-Bengali alphabet is not based on a sound judgement. The well developed Bengali forms which they have seen in the letters *a*, *u*, *ka*, *kha*, *ga*, *ca*, *ja*, *dha* and *ha*, are very much present there in the *siddhamātṛkā* script and with the transition from the *siddhamātṛkā* to the proto-Nāgarī script most of these forms are retained in the latter script. The left-facing curve type of *u*, the looped *ka* with its outer curve elongated, the

28. *JAIH*, 4 (1-2), 120.

opening of the left limb of *kha, ga* (and also of *śa*), the triangular type of *ca* with its tip facing to the left, the doubly curved back of *dha*, the triangular *va*, the tailed *ha*, etc., have already occurred in the older scripts be it exactly in the same or in similar shape. Besides, the letter-forms of *a* and *ja* strictly confirm to their respective proto-Nāgarī forms. Thus the characters of the Bangarh grant cannot be dubbed as proto-Bengali and any attempt to fix the advent of the proto-Bengali from this grant is only to subvert the truth. The same duct of writing continued to be used in the Belwa plates of Mahīpāla I[29] and the Amgachi plate of Vigrahapāla.[30] In the inscriptions of Vigrahapāla III we see the lower limit of the use of the proto-Nāgarī.

The observation of the old palaeographers that the Deopara grant of Vijayasena which is assigned to about the end of the eleventh century or commencement of the twelfth century is the first to exhibit the proto-Bengali characters still holds good. In the use of the "Nepalese hook" on the top of some letters; in the shortening of the outer curve of *ka* and of the left arm of *ṇa* and *la*; in the opening of the loop on the right of *kha*; in the lowering of the horizontal base-line of *na* and *ma*, and in the formation of a solid wedge on the left limb of *sa* we find certain noticeable changes in the existing style of writing in Bengal. These regional deviations are very much a part of the process of palaeographical segmentation that was running parallel to linguistic segmentation in Bengal. There is, therefore, reason to subscribe to the view of the old palaeographers that in the characters of the Deopara grant of Vijayasena we notice the first occurrence of the proto-Bengali. Later on the script is used in the records of the other Sena rulers, the Devas of Samataṭa and Vaṅga, and in those of Vaidyadeva and Vallabhadeva.

From the empirical evidence it is known that some advanced letter-forms or some local peculiarities are bound to occur in the script current in a particular locality because of the idiosyncrasies of the writers, of the so-called "urban strain of palaeography" or of an impingement from outside source. And in such cases, the general duct of writing should be classed under a well-defined palaeographical nomenclature and should not be labelled by a regional appellation. The palaeographers very often ignore this principle and pass on erroneous judgements. More so when it comes to the question of advent of proto-regional script, a tinge of regional chauvinism clouded their judgement. The way in which the palaeographers examined the characters of the Banagarh grant and dubbed them as proto-Bengali does reflect a similar sentiment.

About the origin of the Oriya script scholars are again divided. Ojha has suggested that the Oriya alphabet originated from the proto-Bengali.[31] R.D. Banerji remarked that, "The modern cursive Oriya script developed out of Bengal after the fourteenth century AD like the modern Assamese."[32] D.C. Sircar pointed out that, "the development of Oriya alphabet out of Gauḍī is

29. *EI*, 29, 1.

30. *Ibid.*, 15, 293-301.

31. Ojha, *BPL*, 79.

32. R.D. Banerji, *The Origin of the Bengali Script*, Calcutta, 1919, 6.

complete in the records of about the fourteenth century AD."[33] Grierson wrote in 1932 that, "the Maithili and Bengali alphabets are directly derived from Bühler's proto-Bengali. The Oriya alphabet is on the contrary, derived from Nāgarī and probably reached Orissa directly from the west."[34] Sir Hugh McPherson held, "The Oriyas following their neighbouring nations the Telugus, Tamils, etc., developed a peculiar formation in their provincial "Kuṭila" character."[35] David Diringer believed, "the Oriyas probably developed their written character from the same source as the preceding script (proto-Bengali), under the influence of their south Indian neighbours, the Telugus and Tamils."[36] According to K.B. Tripathi, the Oriya alphabet is "mainly derived from proto-Bengali, although it bears in some cases clear traces of the influence of the Nāgarī and in a few also of the southern alphabets (Bühler's 'later Kaliṅga script')."[37] Thus, the proto-Bengali parentage of the modern Oriya alphabet is the most dominant view expressed by the Indian palaeographers. In the following paragraphs we shall reinvestigate the whole question.

The chief feature that distinguishes the Oriya from the Bengali and Nāgarī scripts is the top curve attached to most of the letters. It has been acknowledged by almost all the authorities that this peculiarity is a modification of the small triangle and the so-called "Nepalese hook." The protagonists of the proto-Bengali parentage of the Oriya script remarked that while the Bengali script has discarded this hook, it has been preserved in Oriya and ultimately contributed to the formation of a shallow curve and then a semi-circle. There is nothing to dispute that the hallow triangular tops and the "Nepalese hooks" are the important features of the proto-Bengali. But the view that these features are borrowed from the proto-Bengali source to develop the Oriya alphabet is not free from suspicion. In the above discussion it has been contended that the hollow triangular head-marks and the "Nepalese hooks" appeared for the first time in the Deopara inscription of Vijayasena belonging to the latter part of the eleventh or early part of the twelfth century, which has also been fixed as the date of beginning of the proto-Bengali. In Nepal, the hooks appeared for the first time in the twelfth-century manuscripts and disappeared in the fifteenth century.[38] Bühler has pointed out that the Nepalese hook is a "cursive substitute for the triangle. The triangle itself is a modification of the top stroke with a semi-circle below. This last mentioned form again is connected with, and gives the outlines of, the thick top-strokes rounded off at both ends."[39]

---

33. D.C. Sircar, "Introduction to Indian Epigraphy and Palaeography," *JAIH*, 4 (1-2), Calcutta, 1970-71, 122.
34. *IA*, Volumes for 1932, 134.
35. *JBORS*, 10 (1-2), 168-70.
36. *The Alphabet*, London, 1953, 287.
37. Tripathi, *EOLS*, 44.
38. Bühler, *op. cit.*, 95.
39. *Ibid.*, 94.

An approximate idea about the evolution of these Nepalese hooks through the stages enumerated by Bühler may be obtained by revisiting the head-marks as appeared in the inscriptions of the Somavaṁśis (*Pl.* X). The solid triangular head-mark of the *siddhamātṛkā* or the *kuṭila* script is either flattened or drawn as a perfect horizontal in the early inscriptions of Janmejaya I (AD 880-920). In his Chaudwar plates of 31st regnal year, the head-mark is seen in the form of a solid triangular wedge with an inward dip at the centre which is the same as Bühler's "thick top-strokes rounded off at both ends." The inverted hollow triangles are seen on the top of the letters in the Kalibhana plates of 34th regnal year of Janmejaya I. The same type of head formation is seen in a few records of Somavaṁśīs up to the time of Dharmaratha (AD 975-95). Later on the "small triangles with the rounded (or straight) lower side" are seen "attached to the left of the tops of various letters" as in the Maranja-Mara plates of Yayāti II (AD 1023-40). This is further modified into a simple horizontal joined to the left of some of the letters as in the Nuapatana plates of the time of Janmejaya II (AD 1065-80) or the so-called "Nepalese hook" as appeared in the Ratnagiri plates of the last Somavaṁśī ruler Karṇadeva (AD 1100-13). Thus the Somavaṁśī records furnish a true index of development of these "Nepalese hooks" from the hollow triangle. Given this index and chronology, it would not be wrong to infer that Orissa is the palaeographical zone where the hook originated and later on it, travelled to Bengal and Nepal. It is probably for this reason the modern Bengali has discarded this hook while it has been preserved in Oriya and has contributed significantly to the development of the horizontal top *mātrā* into a top curve.

The formation of a tick or triangle in the lower extremity of the initial *a* and *ā* is seen as early as the ninth-tenth century (vide *Pl.* IXa.1, *Pl.* Xa.3). In Bengal it is used in the inscriptions of Lakṣmaṇasena belonging to the later part of the twelfth century. The proto-Bengali *i* with a definite right upright is never found used in Orissa. The left-facing curve type of *u* is common to proto-Nāgarī and its off-shoots in a wide area of north India. The Orissa Museum plates of Neṭṭabhañja (AD 949) display one of the earliest examples of the opening of *e*. Later on from the closing decades of the tenth century the letter-form is popularized in the records of the Gaṅgas and their feudatories (*Pl.* XIIa.7-10). The triangular type of the medial *u* appeared optionally in the Somavaṁśī charters as early as the beginning of the tenth century.

Among the consonants, the letter-forms of *kha*, *ga* and *śa* have rounded tops in general. Unlike the proto-Bengali form of a hook or curve at the bottom of the left limb of these letters, in the Orissan inscriptions of the ninth-eleventh centuries a horizontal tick or triangular or circular loop is noticed. The last known feature is continued even in the subsequent centuries along with other feature of slight opening of this loop. Further opening of the loop in the right arm of *kha* and shifting it to the top, which is claimed as proto-Bengali peculiarity, has occurred in the inscriptions of Orissa, long before its advent in those of Bengali. The letter-form in the Patna plates of Yayāti I of 28th regnal year (*Pl.* Xa.4) and the Chicacole plates of Madhukāmārṇava of AD 1024 (*Pl.* XIIa.8) closely resemble to the Oriya *kha*. The *ja* of the Banagarh grant which has been claimed as resembling to its modern Bengali form has appeared at least a century earlier in the records of Orissa (*Pl.* Xa.1). The left-facing curve type of *ta* appeared in the Nuapatana plates of the time of Janmejaya II, the date of which is earlier than the Deopara inscription of Vijayasena. The bipartite *tha* with closed loop on its left limb and a right upright appeared in the official charters of the Bhaumakaras and the Somavaṁśīs from the tenth century. The occurrence of this variety of *tha* in the records of Bengal points to a later date. The triangular type of *ra* is found used in the inscriptions of Orissa (*Pl.* Xb.3) at least two centuries prior to its use in Bengal in the twelfth century. Another proto-Bengali feature of shortening of the outer curve of *ka* and the left arm of *ṇa* and *la* is not favoured in the inscriptions of Orissa.

The above comparison fairly establishes that the prominent features of the proto-Bengali are already current in Orissa long before their occurrence in Bengal. The general consensus among the palaeographers is that the modern Oriya alphabet derived from the proto-Bengali appears to be erroneous, misleading and unconvincing. On the other hand, the process of palaeographical development in Orissa between the ninth and eleventh centuries does not deny the fact that Bengal received most of the important features of its proto-regional script from the proto-Nāgarī script of Orissa. The script has been rightly dubbed as proto-Nāgarī because the process of the formation of the hook continued throughout the period and appeared until the closing decades of the eleventh century and excepting the head-marks, the essential characters of the letter-forms largely conform to their respective proto-Nāgarī counterparts. Moreover, the scribes under the Somavaṁśīs time to time tried to experiment with certain innovations in the sphere of head formation and letter-forms, and thus, the script appears to be unconventional. But the scribes of other localities by and large followed the proto-Nāgarī alphabet during the same period. Judging from the cursive engraving of some of the Somavaṁśī and Eastern Gaṅga records which rendered a few letters like *kha, ga, tha, pa, pha, śa,* etc., resemble to their respective modern Oriya forms, one may tempt to label the script as proto-Oriya, and trace its advent as early as the beginning of the tenth cenuty (in the inscriptions of the Somavaṁśī Janmejaya I and Yayāti I). But except for a few, the essential characters of rest of the letters can clearly be recognized as proto-Nāgarī. The hook, which is so prominently applied to the proto-regional characters, has not developed as yet. The medial vowels are also as usual. It is, therefore, legitimate to conclude that the script as used in the records of the Somavaṁśīs is proto-Nāgarī and that proto-regional characters are essentially a derivative of the proto-Nāgarī script of Orissa of the ninth-eleventh centuries. While the application of ticks or triangles on the lower extremity of *a* and *ā*, the joining of the loops of *i* by a wavy line, the opening of *e*, and the shifting of the horizontal mid-bar of the proto-Nāgarī *ja* to the left are local mannerisms incorporated into the existing proto-Nāgarī script, the rounded top of *kha, ga* and *śa,* and the left-facing curve type of *ta* can be attributed to the extreme cursive engraving that was prevalent in Eastern Gaṅga grants of the same period. Since the local mannerisms as well as the cursive letter-forms as mentioned above are peculiar to the proto-Bengali, the conclusion that the proto-Nāgarī is the parent of the proto-regional scripts of eastern

India holds good even for the advent of proto-Bengali. Thus, the proto-Nāgarī is the common parent of the proto-regional characters of Orissa and Bengal, and both the scripts took their birth in the latter part of the eleventh or beginning of the twelfth century. Moreover, it is perceptible that the proto-Bengali received some impingement from the proto-Oriya source. The instant occurrence of some of the features in the Deopara inscription of Vijayasenā cannot be otherwise explained satisfactorily. The triangular type of *ra* may be one such a case in point. Possibly that is the reason why the hook is so short-lived in the proto-Bengali and finally discarded in the Bengali while it is retained in the proto-Oriya and subsequently contributed to the formation of top curves of the letters, which distinguishes it from the rest of the regional scripts derived from the proto-Nāgarī.

The process of development of a proto-regional script in a definite linguistic segment very much depended on the language medium. In other words, the scriptal development is closely connected with the language medium. Once this undercurrent is noticed, it is easy to appreciate the process and attribute to its slower development, if any. Oriya, as the epigraphical media, for the first time appeared in the Urajam inscription of Ś. 963 (AD 1041). But the influence of this vernacular on Sanskrit epigraphic composition is noticed much before its adoption as the epigraphical media in the middle of the eleventh century. The influence of the vernacular on the inscriptional Sanskrit texts is noticed particularly in the grant portions of the charters. It took nearly three-four centuries of the earliest use of the regional dialects in the midst of inscriptional Sanskrit to draft a record entirely in the vernacular. In spite of its appearance as the epigraphical media, the vernacular could not totally replace the Sanskrit for another few centuries. The copper-plate grants of the Imperial Gaṅgas and their contemporaries are by and large written in Sanskrit language while the stone inscriptions written by the private individuals, officials, etc., are in Oriya language. Like the language, the proto-regional script of Orissa took the field from the closing decades of the eleventh century. The increasing occurrence of the regional features drifted it away from the proto-Nāgarī by this time and finally it developed into an easily identifiable regional script. The process through which the regional features contributed to the formation of a regional script of Orissa has been called here as the proto-Oriya. Unlike the other proto-regional scripts, the proto-Oriya was prevalent for more than three hundred years, roughly from the closing decades of the eleventh century to the beginning of the fifteenth century, and, therefore, the advent of the modern Oriya alphabet is delayed by a couple of centuries.

There is an increasing incidence of the proto-Oriya features in the inscriptions of the later Somavaṁśīs and their contemporaries belonging to the later part of the eleventh and commencement of the twelfth century. The Nuapatana plates of the time of Somavaṁśī Jammejaya II display certain peculiar traits, which can aplty be considered as the beginning of the proto-regional characters of Orissa. The line head-mark attached to the top left of the letters; the inward dip in the left limb of *pa, pha, ya, ṣa* consequent upon the use of the hooked top stroke; the semi-circular type of the medial *i*; etc., are decidedly proto-Oriya characteristics. But we preferred to include it in the proto-Nāgarī script (*Pl.* X.10) chiefly with an intention to establish that the script of this record is a logical evolution from those used in the charters of the Somavaṁśīs. Of course, the medial *i* is an import from the southern sources through Kaliṅga. The proto-Oriya features are more pronounced in the Ratnagiri plates of the last Somavaṁśī ruler Karṇadeva. The hollow triangle and the hook are prominently applied to the top of the letters. The application of the hook to *gha, pa, pha, ya, ṣa, sa, kṣa,* etc., led to an inward dip at the centre of the left limb of these letters. Inital *a, ā, i, u* and the consonants *kha, ga, ṭa, ta, tha, ra, śa* can aptly be called as proto-Oriya. *A* and *ā* have hooks on their top, *i* has joined its arms with the circles, *u* is rounded; *kha, ga* and *śa* have rounded tops and loops on the left limb; *ṭa* is rounded; *ta* is of left-facing curve type; *tha* has retained its earlier form and devoid of any head-mark; and *ra* is of triangular type.

The Kamalpur grant of Jayārṇava is also written in the proto-Oriya. But the proto-Oriya features are not so prominent, except the initial *i,* the consonants *kha, ga, ja, pa, pha, ya, sa,* and medial *i.* Both the Ratnagiri and the Kamalpur plates belong to the same age. But judging from the characters of these two records, one can easily perceive that while the former is written in an ornate style, the latter is in a simplified script and display some archaism, especially in the application of the head-marks. In this connection, the observation of K.V. Ramesh appears to be more convincing. According to him, "a carefully written epigraph and a contemporaneous and carelessly written inscription, when compared with each other, bring to light many palaeographical incompatibilities which would be convincingly explained away only in the light of relativity between urban and rural palaeography."[40] Karṇadeva ruled over north Orissa with his capital at Yayātinagar (Jājpur in Cuttack district), which was not only the political headquarters of Orissa for several centuries but also an important centre of Orissa's socio-cultural activities. It is no wonder, therefore, that the palaeography of the Ratnagiri plates exhibit an urban strain and much developed of its age. But Jayārṇava was a feudatory under Karṇadeva and ruled over Koleḍā-maṇḍala with its centre at Koleḍā identified with Kulada (near Bhajanagar in the Ganjam distirct) which is not known hitherto from any other inscription. The archaism of the characters of the Kamalpur charter of Jayārṇava can be attributed to the rural strain of palaeography. The Sonepur plates of Kumāra Someśvara, who was belonging to a line of the Somavamśī family, are also written in proto-Oriya. He was a contemporary of the latter members of the Somavaṁśī family and was ruling from Suvarṇapura (modern Sonepur). After Someśvara, the Sambalpur-Sonepur tract was ruled by the Telugu-Coḍas with their capital at Suvarṇapura. Like the plates of Someśvara, the characters of the Telugu-Coḍas are also written in the proto-Oriya script. Although the hook is not so frequently seen, yet certain letters like *kha, ga, tha, pa, pha, ṣa, kṣa,* etc., have rounded tops. The occasional rounding of the top of *ma, ra, va,* etc., is significant for the evolution of their respective regional forms. The medial *i* is a semi-circle on most occasions. The medial *e* is indicated by a side stroke or curve. Unlike the other proto-

40. *Indian Epigraphy*, I, Delhi, 1984, 61-62.

regional derivatives from the proto-Nāgarī, the proto-Oriya retained the archaic form of *tha* with a simple circle. The subscript *ta* has already assumed its modern Oriya form in these records. In this context it may be said that the Somavaṁśīs who had earlier ruled over South Kośala with their political headquarters at Suvarṇapura later on subjugated Utkala and ruled from Yayātinagar. Suvarṇapura became a secondary capital of the Somavaṁśīs and the importance of the place as a centre of political and cultural activities did not diminish even after their rule. Like Yayātinagar, the scribes (under Kumāra Someśvara and the Telugu-Coḍas) at Suvarṇapura introduced certain local mannerisms which contributed significantly to the advent of the proto-regional characters.

The palaeography of some of the records of the later Bhañjas is an important step in the development of the Oriya script. The characters of the Adipur plate of Durjayabhañja, the Jurada plates of Neṭṭabhañja, the Baud plates of Saloṇabhañja, the Antirigam plates of Yaśabhañja and the Antirigam plates of Jayabhañja are a further development from those of the Telugu-Coḍas of the Baud-Sonepur tract. Yaśabhañja and Jayabhañja were contemporaries of Gaṅga King Anaṅgabhīmadeva III (AD 1211-28). Palaeographically all these charters can be assigned to a period between the eleventh and thirteenth centuries. The characters of the plates of Saloṇabhañja and Jayabhañja are decidedly more advanced compared to the other charters. The plates referred to above are scattered over a wide area and they aptly demonstrate that the proto-regional characters were gaining popularity among the people in the smaller kingdoms ruled by the local chiefs. In these plates (except in the case of the Antirigam plates of Yaśabhañja), the so-called "Nepalese hook" is tending to form a shallow curve on the top of the letters. The angle of the hook on the left is changed into a gentle curve and thereby making most of the letters such as *ka, ca, da, pa, pha, ya, ra, la, va, ṣa, ha, kṣa*, etc., come closer to the Oriya alphabet. The letter-forms of *kha, ga* and *śa*, look like their respective modern Oriya forms. The letter-forms of *cha, ja, ṭa, ḍa, ta, tha, bha*, etc., are of proto-Oriya type. Among the other proto-Oriya peculiarities mention may be made of the medial *i* denoted by a semi-circle or curve, and *e* by a side stroke. On most occasions the letter *na* is indicated by a circular loop drawn separately to the left of the right upright. In the Antirigam plates of Yaśabhañja, the hooked head-mark with angles on the left are still retained. On some of the letters like *na, la, va*, etc., the head-mark is denoted by a simple line joined to the top of the letters. The letter-form of *ta* has a definite loop on the left and the letter is drawn in one action. Unlike the other plates of the period, the loop of *na* is joined to the right upright as in Nāgarī. Compared to these, the Baud plates of Kanakabhañja are written in a separate style. With the exception of *ra*, the rest of the letters closely resemble to the proto-Nāgarī or Nāgarī script. They are also very carelessly engraved.

In contrast to these advances in the palaeography of the inscriptions of northern and western Orissa, the records of the Gaṅgas of Kaliṅga in southern Orissa, exhibit a slower scriptal development. Rājarāja I (AD 1070-77) and Anantavarman Coḍagaṅgadeva (AD 1077-1147) continued the existing style of writing of Kaliṅga. There is no marked difference between the palaeography of the plates of Vajrahasta III, and that of Rājarāja I and Coḍagaṅgadeva, except that the tail is getting more prominent and the mid-stem connecting the head-mark above and the essential character below is tending to slope to the left. These features are admittedly due to the influence from the Somavaṁśī charters and they made the script come closer to the proto-Oriya. But the essential characters of most of the letters except *a, ā, e, ja* and *na* (optionally) are seen in the proto-Nāgarī script of Kaliṅga in the preceding century. It may be noted here that the same set of officials (*sāndhivigrahī* Dāmodara son of *mahākāyastha sāndhivigrahī* Māvuraya, and *akṣaśāli* Vallemoju, son of Numkamoju) who caused to have the drafted and engraved the plates of Vajrahasta III from Ś. 971 (AD 1049) was also instrumental in preparing the official documents of Coḍagaṅgadeva at least up to Ś. 1007 (AD 1085). The plates of Vajrahasta III have been grouped under the proto-Nāgarī script and as such there is reason to class the alphabet of the record of his successors under the same script. The editors of all these plates have rightly remarked that their characters belong to the old Nāgarī or south Indian Nāgarī script. However, there is a strong preference for cursive engraving. This is mainly perceptible in the tails and the sloping of the mid-stems of the letters. The palaeography of Phulasara plates of Kīrttirājadeva, a member of the collateral line of the Imperial Gaṅgas, closely resemble to the plates of Coḍagaṅgadeva (except that *ra* is of triangular type and the loop of *na* is scooped out). However, these peculiarities are very much short-lived in Gaṅga grants and roughly from the middle of the twelfth century they are not favoured at all. In the recently discovered Chaudwar plates of Kāmārṇava of AD 1147-48 as well as the Polasara plates of Arkeśvaradeva of *Kali* year 4248 (AD 1147-48), these peculiarities are dropped, and their characters closely resemble to the Nāgarī with a sprinkling of proto-Oriya features. The proto-Oriya features are mainly traceable in the occasional use of the hooked head-mark, the initials like *a, ā, i* and *e*; the consonants like *kha, ga, ta, pa, pha, ya, ra, ṣa, śa, ha* and *kṣa*; and in the semi-circular type of the medial *i* and the *pṛṣṭha-mātrā* type of the medial *e*. The letter-forms of *ka, gha, ḍa, ṇa, da, na, ma, la, va*, etc., resemble to their modern Nāgarī forms. In the Polasara plates of Arkeśvaradeva, the letters like, *ka, kha, ta, dha, ma*, etc., have more than one form. Moreover, the letter *ka* has dropped its loop mostly when it is a superscript, *kha* has not opened up its loop on the left, *ta* has developed a loop, *dha* has a slanting stroke on the top left, the line head-mark of *ma* does not join the right upright. Some of these peculiarities, especially the above varieties of the letters like *ka, ta* and *dha* are not met with in the epigraphs of Bengal at this time and their occurrence point to a slightly later date, say the later half of the twelfth century.

The same duct of writing continued even in the Dasgoba plates of Rājarāja III of AD 1198 and in the plates of Anaṅgabhīmadeva III. The characters of all these records are written in a uniform style. The head-marks are denoted by flat tops, but the hook is seen in *gha, pa, pha, ya, ṣa, kṣa*, etc., where the angle is slightly rounded. The forms of these letters as well as the initials *i, e* and the consonants *kha, ga, ṭha, ta, tha, dha, ra*, etc., belong to the proto-Oriya. The forms of the rest of the letters are the same as used in the proto-Nāgarī script of the preceding centuries.

Almost all the medials except *u* are of Nāgarī type. The medial *u* is an angle open to the left. In the Nagari plates of Anaṅgabhīmadeva III, optionally the medial *i* is indicated by a semi-circle. Thus the characters of all these Gaṅga grants up to the reign of Anaṅgabhīmadeva III are of Nāgarī/proto-Nāgarī with an admixture of proto-regional features of Orissa. The opinion of Sircar that they belonged to the proto-Bengali script is, therefore, not tenable.

The palaeography of the plates of Narasiṁha II (AD 1278-1306) and Bhānudeva II (AD 1306-28) display an altogether different look. The hook is uniformly applied throughout. The tails which have been discarded in the latter part of the eleventh century appeared again. The letter-forms of the initial *a* and the consonants *ka* (optionally), *ta*, *na* (optionally) with a dot on the left, the type of *ma* with its loop suppressed and its left arm curving to the left, the type of *kṣa* with its right upright turning to be a curve, and the medial *u* drawn like a small down-facing curve are not seen earlier. The hook is common to both proto-Bengali and proto-Oriya. But the rest of the peculiarities referred to above including the tails are undoubtedly due to an impingement from the proto-Bengali or Bengali source. Some of these features are very much current in the inscriptions of Bengal of the latter part of the twelfth and thirteenth century and also in the manuscripts of Bengal of the thirteenth century. While the tail is dropped in the records of Orissa after the eleventh century, it is retained in the inscriptions of the Senas belonging to the twelfth century and in the manuscripts of Bengal of thirteenth century. The dot on the left of *a*, *ta*, is due to the confusion for the loop at the junction of the hooked head-mark and the curve below. The looped *ta* is traceable in the Polasara plates of Arkeśvaradeva and the Antirigam plates of Yaśabhañja. The loops of *ka*, *na* and *kṣa* often drawn separately in the proto-Bengali are also engraved as dots. The letters *ma* and *kṣa* as appeared in these inscriptions are very similar to those of the modern Bengali. The medial *u* with a down-facing curve is also an import from the same source. The forms of the rest of the letters are so common to proto-Oriya and proto-Bengali that it becomes difficult to group them under any particular palaeographical zone. At any rate, the scribes in the court of Narasiṁha II and Bhānudeva II came under the influence of the proto-Bengali script and introduced certain features peculiar to Bengal. In the official documents of these rulers issued between Ś. 1215 (AD 1293) and Ś. 1234 (AD 1312) there is a strong influence from the proto-regional characters of Bengal. In general appearance, they therefore, differ from the rest of the plates of the Imperial Gaṅgas. However, these influences are very much short-lived and restricted to the time frame noted above, and in the subsequent charters, the Bengali features are gradually given up. In the Kaijang plates of Bhānudeva II of Ś. 1284 (AD 1362) although the hooked head-mark is applied and the tails are still visible, yet there is no trace of the dot to the left of *a*, *ka*, *ta*, *ma* and *kṣa*.

In the case of *ka* and *ra* the loops are often seen drawn separately. The letter-form of *ma* is of proto-Bengali type. But the letter-forms of *i*, *da*, *dha*, *ha*, *kṣa*, as well as conjunct *ṅka*, are distinctly the Oriya type. The characters of the Kaijang plates are an admixture of the proto-regional characters of Bengal and Orissa. Thus, if at all there is any impingement from the proto-Bengali/

Bengali source, it first made its way into Orissa in the latter part of the thirteenth century. It will be shown below that by this time the proto-Oriya script had developed almost independent in the inscriptions of Orissa for more than a couple of centuries and some of its peculiarities distinguished it from the other proto-regional or regional characters.

In this connection, it is profitable to compare the characters of the reverse side of the second plate of the first set of Kendupatana plates of Narasiṁhadeva II of Ś. 1217 (AD 1296) which is written in the proto-Oriya script with the characters of the rest of the inscribed plates of the same set. The shallow top curves applied to the letters like *ka, gha, ca, ja, ṭa, ḍa, ḍha, ta, da, na, pa, pha, bha, ma, ya, ra, la, va, ṣa, ha,* etc., have already rendered the script to come closer to the Oriya. The letter-forms of *na* and *ma* deserve special mention since they are easily recognized as belonging to modern Oriya. There is no trace of the dots in place of the loops of *a, ka, ta, na* and *kṣa*. But the varieties of the medial *u* and the letter-form of *ma* (optionally) and *kṣa* still remind us of the proto-Bengali influence. On the whole it appears that the reverse side of the second plate is written by a separate hand who was more acquainted with the proto-Oriya than with the proto-Bengali script current then.

The characters of the Kenduli and Sankarananda Math plates of Narasiṁhadeva IV of Ś. 1305 (AD 1384) and Ś. 1316 (AD 1394) respectively are written in the Nāgarī script. The hooks are no longer found used and they are replaced by the horizontal top strokes. At times the stroke is joined to the top left of the letters. Head-marks are also seen joined to *ṭa, tha* and *dha*. The test letters *ka, kha, ga, ja, jha, ṭa, ta, tha, na, pa, pha, la, va, ṣa, sa,* etc., can clearly be recognized as Nāgarī. The medial *e* is indicated by a top stroke. This along with the other medials also belong to the Nāgarī script. The initial *i, u* and *e* and the consonants *gha, ṭha,* etc., are of proto-Oriya type while the letter-form of *ma* (optionally) is of proto-Bengali type. The palatal and dental sibilants are denoted by the form of the latter.

So far as the stone inscriptions of time of the Imperial Gaṅgas are concerned they offer a true index of the development of Oriya script. The inscriptions belonging to the reign of Anantavarman Coḍagaṅgadeva found from Mt. Mahendra, Tekkali, Bobbili, Arsavalli, Mukhalingam, Srikurmam, Draksaram and Sarpavaram are written in Telugu or Sanskrit language and Telugu script. Whereas most of the inscriptions belonging to the twelfth century found from the Oriya-speaking tract of this empire such as Puri, Khillor, Algaum, Mukteśvar and Bhubaneswar are written in Sanskrit language and in the proto-Oriya script. The script can aptly be labelled as proto-Oriya because by this time the regional features drifted away from the proto-Nāgarī or Nāgarī. Although the simple line head-mark is still retained optionally, the hooked head formation is more regularly used in these inscriptions. Sometimes the hook is indicated by a shallow curve. This is particularly true in the case of the Jagannāth (Puri), Kedāreśvara (Bhubaneswar) and the Algaum (Puri) temple inscriptions.

The letter-forms of *kha, ga, pa, ya* and *śa* are more rounded and are closely akin to their respective modern Oriya forms. The initial *a, i, e;* the consonants *ka, ca, ḍha, ta, da, ma, ra, va, ha,* and the conjunct *ñca* are decidedly of the proto-Oriya type. The triangular form of the letter *ra* has developed a tail. One possible reason for such development is that the triangular form of *ra* resembled to that of *ca* and that the scribe joined a tail to the former with an intention of distinguishing it from the latter. The medial *i* is often denoted by a semi-circle on the top and the *e* always by a side stroke. The *visarga,* indicated by two loops drawn in one action, is still current in modern Oriya. The same style of writing continued in the inscriptions of the sons of Coḍagaṅgadeva who ruled over the Orissan empire in the latter half of the twelfth century. Of these, the Liṅgarāja temple inscription of the time of Rājarājadeva of Ś. 1049 (AD 1172) display some important proto-Oriya peculiarities. The shallow top curves on *ja, da, va, ma, sa;* the medials *i, e, o, ai;* and the subscripts *ḍa, ta, ṇa* are interesting to note.

The Megheśvara temple inscription of Svapenśvardeva of the time of Anaṅgabhīma II (AD 1194-98) and the eulogy of Bhaṭṭa Bhavadeva are written in ordinary Nāgarī script. The Cāṭeśvara temple inscription of the time of Anaṅgabhīma III (AD 1211-38) is also written in the same script. But in his record the head-marks are indicated either by simple lines as in Nāgarī or by scooped out triangles or hooks as in proto-Bengali. Except in the case of *kha, ga, ta, ra, śa,* etc., the essential characters of the rest of the letters closely resemble to the proto-Nāgarī forms of the preceding centuries or the Nāgarī as current in the northern India in the twelfth-thirteenth centuries.

Among the thirteenth-century stone inscription of Orissa mention may be made of the Puri and Bhubaneswar inscriptions of the time of Anaṅgabhīmadeva III (AD 1211-38), the Bhubaneswar, Kapilas and Mukhalingam inscription of the time of Narasiṁhadeva I (AD 1238-64) and the Bhubaneswar and Sonepur inscription of the time of Bhānudeva I (AD 1264-78). All these inscriptions are written in the proto-Oriya script. It is pertinent to note here that since the time of Narasiṁhadeva I, some of the inscriptions are written in Oriya language and proto-Oriya script. The Kapilas (Śikhareśvara) temple inscriptions and the Bhubaneswar bi-lingual inscription of the time of Narasiṁhadeva I, and the Sonepur inscription of the time of Bhānudeva I are some of the examples of this category. Apart from the proto-regional peculiarities of the preceding century, the other features evolved in this century are : (a) the initial *i* with its loops drawn in one action, (b) the initial *u* has optionally developed a tail, (c) the inward curl in the left limb of *ṇa,* (d) the slanting stroke joined to the top left of *dha,* (e) the opening of the loop of *na,* (f) the shifting of the horizontal bar of *ma* to the left, (g) the tailed *ra,* (h) the round topped *kṣa,* (i) the looped variety of the medial *e* with its bottom curling in. But an interesting point of palaeography of this century is the occurrence of two distinct signs for the letters *ḷa* and *la*. The regular *la* of the proto-Nāgarī is now used for the retroflex *ḷa* while the liquid *la* is distinguished from the retroflex *ḷa* by the addition of a diacritical mark. The Kapilas inscription of Narasiṁhadeva I offer the earliest example of this distinction between the two letters. But the rare use of the

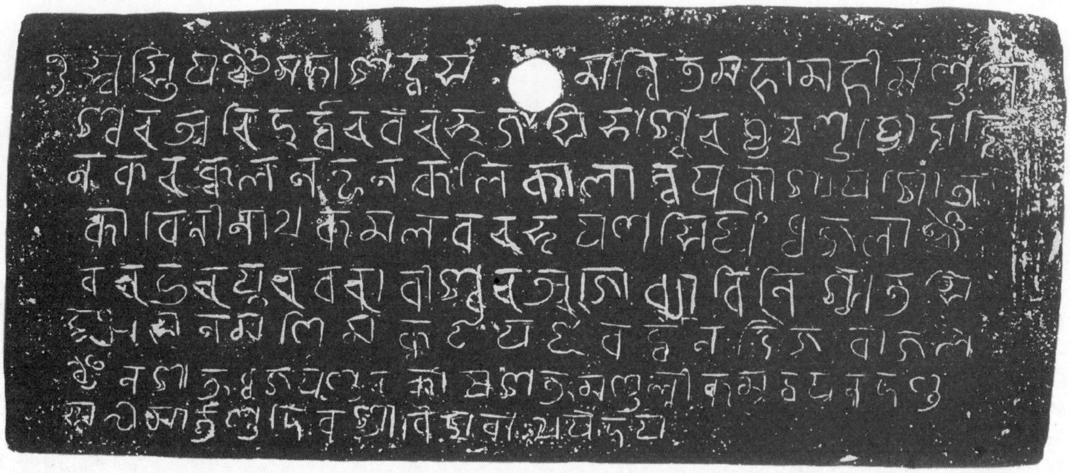

Photo 10.1 (a): Mahada plates of Yogeśvardevavarman (i)

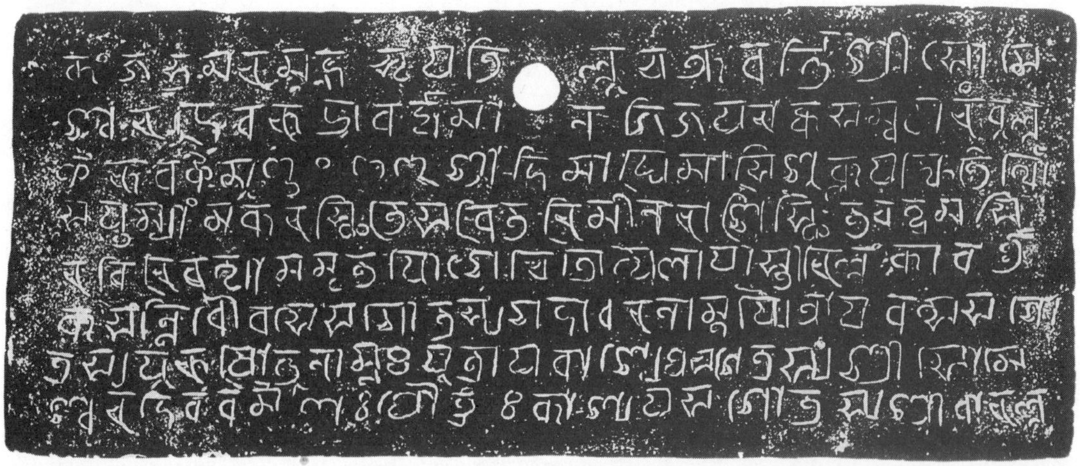

Photo 10.1 (b): Mahada plates of Yogeśvardevavarman (ii a)

Photo 10.1 (c): Mahada plates of Yogeśvardevavarman (ii b)

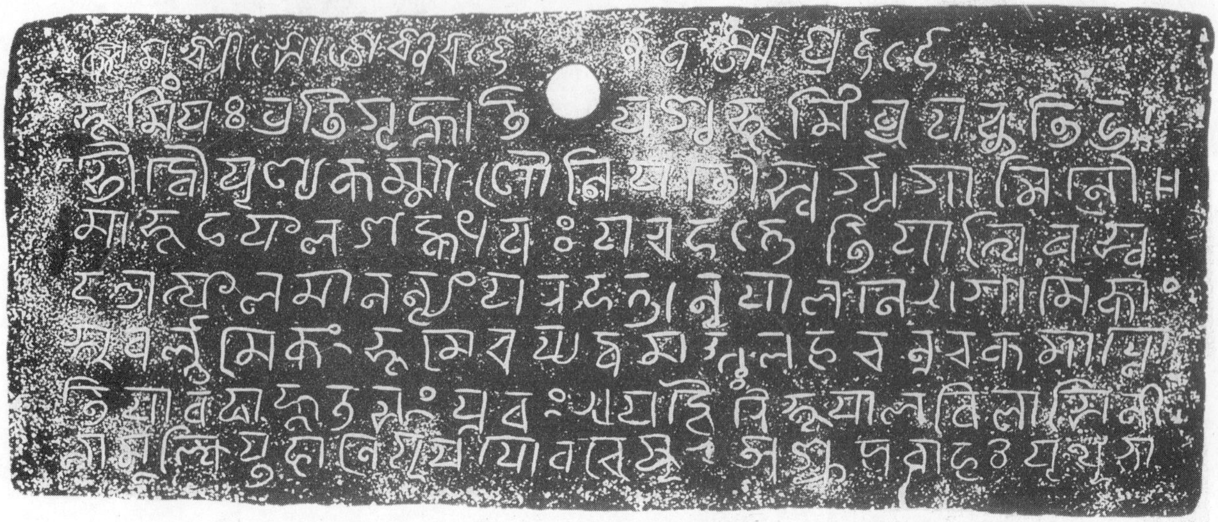

Photo 10.1 (d): Mahada plates of Yogeśvardevavarman (iii a)

Photo 10.1 (e): Mahada plates of Yogeśvardevavarman (iii b)

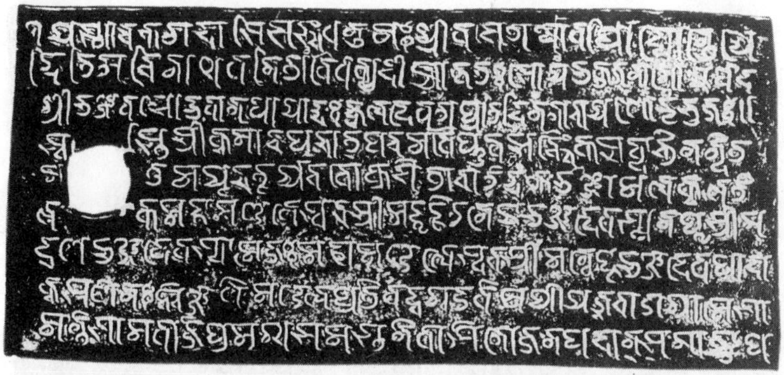

Photo 10.2 (a): Jurada plates of Neṭṭabhañja-deva (i)

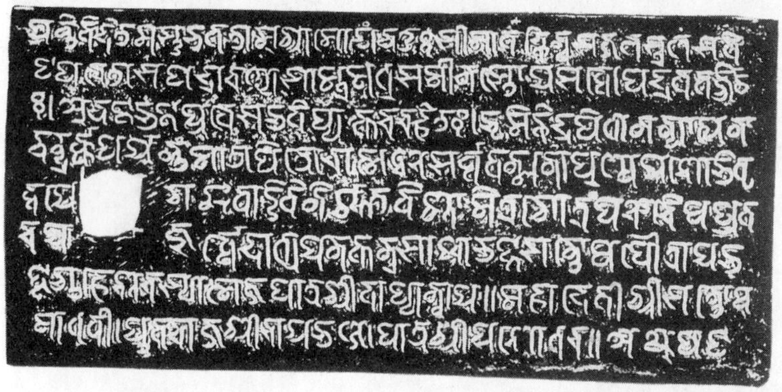

Photo 10.2 (b): Jurada plates of Neṭṭabhañja-deva (ii a)

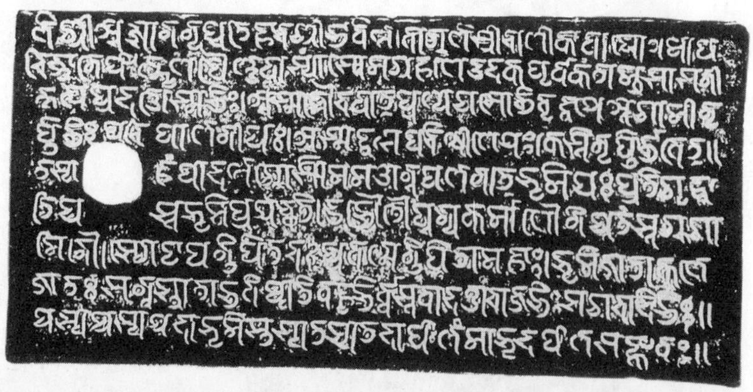

Photo 10.2 (c): Jurada plates of Neṭṭabhañja-deva (ii b)

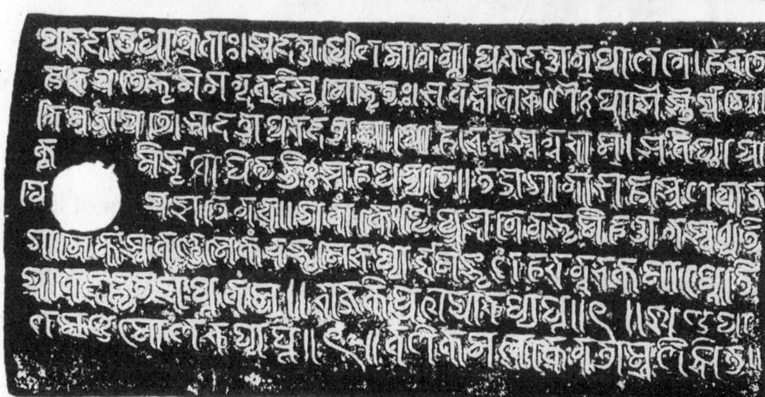

Photo 10.2 (d): Jurada plates of Neṭṭabhañja-deva (iii)

Photo 10.3: Patteśvara temple inscription of Bhānudeva III, Yugābda 4477.

diacritically marked form in the earlier epigraphs suggests the possibility of its standing for *ḷa*. Sircar has rightly pointed out,

> The rare use of the letter in the earlier epigraphs suggests the possibility of its standing for *ḷ*. Otherwise we will have to suppose that it was *ḷ* which was very rarely employed and this seems to be very unlikely especially in view of the fact that the simpler form of the letter stands for *l*, in the other cognate alphabets. It therefore appears to us that originally the diacritical mark was used as the distinguishing sign of *ḷ* but that, at a later date, it came to be generally applied to *l* instead of *ḷ* through confusion.[41]

The fourteenth-century stone inscriptions of Orissa form an important stage in the development of the Oriya script. It is during this period most of the letters of the Oriya alphabet are standardized. The Koṇārka temple inscription, the Paṭṭeśvara (Pottangi, Ganjam district) temple inscription of Bhānudeva III of *Kali* year 4477 (AD 1376) and the Siddheśvara (Jajpur) temple inscription of Narasiṁhadeva IV of *aṅka* 19 (AD 1394) belong to this century while the date of the Narasiṁhanātha (Sambalpur district) temple inscription is fixed at AD 1413. Judging from the characters of these inscriptions it is legitimate to believe that the Paṭṭeśvara temple inscription is the earliest epigraph written in the Oriya script. In this epigraph as well as in the Siddheśvar and Narasimhanatha temple inscriptions the shallow curves are more rounded especially in the case of *u, ka, ca, ja, ḍa, ḍha, ta, da, bha, ḷa, la, va, ha,* etc., and the modern Oriya forms of *a, ā, dha, na, ma, na* (optionally), *sa*, etc., are evolved out of the proto-Oriya. The Oriya forms of these letters are an important addition to the existing Oriya peculiarities current then. The guttural nasal *ṅa* in conjunction with the letters of its class is denoted by a sign resembling to the *anusvāra*. The medial *i* and *ī* are often drawn in continuation with the upper curve of the letters, the medial *u* is looped, and the medial *e* has a definite loop at its bottom as in modern Oriya. Thus, in the characters of the Paṭṭeśvara inscription we come across the true beginning of the modern Oriya script. But we prefer to group this script along with that of the Siddheśvar and Narasiṁhanātha inscriptions under proto-Oriya script on the grounds that the tail of *u* is not uniformly used and that of *i* and *bha* is not yet applied; that the letter-form of *ja, ṭa, ḍa, ta,* etc., are yet to develop their respective Oriya forms; and that the distinction between the palatal semi-vowel *ya* and *ẏa* (pronounced as *ja*) which is peculiar to Oriya alone is yet to appear during this period.

There are a few stone inscriptions of the time of the Imperial Gaṅgas which are written in Oriya language but in Telugu script. They are mostly found in the Telugu-speaking tract of the Gaṅga empire. The trend began roughly from the latter half of the thirteenth century and continued through the fourteenth and fifteenth centuries. Besides, one of the Kūrmeśvar temple inscriptions is written in Oriya language and Nāgarī script. However, palaeographically they have no bearing on the evolution of the regional script of Orissa.

41. *EI*, 33, 41-42.

fig. **I: Head-Marks in the Proto-Oriya Script**

Thus, without fear of contradiction it can be maintained that the proto-Oriya evolved out of the proto-Nāgarī sometime in the latter half of the eleventh century. In the copper-plate grants of the later Somavaṁśīs, the Telugu-Coḍas, the Bhañjas of Baud, Ganjam and Mayurbhanj (all belonging to the eleventh-thirteenth centuries), the proto-regional features are more pronounced compared to those of the Imperial Gaṅgas. Even in the lithic records one can come across a true index of development of the Oriya script. In plate XV, the characters in the copper plate grants of all the ruling houses mentioned above have been reproduced while in plate XVI, the palaeographical features in the stone inscriptions of the period have been illustrated.

The spatio-chronological distribution of the stone inscriptions written in regional language and script reflects that they are mostly located outside the political and cultural base of the Gaṅgas and in the religious centres (like Bhubaneswar, Jajpur, Kapilas, Sonepur, Narasimhanatha, Pottangi and Mukhalingam) scattered over a wide area. That they are the works of small chieftains, subordinate officers working in the periphery of the empire and of the

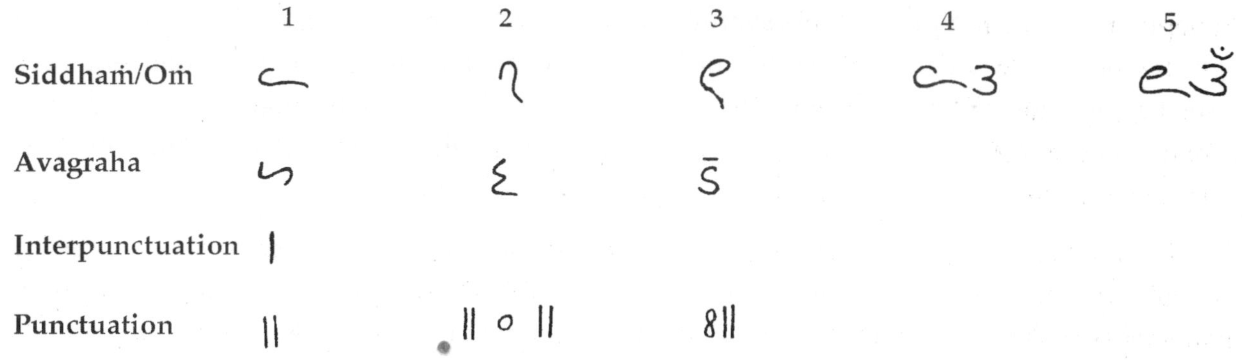

fig. II

ordinary citizens is evidenced by the official designations, personal names and nature of gifts mentioned in the texts. In protest against the language medium and script of the official charters of the Gaṅgas, these agents residing away from the political and cultural centres, braved to experiment with the vernacular and its script. This linguistic movement was basically a resurgence movement projecting the social aspirations of the Oriyas for a separate identity. The agents instrumental in generating the movement made sporadic and isolated efforts from the thirteenth century. But within a couple of centuries the movement graduated and encompassed a larger social space. Among many other factors, the apathy and indifference of the Gaṅga monarchs (who came from the Telugu-speaking tract) towards the language and scripts of the Oriyas largely contributed to this challenge. Instead of giving due recognition to Oriya as the epigraphic medium, they promoted the cause of Telugu and thereby consciously or unconsciously instigated a conflict between the Telugus and the Oriyas. The numerical superiority of the Telugu inscriptions and the engraving of some of the temple inscriptions of Simhancalam and Srikurmam in Oriya language and Telugu script in the latter part of the fourteenth and early fifteenth century can possibly be viewed in the perspective of such a conflict. It was Narasiṁhadeva IV who made an attempt to settle the conflict by allowing Oriya as the epigraphic medium and Telugu as the script. This "compromise formula" might have temporarily settled the language conflict in the Telugu-speaking tract but in the Oriya-speaking tract, the subjects led by many chieftains, royal officers and others continued the struggle and accelerated the pace of disintegration of the Gaṅga empire. Kapilendradeva's usurpation to the throne of Orissa in AD 1435 is a culmination of not only the language movement of the Oriyas but also the fulfilment of their political and social aspirations. The above construction about the slower scriptal (proto-regional) development in Orissa holds good and appears to be more plausible.

The simple line head-mark of the preceding script is now replaced by the angular hook. The hook itself is a modification of the hollow inverted triangle. It is usually seen on the top of the letters. The letter-forms of *i, e, o, kha, ga, ṭa, ṭha, ṇa, tha, dha, śa,* etc., are devoid of the head-mark. The feature is optionally noticed in the plates of the Somavaṁśī Karṇadeva and his times. But it is regularly found used in the official charters of the Telugu-Coḍas and the Imperial Gaṅgas. In the Sonepur plates of Kumāra Someśvaradeva and in a few records of the later Bhañjas, the angle of the hook as well as the flat top of the head formation are rounded. Consequent upon these changes the head-marks resembled to shallow curves (*fig.* I). The shallow curve is more pronounced in the stone inscriptions of the thirteenth-fifteenth centuries. This peculiarity is an important step in the development of the rounded top of the letters.

Another important feature of the proto-Oriya is the strong preference for cursive engraving. The straight and angular portions are invariably rounded. It is very often conjectured that the peculiar shapes of the Oriya letters are due to the scratching of letters by an iron stylus on palm-leaves. According to Diringer,

> The talipot palm-leaves, which are long and narrow, were the only writing material in ancient Odra, as in other parts of the sea-coast provinces of southern India. The local scribes employing an iron stylus to scratch the letters were compelled to avoid straight lines, and particularly the characteristic horizontal *mātrā* of the Devanāgarī and of similar scripts. Indeed any scratch in the direction of the longitudinal fibre, running in the palm leaves from the stalk to the point, would split the palm leaf, which is excessively fragile. Thus, this gave rise to the rounded shapes of Oriya letters.[42]

The technical reasons for the peculiar shape of the Oriya letters may be partly true. Because K.B. Tripathi has recently come across a palm-leaf manuscript with an iron stylus in the Nāgarī script.[43] But more than that it appears that the political and cultural hegemony of the Gaṅgas and Gajapatis of Orissa over their south Indian neighbours, the Telugus and the Tamils, led the Oriyas to prefer and develop the cursive engraving. Almost all the Oriya-speaking tracts of Orissa and parts of the Telugu-speaking tracts of Andhra Pradesh were for long under one administrative system. As such the inspiration for cursive engraving came from their immediate southern neighbours, the Telugus. Apart from the cursive engraving some of the Telugu-Canarese numerals and a few of their medial signs which began to appear in the inscriptions of Orissa from the tenth/eleventh centuries later on became the standard Oriya numerals and medial signs. There is, therefore, reason to believe that although the proto-Oriya script is essentially derived from the proto-Nāgarī, it is strongly influenced by the cursive engraving of the Telugu and other south Indian scripts.

The horn-like protuberance on the right limb and the inward dip at the centre of the left limb of the letters are the other two important features of the Oriya script. While the first peculiarity is only optionally noticed in Oriya inscriptions of the fourteenth-fifteenth centuries, the second feature is almost regularly found used in the records of the period. The inward dip is seen in the letter-form of *ka, gha, ca, ja, ḍa, ḍha, ta, da, na, pa, pha, bha, ma, ya, ra, ḷa, la, va, ṣa, sa, ha* and *kṣa*. Although initially the left half of almost all these letter-forms is drawn in one action, later on with the rounding of the top curves the lower half is drawn first and then the upper

42. Diringer, *op. cit.*, 287-88.

43. *EOLS*, 45, n. 2.

half. This is particularly true in this case of *ka, gha, ja, ḍha, ta, da, na, pa, pha, ma, ya, ḷa, la, va, ṣa, sa, ha,* and *kṣa*.

As in the proto-Nāgarī script of the preceding centuries so also in the proto-Oriya script of the eleventh-thirteenth centuries, the auspicious symbol for *siddhaṁ* is either indicated by a right-facing or a down-facing curve. The sign for *oṁ* is occasionally drawn after the sign for *siddhaṁ* and it is the same as the initial *o* with or without a *candrabindu* on its top. The sign for *avagraha* is either a double-curve as in the Sonepur plates of Kumāra Someśvara (*fig*. II.1) or a double-curve opening to the right as in the Ratnagiri plates of Somavaṁśī Karṇa (*fig*. II.2). In the Algaum inscription of Coḍagaṅgadeva, the sign resembles the English capital letter S with a dash on its top (*fig*. II.3).

The interpunctuation and punctuation marks are usually represented by one and two vertical strokes respectively. In the Imperial Gaṅga grants sometimes the punctuation mark at the end of a verse is seen in the form of a small circle between two double *daṇḍa*s. In the Sonepur inscription of Bhānudeva I a *visarga* like sign is seen before the double *daṇḍa*.

The final forms of *ta, na* and *ma* are used in the inscriptions of the period. The most regular form of indicating the final forms of these letters is an addition of a *halanta* sign at the bottom. In another variety, the letter-forms are drawn without the head-mark. In addition to these, the final *m* is also denoted by a small circle with a *halanta* below it. All these peculiarities have already been noticed in the proto-Nāgarī script of the preceding centuries.

Vowels

Of the initial vowels, *a, ā, i, u, e* and *o* are found used in the inscriptions of the period. The letter-form of *a* is a left-facing curve joined to the right upright with or without having a triangular foot-mark. In course of time the line head-mark and the triangular foot-mark of the letter are turned into curves as in *Pl*. XVIa.2, 3. This is truly the precursor of the modern Oriya *a*. The Oriya *a* is obtained by turning up the left-facing curve and joining it to the upper curve as in *Pl*. XVIa.8. In this case the letter is written in one action. The letter *ā* is the same as *a* with an additional vertical on the right.

The initial *i* is represented by a doubly curved roof with its both ends joining to the circular loops below (*Pl*. XVIa.1, 2). Optionally the right arm of the curve slightly goes up (*Pl*. XVa.1, 6, 8). This variety further progressed in the direction of joining of the loops and lifting up of the right arm of the curve as in *Pl*. XVa.10; XVIa.3, 4, 5, 6, 8, 10, 11. In *Pl*. XVIa.9, the letter-form has obtained a tail on the right and roughly resembles the Oriya *i*. In a few Telugu-Coḍa plates of the eleventh-twelfth centuries, the letter-form resembles to the elliptical *cha* (*Pl*. XVa.3).

The left-facing broad curve type of *u* is still retained. But the hooked head-mark applied to the proto-Nāgarī type of *u* has changed the face of the letter to some extent. In the stone inscriptions of Orissa during the fourteenth-fifteenth century, when the angular hook is transformed into a curve, it almost resembled to the letter-form of *ḍa* current then (cf. *u* and *ḍa* in *Pl.* XVa.5 and XVIa.3). In *Pl.* XVIa.5, 6, 11, it has obtained a tail obviously to distinguish it from *ḍa*.

The initial *e* has at least two broad varieties. In the first variety, a left-facing broad curve is seen joined to the right upright as in *Pl.* XVa.3; XVIa.1, 4. In another variety the letter is opened to the left and it has a cursive top and an angular bottom (*Pl.* XVa.6-11; XVIa.2, 5, 6, 10). The cursive top has occasionally developed into a curve or loop (*Pl.* XVIa.8, 9).

The letter-form of *o* is indicated by two left-facing curves as in *Pl.* XVa.11; XVIa.4.

Consonants

It has been amply demonstrated elsewhere in this chapter that the angular hooked head-marks applied to the existing proto-Nāgarī letter-forms of the ninth-eleventh centuries ultimately gave birth to their respective proto-regional forms of Orissa. Moreover, as a progressive development when the angular hooks got transformed into rounded curves, they ultimately led to the advent of the modern Oriya forms. Since most of the transformation took place in the upper half of the letters, the lower half remained significantly unchanged. This is particularly true in the case of *ka, gha, ca, ḍa, ḍha, da, pa, pha, bha, ya, la, va, ṣa, ha*, etc. Besides, the angular backs of *da, bha*, and *ha* are much more rounded. However, occasionally a few letters have developed their respective secondary forms and they continued to be used side by side with the earlier forms. From the fourteenth century onwards the letter *ka* is often written like the proto-Oriya initial *i* already referred to above. The occurrence of this variety of *ka* can be traced to the Puri and Bhubaneswar inscriptions of the time of Anaṅgabhīmadeva III where the latter-form has loops at the bottom (*Pl.* XVIa.3). The right loop is largely due to the confusion made by the scribe for the outer curve of *ka*. In the Siddheśvara temple inscription of Narasiṁhadeva IV, we come across a secondary from of *pa* that can hardly be distinguished from the Oriya *ga* (*Pl.* XVIb.10). Although the lower half of *ca* is usually found to be drawn in the form of a triangle, optionally it is seen in the form of a beak or it is rounded on left. In the late fourteenth and early fifteenth-century stone inscriptions the triangle is opened up at the top (*Pl.* XVIa.10, 11). Optionally the inward curl or loop on the right of *ḍha* is suppressed (*Pl.* XVIa.3, 4, 6, 8, 9) and the left arm of *ḷa*/*la* has developed an inward curl (*Pl.* XVIb.4, 7, 8, 9). In Oriya, the palatal semi-vowel *ya* is distinguished from *ẏa* (pronounced like *ja*). Although initially they are not distinguished palaeographically yet there are examples which amply prove that they are distinguished at the phonological level. In the Bhubaneswar bi-lingual stone inscription of the time of Narasiṁhadeva, *bije* is written as *biye* (l.2). Similarly, as has been stated above the writers and scribes have made a clear distinction between the retroflex *ḷa* and the liquid *la* on the phonological requirements of the vernacular. While the regular proto-Nāgarī/Nāgarī *la* has come to be known as the proto-Oriya *ḷa*, the liquid *la* is indicated by a diacritical mark resembling to a fork as in *Pl.* XVIa.4, 5. In *Pl.* XVIb.8 & 9, the mark is seen below the medial *ā*. In *Pl.* XVIb.10 & 11 the forked mark is changed into a tail. The letter-forms of *kha, ga* and *śa* are much more rounded compared to their proto-Nāgarī counterparts and are easily recognized as belonging to the Oriya script. The foot-marks on the left limb of the letters are largely represented by closed loops although occasionally they are opened up. The broad curve of *kha* joining the right upright is usually joined at the bottom. But there are cases where it has been shifted to the top (*Pl.* XVa.7, 9, 10; XVIa.3). The letter-form of *cha* is till denoted by an ellipse with a mid-line and on one occasion it resembles the Nāgarī *ka* (*Pl.* XVa.4). *Ṭa* is of double-curved type with a small vertical on the top right and *ṭha* is a simple circle. In the essential characters of the rest of the letters some important changes took place which resulted in the development of the proto-Oriya characteristics.

Ja : The proto-Nāgarī form of *ja* continued to be used in the inscriptions of Orissa during the eleventh-twelfth centuries. But with the application of the angular hooks in place of the simple horizontal line head-marks and with the rounding of the lower half of the letter, its form is slightly changed. The shallow curve on the top of the rounded lower half of *ja* is admittedly the precursor of its modern Oriya form. Although this variety of the letter-form of *ja* appeared as early as Ś. 1094 (AD 1172), the date of the Liṅgarāja temple inscription of the time of Rājarājadeva II (*Pl.* XVIa.2), it has become regular in the stone inscriptions of Orissa after the thirteenth century (*Pl.* XVIa.7, 10, 11). In the Paṭṭeśvara temple inscription, the form of the letter is denoted by two right-facing curves placed one above the other and its lower terminal moves to the left (*Pl.* XVIa. 9). The letter-form of *ja* of this inscription resembles the inital *u* of the same inscription.

Jha : The letter *jha* has at least two broad varieties. The first variety is represented by a vertical with a leftward stroke at the bottom and another small vertical drawn on the right and joined to the main vertical by slanting stroke (*Pl.* XVa.1). In the second variety, the leftward stroke at the bottom is suppressed and is replaced by a small triangle (*Pl.* XVa.4, 11). In *Pl.* XVa.9, the right upright is drawn cursively.

Ṇa : The proto-Nāgarī *ṇa* survived for a longer period. But there has been a tendency to lengthen the left arm and to suppress the horn-like protuberance in the right limb. In the lapidary inscriptions of Orissa of the thirteenth-fifteenth centuries, the body of the letter is bulged and the lower tip of its left arm is curling in as in *Pl.* XVIa.3, 5, 6, 7, 8, 9. This may be termed as proto-Oriya *ṇa*. Its modern Oriya form is obtained by developing a loop at the junction of the two curves and shifting it to the left.

Ta : In the Somavaṁśī grants of the latter half of the eleventh century the letter-form of *ta* is represented by a left-facing curve below the head-mark. Sometimes the upper arm of the curve is seen curling in (*Pl.* XVa.8, 10, XVIa.2-7). In *Pl.* XVa.9, the curve has developed a definite loop on its upper arm and occasionally it has been confused for a dot. However, the left-facing curve type of *ta* with an angular hooked head-mark is the most regular form used during this period and is evidently the precursor of the modern Oriya *ta*. In the stone inscriptions, of the fourteenth-fifteenth century the hook is transformed into a shallow curve and thereby making it come closer to its Oriya form.

Tha **:** The old forms of this letter such as the inward loop type (*Pl.* XVb.5) and the doubly curved back type (*Pl.* XVb.4) survived in the official charters of the minor ruling houses of Ganjam as late as the twelfth-thirteenth centuries. But the most regular form of the letter is the bipartite *tha* with its loop opened and facing left. In the stone inscriptions the base-line is often flattened and drawn angularly and meet the vertical at its lower end (*Pl.* XVIb.3, 4, 5, 6, 10, 11).

Dha **:** The broad-backed and the triangular type of *dha* are still noticed in a few records of the eleventh-twelfth centuries. But there has been a tendency to lower the broad or angular back of the letter as a result of which a horn-like protuberance is seen on the right limb (*Pl.* XVIb.2). Moreover, roughly form the middle of the twelfth century an additional slanting stroke is drawn on the top left which led to the birth of the proto-Oriya *dha*. Chronologically, the Polasara plates of Arkeśvardeva of AD 1147-48 furnish the earliest example of this type of the letter-form of *dha* (*Pl.* XVb.4). Optionally, the slanting stroke crosses the right upright as in *Pl.* XVIb.9. In *Pl.* XVIb.5, 6, 11, the letter-form resembles the modern Oriya *dha*.

Na **:** The Nāgarī form of the letter with a loop joined to the right by a mid-line is regularly found used in the inscriptions of Orissa of the eleventh-thirteenth centuries. Among the other forms of the letter mention may be made of (a) the loop separately placed beside the right upright (*Pl.* XVb.5, 6, 9), and (b) the double-armed variety of *na* with a mid-line (*Pl.* XVb.7, XVIb.4). The proto-Oriya form of the letter is essentially derived from the proto-Nāgarī or Nāgarī *na* where the loop is opened and looked like an inward curl and the mid-line is slightly lifted up and joined to the hooked head-mark as in *Pl.* XVIb.4, 5, 6, 7. The Konarka temple inscription supplies two important proto-Oriya forms of this letter (*Pl.* XVIb.8). In *Pl.* XVIb.11, the inward curl in the left limb of *na* is totally suppressed and the letter-form gets closer to the modern Oriya form of *na*.

Ma **:** Like *na*, the proto-Oriya *ma* is also derived from its Nāgarī counterpart. When the horizontal line is replaced by the angular hooked head-mark, the left arm of *ma* is drawn in a slightly slanting manner and joined to the loop below (*Pl.* XVb.1-8). But in due course of time the stroke is transformed into a curve as in *Pl.* XVI.1, 2, 3. In *Pl.* XVIb.3 (second), although the letter has retained the flat top, its mid-line is shifted to the left. In the fourteenth-fifteenth century stone inscriptions the loop in the left arm is opened as a result of which it looked like an inward curl (*Pl.* XVIb.9, 10, 11). Its modern Oriya form is obtained by suppressing this curl. In the copper-plate grants of the Imperial Gaṅgas of the thirteenth-fourteenth centuries, a peculiar form is seen where the left arm is a curve with its lower tip curling out and the left arm joins the right upright by a mid-line (*Pl.* XVb.9, 10). The letter-form resembles the proto-Bengali *sa*.

Ra **:** The hollow triangular type of *ra* is the most regular form used in the inscriptions of Orissa of the period. When the angular hooked head-mark is joined to the upper tip of the triangular, it resembled to *ca* and, therefore, the scribe made an attempt to distinguish the two by adding a tail beneath the triangle of *ra* as in *raḥ* (*Pl.* XVIb.1). In some of the inscriptions of the thirteenth century the triangle is changed into a beak (*Pl.* XVIb.4, 6). In *Pl.* XVIb.8, 9, 11 the

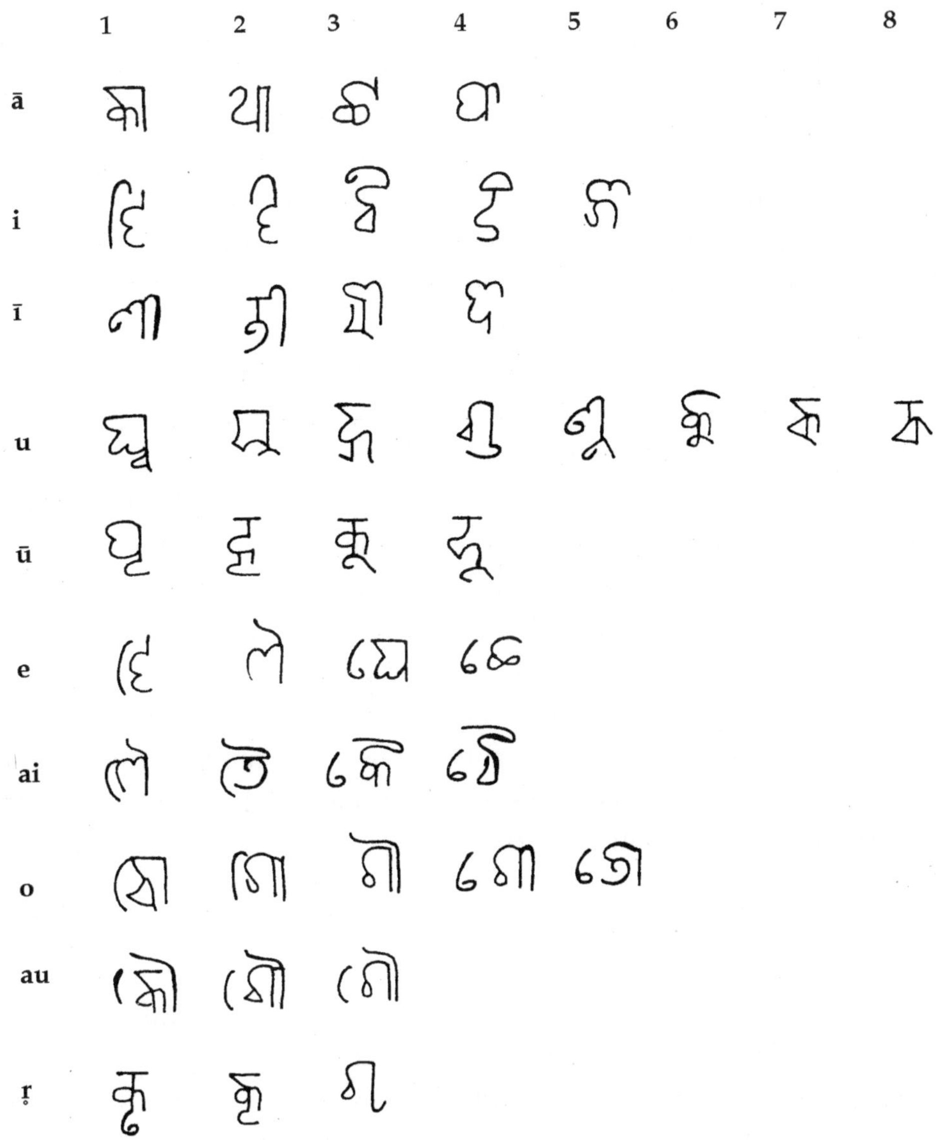

fig. **III: Medials in the Proto-Oriya Script**

triangle is opened at the top. In *Pl.* XVIb.10, the letter-form roughly resembles to the modern Oriya *ra* where the outer curve joins the tail on the right.

Sa **:** The proto-Nāgarī *sa* survived for a couple of centuries more in the inscriptions of Orissa. But gradually a tendency has developed to curve the flat top as in *Pl.* XVb.6; XVIb.2, and to flatten the lower half of the letter as in *Pl.* XVIb.9, 10, 11. These two features led to the birth of the early Oriya *sa*.

Kṣa **:** The letter-form of *kṣa* has undergone certain important changes. The loop of the proto-Nāgarī *kṣa* is now reduced to a small down-facing curve and is outer curve into a mid-line. Moreover, the shallow curve on the top and the definite right upright touching the top curve make it come closer to the Oriya *kṣa* (*Pl.* XVb.3, 5, 10.).

Medials

The medial *ā* is usually a full length vertical on the right. Sometimes it is indicated by a small stroke or a down-facing curve on the right. The old form of the medial *i* with a broad curve covering the entire left half of the letter is still used in the inscriptions of the period. However, the down-facing curve type of the medial sign applied on the top of the letters is the most regular form seen in the records. Towards the end of our period, the curve is drawn in continuation with the letter (especially the letters which have rounded tops and which are without right uprights) as in *fig.* III.5. The tendency of writing the medial *i* in continuation with the letter is still current in modern Oriya and this is chiefly attributed to quick engraving. Its length is denoted by a curve covering the entire right half of the letter. Like the medial *i*, the medial *ī* is also optionally drawn in continuation with the letter and in such cases it becomes quite difficult to distinguish the two. The medial *u* has a number of varieties. The old forms of the medial such as a loop, a triangle, a tick or a left-facing curve at the bottom of the letter are still used in the records of the period. Among the other signs, mention may be made of a down-facing curve as in *fig.* III.2 or an angle as in *fig.* III.3. As in the proto-Nāgarī script so also in proto-Oriya script the medial *u* is seen as a slanting stroke or a curve joined to the right of the letter *ra* (*fig.* III.7, 8). The medial *u* in *mu* (*Pl.* XVb.3) is interesting. The proto-Oriya form of the medial is represented by a loop with an outer curve drawn in continuation with the letter as in *fig.* III.6. The archaic form of the medial *ū* with a right-facing curve at the bottom of the letter is still retained. Occasionally it is seen in the form of a down-facing curve as in the Nāgarī script. The medial *e* is invariably indicated by a *pṛṣṭha-mātrā*. In the thirteenth-fifteenth-century stone inscriptions, it has developed a cursive back and an inward curl or loop at its lower end (*fig.* III.3, 4). This is clearly recognized as belonging to the Oriya script. The medial *ai* is the same as the *pṛṣṭha-mātrā* type of *e* sign together with a *śiro-mātrā* which is a modification of the Nāgarī type of the medial *e* (*fig.* III.3, 4). The medial *o* is again a combination of the *pṛṣṭha-mātrā* type of the medial *e* on the left and a full length vertical type of *ā* sign on the right. The medial *au* is the same as the sing for *ai* with an additional *ā* sign on the right. However, most of the medials excepting the sign for *u* are easily recognized as belonging to the Oriya script.

Conjuncts

The conjuncts do not differ much from the earlier script. The guttural and palatal nasals are never used independently. The guttural nasal *ṅa* when joined to the letters of its class is represented by a right-facing curve with an *anusvāra* sign on the right. In the fourteenth-fifteenth century records, the curve of the nasal is totally suppressed and the *anusvāra* is only retained, e.g., *ṅka*, *ṅgha* and *ṅga* (*Pl.* XVIb.9, 10 and 11). The palatal nasal *ña* as a superscript is the same as seen in the proto-Nāgarī script. As a subscript, the nasal is indistinguishable from the subscript *ṇa*. In *jñā* and *jña* (*Pl.* XVc.6 and 8), the second element *ña* resembles the letter-form of *bha* without its head-mark. As superscripts the cerebral *ṇa* and the dental *na* are expressed fully. But on one occasion, e.g., *ndi* (*Pl.* XVIc.10), the superscript *na* is reduced to a down-facing curve with a small curve on its top. This is an important step in the development of the ligatures like *nda* and *ndha* in Oriya. Subsequently, the down-facing curve is turned into a slanting stroke on the left. The subscripts *da* and *ta* are denoted by one and the same sign. Initially both are seen in the form of a left-facing curve. But later on *ta* has obtained a definite loop at its upper end as in *pti* (*Pl.* XVc.5) and *sta* (*Pl.* XVIc.10). The subscripts *cha* and *tha* look alike. Initially they are written as an ellipse with a mid-line but later on they are represented by double loops drawn in one action as in *cchi* and *sthi* (*Pl.* XIVc.6 and 11). The second *ṭa* in *ṭṭa* is a down-facing curve while the second *ta* in *tta* is a left-facing curve. Thus, so far as the subscripts are concerned, the modified forms of *ḍa*, *ṇa*, *ta*, *tha*, etc., have already appeared and they are still current in the modern Oriya script. The letter *na* as a subscript is represented fully without its head-mark but in *tna* (*Pl.* XVIc.11), only the lower half of the letter is drawn and it is in consonance with the modern Oriya subscript *na*. The subscript *ma* can be recognized as of the Nāgarī type. *Ya*, *ra*, *la*, *va* and the *repha* as second elements do not call for any remark. In the stone inscriptions, the subscript *la* is seen in the form of a down-facing curve (*Pl.* XVIc.3, 4, 9).

Orthography

In the Sanskrit inscriptions of the period the orthographical peculiarities are the same as noticed in the earlier script. As regards the orthography of the Oriya inscriptions, no distinction is made between *r̥* and *ru*, *ba* and *va*, the medial *i* and *ī*, *u* and *ū*; and the dental sibilant is universally used for the other sibilants. From the orthographical point of view, interesting are the words like *āsa* for *āyus*, *āïusva* for *āyuṣya*, *vaïdya* for *vaidya*, *vaïśākha* for *vaīsākha*, *vijaï* for *vijayī*, *vijae* for *vijaye*, *vise* for *viṣaye*, *nāeka* for *nāyaka*, *traodasi* for *trayodaśī*, *kaïlāsa* for *kailāsa*, *sidhesara* for *siddheśvara*, *utresara* for *uttareśvara*, *sarga* for *svarga*, *kātrīka* for *kārttika*, *cataru* for *catur*, *macchya* for *matsya* and so on. Contraction of letters is also found in the records, e.g., *paḍirāṅkra* for *paḍirāṅkara*, *srikraṇa* for *śrīkaraṇa*, *Gajatti/Gajapti* for *Gajapati*, etc. The beginning of such contraction of letters can be traced to some thirteenth-century inscriptions (Kapilas inscriptions of Narasiṁhadeva and Sonepur inscription of Bhānudeva) although the examples of the kind are numerous in the epigraphs of the fifteenth-seventeenth centuries.

Bibliography

PLATE XV

1. Ratnagiri plates of Somavaṁśī Karṇa, D. Mitra, *EI*, 33, 263-68 & pls.; D.C. Sircar, *ibid*., 269-74 & pls.
2. Kamalpur plates of the time of Karṇa, K.C. Panigrahi, *JOH*, 1 (1), 1-5 & pls.
3. Plates of Telugu-Coḍas:

   (a) Mahada plates of Someśvara, D.C. Sircar & M. Venkataramayya, *EI*, 28, 283-92; plates published in B.C. Mazumdar, *ibid*., 12, 218-21 & pls.

   (b) Patna Museum plates of Someśvara, R.D. Banerji, *ibid*., 19, 97-99 & pls.

(c) Kumari-Simha plates of Someśvaradeva, G. Ramdas, *JKHRS*, 1(3), 229-36 & pls.

(d) Sonepur plates of Kumāra Someśvaradeva (belonging to a line of Somavaṁśī rulers), B.C. Mazumdar, *EI*, 12, 237-42 & pls. are also written in this style.

4. Polasara plates of Arkeśvaradeva, *Yugābda* 4248 (AD 1147-48) D.C. Sircar, *ibid.*, 28, 63-67 & pls.
5. Some Bhañja copper-plate grants of eleventh-thirteenth century:

   (a) Adipur plates of Durjayabhañja, K.C. Panigrahi, *ibid.*, 25, 172-73 & pl.

   (b) A Bhañja grant from Khicing, D.C. Sircar, *ibid.*, 30, 220-25 & pl.

   (c) Baud plates of Saloṇabhañja, K.C. Panigrahi, *ibid.*, 26, 276-79 & pls.

   (d) Jurada (also known as Devlapedi) plates of Neṭṭabhañja, C.R. Krishnamacharlu, *ibid.*, 24, 15-20 & pls.
6. (a) Antirigam plates of Yaśabhañja, Hiralal, *ibid.*, 18, 298-99 & pls.

   (b) Antirigam plates of Jayabhañja, T.C. Rath, *ibid.*, 19, 41-45 & pls.

Imperial Gaṅgas

7. Plates of Anantavarman Coḍagaṅgadeva

   (a) Korni plates of Coḍagaṅgadeva, *Ś* .1003, G.V. Sitapati, *JAHRS*, 1, 40-48 & pls.

   (b) Murupaka plates of Coḍagaṅgadeva, *Ś*. 1005, R. Subha Rao, *ibid.*, 12 (1), 9-16 & pls.

   (c) Chicacole plates of Coḍagaṅgadeva, *Ś*. 1006, C.N. Rao & R. Subba Rao, *ibid.*, 8 (2-3), 183-85, 191-92 & pls.

   (d) Danta plates of Coḍagaṅgadeva, *Ś*. 1007, N. Ramesan, *CPIAPGM*, 1, 137-52 & pls.

   (e) Two Vizagapatam plates of Coḍagaṅgadeva, *Ś*. 1003 & *Ś*. 1057, J.F. Fleet, *IA*, 18, 161-65 & 172-76 (without facsimiles).
8. Plates of the successors of Coḍagaṅgadeva up to Anaṅgabhīmadeva III

   (a) Caudwar plates of Kāmārṇava, *Ś*. 1069, Rabi Ray, *Jhaṅkāra* (Oriya), 46 (8), 901-16 & pls.

   (b) Dasgoba plates of Rājarāja, *Ś*. 1120, D.C. Sircar & S.R. Sarma, *EI*, 31, 249-62 & pls.

   (c) Ragolu plates of Anaṅgabhīmadeva III, *Ś*. 1129, N.MN. Rao, *TGR*, 15-32 & pls.

   (d) Nagari plates of Anaṅgabhīmadeva III, *Ś*. 1151 & 1152, D.C. Sircar, *EI*, 28, 235-58 & pls.

   (e) Orissa State Museum (also known as Kapoteśvara) plates of Anaṅgabhīmadeva III, A.K. Rath, *OHRJ*, 12 (4), 164-96 & pls.
9. Plates of Narasiṁha II and Bhānudeva II.

   (a) Alalpur plates of Narasiṁha II, *Ś*. 1215, D.C. Sircar & P. Acharya, *EI*, 31, 17-24 & pls.

   (b) Kendupatana plates (Set I) of Narasiṁha II, *Ś*. 1217, D.C. Sircar, *JAS*, L, 17 (1), 33-39 & pls.

   (c) Kendupatana plates (Set II & III) of Narasiṁha II, *Ś*. 1217, D.C. Sircar, *EI*, 28, 185-95 & pls.

   (d) Asankhali plates of Narasiṁha II, *Ś*. 1225, D.C. Sircar, *ibid.*, 31, 109-28 & pls.

   (e) Punjabi Math (Puri) plates of Bhānudeva II, *Ś*. 1234, D.C. Sircar, *JAS, L*, 17 (1), 19-26 & pls.
10. Kaijang plates of Bhānudeva III, *Ś*. 1284, S.N. Rajaguru & B. Mohanty, *OHRJ*, 14 (3-4), 11-12 & pls.
11. Plates of Narasiṁha IV

    (a) Trimali Math (Puri) (also known as Kenduli) plates of Narasiṁha IV, *Ś*. 1305, S.N. Rajaguru, *ibid.*, 5, 1-100 & pls.

(b) Sankarananda Math (Puri) plates of Narasiṁha IV, Ś. 1316, D.C. Sircar, *EI*, 28, 302-12 & pls.

PLATE XVI

1. Later stone inscriptions of Anantavarman Coḍagaṅgadeva

   (a) Liṅgarāja temple inscriptions, D.C. Sircar, *EI*, 30, 29-32 & pls.

   (b) Jagannāth temple inscription, A. Joshi, *OHRJ*, 9 (3-4), 47-50 & pl.

   (c) Mārkaṇḍeśvara temple inscription, D.C. Sircar, *EI*, 33, 181-84 & pl.

   (d) Algaum (Puri) inscription of the time of Coḍagaṅgadeva, D.C. Sircar & S.R. Sarma, *ibid.*, 29, 44-48 & pl.

   (e) Kedāreśvara temple (Bhubaneswar) inscription of Pramāḍi, Ś. 1064, D.C. Sircar, *ibid.*, 30, 90-94 & pl.

   (f) Mukteśvara (near Khallikote, Ganjam district) temple inscription of the time of Coḍagaṅgadeva, A. Joshi, *OHRJ*, 10 (1-2), 14-16 (without facsimile).

   (g) S.N. Rajaguru, *ITPOSPJ*, Nos. 1-15 & pls may be consulted for the Puri temple inscriptions of the time of Coḍagaṅgadeva.

2. Inscriptions of the sons and successors of Anantavarman Coḍagaṅgadeva

   (a) Khilor (Puri) inscription of Kāmārṇava, Ś. 1075, and Liṅgarāja (Bhubaneswar) temple inscription of Rājarāja II, Ś. 1094,(D.C. Sircar, *EI*, 35, 115-20 & pls.

   (b) Two Liṅgarāja temple inscriptions of Rāghava, S.N. Rajaguru, *OHRJ*, 5 (3-4), 179-82 & pls.

   (c) Puri temple inscriptions of Kāmārṇava and Rāghava, S.N. Rajaguru, *ITPOSPJ*, Nos. 17 and 18 & pls.

3. Inscriptions of the time of Anaṅgabhīmadeva III

   (a) Puri inscriptions of Anaṅgabhīmadeva, Ś. 1147 and 1158, D.C. Sircar, *EI*, 30, 197- 203 & pls.

   (b) Liṅgarāja temple inscription of Bhīmadeva, D.C. Sircar, *ibid.*, 232-36 & pls.

   (c) Bhubaneswar inscription of Anaṅgabhīmadeva, *aṅka* 34, D.C. Sircar, *ibid.*, 17-23 & pls.

   (d) S.N. Rajaguru, *ITPOSPJ*, Nos. 19-25 & pls. may also be consulted for the Puri temple inscriptions of Anaṅgabhīmadeva III.

   (e) Liṅgarāja temple inscriptions of Narasiṁha I, D.C. Sircar & J.C. Ghosh, *IC*, 3, 121-25 (Nos. 1 & 2) & pls. are also written in this style.

4. Śikhareśvara (Kapilas) temple inscriptions of the time of Narasiṁha I, D.C. Sircar, *EI*, 33, 41-45 & pls.
5. Bhubaneswar bilingual inscription of Narasiṁha (I), D.C. Sircar & K.G. Krishnan, *ibid.*, 32, 229-38 & pl.
6. Sonepur inscription of the time of Bhānudeva I, D.C. Sircar, *ibid.*, 32, 325-28 & pl.
7. Pārvati temple inscription of Bhānudeva I, B.V. Nath, *OHRJ*, 3 (3), 146-49 & pl.
8. Konarka temple inscription, M.M. Chakravarti, *JBORS*, 3 (2), 282-83 & pl.
9. Paṭṭeśvara temple inscription of Bhānudeva III, Yugābda 4477, L.N.H. Jagadeb, *JAHRS*, 6, 51-52 (without facsimile). Impression is consulted in the office of the Director (Epigraphy), Mysore.
10. Siddheśvara temple inscription of Narasiṁha IV, *aṅka* 19, D.C. Sircar & K.B. Tripathi, *EI*, 29, 105-08 & pl.
11. Narasimhanath temple inscription of Vaijaladeva, B. Mishra, *IHQ*, 12, 485-88 & pl.

11

Early and Modern Oriya Script

KAPILENDRADEVA who ousted the last Gaṅga ruler and usurped the throne in AD 1435 was a patron of Oriya language and culture. He seems to be the product of the prevailing spirit of revolt directed against the reactionary court and priestly orthodoxy. The mass of conscious people who were against these institutions lent enthusiastic support to the new ruler. This new ruler was very much a "son of soil" and had a greater perception of the "spirit of the revolt." The mass of conscious population had, therefore, reposed confidence on him to lead them in achieving their socio-political aspirations. During his reign, Kapilendradeva (AD 1435-66) reversed the ideologies of the later Gaṅga rulers to soothe the popular conscience. It was from this time onwards that Oriya language was recognized as the official medium in place of Sanskrit. The royal proclamations were issued in Oriya language and script. They were incised on the doors of the Jagannāth temple at Puri. Lord Jagannāth was declared as the state deity. These ideologies set an example for the future rulers to emulate, and proved beneficial for the emergence of a regional consciousness among the natives.

The Oriya inscriptions of the kings of this dynasty, popularly known as the Sūryavaṁśī Gajapati dynasty (AD 1435-1540) and those of the ministerial dynasties (AD 1540-68), numbering more than fifty have been discovered so far. The earlier practice of engraving Oriya inscriptions in Telugu script is no longer favoured, although there are a couple of similar examples in the time of Kapilendradeva[1] and Pratāparudradeva.[2] In the two trilingual plates (Veligalani, Ś. 1380 and Chiruvroli, Ś. 1383) of the time of Kapilendradeva, discovered from the Guntur district of Andhra Pradesh, a gist of the grant portion is given at the end of each of the charters in Oriya language and script. Besides, the Balasore copper axe-head inscription of Puruṣottamadeva is the only copper-plate grant of the Sūryavaṁśīs written in Oriya language and script. However, a majority of the Oriya inscriptions of the period are engraved on stones. They are mostly incised

---

1. The Simhanchalam temple inscription of the 32 *aṅka* of Kapilendradeva, *SII*, 6, No. 793. Also see K.B. Tripathi, *EOLS*, No. 20. 266-67 and R. Subrahmanyam, *ISGO*, No. 10, 17-18. The Gopinathpur (Cuttack district) temple inscription of the time of Kapilendradeva is written in Sanskrit language but the characters are Oriya. According to M.M. Chakravarti, "As yet this appears to be the earliest known inscription of such a kind" (*JASB*, LXIX, 1900, 173).
2. A. Butterworth & Venugopal Chetty, *A Collection of the Inscriptions on Copper-plates and Stones in the Nellor District*, 3 parts, Madras, 1905, CP Nos. 21 & 22.

on the door-jambs, pillars and in the *maṇḍapa*s of different shrines. There are twelve such inscriptions on the left and right sides of the Jaya-Vijaya doorway in the Jagannāth temple at Puri, two on the right side of the doorway in the Liṅgarāja temple at Bhubaneswar, one on the western wall of the Jagamohana of the Madhukeśvara temple of Bhanragada (in Balipatna block of Puri district), one on a stone slab and another on a pillar to the right of the entrance into the central shrine of the Madhukeśvara temple at Mukhalingam, two on the square pillars of the Tirucuttu-*maṇḍapa* of the Kūrmeśvara temple at Srikurmam, twenty-eight on the walls and round pillars of the *maṇḍapa* in front of Ālāvar shrine of the Lakṣmī-Narasiṁha temple at Simhanchalam and one on a stone slab set-up in the eastern courtyard of the Mallikārjuna temple at Sri Sailam. In addition to these, a few Oriya inscriptions are also found from Gaganeśvar (Midnapur district), Trisilia (Balasore district), Indupur (Cuttack district), Tekkali (Srikakulam district), Chitrakote (Visakhapatanam district), Kondavidu (Guntur district) and Kondapalli (Krishna district). They are mostly fragmentary and incomplete. Moreover, there are more than 10 Oriya inscriptions belonging to the latter part of the sixteenth and early seventeenth century. They are all engraved on stone and distributed over a wide area extending from Kesiari (Midnapur district) in the north to Athagarh (Ganjam district) in the south. Three inscriptions are found from the Sarvamaṅgala temple at Kesiari, two each from Srijanga and Sthāneśvar (both in Balasore district), one each from Athagarh (Ganjam district), Deulbarh (Midnapur district) and Baripada Museum (Mayurbhanj district). Most of these inscriptions are dated and one of the Kesiari inscriptions furnishes the latest date, i.e., AD 1615 in the series.[3] Besides, we have also taken into account the Kechala copper-plate grant of Kṛṣṇadeva, a ruler of Nandapura (Jeypur, Koraput district) which was issued in AD 1698. The study of all these inscriptions is of absorbing interest from the linguistic and palaeographical point of view. According to S.K. Chatterji, "The early Oriya of these inscriptions is a living speech . . . and that in quantity it is quite a respectable body of national literature in the language."[4] However, it was during this period the Oriya language and script entered into the mature phase.

The script used in the inscriptions of Orissa of the fifteenth-seventeenth centuries essentially evolved out of the proto-Oriya can be called as "early Oriya script." In *Pl.* XVII all the Oriya inscriptions of the Sūryavaṁśī Gajapatis, the ministerial dynasties and those of the subsequent period up to the end of the seventeenth century have been included.

The chief feature which distinguishes the early Oriya from the proto-Oriya is its extreme cursive forms. The shallow top-curves of most of the proto-Oriya letters are now rounded off and divide them into two distinct parts — an upper and a lower. The actual letter forms the lower part while a great space above is occupied by the ornamental top-curve. Thus, the circular top-curve is an ornamental adjunct of the letters and developed out of the serif applied to the

3. P. Acharya, Kesiari Inscription of Raja Kalyana Mal, *IHRC*, 21, 88-90.

4. S.K. Chatterji, *The Origin and Development of the Bengali Language*, 2 vols., Calcutta, 1926, 107.

transitional/later Brāhmī letters through various intermediate stages. The initial *u* and the consonansts *ka, gha, ca, cha, ja, ḍa, ḍha, ta, da, na, pa, pha, bha, ma, ya, ẏa, ra, ḷa, la, va, ṣa, sa, ha, kṣa,* etc., are some of the letters having this top-curve. In the early Oriya script most of these letters have obtained an inward dip at the centre of the left limb. Another feature that distinguishes the early Oriya from the proto-Oriya is the compression of the lower part of the letters. Since the top-curve occupied a greater space above, the lower part of the letters is compressed. The letter-forms of *i, e, o, kha, ga, ṭa, ṇa, tha, dha, śa,* etc., which were devoid of the head-marks in the earlier scripts are also seen rounded. The initial *a* and *ā* have obtained double curves. The letter-form of *ṭha* is the same old Brāhmī form preserved in the Oriya script. Excepting a few instances, the loop of *kha, ga, tha* and *śa* is mostly seen opened up.

Most of the letters are considerably rounded on the left side and have the vertical at the right. The initial *a, ā,* and the consonants *kha, ga, gha, ṇa, tha, dha, pa, bha, ma, ya, ẏa, śa, ṣa, sa, kṣa,* etc., are some of the letters having a vertical on the right. In the case of *a, ā, tha* and *dha* the rounded left limb joins the right upright at the bottom while the left limb of *kha, ga, ṇa, ma,* etc., joins the right upright at the top. In the case of the rest of the letters the top curve joins the vertical at the top while the cursive lower part joins the vertical at the bottom. Although initially, the vertical does not go beyond the point of junction either at the top or bottom, later on a horn-like protuberance is seen at the top and a slight projection is also seen at the bottom.

In the early Oriya script, a tail is found added to the letters like *i, u, bha, ya, ra, la,* etc. Of course, the practice had already started in the earlier script. The proto-Oriya *u* (optionally), *ra* and *la* are having this tail. The reason behind the addition of a tail is that when the form of two letters resemble closely and become indistinguishable the scribes preferred to put a tail to one to distinguish it from the other. The initial *i* is not easily distinguished from the double-looped variety of *ka*. Similarly the proto-Oriya forms of *u* and *ḍa, bha* and *ja, ra* and *ca* look alike and cannot be distinguished easily, and, therefore, a tail is seen joined to *u* to distinguish it from *ḍa, bha* from *ja,* and *ra* from *ca*. The linguistic requirement of two separate letters such as the retroflex *ḷa* and the liquid *la* led to their palaeographical separation by the addition of a diacritical mark to the latter. Although initally there was some confusion in the use of these two letter-forms (as noticed in the proto-Oriya), later on the confusion was avoided, and the original sign of *la* which came through an evolutionary process stood for the retroflex *ḷa* while the liquid *la* received a diacritical mark. Similarly, in modern Oriya there are two distinct signs for the semi-vowel *ya* and *ẏa* (pronounced like *ja*). The use of distinct signs for these two letters can be traced to the records of Puruṣottamadeva. In the Balasore copper axe-head inscription, the letter *ya* is used for *ja* as in *yāvacandrārke*[5] but in one of the inscriptions of Lakṣmī-Narasiṁha temple of Simhanchalam the semi-vowel is seen with a tail as in *jāyate*.[6] The proto-Oriya *ya* which is a

5. P. Mukherji, *OHRJ*, 2 (3-4), 37-41.

6. *SII*, 6, No. 703.

derivative of the proto-Nāgarī actually stood for *ẏa* while a diacritical mark is added to it to indicate the semi-vowel *ya*. However, unlike the other letters where the tail is separated from the bottom to join the top-curve of the letters, the diacritical mark of *ya* grew into a left-facing curve with a tail in modern Oriya.

Another important feature of the early Oriya script is that there are several alternative forms of one and the same letter. *Ka, gha, cha, ja, pa, bha, ra, śa, ha*, etc., are some of the letters which have more than one form (*fig*. I). The double-looped type of *ka* resembling the initial *i* and the type of *pa* resembling to the modern Oriya *ga* are already noticed in the proto-Oriya Script. These peculiarities continued to be used during this period along with their modern Oriya forms. In another variety the double-looped *ka* has a small vertical tick at its bottom. It may be noted here that when the double-looped *i* and *ka* resembled each othter, the scribes of some localities preferred to add a tick to *ka* with an intention to distinguish it from *i*. It is for the same reason the scribes of other localities added a tail to *i* to separate it from the double-looped *ka*. However,

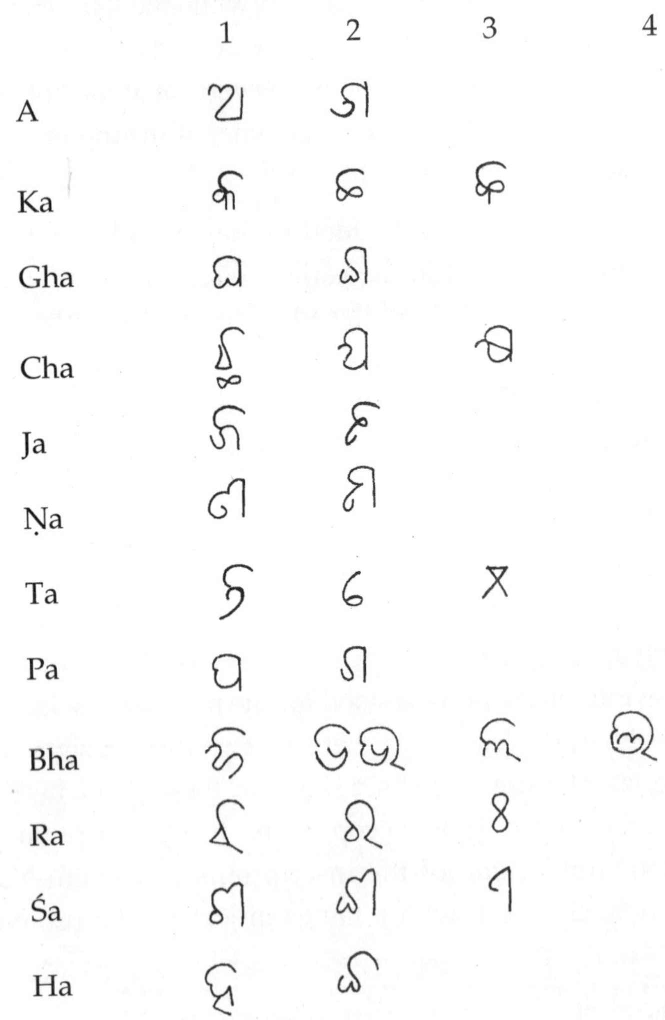

fig. **I: Letters having more than one form.**

this variety of *ka* is not so much popularized in the inscriptions of the period. Although the letters such as *gha, śa,* and *ha* have already obtained their respective modern Oriya forms, yet optionally these letters are also seen in their secondary forms where the base is doubly curved and opened at the top. The secondary form of *gha* looks like *ṅga* without the small circle on the top right. A third is only having variety of *śa* is also noticed where the left limb is only having a down-facing curve. The proto-Oriya *ja* is still predominant throughout the period. A secondary form of *ja* is also noticed which is drawn in one action with a loop in the middle. Apart from the proto-Oriya and modern Oriya forms of *ra,* another peculiar form of *ra* is found which is

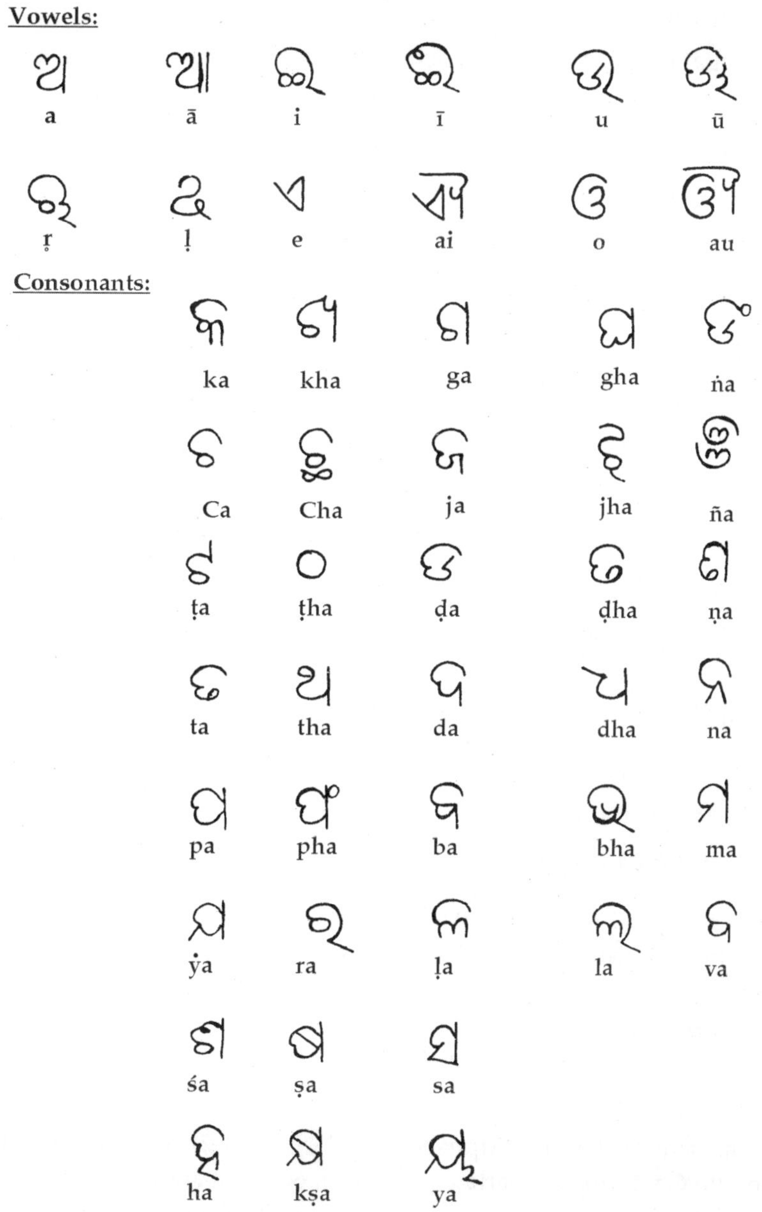

fig. **II: Modern Oriya Alphabet**

represented by two loops entwining and standing heightwise with the usual tail at the bottom. But of all these letters, the letter *bha* has a number of varieties. In addition to its proto-Oriya form, the letter is noticed in the form of two down-facing curves covered by a rounded curve and a tail is added at the bottom. In another variety the letter-form resembles to the liquid *la*. Besides, optionally the initial *a* is written like *tā*, *cha* like *ya* or *kṣa*, *ṇa* like *ma* and *ta* like the medial *e*.

It is significant to note that there are two varieties of scripts such as the Brāhmaṇī and Karaṇī used in modern Oriya. It is generally believed that the former is used by the brāhmaṇas for writing the texts in the palm-leaf manuscripts while the latter is popularized among the professional scribes engaged in drafting official documents, deeds and records.[7] However, the Karaṇī script was not evolved out of any script; it is rather created to suit to quick engraving. Since the secondary forms of some of the letters such as the double-looped type of *ka*, the double-curved base type of *ha*, etc., as well as the peculiar forms of the medial vowels and ligatures (as will be discussed below) have already appeared in the inscriptions of the period, the antiquity of the use of the Karaṇī script can be traced to the early Oriya script of the fifteenth-seventeenth centuries. In the opinion of S.N. Rajaguru, after the sixteenth-seventeenth centuries, the popularization of this script was mainly confined to Cuttack and Puri districts of Orissa for the capital of Orissa was located there and most of the professional scribes were residents of that locality.[8] Rajaguru further opines that it is for these reasons the scribes of other parts of Orissa are still ignorant about the script.

Thus, the early Oriya script is essentially a derivative of the proto-Oriya as used in the inscriptions of Orissa of the eleventh-fourteenth centuries. In the early Oriya script almost all the letters excepting *ja*, *la* and *bha* have obtained their respective modern Oriya forms (fig. II). It should be remembered here that in spite of the fully developed forms of the Oriya letters, their proto-Oriya forms still retained popularity and are current in the inscriptions up to the seventeenth century.

The Oriya inscriptions of the period normally do not follow any system of punctuation. K.B. Tripathi has rightly observed,

> Most of the inscriptions do not follow any system of punctuation whatsoever. From the beginning to the end, the letters are inscribed without indicating the beginning and end of a word or a clause or a sentence. . . . In some inscriptions, however, we find punctuation marks, which consist of either one or two *daṇḍa*s (vertical strokes).[9]

---

7. Sir Hugh McPherson, "The Oriya Alphabet," *JBORS*, 10 (1-2), 168-70 & pls. Pt. Nilamani Mishra, "Tālapatra Pothire Oḍiā Lipira Bibartana," *Koṇārka*, 66, Bhubaneswar, 1988, 17-23 & pls.
8. S.N. Rajaguru, *Oḍiā Lipira Kramavikāsa*, Bhubaneswar, 1960, 27-28.
9. K.B. Tripathi, *EOLS*, 34.

One of the inscriptions of the time of Kapilendradeva uses the single vertical stroke throughout. A sentence is divided into many parts and sometimes individual words are flanked by stroke marks.[10] A few inscriptions of the Lakṣmi-Narasiṁha temple at Simhanchalam use single *daṇḍa* marks in the text but the end of the texts is indicated by double *daṇḍa* marks.[11] This is also true in the case of the Kechala copper-plate grant of Kṛṣṇadeva. Another inscription of the same temple furnish an interesting information about corrections in the body of the text by putting a cross-mark.[12]

At the end of the reverse side of the Balasore copper axe-head inscription of Puruṣottamadeva there are line drawing of *pāśa*, *aṅkuśa* and *śaṅkha*, and two swords, one with a long blade widest at the top and other smaller one with a tapering and bent blade. In the Kechala grant of Kṛṣṇadeva, a similar *pāśa* and a daggar-like object are drawn at the end. G. Ramdas, the editor of the plates, takes these drawings as sign manuals of the rulers and believes that they signify a feudal ranking in the political structure of the then Orissa.

Moreover, the final forms of the consonants are wanting in the vernacular inscriptions of the period. Since in modern Oriya as a general rule every word ends in a vowel, it may be persumed that in early Oriya too words normally ended in a vowel. In this respect Oriya differs from almost all the Neo Indo-Āryan languages.

Vowels

Of the initial vowels, *a*, *ā*, *i*, *u*, *e* and *o* are found used in the inscriptions of the period. The initial *i* is not properly distinguished from *ī* and the letter-form resembles more to *ī* than to *i*. The difference between the two initials in a modern Oriya lies in the loop in the upper curve. Since the loop itself is a modification of the notch and the letter-form is seen with the notch throughout, it appears that the sign stands for *ī*. But the same sign is used for both *i* and *ī*. Similarly, in modern Oriya the length of *u* is indicated by the addition of a loop in the upper curve of the letter. But in the inscriptions of the period there is no trace of the loop or notch and, therefore, the same sign represents both *u* and *ū*. The diphthongs *ai* and *au* do not occur at all. The modern Oriya forms of the initial *ṛ* and the liquid vowel *ḷ* are noticed in a few inscriptions of the Lakṣmī-Narasiṁhan temple at Simhanchalam of the time of Govindadeva (AD 1541-49). But they are not used as initials. The signs for *ṛ* and *ḷ* are used for *ru* and *lu* respectively.[13]

---

10. K.B. Tripathi, *EOLS*, 272.
11. *Ibid.*, Nos. 35, 41, 49.
12. In line 9 of the inscription (*SII*, 6, No. 895), the word *karibo* is engraved below the line by putting a cross-mark between the words *sebā* and *e dharma*, evidently indicating that the word should be inserted in the space marked.
13. The letter-form of *ru* in the word *desaru* (l.13) and that of *lu* in the word *dhīlu* (l.7) in the LN temple inscriptions of the 8th and 5th *aṅka* of Govindadeva (*SII*, 6, No. 749 and No. 927) look like the modern Oriya form of the initial vowel *ṛ and ḷ* respecitvely.

The down-facing upper curve of *a* is notched in the middle and it is joined to the right upright by a slanting line or a curve. Whenever a slanting line is drawn it forms an acute angle on the left and this is more pronounced in *Pl.* XVIIa.4, 5, 6. But the other form with a rounded base is also used side by side and it is more nearer to the modern Oriya form. Another important development is that although the base-line joins the right upright at the bottom, later on it joins the right arm medially. A secondary form of *a* is seen in *Pl.* XVIIa.3, where the letter-form looks like the proto-Oriya *tā*. According to K.B. Tripathi, the letter-form is a derivative of the proto-Bengali *a* by turning the horizontal top-curve of *a* into a curve. However, this is the solitary example of its kind in the Oriya inscriptions examined here. The initial *ā* is the same as *a* with an additional vertical on the right. In *Pl.* XVIIa.2, the two right verticals of the letter are joined together by a horizontal or slanting bar.

The proto-Oriya type of the initial *i* with the two loops entwined at the base, the upper curve notched in the middle and a tail-like mark on the right is still current throughout the period. But at the same time its modern Oriya form is also obtained by separating the tail from the entwined loops and joining it to the terminal of the top curve as in *Pl.* XVIIa.1, 2 (second), 4 (second), 5 (second), 6 (second). However, as has been stated above, there is no distinction between *i* and *ī* at this stage of development but later on the present sign denoted the length of *i* while the notch is suppressed to indicate *i*.

The proto-Oriya form of *u* with a broad left-facing curve, a top curve and a tail on the right is still retained and popularly used throughout the period. In the modern Oriya form of *u* the top curve joins the terminal of the left-facing curve on the left and the tail is merged with the terminal of the top-curve on the right. The letter-form in *Pl.* XVIIa.1 (second) is reproduced form of the Veligalani plates of Kapilendradeva (vide *Gauḍeśvara*, l.5). In *Pl.* XVIIa.4 (second), 5 (second) and 6 (second), the letter is devoid of the inward dip on the left which is normally met with the junction of the two curves in the modern Oriya *u*. The length of *u* is indicated by the formation of an inward loop on the right. But it does not occur in the Oriya inscriptions of the period under review.

The initial vowels *e* and *o* do not exhibit any marked development down to the seventeenth century. The vowel *e* is still represented by the same old form where the letter is opened on the left and has a cursive top and an angular bottom while *o* is still indicated by two left-facing curves.

Consonants

In the early Oriya script, although a number of letters have already obtained their respective modern Oriya forms, yet their proto-Oriya forms continued to be used in the inscriptions. The loop in the left limb of *kha, ga, tha, śa* is still open in a majority of cases. But towards the end of the sixteenth century it is closed (*Pl.* XVIIa.& b.8). Similarly the loop at the base of *ca, ta, ra* and *va* is open on a number of occasions while the close looped forms of these letters are also noticed in the epigraphs of the period. Thus, the letter-form of *ca* in *Pl.* XVIIa.2 (second), 5, 8, 9 (first), 11; *ṭa* in *Pl.* XVIIa.5 (second) 6 (third), 10 (third), 11; *ra* in *Pl.* XVIIb.3 (second), 5 (first & third), 6 (first), 8, 10, 11; and that of *va* in *Pl.* XVIIb.1, 2 (first), 4 (second), 5, 6, 10, 11 have closed loops and they closely resemble to their modern Oriya forms. In the case of *ra* the tail is separated from the loop and joined to the terminal of the outer curve to complete the evolution of its Oriya form. The archaic forms of *ka, ṭa, ḍa, ta, dha, na, ma, ḷa,* etc., are noticed along with their modern Oriya forms. Of these, the modern Oriya forms of *kha* and *dha* are already noticed in the proto-Oriya script (*Pl.* XVIa.8, 9; and b.11) and that of the other letters have been evolved in the records of Kapilendradeva (*Pl.* XVII.1, 2). The letter *ṭa* has developed a loop at the base with a top-curve; a small vertical stroke being added to it on the right as in *Pl.* XVIIa.5 (second), 6 (second & third), 10, 11. The letter-form is a modification of the proto-Oriya *ṭa* by the formation of a loop at the base; the top-curve and the small vertical remained unchanged. In the letter-form of *ḍa*, the top-curve is shifted from the slanting stroke of its proto-Oriya form and joined to the terminal of the left-facing broad curve on the left as in *Pl.* XVIIa.2, 4 (second), 6 (second), 8. The letter *ta* in *Pl.* XVIIa.1 (second) can clearly be recognized as the modern Oriya *ta* and the same form is used in subsequent records along with its proto-Oriya form. In the case of *na*, the curl at the bottom of the left arm is suppressed and the lower half is angularly drawn as in *Pl.* XVIIb.1, 3, 4 (third), 6 (second), 7, 8 (second), 9 (first), 10. These changes render the letter to resemble to its modern Oriya form. Similarly, the curl at the bottom of the left arm of the proto-Oriya *ma* is suppressed to obtain its Oriya form as in *Pl.* XVIIb.2 (second), 4 (second), 5 (second), 6 (second), 7, 9, 10 (second), 11. Although the top-curve of *ḷa* is fully rounded in the early Oriya script, by the end of the seventeenth century (*Pl.* XVIIb.11) it is drawn from the left arm instead of drawing it from the right arm of the lower limb. Besides, the letters *ṭha, da, pha, ṣa* and *sa* closely resemble to their respective modern Oriya forms and, therefore, do not call for special remark. *Ṭha* is a simple circle throughout. The rest of the letters have full grown top-curves which rendered their Oriya forms. *Pha* has developed a small circle on the top right as in *Pl.* XVIIb.2, 4.

As has been mentioned above, each of the letters like *ka, gha, cha, ja, ṇa, ta, pa, bha, ra, śa, ha,* etc., has a secondary form in addition to its regular form and on most occasions the secondary forms are created by the scribes for some reason or other. They need to be discussed at some length in the following. Moreover, there are few letters such as *jha, ḍha, ẏa, ya, la,* etc., which merit attention because they took some more time to obtain their respective modern Oriya forms.

Ka : The letter-form of *ka* has at least three important varieties:

(a) The first variety is represented by its modern Oriya form as in *Pl.* XVIIa.2 (second), 3, 4, (third), 5 (second), 6 (third), 7 (second), 8 (first), 9, 11.

(b) The second variety is indicated by two loops joined together with the usual top curve. This has already been termed a double-looped type of *ka* and has also occurred optionally in the proto-Oriya script. It resembles the letter-form of *i* and appears throughout the period, vide *Pl.* XVIIa.2 (first), 4 (first), 5 (first), 6 (first), 7 (first), 8 (second). This form of *ka* is also seen in the Karaṇī script.

(c) The third variety of the letter is the same as the double-looped type of *ka* with an additional vertical line at the bottom as in *Pl.* XVIIa.1, 4 (second), 6 (second), 7 (first), 10. As has already been observed earlier, the application of an additional vertical to the double-looped type of *ka* is to distinguish it from the letter-form of *i*.

Gha : The modern Oriya form of *gha* is almost regular in the records of the period. Optionally it is represented by a peculiar form where its rounded top curve instead of starting from the left arm moves from the right in one action and the right upright is drawn separately (*Pl.* XVIIa.4, 6).

Cha : In the inscriptions of the period the earlier forms of the letter are no longer favoured and some new types have occurred. In the first variety the letter-form is the same as the proto-Oriya *ca* with an ellipse at its bottom (*Pl.* XVIIa. 2, first). In the second variety it resembles to the Oriya *ẏa* (cf. *Pl.* XVIIb.3) as in *Pl.* XVIIa.2 (second), 4. In yet another variety a slanting mid-line is joined to the second variety of *cha* (*Pl.* XVIIa.1, 5, 11) and thereby it roughly resembles to the Oriya *kṣa* current then. Of these, the first variety is subsequently developed into the modern Oriya form of *cha* and the other two varieties are discarded.

Ja : The letter-form of *ja* has two important varieties. In the first variety the proto-Oriya form of the letter is much more rounded and frequently found used in the epigraphs of the period. Its modern Oriya form has not appeared until a century or so. In the modern Oriya form the rounded top curve instead of starting from the middle of the lower limb, starts from the terminal of the upturned curve on the left. In another variety, the letter is seen in the form of a hook at the bottom, a loop in the middle and a curve on the top, and the whole sign is drawn in one action as in *Pl.* XVIIa.1, 2 (second), 4 (first), 6 (first), 7, 10 (first), 11. It seems that this is a corrupt form of the proto-Oriya *ja* by joining the right arm of the lower limb with the top curve and turning the upturned left arm into a hook.

Jha : The rare letter *jha* has occurred only on a couple of occasions. In one of the LN temple inscriptions of the time of Govindadeva of AD 1547 (*majhira*, l.6), the letter has retained its triangle with a tail at the base and the right upright is substituted by a down-facing curve. Besides, the upper limb is totally rounded (*Pl.* XVIIa.6). A comparison of this form of the letter with the one used in *Pl.* XVa.9 makes it evident that the former is derived from the latter. But it took some more time to develop its modern Oriya form.

Ḍha : The right arm in the lower limb of *ḍha* curls in as in *Pl.* XVIIa.4 (first). In the modern Oriya script, the curl is seen in the form of a loop and, therefore, the letter-form resembles *ta*. The letters are distinguished by putting a dot at the bottom of *ḍha*. However, the dot is not applied to *ḍha* by the seventeenth century.

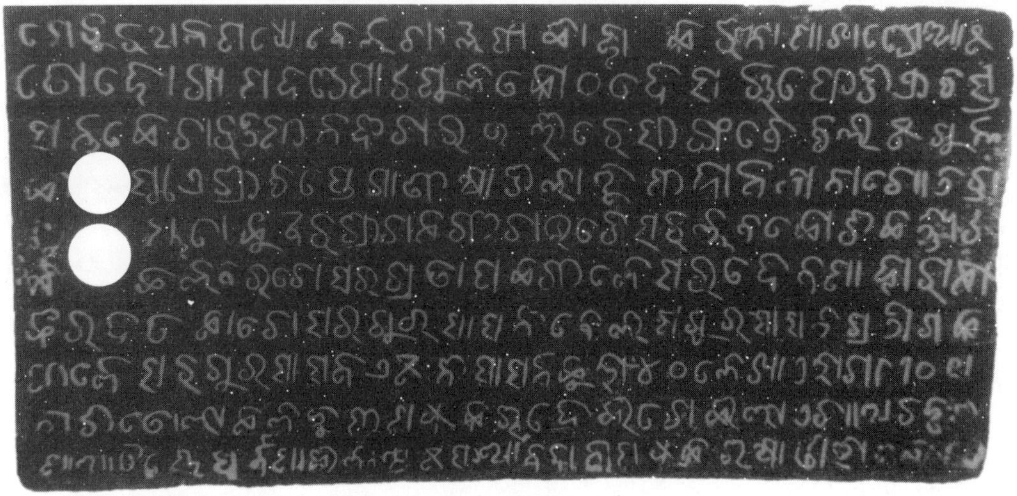

Photo 11.1: Veligalani plates (Oriya portion) of Kapilendradeva, Ś. 1380.

Photo 11.2: Kurmeśvara temple inscription of the time of Pratāparudradeva

Photo 11.3: Kesiari Sarvamangala temple inscription, Ś. 1537.

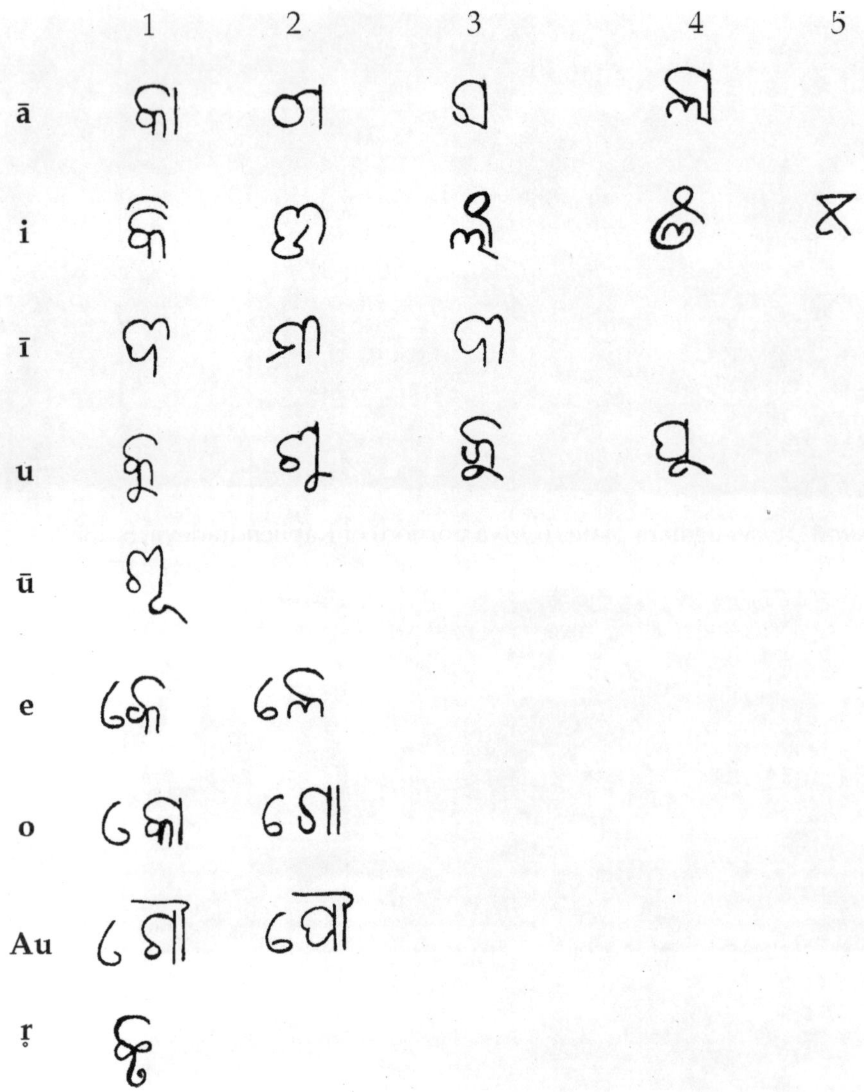

fig. **III: Medials in the Early and Modern Oriya Script**

Ṇa : The proto-Oriya form of *ṇa* with a bulged body is still frequently noticed in the epigraphs of the period. In *Pl.* XVIIa.5, 11, the curl in its left arm is turned into a small loop and the so-called "horn-like protuberance" in the right arm. A secondary form of the letter is found in the Athagarh rock inscription of Narasiṁha Gajapati (*Pl.* XVIIa.8) where it looks like the proto-Oriya *ma*.

Ta : As has already been stated above, the proto-Oriya form of *ta* continued to be used along with its modern Oriya form in the records of the period. Another peculiar form of the letter is seen in one of the LN temple inscriptions of the time of Govindadeva of AD 1547 (vide, *nimate*, l.7) where the letter-form is represented by an inverted triangle with its side arms elongated. This is the only example of its kind and not traced in any other regional script of the period. It may, therefore, be attributed to the writer's fancy and nothing else. In fact, the inscription in question has a number of such peculiar forms for the letters like *na*, *bha*, *ra*, etc.

Na : The proto-Oriya form of *na* with a curl or loop in the left arm is still noticed optionally as in *Pl.* XVIIb.2 (first), 4 (second), 5 (second), 8 (first). The other variety in which the rounded top curve emerges from the right upright as in *Pl.* XVIIb.2 (second), 6 (first), 9 (second) is also found occasionally. In *Pl.* XVIIb.4 (first), the top curve is suppressed. In addition to these, the modern Oriya form of the letter has appeared throughout the period where the curl or loop in the left arm as well as the right upright are totally suppressed, and the rounded top curve moves from the angle of the lower limb, e.g., *ne* in *Pl.* XVIIb.10. In yet another peculiar variety the letter-form is seen in the form of an inverted triangle with its side arms elongated and the left arm curling in .. This has been reproduced from l.7 of the LN temple inscription of Govindadeva referred to above and it stands for *ni*.

Pa : The modern Oriya form of *pa* is regularly found used throughout the period. The other variety resembling to the Oriya *ga* is also noticed optionally as in *Pl.* XVIIb.1 (second), 5 (second), 6 (second), 7. However, this form of the letter is not favoured in the epigraphs after the sixteenth century.

Bha : Of all the consonants, the letter-form of *bha* has a number of varieties. The archaic form of the letter with an angular back is still noticed. But it has obtained a top curve and a tail, vide *Pl.* XVIIb.2. In another variety, the angular back of the letter is much more rounded and the letter-form looks like the proto-Oriya *ja* with or without a tail as in *Pl.* XVIIb.1. Both these varieties have been occurred in the proto-Oriya script. The modern Oriya form of the letter is derived by extending its lower limb to the left and joining it to the top curve as in *Pl.* XVIIb.10 (second). The letter-form in *Pl.* XVIIb.3, 8, 9 are some of the intermediate stages through which the modern Oriya *bha* is derived. In yet another variety the letter-form resembles to that of *la* as in *Pl.* XVIIb.4 (first), 5 (first). In the inscriptions of the ministerial dynasties, a few other peculiar forms of *bha* are noticed as in *Pl.* XVIIb.6 (first and second). However, all these peculiarities are discarded in favour of its modern Oriya form roughly after the middle of the sixteenth century.

Ẏa & Ya : It has already been referred to above that in modern Oriya there are two distinct signs for the semi-vowel *ẏa* and *ya*. Its beginning is traced to the inscriptions of Gajapati Puruṣottamadeva. The letter-form *ẏa* is basically a derivative of the proto-Oriya *ya* which is itself a derivative of its proto-Nāgārī form. In the early Oriya script it is fully rounded and has developed a down-facing curve in the left limb as in *Pl.* XVIIb.3, 8. *Ya* is distinguished from *ẏa* by adding a tail or a diacritical mark to the letter-form of *ẏa*. In *Pl.* XVIIb.4, the diacritical mark of *ya* slightly curves and faces left. This further blossomed into a full left-facing curve with a slanting stroke at the bottom. This feature is much more pronounced in the Kechala plates as in *yāṁ* (*Pl.* XVIIb.11). It merits attention here that the down-facing curve of *ẏa* and *ya* is further reduced to a small tick or a slanting stroke as in *Pl.* XVIIb.10, 11.

Ra : The proto-Oriya forms of *ra* either with a closed or opened triangular loop are still current in the inscriptions of the period. But in all such cases the top curve is extremely rounded and the tail is invariably applied as in *Pl.* XVIIb.2, 3 (first), 4 (second), 9. These proto-Oriya forms further progressed in the direction of forming a closed circular loop at the base as in *Pl.* XVIIb.1 (first), 3 (second), 5 (first), 6 (first), 8, 10 (first). Further, the tail is separated from the loop and joined to the terminal of the top curve on the right to complete its modern Oriya form. Although in *Pl.* XVIIb.1 (second), the loop is opened up; in *Pl.* XVIIb.5 (third) it is closed and the letter-form strictly conforms to the modern Oriya *ra*. Apart from these, in the temple inscriptions of the fifteenth-sixteenth centuries we come across another peculiar variety of the letter where two loops entwin and stand heightwise with a tail as in *Pl.* XVIIb.4 (first), 6 (second). This seems to be a corrupt form and never repeated after the sixteenth century.

Ḷa & La : As in *ẏa* and *ya* so also in *ḷa* and *la*, the latter is distinguished from the former by an addition of a tail. Although the letter-form of *ḷa* can be easily recognized as Oriya *ḷa*, yet its rounded top curve instead of starting from the left starts from the right. In the Kechala grant this feature is met with for the first time (*Pl.* XVIIb.11) and thus completes the formation of the modern Oriya *ḷa*. The tail of *la* is not yet separated from the bottom to join it to the terminal of the top curve on the right.

Śa : The proto-Oriya *śa* with an open loop at the base survived for sometime but later on it developed into a closed circular loop to represent its modern Oriya form (*Pl.* XVIIb.4, 8, 10, 11). Optionally the open loop is doubly curved as in *Pl.* XVIIb.7. In *Pl.* XVIIb.1 (second), the letter-form is drawn half; its left curve and loop being omitted. This may be due to the carelessness on the part of the engarver. In another variety, the palatal *śa* has an altogether different form, e.g., *śrī* in *Pl.* XVIIc.7 and 11. This peculiar form was current in the Telugu script.

Ha : With the rounding of the top curve and with the formation of an angle in its tail, the letter-form of *ha* has come closer to the modern Oriya *ha* (*Pl.* XVIIb). In another variety, the letter is represented by a doubly curved base with the usual top curve as in *Pl.* XVIIb.1 (second), 4 (second), 5 (second), 6 (second), 10 (second), 11 (first). In all such cases, the letter-form is drawn in one action. This has not come through an evolutionary process, but has been created to suit quick engraving. In *Pl.* XVIIb.11 (second), a tail is added to this peculiar variety. However, these peculiar varieties are also met with in the Karaṇī script.

Kṣa : The proto-Oriya *kṣa* is still retained for sometime but later on its down-facing curve in the left arm is reduced to a small tick (*Pl.* XVIIb.8). This resulted in the formation of the Oriya *kṣa*. The letter-form is the same as Oriya *ẏa* with a mid-line.

Medials

Most of the Oriya medials used today are standardized during this period. The medial *ā* is a full length vertical on the right. In the case of *ṭhā*, the medial is joined to the letter by an additional curve or line. In the case of letters having a tail such as *bha*, *ra*, *la*, etc., it joins the terminal of the top curve and tail (*fig.* III.3). This practice is still current in modern writings.

The medial *i* represented by a down-facing curve on the top of the letters is the regular type used throughout the period. In addition to this, the medial is also denoted by an inward dip in the rounded top curve of the letters (*fig.* III.2). This practice has already been noticed in the proto-Oriya script and is still current in modern Oriya. This type of the medial is never applied to the letters having a right upright such as *dha, ga, gha,* etc. We have another variety of the medial where it is seen in the form of a loop as in *bhi* and *li* in *fig.* III.3 and 4. The letter-form in *fig.* III.5 is reproduced from the word *nimate* in the LN temple inscription of Govindadeva of AD 1547. Here the medial is a curve on the right drawn in continuation with the top curve of the letter. At times it becomes difficult to distinguish between the medial *i* and *ī* when both of them are applied in the same manner. In another variety, the curve narrows down and its right arm is lengthened like a full length vertical as in *fig.* III.2. On most occasions it resembles the vertical type of the medial *ā*. In *fig.* III.3, the vertical is suspended mid-way.

The looped variety of the medial *u* which appeared in the proto-Oriya script is the regular type used in the early Oriya script. It is usually seen at the bottom of the consonants but in the case of the letters having right upright it is drawn in continuation with the upright as in *fig.* III.2. In another variety, the loop is drawn differently (*fig.* III.3). The medial *u* is denoted by a curve open at the top and a stroke added to it on the right (*fig.* III).

The inward curl in the *pr̥ṣṭha mātrā* type of the medial *e* gradually turned into a loop. The medial *ai* does not occur medially. The medial *o* consists of the *pr̥ṣṭha mātrā* type of *e* and the vertical type of *a*. *Au* is the same as *o* with an additional left going stroke on the top as in *gau* and *pau* in *fig.* III.1 and 2 respectively.

The medial *r̥* is a curve with an inward curl or loop drawn at the bottom of the consonants.

Thus, by the close of the seventeenth century almost all the medials have obtained their respective modern Oriya forms. The only exception is that the medial *ī* and *u* are drawn in continuation with the consonants while in modern Oriya they are drawn separately.

Conjuncts

As regards the conjuncts, the guttural nasal *ṅa* is indicated by a small circle on the top right of the letters of its class and the palatal nasal *ña* by the sign for the medial *o*. The second element *ca* in conjunction with *ña* looks like *tha* (*Pl.* XVIIb.8). The other nasals as superscripts are drawn fully. The right arm of the cerebral *ṇa* is often rounded but the second element *ḍa* in conjunction with *ṇa* is still denoted by left-facing curve. The down-facing curve of the dental *na* in conjunction with *da* (and also *dha*) is still retained as in *Pl.* XVIIc.2, 3, 6, 7, 10, but later on it has been reduced to a small tick or stroke as in modern Oriya (*Pl.* XVIIc.8, 9, 11). The second element *bha* in conjunction with *ma* is a left-facing curve with a slanting or straight stroke as in modern Oriya (*Pl.* XVIIc.6, 10, 11). As in the proto-Oriya so also in the early Oriya script, the subscripts *ḍa* and *ta* are indicated by one and the same sign which is usually a left-facing curve. But gradually a loop is formed in the top arm of the curve of the subscript *ta* as in *nti, pti* and *sti* in *Pl.* XVIIc.6. This modified form of *ta* is also current in modern Oriya. Another form of the subscript *ta* represented by a right-going slanting stroke current in modern Oriya can be traced to the type used in the conjuncts *tma* and *tna* in *Pl.* XVIIc.4. In both the examples, the subscript *ta* is a right-facing curve moving from the middle of the left limb. In course of time, the same sign is placed at the bottom of the superscript. The conjunct *tta* is drawn variously. The subscript *ta* is simply a left facing curve under the letter *ta* (*Pl.* XVIIc.3, 6). In another variety the lower limb of the superscript *ta* is shortened and joined to the left facing curve type of the subscript *ta* with the usual top curve as in *Pl.* XVIIc.8, 11. In *Pl.* XVIIc.7 (first) and 10, it has obtained a tail and can truely be recognized as the precursor of the modern Oriya *tta*. In yet another variety, the conjunct resembles the modern Oriya initial *o* with an extended outer curve. When the letter *da* is doubled, its lower curve is also doubled. The conjunct *dda* in *ddu* (*Pl.* XVIIc.11) resembles its modern Oriya form. But the subscript *da* in conjunction with *va* (*ba*) is still placed below the latter. The subscripts *ca, ma,* and *la* are still archaic. The subscript *ṭa* in *ṣṭha* is a small circle. The modified forms of the subscripts *ṇa, tha,* etc., as noticed in the proto-Oriya survived in early and modern Oriya script as well. In *kka* (*Pl.* XVIIc. 8) and *ska* (*Pl.* XVIIc.9), the subscript *ka* is devoid of the top curve. In *spha* (*Pl.* XVIIc.11), the subscript *pha* is written like *pa* and its circular loop is placed on the top right of the superscript *sa*. The old form of *ya* survived as late as the fifteenth century, e.g., *lya* and *jye* (*Pl.* XVIIc.2 and 5). But its modern Oriya form represented by a curve opening up and joining to a right upright has already been developed by the fifteenth century, vide *gya* (*Pl.* XVIIc.1). Optionally it is either drawn in continuation with the rounded top curve of the superscript as in *Pl.* XVIIc.6, 11, or placed on the bottom right of the superscript as in *Pl.* XVIIc.3 and 4. In *Pl.* XVIIc.10, it looks like the modified form of the subscript *va*. The palaeographical peculiarity of the conjunct *tye* (*Pl.* XVIIc.2) is interesting. In this example, the modified form of *ta* is joined to the letter-form of *ya* drawn in full. However, this practice is not favoured in modern Oriya. The subscript *ra* and the *repha* do not call for remark. The modified form of the subscript *va* is regularly found used in the epigraphs of the period with a few exceptions. In *śva* (*Pl.* XVIIc.4), it is seen in the form of an upturned angle and in *mve* (*Pl.* XVIIc.6) it right upright is drawn in a slanting manner.

Orthography

The orthographical peculiarities of the Oriya inscriptions of the period are so vast that it becomes difficult to make a comprehensive treatment of all of them in this limited space. K.B. Tripathi, however, has examined the orthography of the Oriya inscriptions up to AD 1568 in his book and it would be a repetition to re-examine them here. However, some broad features may be outlined in the following. No distinction is found between *va* and *ba*, *i* and *ī*, and *u* and *ū*. The sibilants are sometimes confused and the cerebral *ṣa* is never used independently. *Ṛ* is occasionally confused with *ru* or *ri* (as in *Kruṣṇa* or *Kriṣṇa*). The letters *da* and *dha* as well as *ja* and *ẏa* are interchanged on several occasions. Consonants which are usually doubled such as *ṭ* (in *bhaṭṭa*), *t* (*uttara*), etc., are often left single. The letters or group of letters such as *kṣa*, *kṣma*, *jña* and *hma* are changed into *khya*, *kha*, *gya* and *mbha* respectively as in *dakhya* (for *dakṣa*), *lakhaṇa* (for *Lakṣmaṇa*), *gyāti* (*jñāti*) and *brāmbhana* (for *brāhmaṇa*). This list of such letters or group of letters can be multiplied.

The practice of contracting simple letters into complex compounds which had started roughly from the thirteenth century has been widely popularized among the scribes of the fifteenth-seventeenth centuries. According to this practice *gajapati* is written as *gajapti*, *marakata* as *marakta*, *guruvāra* as *gruvāra*, *parameśvara* as *prameśvara* or *prameśvra*, *tāhāṅkara* as *tāṅkra*, *puruṇā* as *pr̥ṇā*, *mahārājā* as *mahārjā*, *puruṣottama* as *pr̥sotma* and so on. Such contraction of letters led to the creation of certain new conjuncts in the Oriya alphabet. But after testing their suitability or otherwise from linguistic and palaeographical point of view, the practice was discarded after the seventeenth century. In the eighteenth-cenutury writings we normally do not come across such contraction of letters. It seems that the professional scribes made an experiment with the practice and on getting confirmed about its unsuitability in linguistic and palaeographical formulations discarded it subsequently.

Bibliography

PLATE XVII

1. Plates of the time of Kapilendradeva

   (a) Veligalani plates of Kapilendradeva, Ś. 1380, D.C. Sircar, *JAS*, *L*, 23 (1), 13-17 & pls.

   (b) Chiruvroli plates of Hamvira, Ś. 1383, D.C. Sircar & K.H.V. Sharma, *EI*, 34, 177-88 & pls.

2. (a) Temple inscriptions of the time of Kapilendradeva, K.B. Tripathi, *EOLS*, Nos. 11-18, 21-26. Impressions in possession of K.B. Tripathi have been consulted.

   (b) Mallikārjuna (Sri Sailam) temple inscription of the time of Kapilendradeva, D.C. Sircar, *EI*, 36, 75-80 & pl.

   (c) Kapali Math (near Liṅgarāja temple in Bhubaneswar) temple inscription of Kapilendradeva, K.C. Panigrahi, *OHRJ*, 1 (2), 8-9, Inscription No. C & pl.

   (d) Tekkali Stone Inscription of Kapilendradeva, S.K. Acharya, *JESI*, 26, 102-03. Estampage preserved in the office of the Director (Epigraphy).

   (e) Gopinathpur temple inscription of the time of Kapilendradeva, M.M. Chakravarti, *JASB*, 69, 173-89 (without facsimile).

3. Balasore copper axe-head inscription of Puruṣottamadeva, K.B. Tripathi, *EOLS*, No. 31. Plate published in Artaballabh Mohanti, *Prācīna Oḍia Gadyapadyādarśa* (Oriya), pl. facing p. 42.

4. (a) Temple inscriptions of the time of Puruṣottamadeva, K.B. Tripathi, *EOLS*, Nos. 27-29, 30, 32-41. Impressions in possession of K.B. Tripathi have been consulted.

   (b) An Oriya inscription from Trisilia near Agarpara, B.V. Nath, *OHRJ*, 2 (1), 61-64 & pl.

   (c) Liṅgarāja temple inscription of the time of Puruṣottamadeva, P.K. Ray, *ibid.*, 15 (1-2), 113-14 & pl.

   (d) Madhukeśvara (Bhanragada) temple inscription of the time of Puruṣottamadeva, K.S. Behera, *Orissa Review*, 52 (5), 3-6 & pl.

5. (a) Temple inscriptions of the time of Pratāparudradeva, K.B. Tripathi, *EOLS*, Nos. 42-48. Impressions in possession of K.B. Tripathi have been consulted.

   (b) An Oriya inscription from Indupur, B.V. Nath, *OHRJ*, 3 (3), 163-64 (without facsimile).

6. Inscriptions of the ministerial dynasties, K.B. Tripathi, *EOLS*, Nos. 49-55. Impressions in possession of K.B. Tripathi have been consulted.

7. Bilingual stone inscription of Baripada Museum, Ś. 1509, S.C. De, *OHRJ*, 2 (3 & 4), 94-98 & pl.

8. Athgarh rock inscription of Narasiṁha Gajapati, Ś. 1512, S.N. Rajaguru, *ibid.*, 6 (1), 23-28 & pl.

9. Srijang inscriptions of Acyuta Baliār Siṅgh Mohāpātra, Ś. 1520, Sudhakar Patnaik, *JOA*, 2, 21-32 & pls.

10. (a) Sthāneśvar (Manjuri) temple inscription of the time of Puruṣottamdeva of Bhoi dynasty, *aṅka* 8, Ekadasi Padhi, *Proceedings of the Orissa History Congress*, 1995 session, 85-91. (without facsimile).

    (b) Kesiari Sarvamaṅgala temple inscriptions, Ś. 1526 & 1537, P. Acharya, *IHRC*, 21, 1-3; 22, 86-89. Estampages preseved in the office of the Director (Epigraphy) have been consulted.

    (c) Deulbarh temple inscription, A.K. Bhattacharya, *A Corpus of Dedicatory Inscriptions from Temples of West Bengal*, Calcutta, 1982, Inscription No. 4, pl. III.

11. Kechala plate of Kṛṣṇadeva, G. Ramdas, *JAHRS*, 6 (1), 8-14 & pl.

12

Conclusion

THE Imperial Brāhmī script diffused to a wider region is thus an originally homogeneous script and became the parent of most of the proto-regional and regional scripts used in India. The peculiar reversible characters of the letters such as *o*, *dha*, *na*, etc., and the juxtaposition of both angular and cursive style of engraving in the edicts at Dhauli and Jaugada are not regional peculiarities. The Brāhmī script as noticed in the Orissa edicts, therefore, can hardly be reduced to a regional variety merely on the strength of the above digressions. A majority of the letter-forms and medial vowels strictly conform with the standard Aśokan Brāhmī script. Whatever digression have been found are possibly due to the carelessness on the part of the engraver or due to the surface of the rock on which the writing is made.

In the next stage of development the Imperial Brāhmī script entered into a stage of transition from royalty to popularity. During this time a "new-edged pen" was discovered which imparted altogether new features to the letter forms. In HI and other contemporary inscriptions of Orissa the new pen was not employed but from the occurrence of both the advanced and archaic letter-forms it appears that more than one scribe representing different localities were instrumental in inscribing the epigraphs.

There is a clear gap of about two or three centuries between the transitional and the later Brāhmī scripts in Orissa. The dearth of epigraphical sources during the early centuries of the Christian era makes it difficult to trace the connective link between the two groups of writing. When we come across the later Brāhmī script in the lithic records, the alphabet has undergone rapid changes and given place to certain new varieties, whose parentage is undisputed. However, in the head-marks, the medial signs and in the essential characteristics no uniform pattern of development is noticed. While the characters of the Bhadrak inscription of Mahārāja Gaṇa and the Sitabinji inscriptions developed locally, the characters of the Asanapat stone inscription appear to have been the earliest specimen of the western variety of alphabet in eastern India.

In the early medieval and medieval times the historical geography of Orissa was characterized by different territorial units with their boundaries frequently fluctuating from time to time. Many of the early dynasties ruled over parts of Orissa as well as of other territories in the adjoining states of Orissa. Contemporaneous with these ruling families a number of important dynasties flourished in close neighbourhood and they had considerably influenced the polity and culture of the different political entities of Orissa. Therefore, in the sphere of the cultural life, Orissa exhibits an admixture of different elements from the north, south and central India.

During this time, Kaliṅga under the minor ruling families and the Eastern Gaṅgas borrowed certain new features from the south which later on served as a permanent source region from which the writing styles made a constant flow to this sub-region and considerably reinforced the existing local style. The letter-forms are, therefore, pre-eminently south Indian. In the essential characters of *a, ka, ma, ra, la,* etc., the medial *ï,* the notched base-line of some of the letters, and in the general cursive engravings an unmistakable imprint of the south Indian characters is noticed. However, the script continued to be used in the locality right up to the close of the seventh century whereafter a mixed style of engraving which derived its source from different palaeographical zones began to exert considerable influence on the existing style of the locality. The inextricable admixture of the Telugu-Canarese, the Grantha, the *kuṭila* and the the proto-Nāgarī features with the existing local peculiarities not only display the proficiency of the scribes and engravers in the scripts of other palaeographical zones of India but also portray a truely cosmopolitan character of the sub-regional kingdom of Kaliṅga in the eighth-ninth centuries.

The Nalas and the Śarabhapurīyas who held sway over South Kośala used a type of script which is more akin to the box-headed characters of central India. The Nala-Vākāṭaka struggle in the fourth-fifth centuries is mainly responsible for the flow of this technical skill to this region. The box-headed variety is a highly ornamental script that needed great draftmanship in execution. The script is distinguished by the addition of hollow box head-marks on the top of the verticals and extreme angularization of the letter-forms in general. There is often the possibility of confusing the script of South Kośala with that of the Eastern Gaṅgas of Kaliṅga of the sixth-seventh centuries. In the essential characters, the scripts of Kaliṅga and South Kośala can hardly be distinguished, because for sometime the Eastern Gaṅgas also angularized the letter-forms. But the only distinguishing feature is the hollow box head-marks that separates the style from the median Kaliṅga script. Moreover, there is no positive evidence regarding the political and cultural relationship of South Kośala with Kaliṅga in the days prior to the Eastern Gaṅgas. It is, therefore, legitimate to infer that the box-headed variety of South Kośala is indebted more to Central India than to any other source region. But one of the most astonishing facts is that once the style penetrated into the region it could hardly be outlived by any other character and continued to be used in this region for a fairly long time. The script survived in the inscriptions of the Pāṇḍuvaṁśīs right up to the time of Mahāśivagupta Bālārjuna. This reflects the insular character of the sub-regional kingdom of South Kośala in the seventh-ninth centuries and also the conservatism of the professional scribes of the locality.

While Kaliṅga and South Kośala received inspiration from south and central India respectively, Toṣalī or Utkala came under the influence of north India. By this time the first wave of displacement of the eastern variety of alphabet had been completed by the western variety and the Middle Ganges valley served as the spring-board from where the style diffused to different parts of eastern India. Though it is difficult to ascertain the process of displacement in the inscriptions of the Dattas, the Vigrahas and the Mudgalas, the letter-forms of *ma, la, ṣa* and *ha* stand the test very well for the advancement in the palaeography of the region.

The second wave of displacement took place in eastern India sometime in the last quarter of the sixth century. The new style of acute-angled alphabet that infiltrated as far south as Koṅgoda along the routes of Śaśāṅka's invasion became the epigraphic alphabet of the Śailodbhavas. In the application of the solid triangular head-marks and in turning the right angles into acute angles the Śailodbhava charters betrayed the perfection of the style and preferred to use the existing local style which closely resembles the sixth-century alphabet of Toṣalī or Utkala. The advanced palaeography in some of the grants of the Śailodbhavas, which invited serious speculations from scholars, may be due to the fact that they have been copied from the original at a later date due to some reason or other. The *kuṭila* style which is only a logical sequel to the acute-angled alphabet found its way to Toṣalī again from eastern India. In the application of the head-marks, medial vowels and in the twisting of the right verticals, the *kuṭila* variety exihibited highly ornamental characters. The occurrence of this stylized form exclusively in the stone inscriptions of the Pāṇḍuvaṁśī king Mahāśivagupta Bālārjuna admits of the fact that South Kośala borrowed the style from the Bhaumakaras of Toṣalī.

In the ninth century while the highly stylized *kuṭila* script was current in the inscriptions of the Bhaumakaras, the feudatories under them considerably simplified the script. The simplification was a never a conscious attempt on the part of the engraver but it was largely due to inferior draftmanship. The dichotomy between the ornamental calligraphy of the early Bhaumakaras charters and the simplified calligraphy of their subordinates and contemporaries can also be viewed from the standpoint of urban and rural strain of palaeography. But what was simple, inferior and rural was gradually adopted by a majority as the most favoured script. Its popularity was because of quick engraving. This simplified script is termed as the proto-Nāgarī and is evidently the precursor of the Nāgarī and other proto-regional and regional scripts of eastern India. The Somavaṁśīs who inherited the writing style from their predecessors, the Pāṇḍuvaṁśīs, at first introduced this simplified script in their charters in South Kośala. The political fusion of South Kośala and Utkala under the Somavaṁśīs sometime in the tenth century fostered a uniform pattern of development of the alphabet in the region. The script was also current in the eleventh-century records of Kaliṅga. In Orissa, the proto-Nāgarī survived for more than two hundred years and by the closing decades of the eleventh century showed the signs of the advent of the proto-regional characters.

The proto-Oriya script is a derivative of the proto-Nāgarī. The real beginning of the proto-Oriya characters can be traced to the advent of the so-called "Nepalese hook" on the top of the letters. In the whole range of the epigraphic alphabet of eastern India, the Somavaṁśī charters demonstrate the different stages through which the "hook" was evolved. From the closing decades of the eleventh century the hook began to be rounded and an inward dip was formed in the left half of some of the letters. Besides, the rounding of the letter-forms, the development of a definite right upright with a "horn-like protuberance" and the type of some of the medial vowels borrowed from the Telugu-Canarese script are the other distinctive features the proto-Oriya. The script was regular in the charters of the later Somavaṁśīs, the Telugu-Coḍas, the later Bhañjas of different administrative units and those of the Imperial Gaṅgas. It was also frequent in the numerous lithic records of the time of the Imperial Gaṅgas. But in the official charters belonging to the thirteenth-fourteenth centuries, the script was never favoured and the proto-Bengali or the Nāgarī scripts were used instead. Thus, the proto-Oriya survived long in the records of Orissa at least up to the early part of the fifteenth century and hence the advent of modern Oriya was delayed by a couple of centuries. The apathy and indifference of the later Imperial Gaṅgas towards the growing proto-Oriya script was chiefly responsible for this delay. During this time, the local chieftains, the native pilgrims, private individuals and some of the officials of the court circle took genuine interest in making the Oriya language and script a living language and a living script. The language movement was thus very much a part of the socio-political tension that was mounting in the fourteenth-fifteenth centuries.

With the commencement of the Gajapati rule in Orissa, there was a remarkable change in the ideologies of the ruling class towards the native language and script. It was in the fifteenth-sixteenth centuries, that the Oriya language was recognized as the official medium, the royal proclamations were drafted in this language and the regional script of Orissa entered into its mature phase. During this period the shallow top curves of the proto-Oriya letters are fully rounded, the inward dip at the centre of the left limb as well as the right upright get prominent, and the medial vowels are standardized. Although in the early Oriya script some of the individual letters exhibited more than one form, subsequently in the modern Oriya script most of the peculiar varieties of the individual letters are suppressed in favour of the standard modern Oriya alphabet. Thus, by the close of the seventeenth century almost all the vowels, consonants, conjuncts and medials are fully grown into their respective modern Oriya forms.

Plates

PLATE Ia : Imperial Brāhmī Script in Orissa .

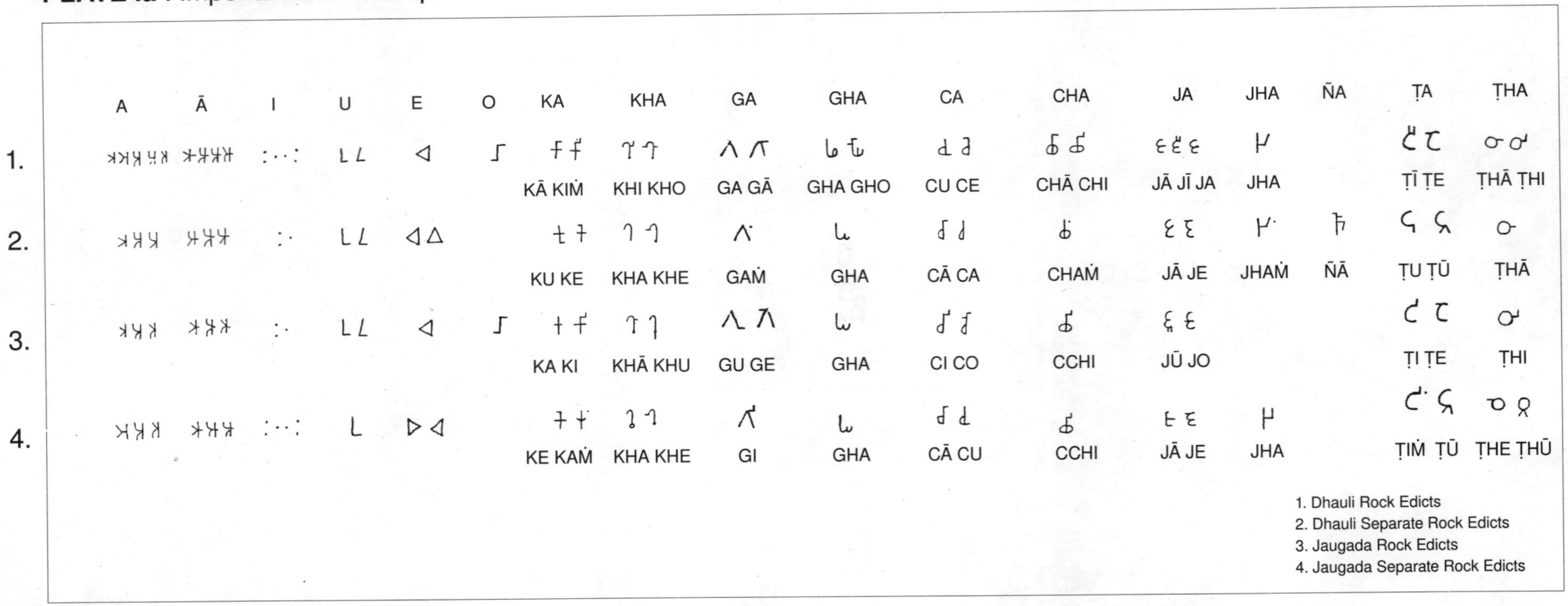

PLATE III b : Median Kaliṅga Script : Inscriptions of the Minor Ruling Families of Kaliṅga .

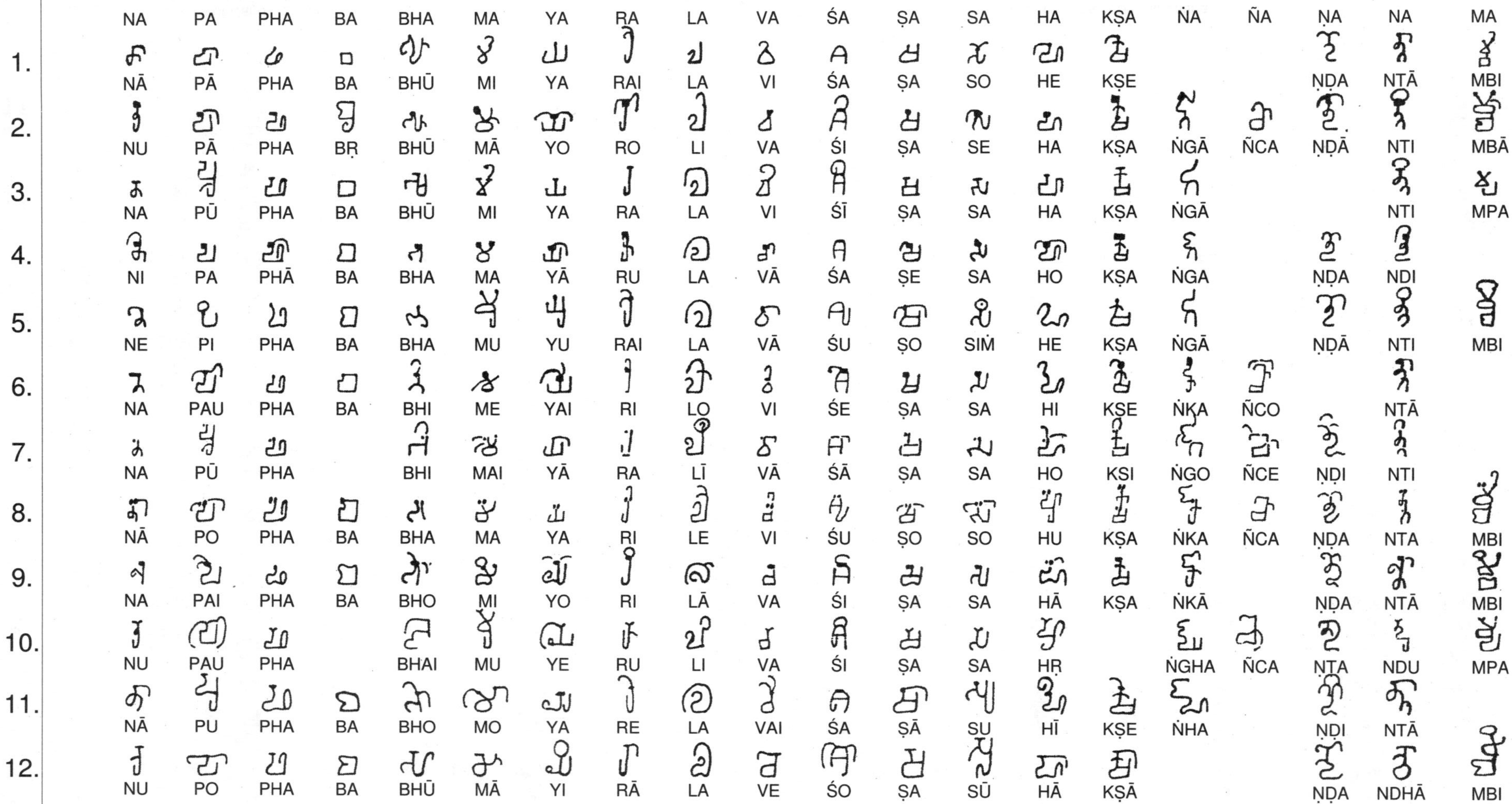

Minor Ruling Families of Kaliṅga (4th-6th century AD)

1.Koroshonda plates of Viśākhavarman
2.Plates of Umāvarman
3.Baranga and Chicacole plates of Nanda-Prabhañjanavarman
4.Ragolu plates of Nanda-Prabhañjanavarman
5.Plates of Caṇḍavarman
6.Ragolu plates of Śaktivarman
7. Ningondi plates of Prabhañjanavarman
8. Andhavaram plates of Anantaśaktivarman
9. Madras Museum plates of Anantaśaktivarman
10. Pates of Anantavarman
11. Pedda-Dugam plates of Śatrudamana
12. Plates of Pṛthivī Mahārāja

PLATE III c : Median Kaliṅga Script : Inscriptions of the Minor Ruling Families of Kaliṅga .

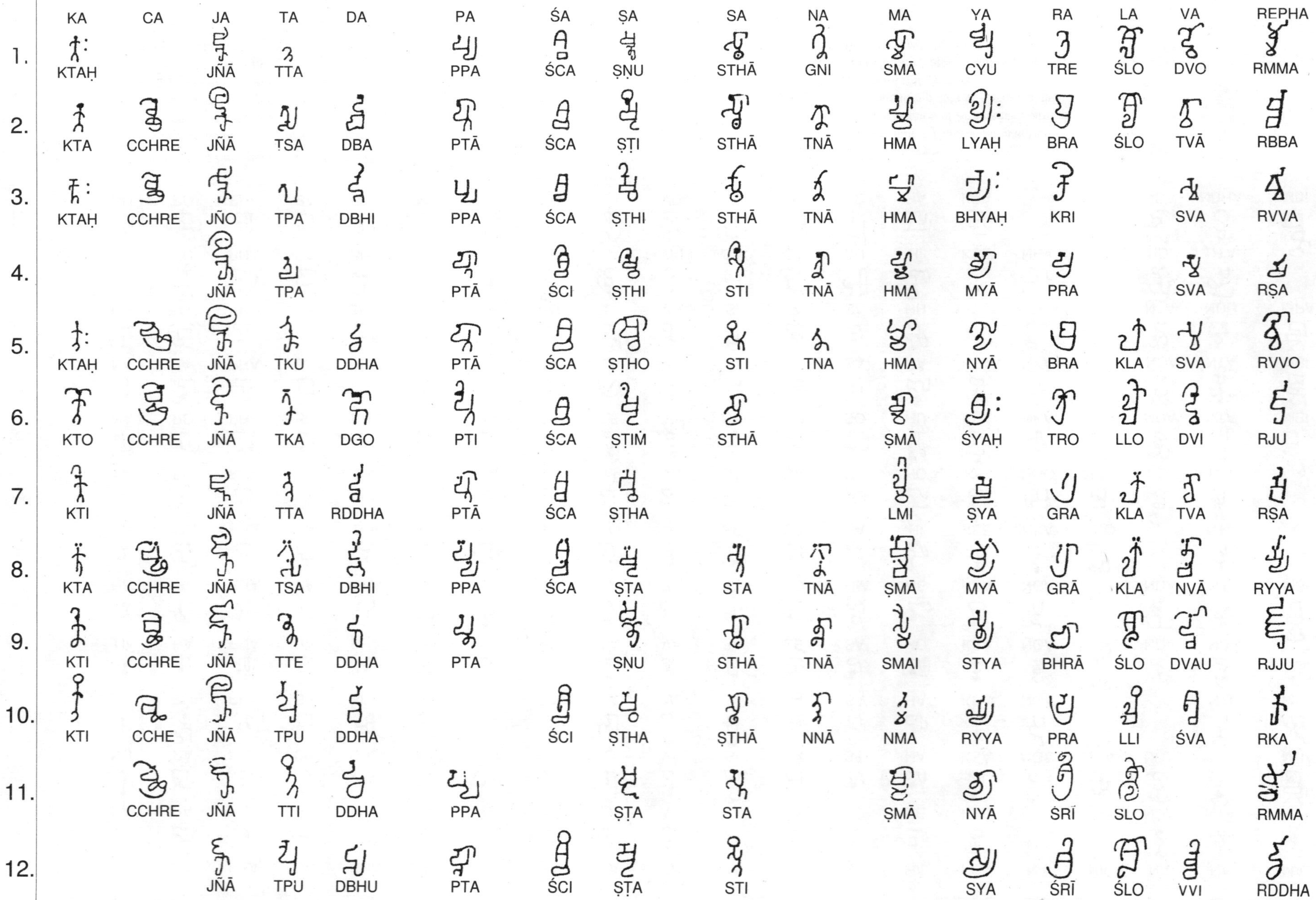

Minor Ruling Families of Kaliṅga (4th-6th century AD)

1. Koroshonda plates of Viśākhavarman
2. Plates of Umāvarman
3. Baranga and Chicacole plates of Nanda-Prabhañjanavarman
4. Ragolu plates of Nanda-Prabhañjanavarman
5. Plates of Chaṇḍavarman
6. Ragolu plates of Śaktivarman
7. Ningondi plates of Prabhañjanavarman
8. Andhavaram plates of Anantaśaktivarman
9. Madras Museum plates of Anantaśaktivarman
10. Pates of Anantavarman
11. Pedda-Dugam plates of Śatrudamana
12. Plates of Pṛthvī Mahārāja

PLATE IV a : Median Kaliṅga Script : Inscriptions of the Eastern Gaṅgas .

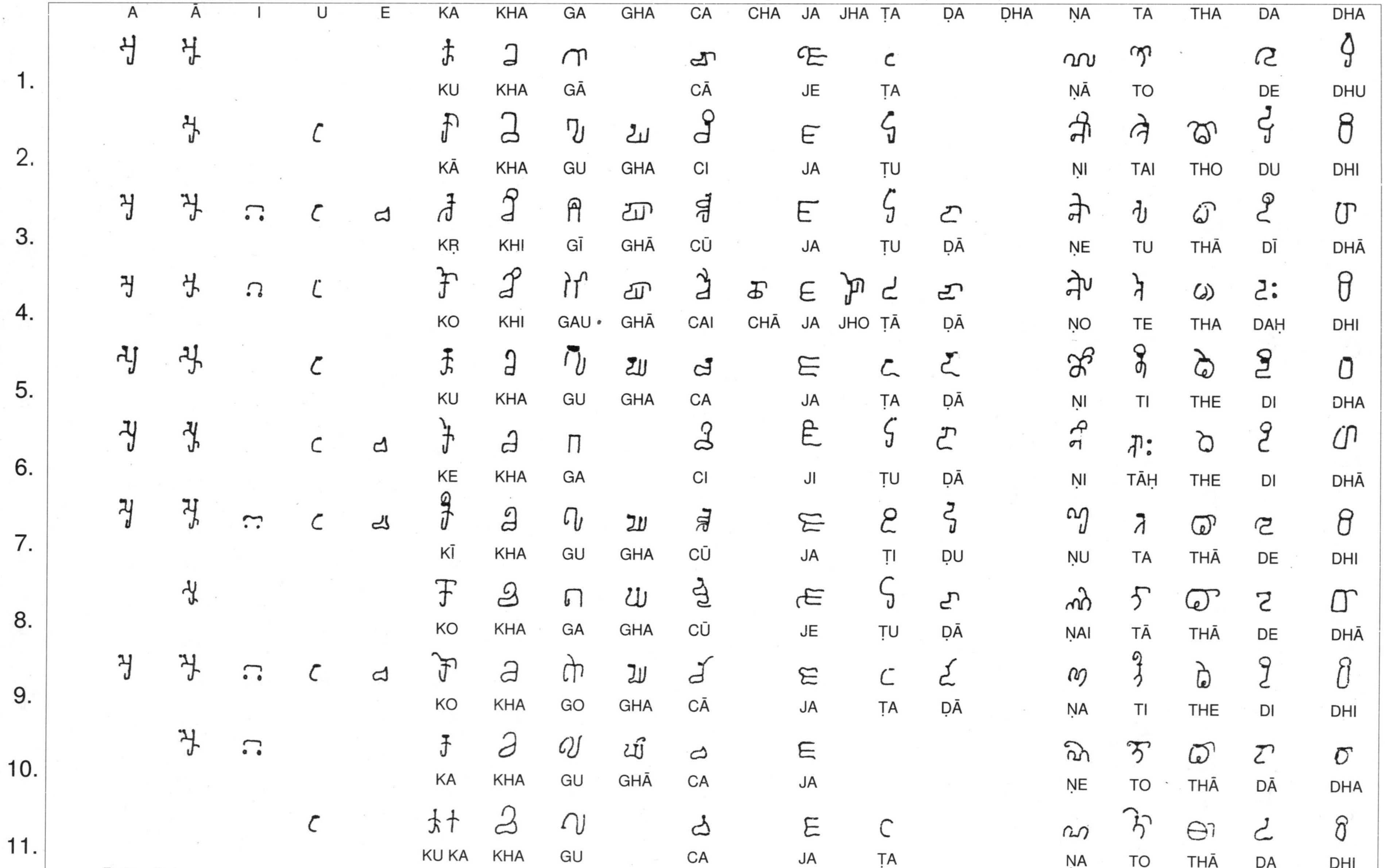

Eastern Gaṅgas

1. Jirjingi plates of Indravarman, GY 39
2. Ponnuturu plates of Sāmantavarman, GY 64
3. Plates of Hastivarman, GY 79, 80
4. Plates of Indravarman, GY 87, 97
5. Chicacole plates of Indravarman, GY 128
6. Andhavaram plates of Indravarman, GY 133
7. Purle and Tekkali plates of Indravarman, GY 137, 154
8. Chicacole plates of Indravarman, GY 138
9. Chicacole and Dharmalingesvara plates of Devendravarman, GY 183, 184
10. Trilingi plates of Devendravarman, GY 192

Svetaka Gaṅgas:

11. Pherava plates of Sāmantavarman, (GY) 185

PLATE IV b : Median Kaliṅga Script : Inscriptions of the Eastern Gaṅgas .

	NA	PA	PHA	BA	BHA	MA	YA	RA	LA	VA	ŚA	ṢA	SA	HA	KṢA	ṄA	ÑA	ṆA	NA	MA
1.	NṚ	PU			BHŪ	MI	YŪ	RA	LA LA	VO	ŚI	ṢA	SAṀ	HĪ	KṢA	ṄGHA	ÑCA	ṆḌA	NDHA	MPA
2.	NO	PA	PHA	BO	BHA	MU	YAṀ	RĀ	LAI	VA	ŚE	ṢO	SE	HA	KṢE	ṄKṚ	ÑCE	RṆṆA	NDĀ	MBI
3.	NU	PĀ	PHA	BA	BHIḤ	MI	YO	RA	LI	VA	ŚĀ	ṢA	SŪ	HĪ	KṢE	ṄKO	ÑJA	ṆḌE	NTA	MBI
4.	NA	PU	PHA	BA	BHU	MĀ	YU	RU	LĪ	VA	ŚĀ	ṢA	SĪ	HE	KṢO	ṄGA	ÑJI	ṆḌA	NDI	MPA
5.	NU	PAU	PHA	BĀ	BHA	ME	YU	RO	LĀ	VI	ŚI	ṢA	SŪ	HĀ	KṢA	ṄKO		RṆṆA	NDĀ	MBA
6.	NĀ	PI	PHA	BĀ	BHŪ	MI	YE	RA	LO	VI	ŚA	ṢA	SU SŪ	HA	KṢA	ṄKI	ÑJI		NTI	MPA
7.	NUḤ	PO	PHA	BO	BHO	MA	YA YA	RAI	LI	VĀ	ŚĀ	ṢA	SĀ	HU	KṢE	ṄGA	ÑJI	ṆḌI	NDHI	MPA
8.	NI	PŪ	PHA	BU	BHI	MU	YO	RO	LĀ	VṚ	ŚA	ṢA	SA	HĪ	KṢE	ṄGA			NTA	MBI
9.	NI	PU	PHA	BA	BHA	MA	YU	RĪ	LA	VI	ŚĪ	ṢA	SU	HE	KṢA	ṄGA	ÑJA		NTI	MBI
10.	NĀ	PI	PHA		BHŪ	MA	YE	RO	LA LA	VṚ	ŚE ŚA	ṢA	SĀ	HE	KṢA	ṄKA	ÑJI	RṆṆE	NDHA	MBA
11.	NU	PŪ	PHA		BHĀ	MA MA	YA	RA RA	LA	VA	ŚE	ṢA	SI	HE	KṢI	ṄKA		ṆḌĀ	NTA	

Eastern Gaṅgas

1. Jirjingi plates of Indravarman, GY 39
2. Ponnuturu plates of Sāmantavarman, GY 64
3. Plates of Hastivarman, GY 79, 80
4. Plates of Indravarman, GY 87, 97
5. Chicacole plates of Indravarman, GY 128
6. Andhavaram plates of Indravarman, GY 133
7. Purle and Tekkali plates of Indravarman, GY 137, 154
8. Chicacole plates of Indravarman, GY 138
9. Chicacole and Dharmalingesvara plates of Devendravarman, GY 183, 184
10. Trilingi plates of Devendravarman, GY 192

Svetaka Gaṅgas:

11. Pherava plates of Sāmantavarman, (GY) 185

PLATE IV c : Median Kaliṅga Script : Inscriptions of the Eastern Gaṅgas .

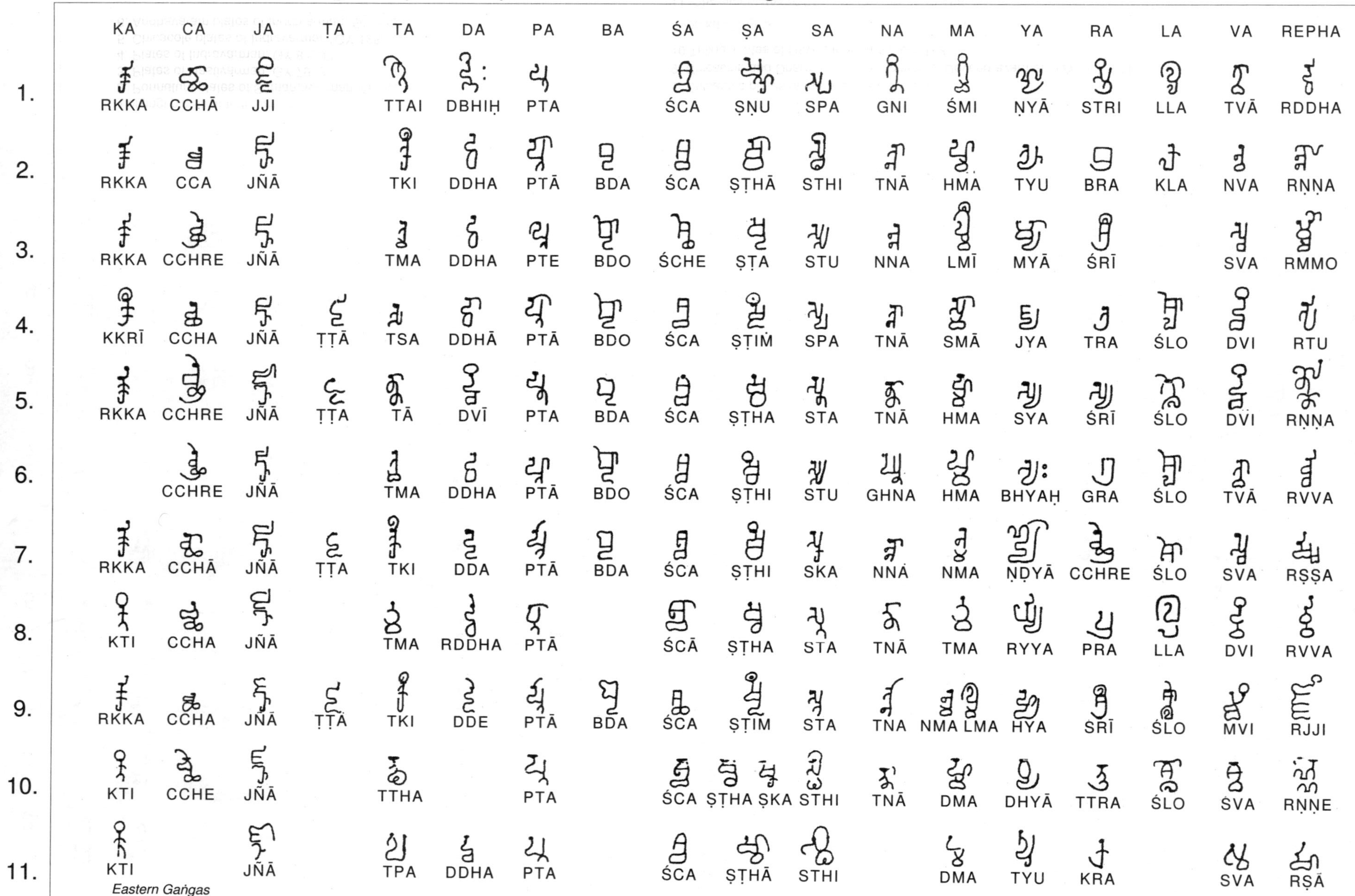

Eastern Gaṅgas

1. Jirjingi plates of Indravarman, GY 39
2. Ponnuturu plates of Sāmantavarman, GY 64
3. Plates of Hastivarman, GY 79, 80
4. Plates of Indravarman, GY 87, 97
5. Chicacole plates of Indravarman, GY 128
6. Andhavaram plates of Indravarman, GY 133
7. Purle and Tekkali plates of Indravarman, GY 137, 154
8. Chicacole plates of Indravarman, GY 138
9. Chicacole and Dharmalingesvara plates of Devendravarman, GY 183, 184
10. Trilingi plates of Devendravarman, GY 192

Svetaka Gaṅgas:

11. Pherava plates of Sāmantavarman, (GY) 185

PLATE V a : Box-headed characters in South Kośala : Inscriptions of the Nalas, the Śarabhapurīyas and the Pāṇḍuvaṁśīs

Nalas : (4th-5th century AD)

1. Rithapur plates of Bhavattavarman
2. Kesaribeda plates of Arthapati
3. Podagadh stone inscription of Skandavarman

Śarabhapurīyas (5th-7th century AD)

4. Pipardula stone inscription of Narendra
5. Khurud and Rawan plates of Narendra
6. Plates of Jayarāja and Sudevarāja I
7. Plates of Pravararāja and Sudevarāja II
8. Adhabhara plates of Nannarāja

Pāṇḍuvaṁśīs : (7th-9th century AD)

9. Plates of Tīvaradeva
10. Plates of Mahāśivagupta Bālārjuna

Plate V b : Box-headed characters in South Kośala : Inscriptions of the Nalas, the Śarabhapurīyas and the Pāṇḍuvaṁśīs.

Nalas : (4th-5th century AD)

1. Rithapur plates of Bhavattavarman
2. Kesaribeda plates of Arthapati
3. Podagadh stone inscription of Skandavarman

Śarabhapurīyas (5th-7th century AD)

4. Pipardula stone inscription of Narendra
5 Khurud and Rawan plates of Narendra

6. Plates of Jayarāja and Sudevarāja I
7. Plates of Pravararāja and Sudevarāja II
8. Adhabhara plates of Nannarāja

Pāṇḍuvaṁśīs : (7th-9th century AD)

9. Plates of Tīvaradeva
10. Plates of Mahāśivagupta Bālārjuna

Plate V c : Box-headed characters in South Kośala : Inscriptions of the Nalas, the Śarabhapurīyas and the Pāṇḍuvaṁśīs.

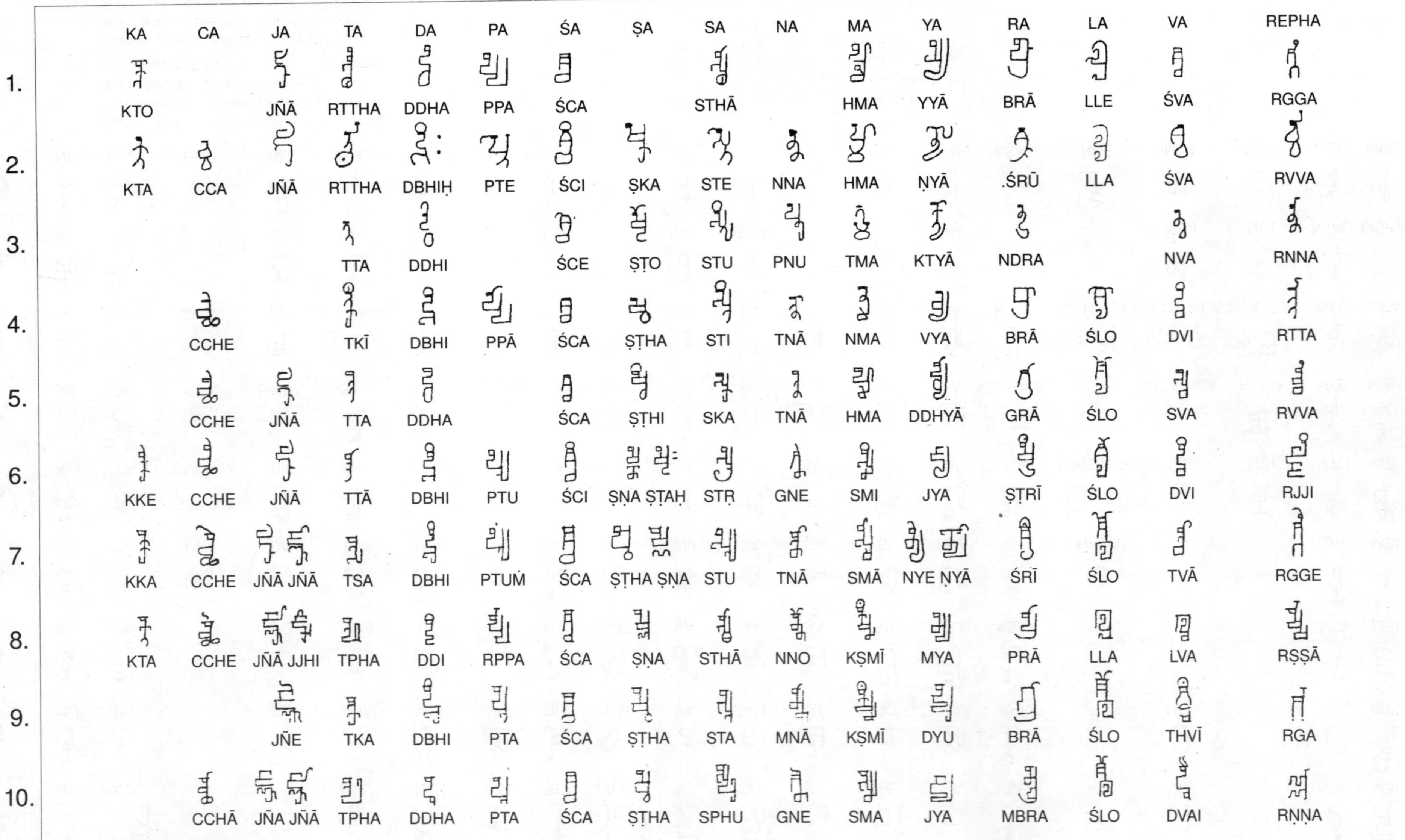

Nalas :(4th-5th century AD)

1. Rithapur plates of Bhavattavarman
2. Kesaribeda plates of Arthapati
3. Podagadh stone inscription of Skandavarman

Śarabhapurīyas (5th-7th century AD)

4. Pipardula stone inscription of Narendra
5 Khurud and Rawan plates of Narendra
6. Plates of Jayarāja and Sudevarāja I
7. Plates of Pravararāja and Sudevarāja II
8. Adhabhara plates of Nannarāja

Pāṇḍuvaṁśīs : (7th-9th century AD)

9. Plates of Tīvaradeva
10. Plates of Mahāśivagupta Bālārjuna

Plate VI a : Acute-angled Script in Toṣalī, Utkala and Koṅgoda : Inscriptions of the minor ruling families

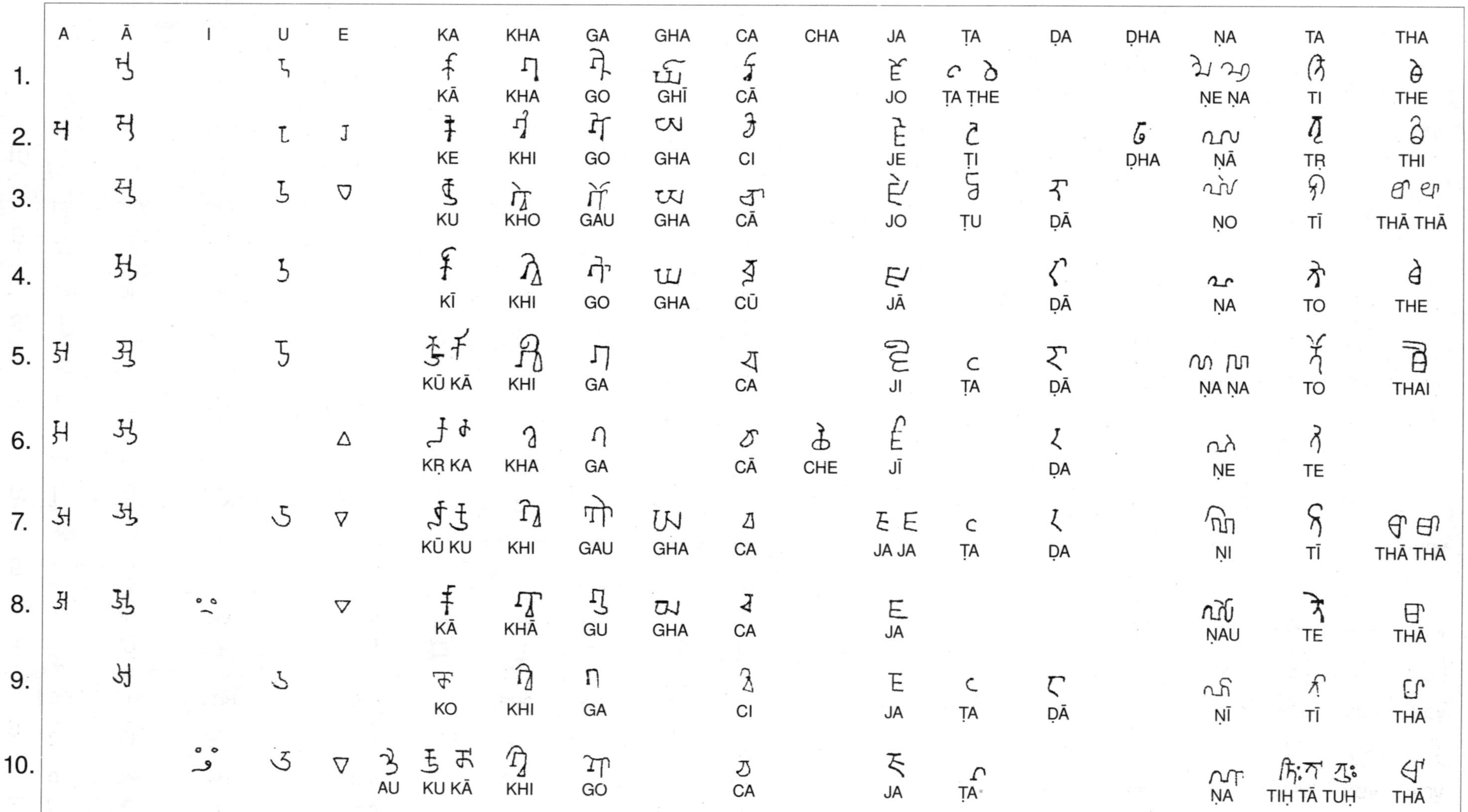

Minor Ruling Families of Toṣalī and Utkala : (5th-7th century AD)

1. Asanapat Naṭarāj image inscription (5th-6th century AD)
2. Jeyrampur plate of the time of Gopachandra (early 6th century AD)
3. Sumandala plates of the time of Pṛithivīvigraha, GE 250
4. Soro plate of Śambhuyaśa, GE 260
5. Erbang plate of Śambhuyaśa
6. Kanas plate of Lokavigraha, GE 280 and Patiakella plate of Śivarāja
7. Two Soro plates of Somadatta
8. Midnapur plates of Somadatta and Śubhakīrtti
9. Plates of Bhānudatta
10. Dhenkanal plate of Jayasiṁha

Plate VI b : Acute-angled Script in Toṣalī, Utkala and Koṅgoda : Inscriptions of the minor ruling families

Minor Ruling Families of Toṣalī and Utkala : (5th-7th century AD)

1. Asanapat Naṭarāj image inscription (5th-6th century AD)
2. Jeyrampur plate of the time of Gopachandra (early 6th century AD)
3. Sumandala plates of the time of Pṛithivīvigraha, GE 250
4. Soro plate of Śambhuyaśa, GE 260
5. Erbang plate of Śambhuyaśa
6. Kanas plate of Lokavigraha, GE 280 and Patiakella plate of Śivarāja
7. Two Soro plates of Somadatta
8. Midnapur plates of Somadatta and Śubhakīrtti
9. Plates of Bhānudatta
10. Dhenkanal plate of Jayasiṁha

Plate VI c : Acute-angled Script in Toṣalī, Utkala and Koṅgoda : Inscriptions of the minor ruling families

	ṆA	NA	MA	KA	CA	JA	ṬA	TA	DA	PA	ŚA	ṢA	SA	NA	MA	YA	RA	LA	VA	REPHA
1.	ṆḌA	NTA			CCHA	JÑE		TTI		PTA	ŚLĀ		STHĀ		HMA	ṆYA	BRA	ŚLĀ	SVA	RNNI
2.	ṆḌA	NTI			CCHA		ṬṬA	TSA		PTĀ	ŚCI	ṢṬA	STU	TNA	SMṚ	DYU ŚYA	DRA		DVI	RṆṆI
3.	ṆḌU	NDHA		KTO			ṬṬĀ	TPA	DDHA	PPA	ŚCA	ṢṆA	STHI	NNA	DMA	SYAI	BRĀ	LLA	MVA	RTHI RKKA
4.	ṆṬĀ	NDU	MPA	KTA		RJJI		TTA	DGA	PPA	ŚCA	ṢṬAU	SKA	NNĀ	SMA	ṆYA	KRA	LLA	ṆVE	RVVA
5.	ṆḌA	NDU	MBHU	KTA	CCHRU		ṬṬA	RTTA		PPA	ŚCĀ	ṢṬA	STU	NNA	SMA	LYĀ	PRA	LLA	SVĀ	RVVA
6.	ṆḌRA	NTA		KTA			ṬṬĀ	TPA	DGA	PTĀ	ŚCA	ṢṬHA	STI		SMĀ	ṢYA	ŚRĀ		ŚVA	RHA
7.	ṆḌA	NDHI	MPA	KTA			ṬṬĀ	TKT		PTĀ	ŚCA	ṢṬĪ	STHI		NMA	LYĀṂ	DHRU	LLA	NVI	RTHI
8.	ṆḌA	NTA	MBHĪ	KTI		JÑĀ	ṬṬE	TKA	DDHA			ṢṬA	STHI	TNA	SMA	TYO	STRA	ŚLO	DVI	RGAḤ
9.	ṆḌA	NTA		KTA			ṬṬĀ	TSA	DBHO		ŚCA	ṢṬHI	STHĀ		NMA	ṆYĀ	PRI		SVA	RTHI
10.		NTHI					ṬṬA	TPA	DDHA	PTA	ŚCA	ṢṬA	SKA		SMĀ	NYĀ	GRĀ		DVI	RYĀ

Minor Ruling Families of Toṣalī and Utkala : (5th-7th century AD)

1. Asanapat Naṭarāj image inscription (5th-6th century AD)
2. Jeyrampur plate of the time of Gopachandra (early 6th century AD)
3. Sumandala plates of the time of Pṛithivīvigraha, GE 250
4. Soro plate of Śambhuyaśa, GE 260
5. Erbang plate of Śambhuyaśa
6. Kanas plate of Lokavigraha, GE 280 and Patiakella plate of Śivarāja
7. Two Soro plates of Somadatta
8. Midnapur plates of Somadatta and Śubhakīrtti
9. Plates of Bhānudatta
10. Dhenkanal plate of Jayasiṁha

Plate VII a : Acute-angled Script in Toṣalī, Utkala and Koṅgoda : Inscriptions of the Śailodbhavas, Bhañjas and others

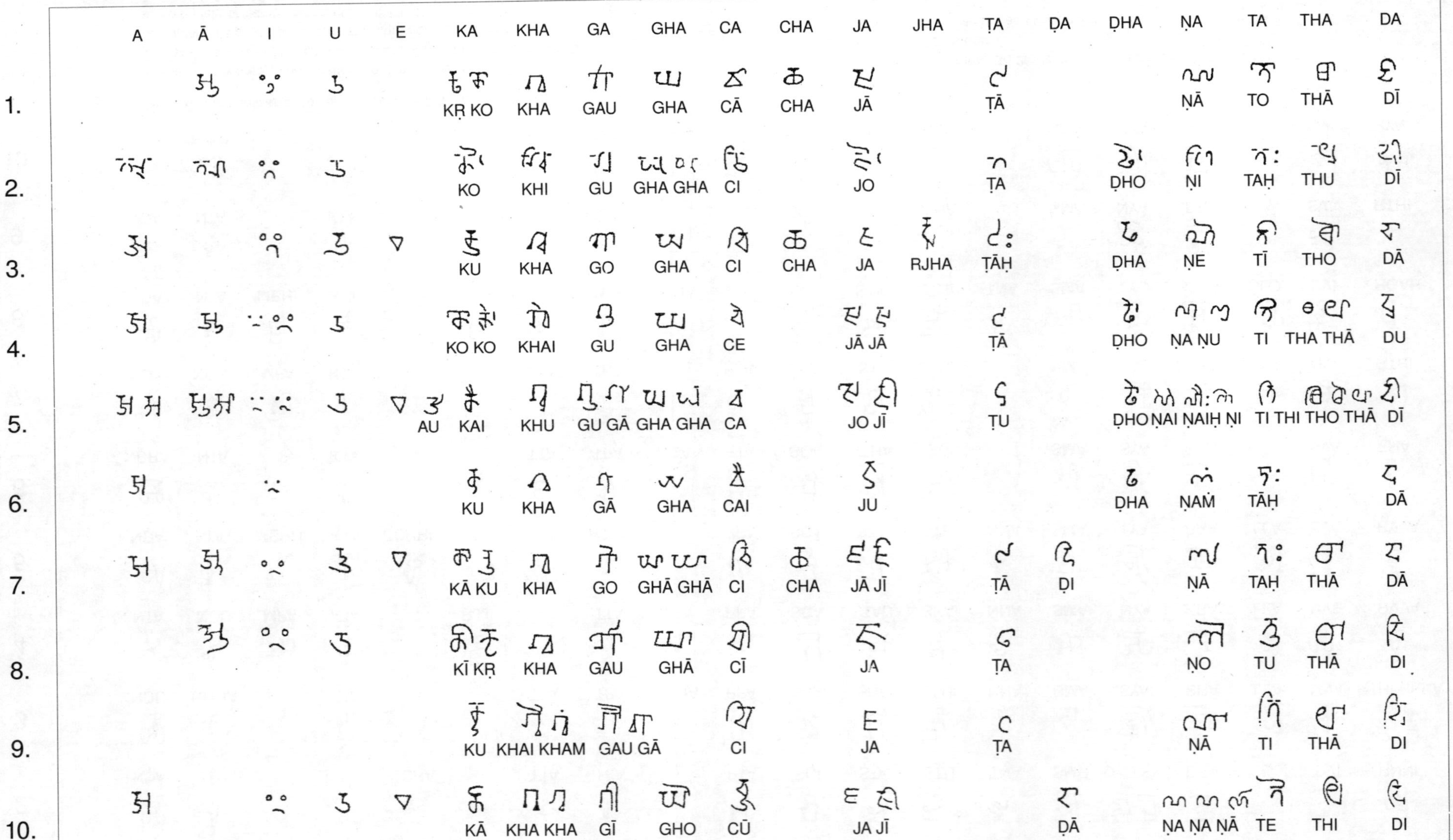

Śailodbhavas : (7th-8th century AD)

1. Ganjam (GE 300) & Khurda plates of Mādhavarāja
2. Purusottampur & Puri plates of Mādhavavarman
3. Orissa Museum plates of Mādhavavarman
4. Plates of Madhyamarāja I
5. Plates of Dharmarāja
6. Tekkali plates of Madhyamarāja III

Other Contemporary Records : (6th-8th century AD)

7. Russelkonda plates of Neṭṭabhañja
8. Baud plates of Neṭṭabhañja
9. Pipalpadar plates of Nandarājadeva
10. Stone inscriptions from Bhubaneswar and Bankada

Plate VII b : Acute-angled Script in Toṣalī, Utkala and Koṅgoda : Inscriptions of the Śailodbhavas, Bhañjas and others

	DHA	NA	PA	PHA	BHA	MA	YA	RA	LA	VA	ŚA	ṢA	SA	HA	KṢA	ṄA	ÑA	ṆA	NA	MA
1.	DHI	NU	PAI	PHA	BHU	MO	YU	RU	LĪ	VṚ	ŚA ŚĀ	ṢA	SŪ	HI	KṢE	ṄGE	ÑCHA	ṆṬHĀ	NDHA	MPA
2.	DHA	NE	PŪ	PHA	BHU	MĀ	YO	RU	LI	VI	ŚO	ṢA	SI	HA	KṢE	ṄGA	ÑCHĀ	ṆḌA	NTHI	MBHI
3.	DHI	NU	PĪ	PHA	BHŪ	MU	YU	RI RA	LĪ	VṚ VĀ	ŚĀ	ṢU	SAI	HUḤ	KṢI	ṄKĀ	ÑCA	ṆḌA	NDA	MBHO
4.	DHŪ	NI NU	PU PI	PHA	BHU	MA	YE	RE RĪ	LO	VO	ŚAḤ	ṢA	SU	HE HI	KṢI	ṄKĀ	ÑCA	ṆḌA	NDHA	MBHŪ
5.	DHŪ	NO NĀ NO	PI PĀ	PHĀ	BHĪ	MĀ MU	YI	RAI RI	LAU LĪ	VE VĀ	ŚAI ŚU	ṢA ṢAI	SE SI	HE HA	KṢĀ	ṄGA	ÑCĀ ÑCHĀ	ṆḌA ṆḌĀ	NTU	MPI
6.	DHṚ	NU	PI	PHA	BHŪ	MĀ	YI	RA	LO LAṀ	VAI	ŚE	ṢA	SA	HĀ	KṢI	ṄGO		ṆḌA		MBHĀ
7.	DHŪ	NI NĪ	PĀ PU	PHA	BHU	MO	YĪ	RU	LĀ	VO	ŚU	ṢAI	SA SA	HṚ	KṢO	ṄKA	ÑJA	ṆḌA	NDU	MPA
8.	DHĀ	NĀ NU	PĀ PU	PHA	BHO BHŪ	MU	YU	RĀ	LO	VI	ŚA	ṢAI ṢA	SĀ	HE	KṢA	ṄGA	ÑJA	ṆḌA	NTA	MBHṚ
9.	DHA	NU	PĀ		BHO	MU MĀ	YA	RĀ	LĪ	VA	ŚĀ	ṢA	SA SU			ṄKĀ			NDA	
10.	DHAU	NĀ	PU PU	PHA	BRHṚ	MŪ	YI	RU	LO	VI	ŚA ŚA	ṢO	SU	HI	KṢA	ṄKĪ	ÑCA		NDI	MPA

Śailodbhavas : (7th-8th century AD)

1. Ganjam (GE 300) & Khurda plates of Mādhavarāja
2. Purusottampur & Puri plates of Mādhavavarman
3. Orissa Museum plates of Mādhavavarman
4. Plates of Madhyamarāja I
5. Plates of Dharmarāja
6. Tekkali plates of Madhyamarāja III

Other Contemporary Records : (6th-8th century AD)

7. Russelkonda plates of Neṭṭabhañja
8. Baud plates of Neṭṭabhañja
9. Pipalpadar plates of Nandarājadeva
10. Stone inscriptions from Bhubaneswar and Bankada

Plate VII c : Acute-angled Script in Toṣalī, Utkala and Koṅgoda : Inscriptions of the Śailodbhavas, Bhañjas and others

Śailodbhavas : (7th-8th century AD)

1. Ganjam (GE 300) & Khurda plates of Mādhavarāja
2. Purusottampur & Puri plates of Mādhavavarman
3. Orissa Museum plates of Mādhavavarman
4. Plates of Madhyamarāja I
5. Plates of Dharmarāja
6. Tekkali plates of Madhyamarāja III

Other Contemporary Records : (6th-8th century AD)

7. Russelkonda plates of Neṭṭabhañja
8. Baud plates of Neṭṭabhañja
9. Pipalpadar plates of Nandarājadeva
10. Stone inscriptions from Bhubaneswar and Bankada

Plate VIII a : Kuṭila Script : Inscriptions of the Bhaumakaras and the Pāṇḍuvaṁśīs.

Bhaumakaras :

1. Neulpur plate of Śubhākara (8th century AD)
2. Plates of Śubhākara, BE 100, 103
3. Dhenkanal plate of Tribhuvanamahādevī, BE 110
4. Two Talcher plates of Śivakaradeva, BE 149
5. Two Baud plates of Tribhuvanamahādevī, BE 158
6. Kumurang plate of Daṇḍīmahādevī, BE 187
7. Two inscriptions from Jajpur (8th-9th century AD)

Contemporaries of the Bhaumakaras : (8th-9th century AD)

8. Jangalpadu plates of Śatrubhañja
9. Rajim stone inscription of Vilāsatuṅga
10. Sirpur inscriptions of the time of Mahāśivagupta Bālārjuna
11. Senakapat inscription of the time of Mahāśivagupta Bālārjuna

Plate VIII b : Kuṭila Script : Inscriptions of the Bhaumakaras and the Pāṇḍuvaṁśīs.

Bhaumakaras :

1. Neulpur plate of Śubhākara (8th century AD)
2. Plates of Śubhākara, BE 100, 103
3. Dhenkanal plate of Tribhuvanamahādevī, BE 110
4. Two Talcher plates of Śivakaradeva, BE 149
5. Two Baud plates of Tribhuvanamahādevī, BE 158
6. Kumurang plate of Daṇḍīmahādevī, BE 187
7. Two inscriptions from Jajpur (8th-9th century AD)

Contemporaries of the Bhaumakaras : (8th-9th century AD)

8. Jangalpadu plates of Śatrubhañja
9. Rajim stone inscription of Vilāsatuṅga
10. Sirpur inscriptions of the time of Mahāśivagupta Bālārjuna
11. Senakapat inscription of the time of Mahāśivagupta Bālārjuna

Plate VIII c : Kuṭila Script : Inscriptions of the Bhaumakaras and the Pāṇḍuvaṁśīs

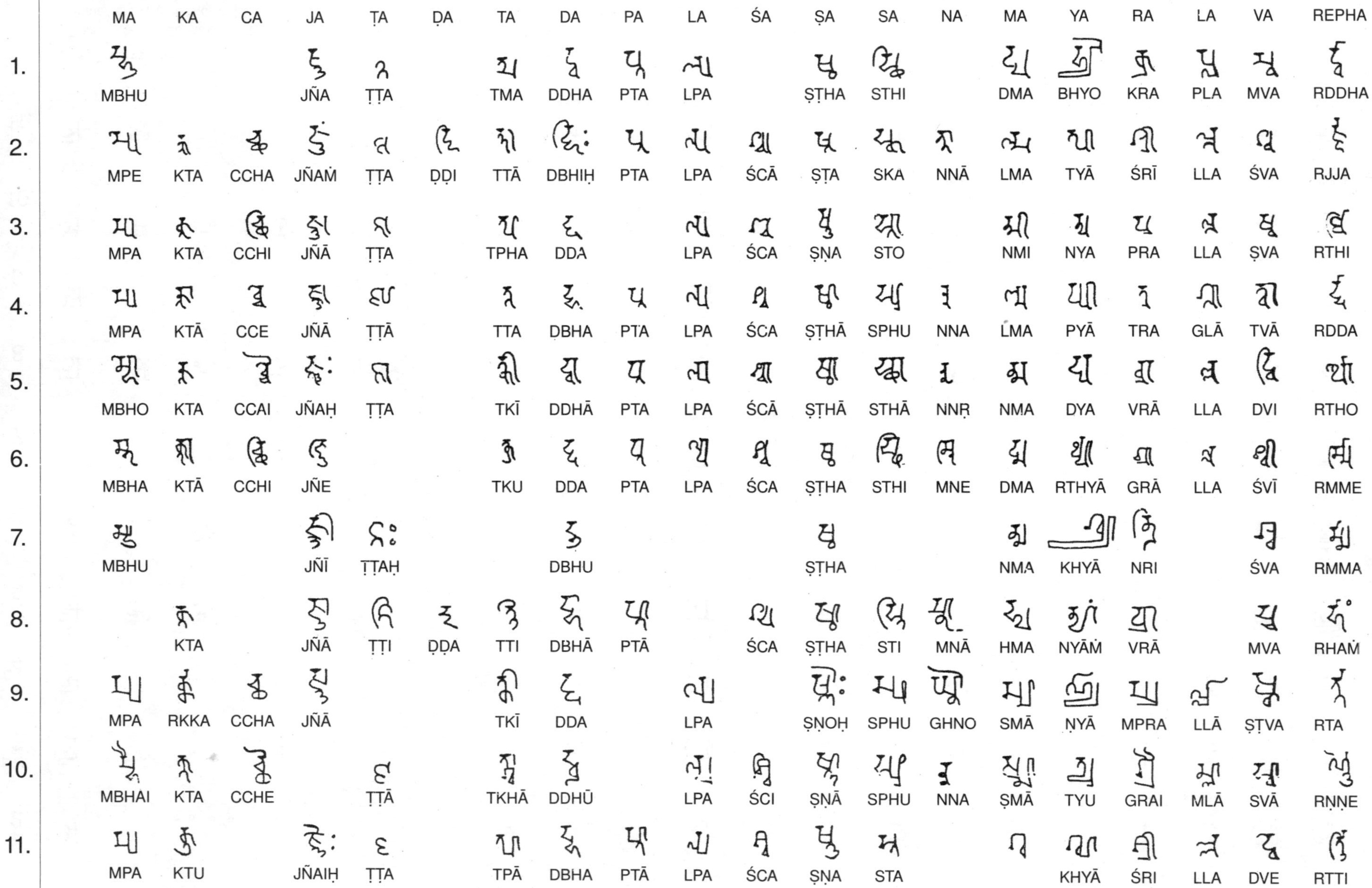

Bhaumakaras :

1. Neulpur plate of Śubhākara (8th century AD)
2. Plates of Śubhākara, BE 100, 103
3. Dhenkanal plate of Tribhuvanamahādevī, BE 110
4. Two Talcher plates of Śivakaradeva, BE 149
5. Two Baud plates of Tribhuvanamahādevī, BE 158
6. Kumurang plate of Daṇḍīmahādevī, BE 187
7. Two inscriptions from Jajpur (8th-9th century AD)

Contemporaries of the Bhaumakaras : (8th-9th century AD)

8. Jangalpadu plates of Śatrubhañja
9. Rajim stone inscription of Vilāsatuṅga
10. Sirpur inscriptions of the time of Mahāśivagupta Bālārjuna
11. Senakapat inscription of the time of Mahāśivagupta Bālārjuna

Plate IX a : Proto-Nāgarī Script in Orissa : Inscriptions of the later Bhauma-Karas, the Śulkis, the Tuṅgas and the Nandas

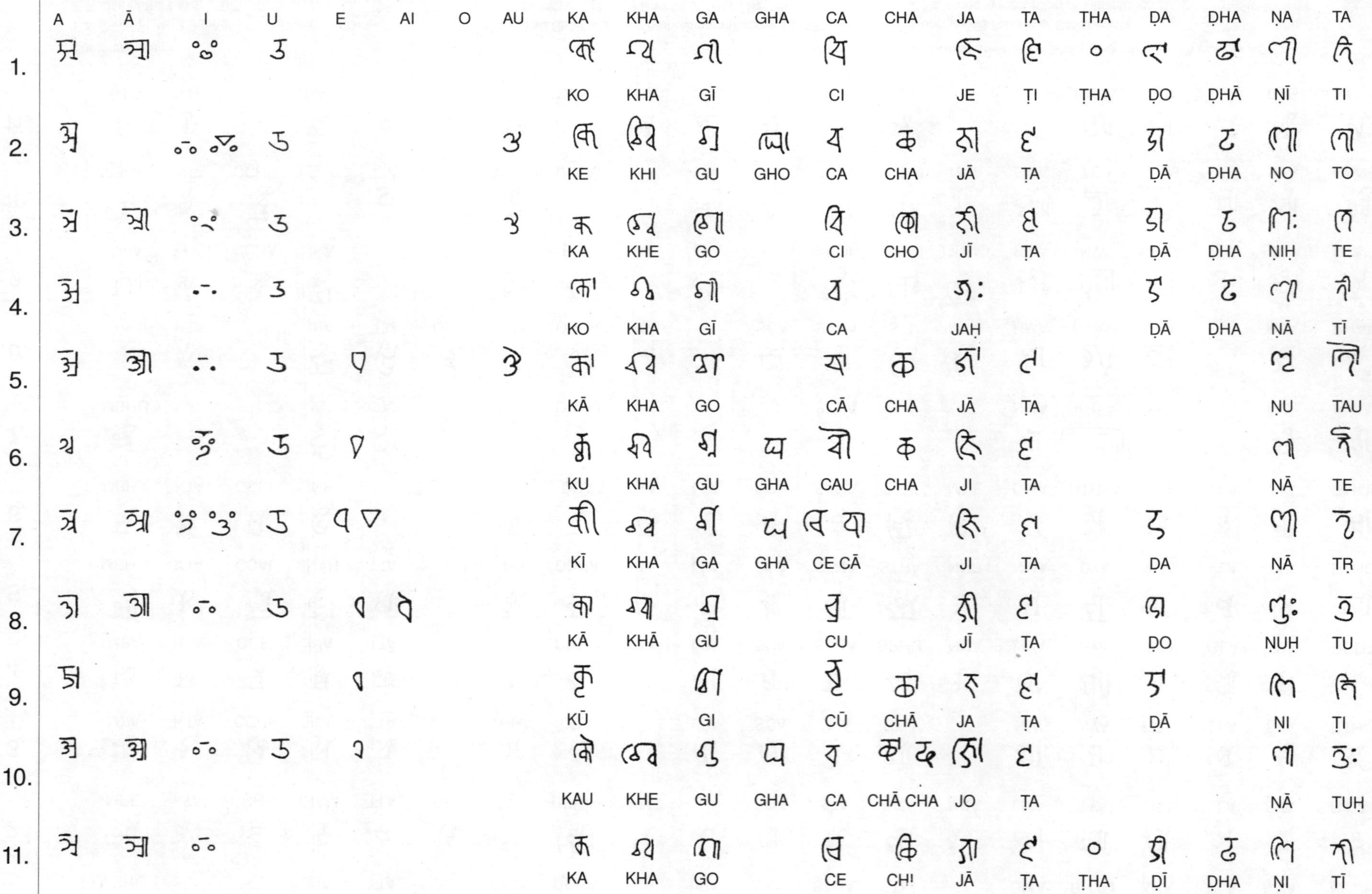

Later Bhaumakaras :

1. Talcher plate of Śubhākara, BE 141(5)
2. Plates of Daṇḍimahādevī, BE 180, 183
3. A grant of Vakulamahādevi, BE 204
4. Plates of Dharmmamahādevī (10th century AD)

Contemporaries of the Bhaumakaras : (9th-10th century AD)

5. Plates of the Śulkis
6. Dhenkanal plate of Jayastambha and Puri plate of Kulastambha
7. Plates of the Tuṅgas
8. Plates of the Nandas
9. Hindol plate of Vīrapracaṇḍadeva
10. Bonai plate of Udayavarāha
11. Angul plates of Śāntikaradeva

Plate IX b : Proto-Nāgarī Script in Orissa : Inscriptions of the later Bhauma-Karas, the Śulkis, the Tuṅgas and the Nandas

Later Bhaumakaras :

1. Talcher plate of Śubhākara, BE 141(5)
2. Plates of Daṇḍimahādevī, BE 180, 183
3. A grant of Vakulamahādevi, BE 204
4. Plates of Dharmmamahādevī (10th century AD)

Contemporaries of the Bhaumakaras : (9th-10th century AD)

5. Plates of the Śulkis
6. Dhenkanal plate of Jayastambha and Puri plate of Kulastambha
7. Plates of the Tuṅgas
8. Plates of the Nandas
9. Hindol plate of Vīrapracaṇḍadeva
10. Bonai plate of Udayavarāha
11. Angul plates of Śāntikaradeva

Plate IX c : Proto-Nāgarī Script in Orissa : Inscriptions of the later Bhauma-Karas, the Śulkis, the Tuṅgas and the Nandas

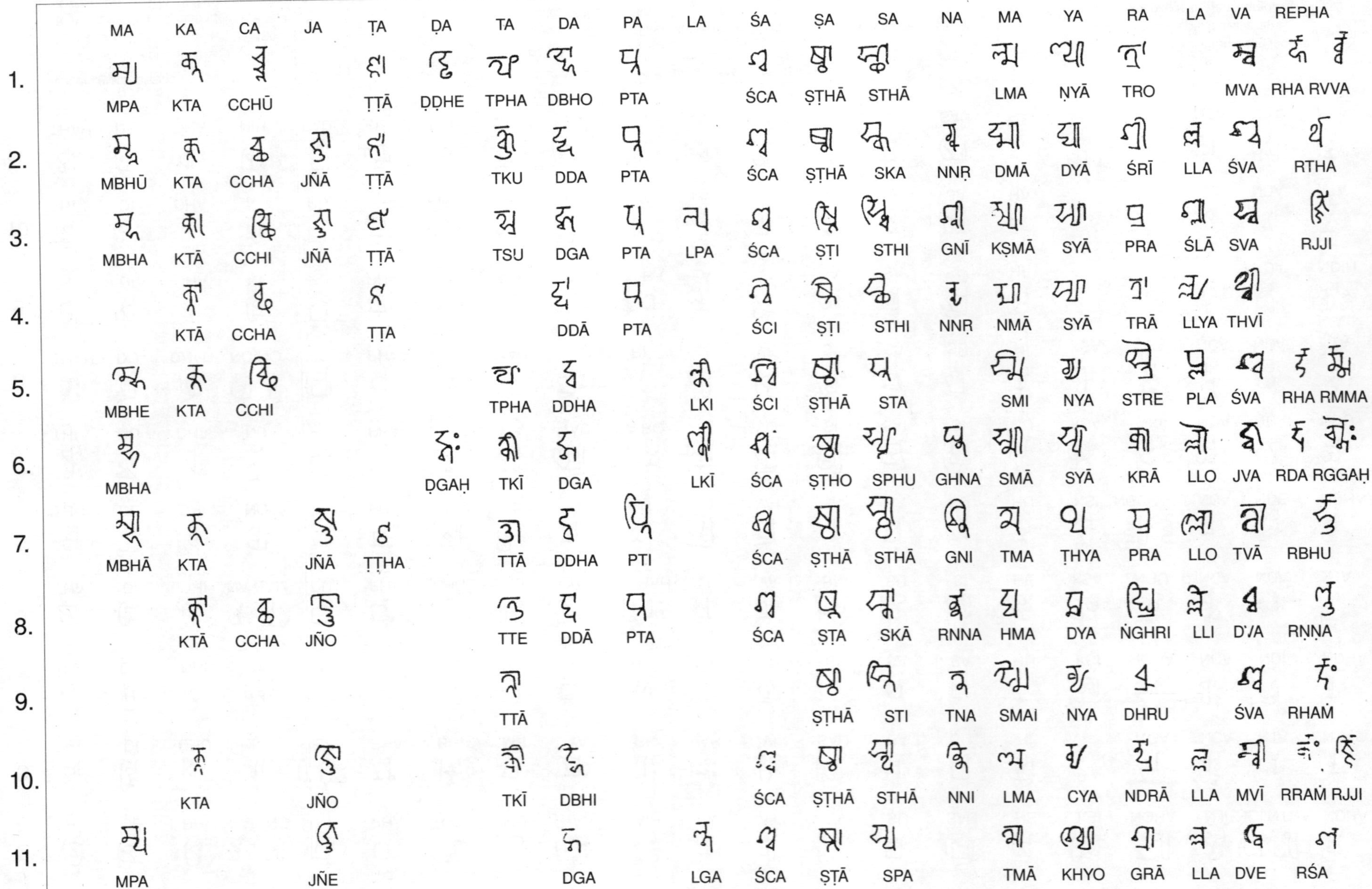

Later Bhaumakaras :

1. Talcher plate of Śubhākara, BE 141(5)
2. Plates of Daṇḍimahādevī, BE 180, 183
3. A grant of Vakulamahādevi, BE 204
4. Plates of Dharmmamahādevī (10th century AD)

Contemporaries of the Bhaumakaras : (9th-10th century AD)

5. Plates of the Śulkis
6. Dhenkanal plate of Jayastambha and Puri plate of Kulastambha
7. Plates of the Tuṅgas
8. Plates of the Nandas
9. Hindol plate of Vīrapracaṇḍadeva
10. Bonai plate of Udayavarāha
11. Angul plates of Śāntikaradeva

Plate X a : Proto-Nāgarī Script in Orissa : Inscriptions of the Somavaṁśīs

Somavaṁśīs : (9th-11th century AD)

1. Plates of Janmejaya I (upto RY 23)
2. Three Cuttack plates of Janmejaya I
3. Kalibhana plates of Janmejaya I & plates of Yayāti I (upto RY 24)
4. Patna plates of Yayāti I, Cuttack plates of Bhīmaratha and Banpur plates of Indraratha
5. Mahakosala Historical Society's plates of Bhīmaratha
6. Kudopali plates of the time of Bhīmaratha
7. Mahulpara plates of the time of Bhīmaratha
8. Maranja-Mura plates of Yayāti II
9. Plates of Uddyotakeśarī
10. Temple and cave inscriptions of the time of Uddyotakeśarī
11. Nuapatana plates of Janmejaya II

Plate X b : Proto-Nāgarī Script in Orissa : Inscriptions of the Somavaṁśīs

Somavaṁśīs : (9th-11th century AD)

1. Plates of Janmejaya I (upto RY 23)
2. Three Cuttack plates of Janmejaya I
3. Kalibhana plates of Janmejaya I & plates of Yayāti I (upto RY 24)
4. Patna plates of Yayāti I, Cuttack plates of Bhīmaratha and Banpur plates of Indraratha
5. Mahakosala Historical Society's plates of Bhīmaratha
6. Kudopali plates of the time of Bhīmaratha
7. Mahulpara plates of the time of Bhīmaratha
8. Maranja-Mura plates of Yayāti II
9. Plates of Uddyotakeśarī
10. Temple and cave inscriptions of the time of Uddyotakeśarī
11. Nuapatana plates of Janmejaya II

Plate X c : Proto-Nāgarī Script in Orissa : Inscriptions of the Somavaṁśīs

Somavaṁśīs : (9th-11th century AD)

1. Plates of Janmejaya I (upto RY 23)
2. Three Cuttack plates of Janmejaya I
3. Kalibhana plates of Janmejaya I & plates of Yayāti I (upto RY 24)
4. Patna plates of Yayāti I, Cuttack plates of Bhīmaratha and Banpur plates of Indraratha
5. Mahakosala Historical Society's plates of Bhīmaratha
6. Kudopali plates of the time of Bhīmaratha
7. Mahulpara plates of the time of Bhīmaratha
8. Maranja-Mura plates of Yayāti II
9. Plates of Uddyotakeśarī
10. Temple and cave inscriptions of the time of Uddyotakeśarī
11. Nuapatana plates of Janmejaya II

Plate XI a : Proto-Nāgarī Script in Orissa : Inscriptions of the Bhañjas of Khiñjali-maṇḍala and Khijjiṅgakoṭṭa

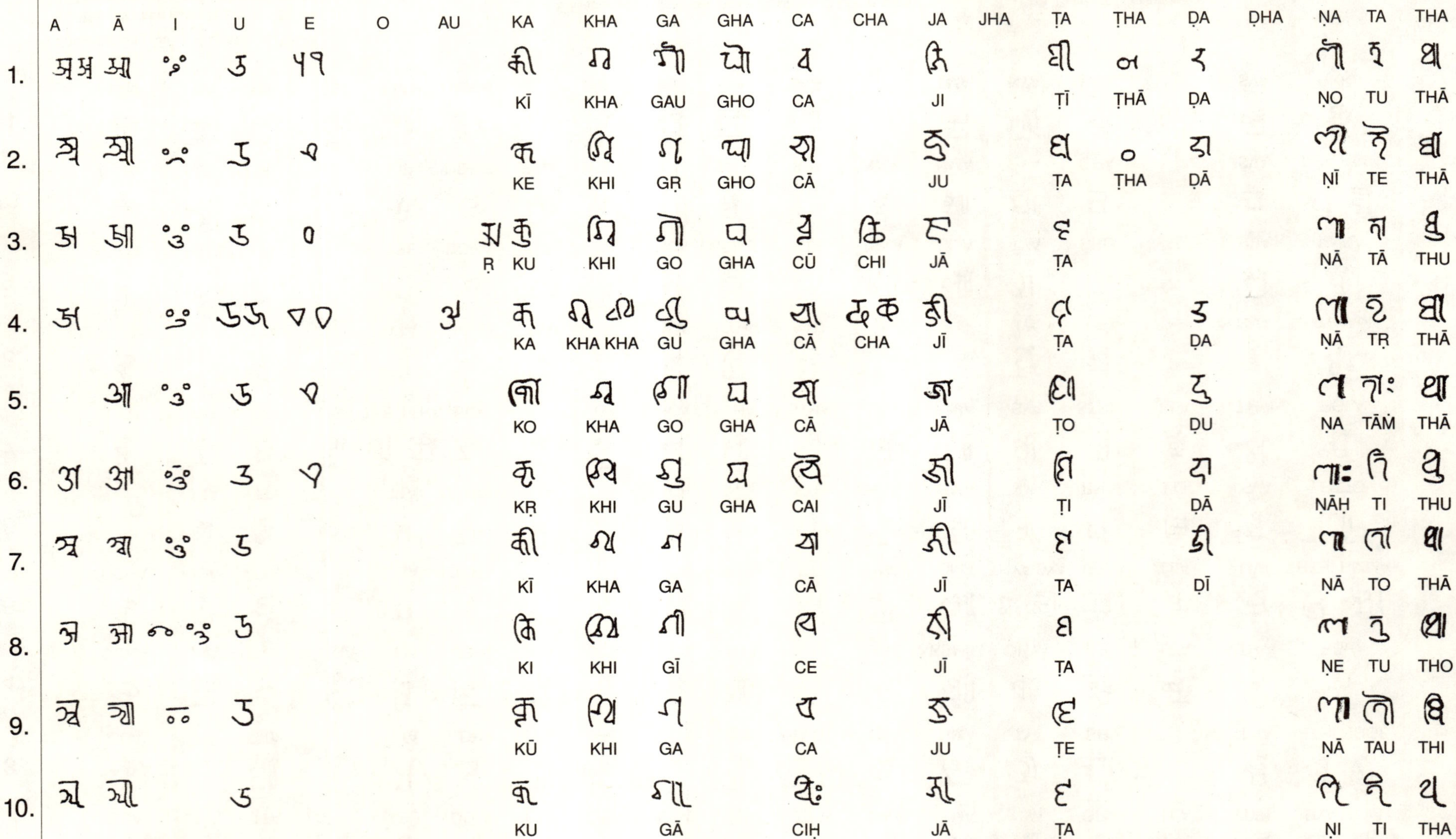

Bhañjas of Khiñjali-maṇḍala : (9th-10th century AD)

1. Kumurukela plates of Śatrubhañja
2. Sonepur plates of Śatrubhañja and plates of Raṇabhañja (upto RY 50)
3. Later grants of Raṇabhañja, RY 52-58
4. Plates of Neṭṭabhañja I, Śilābhañja, Vidyādharabhañja and Neṭṭabhañja II
5. Plates of Śatrubhañja, (BE) 198
6. Orissa Museum plates of Neṭṭabhañja III, (BE) 213

Bhañjas of Khijiṅgakotta : (10th-11th century AD)

7. Plates of Raṇabhañja
8. Adipur plates of Narendrabhañja, (BE) 193
9. Plates of Rāyabhanja and Pṛithvībhañja
10. Plates of Śatrubhañja and Rāyabhañja

Plate XI b : Proto-Nāgarī Script in Orissa : Inscriptions of the Bhañjas of Khiñjali-maṇḍala and Khijjiṅgakoṭṭa

Bhañjas of Khiñjali-maṇḍala : (9th-10th century AD)

1. Kumurukela plates of Śatrubhañja
2. Sonepur plates of Śatrubhañja and plates of Raṇabhañja (upto RY 50)
3. Later grants of Raṇabhañja, RY 52-58
4. Plates of Neṭṭabhañja I, Śīlābhañja, Vidyādharabhañja and Neṭṭabhañja II
5. Plates of Śatrubhañja, (BE) 198
6. Orissa Museum plates of Neṭṭabhañja III, (BE) 213

Bhañjas of Khijjiṅgakotta : (10th-11th century AD)

7. Plates of Raṇabhañja
8. Adipur plates of Narendrabhañja, (BE) 193
9. Plates of Rāyabhanja and Pṛithvībhañja
10. Plates of Śatrubhañja and Rāyabhañja

Plate XI c : Proto-Nāgarī Script in Orissa : Inscriptions of the Bhañjas of Khiñjali-maṇḍala and Khijjiṅgakoṭṭa

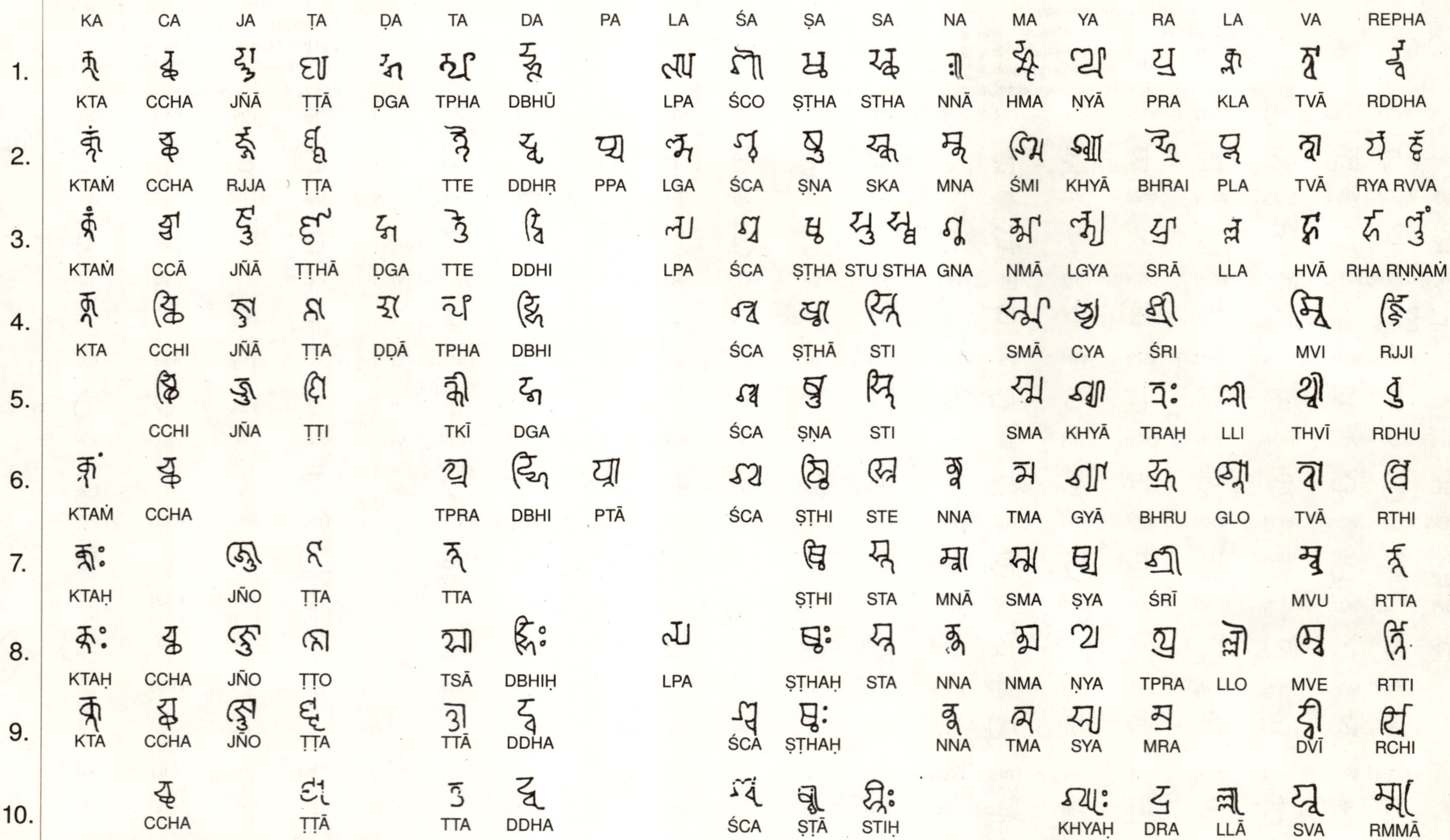

Bhañjas of Khiñjali-maṇḍala : (9th-10th century AD)

1. Kumurukela plates of Śatrubhañja
2. Sonepur plates of Śatrubhañja and plates of Raṇabhañja (upto RY 50)
3. Later grants of Raṇabhañja, RY 52-58
4. Plates of Neṭṭabhañja I, Śilābhañja, Vidyādharabhañja and Neṭṭabhañja II
5. Plates of Śatrubhañja, (BE) 198
6. Orissa Museum plates of Neṭṭabhañja III, (BE) 213

Bhañjas of Khijjiṅgakotta : (10th-11th century AD)

7. Plates of Raṇabhañja
8. Adipur plates of Narendrabhañja, (BE) 193
9. Plates of Rāyabhanja and Pṛithvībhañja
10. Plates of Śatrubhañja and Rāyabhañja

PLATE XII a : Proto-Nāgarī Script in Orissa : Inscriptions of the Nalas, the Śvetaka Gaṅgas & the later Eastern Gaṅgas

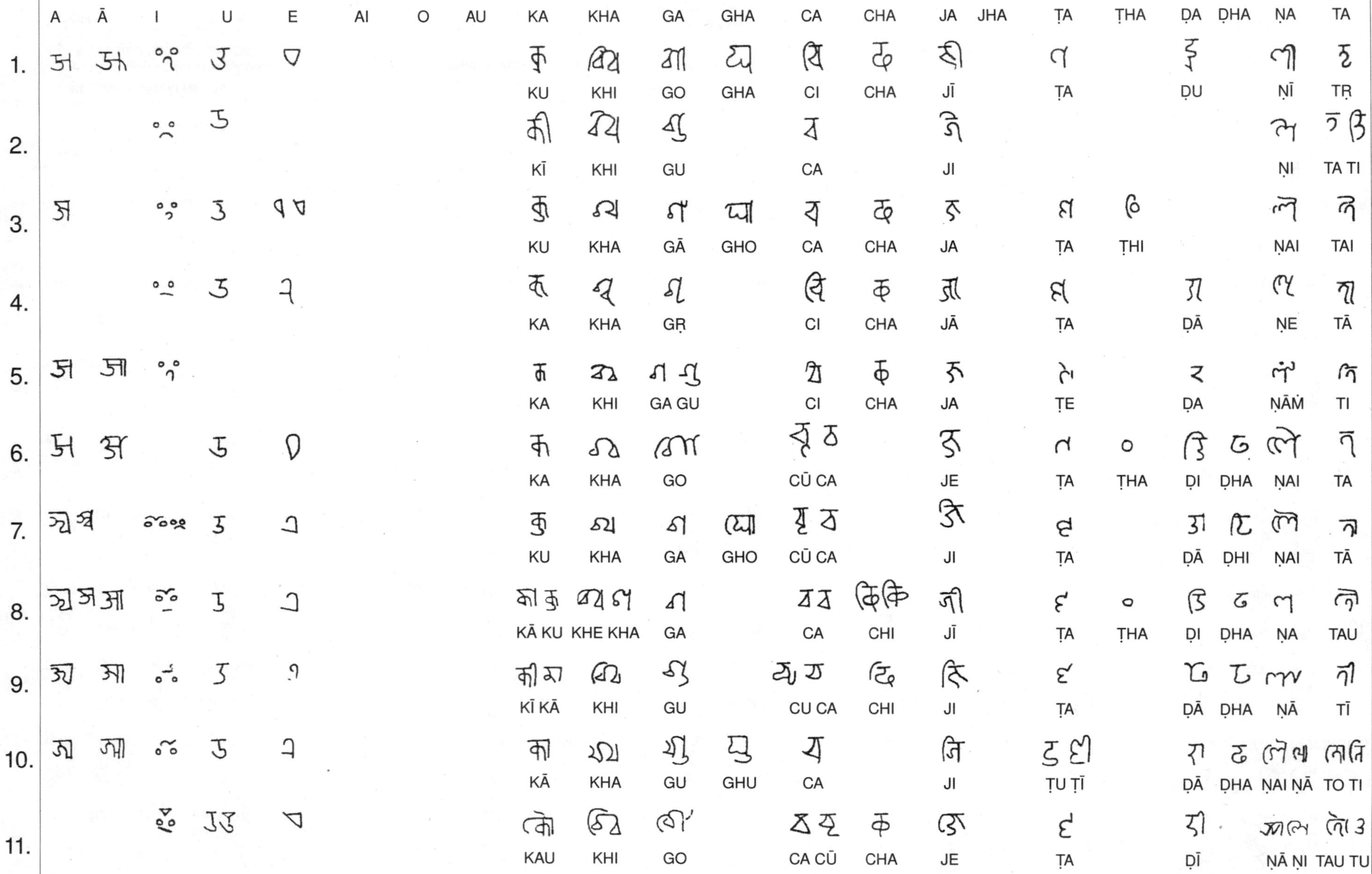

Nalas : (9th-10th century AD)

1. Pandiapathar plates of Bhīmasena, (BE) 159
2. Plates of Narendradhavala

Śvetaka Gaṅgas : (9th-10th century AD)

3. Indian Museum plates of Indravarman
4. Ganjam plates of Dānārṇava

Eastern Gaṅgas : (9th-11th century AD)

5. Chidivalasa plates of Devendravarman, GY 397
6. Nirakarpur plates of the time of Devendravarman and Doora plates of Udayakheḍi
7. Ponduru and Andhavaram plates of Vajrahasta II
8. Simhipura plates of Dharmakheḍi and Chicacole plates of Madhukāmārṇava
9. Narasapatam plates of Vajrahasta III, Ś. 967
10. Plates of Vajrahasta III and Rājarāja I
11. Gunupur plates of *Rāṇaka* Dānārṇava

PLATE XII b : Proto-Nāgarī Script in Orissa : Inscriptions of the Nalas, the Śvetaka Gaṅgas & the later Eastern Gaṅgas

Nalas : (9th-10th century AD)

1. Pandiapathar plates of Bhīmasena, (BE) 159
2. Plates of Narendradhavala

Śvetaka Gaṅgas : (9th-10th century AD)

3. Indian Museum plates of Indravarman
4. Ganjam plates of Dānārṇava

Eastern Gaṅgas : (9th-11th century AD)

5. Chidivalasa plates of Devendravarman, GY 397
6. Nirakarpur plates of the time of Devendravarman and Doora plates of Udayakheḍi
7. Ponduru and Andhavaram plates of Vajrahasta II
8. Simhipura plates of Dharmakheḍi and Chicacole plates of Madhukāmārṇava
9. Narasapatam plates of Vajrahasta III, Ś. 967
10. Plates of Vajrahasta III and Rājarāja I
11. Gunupur plates of *Rāṇaka* Dānārṇava

PLATE XII c : Proto-Nāgarī Script in Orissa : Inscriptions of the Nalas, the Śvetaka Gaṅgas & the later Eastern Gaṅgas

Nalas : (9th-10th century AD)

1. Pandiapathar plates of Bhīmasena, (BE) 159
2. Plates of Narendradhavala

Śvetaka Gaṅgas : (9th-10th century AD)

3. Indian Museum plates of Indravarman
4. Ganjam plates of Dānārṇava

Eastern Gaṅgas : (9th-11th century AD)

5. Chidivalasa plates of Devendravarman, GY 397
6. Nirakarpur plates of the time of Devendravarman and Doora plates of Udayakheḍi
7. Ponduru and Andhavaram plates of Vajrahasta II
8. Simhipura plates of Dharmakheḍi and Chicacole plates of Madhukāmārṇava
9. Narasapatam plates of Vajrahasta III, Ś. 967
10. Plates of Vajrahasta III and Rājarāja I
11. Gunupur plates of *Rāṇaka* Dānārṇava

PLATE XIII a : Mixed Kaliṅga Script : Inscriptions of the Eastern Gaṅgas

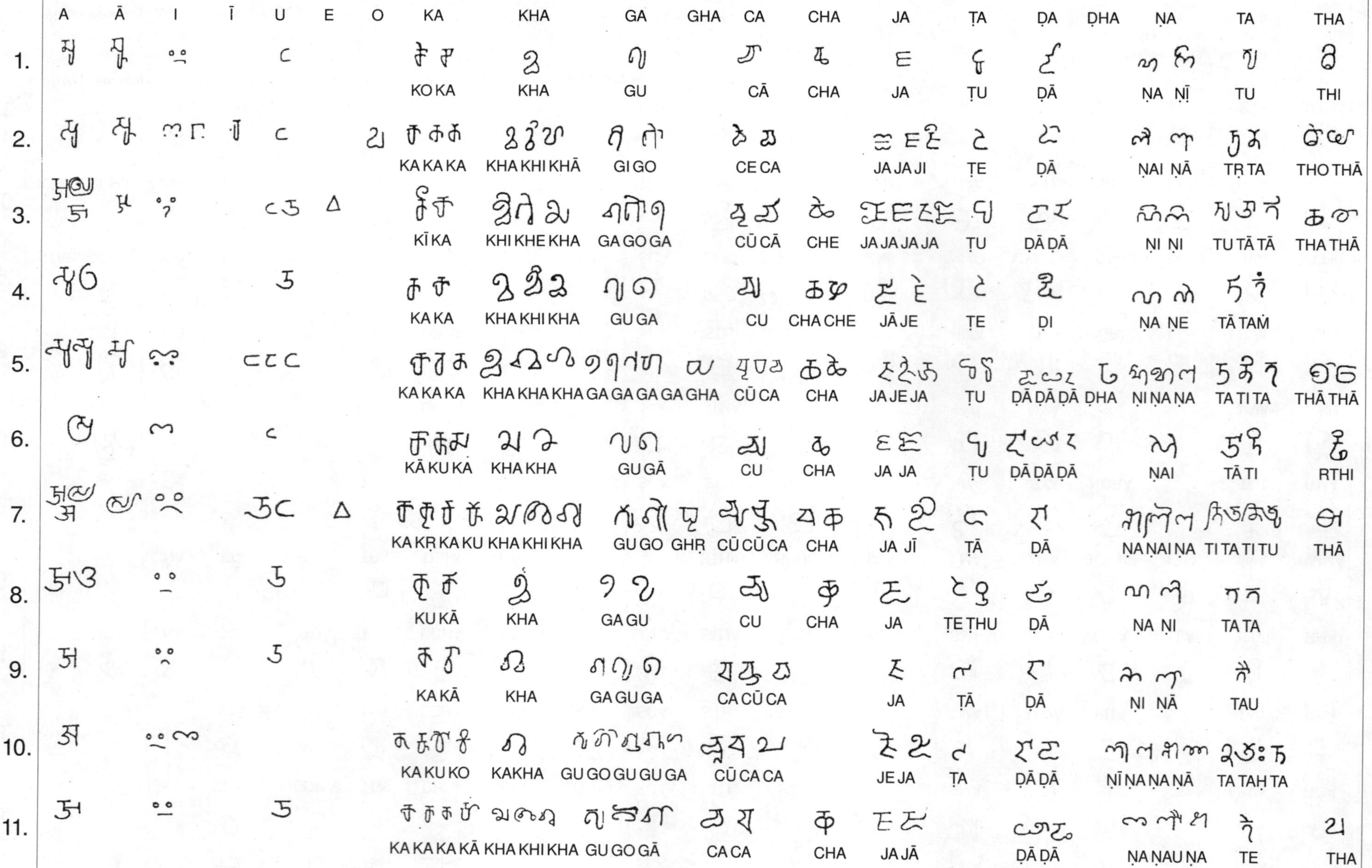

Eastern Gaṅgas :

1. Siddhantam plates of Devendravarman, GY 195
2. Dharmlingeswar & Andhavaram plates of Anantavarman, GY 204 & 216
3. Chicacole & Visakhapatanam plates of Devendravarman, GY 251& 254
4. Alamanda (GY 304) & Munjeru plates of Anantavarman
5. Plates of Devendravarman, GY 306-10
6. Plates of Yuvarāja Rājendravarman, GY 313-314
7. Chicacole plates of Satyavarman, GY 351
8. Tekkali plates of Anantavarman, GY 358
9. Chipurupalli plates of Anantavarman, GY 383
10. Gallavalli plates of Manujendravarman, GY 393
11. Undated Chicacole plates of Anantavarman

PLATE XIII b : Mixed Kaliṅga Script : Inscriptions of the Eastern Gaṅgas

Eastern Gaṅgas :

1. Siddhantam plates of Devendravarman, GY 195
2. Dharmlingeswar & Andhavaram plates of Anantavarman, GY 204 & 216
3. Chicacole & Visakhapatanam plates of Devendravarman, GY 251& 254
4. Alamanda (GY 304) & Munjeru plates of Anantavarman
5. Plates of Devendravarman, GY 306-10
6. Plates of Yuvarāja Rājendravarman, GY 313-314
7. Chicacole plates of Satyavarman, GY 351
8. Tekkali plates of Anantavarman, GY 358
9. Chipurupalli plates of Anantavarman, GY 383
10. Gallavalli plates of Manujendravarman, GY 393
11. Undated Chicacole plates of Anantavarman

PLATE XIII c : Mixed Kaliṅga Script : Inscriptions of the Eastern Gaṅgas

Eastern Gaṅgas :

1. Siddhantam plates of Devendravarman, GY 195
2. Dharmlingeswar & Andhavaram plates of Anantavarman, GY 204 & 216
3. Chicacole & Visakhapatanam plates of Devendravarman, GY 251& 254
4. Alamanda (GY 304) & Munjeru plates of Anantavarman
5. Plates of Devendravarman, GY 306-10
6. Plates of Yuvarāja Rājendravarman, GY 313-314
7. Chicacole plates of Satyavarman, GY 351
8. Tekkali plates of Anantavarman, GY 358
9. Chipurupalli plates of Anantavarman, GY 383
10. Gallavalli plates of Manujendravarman, GY 393
11. Undated Chicacole plates of Anantavarman

PLATE XIV a : Mixed Kaliṅga Script : Inscriptions of the Kadambas and the Śvetaka Gaṅgas

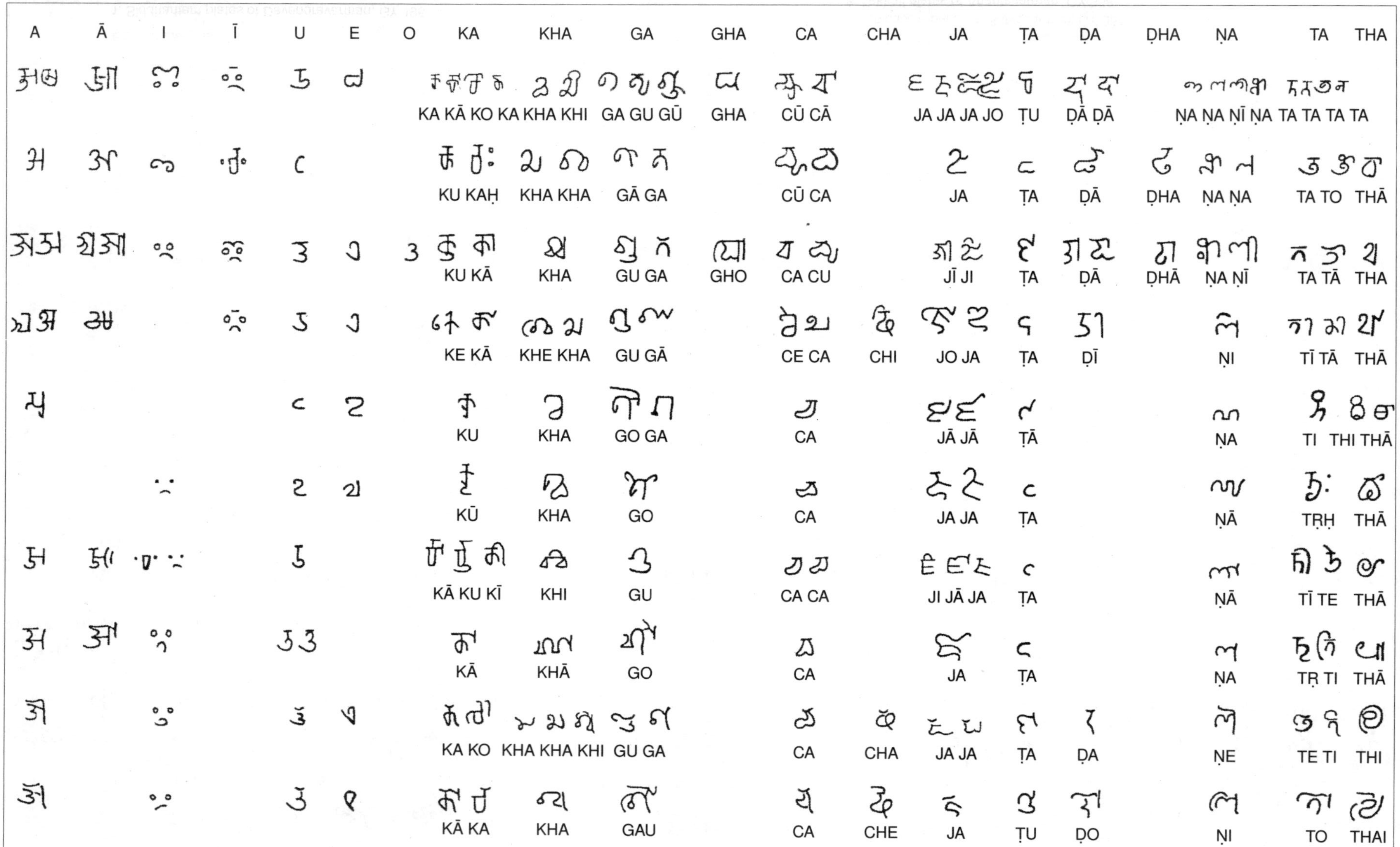

Kadambas : (10th-11th century AD)

1.Parlakimedi plates of Vajrahasta
2. Napitavataka plates of Devendravarman
3. Ramapuram plates of the time of Vajrahasta II, GY 495
4. Mandasa plates of the time of Vajrahasta II, Ś.917

Śvetaka Gaṅgas : (8th-9th century AD)

5. Gautami plates Indravarman
6. Badakhemundi plates of Jayavarman
7. Svalpavelura plates of Anantavarman
8. Vishmagiri plates of Indravarman
9. Indian Museum plates of Jayavarman, (BE)100
10. Badakhemundi plates of Bhūpendravarman

PLATE XIV b : Mixed Kaliṅga Script : Inscriptions of the Kadambas and the Śvetaka Gaṅgas

Kadambas : (10th-11th century AD)

1. Parlakimedi plates of Vajrahasta
2. Napitavataka plates of Devendravarman
3. Ramapuram plates of the time of Vajrahasta II, GY 495
4. Mandasa plates of the time of Vajrahasta II, Ś.917

Śvetaka Gaṅgas : (8th-9th century AD)

5. Gautami plates Indravarman
6. Badakhemundi plates of Jayavarman
7. Svalpavelura plates of Anantavarman
8. Vishmagiri plates of Indravarman
9. Indian Museum plates of Jayavarman, (BE)100
10. Badakhemundi plates of Bhūpendravarman

PLATE XIV c : Mixed Kaliṅga Script : Inscriptions of the Kadambas and the Śvetaka Gaṅgas

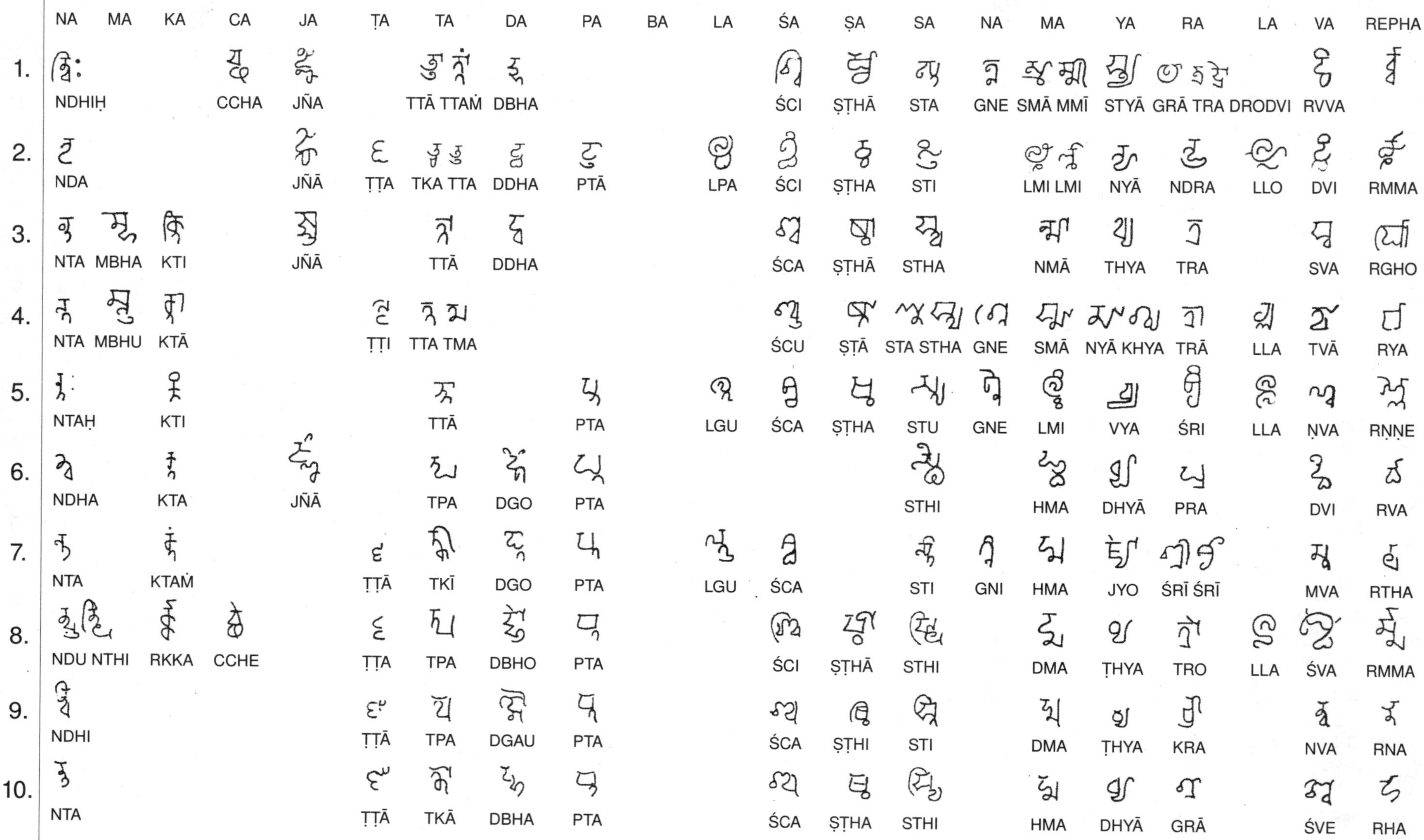

Kadambas : (10th-11th century AD)

1. Parlakimedi plates of Vajrahasta
2. Napitavataka plates of Devendravarman
3. Ramapuram plates of the time of Vajrahasta II, GY 495
4. Mandasa plates of the time of Vajrahasta II, Ś.917

Śvetaka Gaṅgas : (8th-9th century AD)

5. Gautami plates Indravarman
6. Badakhemundi plates of Jayavarman
7. Svalpavelura plates of Anantavarman
8. Vishmagiri plates of Indravarman
9. Indian Museum plates of Jayavarman, (BE)100
10. Badakhemundi plates of Bhūpendravarman

PLATE XV a : Proto-Oriya Script : Inscriptions of later Somavaṁśīs, Telugu-Coḍas, Bhañjas, Imperial Gaṅgas, etc.

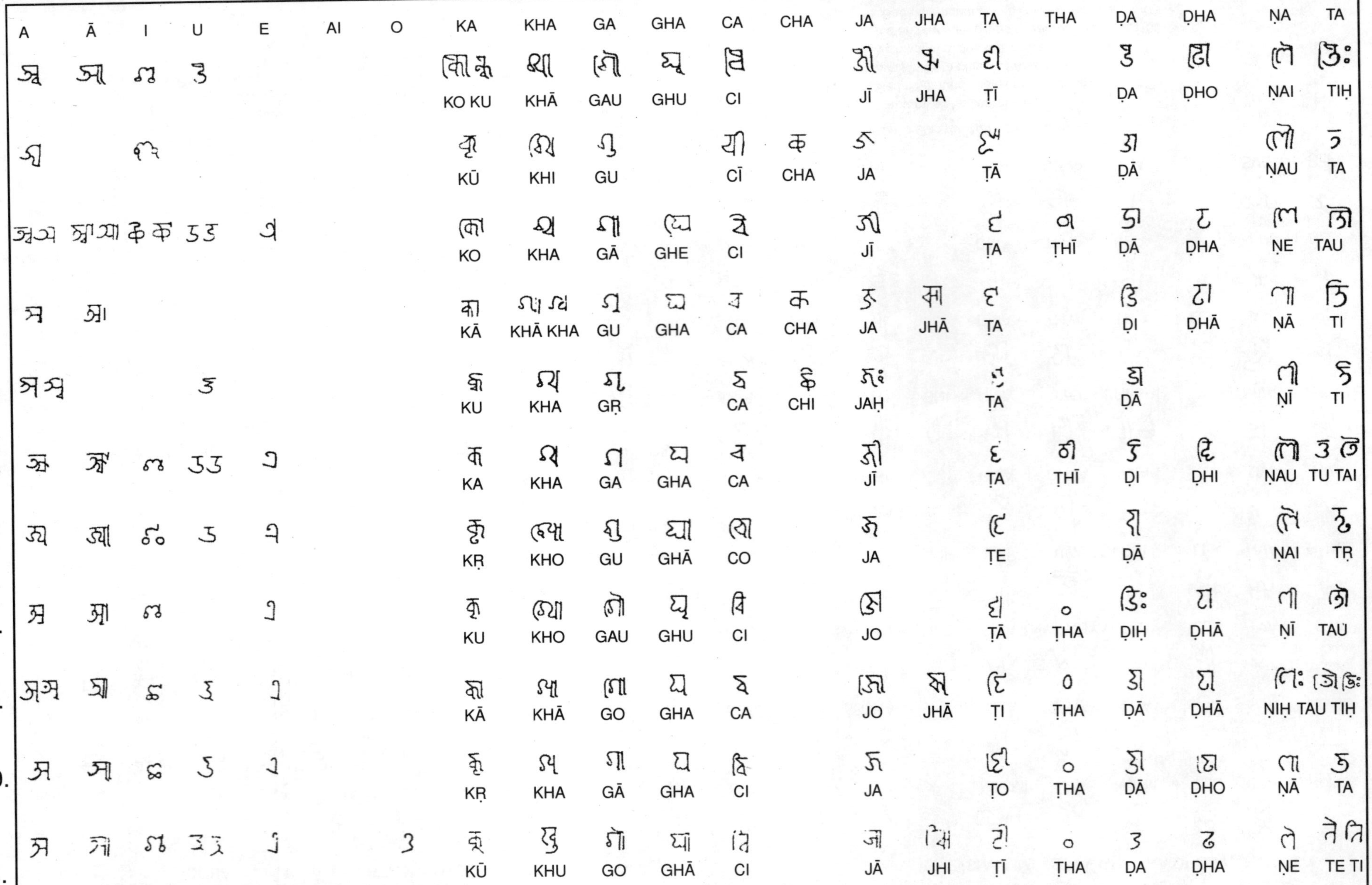

Later Somavaṁśīs, Telugu-Coḍas and others : (11th-13th century AD)

1. Ratnagiri plates of Somavaṁśī Karṇa
2. Kamalpur plates of the time of Karṇa
3. Plates of the Telugu-Coḍas
4. Polasara plates of Arkeśvaradeva, Yugābda 4248
5. Some Bhañja records of the 11th-13th century
6. Antirigam plates of Yaśabhañja and Jayabhañja

Imperial Gaṅgas :

7. Plates of Anantavarman Coḍagaṅgadeva (AD 1077-1147)
8. Plates of the successors of Coḍagaṅgadeva upto Anaṅgabhīmadeva III (AD 1147-1238)
9. Plates of Narasiṁha II (AD 1278-1306) and Bhānudeva II (AD 1306-28)
10. Kaijang plates of Bhānudeva III, Ś.1248
11. Plates of Narasiṁha IV, Ś.1305 & 1316

PLATE XV b : Proto-Oriya Script : Inscriptions of later Somavaṁśīs, Telugu-Coḍas, Bhañjas, Imperial Gaṅgas, etc.

Later Somavaṁśīs, Telugu-Coḍas and others : (11th-13th century AD)

1. Ratnagiri plates of Somavaṁśī Karṇa
2. Kamalpur plates of the time of Karṇa
3. Plates of the Telugu-Coḍas
4. Polasara plates of Arkeśvaradeva, Yugābda 4248
5. Some Bhañja records of the 11th-13th century
6. Antirigam plates of Yaśabhañja and Jayabhañja

Imperial Gaṅgas :

7. Plates of Anantavarman Coḍagaṅgadeva (AD 1077-1147)
8. Plates of the successors of Coḍagaṅgadeva upto Anaṅgabhīmadeva III (AD 1147-1238)
9. Plates of Narasiṁha II (AD 1278-1306) and Bhānudeva II (AD 1306-28)
10. Kaijang plates of Bhānudeva III, Ś.1248
11. Plates of Narasiṁha IV, Ś.1305 & 1316

PLATE XV c : Proto-Oriya Script : Inscriptions of later Somavaṁśīs, Telugu-Coḍas, Bhañjas, Imperial Gaṅgas, etc.

Later Somavaṁśīs, Telugu-Coḍas and others : (11th-13th century AD)

1. Ratnagiri plates of Somavaṁśī Karṇa
2. Kamalpur plates of the time of Karṇa
3. Plates of the Telugu-Coḍas
4. Polasara plates of Arkeśvaradeva, Yugābda 4248
5. Some Bhañja records of the 11th-13th century
6. Antirigam plates of Yaśabhañja and Jayabhañja

Imperial Gaṅgas :

7. Plates of Anantavarman Coḍagaṅgadeva (AD 1077-1147)
8. Plates of the successors of Coḍagaṅgadeva upto Anaṅgabhīmadeva III (AD 1147-1238)
9. Plates of Narasiṁha II (AD 1278-1306) and Bhānudeva II (AD 1306-28)
10. Kaijang plates of Bhānudeva III, Ś.1248
11. Plates of Narasiṁha IV, Ś.1305 & 1316

PLATE XVI a : Proto-Oriya Script : Inscriptions (stone) of the time of the Imperial Gaṅgas

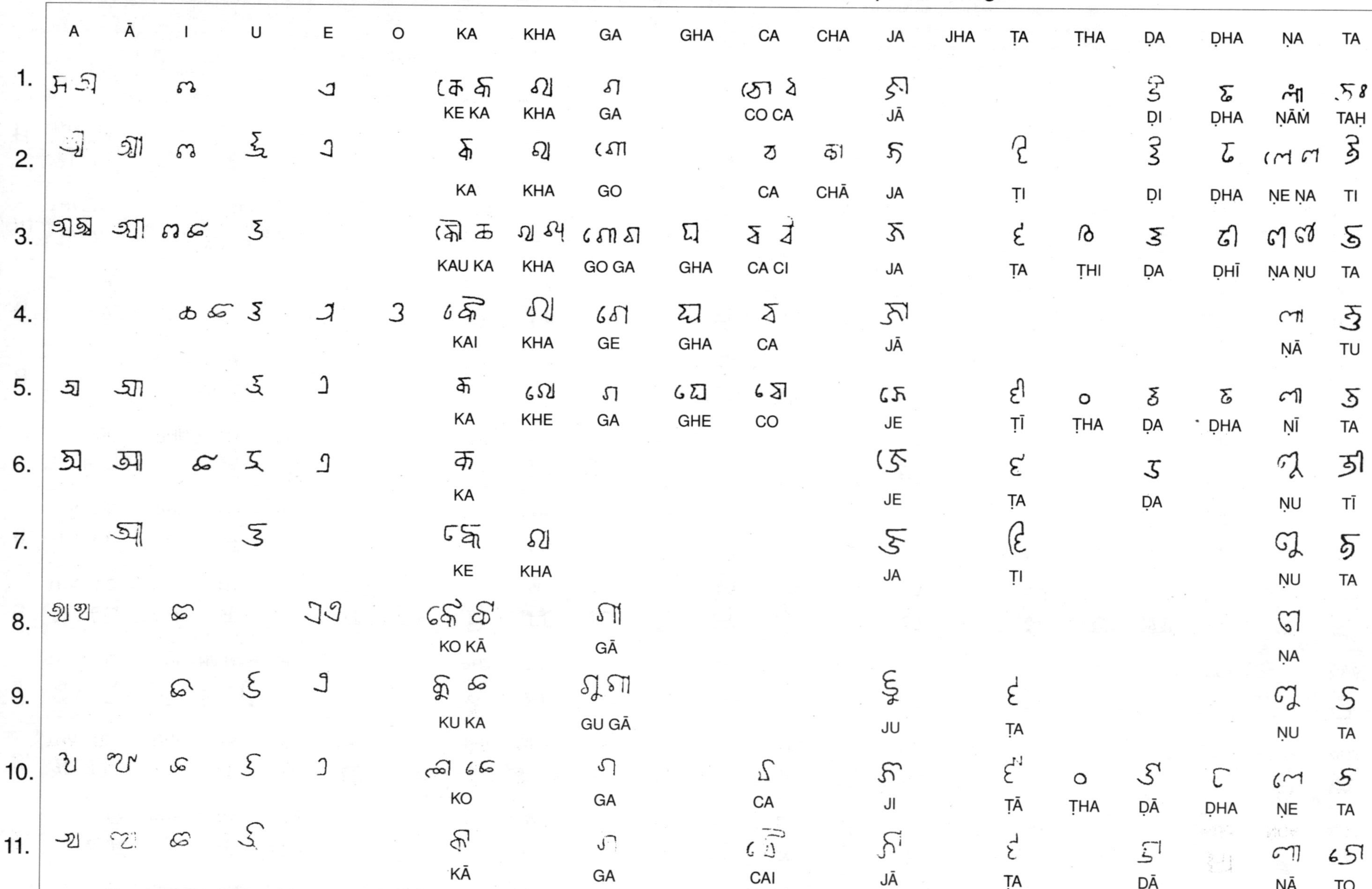

Stone Inscriptions of the time of the Imperial Gaṅgas (12th-15th century AD)

1. Later stone inscriptions of Coḍagaṅgadeva
2. Inscriptions of the sons and successors of Coḍagaṅgadeva
3. Inscriptions of the time of Anaṅgabhīma III
4. Śikhareśvara temple inscriptions of the time of Narasiṁha I
5. Bhubaneswar bilingual inscription of Narasiṁha (I)
6. Sonepur inscription of the time of Bhānudeva I
7. Parvati temple inscription of Bhānudeva I
8. Konarka temple inscription
9. Paṭṭeśvara temple inscription of Bhānudeva III, Yugābda 4477
10. Siddheśvara temple inscription of Narasiṁha IV
11. Narasinghnath temple inscription of Vaijaladeva

PLATE XVI b : Proto-Oriya Script : Inscriptions (stone) of the time of the Imperial Gaṅgas

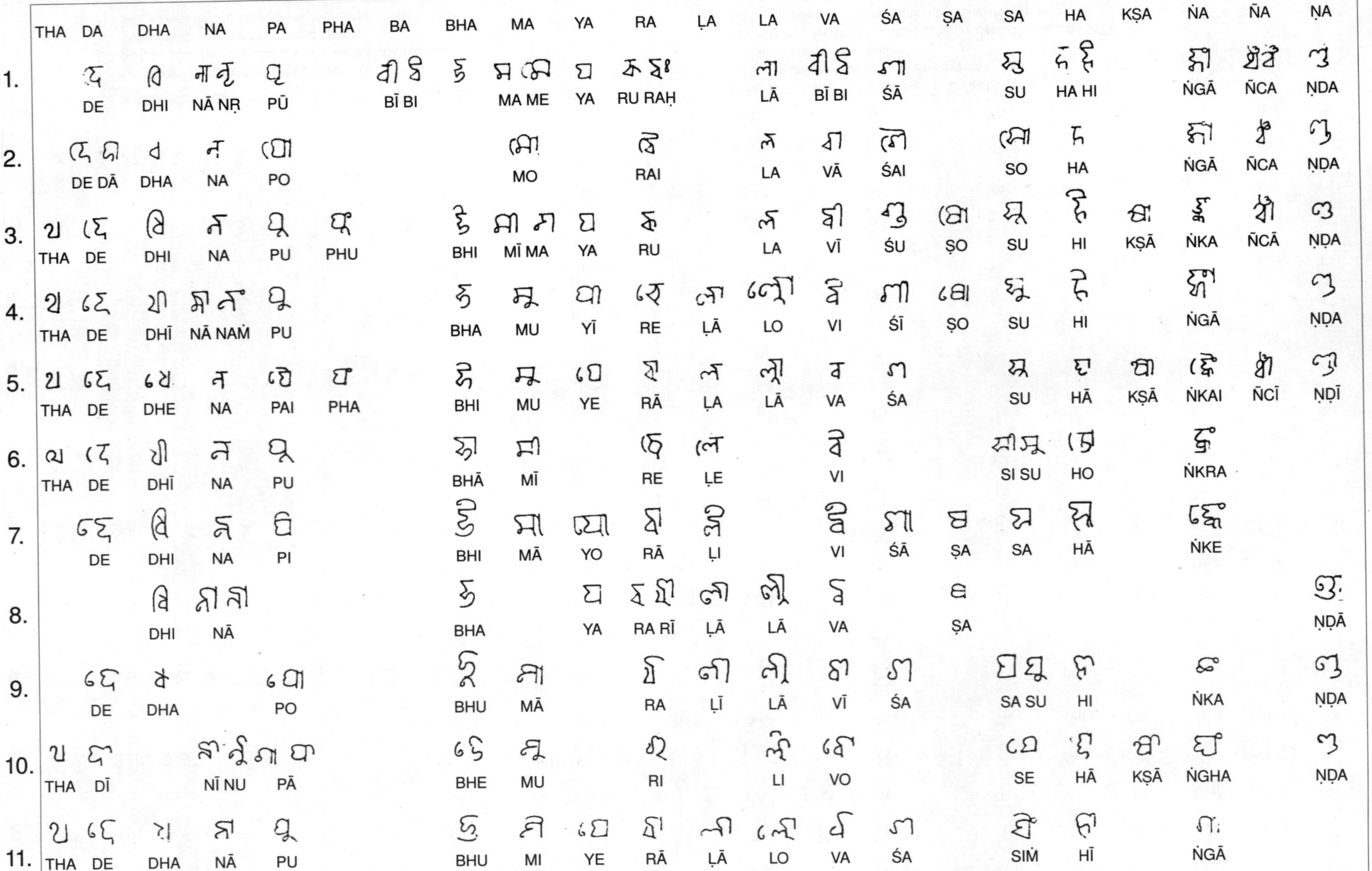

Stone Inscriptions of the time of the Imperial Gaṅgas (12th-15th century AD)

1. Later stone inscriptions of Coḍagaṅgadeva
2. Inscriptions of the sons and successors of Coḍagaṅgadeva
3. Inscriptions of the time of Anaṅgabhīma III
4. Śikhareśvara temple inscriptions of the time of Narasiṁha I
5. Bhubaneswar bilingual inscription of Narasiṁha (I)
6. Sonepur inscription of the time of Bhānudeva I
7. Parvati temple inscription of Bhānudeva I
8. Konarka temple inscription
9. Paṭṭeśvara temple inscription of Bhānudeva III, Yugābda 4477
10. Siddheśvara temple inscription of Narasiṁha IV
11. Narasinghnath temple inscription of Vaijaladeva

PLATE XVI c : Proto-Oriya Script : Inscriptions (stone) of the time of the Imperial Gaṅgas

Stone Inscriptions of the time of the Imperial Gaṅgas (12th-15th century AD)

1. Later stone inscriptions of Coḍagaṅgadeva
2. Inscriptions of the sons and successors of Coḍagaṅgadeva
3. Inscriptions of the time of Anaṅgabhīma III
4. Śikhareśvara temple inscriptions of the time of Narasiṁha I
5. Bhubaneswar bilingual inscription of Narasiṁha (I)
6. Sonepur inscription of the time of Bhānudeva I
7. Parvati temple inscription of Bhānudeva I
8. Konarka temple inscription
9. Paṭṭeśvara temple inscription of Bhānudeva III, Yugābda 4477
10. Siddheśvara temple inscription of Narasiṁha IV
11. Narasinghnath temple inscription of Vaijaladeva

PLATE XVII a : Early and Modern Oriya Script : Inscriptions of Sūryavaṁśī Gajapatis, Ministerial Dynasties and others .

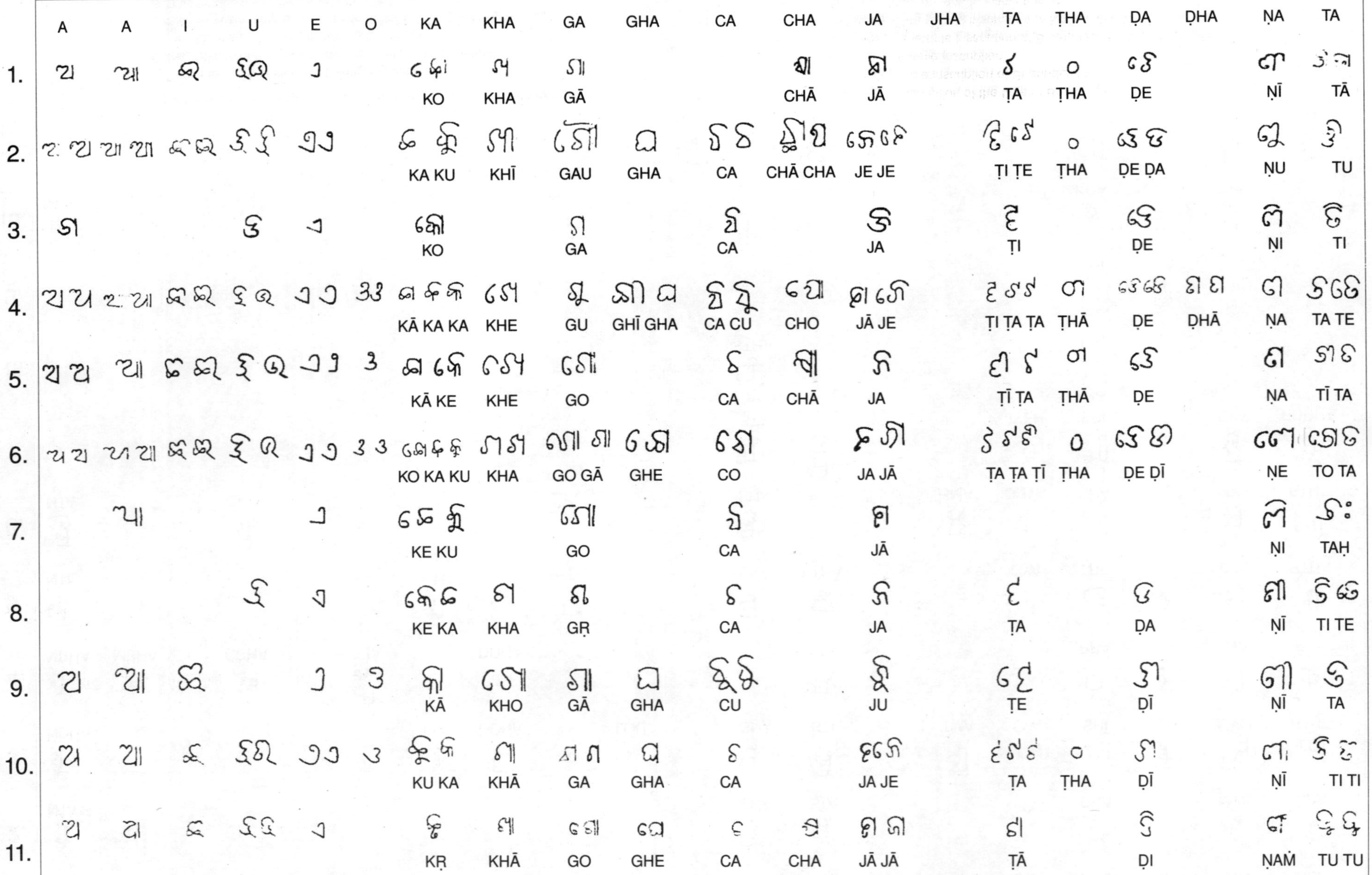

Sūryavaṁśī Gajapatis :

1. Plates of the time of Kapilendradeva (AD 1435-68)
2. Temple inscriptions of the time of Kapilendradeva
3. Balasore copper axe-head inscription of Purṣottamadeva (AD 1468-97)
4. Temple inscriptions of the time of Puruṣottamadeva
5. Temple inscriptions of the time of Pratāparudradeva (AD 1497-1538)

Ministerial Dynacties and others :

6. Inscriptions of the ministerial dynasties (AD 1538-68)
7. Bilingual stone inscription of Baripada Museum, Ś.1509
8. Athgarh rock inscription of Narasiṁha Gajapati, Ś. 1512
9. Srijang inscriptions of Acyuta Baliār Singh Mahāpātra, Ś. 1520
10. Sthānesvar and Kesiari Sarvamaṅgalā (Ś, 1526 & 1537) temple inscriptions
11. Kechala plate of Kṛṣṇadeva (late 17th century AD)

PLATE XVII b : Early and Modern Oriya Script : Inscriptions of Sūryavaṁśī Gajapatis, Ministerial Dynasties and others .

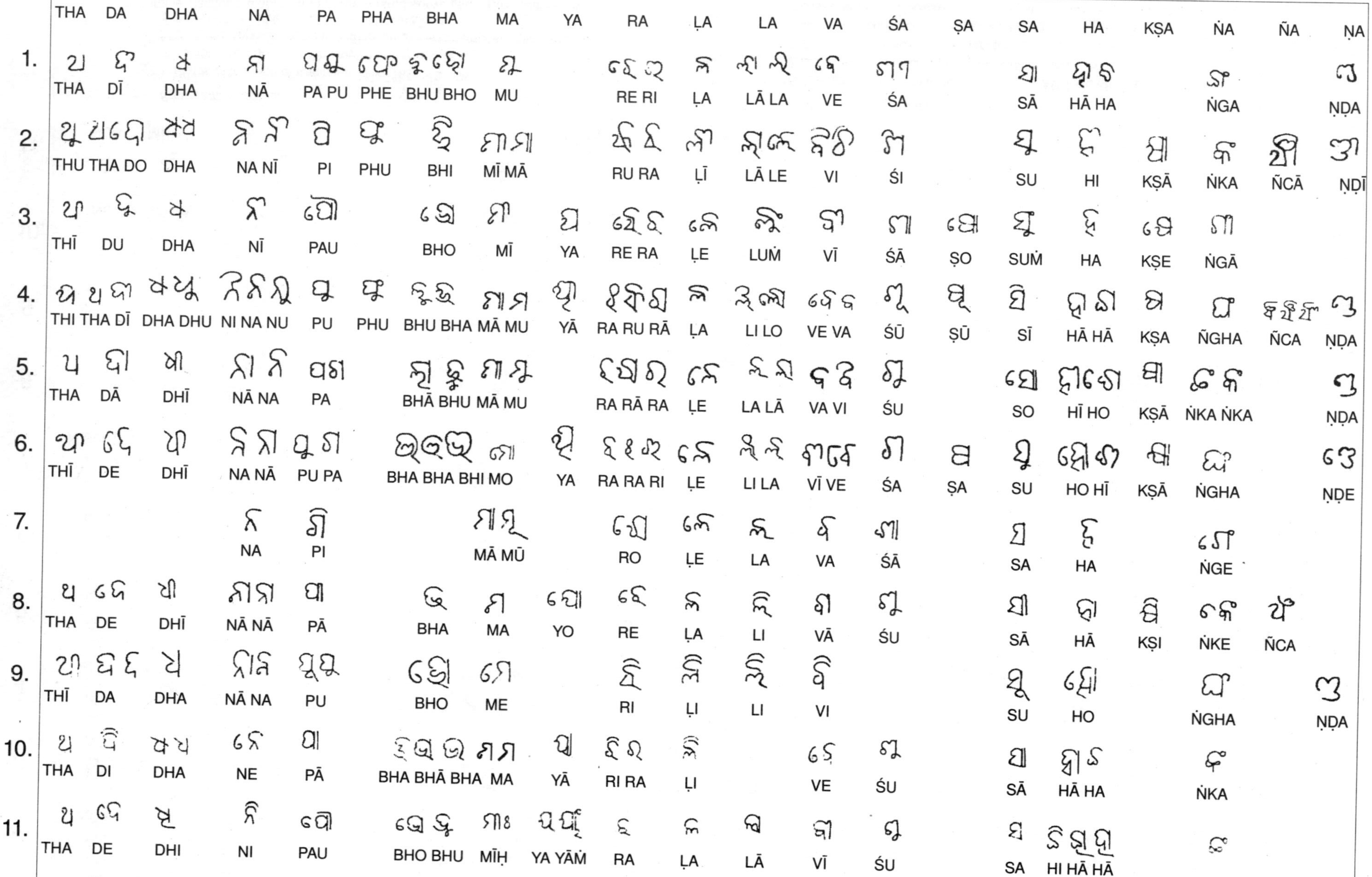

Sūryavaṁśī Gajapatis :

1. Plates of the time of Kapilendradeva (AD 1435-68)
2. Temple inscriptions of the time of Kapilendradeva
3. Balasore copper axe-head inscription of Purṣottamadeva (AD 1468-97)
4. Temple inscriptions of the time of Puruṣottamadeva
5. Temple inscriptions of the time of Pratāparudradeva (AD 1497-1538)

Ministerial Dynacties and others :

6. Inscriptions of the ministerial dynasties (AD 1538-68)
7. Bilingual stone inscription of Baripada Museum, Ś.1509
8. Athgarh rock inscription of Narasiṁha Gajapati, Ś. 1512
9. Srijang inscriptions of Acyuta Baliār Singh Mahāpātra, Ś. 1520
10. Sthāneśvar and Kesiari Sarvamaṅgalā (Ś, 1526 & 1537) temple inscriptions
11. Kechala plate of Kṛṣnadeva (late 17th century AD)

PLATE XVII c : Early and Modern Oriya Script : Inscriptions of Sūryavaṁśī Gajapatis, Ministerial Dynasties and others

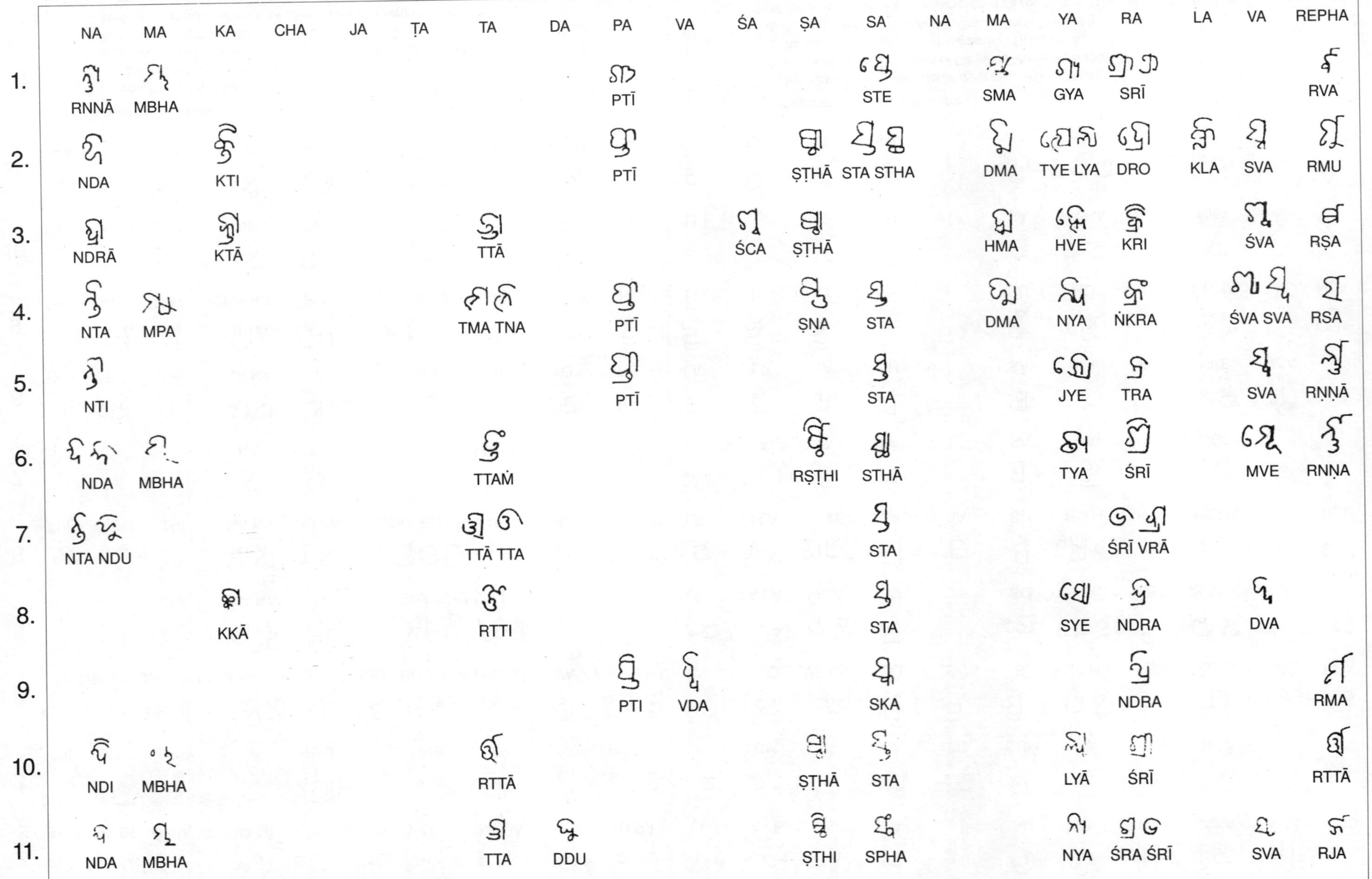

Sūryavaṁśī Gajapatis :

1. Plates of the time of Kapilendradeva (AD 1435-68)
2. Temple inscriptions of the time of Kapilendradeva
3. Balasore copper axe-head inscription of Purṣottamadeva (AD 1468-97)
4. Temple inscriptions of the time of Puruṣottamadeva
5. Temple inscriptions of the time of Pratāparudradeva (AD 1497-1538)

Ministerial Dynacties and others :

6. Inscriptions of the ministerial dynasties (AD 1538-68)
7. Bilingual stone inscription of Baripada Museum, Ś.1509
8. Athgarh rock inscription of Narasiṁha Gajapati, Ś. 1512
9. Srijang inscriptions of Acyuta Baliār Singh Mahāpātra, Ś. 1520
10. Sthāneśvar and Kesiari Sarvamaṅgalā (Ś, 1526 & 1537) temple inscriptions
11. Kechala plate of Kṛṣṇadeva (late 17th century AD)

Glossary of Terms

a, ā

 angular *a*

 angular *a* with a small horizontal dash

 cursive *a* with the two curves meet the vertical at a point

 cursive *a* with the two curves meet the vertical at two different points

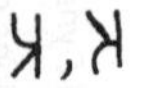 mixed type of *a*

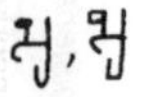 upturned curve type of *a*

 left-facing curve type

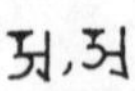 left-facing curve with a tick type

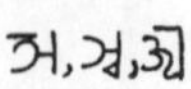 proto-Nāgarī type

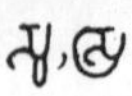 Telugu-Canarese type

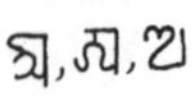 proto-Oriya type

 *kā* with the horizontal dash type of the medial *ā*

 *kā* with the horizontal dash with a downward tick type of the medial *ā*

 *kā* with the slanting stroke type of the medial *ā*

jā with the upturned curve type of the medial *ā*

 *jā* with the broad curve type of the medial *ā*

 *rā* with the twisted curve type of the medial *ā*

 *dhā* with the vertical type of the medial *ā*

 *kā* with the full length vertical type of the medial *ā*

 *lā* with the angle on the right type of the medial *ā*

i, ī

 three-dotted type of *i* arranged trianglewise

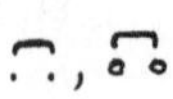 roof type

 notched roof type

 two dots or circles with a bottom element type

 two circles with a top element type

 two circles with both top and bottom element type

 proto-Oriya type

 *ki* with the angular type of the medial *i*.

 *di* with the circular type of the medial *i*.

 *khi* with the semi-circular type of the medial *i*.

 *ji* with the broad curve type of the medial *i*.

 *ri* with a curve falling to the left type of the medial *i*.

 *ri* with a full length curve falling to the left type of the medial *i*.

 *kī* with the angular type of the medial *ī*.

 *kī* with two slanting bar or curve type of medial *ī*.

 *gī* with the circular type of the medial *ī* in which a tick, hook, curl or a semi-circle in the middle.

 *rī* with the curve falling to the the right type of the medial *ī*.

 *rī* with the full length curve falling to the right type of the medial *ī*.

u, ū

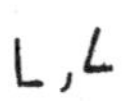 angular type.

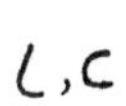 broad-backed *u*.

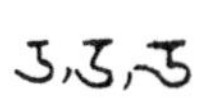 left-facing broad curve type.

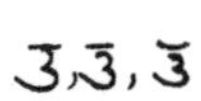 proto-Nāgarī type.

 proto-Oriya type.

 *ku* with the horizontal type of the medial *u*.

 *mu* with the vertical type of the medial *u*.

 *mu* with the upturned curve type of the medial *u*.

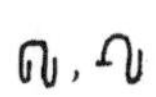 *gu* with the upturned curve type of the medial *u*.

 *ku* with the angular hook type of the medial *u*.

 *pu* with the vertical and tick type of the medial *u*.

 *su* with the triangular type of the medial *u*.

 *nu* with the left-facing curve type of the medial *u*.

 *mu* with the upturned curve touching the base type of the medial *u*.

 *ku* with the looped type of the medial *u*.

 *kū* with the double horizontal type of the medial *ū*.

 *mū* with the double vertical type of the medial *ū*.

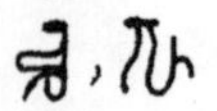 *cū* and *bhū* with the upturned curve and a slanting stroke type of the medial *ū*.

 *yū* with the right-facing broad curve type of the medial *ū*.

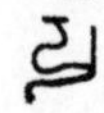 *yū* with the down-facing broad curve type of the medial *ū*.

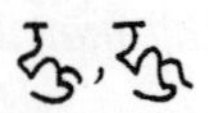 *bhū* with the left-facing curve with a stroke or curve to right type of the medial *ū*.

 *ṣū* with the curve opened at the top and a stroke added to it on the right type of the medial *ū*.

ṛ

 *vṛ* with the left-going broad curve type of the medial *ṛ*.

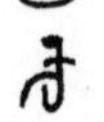 *kṛ* with down-facing curve type of the medial *ṛ*.

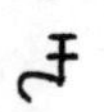 *kṛ* with the down-facing broad curve type of the medial *ṛ*.

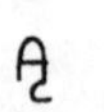 *śṛ* with the curve opened to the right type of the medial *ṛ*.

 *kṛ* with the curve opened to the right with a loop at the bottom type for the medial *ṛ*.

e, ai

▷,◁,△,▽ triangular type.

 broad-looped *e*.

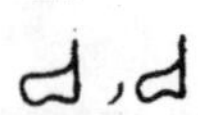 broad-looped *e* with its base-line notched.

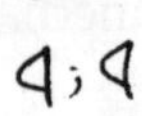 round-topped *e*.

 round-topped *e* with a projection on the left; proto-Oriya type.

 round-topped *e* with an opening on the left; proto-Oriya type.

 proto-Nāgarī type.

 left-facing curve and right upright type.

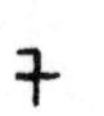 *ke* with the horizontal type of the medial *e*.

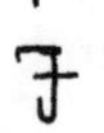 *ke* with the horizontal with a downward tick type of the medial *e*.

 *ke* with the slanting stroke type of the medial *e*.

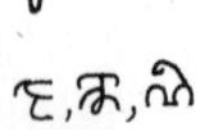 *je*, *ṇe*, and *ṇe* with the curve type of the medial *e*.

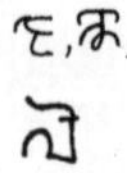 *le* with the twisted type of the medial *e*.

 *le* with the left-going top curve (*śiro-mātrā*) type of medial *e*.

 *ge* with the broad curve covering the left half (*pṛṣṭha-mātrā*) type of the medial *e*.

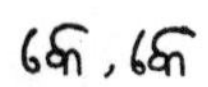 *ke* with the broad curve on the left obtaining a curl or loop at the bottom type of the medial *e*.

 proto-Nāgarī type of *ai*.

 *cai* with the double slanting stroke for the medial *ai*.

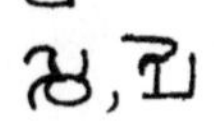 *mai* with the double curve for the medial *ai*.

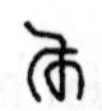 *kai* with the top stroke (*śiro-mātrā*) and the broad curve on the left (*pṛṣṭha-mātrā*) for the medial *ai*.

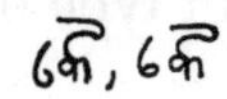 *kai* with the left going top curve and the broad curve with a curl or loop at the bottom for the medial *ai*.

o, au

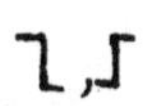 angular *o*

 angular *o* with its vertical slanting

 double-curved type

 proto-Nāgarī type

 Telugu-Canarese type

 *ko* with the two horizontal stroke type of the medial *o*.

 *ko* with the single horizontal stroke type of the medial *o*.

 *po* with the double curve type of the medial *o*.

 *jo* with the double stroke type of the medial *o*.

 *do* with the leftward curve and a right vertical drawn in one action for the medial *o*.

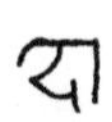 *do* with the small curve and a right vertical for the medial *o*.

 *lo* with the leftward curve on the top (*śiro-mātrā*) and a right vertical for the medial *o*.

 *yo* with the broad curve on the left (*pṛṣṭha-mātrā*) and a right vertical for the medial *o*.

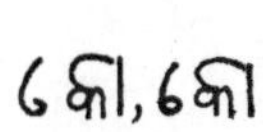 *ko* with the broad curve on the left obtaining a curl or loop at the bottom and a right vertical for the medial *o*.

 double-curved *au* with an additional stroke type.

 proto-Nāgarī type.

 *kau* with the left curve and the right hook for the medial *au.*

 *gau* with three top strokes for the medial *au.*

 *kau* with the two side strokes and a top curve for the medial *au.*

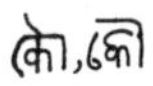 *kau* with a curve on each side (*pṛṣṭha-mātrā*) and a top curve (*śiro-mātrā*) for the medial *au.*

ka

 simple cross type

 simple cross type of *ka* with an elongated vertical

 simple cross type of *ka* with its horizontal bar curved

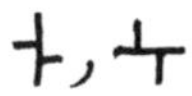 corrupt forms of the cross type of *ka*

 simple cross type of *ka* with its vertical reduced in size

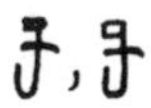 upturned curve type

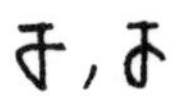 looped type

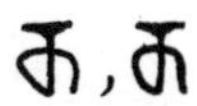 looped *ka* with an elongated outer curve

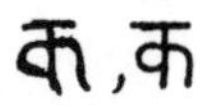 proto-Nāgarī *ka*

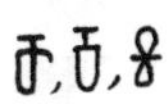 Telugu-Canarese type

 Grantha type

 Tamil type

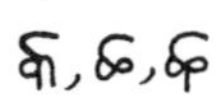 proto-Oriya type

kha

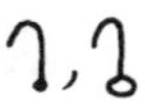 hooked *kha* with a dot or circle

 hooked *kha* without a dot or circle

 triangular loop type of *kha*

 hooked *kha* with a line

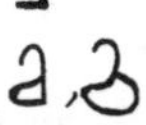 broad-looped type

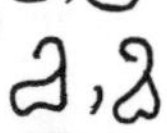 broad-looped *kha* with a notched base-line

 flat-topped *kha* with a triangular loop on the right

 round-topped *kha* with a solid triangular foot-mark

 round-topped *kha* with a looped foot-mark

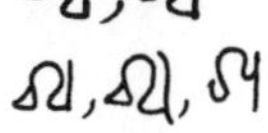 open-mouthed type; proto-Oriya type.

 Telugu-Canarese type.

ga

 angular type

 round-topped *ga*

 flat-topped *ga*

 round-topped *ga* with its left foot curling in

 flat-topped *ga* with its left foot curling in

 flat-topped *ga* with an extended right arm

 round-topped *ga* with a solid foot-mark

 round-topped *ga* with a close looped foot-mark

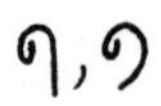 Telugu-Canarese type

 Grantha type

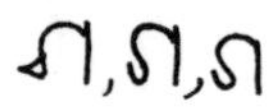 proto-Oriya type

gha

 three-pronged *gha*

 three-pronged *gha* with a flattened base

 bent arm type of *gha*

 acute-angled *gha*

 bipartite *gha*

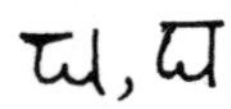 proto-Nāgarī *gha*

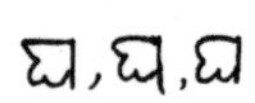 proto-Oriya type

ṅa

 simple type of *ṅa* with an opening to the right type

 square type of *ṅa*

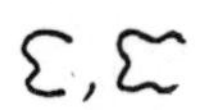 broad curve type of *ṅa* with its arms notched

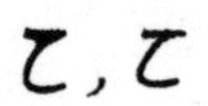 simple curve type of *ṅa* with its upper arm merged with the head-mark

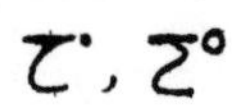 simple curve type of *ṅa* with a dot or circle on top right

 acute-angled *ṅa*.

ca

	semi-circular loop type
	triangular loop type
	square loop type
	broad-looped type
	broad-looped *ca* with a notched base-line
	triangular type
	beaked type
	triangular *ca* with its tip facing left
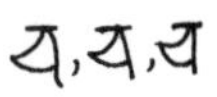	inward and outward curve type
	bipartite *ca*
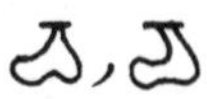	Telugu-Canarese type
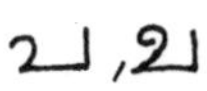	Grantha type
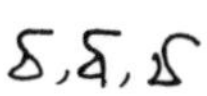	proto-Oriya type

cha

	circular base type
	elliptical *cha*
	butter-fly type
	elliptical *cha* with its middle arm drawn in *kuṭila* fashion
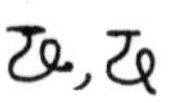	open-mouthed type
	Telugu-Canarese type

ja

	three-armed *ja*
	doubled-curved *ja*
	doubled-curved *ja* with a dot/knob in the middle
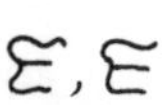	three armed *ja* with its arms notched
	suppressed upper arm type
	*kuṭila* type
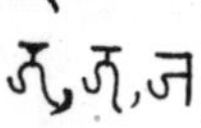	proto-Nāgarī type
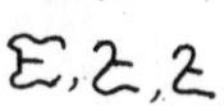	Telugu-Canarese type

	Grantha type
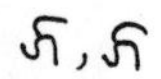	proto-Oriya type

jha

	angular *jha*
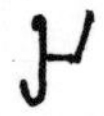	angular *jha* with an upturned curve to left
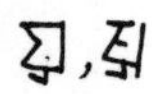	tailed *jha*
	left-going stroke type
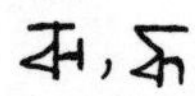	triangular type

ña

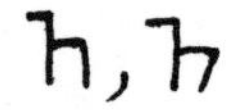	angular *ña*
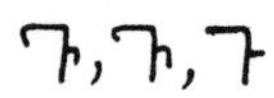	flat-topped *ña*
	upturned curve type
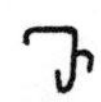	notched type
	double-curved type of *ña* with a firm base-line
	double-curved type
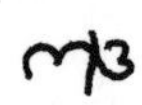	double-curved *ña* with the initial *o* on the right type
	down-facing curve with the initial *o* on the right type

ṭa

	semi-circular type
	flattened arm type
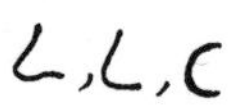	broad-backed *ṭa*
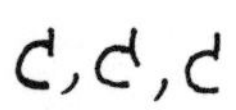	semi-circle with a vertical type
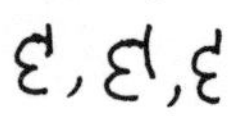	two semi-circles with a vertical type

ṭha

	circular type

ḍa

	angular *ḍa*
	broad-backed *ḍa*
	broad-backed *ḍa* with its base notched

 angular-backed type
 round-backed *ḍa* with a cursive appendage
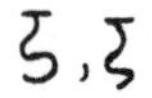 proto-Nāgarī type
 Telugu-Canarese type
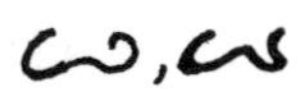 Grantha type
 proto-Oriya type

ḍha

 round-backed *ḍha*
 round-backed *ḍha* with a loop to the right
 round-backed *ḍha* with an inward curl
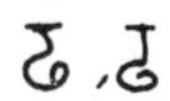 proto-Nāgarī type
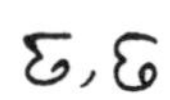 proto-Oriya type

ṇa

 angular *ṇa*
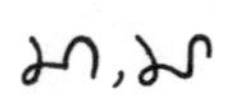 looped variety of *ṇa* of the north
 double-curved type
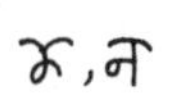 looped *ṇa*
 acute-angled *ṇa*
 transitional *ṇa*
 *kuṭila* type of *ṇa*
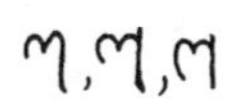 proto-Nāgarī type
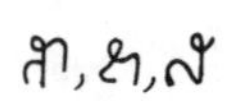 Telugu-Canarese type
 Grantha type
 proto-Oriya type

ta

 angular *ta* with two slanting strokes
 *ta* with an inclining straight line and a slanting stroke on the right
 *ta* with an inclining straight line and a slanting stroke on the left
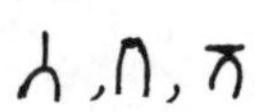 down-facing curve type

 looped *ta*

 *kuṭila* type

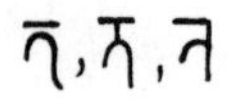 proto-Nāgarī type

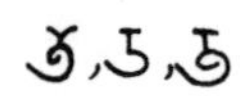 Telugu-Canarese type

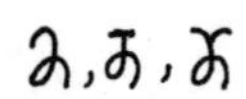 Grantha type

 proto-Bengali type

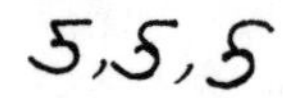 proto-Oriya type

tha

 circle with a dot in the middle type

 looped *tha*

 broad-backed *tha* with a mid-line

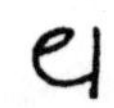 inward curl or loop type

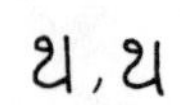 bipartite *tha*

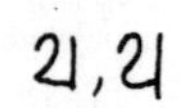 bipartite *tha* with its loop opened

 elliptical *tha*

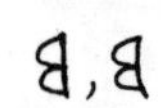 double-curved back type

da

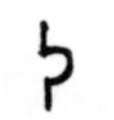 round-backed type

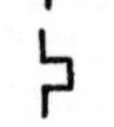 angular-backed type

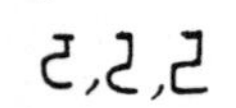 broad-backed type

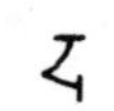 angular *da*

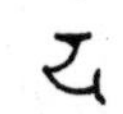 *kuṭila* type

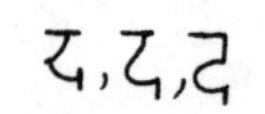 proto-Nāgarī type

 Telugu-Canarese type

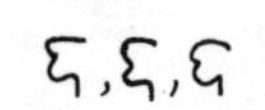 proto-Oriya type

dha

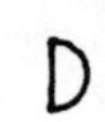 semi-circular type of *dha* with its diameter to left

 semi-circular type of *dha* with its diameter to right

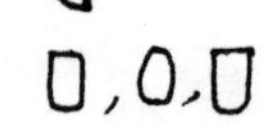 corrupt forms of *dha*

 broad-backed type

 open-mouthed *dha*

 double-curved type

 Telugu-Canarese type

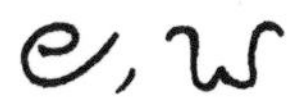 Grantha type

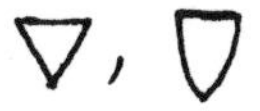 triangular type

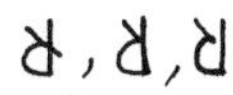 proto-Oriya type

na

 horizontal base types

 looped *na*

 looped *na* with a definite right upright

 double-armed *na*

 transitional *na*

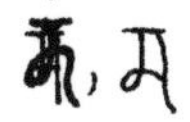 looped *na* with its outer curve drawn in *kuṭila* fashion

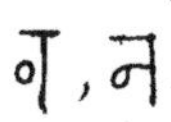 double armed *na* with a mid-line

 proto-Nāgarī type

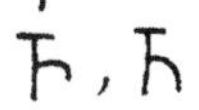 Telugu-Canarese type

 Grantha type

proto-Oriya type

pa

 hooked *pa*

 firm base-line type

 firm base-line type of *pa* with equal arms

 bent arm type

 bent arm type of *pa* with its base-line notched

 acute-angled *pa*

 *kuṭila* type

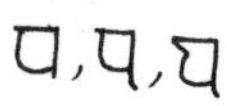 proto-Nāgarī type

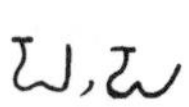 Telugu-Canarese type

 Grantha type

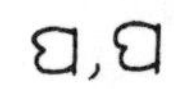 proto-Oriya type

pha

 hooked *pha*

 bent arm type

 bent arm type of *pha* with its base-line notched

 acute-angled *pha*

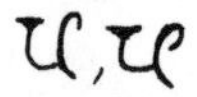 *kuṭila* type

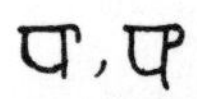 proto-Nāgarī type

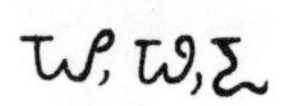 Telugu-Canarese type

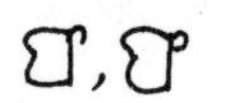 proto-Oriya type

ba

 square type

 square type of *ba* with an inward dip in its left arm

 Telugu-Canarese type

bha

 angular type

 angular *bha* with a definite right upright

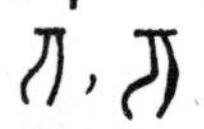 double-curved type

 broad type

 solid triangular type

 triangular loop type

 open-mouthed type

 open-mouthed *bha* with its outer curve drawn in *kuṭila* fashion

 open-mouthed *bha* with its outer curve facing down

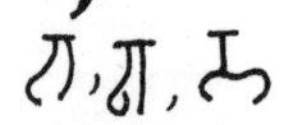 Telugu-Canarese type

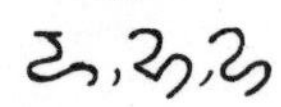 Grantha type

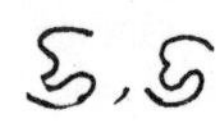 proto-Oriya type

ma

 circular loop type

 triangular loop type

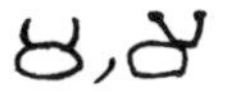 broad-looped type

 broad-looped *ma* with a notched base-line

 tailed *ma*

 acute-angled *ma*

 looped *ma*

 *kuṭila* type

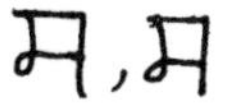 proto-Nāgarī type

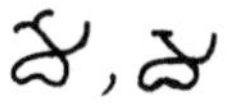 Telugu-Canarese type

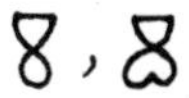 Grantha type

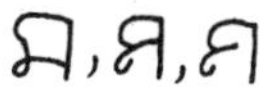 proto-Oriya type

ya

 crescentic *ya*

 segmented *ya*

 tripartite *ya*

 tripartite *ya* with its left arm curling in

 looped *ya*

 doubled-armed *ya*

 acute-angled *ya*

 bipartite *ya*

 *kuṭila* type

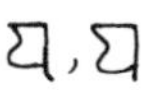 proto-Nāgarī type

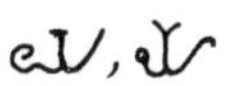 Telugu-Canarese type

 proto-Oriya type

ra

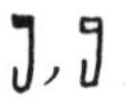 upturned curve type

 vertical type

 vertical with a tick type

 vertical with a slanting stroke type

 proto-Nāgarī type

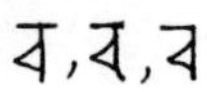 hollow triangular type

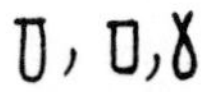 Telugu-Canarese type

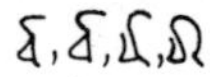 proto-Oriya type

la

 round-bottomed *la*

 flattened base-line type

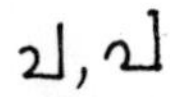 hooked *la*

 hooked *la* with an extended upper curve

 circular type; Telugu-Canarese type

 acute-angled *la*

 double-curved type

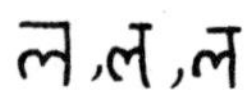 proto-Nāgarī type

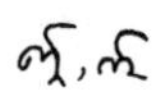 proto-Oriya type

va

 circular base type

 triangular loop type

 triangular looped *va* with its vertical reduced in size

 broad-looped type

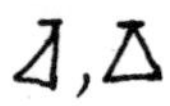 triangular type

 broad curve with a definite right upright type

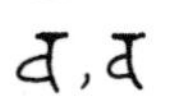 *kuṭila* type

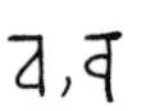 proto-Nāgarī type

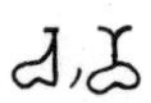 Telugu-Canarese type

 Grantha type

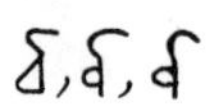 proto-Oriya type

śa

 round-topped *śa*

 flat-topped *śa*

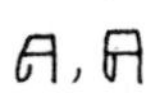 flat-topped *śa* with its left arm curling in

 looped type

 round-topped *śa* with a solid triangular foot-mark

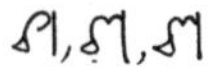 round-topped *śa* with a close looped foot-mark

 round-topped *śa* with its looped foot-mark opened up

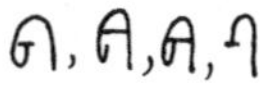 Telugu-Canarese type

 proto-Oriya type

ṣa

 bent arm type

 equal arm type

 acute-angle type

 *kuṭila* type

 proto-Nāgarī type

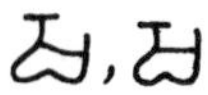 Telugu-Canarese type

 Grantha type

 proto-Oriya type

sa

 doubled-curved type

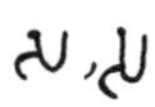 hooked *sa*

 looped *sa*

 close triangular loop type

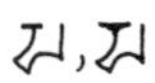 open-mouthed type

 proto-Nāgarī type

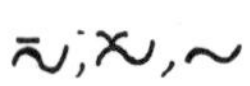 Telugu-Canarese type

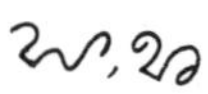 Grantha type

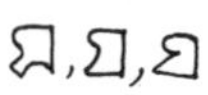 proto-Oriya type

ha

 round-bottomed *ha*

 flattened base-line type

 flattened base-line type of *ha* with equal arms

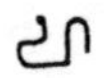 bent arm type

 bent arm type of *ha* with its base-line notched

 acute-angled *ha*

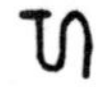 round bottomed *ha* with an extended right arm

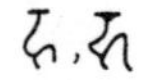 tailed *ha*

 proto-Nāgarī type

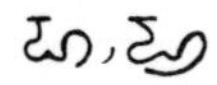 Telugu-Canarese type

 Grantha type

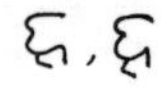 proto-Oriya type.

Bibliography

Acharya, P., *Studies in Orissan History, Archaeology and Archives*, Cuttack, 1969.

Acharya, S.K., *Numerals in Orissan Inscriptions*, Simla, 2002.

Asher, F.M. & Gai, G.S., *Indian Epigraphy: Its bearing on the History of Art*, New Delhi, 1985.

Banerji, R.D., *The Origin of the Bengali Script*, Calcutta, 1919.

———, "The Palaeography of the Hāthīguṁphā and the Nanaghat Inscriptions," *MASB*, 11 (3), 113-46.

———, *History of Orissa*, 2 vols., Calcutta, 1930-31.

Banerji Sastri, A.P., *Early Inscriptions of Bihar and Orissa*, Patna, 1927.

Barua, B.M., *Old Brahmi Inscriptions in the Udayagiri and Khandagiri Caves*, Calcutta, 1929.

———, *Asoka and His Inscriptions*, 3rd edn., 2 parts, Calcutta, 1969.

Basak, R.G., *The History of North-Eastern India*, Calcutta, 1934.

———, *Asokan Inscriptions*, Calcutta, 1959.

Beal, S. (ed.), *The Life of Hiuen-Tsang*, London, 1911.

Beams, John, *A Comparative Grammar of the Modern Aryan Languages of India*, 3 vols., London, 1872-79.

Behera, S.C., *Rise and Fall of the Śailodbhavas*, Calcutta, 1982.

Bhandarkar, D.R., *List of Inscriptions of North India*, Appendix to *EI*, 21.

Bhattacharya, A.K., *A Corpus of Dedicatory Inscriptions from Temples of West Bengal*, Calcutta, 1982.

Bhattacharya, H.K., *The Language and Scripts of Ancient India*, Calcutta, 1959.

Bose, Susil K., "Studies in Gupta Palaeography," *Indian Culture*, 4, 181-88 & 325-46.

Bühler, J.G., *Indian Palaeography*, reprinted in *Indian Studies: Past & Present*, I, 3, Calcutta, 1959.

———, *On the Origin of the Brahma Alphabet*, Indian Studies, III, 2nd edn., Varanasi, 1963.

Burnell, A.C., *Elements of South Indian Palaeography*, London, 1878.

Butterworth, A. & V. Venugopal Chetty, *Nellor District Inscriptions*, 3 parts, Madras, 1905.

Chakravarti, S.N., "Development of the Bengali Alphabet," *JRASB*, *L*, 4, 1938, 351-91.

Chatterji, Suniti Kumar, *The People, Language and Culture of Orissa, Artavallabh Mahanty Memorial Lectures*, Bhubaneswar, 1966.

———, *The Origin and Development of the Bengali Language*, 2 vols., 2nd edn., London, 1970.

Clodd, E., *The Story of Alphabet*, 2nd edn., New York, 1938.

Cunningham, A. (ed.), *Corpus Inscriptionum Indicarum*, I, *Inscriptions of Asoka*, (reprint), Varanasi, 1961.

Dani, A.H., *Indian Palaeography*, 2nd edn., Delhi, 1986.

Das, B.S., "Dynamics of Changes in the Social Framework, Religion and Language in Eastern India (eighth-twelfth Century)," *JOH*, 1 (2), 1980, 44-59.

Das, Bisvarup, *The Bhauma-Karas and Their Times*, New Delhi, 1978.

———, *Orissa : Social, Cultural and Religious Aspects*, Delhi, 1985.

Das, C.R., *Studies in Medieval Religion and Literature of Orissa*, Santiniketan, 1951.

Das, D.N., *The Early History of Kaliṅga*, Calcutta, 1977.

Das, H.C., S. Tripathy & B.K. Rath (eds.), *Kṛṣṇa Pratibhā, Studies in Indology* (*Prof. Krishna Chandra Panigrahi Commemoration Volume*), 2 vols., Delhi, 1994.

Das, M.N., (ed.), *Sidelights on History and Culture of Orissa*, Cuttack, 1978.

Das, Pt. N.K., "Oriya Language and Culture," *OHRJ*, 8 (1), 1959, 1-40.

Das Gupta, C.C., *The Development of the Kharoṣṭhi Script*, Calcutta, 1958.

Dash, K.C., *Legend, History and Culture of India*, Calcutta, 1997.

Datta, Swati, *Migrant Brāhmaṇas in Northern India, Their Settlement and General Impact, c.* AD *475-1030*, Delhi, 1989.

Dehejia, V., *The Early Stone Temples of Orissa*, New Delhi, 1979.

Diringer, D., *The Alphabet*, London, 1953.

Disalkar, D.B., "Inscriptions in the Sanskritic Provincial Languages," *OHRJ*, 5 (1-2), 1956, 101-03.

De, S.C., *Descriptive Catalogue of the Copper Plate Inscriptions of Orissa*, Bhubaneswar, 1961.

Eschmann, A., H. Kulke & G.C. Tripathy (eds.), *The Cult of Jagannath and the Regional Tradition of Orissa*, New Delhi, 1978.

Fleet, J.F., *Corpus Inscriptionum Indicarum*, III, *Inscriptions of Early Gupta Kings and their Successors* (rev. edn.), Calcutta, 1971.

Ganguly, D.K., *Historical Geography and Dynastic History of Orissa*, Calcutta, 1975.

Ganguly, M.M., *Orissa and Her Remains*, Calcutta, 1912.

Gelb, I.J., *A Study of Writing*, London, 1962.

Gnoli, Ramiero, *Nepalese Inscriptions in Gupta Characters*, 2 parts, Roma, 1956.

Grierson, G.A., "Specimens of Bihari and Oriya Languages," *Linguistic Survey of India*, 5 (2), Calcutta, 1903, 367-441.

———, "On the Modern Indo-Aryan Vernaculars," *IA*, 1931-32 (Supplement), 57-67 & pls.

Gupta, S.P. & K.S. Ramachandran, *The Origin of the Brāhmī Script*, New Delhi, 1979.

Hiralal, *List of Inscriptions of the Central Provinces and Berar*, 2nd edn., Nagpur, 1932.

Hoernle, Rudolf, "The Bower Manuscript," *JASB*, 60, 92 ff; *IA*, 21, 29-45.

Hultzsch, E., *Corpus Inscriptionum Indicarum*, I, *Inscriptions of Aśoka*, 2nd edn., Varanasi, 1969.

Hunter, W.W., *Orissa*, I, London, 1880.

Jansen, Hans, *Sign, Symbol and Script*, London, 1970.

Joshi, A., *New Light on the Cultural Heritage of Orissa*, Cuttack, 1979.

Jauvean-Dubreuil, G., *Ancient History of the Deccan*, Pondichery, 1920.

Kannaiyan, V, *Scripts in and around India*, Madras, 1960.

Kant, Sashi, *Hātīguṁphā Inscription of Khāravela and the Bhabru Edicts of Aśoka — A Critical Study*, Delhi, 1971.

Krishna Rao, B.V., *A History of the Early Dynasties of Andhradesa, Cir, 200-625 AD*, Madras, 1942.

———, *History of the Eastern Chālukyas of Veṅgi*, Hyderabad, 1973.

Kulke, Hermann, *Kings and Cults, State Formation and Legitimation in India and South-East Asia*, New Delhi, 1993.

Lohuizen De Leeuw, J.E. Von, *The Scythian Period*, Leiden, 1949.

Mahalingam, T.V., *Early South Indian Palaeography*, Madras, 1967.

Mahanty, A.B., *Prācīna Oḍiā Gadyapadyādarśa* (Oriya), Cuttack, 1940.

Mahapatra, R.P., *Udayagiri and Khandagiri Caves*, Delhi, 1981.

———, *Archaeology in Orissa*, 2 vols., Delhi, 1986.

Majumdar, B.C., *Orissa in the Making*, Calcutta, 1925.

———, (ed.), *Typical Selections from Oriya Literature*, 3 vols., Calcutta University, Calcutta, 1921, 1923 & 1925.

Majumdar, N.G. (ed.), *Inscriptions of Bengal*, III, Rajasahi, 1929.

Majumdar, R.C. (ed.), *The History of Bengal*, I, Dacca, 1943.

McPherson, Sir Hugh, "The Oriya Alphabet," *JBORS*, 10 (1-2), 168-70 & pls.

Mirashi, V.V. (ed.), *Corpus Inscriptionum Indicarum*, IV, 2 parts, Inscriptions of Kalachuri Chedi era. Ootacamund, 1955.

———, (ed.), *Corpus Inscriptionum Indicarum*, V, Inscriptions of the Vākāṭakas, Ootacamund, 1963.

———, (ed.), *Corpus Inscriptionum Indicarum*, VI, Inscriptions of the Śilāhāras, New Delhi, 1977.

———, *The History and Inscriptions of the Sātavāhanas and the Western Kshatrapas*, Bombay, 1981.

Misra, B., *Dynasties of Medieval Orissa*, Calcutta, 1933.

———, *Orissa Under the Bhauma Kings*, Calcutta, 1934.

Mishra, N., "Tālapatra Pothire Oḍiā Lipira Bibartana," *Konarka* (a quarterly Oriya Journal of Orissa Sahitya Academy), No. 66, Bhubaneswar, 1988, 17-23.

Mishra, P.K. & J.K. Samal (eds.), *Comprehensive History and Culture of Orissa*, 2 vols., New Delhi, 1997.

Mitra, D., *Ratnagiri*, 2 vols., New Delhi, 1981 & 1983.

Mitra, R.L., *Antiquities of Orissa*, 2 vols. (reprint), Calcutta, 1961.

Mittal, A.C., *Early History of Orissa*, Varanasi, 1962.

Mukherjee, P., *The History of the Gajapati Kings of Orissa and Their Successors*, Calcutta, 1953.

Nagaraju, S., "Emergence of Regional Identity and Beginnings of Vernacular Literature: a case study of Telugu," *Social Scientist*, 23 (10-12), Oct.-Dec. 1975, 8-23.

Nema, S.R., *Political History of the Somavaṁśī Kings of South Kośala and Orissa*, New Delhi, 1978.

Naik, A.V., *Inscriptions of Deccan*, Mysore.

Ojha, G.H., *Bhāratīya Prācīna Lipimālā* (*The Palaeography of India*), (Hindi), 3rd edn, Delhi, 1959.

Panda, S.K., *Medieval Orissa A Socio-Economic Study*, New Delhi, 1991.

———, *The State and the Statecraft in Medieval Orissa under the Later Eastern Gaṅgas*, AD *1038-1434*, Calcutta, 1995.

Pandey, R.B., *Indian Palaeography*, part I, Varanasi, 1952.

Panigrahi, K.C., *Archaeological Remains at Bhubaneswar*, Calcutta, 1961.

———, *Chronology of the Bhauma-Karas and Somavaṁśīs of Orissa*, Bhopal, 1961.

Pargiter, F.E. (ed.), *Purāṇa Texts of the Dynasties of the Kali Age*, Oxford, 1913.

Paul, P.L., "The Development of the Bengali Script," *IHQ*, 12, 1936, 308-34.

Pillai, L.D.S., *Indian Ephemeris, 700* AD *to 2000* AD, Madras, 1922.

Prinsep, J., *Essays on Indian Antiquity*, London, 1968.

Rajaguru, S.N. (ed.), *Inscriptions of Orissa*, 5 vols., Berhampur and Bhubaneswar, 1958-76.

———, *Oḍiā Lipira Krama Vikāsa* (Oriya), Bhubaneswar, 1960.

———, *History of the Gaṅgas*, 2vols., Bhubaneswar, 1968 & 1972.

———, "Oḍiā Lipi," *Koṇārka* (a quarterly Oriya journal of Orissa Sahitya Academy), 4 (3), Bhubaneswar, 1969, 43-60.

———, (ed.), *Inscriptions of the Temples of Puri and Origin of Śrī Puruṣottama Jagannāth*, I, Puri, 1992.

Ramesan, N. (ed.), *Copper Plate Inscriptions of Andhra Pradesh Government Museum, Hyderabad*, 2 vols., Hyderabad, 1962 & 1970.

Ramesh, K.V. (ed.), *Inscriptions of the Western Gaṅgas*, New Delhi, 1984.

———, *Indian Epigraphy*, I, Delhi, 1984.

Ramesh, K.V. and S.P. Tiwari (eds.), *A Copper-Plate Hoard of the Gupta Period from Bagh, Madhya Pradesh*, New Delhi, 1990.

Rangacharya, V., *Topographical List of Inscriptions of the Madras Presidency*, 3 vols., Madras, 1919.

Sewell, R. & S.K. Aiyangar, *Historical Inscriptions of South India*, Madras, 1932.

Rao, C.V.R., *Administration and Society in Medieval Andhra under the Later Eastern Gaṅgas and Sūryavaṁśī Gajapatis*, Nellor, 1976.

Rao, N.M., *Three Grants from Ragolu*, Hyderabad, 1982.

———, *Kaliṅga Under the Eastern Gaṅgas Ca. 900 AD-1200 AD*, Delhi, 1991.

Rath, B.K., *Cultural History of Orissa (AD 885-1110)*, Delhi, 1983.

Regmi, D.R. (ed.), *Inscriptions of Ancient Nepal*, 3 vols., New Delhi, 1983.

Sachau, E.C. (ed.), *Alberuni's India*, Ist Indian reprint, New Delhi, 1964.

Sah, A.P., *Life in Medieval Orissa (Cir AD 600-1200)*, Varanasi, 1976.

Sahu, J.K., *Historical Geography of Orissa*, New Delhi, 1998.

Sahu, N.K., *Buddhism in Orissa*, Utkal University, 1958.

———, *Utkal University History of Orissa*, I, Utkal University, 1964.

———, *Khāravela*, Bhubaneswar, 1984.

Sankarnarayanan, S., *The Viṣṇukuṇḍins and Their Times*, Delhi, 1977.

Sastri, Hiranand, "Nalanda and its Epigraphical Materials," *Memoirs of the Archaeological Survey of India*, No. 66, Calcutta, 1942.

Sastri, K. A.N. (ed.), *A Comprehensive History of India*, II, Calcutta, 1957.

———, *A History of South India*, 4th edn., Madras, 1976.

Sharma, R.S., *Urban Decay in India (c. 300-c. 1000)*, New Dehi, 1987.

Shastri, A.M. (ed.), *Inscriptions of the Śarabhapurīyas, Pāṇḍuvaṁśīns and Somavaṁśīns*, 2 parts, New Delhi, 1995.

Shrava, Satya (ed.), *Dated Kuṣāṇa Inscriptions*, New Delhi, 1993.

Singh, A.K., *Development of Nāgarī Script*, Delhi, 1991.

Singh, U., *Kings, Brāhmaṇas and Temples in Orissa, An Epigraphic Study AD 300- 1147*, New Delhi, 1994.

Singh Deo, J.P., *Cultural Profile of South Kośala*, Delhi, 1987.

Sircar, D.C. (ed.), *The Successors of the Sātavāhanas*, Calcutta, 1939. *Select Inscriptions Bearing on Indian History and Civilization*, I, Calcutta, 1942; II, Delhi, 1983.

———, "Palaeography of the Śailodbhava Grants," *OHRJ*, 3 (1), 1954, 31-34.

———, *Indian Epigraphy*, Delhi, 1965.

———, *Indian Epigraphical Glossary*, Delhi, 1966.

———, "Introduction to Indian Epigraphy and Palaeography," *JAIH*, 4, 1970-71, 72-136.

———, *Epigraphic Discoveries in East Pakisthan*, Calcutta, 1973.

———, *Some Epigraphical Records of the Medieval Period from Eastern India*, New Delhi, 1979.

Sivarammurti, C., *Indian Epigraphy and South Indian Scripts*, Madras, 1966.

Subrahmanyam, R., *The Sūryavaṁśī Gajapatis of Orissa*, Waltair, 1957.

———, *The Guntupally Brāhmī Inscriptions of Khāravela*, Epigraphical Series No. 3, Hyderabad, 1968.

———, (ed.), *Inscriptions of the Sūryavaṁśī Gajapatis of Orissa*, Delhi, 1986.

Subudhi, U.K., *The Bhauma-Kara Kings of Orissa*, Calcutta, 1978.

Sukthankar, V.S., "Palaeographic Notes," *R.G. Bhandarkar Commemoration Volume*, Poona, 1917, 309-22.

Suryanarayana, K., (ed.), *Inscriptions of the Minor Chālukya Dynasties of Andhra Pradesh*, New Delhi, 1993.

Thaplyal, K.K. (ed.), *Inscriptions of the Maukharis, Later Guptas, Puṣpabhutis and Yaśovarman of Kanauj*, Delhi, 1985.

Tiwari, S.P., *Comprehensive History of Orissa*, Calcutta, 1985.

Tripathi, K.B., "The Palaeography of early Oriya Inscriptions," *OHRJ*, 4 (1-2), 1955, 11-27; 5 (3-4), 1956, 144-55.

———, *The Evolution of Oriya Language and Script*, Cuttack, 1962.

———, *Prācīna Oḍiā Abhilekha* (Oriya), Bhubaneswar, 1965.

Tripathy, S. (ed.), *Inscriptions of Orissa*, 6, Bhubaneswar, 1974.

———, *Early and Medieval Coins and Currency System of Orissa* (*Circa 300 BC to AD 1568*), Calcutta, 1985.

———, (ed.), *Inscriptions of Orissa*, I (*circa* Fifth-Eighth Centuries AD), Delhi, 1997.

———, (ed.), *Inscriptions of Orissa*, II (Inscriptions of the Bhauma-Karas), New Delhi, 2000.

Upasak, C.S., *The History and Palaeography of Mauryan Brāhmī Script*, Nalanda, 1960.

Vasu, N.N., *The Archaeological Survey of Mayurabhanja*, I, rare reprints, Delhi, 1981.

Verma, T.P., *The Palaeography of Brāhmī Script in North India*, Varanasi, 1971.

———, *Development of Script in Ancient Kāmarūpa*, Jorhat, 1976.

Walawalkar, A.B., *Pre-Asokan Brāhmī—A Study on the Origin of the Indian Alphabet*, Bombay, 1951.

Warder, A.K., *Introduction to Pali*, London, 1963.

Woolner, A.C., *Introduction of Prakrit*, Lahore, 1939.

Yazdani, G., *Early History of the Deccan*, Oxford, 1960.

Index
(Omitting bibliographical lists, glossary and plates)